THE SHORTER
COLUMBIA ANTHOLOGY
OF TRADITIONAL CHINESE
LITERATURE

TRANSLATIONS FROM THE ASIAN CLASSICS

TRANSLATIONS FROM THE ASIAN CLASSICS

THE SHORTER
Columbia Anthology of Traditional Chinese Literature

Victor H. Mair, editor

COLUMBIA UNIVERSITY PRESS / NEW YORK

Columbia University Press
New York   Chichester, West Sussex
Copyright © 2000 Columbia University Press
All rights reserved

Library of Congress Cataloging-in-Publication Data

The shorter Columbia anthology of traditional Chinese literature / Victor H. Mair, editor.
      p.   cm.— (Translations from the Asian classics)
   Includes bibliographical references.
   ISBN 0-231-11998-4 (alk. paper)—ISBN 0-231-11999-2 (pbk. : alk. paper)
   1. Chinese literature—Translations into English.   I. Title: Columbia anthology of
traditional Chinese literature.   II. Mair, Victor H., 1943–   III. Series.
PL2658.E1 S53 2000
895.1'08—dc21

00-035878

For Tom and Taunja

CONTENTS

Introduction xvii
Bibliographical Note xxvii
Acknowledgments xxix
Map of the Provinces of China xxxi

PART I. FOUNDATIONS AND INTERPRETATIONS

Divinations and Inscriptions

1. A Late Shang Divination Record 3
2. A Bronze Inscription of the Western Chou 4
3. The Book of Changes of the Chou People 5
4. An Early Commentary on the *Classic of Changes* 10

Philosophy, Thought, and Religion

5. Attributed to Kuan Chung, *Kuan Tzu*, "Duties of the Student" 12
6. Anonymous, Confucian *Analects*, Book 2 17
7. Meng K'o, *Mencius*, "Bull Mountain" and "Fish and Bear's Paws" 20
8. Chuang Chou, *Chuang Tzu*, Chapter 17 and other passages 22
9. Attributed to Lao Tzu, The Classic Book of Integrity and the Way: *Tao te ching* 32
10. Attributed to Lieh Yü-k'ou, *Lieh Tzu*, "The Stupid Old Man Who Moved a Mountain" 37
11. Translated by Hsüan-tsang, *Abhidharma-mahāvibhāṣā-śāstra*, Chapter 99: "The Sins of Mahādeva" 39

Criticism and Theory

12. Hsiao T'ung, Preface to *Literary Selections* 46
13. Hsieh Ho, Preface to *Record of the Classification of Old Painters* 51

14. Yen Yü, *Ts'ang-lang's Discussions of Poetry*, "An Analysis of Po-
       etry"   52
15. Yüan Hao-wen, "Poems on Poetry, No. 30"   58

PART II. VERSE

Classical Poetry

16. Anonymous, *Classic of Odes*   61
17. Liu Chen, "Cockfight"   73
18. Juan Chi, "Songs of My Soul"   74
19. Kuo P'u, "Poem on the Wandering Immortal"   77
20. T'ao Ch'ien "Poems After Drinking Wine" (No. 5)   77
       "On Reading the *Mountains and Seas Classic*"   79
21. Hsieh Ling-yün, "On My Way from South Mountain to North
       Mountain, I Glance at the Scenery from the Lake"   80
22. Shen Yüeh, "Harmonizing with a Poem by Left Assistant Yü
       Kao-chih Requesting Sick Leave"   81
       "Listening to Gibbons at Rock-Pool Creek"   81
23. Wang Seng-ju, "Describing a Dream for Someone"   82
24. Yü Chien-wu, "Spring Day"   82
25. Hsiao Kang, "A Pheasant on His Morning Flight"   83
26. Brahmacārin Wang, [Untitled]   83
27. Lo Pin-wang, "On the Cicada: In Prison"   84
28. Ho Chih-chang, "Written Impromptu upon Returning to My
       Hometown"   85
29. Ch'en Tzu-ang, "Poems of Reflection on the Vicissitudes of
       Life"   85
30. Chang Chiu-ling, "Poems of Reflection on the Vicissitudes of
       Life"   87
31. Wang Chih-huan, "Climbing the Stork Pavilion"   87
32. Meng Hao-jan, "Seeking Out Master Chan on Incense
       Mountain"   88
       "Spring Dawn"   89
       "Passing Seven-League Rapids"   89
33. Wang Ch'ang-ling, "Silent at Her Window"   90
34. Wang Wei, "Climbing Pien-chüeh Temple"   90
       "Second Song for the Worship of the Goddess at Yü
       Mountain: 'Bidding the Goddess Farewell' "   91
       "Deer Enclosure"   92
35. Li Po, "To Meng Hao-jan"   92
       "Late Bloomer at the Front of My Garden"   93
       "To Send to Tu Fu as a Joke"   93
       "Drinking Alone in the Moonlight" (No. 1)   94
       "Still Night Thoughts"   94
       "Poems in an Old Style"   95

36. Ch'u Kuang-hsi, "The Streets of Ch'ang-an"   96
37. Tu Fu, "Spring View"   97
    "A Guest Arrives"   97
    "Recruiting Officer of Shih-hao"   98
    "At the Sky's End, Thinking of Li Po"   98
38. Chang Chi, "Maple Bridge Night Mooring"   100
39. Ts'en Shen, "A Song of the Running Horse River: Presented on
        Saying Farewell to the Army Going on Campaign to the
        West"   101
40. Ssu-k'ung Shu, "In Illness, Dismissing My Singing Girl"   102
41. Meng Chiao, "On Failing the Examination"   103
42. Han Yü, "The Girl of Mount Hua"   103
43. Hsüeh T'ao, "Listening to a Monk Play the Reed Pipes"   105
    "Lotus-Gathering Boat"   106
44. Liu Tsung-yüan, "River Snow"   106
45. Cold Mountain, [Untitled Poems]   107
46. Chia Tao, "Looking for a Recluse but Failing to Find Him"   111
47. Li Shen, "Pitying the Farmer"   111
48. Li Te-yü, "To Patriarch Sun at Hua-yang Grotto"   112
49. Li Ho, "At Ch'ang-ku, Reading: To Show to My Man Pa"   113
    "My Man Pa Replies"   113
    "Ravine on a Cold Evening"   113
50. Autumn Maid Tu, "The Robe of Golden Thread"   114
51. Li Shang-yin, "Master Chia"   114
52. P'i Jih-hsiu, "Impromptu on a Hangover"   115
53. Yü Hsüan-chi, "On a Visit to Ch'ung-chen Taoist Temple I See
        in the South Hall the List of Successful Candidates in the
        Imperial Examinations"   116
54. Mei Yao-ch'en, "Sharing Lodging with Hsieh Shih-hou in the
        Library of the Hsü Family and Being Much Bothered by
        the Noise of Rats"   116
    "Shih-hou Pointed Out to Me That from Ancient Times
        There Had Never Been a Poem on the Subject of Lice,
        and Urged Me to Try Writing One"   117
55. Wang An-shih, "Bald Mountain"   118
56. Su Shih, "When Yü-k'o Painted Bamboo"   119
    "Reading the Poetry of Meng Chiao"   119
    "Lament of the Farm Wife of Wu"   120
57. Huang T'ing-chien, "To Go with Shih K'o's Painting of an Old
        Man Tasting Vinegar"   121
58. Yang Wan-li, "Watching a Village Festival"   122
    "Songs of Depression" (two selections)   122
59. Lu Yu, "The Merchant's Joy"   123
    "Written in a Carefree Mood"   124
    "To Show to My Sons"   124
60. Wen T'ien-hsiang, "Chin-ling Post Station"   125

61. Chao Meng-fu, "To a Pyrotechnist"   125
62. Yang Wei-chen, "Mating"   126
63. Ni Tsan, "Inscribed on a Painting by Myself"   127
64. Hsü Pen, "Saying Goodbye to a Monk from Japan"   127
65. Kao Ch'i, "Written on Seeing the Flowers, and Remembering
        My Daughter"   128
      "Silkworm Song of Torchlit Fields"   129
66. Yang Shih-ch'i, "Night Rain: A Wall Collapses"   129
67. Shen Chou, "The Taoist Huang Has Died of Alcoholism"   130
68. Yang Hsün-chi, "Inscribed on the Doors of My Bookshelves"   130
69. Chu Yün-ming, "A Fan from Korea"   131
70. Wang Chiu-ssu, "Ballad of Selling a Child"   132
71. Ho Ching-ming, "Ballad of the Government Granary Clerk"   133
72. Huang Ě, [Title Lost]   134
73. Li K'ai-hsien, "A Parable"   135
      "Earthquake"   136
74. Hsü Wei, "A Buddhist Monk Cut and Burned His Own Flesh
        to Make the Rains Stop—a Man from His Native Place
        Asked Me to Write a Poem to Send to Him"   137
      "A Kite"   138
75. Tsung Ch'en, "Song of Selling Flowers"   138
76. Mo Shih-lung, "Saying Good-bye to a Singing Girl Who Has
        Decided to Become a Nun"   139
77. T'ang Hsien-tsu, "Twenty-Two Quatrains on Receiving the
        Obituary Notice for My Son Shih-ch'ü"   139
78. Yüan Hung-tao, "The 'Slowly, Slowly' Poem"   140
      "On Receiving My Letter of Termination"   141
79. Wu Chia-chi, "The Grain-Barge Wife"   141
80. Wu Li, "Singing of the Source of Holy Church"   143
81. Wang Shih-chen, "Medicine"   144
82. K'ang-hsi, "Lines in Praise of a Self-Chiming Clock"   144
83. Cheng Hsieh, "Song of Surfing on the Bore"   145
84. Yüan Mei, "On the Way to Pa-ling"   145

Lyrics and Arias

85. Attributed to Li Po, "A Suite in the *Ch'ing-p'ing* Mode"   147
86. Anonymous, Tune: "Magpie on the Branch"; a Lyric from
        Tun-huang   149
87. Liu Yü-hsi, Tune: "Memories of the South"; a Spring Lyric
        After Po Chü-yi   150
88. Wen T'ing-yün, Tune: "Deva-Like Barbarian"   150
89. Wei Chuang, Tune: "The Bodhisattva Foreigner"   151
90. Ou-yang Chiung, Tune: "Offering Congratulations to the
        Enlightened Reign"   152
91. Li Yü, Tune: "The Crow's Nocturnal Cry"   153
      Tune: "New Bounty of Royalty"   154

	Tune: "Pure Serene Music"	154
	Tune: "Memories of the South"; A Reminiscence	155
92.	Liu Yung, Tune: "Bells Ringing in the Rain"; Sadness of Parting	155
93.	Fan Chung-yen, Tune: "Sumuche Dancers"	156
94.	Yen Shu, Tune: "Spring in the Jade House"	157
95.	Ou-yang Hsiu, Tune: "Drunk in Fairyland"	158
96.	Su Shih, Tune: "Partridge Sky"; Written While Banished to Huang-chou	158
	Tune: "Fragrance Fills the Courtyard"	159
	Tune: "Immortal by the River"	160
97.	Huang T'ing-chien, Tune: "The Courtyard Full of Fragrance"; Tea	160
	Tune: "A Thousand Autumns"	161
98.	Ch'in Kuan, Tune: "Sand of Silk-Washing Brook"; A Spring Morning	162
	Tune: "Perfumed Garden"; Bidding Adieu	163
99.	Li Chih-yi, Tune: "The Diviner"	163
100.	Chu Tun-ju, Tune: "Nien-nu Is Charming"	164
101.	Li Ch'ing-chao, Tune: "Rouged Lips"; Naïveté	165
	Tune: "Magnolia Flowers" (short version)	166
	Tune: "Fisherman's Pride"; A Dream	166
	"A Long Melancholy Tune (Autumn Sorrow)"; Despair	167
	Tune: "Spring at Wu Ling"; Spring Ends	168
102.	Hsin Ch'i-chi, Tune: "Spring in the Ch'in Garden" (About to swear off drinking, he warns the wine cup to go away)	169
	Tune: "Pure Serene Music"; Rural Life	170
103.	Wu Wen-ying, Tune: "Rouged Lips"; Rain Just Over on the Night of the Lantern Preview	171
104.	Chang Yen, Tune: "Pure Serene Music"	171
105.	Kuan Han-ch'ing, In the Southern Mode, to the Tune of "A Sprig of Flowers"; The Refusal to Get Old	172
106.	Tu Shan-fu, Tune, "Shua Hai-erh"; Country Cousin at the Theater	174
107.	Ma Chih-yüan, Tune: "Heaven-Cleansed Sands"; Autumn Thoughts	176
108.	Chang Yang-hao, [Untitled]	177
109.	Kuan Yün-shih, Tune: "Rapt with Wine, Loudly Singing—Joy in Spring's coming"; My Love	178
110.	Wang Ho-ch'ing, Tune: "Tsui-chung T'ien"; To the Giant Butterfly	179
	Tune: "Po Pu-tuan"; Long-Haired Little Dog	179
	Tune: "Po Pu-tuan"; Fat Couple	180
111.	Anonymous, Tune: "San-fan Yü-lou Jen"	180
112.	Yang Na, Tune: "Hung Hsiu-hsieh"; To a Flea	181
113.	Anonymous, Tune: "Wu Yeh-erh"; Twitting the Teller of Tall Tales	181

114. Anonymous, In the Chung Mode, to the Tune of "P'u T'ien
Lo"   182
115. Yün-k'an Tzu, [Untitled]   182
116. Ali Hsiying, "Lazy Cloud's Nest" 1 and 2   183
117. Yang Shen, Tune: "Moon Over West River"   184
118. Liu Shih, Tune: "Dreaming of Southland"; Thinking of
Someone   184
119. Wu Li, Tune: "Happily Flitting Oriole"; From Music of
Harmonious Heaven in Reverent Thanks to the Lord
of Heaven   189
120. Nara Singde, Tune: "As If in a Dream"   189
121. Wang Kuo-wei, Tune: "Sand of Silk-Washing Brook"   190

Elegies and Rhapsodies

122. Attributed to Ch'ü Yüan, "Heavenly Questions"   192
123. Chia Yi, "The Owl"   208
124. Mei Ch'eng, "Seven Stimuli"   211
125. Ch'eng-kung Sui, "Rhapsody on Whistling"   229
126. T'ao Ch'ien, "The Return"   235
127. Su Shih, "Red Cliff Rhapsody"   238

Folk and Folklike Songs, Ballads, and Narrative Verse

128. Liu Pang, "Song of the Great Wind"   241
129. Ssu-ma Hsiang-ju, "Cock-Phoenix, Hen-Phoenix"   241
130. Anonymous, "Ground-Thumping Song"   242
131. Li Yen-nien, "A Song"   243
132. Attributed to Hsi-chün, "Lost Horizon"   243
133. Anonymous, "Song of the Viet Boatman"   244
134. Anonymous, "Mulberry Up the Lane"   245
135. Anonymous, From the "Nineteen Old Poems"   247
"Green, Green Riverside Grass"   247
136. Anonymous, "They Fought South of the Wall"   247
137. Anonymous, "Crows on City Walls"; a Children's Ditty from
the Early Years of the Reign of the Later Han Emperor
Huan   248
138. Anonymous or attributed to Ts'ai Yung, "Watering Horses at a
Long Wall Hole"   249
139. Ts'ao Ts'ao, "Song on Enduring the Cold"   250
140. Fu Hsüan, "Pity Me!"   251
141. Anonymous, "Midnight Songs"   253
142. Anonymous, "A Peacock Southeast Flew"   255
143. Pao Chao, "Magic Cinnabar"   265
144. Pao Ling-hui, "Added to a Letter Sent to a Traveler"   266
145. Anonymous, "The Ballad of Mulan"   267
146. Hulü Chin, "Song of the Tölös"   269

147. Anonymous, "Song of the Breaking of the Willow"   269
148. Wang Wei, "Army Ballad"   270
149. Po Chü-yi, "The Song of Lasting Regret"   270
150. Po Chü-yi and Yüan Chen, "Iranian Whirling Girls"   278
151. Anonymous, "Poem of Medicine Puns"   281
152. Yao Chen, "Ballad on the Investigation of a Disaster"   283
153. Li Mi-an, "The Half-and-Half Song"   284
154. Feng Meng-lung, "Mountain Songs"   285
155. Chiu Tsz-yung, "A Lament for Fortune's Frailty"   287
156. Chin Ho, "Ballad of the Maiden of Lan-ling"   290

PART III. PROSE

Documents

157. Anonymous, "The Great Announcement," from the *Classic of
        Documents*   301
158. Wang Pao, "The Contract for a Youth"   304

History

159. Attributed to Tso Ch'iu-ming, "Two Brothers of Cheng and
        the Mother Who Doted on the Younger," from *The
        Commentary of Mr. Tso*   308
160. Pan Ku, "The Passing of Kung Sheng," from *History of the Han*   312

Moral Lessons

161. Yang Hsiung, Exemplary Sayings, Chapter 2   316
162. Pan Chao, Lessons for Women   320

Parallel Prose

163. Jen Fang, "Memorial of Indictment Against Liu Cheng"   328
164. Wang Po, Preface to "Ascending the Pavilion of King T'eng in
        Hung-chou on an Autumn Day for a Parting Feast"   333

Letters

165. Li Po, "Letter to Han Ching-chou"   342
166. Tsung Ch'en, "Letter in Reply to Liu Yi-chang"   345

Prefaces and Postfaces

167. Hsü Shen, Postface to *Explanation of Simple and Compound
        Graphs*   348
168. Wang Hsi-chih, Preface to *Collected Poems from the Orchid
        Pavilion*   351

169. Liu Tsung-yüan, Preface to the "Foolish Brook Poems"   353
170. Li Ch'ing-chao, Postface to a Catalog on a Collection of Bronze
    and Stone Inscriptions   355

Discourses, Essays, and Sketches

171. Hsi K'ang, "Discourse on Nourishing Life"   359
172. T'ao Ch'ien, "The Peach Blossom Spring"   364
173. Han Yü, An Explication of "Progress in Learning"   366
174. Ou-yang Hsiu, "The Three Zithers"   375
    "A Record of the Pavilion of an Intoxicated Old Man"   376
175. Shen Kua, ["On a UFO"], from *Brush Talks from Dream Brook*   377
176. Chang Tai, "Liu Ching-t'ing the Storyteller"   378
    "Professional Matchmakers," from *Dream Memories of West
    Lake*   380
177. Wei Hsüeh-yi, "Account of a Peach-Stone Boat"   382
178. Lin Ssu-huan, "The Vocal Mimic"   384
179. Li Yü, "The Arts of Sleeping, Walking, Sitting, and Standing,"
    from *The Arts of Living*   386
180. Yüan Mei, "Thoughts upon Student Huang's Borrowing of
    Books"   390

Travelogues and Scenic Descriptions

181. Laymen of Mount Lu Associated with Hui-yüan, "A Poem on
    Wandering at the Stone Gate," with Introduction   392
182. Yang Hsüan-chih, "The Establishment of the White Horse
    Temple," from *The Record of the Monasteries of Loyang*   395
183. Fan Ch'eng-ta, "A Climb Up Mount Omei," from *Diary of a
    Boat Trip to Wu*   397
184. Chou Mi, "Observing the Tidal Bore," from *Reminiscences of
    Wu-lin*   405

Miscellanea

185. Fan Sheng-chih, *Fan Sheng-chih's Book*, Chapter 1: "Basic
    Principles of Farming"   407
186. Anonymous, "Miscellanies, Secret H," A Fragment   410
187. Li Shang-yin, *Li Shang-yin's Miscellany*   412
188. Anonymous, Lay Student Notations from Tun-huang   425
189. Ch'ü Ching-ch'un, "That Which Is Mandated by Heaven Is
    Called Nature"   426
190. Jokes   430

Biographies, Autobiographies, and Memoirs

191. Ch'en Shou, "The Biography of Hua-t'o," from *History of the
    Three Kingdoms*   441

192. Yeh Meng-te, "Physicians Cannot Raise the Dead"   450
193. Lu Yü, "The Autobiography of Instructor Lu"   452
194. Liu Tsung-yüan, "Biography of the Child Ou Chi"   456
195. P'i Jih-hsiu, "Biography of a Girl Surnamed Chao"   458
196. Lu Jung, "The Biography of A-liu"   459
197. Hou Fang-Yü, "The Biography of Actor Ma"   460

Fictional and Fictionalized Biographies and Autobiographies

198. Han Yü, "The Biography of Fur Point"   463
199. Lu Kuei-meng, "Biography of the Vagrant of Rivers and Lakes"   466

PART IV. FICTION

Rhetorical Persuasions and Allegories

200. Compiled by Liu Hsiang, *Intrigues of the Warring States*   471
201. Liu Tsung-yüan, "The Donkey of Ch'ien"   474

Anecdotal Fiction

202. Liu Yi-ch'ing, *A New Account of Tales of the World*   476

Tales of the Strange

203. Attributed to Liu Hsiang, *Biographies of Transcendents*   479
204. Kan Pao, Preface to and Tales from *Search for the Supernatural* 480
205. P'u Sung-ling, *Strange Tales from Make-Do Studio*   485
206. Chi Yün, *Sketches from the Cottage for the Contemplation of
         Subtleties*   496

Classical-Language Short Stories

207. Yüan Chen, "The Story of Ying-ying"   507
208. Li Kung-tso, "An Account of the Governor of the Southern
         Branch"   517

Vernacular Short Stories

209. Anonymous, "The Shrew: Sharp-Tongued Ts'ui-lien"   529
210. Feng Meng-lung, "The Canary Murders"   551

Novels

211. Attributed to Wu Ch'eng-en, *The Journey to the West*, Chapter 7 566
212. Anonymous, "Wu Sung Beats the Tiger," from *Water Margin*,
         with Commentary by Chin Sheng-t'an   581
213. Ts'ao Hsüeh-ch'in, "A Burial Mound for Flowers," from *Dream
         of Red Towers*   591

PART V. ORAL AND PERFORMING ARTS

Prosimetric Narratives

214. Anonymous, "Transformation Text on Mahāmaudgalyāyana
        Rescuing His Mother from the Underworld with Pictures,
        One Scroll, with Preface"   607
215. Tung Chieh-yuan, *Master Tung's Western Chamber Romance*,
        Chapter 2   643

Drama

216. Kuan Han-ch'ing, *Injustice to Tou Ŏ*   673
217. T'ang Hsien-tsu, *The Peony Pavilion*, Scene 7   713
218. Anonymous, "The Mortal Thoughts of a Nun," from a Popular
        Drama   721

  Principal Chinese Dynasties and Periods   725
  Romanization Schemes for Modern Standard Mandarin   727
  List of Permissions   732

INTRODUCTION

This *Shorter Columbia Anthology of Traditional Chinese Literature* is based on *The Columbia Anthology of Traditional Chinese Literature*, which first appeared in 1994. After the original anthology was published, the need for a streamlined edition was repeatedly expressed to the editor and to the press. In particular, many teachers at community colleges and liberal arts colleges found the original anthology too lengthy for the type of courses they offered. They liked the commentaries and the contents but regretted that there was too much of both for their students to digest. In response to their requests, we are offering this revised and abridged version.

In this new work, the basic conceptual structure of the original is retained. The arrangement of the texts and commentaries remains the same. The major difference is that the size of the book has been reduced by almost half. The scope of the *Shorter Anthology* is still quite generous, however, with 218 selections (compared to 278 in the original, unabridged anthology). This reduction of size but retention of overall scope and maintenance of general nature has been achieved in the following ways: some of the longer fiction has been removed; where the original anthology gave four or five parallel examples of a given genre, the number has now been reduced to two or three; the amount of poetry representing each poet has been cut by one- to two-thirds; and several of the more esoteric texts and obscure authors have been eliminated. In the spirit of the original, I have striven to use only integral texts. Nothing is more annoying to a reader of translated literature than encountering ellipses at every turn, causing him or her to wonder what was left out and why.

Although every effort has been made to pare down the liberal dimensions of the original anthology to a more manageable and portable size, all the special favorites have been kept, such as the jokes, medieval doodles, the aphorisms of Li Shang-yin, the raucous tale of the sharp-tongued shrew, and the poem consisting of puns on the names of medicines. The sole addition has been the inclusion of the complete play *Injustice to Tou Ŏ*, of which formerly only one act was included. This most beloved and revealing of Yüan dramas thus takes the place of a rare comedy with a slight anti-Buddhist tinge.

The primary purpose of this anthology is to provide a broad selection of expertly translated texts from the widest possible variety of sources while staying within the limits of a portable text. My aim throughout has been to give a sense of the full range of Chinese literature. The editorial principles I have employed do not restrict literature to belles lettres in the narrowest sense. For the purposes of this anthology, literature is construed very broadly as writing that is vivid or imaginative. Literature may be driven by a lyrical impulse or generated by a narrative intent; it may even be chiefly descriptive or expository. A text might be concerned with any sort of subject matter or be written in virtually any genre or form; so long as it has esthetic merit or genuine emotional appeal (apart from whatever its original purpose may have been), it can be considered literature. This anthology attempts to show that many different types of written texts might be thought of as literature.

The rather narrow limits that have heretofore been used with regard to "Chinese literature" necessitate an enlargement of the canon. To a certain extent, then, this is meant to be an iconoclastic anthology. As soon as we free ourselves from the customary constraints imposed by the concept of what is "classical," we discover that an enormous number of interesting texts are available for consideration. Throughout history, the tradition was constantly reshaped in response to a host of literary and nonliterary factors. And, in retrospective fashion, it will go on being remade in response to similar factors. Chinese literature, like Chinese culture as a whole, is not a seamless, monochromatic fabric. Anthologists and literary historians who emphasize only standard genres and elite writers are responsible for perpetuating a false image of what Chinese literature might be for our own age.

I have attempted to choose texts that reveal what people from all levels and sectors of society in China thought, felt, believed, and did. The China of this anthology is not an idealized land conceived of by thinkers and scholars isolated from the lives of the masses. The full literary record in China offers a rich source of information, images, and impressions to complement those of the official historiographers and the Confucian bureaucrats. A conscious effort has been made to include material by and about women, minority nationalities, farmers, soldiers, merchants, physicians, and others, to comprise people from all walks of life.

On the other hand, I have by no means avoided the most sophisticated, mannered, and abstruse kinds of texts, which were an important part of Chinese culture as a whole. China's literati-officials were the greatest bureaucrats the world has ever seen. They created a stable institutional system that, despite the vicissitudes of periodic war and recurrent dynastic change, persisted for more than two thousand years, until 1911. They were also accomplished poets and essayists who had their roots in the social and political thinkers of the Warring States period, among whom the most distinguished were Confucius, Mencius, Hsün Tzu, Han Fei Tzu, and the like. An abiding characteristic of premodern China was that the bureaucracy and the intelligentsia overlapped almost completely. To be a respected statesman, one was almost always required to be a passable poet. It was only with the intrusion of Western ways that the old institutions of literati dominance and control disintegrated beyond all hope of repair.

Before China was confronted by Western ideas and objects in the late nineteenth and twentieth centuries, with a nearly complete capitulation to such notions as science, democracy, and communism and the resultant collapse of literati authority, the West had already begun to influence Chinese thought, learning, literature, and technology by the sixteenth century. Indeed, I have tried to show in this volume that China was never separated from the rest of the world. China-watchers (and many Chinese themselves) have long accepted a Middle Kingdom mentality according to which this great East Asian empire was allegedly sealed off from the rest of the world. Nothing could be further from the truth, as is amply shown by the cosmopolitan character of many of the texts collected here.

A third guideline in the compilation of this anthology was to avoid a preponderance of works that have been overanthologized in the past. I have assiduously sought out previously untranslated works, although a few old favorites (such as T'ao Ch'ien's famous essay on "The Peach Blossom Spring" and Su Shih's inimitable Red Cliff rhapsody) were inevitable. This reader offers many exciting items that have never before been made available in the West and others that are scarcely known even in China but richly deserving of fuller recognition.

A fourth goal of this anthology is to introduce new and different translators. I did not wish to reprint once again translations by those whose works have been anthologized repeatedly. Aside from a few instances where earlier translators have been chosen for special effect, all the translators in this volume are attuned to the spirit and needs of students at the turn of the twenty-first century. This choice is by no means to denigrate the splendid achievements of our predecessors, but I see little reason to anthologize yet again translations of a century or half-century ago that have already been offered to the public in one guise or another.

A fifth principle for the compilation of this reader is that integral texts are used as much as possible in order not to mystify the reader with omissions and paraphrases at every turn. Hence, an entire chapter of a novel is included to give the reader an idea of how Chinese narrative progresses, as well as an entire play, rather than bits and pieces. Chinese verse being what it is, most of the poems gathered here are short, although I have made a special effort to include some of the longest poems in Chinese literature. This anthology strives to strike a balance between long and short pieces so as not to give a false impression of the character of Chinese literature and to prevent monotony.

As shown in the table of contents, the works included here have been divided into several broad categories and a larger number of subcategories. These categories and subcategories should be considered only one possible scheme among many that may be employed for the classification of Chinese literature. Even a distinction between prose and poetry is inadequate when attempting to deal with Chinese literary texts. There are, for instance, genres such as the rhapsody (*fu*) and parallel prose (*p'ien-t'i-wen*), which seem to straddle the boundary between prose and poetry. And what do we do with the ubiquitous prosimetric or *chantefable* form of popular literary texts in which verse sections regularly alternate with prose? Such problems are the despair of theorists and historians who aspire to a neat classification scheme embracing the whole of Chinese literature. Nonetheless, the arrangement of this anthology according to type and genre instead of stubbornly following a chronological scheme enables students to grasp more readily the reality that Chinese literature is not an indistinguishable mass of unfamiliar names and titles. Within the various sections of the anthology, works are arranged by date and by author. Particularly for the earlier texts, however, dating is uncertain and authorship is often unknown.

The reader will note that biography and autobiography are particularly well represented in this anthology. The reasons for this are many, chiefly the fact that much of the finest literature in China was written in the form of biography; strictly in terms of sheer literary merit, biography deserves to occupy a prominent position in any anthology of Chinese literature. Furthermore, a large proportion of Chinese history—both official and unofficial— was written in the form of biography. Consequently, several of the biographical pieces selected in this anthology could also have been placed under that category.

Three other types of literature that are well represented in the present anthology are the rhapsody and various popular genres derived from prosimetric oral storytelling. The former is stressed because it constitutes the first flowering of descriptive and imaginative literature, albeit one that is often issued under a thin veil of didacticism. The latter is emphasized because it was from the oral and performing arts that fiction and drama in China took their lifeblood. Aside from a generous selection of works that derive from the oral and performing arts, I have also included texts in other genres that describe performers and their profession. And, although next to nothing survives of genuine, unadulterated folk literature from the premodern period, I have selected some texts that adumbrate its qualities and concerns. Due consideration for folk and popular literature is a fundamental premise of this anthology because it is through them that the tradition was continuously rejuvenated and rescued from stultification and stasis.

Chinese literature was overwhelmingly dominated by men until the twentieth century. Nonetheless, I have made a special attempt to include works by and about women. Except where noted, however, all authors in this volume are male — even in many cases where the poetic voice is female.[1]

This is an integrated reader in the sense that the various works collected here are viewed not as separate entities but as part of an organic whole. Each text or group of texts is numbered for ease of reference. Extensive cross-referencing is provided, for most of the texts in this anthology refer or allude to one or more of the other texts. By structure and design, the entire anthology is an exercise in intertextual analysis. The notes indicate themes and images that recur in different genres dating from different periods. It is surprising, for example, how often tidal bores and cockfighting reappear in texts that are widely separated in time. But the fact that such motifs and allusions (as well as hundreds of others) recur time and time again in a self-referential way is an interesting feature of Chinese literature that should not be overlooked. It should also be pointed out that the notes, *in toto*, amount to an introduction to the history of Chinese literature.

Another facet of Chinese literature to which this anthology pays particular attention is its interrelationship with the other arts. For example, poems are included about paintings and other poems that were actually inscribed on objects, as are poems and essays that discuss the subject of painting and the arts in general. There are also reactions to different kinds of music and dance and appreciations of the skill of craftsmen. The anthology also includes a section on literary criticism and theory. This is somewhat unusual in an anthology of Chinese literature but nonetheless vital for understanding what the Chinese themselves thought of their own literary tradition.

Many of the texts in this anthology have been chosen for their potential to stimulate classroom discussion. There are many reasons for college and university students to become excited by reading a Chinese text. One of these is its similarity to or contrast with something from their own tradition. For example, the transformation text on Maudgalyāyana's journey to hell in search of his mother bears fruitful comparison with Dante's *Inferno* and parts of Milton's *Paradise Lost*. The narrative poem about the female warrior Mulan immediately calls to mind Joan of Arc. Parts of *The Journey to the West* are reminiscent of Rabelais. And so on.

This anthology presupposes no prior knowledge of Chinese languages, writing, or history. It has been purposely designed not just for students at large research universities with many sinologists on the faculty and extensive

---

1. The principles concerning the matters discussed in the above paragraphs used in this reader are more fully developed in my "Anthologizing and Anthropologizing: The Place of Nonelite and Nonstandard Culture in the Chinese Literary Tradition," in Eugene Eoyang and Lin Yao-fu, ed., *Translating Chinese Literature* (Bloomington and Indianapolis: Indiana University Press, 1995), pp. 231–261.

library resources. Rather, it has been expressly created to satisfy the needs of students at small colleges, which have only one faculty member handling all aspects of Chinese civilization (and often of other Asian civilizations as well). To be sure, I would be most gratified if readers who do not have any academic affiliation became acquainted with and learned to appreciate Chinese literature through this book.

Three decades of teaching Chinese literature to undergraduates at Tunghai, Harvard, and Penn have taught me that it does not pay to overwhelm students with too much material. A deluge of texts by a host of authors is not nearly so effective as a few carefully chosen items by a smaller number of the most interesting writers. Students absorb a limited dose of material from an unfamiliar culture much better this way than when a massive quantity of it is thrown at them. It makes no sense to strive for comprehensiveness in a book of this sort. This is, after all, an anthology, and it is the job of the anthologist to pick and choose. At the same time, I recognize the existence of two counterpoised demands: the obligation to provide a representative sample of the entire breadth of Chinese literature in all its abundance, and the desire to satisfy the special interests of as many instructors and students as possible. Beyond striving judiciously to meet both demands, I wish to offer a few pleasant surprises for those who may already have become somewhat jaded by reading too much in one small corner of the universe of Chinese literature or who have prematurely succumbed to stereotypes about its supposed exoticism and overrefinement. My hope is that this anthology will be one from which everyone will be enticed to taste, not necessarily devour from cover to cover (although that, too, would be gratifying).

In the end, the responsible anthologist can do no more than select from the vast abundance that confronts him those items that he is prepared to justify on the grounds of sheer literary excellence or lasting significance. While trying to cover as many different genres and types of subject matter as feasible within the confines of approximately 725 pages, I have also kept a sharp lookout for quality. I have searched for pieces that are animated and esthetically pleasing, since these are the most attractive and memorable for undergraduates. Unless a text has demonstrable literary virtues or provides valuable insights and remarkable impressions (whether social or intellectual), I have not considered it for inclusion. The same holds for the most sophisticated examples of belles lettres and for the most vibrant, earthy texts from the folk and popular realms. Above all, I did not want this anthology to be a stale collection of the same old chestnuts that have been presented repeatedly as the quintessence of Chinese literature. I hope that readers of this anthology will for the first time be exposed to the true richness of the Chinese literary tradition, not just a preconceived notion of what is "elevated."

I view this anthology as a companion volume to the venerable *Sources of Chinese Tradition*, also published by Columbia University Press and now in a totally revised second edition. As such, it avoids duplicating the types of material available in *Sources*. Texts dealing with religion, thought, philosophy, and institutions are not included in this volume unless they have demonstrated literary merit or significance. This anthology could very well be used as the primary textbook for a one-semester general course on traditional Chinese literature or as an ancillary text for introductory courses on Chinese history, civilization, society, and culture. Nevertheless, because of the high literary quality and unavailability elsewhere of the translations that this volume offers, many instructors may wish to assign it, perhaps together with other materials, for more specialized courses on Chinese literature (poetry, prose, fiction, and drama) as well.

Apart from a couple of texts (specified in the annotations), all selections in this anthology were originally written in one of the following languages:

1. Classical Chinese (also sometimes called Literary Chinese or Literary Sinitic) in a wide variety of styles
2. Medieval Vernacular Sinitic, also in several variants
3. Early Mandarin, with extremely rare admixtures from the non-standard Sinitic topolects and from non-Sinitic languages
4. Buddhist Hybrid Sinitic

The task of preparing another anthology of Chinese folk, popular, and "minority" literature that will include texts written in the many other Sinitic and non-Sinitic languages of China remains to be fulfilled, although Mark Bender and I are more than halfway through its compilation.

With a handful of exceptions (e.g., a retired school teacher from Shanghai, two distinguished American poets, a deceased British missionary-sinologist, a Chinese author of international stature, and so on), the majority of translators whose works are included in this volume are professional sinologists teaching in American universities. Although they are all highly skilled, each has his or her own style of translation, some striving more for accuracy while others are more concerned with felicity. No matter what their preferences, however, all are subject to a universal rule for translators of Chinese texts. Namely, the highly elliptical nature of written Sinitic languages, especially Classical Chinese, makes it necessary for any translator of a work of Chinese literature to add numerous components for the product of his or her labor to make sense in English. Where a Chinese sentence will often omit the subject or another part of speech in a sentence and may not specify sex, number, tense, or mood, the requirements of English grammar generally demand that such elements be supplied. Strict translation has precise conventions (mainly the use of parentheses and brackets) for designating which elements have been added and which were already present in the original text. So as not to interfere with the smooth reading of these texts by nonspecialists, all such technical apparatuses have been removed, except in rare circumstances where their retention is deemed appropriate to convey information that is significant for the general reader. Occasionally, it has also been necessary to make other minor changes in the translations so that readers will not be confused by varying conventions.

Similarly, translations from Chinese are often studded with Chinese characters (i.e., sinographs). Since they would clearly be useless and out of place in an anthology of this nature, all sinographs have been removed except in one text that deals with the nature of the writing system itself. Likewise, there is no point in providing long strings of transcribed Chinese syllables for readers to whom they would only be so many meaningless sounds. Hence, titles of poems or essays are normally given only in translation, although the titles of important books are also provided in romanized form for ease of reference.

Save when a consecutive group of translations has been done by one person (in which case her or her name appears at the end of the series in question), the names of the translators of all the selections in this anthology are given at the bottom of each piece.

Aside from half a dozen special cases (to be discussed below), annotations have been kept to a bare minimum. This is in part to prevent the book from becoming too bulky, but also because overly detailed notes and commentaries would only distract from the pleasure of reading the works themselves and, in any event, would not be easily assimilated by the typical reader. Indeed, the constant purpose of the editor has been to devise translations that can stand on their own as literary texts in English without elaborate notes. There are, however, two situations in which fuller annotations are called for and for which a relatively greater number of explanatory notes are provided. The first is for the heuristic purpose of demonstrating how traditional Chinese commentators read and explicated literary texts. The second is when the original work is so densely allusive or highly symbolic that it is virtually impossible to understand without extensive commentary. In general, the notes avoid technicalities and do not deal with such narrow matters as textual emendations and identifications of place names.

In this and the following few paragraphs, I shall discuss several additional technical and mechanical aspects of this anthology. First is the question of how to represent the sounds of sinographs. It should be stated emphatically that the pronunciation of Chinese characters has varied greatly through history and across the geographic expanse of this great empire. It is only a convention that we use Modern Standard Mandarin (hereafter MSM) to represent the sinographs in our writings about China. In many ways, MSM is the least satisfactory of all Sinitic languages for reading aloud traditional Chinese texts. Certainly it would be better to recite early poetry in Cantonese or Fukienese, which preserve significant features of the ancient phonology. This is ironic since languages such as Cantonese and Fukienese are farther removed from the center of Sinitic civilization and were incorporated into the cultural sphere of China relatively late. The main explanation for this phenomenon is that peripheral extensions of a cultural entity frequently tend to be the most conservative. Furthermore, north China was often dominated to some extent by non-Sinitic peoples. Särbi, Tibetan, Tabgatch, Tangut, Khitan, Jürchen, Mongol, and Manchu rulers (to name a few) established dynasties or kingdoms that controlled all or part of north China. The latter two groups, in fact, succeeded in gaining control over the whole of China for considerable periods and expanded the military and political might of the empire beyond the limits of what it had been under ethnic Han rulers. Under such circumstances, a heavy Altaic impact (lexical, grammatical, phonological, and otherwise) on northern Sinitic languages such as Mandarin was unavoidable. Consequently, Mandarin as it is spoken today is furthest removed from the older stages of Sinitic and thus least suitable for representing the sounds of most of the works of literature collected in this volume. Yet there is a nearly universal practice among scholars who write about Chinese history in alphabetic languages to use the sounds of MSM as the sole phonetic realization of the sinographs. I believe that Sinology in the twenty-first century will almost certainly progress to a stage where references to proper nouns relating to earlier periods and regional cultures will routinely be provided in the reconstructions or transcriptions that appropriately and accurately reflect their actual pronunciation instead of in the artificial construct of MSM.

Granting that at present we are obliged (because of inadequate historical reconstructions and a paucity of topolectal handbooks) to use MSM as the sole phoneticization of the sinographs, we are faced with the necessity of making a choice among numerous competing transcriptions of MSM. The one adopted for this anthology is a slightly modified form of Wade-Giles, the old sinological standard.[2] Wade-Giles romanization of MSM is still used by the overwhelming majority of sinologists and nearly all major academic research libraries in English-speaking countries. Furthermore, the vast bulk of accumulated scholarly writing in English about Chinese literature employs the Wade-Giles system. It would be terribly confusing and difficult for students

2. A few special spellings have been adopted. Chow is used to transcribe the name of the depraved and tyrannical last emperor of the Shang dynasty in order to distinguish him from the succeeding Chou dynasty. Wey is used to differentiate the Chou dynasty state from the Warring States kingdom Wei. Yi is used throughout instead of I so as not to be confused with the first-person English pronoun (except for Yee, which signifies the name of a freehold during the Shang period, and Yih, which stands for the name of a high official of the legendary ruler Yü, to distinguish him from the famous archer Yi). Yüh is used as the alternative name for the legendary ruler Shun in order to distinguish him from Yü, who controlled the flood. Viet and Ngwa are used to signify the states of Yüeh and Wu in order to distinguish them from other names that are homophonous in MSM or to emphasize that the people of these ancient, southern states originally spoke non-Sinitic languages.

without any background in the study of Mandarin (the typical sort of student who will use this book) to try to follow up the readings herein with any sort of research whatsoever if another romanization system were chosen. Pinyin (the official romanized script of the People's Republic of China), however, has lately become widely current in the mass media and many introductory Mandarin courses use it exclusively, so I have included a conversion chart from Wade-Giles to pinyin for those who may already happen to be familiar with the latter. It should be noted that a few of the translations selected here originally employed pinyin or other transcription systems; these have uniformly been converted to Wade-Giles for the sake of consistency. Because scores of translators were involved in the making of this anthology, it has been virtually impossible to attain absolute uniformity with regard to such matters as capitalization, hyphenation, and diacriticals. Each individual brings to the task of translation his or her own expertise and style. This is a distinct advantage for a work in which a wide variety of literary texts must be interpreted, but it does pose the difficulty of dissimilarities in usage that cannot always be overcome with complete satisfaction for all parties concerned.

For ease of reference, line numbers are usually provided for poems eight or more lines in length except when they are clearly divided into easily identifiable stanzas or when they possess a strong narrative content. The lines of lyrics and arias have not been numbered, nor have those of rhapsodies unless the translator has specifically requested that they be so treated.

Chinese authors may have many different names, such as soubriquets, styles, studio names, pen names, nicknames, fancy names, cognomens, milk (i.e., baby) names, and so on. Even in the last century, a well-known author like Lu Hsün (not his real name!) employed more than a hundred aliases. To avoid hopeless confusion, I have usually referred to authors and other individuals only by the name by which they are best known.

I have found it convenient to introduce one new English word in the translations, namely "tricent." This means "three hundred [paces]" (approximately a third of a mile) and is modeled on the word "mile" (from Latin *mille*, i.e., "[a] thousand [paces]"). Sinologists have long felt the need for such a word to render accurately the Chinese unit of length *li* because the same syllable is also used to transcribe the following frequently cited terms: "principle," "rites/ritual/etiquette/ceremony/civility," "benefit/profit/gain," "ward," as well as another smaller unit of length (1/3 millimeter), a unit of weight (.05 grams), a unit of area (.666 square meters), a monetary unit (one-thousandth of a Chinese dollar), a unit of monthly interest (0.1 percent), and so forth. Simply to transcribe *li* would, at best, be meaningless for an American reader and, at worst, ambiguous or misleading. "Tricent" is an exact equivalent of *li* in the sense of a third of a mile, and it represents a happy solution to a difficult problem in sinological translation that the majority of contributors whom I have consulted welcome warmly.

BIBLIOGRAPHICAL NOTE

The most important source of information for the brief introductory notes has been *The Indiana Companion to Traditional Chinese Literature* (Bloomington: Indiana University Press, 1986), William H. Nienhauser Jr. (Editor and Compiler), Charles Hartman (Associate Editor for Poetry), Y. W. Ma (Associate Editor for Fiction), and Stephen H. West (Associate Editor for Drama). This is a magnificent reference tool and the first one to which readers should turn when they wish to pursue questions raised by the texts in this anthology. The entries in Nienhauser et al. are succinct and authoritative; in many cases it has been impossible to simplify them further. The bibliographies are ample and provide citations to the best available scholarship in English, French, German, Russian, Chinese, Japanese, and other languages. A second volume of the *Indiana Companion* (1998), edited by Nienhauser with the assistance of Hartman and Scott W. Galer, has many new and substantial entries, plus hugely expanded and updated bibliographies. My debt to *The Indiana Companion* is great, and I wish to acknowledge it explicitly.

Another very valuable source of bibliographical information may be found on pages 303–446 of Wilt Idema and Lloyd Haft, *A Guide to Chinese Literature* (Ann Arbor: Center for Chinese Studies, University of Michigan, 1997). Also helpful for students who wish to do research on selected topics are the guides to Chinese prose, poetry, drama, and fiction published by G. K. Hall.

Other works frequently consulted in drawing up the annotations include Helwig Schmidt-Glintzer's *Geschichte der chinesischen Literatur: Die 3000jährige Entwicklung der poetischen, erzählenden und philosophisch-religiösen Literatur Chinas von den Anfängen bis zur Gegenwart* (Bern, Munich, Vienna: Scherz, 1990; Munich: C. H. Beck, 1999). This is the most comprehensive single-volume history of Chinese literature currently available in a Western language. It is up-to-date, full of valuable insights, and extensively documented. Also useful has been Eugen Feifel, *Geschichte der chinesischen Literatur: Mit Berücksichtigung ihres geistesgeschichtlichen Hintergrundes* (Hildesheim, Zurich, New York: Georg Olms, 1982). This compact volume, which is packed with detailed information, is based on Nagasawa Kikuya's *Shina gakujutsu bungeishi* (A *History of Chinese Scholarship and Literary Arts*, 3d ed. [Tokyo: Sanseidō), 1957]) but has expanded upon it considerably. Relying heavily on the excellent Czech school of sinology is the *Dictionary of Oriental Literatures*, vol. I, East Asia (New York: Basic Books, 1974), Jaroslav Průšek (General Editor) and Zbigniew Słupski (Volume Editor). Although the coverage of this volume is limited and the bibliographies are minimal, the quality of the entries is high and merits careful reading. Finally, there is the old standby James Robert Hightower, *Topics in Chinese Literature: Outlines and Bibliographies*, Harvard-Yenching Institute Studies, vol. III, rev. ed. (Cambridge: Harvard University Press, 1953). Although the bibliographies are out of date, the series of seventeen essays on various genres reveals the hand of a master. This remains the best survey of Chinese literature in brief compass for someone who desires a perceptive overview of the field.

Certain annotations have also been based on more specialized works. Among these are John Timothy Wixted's translation of Yoshikawa Kōjirō, *Five Hundred Years of Chinese Poetry, 1150–1650: The Chin, Yuan and Ming Dynasties* (Princeton: Princeton University Press, 1989), and Lois Fusek, *Among the Flowers* (New York: Cambridge University Press, 1982). I am especially indebted to the rich fund of folklore and historical data in Anne Birrell's two volumes *Popular Songs and Ballads of Han China* (London, Sydney, Wellington: Unwin Hyman, 1988) and *New Songs from Jade Terrace: An Anthology of Early Chinese Love Poetry* (London: George Allen and Unwin, 1982); they have served as the basis for a number of the annotations in this anthology, and both are available in more recent reprints. The commentaries and notes in Harold Shadick, *A First Course in Literary Chinese*, 3 vols. (Ithaca, London: Cornell University Press, 1968), have also been helpful. For the brief biographical notices of poets, I have relied heavily on Burton Watson, *The Columbia Book of Chinese Poetry: From Early Times to the Thirteenth Century* (New York: Columbia University Press, 1984), and Jonathan Chaves, *The Columbia Book of Later Chinese Poetry* (New York: Cambridge University Press, 1986). The introductions to and commentaries in Professor Watson's numerous other translations of Chinese literary texts have also been utilized extensively.

Finally, it should be noted that *The Columbia History of Chinese Literature*, by this volume's editor, is now in preparation. This is a comprehensive, one-volume treatment of all significant aspects of Chinese literature from the very beginning up to the present moment. Consisting of more than fifty authoritative chapters, the *Columbia History* is designed to complement this anthology and the original upon which it is based.

ACKNOWLEDGMENTS

Many colleagues offered their opinions for what should be deleted and what should be retained in this *Shorter Anthology*. While I have done my best to take their advice into account, it has not been possible to do so in every instance. Nonetheless, I deeply appreciate the detailed comments and thoughtful suggestions that were so generously proffered. Among those who responded to my request for advice about how to reduce the length of the original anthology, I am particularly grateful to Philip F. C. Williams, Robert Joe Cutter, Carrie E. Reed, David Prager Branner, and, above all, Anne Birrell, who sent in twenty handwritten pages of detailed comments. Several anonymous respondents also delivered useful lists of suggestions; I regret that I am unable to acknowledge them by name.

I am deeply grateful to all those individuals, including the translators, who have contributed annotations for the various selections in the anthology or who made suggestions about how to improve the annotations. In many instances where a translation was previously published, I have adapted the introductory note and annotations from the source in which it originally appeared. Often, however, the translator provided a completely new set of notes or I have written them myself because the old ones were not suitable for the purposes of this anthology.

Without naming each of them individually, I wish to thank en masse all those who made suggestions for improvements to the notes or for occasional corrections to the translations.

Some selections were made by popular acclaim. Many of the selections, however, purely reflect my own preferences and strong desire to represent all segments of society and all parts of the Chinese empire.

Naturally, an anthology of this scope would not have been possible without the cooperation of the numerous contributors. My thanks go out to each of them for kindly consenting to let their work become a part of this anthology. I am especially indebted to those contributors who prepared new translations or who permitted me to use translations that they hoped to publish themselves later on. Many of the works appearing here are available nowhere else.

Some of the translations have already appeared in various books and journals. I wish to register here my particular gratitude to their publishers and editors for granting permission to reprint in this anthology.

Most of the editorial work on this volume was carried out while I was a member of the Institute for Advanced Study (1998–1999) in Princeton, New Jersey. The Institute is a scholar's heaven. It provided the perfect environment in which to work on this anthology and on other projects.

I would like to express my particular gratitude to Jennifer Crewe, Editorial Director at Columbia University Press, for encouragement, support, and, most of all, sage guidance in the preparation of this volume. A roundtable on tools for teaching Chinese literature that she organized for a meeting of the Association for Asian Studies in Washington, DC, in 1997 was extremely valuable in helping me to formulate plans for the design of the *Shorter Anthology*.

Victor H. Mair
Swarthmore, Pennsylvania
June 21, 1999

HEILUNGKIANG

KIRIN

MONGOLIA

NNER

LIAONING

River

KOREA

Peking
Tientsin
HOPEI

Taiyuan
SHANSI

Tsinan Tsingtao
SHANTUNG
Mt. T'ai

Yellow Kaifeng
Sian Loyang Chengchow
Ch'ang-an)
ENSI HONAN
Huai R.
Nanking
HUPEI ANHWEI
Yangtze River
Ch'ien-
t'ang
R.
ngking Tung-t'ing
Lake CHEKIANG
Mt. P'o-
Lu yang
Lake
WEI— Changsha KIANGSI
OW HUNAN

FUKIEN

Chuanchow

KWANGSI KWANGTUNG
Canton

Yangchow
Soochow
Shanghai
Hangchow

KIANGSU

JAPAN

TAIWAN

HAINAN

CHINA

ᘉᘉᘉ Long   ᴜᴜᴜ Grand
Walls   Canal

PART I

Foundations and Interpretations

Divinations
and Inscriptions

1
A Late Shang Divination Record

Oracle Bone (early 12th century B.C.E)

(Preface:) Crack-making on *chia-shen* (day twenty-one), Ch'üch divined: **(Charge:)** "Lady Hao will give birth and it will be good." **(Prognostication:)** The king read the cracks and said: "If it be on a *ting* day that she give birth, it will be good. If it be on a *keng* day that she give birth, there will be

The kings of the late Shang period (c. 1200–1050 B.C.E.) attempted to communicate with the spiritual forces that ruled their world by reading the stress cracks in cattle scapulas and turtle plastrons. They and their diviners produced these cracks by applying a heated brand or poker to the bones or shells, intoning, as they did so, a charge that conveyed their intentions, wishes, or need to know. After the divination ritual was over, a record of the topic and, sometimes, of the prognostication and the result, was engraved into the bone. Those inscriptions, recovered only within the last hundred years by archeologists and painstakingly deciphered by paleographers, provide a direct contact with many of the Shang kings' daily activities and concerns. This inscription, like many, shows that the Shang king himself, in this case Wu Ting (ca. 1200–1180 B.C.E.), read the oracle. The ritual and spiritual ability to foretell the future was generally a royal monopoly; the diviners, such as Ch'üeh, rarely prognosticated in this way.

The inscriptions on the oracle bones represent the earliest written Sinitic texts. Since the script is in essence fully formed when it first appears and there are few if any indigenous precursors in the rich archeological record for the preceding millennia that reveal its gradual development, the origins of writing in China remain deeply puzzling. New discoveries and directions in research, however, are expected to throw light on this question.

For more information on the Chinese writing system, see selection 167.

prolonged luck." (**Verification:**) After thirty-one days, on *chia-yin* (day fifty-one), she gave birth. It was not good. It was a girl.

(**Preface:**) Crack-making on *chia-shen* (day twenty-one), Ch'üeh divined: (**Charge:**) "Lady Hao will give birth and it may not be good." (**Verification:**) After thirty-one days, on *chia-yin* (day fifty-one), she gave birth. It really was not good. It was a girl.

Translated by David N. Keightley

2

A Bronze Inscription of the Western Chou

To Yu ting [Tripod]

To Yu (Late Western Chou)

It was the tenth month; because the Hsien-yün arose and broadly attacked the Ching Garrison it was reported back to the king, who commanded Duke Wu: "Dispatch your premier troops and pursue at Ching Garrison." Duke Wu commanded To Yu to lead the duke's chariotry in pursuit at Ching Garrison. On *kuei-wei* (day twenty), the belligerents attacked Hsün, taking captives. To Yu westwardly pursued. On the morning of *chia-shen* (day twenty-one), striking at Mai, To Yu cut off heads and manacled prisoners to be interrogated; in all, using the duke's chariotry to cut off the heads of two hundred and . . . five men, manacling twenty-three prisoners to be interrogated, capturing one hundred and seventeen of the belligerents' chariots, and taking back the captives from among the people of Hsün. And then striking at Kung, he cut off the heads of thirty-six men, manacled two prisoners to be interrogated, and captured ten chariots. Following in pursuit and striking at Shih, To Yu again cut off heads and manacled prisoners to be interrogated. Then he raced in chase as far as Yang-chung, where the duke's chariotry cut off the heads of one hundred and fifteen men and manacled three prisoners to be interrogated. The captured chariots could not be taken and were burned, with only the horses driving the wounded and the recovered prison-

This recently discovered inscription dates toward the beginning of the reign of King Hsüan (r. 827–782 B.C.E.; the exact date may be 816 B.C.E.) of the Chou dynasty and commemorates quite graphically a series of battles between a Chou army and a Hsien-yün army. It should be noted that this text is not really representative of the great majority of early inscriptions on bronze artifacts in terms of its rather unusual length and narrative quality.

ers from the Ching Garrison. To Yu then presented to the duke the captives, heads, and prisoners to be interrogated. Duke Wu then presented them to the king, who addressed Duke Wu, saying: "You have pacified the Ching Garrison; I enrich you, awarding you lands and fields." On *ting-yu* (day thirty-four), Duke Wu was at the Presentation Hall and commanded Hsiang-fu to summon To Yu, who then entered the Presentation Hall. The duke personally addressed To Yu, saying: "I began by giving you sanctuary; you have not transgressed but have succeeded in affairs and made a great catch. You have pacified the Ching Garrison; I award you one tessera, one set of golden bells, and one hundred catties of *hao-yu*-bronze." To Yu dares to respond to the duke's beneficence and herewith makes this precious cauldron with which to befriend him; may [my] sons and grandsons eternally treasure and use it.

Translated by Edward L. Shaughnessy

3

The Book of Changes of the Chou People

1. *Ch'ien (Heaven)* [1]

Anonymous (Western Chou?)

1.0 Grand treat.[2]
    A favorable determination.[3]

The *Changes*, known in modern Chinese as *Yi-ching (I-ching)*, *The Classic of Changes*, or *Chou-yi (The Changes of Chou)*, is one of China's oldest books. Originally a diviner's manual, it was used in conjunction with a type of divination in which stalks of the yarrow plant were manipulated in groups of four to arrive at a series of numbers that were keys to lines in the text. The text itself was probably orally transmitted and elaborated by many generations of diviners in the Shang and Chou dynasties in the first two millennia B.C.E. and came to be written down in substantially its present form in the early centuries of the Chou dynasty, which nominally ruled from about 1100 B.C.E. until about 200 B.C.E. The oldest known version of the text, which is the basis of this translation, consists of sixty-four brief "chapters" associated with sixty-four hexagrams as identifying labels, each hexagram being one of the sixty-four possible combinations of six solid or broken lines. Each hexagram-chapter is composed of a hexagram text and six (or, in two cases, seven) line texts. The texts are filled with a variety of omens and images which, often in rhyme and probably involving word-magic, are based upon puns on like-sounding words, obscure allusions to historical episodes such as "curiosity killed the cat," and folk wisdom such as "step on a crack and break your mother's back." Perhaps, as the diviners manipulated the yarrow stalks and kept obtaining the same hexagrams and lines in connection with certain omens or situations of their clients, they might have begun to keep track of these *synchronicities*, along with their actual outcomes—auspicious, threatening, unfortunate, and so

1.1 A submerged dragon.[4]
    Do not use it.[5]

1.2 See a dragon in a field: it will be favorable to see a big man.[6]

1.3 Nobles throughout the day are *g'ian-g'ian* vigorous, but at night they
    are wary.[7]

---

on—so as to improve their predictive power. These diviners' notes formed the core of the
Changes.

Centuries later, in the Warring States period of the late Chou dynasty and Han dynasty,
commentaries were added to the original text by urbane scholars of the day to explain the
meaning of what had become a very archaic and obscure work in terms comprehensible to the
more sophisticated Chinese society of their day. These commentaries gradually found their way
into the canon itself, adding a new and more philosophical layer of meaning to the once simple
classic. One of the most important of these commentaries is offered in selection 4. This sort of
reinterpretation continued through the centuries; important commentaries were written that
recast the *Changes* in a Taoist, Buddhist, or Neo-Confucian light, with the *Changes* reaching
a pinnacle of importance in the Neo-Confucian thought of the Sung dynasty. Art, literature,
natural philosophy, and even the martial arts have all drawn heavily from the tradition of the
Changes for their theoretical framework and terminology.

1. Almost all the names of the sixty-four hexagram-chapters in the *Changes* originated as
tags designating a hexagram by selecting a prominent word in the hexagram or line texts and
writing it at the beginning of the hexagram text if it did not already occur at that position. Thus
Ch'ien occurs in the line text 1.3 reduplicated as an echoic adverb of manner, describing the
vigorous appearance of a nobleman. In later eras each hexagram name took on a rich symbolic
significance. The most famous pair of these symbols were Ch'ien and K'un. Ch'ien became
the symbol of Heaven, the yang principle, the active and creative, while K'un became its
counterpart, the symbol of Earth, the yin principle, the passive and receptive.

2. The "grand treat" was a sacrificial offering accepted by the gods. The notation "grand
treat" or just "treat" appears frequently throughout the *Changes*, particularly in the hexagram
texts which begin each hexagram-chapter. It is a mildly imperative "treat!," which is a mandate
to the diviner consulting the stalks to offer a sacrificial treat.

3. The word translated here as "determination" occurs often in the text of the *Changes*. It
started out as a technical term inherited from the oracular tradition of the Shang dynasty, in
which it always preceded a divinatory charge to the oracle bone or turtle plastron involving a
proposition to be tested, an issue to be settled. From this original sense of "resolution of doubt,"
referring to a divinatory determination, it later evolved into a personal moral quality of "firm
resolution" or "perseverance." Note that the English words "determination" and "resolution"
themselves wear these two semantic hats. "Favorable determination" came to mean that when
this line was encountered in manipulating the stalks, it would be favorable to be firm and
determined.

4. The Chinese dragon was overall an auspicious beast which usually dwelt in water. We
are free to understand the dragons here as powerful mythic symbols, as do the Chinese.

5. This probably means that one should not use the outcome of the divinatory determination in action.

6. The society of the early Chou dynasty was divided into an aristocratic class, referred to
in the *Changes* as "nobles" or "big men," and the common people, referred to as "small men."
The class society of early Chou was later reinterpreted by Confucius and his contemporaries in
ethical terms, just like the word "noble" in English. "Noble" came to mean noble in behavior,
not in birth, while a small man was mean-spirited and lacking in the Confucian virtues.

7. *G'ian-g'ian* is the reduplicated Old Chinese pronunciation of the hexagram name
Ch'ien.

Threatening, but there will be no misfortune.

1.4 Or it leaps in the deep: no misfortune.

1.5 A dragon flying in the sky: it will be favorable to see a big man.

1.6 A dragon in a gully: there will be trouble.

1.7 See a group of dragons without heads: auspicious.[8]

2. *K'un (Earth)*

2.0 Grand treat.

A determination favorable for a mare.

A noble who is going somewhere will first lose his way and later find a host.

Favorable to the west and south — one will find a friend. To the east and north he will lose a friend.

Auspicious in a determination about security.

2.1 When one steps on the frost, the solid ice is coming.[9]

2.2 Straight and square, big and not doubled up:[10] there is nothing for which this is unfavorable.

2.3 Hold a jade talisman in the mouth.

Can be determined.[11]

If someone pursues the service of the king, there will be no completion; there will be an end.

2.4 Bind up a pouch: there will be no misfortune and no honor.

2.5 A yellow skirt: very auspicious.

---

8. The first two hexagram-chapters in the traditional order, Ch'ien and K'un, both have an extra—seventh—line text, the original purpose of which is not clear. These lines are labeled "use nine" and "use six" in the text. One explanation of this usage is that the seventh line is consulted when all the lines one obtains in manipulating the yarrow stalks are "nines" (in the first hexagram, Ch'ien) or "sixes" (in the second hexagram, K'un).

9. Many of the line texts of the *Changes* are in rhyme, either internally or with a rhyming word in each of successive line texts. In the hexagram-chapter K'un, the words "frost" in 2.1, "square" in 2.2, "jade talisman" in 2.3, "pouch" in 2.4, "skirt" in 2.5, and "yellow-bright" in 2.6 all rhyme—even in modern Mandarin. The rhyme is also echoed by the notation "grand treat" and the word "going" in the hexagram text 2.0. Sound symbolism could have led to each of the rhyming emblems being collected in this hexagram-chapter, all linked by their sound with one another and with the "grand treat" sacrifice.

10. This might have been a description of the shape of a crack made by a diviner in an oracle bone. One scholarly view holds that the tradition of the *Changes* originated as a supplement to the oracle bone divination of the Shang and early Chou dynasties. Thus the *Changes* was a quick and literally "easy" (*yi*) way to prognosticate a crack.

11. This is the strict grammatical sense, but the line may simply mean "an acceptable determination," i.e., the action divined about can be taken.

2.6 Dragons battle in the open country. Their blood is dark and yellow-bright.[12]

2.7 Favorable in a long-range determination.[13]

63. *Chi-chi (Already across the stream)*

63.0 Treat.

A somewhat favorable determination.

Auspicious for the beginning, but a tangle at the end.[14]

63.1 He trails along the spun thread.[15]

It wets its tail.[16]

There will be no misfortune.

63.2 A matron loses her wig. Do not search for it. She will get it in seven days.

63.3 The High Ancestor[17] attacked the Kuei[18] border tribe and conquered it in three years.

A small man should not use this.

63.4 For a jacket there are those who wear worn-out silk floss.

Be cautious throughout the day.

12. The hexagram-chapters of the *Changes* are divided into odd-and-even pairs, which are linked through their hexagram signs. The signs are related either by being reverse images of each other, with the yin-yang polarity of unbroken and broken lines reversed, as is the case with Ch'ien and K'un, or by being inverse, top-to-bottom mirror images of each other, as is the case with the last two hexagram chapters, no. 63 (Chi-chi) and no. 64 (Wei-chi) below. The pairs are sometimes semantically linked through common images in the line texts. Here the dragon image continues the imagery of the Ch'ien hexagram-chapter.

13. See note 8.

14. The word translated as "tangle" originally meant a tangle of thread, from which a general sense of "disorder" or "chaos" was derived. The Chinese character used to write this word shows two hands separating tangled silk threads on a frame. The omen of the tangled ends of silk strands, symbolic of disorder at the end of one's affairs, fits in with the images taken from spinning in the following line texts.

15. This must have been an omen associated with spinning technology. Spun or twisted thread could be a fishing line, as in song 226 of the *Classic of Odes* (*Shih ching*), in which there is the line "This gentleman went fishing; I twisted the line for him." "He trails the line" would be a parallel image with the fox wetting his tail. Spinning images appear as a leitmotif throughout the line texts of the pair of hexagram-chapters composed of this and the following one, mingled with the images of the fox crossing the stream and various other historical anecdotes.

16. This probably refers to the "small fox" which is explicitly named in the hexagram text 64.0 of the paired hexagram below.

17. Probably a reference to the greatest king of the preceding Shang dynasty, King Wu-ting, who reigned c.1200 B.C.E. See selection 1.

18. Although the character *kuei* later was used to write a word meaning "devil" or "ghost," it probably refers here to the historically documented Hsien-pei (Šärbi) Altaic tribe, the Kuei, or Kuei-jung.

63.5 The neighbors to the east slaughter an ox. It does not compare with the summer sacrifice of the neighbors to the west in really receiving their blessings.

63.6 It gets its head wet. Threatening.

64. *Wei-chi (Not yet across the stream)*

64.0 Treat.

The small fox is on the point of crossing the stream and wetting its tail: there is nothing for which this is favorable.

64.1 It wets its tail: distress.

64.2 He trails along the spun thread.

The determination is auspicious.

64.3 It has not yet crossed the stream.

Ominous for an attack.

Favorable for wading across a big river.

64.4 The determination is auspicious. Troubles will go away.

Chen [19] used this to attack the Kuei border tribe and in three years was rewarded in the great state.[20]

64.5 The determination is auspicious. There will be no trouble.

It will be glory for the nobles. There will be a capture.[21]

19. *Chen* means "to thunder," "to shake." Here it appears to be the name of a historical figure ("The Shaker"?), perhaps a general who took part in the attack referred to in lines 63.3 and 64.4. In the annals of the Shang dynasty, recorded more than a thousand years later in the Han period history *Records of the Grand Historian* (*Shih chi*), a certain Chen is cited as an ancestral king of the Shang, while in a later history, the *Bamboo Annals,* quoted in the *History of the Later Han* (*Hou Han shu*), it is recorded that "in the thirty-fifth year of the reign of Wu-yi, the Chou duke Chi-li attacked the western tribe, the Kuei-jung, and captured twenty Ti tribe chieftains." The Shang king Wu-yi was great-grandson to King Wu-ting. So Chen the Shaker might also have been the Chou chieftain Chi-li, who, generations before the Chou people conquered the Shang and founded their own dynasty, helped the Shang attack the Kuei and was subsequently rewarded by the Shang, referred to here as "the great state." Most likely, this line is a conflation of several historical traditions.

20. Perhaps a reference to the state of Shang, the dominant state in north China in the late second millennium B.C.E.

21. The word *fu,* rendered here as "capture," is used frequently in bronze inscriptions and other early Chou period texts to refer to the capture in battle of enemy prisoners or booty. Captives in the Shang and early Chou often became either sacrificial victims or forced labor. Later in the tradition of the *Changes,* the same word, still written with its archaic form now unique to the *Changes,* is invariably interpreted as meaning "trustworthiness" or "sincerity." The link between the older and later usage is vague, but seems to turn on the concept of "reliability." Perhaps "capture" became "be captured," which became "be captivated by," which became "regard as reliable, trustworthy," which became "trustworthy, sincere." The transitional stage could be reflected in this line from the *Classic of Documents* (or *Book of History* [*Shu ching*]) (Chün-shih, 9): "Therefore, when the One Man (the king) had sacrificial services to the four quarters, if he performed the divinations with oracle bones and yarrow stalks, there

Auspicious.
64.6 There will be a capture while drinking wine.
There will be no misfortune.
It gets its head wet.
There will be a capture.
He will lose the ladle.[22]

Translated by Richard A. Kunst

---

were none which did not captivate him," i.e., there were none which were not reliable. It has also been proposed that this semantic shift might have been based on the ancient Chinese practice of taking hostages to ensure the reliability of one's enemies.

22. Reading the character *shih* of the received text as the original form of the word *ch'ih* (ladle) would make this line similar to the earlier line "Do not lose ladle and aromatic spirits" (51.0). Retaining the common sense of *shih*, the phrase would instead mean "He will lose his decorum."

4

An Early Commentary on the *Classic* of *Changes*

The Great Treatise (Appended Phrases)

Anonymous (Warring States or Early Western Han)

Part I, Chapter 12 (Summary)

The *Changes* says: "Heaven will assist him as a matter of course; this is good fortune, and nothing will be to his disadvantage." The Master said: "*Yu* [divine assistance] means help." One whom Heaven helps is someone who is in accord with It. One whom people help is someone who is trustworthy. Such a person treads the way of trustworthiness, keeps his thoughts in accord with Heaven, and also thereby holds the worthy in esteem. This is why "Heaven will assist him as a matter of course; this is good fortune, and nothing will be to his disadvantage."

The Master said: "Writing does not exhaust words, and words do not exhaust ideas. If this is so, does this mean that the ideas of the sages cannot be discerned?" The Master said: "The sages established images in order to express their ideas exhaustively. They established the hexagrams in order to treat exhaustively the true innate tendency of things and their counter tendencies to spuriousness. They attached phrases to the hexagrams in order to exhaust what they had to say. They let flux occur and achieve free flow in order to exhaust the potential of the benefit involved. They made a drum of it, made a dance of it, and so exhausted the potential of its numinous power."

Ch'ien and *K'un*, do they not comprise the arcane source for change? When *Ch'ien* and *K'un* form ranks, change stands in their midst, but if *Ch'ien* and *K'un* were to disintegrate, there would be no way that change could manifest itself. If change could not manifest itself, this would mean that *Ch'ien* and *K'un* might almost be on the verge of extinction!

Therefore, what is prior to physical form pertains to the Way, and what is subsequent to physical form pertains to concrete objects. That which transforms things and regulates them is called flux. By extending this to practical action one may be said to achieve complete success. To take this up and integrate it into the lives of the common folk of the world is called the great task of life.

Therefore, as for the images, the sages had the means to perceive the mysteries of the world and, drawing comparisons for them with analogous things, made images out of those things which seemed appropriate. In consequence of this, they called these "images." The sages had the means to perceive the activities taking place in the world and, observing how things come together and go smoothly, enacted statutes and rituals accordingly. They appended phrases to the hexagram lines in order to judge the good and bad fortune involved. This is why these are called line phrases. These line phrases speak to the most mysterious things in the world, and yet one may not feel aversion toward them; they speak to the things in the world which are most fraught with activity, and yet one may not feel confused about them.

To plumb the mysteries of the world to the utmost is dependent on the hexagrams; to drum up people to action all over the world is dependent on the phrases; to transform things and regulate them is dependent on flux; to start things going and carry them out is dependent on the free flow of flux; to be aware of the numinous and bring it to light is dependent on the men involved; to accomplish things while remaining silent and to be trusted without speaking is something intrinsic to virtuous conduct.

Translated by Richard John Lynn

Philosophy, Thought, and Religion

5
Kuan Tzu

Duties of the Student

Attributed to Kuan Chung (?–645 B.C.E.)

> The teacher presents his teachings; students take them as their
> standards.
> By being docile and reverential, and keeping their minds completely
> open, their learning is maximized.
> On seeing goodness, they follow it; on hearing of righteousness, they
> submit to it.

The *Kuan Tzu* is an enormous, heterogeneous work attributed to Kuan Chung, an illustrious prime minister who served under Duke Huan of the state of Ch'i. The text as we have it now, however, was largely put together by the busy Han period editor, Liu Hsiang (see selections 200 and 203). Although the *Kuan Tzu* is difficult to characterize and date, it is a treasury of Warring States thought, including the earliest economic theory from China and discernible strands of proto-Confucian political ideals.

This essay constitutes chapter 59 of the *Kuan Tzu*, but it also circulated independently. "Duties of the Student" has received considerable attention from Chinese scholars ever since Han times. It is one of the earliest discussions on education in China. The nature of the ritual described is rudimentary compared with the detailed works of Han Confucianists, such as the *Record of Rites (Li chi)*. Several phrases incorporated from the *Classic of Odes (Shih ching)* indicate that the text probably dates from the third or fourth century B.C.E. and represents a common tradition that was operative in the thousands of local schools and larger academies functioning during that period, rather than being a specifically Confucian statement.

Docile and compliant, filial and respectful toward their elders, they
never display arrogance or resort to physical force.
5 Never false or depraved in purpose, their conduct is certain to be
correct and straightforward.
Observing constant standards whether abroad or at home, they are
certain to seek out those who are virtuous.
Their features being well composed, their inner thoughts are certain to
be exemplary in their correctness.
Though they awaken early and go to bed late, their dress is certain to
be tidy.
Mornings being devoted to enhancing their learning and evenings to
practicing what they have learned, they are ever cautious of doing
anything wrong.
10 Being ever diligent in concentrating on these things, such are the
standards for study.

Young students in rendering service are late to bed and early to rise.
When sweeping the floor in front of the teaching mat, washing their
hands, and rinsing their mouths, they conduct themselves in a
respectful manner.
Once they have finished dressing and prepared the wash-basin for the
teacher, he also rises.
When he has completed his toilet, the students remove the basin,
sprinkle and sweep the floor, and adjust the teacher's mat.
15 The teacher then seats himself, and the students in going out or
coming in are as respectful as if they were greeting guests.
They sit in a dignified manner facing the master, their features
composed and never changing.

For receiving instruction, there are guidelines:
The eldest student must come first.
The first time around, it is like this, but thereafter it is not.
20 The first time students recite their lessons, they must stand, but
thereafter they do not.
If a student arrives late, his fellow students on either side will stand.
Should there appear a guest,
A student will immediately arise.
Since a guest cannot be denied,
25 The student will welcome him and hurry to carry out his wishes,
Rushing to the teacher for instruction.
Even though the person the guest seeks is not there, the student will
still report back to him.
He then returns to his seat and resumes his studies.

If a student has a question,
30   He will raise his hand to ask it.
When the master leaves, everyone stands.
In his every word and action, the student takes moderation as his
  guide.
Those who were to flourish in the past were certain to begin like this.

At mealtimes, when the teacher is about to eat, a student prepares food
  for him.
35   Having pulled up his sleeves, washed his hands, and rinsed his mouth,
  the server then kneels down to present the food.
When the sauces, grain, and various dishes are set forth, it must be
  done in an orderly fashion.
Vegetable stews are served before dishes of fowl, meat, fish, or turtle.
Both the stews and sliced meat dishes are placed in the middle but
  kept separate.
Meat dishes having been placed in front of the sauces, the entire
  setting forms a square.
40   The grain is served last; on the left is the wine, on the right is the soy.[1]
Having reported that everything is ready, the student withdraws and,
  cupping his hands before him in obeisance, stands to one side.
The normal meal consists of three servings of grain and two dippers of
  wine,
The student holds in his left hand a pottery serving dish, in his right
  chopsticks or a ladle.
He refills the various dishes in order as soon as he sees they are
  becoming empty.
45   If two dishes become empty at the same time, he refills them in the
  order they were originally served.
Having refilled all the dishes, he begins the cycle again.
Since his serving implement has a foot-long handle, he does not need
  to kneel. Such are the guidelines for making refills.

When the teacher has finished eating, the student clears everything
  away,
And hastens to bring in a basin for the teacher to rinse his mouth,
  sweeps the floor in front of the mat, and gathers together the
  sacrificial utensils.
50   Once the teacher gives the order, the students then begin their meal.

1. This may, however, refer to another word that is homophonous and is written with a
similar graph. This alternative reading signifies water in which a little rice or millet has been
boiled for some time and which is used for rinsing the mouth after a meal.

They arrange themselves properly according to age and are certain to
    sit at the very front of the mat.
Grain must be picked up and eaten with the fingers, but stews are not
    eaten with the hands.
It is permissible for them to rest their hands on their knees, but not to
    lean on their elbows.
Having eaten to the full, they should cup their hands and touch the
    edges of their mouths to see if any food particles remain there,

55   Shake their skirts to get rid of any food crumbs, brush them off the
    mat, and, having completed their meal, rise from their places.
Gathering up their clothing, they step down from the mat and turn to
    face it.
Each person then clears away the remains of his food as though he
    were a guest.
Having cleared the food, they put away the utensils,
And then return to their positions before the mat.

60   Whenever sweeping the floor in front of the teaching mat, students
    should use the following method:
They should fill a basin with water and roll up their sleeves to the
    elbow.
In a large hall, they may sprinkle the water by tossing it widely about;
    in a small room, they should sprinkle by taking only a little in their
    hands.
When holding the dustpan, the handle should be pointed toward the
    sweeper; in the middle is placed the broom.
The sweeper, on entering the door, stands for a while to make sure his
    demeanor is without fault.

65   He holds the broom in his hand and lowers the dustpan, leaning it
    against the doorjamb.
For sweeping in front of the teaching mat, there are guidelines:
The sweeper must begin with the southwest corner;
Moving back and forth with his back bent in the shape of a bent
    chime,
He makes certain that he does not knock into anything;

70   From the front of the room, he works backward,
Collecting the dirt just inside the door.
Then squatting down, he gathers up the dirt by pushing it into the
    dustpan with his hand.
He points the handle of the dustpan toward himself and places the
    broom across it.
Should the teacher rise from his place on the mat, the sweeper will
    straighten up and excuse himself.

75   Then, after squatting down to grasp the dustpan and broom, he
            reassumes a standing position and proceeds to remove them.
        Having finished with his sweeping, the sweeper then returns to his
            position—this all being in accord with the object of his studies.

        During the evening meal, the students repeat the morning's ritual.
        At dusk they light the torches, in each corner sitting and holding
            them.
        The method for placing the faggots is to lay them crosswise to the
            torch holder's sitting position.
80   When the torch has burned down to an appropriate length, he lights a
            new one by pacing it at right angles to the old one like a carpenter's
            square.
        He leaves a faggot's width between them, the one that is already
            burning being just below the one being lit.
        At the same time he holds up a basin to catch falling embers.
        Then with his right hand grasping the old torch,
        He trims the burning end with his left, but should any embers be
            about to drop, another student will replace him in holding the
            torch.
85   When exchanging seats, students must not turn their backs on those
            who hold positions of honor.
        Subsequently, the burned ends are taken out and discarded.

        When the teacher is about to retire, the students all stand.
        They respectfully present him with his pillow and mat, and ask him
            where he would like to place his feet.
        The first time they arrange his sleeping mat, they request this
            information, but once the pattern has been established, they do not.
90   After the teacher has retired, each student seeks out his friends;
        Dissecting and polishing,
        Each one strengthens his arguments.
        The day's routine having been completed, the next day it begins anew.
        Such are the guidelines for students.

Translated by W. Allyn Rickett

6
Confucian *Analects*

Book 2

Anonymous (5th–4th centuries, B.C.E.)

I

1. Governing by the light of one's conscience is like the pole star which dwells in its place, and the other stars fulfill their functions respectfully.

II

1. He [1] said: The anthology of three hundred poems can be gathered into the one sentence: Have no twisty thoughts.

III

1. He said: If in governing you try to keep things leveled off in order by punishments, the people will, shamelessly, dodge.

2. Governing them by looking straight into one's heart and then acting on it (on conscience) and keeping order by the rites, their sense of shame will bring them not only to an external conformity but to an organic order.

IV

1. He said: At fifteen I wanted to learn.
2. At thirty I had a foundation.
3. At forty, a certitude.
4. At fifty, knew the orders of heaven.
5. At sixty, was ready to listen to them.
6. At seventy, could follow my own heart's desire without overstepping the T-square.

V

1. Meng Yi-tzu asked about filiality. He said: Don't disobey.
2. Fan Ch'ih was driving him, and he said: Meng-sun asked me about filiality, I said: It consists in not disobeying (not opposing, not avoiding).
3. Fan Ch'ih said: How do you mean that? He said: While they are alive,

The *Analects* is a body of sayings, brief discourses, and conversations attributed primarily to Confucius and secondarily to his disciples. Although the words of Confucius and his disciples reported are sometimes accompanied by short anecdotes, the collection otherwise provides very little context for the occasions upon which they were spoken. Critical scholarship has shown that the *Analects* is as multifarious in its origins and dating as the Bible.

1. Confucius.

be useful to them according to the proprieties; when dead, bury them according to the rites, make the offerings according to the rites.

VI

1. Meng Wu the elder asked about filiality. He said: A father or mother is only worried as to whether a child is sick.

VII

1. Tzu-yu asked about filiality. He said: Present-day filial piety consists in feeding the parents, as one would a dog or a horse; unless there is reverence, what difference is there?

VIII

1. Tzu-hsia asked about filiality. He said: The trouble is with the facial expression. Something to be done; the junior takes trouble, offers food first to his elders; is that all there is to filiality?

IX

1. He said: I have talked a whole day with Hui and he sits quiet as if he understood nothing, then I have watched what he does. Hui is by no means stupid.

X

1. He said: Watch a man's means, what and how.
2. See what starts him.
3. See what he is at ease in.
4. How can a man conceal his real bent?

XI

1. If a man keep alive what is old and recognize novelty, he can, eventually, teach.

XII

1. The proper man is not a dish.

XIII

1. Tzu-kung said: What is a proper man? He said: He acts first and then his talk fits what he has done.

XIV

1. He said: A proper man is inclusive, not sectary; the small man is sectarian and not inclusive.

XV

1. He said: Research without thought is a mere net and entanglement; thought without gathering data, a peril.

XVI

1. He said: Attacking false systems merely harms you.

XVII

1. He said: Yu, want a definition of knowledge? To know is to act knowledge, and when you do not know, not to try to appear as if you did, that's knowing.

XVIII

1. Tzu-chang was studying to get a paid job.
2. He said: Listen a lot and hide your suspicions; see that you really mean what you say about the rest, and you won't get into many scrapes. Look a lot, avoid the dangerous and be careful what you do with the rest, you will have few remorses. Salary is found in a middle space where there are few words blamed, and few acts that lead to remorse.

XIX

1. Duke Ai asked how to keep the people in order. He said: Promote the straight and throw out the twisty, and the people will keep order; promote the twisty and throw out the straight and they won't.

XX

1. Chi K'ang asked how to instill that sincere reverence which would make people work. He said: Approach them seriously [*verso il popolo*]; be respectful and deferent to everyone; promote the just and teach those who just cannot, and they will try.

XXI

1. Someone asked Confucius why he was not in the government.
2. He said: The Historic Documents say: filiality, simply filiality and the exchange between elder and younger brother that spreads into government; why should one go into the government?

XXII

1. He said: Men don't keep their word. I don't know what can be done for them: a great cart without a wagon-pole, a small cart and no place to hitch the traces.

XXIII

1. Tzu-chang asked if there were any knowledge good for ten generations.

2. He said: Yin, because there was wisdom in the rites of Hsia, took over some and added, and one can know this; Chou, because it was in the rites of Yin, took over some and added, and one can know what; someone will thread along after Chou, be it to an hundred generations one can know.

XXIV

1. He said: To sacrifice to a spirit not one's own is flattery.

2. To see justice and not act upon it is cowardice.

Translated by Ezra Pound

7

Mencius

Bull Mountain

Meng K'o (372–289 B.C.E.)

Mencius said, "Bull Mountain was once beautifully wooded. But, because it was close to a large city, its trees all fell to the axe. What of its beauty then? However, as the days passed things grew, and with the rains and the dews it was not without greenery. Then came the cattle and goats to graze. That is why, today, it has that scoured-like appearance. On seeing it now, people imagine that nothing ever grew there. But this is surely not the true nature of a mountain? And so, too, with human beings. Can it be that any man's mind naturally lacks Humanity and Justice? If he loses his sense of the good, then he loses it as the mountain lost its trees. It has been hacked away at—day after day—what of its beauty then?

"However, as the days pass he grows, and, as with all men, in the still air of the early hours his sense of right and wrong is at work. If it is barely perceptible, it is because his actions during the day have disturbed or destroyed it. Being disturbed and turned upside down the 'night airs' can barely

---

The *Mencius* consists of the rather full discussions of the "Second Sage" (Mencius) of Confucianism with rulers and rival thinkers. The present edition was established by Chao Ch'i in 201 B.C.E. This text has greater literary value but less authority than the *Analects* (see preceding selection), which is supposed to represent the words and thoughts of the "First Sage" (Confucius) himself.

The two section titles are supplied by the editor.

sustain it. If this happens he is not far removed from the animals. Seeing a man so close to an animal, people cannot imagine that once his nature was different—but this is surely not the true nature of the man? Indeed, if nurtured aright, anything will grow, but if not nurtured aright, anything will wither away. Confucius said, 'Hold fast to it, and you preserve it; let it go and you destroy it; it may come and go at any time—no one knows its whereabouts.' Confucius was speaking of nothing less than the mind."

Translated by W. A. C. H. Dobson

Fish and Bear's Paws

Mencius said, "I am fond of fish, but, too, I am fond of bear's paws. If I cannot have both, then I prefer bear's paws. I care about life, but, too, I care about Justice. If I cannot have both, then I choose Justice. I care about life, but then there are things I care about more than life. For that reason I will not seek life improperly. I do not like death, but then there are things I dislike more than death. For that reason there are some contingencies from which I will not escape.

"If men are taught to desire life above all else, then they will seize it by all means in their power. If they are taught to hate death above all else, then they will avoid all contingencies by which they might meet it. There are times when one might save one's life, but only by means that are wrong. There are times when death can be avoided, but only by means that are improper. Having desires above life itself and having dislikes greater than death itself is a type of mind that all men possess—it is not only confined to the worthy. What distinguishes the worthy is that he ensures that he does not lose it.

"Even though it be a matter of life or death to him, a traveler will refuse a basket of rice or a dish of soup if offered in an insulting manner. But food that has been trampled upon, not even a beggar will think fit to eat. And yet a man will accept emoluments of ten thousand *chung* regardless of the claims of Propriety and Justice. And what does he gain by that? Elegant palaces and houses, wives and concubines to wait on him, and the allegiance of the poor among his acquaintance! I was previously speaking of matters affecting life and death, where even there under certain conditions one will not accept relief, but this is a matter of palaces and houses, of wives and concubines, and of time-serving friends. Should we not stop such things? This is what I mean by 'losing the mind with which we originally were endowed.' "

Translated by W. A. C. H. Dobson

8

Chuang Tzu

Chuang Chou (355?–275 B.C.E.)

Once upon a time, Chuang Chou [1] dreamed that he was a butterfly, a butterfly flitting about happily enjoying himself. He didn't know that he was Chou. Suddenly he awoke and was palpably Chou. He didn't know whether he were Chou who had dreamed of being a butterfly, or a butterfly who was dreaming that he was Chou. Now, there must be a difference between Chou and the butterfly. This is called the transformation of things.

> Of all early Chinese thinkers, Master Chuang possessed the most fertile imagination, and his highly creative literary style had a greater impact on later writers throughout history than any other figure from the pre-Ch'in period. While the *Chuang Tzu* is invariably characterized as a Taoist text both by Taoists and by others, the positions espoused in the book are so diverse and protean that they defy easy classification. Certainly the book is not by one author. The seven "Inner Chapters" are generally considered most clearly associated with the shadowy individual named Chuang Chou. While some of the fifteen "Outer Chapters" and eleven "Miscellaneous Chapters" also include passages of great interest, much of the material in them consists of thinly disguised Confucianism and Legalism, as well as other more conventional ideologies that are at odds with the unconstrained playfulness of the more genuine chapters.
>
> 1. Master Chuang (Chuang Tzu). The surname Chuang means "sedate" and Chou, his personal name, signifies "[all] round" or "whole."

The emperor of the Southern Sea was Lickety, the emperor of the Northern Sea was Split, and the emperor of the Center was Wonton. [1] Lickety and Split often met each other in the land of Wonton, and Wonton treated them very well. Wanting to repay Wonton's kindness, Lickety and Split said, "All people have seven holes for seeing, hearing, eating, and breathing. Wonton alone lacks them. Let's try boring some holes for him." So every day they bored one hole, and on the seventh day Wonton died.

> 1. The undifferentiated soup of primordial chaos. As it begins to differentiate, dumpling-blobs of matter coalesce. Wonton soup probably came first as a type of simple early fare. With the evolution of human consciousness and reflectiveness, the soup would have been adopted as a suitable metaphor for chaos.

Chapter 17: Autumn Floods

When the time of the autumn floods arrived, the hundred tributaries poured into the Yellow River. Its onrushing current was so huge that one could not discern an ox or a horse on the opposite side or on the banks of its islets. Thereupon the Earl of the River [1] delightedly congratulated himself at having

> 1. The god of the Yellow River.

complete and sole possession of all excellences under heaven. Following along with the current, he went east until he reached the North Sea. There he looked eastward but could not see the water's end, whereupon he crestfallenly gazed across the surface of the sea and said with a sigh toward its Overlord,[2] "There is a proverb which says, 'He who has heard the Way a hundred times believes no one may be compared with himself!' This applies to me. Furthermore, when I first heard those who belittle the learning of Confucius and disparage the righteousness of Po-yi, I did not believe them. But now that I behold your boundlessness, I realize that, had I not come to your gate,[3] I would have been in danger[4] and ridiculed forever by the practitioners of the great method."[5]

The Overlord of the North Sea said, "You can't tell a frog at the bottom of a well about the sea because he's stuck in his little space. You can't tell a summer insect about ice because it is confined by its season. You can't tell a scholar of distorted views about the Way because he is bound by his doctrine. Now you have ventured forth from your banks to observe the great sea and have recognized your own insignificance, so that you can be told of the great principle.

"Of all the waters under heaven, none is greater than the sea. The myriad rivers return to it ceaselessly, but it never fills up; the drain[6] at its bottom endlessly discharges, but it never empties. Spring and autumn it never varies, and it knows nothing of flood and drought. Its superiority to such streams as the Yangtze and the Yellow River cannot be measured in numbers. Yet the reason I have never made much of myself on this account is because I compare my own form to that of heaven and earth and recall that I received my vital breath from yin and yang. Midst heaven and earth, I am as a little pebble or tiny tree on a big mountain. Since I perceive of myself as being small, how then can I make much of myself? May we not reckon that the four seas in the midst of heaven and earth resemble the cavity in a pile of stones lying in a huge marsh? May we not reckon that the Middle Kingdom[7] in the midst of the sea is like a mustard seed[8] in a huge granary? When we designate the number of things there are in existence, we refer to them in terms of myriads, but man occupies only one place among them. The masses of men occupy the nine regions,[9] but wherever grain grows and wherever

2. Whose name was Jo.
3. To learn from you instead of from the Confucians.
4. Of continuing in my delusion.
5. The Way (Tao).
6. More literally, "tail-confluence" (*wei-lü*), a hole with a gigantic stone plug at the bottom of the sea whence its waters are removed.
7. To this day, this is still China's name for itself.
8. The Chinese text has a bisyllabic term meaning "tares" or "panic grass."
9. The ancient Chinese conceived of their realm as being divided into nine sections, somewhat like a tic-tac-toe diagram.

boats and carriages reach, the individual occupies only one place among them. In comparison with the myriad things, would he not resemble the tip of a downy hair on a horse's body? The succession of the five emperors, the contention of the three kings, the worries of humane men, the labors of the committed scholars all amount to no more than this. Po-yi declined it for the sake of fame. Confucius lectured on it for the sake of his erudition. This is because they made much of themselves. Is this not like you just now making much of yourself because of your flooding waters?"

"This being so," asked the Earl of the River, "may I take heaven and earth as the standard for what is large, and the tip of a downy hair as the standard for what is small?"

"No," said the Overlord of the North Sea. "Things are limitless in their capacities, incessant in their occurrences, inconstant in their portions, uncertain in their beginning and ending. For this reason, great knowledge observes things at a relative distance; hence it does not belittle what is small or make much of what is big, knowing that their capacities are limitless. It witnesses clearly the past and the present; hence it is not frustrated by what is far off or attracted by what is close at hand, knowing that their occurrences are incessant. It examines fullness and emptiness; hence it is not pleased when it obtains or worried when it loses, knowing that their portions are inconstant. It understands the level path; hence it is not enraptured by life or perturbed by death, knowing that beginnings and endings are uncertain. We may reckon that what man knows is less than what he doesn't know; the time when he is alive is less than the time when he is not alive. When he seeks to delimit the boundaries of the extremely large with what is extremely small, he becomes disoriented and can't get hold of himself. Viewed from this vantage, how do we know that the tip of a downy hair is adequate to determine the parameters of the extremely small? And how do we know that heaven and earth are adequate to delimit the boundaries of the extremely large?"

"The deliberators of the world," said the Earl of the Yellow River, "all say, 'That which is extremely minute has no form; that which is extremely large cannot be encompassed.' Is this true?"

"If we look at what is large from the viewpoint of what is minuscule," said the Overlord of the North Sea, "we won't see the whole. If we look at what is minuscule from the viewpoint of what is large, we won't see the details. Now, that which is minute is the smallest of the small; that which is enormous is the largest of the large. Hence their differences are suitable and in accord with their circumstances. Yet, the minute and the coarse are both dependent upon their having a form. That which has no form is numerically indivisible; that which cannot be encompassed is numerically undelimitable. That which can be discussed in words is the coarseness of things; that which can be conceived of in thought is the minuteness of things. That which can neither be discussed in words nor conceived of in thought is independent of minuteness and coarseness." [10]

"How, then," asked the Earl of the Yellow River, "are we to demarcate the value and magnitude of a thing, whether it be intrinsic or extrinsic?"

The Overlord of the North Sea said, "Observed in the light of the Way, things are neither prized nor despised; observed in the light of things, they prize themselves and despise others; observed in the light of the common lot, one's value is not determined by oneself. Observed in the light of gradations, if we consider to be large that which is larger than something else, then the myriad things are without exception large; if we consider to be small that which is smaller than something else, then all the myriad things are without exception small. If we regard heaven and earth as a mustard seed and the tip of a downy hair as a mountain, we can perceive the numerousness of their relative gradations. Observed in the light of merit, if we grant whatever merit they have, then the myriad things without exception have merit; if we point to whatever merit they lack, then the myriad things lack merit. If we recognize that east and west, though opposites, cannot be without each other, their shared merit will be fixed. Observed in the light of inclination, if we approve whatever they approve, then the myriad things without exception may be approved; if we condemn whatever they condemn, then the myriad things without exception may be condemned. If we recognize that Yao and Chieh approved of themselves but condemned each other, we can perceive their controlling inclinations.

"Long ago, Yao yielded his throne to Shun and the latter became emperor, but when K'uai yielded his throne to Tzu Chih [11] they were both cut down.

10. The following lengthy paragraph has been inappropriately inserted at this point:

> Therefore the conduct of the great man is not aimed at hurting others, yet he does not make much of his humaneness and kindness. When he moves, it is not for profit, but he does not despise the porter[a] at the gate. He does not wrangle over goods and property, yet he does not make much of his declining and yielding. In his affairs, he does not rely upon others and does not make much of utilizing his own strength, but he does not despise those who are avaricious and corrupt. His conduct may differ from that of the common lot, but he does not make much of his eccentricity. His behavior may follow that of the crowd, but he does not despise the glib flatterer. All the titles and emoluments in the world are not enough to encourage him, nor are penalties and shame enough to disgrace him. He knows that right and wrong are indivisible, that minuscule and large are undemarcatable. I have heard it said, "The Man of the Way is not celebrated; the man of ultimate virtue is not successful; the great man has no self." This is the pinnacle of restraint.
>
> a. Who is always looking out for a tip or a bribe.

11. In the year 316 B.C.E., King K'uai of Yen yielded his throne to his minister, Tzu Chih, in conscious imitation of Yao handing over his throne to Shun. This led to three years of internal strife and the invasion of Yen by the state of Ch'i.

T'ang and Wu became kings through contention, but the duke of Po contended and was destroyed.[12] Viewed in this light, the etiquette of contending and yielding, the conduct of Yao and Chieh, may be either prized or despised in accord with the times, but may not be taken as constants. A beam or a ridgepole may be used to breach a city wall, but it cannot be used to plug a hole, which is to say that implements have specific purposes. A Ch'i-chi or a Hua-liu[13] may gallop a thousand tricents in a day, but for catching rats they're not as good as a wild cat or a weasel, which is to say that creatures have different skills. An owl can catch fleas at night and discern the tip of a downy hair, but when it comes out during the day it stares blankly and can't even see a hill or a mountain, which is to say that beings have different natures. Therefore, when it is said 'Make right your teacher, not wrong; make good government your teacher, not disorder,' this is to misunderstand the principle of heaven and earth and the attributes of the myriad things. It would be like making heaven your teacher and ignoring earth, like making yin your teacher and ignoring yang. The unworkability of this is clear. Still, if one goes on talking like this and does not give it up, one is either being stupid or deceptive. The emperors and kings of old had different modes of abdication, and the rulers of the three dynasties had different modes of succession. He who acts contrary to the times and contravenes custom is called a usurper; he who accords with the times and conforms to custom is called a disciple of righteousness. Keep silent, oh Earl of the Yellow River! How could you know about the gate of honor and baseness and about the practitioners of small and large?"[14]

"Then what am I to do?" asked the Earl of the Yellow River, "and what am I not to do? With regard to rejecting and accepting, taking and giving, how should I behave?"

"Viewed in the light of the Way," said the Overlord of the North Sea,

> "What is prized and what is despised
> May be referred to as alternating developments of each other.
> Do not persist in following the dictates of your will,
> For it will bring you into great conflict with the Way.

> 5   What is few and what is many
> May be referred to as reciprocal extensions of each other.

12. T'ang and Wu were the founding kings of the Shang and Chou dynasties respectively. The duke of Po was the grandson of King P'ing of Ch'u. His father, the crown prince, was demoted when the king became infatuated with a woman from the state of Ch'in. He fled to Cheng and married a woman who gave birth to the duke of Po. When the latter grew up, he returned to Ch'u and raised an armed insurrection in 479 B.C.E. to take revenge for his father, but was defeated and eventually committed suicide.

13. The Chinese counterparts of Bucephalus and Pegasus.

14. The words "gate" and "practitioners" here are resonant with their occurrence in the Earl of the Yellow River's first speech at the beginning of the chapter.

Do not be inflexibly monotonous in your behavior,
For it will put you at odds with the Way.

Be solemn as the lord of a state
10   Whose integrity is impartial;
Be self-composed as the officiant of a sacrificial altar
      Whose blessings are impartial;
Be broad-minded as the immensity of the four directions
      Which have no borders.

15   Embosom all the myriad things,
Taking each one under your protective wings.
This may be referred to as universality.[15]
The myriad things will be equally regarded,
There being no long or short among them.

20   The Way has neither beginning nor end,
But things have life and death.
Not being able to presume upon their completion,
They are now empty, now full,
Without stability in form.

25   The years cannot be advanced,
Nor can time be stayed.
Dissolution and generation, fullness and emptiness—
Whatever ends has a beginning.

Thus may we
Speak of the secret of the great purport,[16]
30   Discuss the principle of the myriad things.

The life of things
Is like the cantering and galloping of a horse—
They are transformed with each movement,
They change with each moment.
35   What are you to do?
What are you not to do?
Just let things evolve by themselves."

   "Then what is to be prized about the Way?" asked the Earl of the Yellow
River.
   The Overlord of the North Sea said, "She who knows the Way must

   15. More literally, the text has "nonlocality."
   16. It would be totally out of keeping with this magnificent dialogue between the Overlord
of the North Sea and the Earl of Yellow River to translate *yi* here in its restricted Confucian
sense of "righteousness."

apprehend principle; she who apprehends principle must be clear about contingency; she who is clear about contingency will not harm herself with things. She who has ultimate integrity will neither be burned by fire nor drowned in water, will neither be harmed by cold and heat nor injured by bird and beast. This does not mean that she belittles these things, but rather that she examines where she will be safe or in danger. She is tranquil in misfortune or in fortune; she is careful about her comings and goings, so that nothing can harm her. Therefore it is said, 'The heavenly is within, the human is without; integrity lies in heaven.' When you know the operation of the heavenly and the human, you will root yourself in heaven and position yourself in contentment. Then you will be hesitant and flexible, reverting to what is important and bespeaking perfection."

"What do you mean by heavenly, and what do you mean by human?"

The Overlord of the North Sea said, "Oxen and horses having four feet is what is meant by 'heavenly.' Putting a halter over a horse's head or piercing through an ox's nose is what is meant by 'human.' Therefore it is said,

'Do not destroy the heavenly with the human;
Do not destroy destiny with intentionality;
Do not sacrifice your good name for attainments.' [17]
If you guard this carefully and do not lose it,
You may be said to have returned to the truth."

The unipede envies the millipede; the millipede envies the snake; the snake envies the wind; the wind envies the eye; the eye envies the mind.

The unipede said to the millipede, "I go hippity-hopping along on my one foot but barely manage. How is it, sir, that you can control myriad feet?"

"It's not so," said the millipede. "Haven't you seen a person spit? When they spew forth, the big globs are like pearls, the droplets are like a mist. All mixed up together, the number that falls is immeasurable. Now, I just move by my natural inner workings but don't know why it is so."

The millipede said to the snake, "I go along on my multitudinous feet, but I'm not as fast as you who have no feet. How come?"

"How could we change the movements of our natural inner workings?" asked the snake. "What use do I have for feet?"

The snake said to the wind, "I go along by moving my spine and ribs, thus I have a shape. But you, sir, who arise with a whoosh from the North Sea

---

17. Most commentators interpret the last clause as meaning "do not sacrifice yourself for the sake of fame," but this totally ignores both the syntax and diction of the sentence. The problem with the present interpretation is that we would not expect the Overlord of the North Sea to care the slightest about name or fame. One suspects, therefore, a lapse on the part of the author.

and alight with a whoosh in the South Sea, have no shape at all. How can this be?"

"It's true that I arise with a whoosh from the North Sea and alight in the South Sea," said the wind, "but whoever points at me vanquishes me, and whoever treads upon me vanquishes me. Nonetheless, only I can snap big trees and blow down big houses. Therefore, the great vanquishing depends upon a host of minor defeats. It is only the sage who can be a great vanquisher."

Master Chuang was fishing in the P'u River.[18] The king of Ch'u dispatched two high-ranking officials to go before him with this message: "I wish to encumber you with the administration of my realm."

Without turning around, Master Chuang just kept holding on to his fishing rod and said, "I have heard that in Ch'u there is a sacred tortoise that has already been dead for three thousand years. The king stores it inside a hamper wrapped with cloth in his ancestral temple. Do you think this tortoise would rather be dead and have its bones preserved as objects of veneration, or be alive and dragging its tail through the mud?"

"It would rather be alive and dragging its tail through the mud," said the two officials.

"Begone!" said Master Chuang. "I'd rather be dragging my tail in the mud."

When Master Hui was serving as the prime minister of Liang, Master Chuang set off to visit him. Somebody said to Master Hui, "Master Chuang is coming and he wants to replace you as prime minister." Whereupon Master Hui became afraid and had the kingdom searched for three days and three nights.

After Master Chuang arrived, he went to see Master Hui and said, "In the south there is a bird. Its name is Yellow Phoenix.[19] Have you ever heard of it? It takes off from the South Sea and flies to the North Sea. It won't stop on any other tree but the kolanut; won't eat anything else but bamboo seeds;[20] won't drink anything but sweet spring water. There was once an owl which,

18. In Shantung.

19. The precise meaning of the name *yüan-ch'u* is uncertain, although the second graph seems to indicate that the bird in question was young.

20. Since bamboo flowers (and hence produces seeds) only rarely—some species as seldom as once a century—the implication is that the Yellow Phoenix (which itself only appears at great intervals) is very particular about its food. Another interpretation of the sinographs in question yields "fruits of the *Melia azedarach*," said to be favored by the phoenix and the unicorn but shunned by the dragon. Common names for this plant are pride of India, pride of China, and chinaberry.

having got hold of a putrid rat, looked up at the Yellow Phoenix as it was passing by and shouted 'shoo!' Now, sir, do you wish to shoo me away from your kingdom of Liang?"

Master Chuang and Master Hui were strolling across the bridge over the Hao.[21] "The hemiculters [22] have come out and are swimming [23] so leisurely," said Master Chuang. "This is the joy of fishes."

"You're not a fish," said Master Hui. "How do you know what the joy of fishes is?"

"You're not me," said Master Chuang, "so how do you know that I don't know what the joy of fishes is?"

"I'm not you," said Master Hui, "so I certainly do not know what you do. But you're certainly not a fish, so it is irrefutable that you do not know what the joy of fishes is."

"Let's go back to where we started," [24] said Master Chuang. "When you said, 'How do you know what the joy of fishes is?', you asked me because you already knew that I knew. I know it by strolling over the Hao." [25]

21. In Anhwei.

22. Small fish found in rivers and lakes. They are only a few inches long with thin, flat bodies that, according to old Chinese texts, are "shaped like a willow leaf."

23. Note that this is a rendering of the same graph translated in the previous sentence as "strolling" and elsewhere in the *Chuang Tzu* as "wandering" or occasionally as "traveling."

24. More literally, "to the root [of the problem/argument]."

25. Although not so protracted and elaborate, the entire style of argumentation in this famous passage bears an uncanny resemblance to many philosophical arguments found in the works of Plato. Chapter 17 ends here.

In seeds there are germs. When they are found in water they become filaments. When they are found at the border of water and land they become algae.[1] When they germinate in elevated places they become plantain. When the plantain is found in fertile soil it becomes crow's foot.[2] The crow's foot's roots become scarab grubs and its leaves become butterflies. The butterflies soon evolve into insects that are born beneath the stove. They have the appearance of exuviae and are called "house crickets." After a thousand days the house crickets became birds called "dried surplus bones." [3] The spittle of the dried surplus bones becomes a misty spray and the misty spray becomes mother of vinegar. Midges are born from mother of vinegar; yellow whirligigs

1. The Chinese expression may be rendered more literally as "clothing of frogs and oysters."

2. This is a literal translation of the two sinographs forming the name. The plant in question is commonly called blackberry lily in English.

3. The precise identification of this and several of the following terms is impossible because they are colloquial names lost to the tradition of classical explication.

are born from fetid wine; blindgnats are born from putrid slimebugs. When goat's queue couples with bamboo that has not shooted for a long time, they produce greenies. The greenies produce panthers; panthers produce horses; horses produce men; and men return to enter the wellsprings[4] of nature. The myriad things all come out of the wellsprings and all reenter the wellsprings.

4. The sinograph for "wellsprings [of nature]" includes within it the graph for "germs," which occurs at the beginning of this bizarre romp through evolution. There is little doubt that the two words are etymologically related in Sinitic. This has prompted many scholars to equate the two as they occur in the passage.

Duke Huan[1] was hunting in the marshes with Kuan Chung[2] as his charioteer when he saw a ghost. Grabbing hold of Kuan Chung's hand, he asked, "Did you see something, Father[3] Chung?"

"Your servant saw nothing," was the reply.

After the duke returned he babbled incoherently and became ill, so that he did not go out for several days. There was a scholar of Ch'i named Master Leisurely Ramble who said to him, "Your Highness is harming yourself. How could a ghost harm you? If an embolism of vital breath caused by agitation disperses and does not return, what remains will be insufficient; if it rises and does not come back down, it will cause a person to be easily angered; if it descends and does not come back up, it will cause a person to forget easily; if it neither rises nor descends, it will stay in the center of a person's body, clogging his heart, and he will become ill."

"Yes," said Duke Huan, "but are there ghosts?"

"There are. In pits there are pacers; around stoves there are tufties. Fulgurlings frequent dust piles inside the door; croakers and twoads hop about in low-lying places to the northeast; spillsuns frequent low-lying places to the northwest. In water there are nonimagoes; on hills there are scrabblers; on mountains there are unipedes; in the wilds there are will-o'-the-wisps; and in marshes there are bendcrooks."

"May I ask what a bendcrook looks like?" said the duke.

"The bendcrook," said Master Ramble, "is as big around as the hub of a chariot wheel and as long as the shafts. It wears purple clothes and a vermilion cap. This is a creature that hates to hear the sound of rumbling chariots. When it does, it stands up holding its head in its hands. He who sees it is likely to become hegemon."

Duke Huan erupted in laughter and said, "That was what I saw." Whereupon he adjusted his clothing and cap, and had Master Ramble sit

1. Of the state of Ch'i, the first of the five hegemons who imposed their will on the other feudal states.

2. Prime minister of Duke Huan and the ostensible author of the book entitled *Master Kuan (Kuan Tzu,* see selection 5).

3. A term of address used to show respect.

down with him. Before the day was over, his illness left him without his even being aware of it.

Translated by Victor H. Mair

9

The Classic Book of Integrity and the Way: *Tao te ching*

Attributed to Lao Tzu (c. 250 B.C.E.?)

1
(38)

> The person of superior integrity
> > does not insist upon his integrity;
> For this reason, he has integrity.
> The person of inferior integrity
> > never loses sight of his integrity;
> For this reason, he lacks integrity.

> The person of superior integrity takes no action,
> > nor has he a purpose for acting.
> The person of superior humaneness takes action,
> > but has no purpose for acting.

The *Tao te ching* is probably the best-known Chinese book in the world, having been translated hundreds of times into dozens of languages. This slender tome of approximately five thousand sinographs divided—sometimes rather arbitrarily—into eighty-one brief "chapters," has had an important influence on religion and thought that is hugely out of proportion to its size. Although the text is held by Taoist believers to have been composed by Lao Tzu in the sixth century B.C.E., the available evidence indicates that it was actually not committed to writing until sometime in the third century. Furthermore, there is no reliable biographical information concerning Lao Tzu. The name, which means "Old Master," is most likely a general designation for a number of venerable sages who actively promoted one brand or another of quietist thought. The authorship of the *Tao te ching* may thus be said to be composite in nature.

The word translated as "integrity" here is *te*. It is usually rendered as "virtue" and has also been interpreted as "power." Etymologically speaking, perhaps the closest equivalent is "doughtiness."

The present translation is based on silk manuscripts discovered in 1973 at Ma-wang-tui in Hunan province. These, approximately half a millennium older than the earliest editions previously available, permit the solution of many difficult textual problems. The chapter numbers are those of the Ma-wang-tui manuscripts; the traditional chapter numbers are given in parentheses.

The person of superior righteousness takes action,
    and has a purpose for acting.
The person of superior etiquette takes action,
    but others do not respond to him;
Whereupon he rolls up his sleeves
    and coerces them.

Therefore,
    When the Way is lost,
        afterward comes integrity.
    When integrity is lost,
        afterward comes humaneness.
    When humaneness is lost,
        afterward comes righteousness.
    When righteousness is lost,
        afterward comes etiquette.

10
(47)

Without going out-of-doors,
    one may know all under heaven;
Without peering through windows,
    one may know the Way of heaven.

The farther one goes,
The less one knows.

For this reason,
    The sage knows without journeying,
        understands without looking,
        accomplishes without acting.

24
(61)

A large state is like a low-lying estuary,
    the female of all under heaven.
In the congress of all under heaven,
    the female always conquers the male through her stillness.
Because she is still,
    it is fitting for her to lie low.
By lying beneath a small state,
    a large state can take over a small state.
By lying beneath a large state,
    a small state can be taken over by a large state.

Therefore,
> One may either take over or be taken over by lying low.

Therefore,
> The large state wishes only to annex and nurture others;
> The small state wants only to join with and serve others.

Now,
> Since both get what they want,
> It is fitting for the large state to lie low.

30
(80)

Let there be a small state with few people,
> where military devices find no use;
Let the people look solemnly upon death,
> and banish the thought of moving elsewhere.

They may have carts and boats,
> but there is no reason to ride them;
They may have armor and weapons,
> but there is no reason to display them.

Let the people go back to tying knots
> to keep records.
Let their food be savory,
> their clothes beautiful,
> their customs pleasurable,
> their dwellings secure.

Though they may gaze across at a neighboring state,
> and hear the sounds of its dogs and chickens,
The people will never travel back and forth,
> till they die of old age.

41
(76)

Human beings are
> soft and supple when alive,
> stiff and straight when dead.

The myriad creatures, the grasses and trees are
> soft and fragile when alive,
> dry and withered when dead.

Therefore, it is said:
> The rigid person is a disciple of death;
> The soft, supple, and delicate are lovers of life.

An army that is inflexible will not conquer;
A tree that is inflexible will snap.

The unyielding and mighty shall be brought low;
The soft, supple, and delicate will be set above.

45
(1)

The ways that can be walked are not the eternal Way;
The names that can be named are not the eternal name.
The nameless is the origin of the myriad creatures;
The named is the mother of the myriad creatures.

Therefore,
    Always be without desire
        in order to observe its wondrous subtleties;
    Always have desire
        so that you may observe its manifestations.

Both of these derive from the same source;
They have different names but the same designation.

Mystery of mysteries,
The gate of all wonders!

50
(6)

The valley spirit never dies—
    it is called "the mysterious female";
The gate of the mysterious female
    is called "the root of heaven and earth."
Gossamer it is,
    seemingly insubstantial,
    yet never consumed through use.

54
(10)

While you
    Cultivate the soul and embrace unity,
        can you keep them from separating?
    Focus your vital breath until it is supremely soft,
        can you be like a baby?
    Cleanse the mirror of mysteries,
        can you make it free of blemish?

Love the people and enliven the state,
    can you do so without cunning?
Open and close the gate of heaven,
    can you play the part of the female?
Reach out with clarity in all directions,
    can you refrain from action?

It gives birth to them and nurtures them,
It gives birth to them but does not possess them,
It rears them but does not control them.
    This is called "mysterious integrity."

55
(11)

Thirty spokes converge on a single hub,
    but it is in the space where there is nothing
        that the usefulness of the cart lies.
Clay is molded to make a pot,
    but it is in the space where there is nothing
        that the usefulness of the clay pot lies.
Cut out doors and windows to make a room,
    but it is in the spaces where there is nothing
        that the usefulness of the room lies.
Therefore,
    Benefit may be derived from something,
        but it is in nothing that we find usefulness.

72
(28)

Know masculinity,
Maintain femininity,
    and be a ravine for all under heaven.
By being a ravine for all under heaven,
Eternal integrity will never desert you.
If eternal integrity never deserts you,
You will return to the state of infancy.

Know you are innocent,
Remain steadfast when insulted,
    and be a valley for all under heaven.
By being a valley for all under heaven,
Eternal integrity will suffice.
If eternal integrity suffices,
You will return to the simplicity of the unhewn log.

Know whiteness,
Maintain blackness,
    and be a model for all under heaven.
By being a model for all under heaven,
Eternal integrity will not err.
If eternal integrity does not err,
You will return to infinity.

When the unhewn log is sawn apart,
    it is made into tools;
When the sage is put to use,
    he becomes the chief of officials.

For

    Great carving does no cutting.

Translated by Victor H. Mair

10
Lieh Tzu

The Stupid Old Man Who Moved a Mountain

Attributed to Lieh Yü-k'ou (3d century B.C.E.?)

The mountains T'ai-hsing and Wang-wu are seven hundred miles square and seven hundred thousand feet high. They stood originally between Chi-chou on the north and Ho-yang on the south. When Mister Simple of North

Master Lieh and his text, traditionally dated to the fourth century B.C.E., are both doubtful, although we do find references to a Lieh Yü-k'ou as early as the third century B.C.E. The book that carries his name is a collection of stories, sayings, and brief essays grouped in eight chapters, each loosely organized around a single theme. Among these, the "Yang Chu" chapter preaches a hedonism out of keeping with the rest of the book, but the remaining seven chapters constitute the most important Taoist document after the *Tao te ching* (see selection 9) and *Chuang Tzu* (see selection 8). While the book does contain material dating to around the third century B.C.E., the scholarly consensus is that it assumed its present form as late as 300 C.E. or even later. One of the reasons for this consensus is that the book contains Indian tales that can be traced to specific Buddhist works introduced to China only after that date.

The *Lieh Tzu* is the most easily intelligible of the Taoist classics for its straightforward prose style. When the same story appears in both the *Lieh Tzu* and the *Chuang Tzu* (as is often the case), the version in the *Lieh Tzu* is inevitably easier to understand.

The section title is supplied by the editor.

Mountain was nearly ninety, he was living opposite them. It vexed him that, with the north flank of the mountains blocking the road, it was such a long way round to come and go. He called together the family and made a proposal: "Do you agree that we should make every effort to level the high ground, so that there is a clear road straight through to South of Yü and down to the south bank of the Han river?"

They all agreed. But his wife raised difficulties: "You are too weak to reduce even the smallest hillock; what can you do with T'ai-hsing and Wang-wu? Besides, where will you put the earth and stones?"

They all answered: "Throw them in the tail of the gulf of Chih-li, north of Yin-t'u."

Then, taking his son and grandson as porters, he broke stones and dug up earth, which they transported in hods and baskets to the tail of the gulf of Chih-li. The son of their neighbor Mr. Ching-ch'eng, born to his widow after his death and now just cutting his second teeth, ran away to help them.

Mister Simple did not come home until the hot season had given way to the cold. Old Wiseacre of River Bend smiled and tried to stop him, saying: "How can you be so unwise? With the last strength of your declining years, you cannot even damage one blade of grass on the mountains; what can you do to stones and earth?"

Mister Simple of North Mountain breathed a long sigh, and said: "Certainly your mind is set too firm for me ever to penetrate it. You are not even as clever as the widow's little child. Even when I die, I shall have sons surviving me. My sons will beget me more grandsons, my grandsons in their turn will have sons, and these will have more sons and grandsons. My descendants will go on forever, but the mountains will get no bigger. Why should there be any difficulty about leveling them?"

Old Wiseacre of River Bend was at a loss for an answer.

The mountain spirits, which carried snakes in their hands, heard about it, and were afraid he would not give up. They reported it to God, who, moved by his sincerity, commanded the two sons of K'ua-erh to carry the mountains on their backs. They put one in Shuo-tung and the other in Yung-nan. Since then there has been no high ground from Chi-chou in the north to the south bank of the Han river.

Translated by A. C. Graham

11
Abhidharma-mahāvibhāṣā-śāstra

Chapter 99: The Sins of Mahādeva

Translated by Hsüan-tsang (600–664)

Once upon a time, there was a merchant in the kingdom of Mathurā. He married while still a youth and soon his wife gave birth to a baby boy. The child, who had a pleasing appearance, was given the name Mahādeva.

Before long, the merchant went on a long journey to another country, taking with him rich treasures. As he engaged in commercial ventures while wending his way, a long time passed without his return. The son, meanwhile, had grown up and committed incest with his mother. Later on, he heard that his father was returning and he became fearful at heart. Together with his mother, he contrived a plan whereby he murdered his father. Thus did he commit his first cardinal sin.[1]

This deed of his gradually came to light, whereupon, taking his mother, he fled to the city of Pāṭaliputra where they secluded themselves. Later, he encountered a monk-arhat from his native land who had received the support of his family. Again, fearing that his crime would be exposed, he devised a plan whereby he murdered the monk. Thus did he commit his second cardinal sin.

Mahādeva became despondent. Later, when he saw that his mother was having illicit relations, he said to her in a raging anger: "Because of this affair, I have committed two serious crimes. Drifting about in an alien land, I am forlorn and ill at ease. Now you have abandoned me and fallen in love with another man. How could anyone endure such harlotry as this?" Thereupon he found an opportune time to murder his mother. He had committed his third cardinal sin.

Inasmuch as he had not entirely cut off the strength of his roots of goodness, Mahādeva grew deeply and morosely regretful. Whenever he tried to sleep, he became ill at ease. He considered by what means his serious

---

This text, the title of which has been supplied by the editor, is taken from chapter 99 of the *Abhidharma-mahāvibhāṣā-śāstra*, which is said to have been compiled 400 years after the Buddha entered Nirvana. It was translated from Sanskrit into Chinese by the famous pilgrim Hsüan-tsang (see selection 211) during the years 656–659. The Chinese title of the scripture is *A-p'i-ta-mo ta-p'i-p'o-sha lun*.

The oedipal dimensions of the Mahādeva story are fascinating, but its main import is as a vivid narrative statement of sectarian differences.

1. There are five such sins altogether: parricide, matricide, killing an arhat (advanced Buddhist disciple or saint), injuring the body of Buddha, and causing disunity in the *saṃgha* (community of monks).

crimes might be eradicated. Later, he heard that Buddhist monks were in possession of a method for eradicating crimes. So he went to the monastery known as Kukkuṭārāma.[2] Outside its gate, he saw a monk walking slowly and meditating. The monk recited a hymn which went:

If someone has committed a serious crime,
He can eradicate it by cultivating goodness;
He could then illuminate the world,
Like the moon emerging from behind a screen of clouds.

When Mahādeva heard this, he jumped for joy. He knew that, if he converted to Buddhism, his crimes could certainly be eradicated. Therefore he went to visit a monk in his quarters. Earnestly and persistently, Mahādeva entreated the monk to ordain him as a novice. When the monk saw how persistent Mahādeva's entreaties were, he ordained him as a novice without making an investigation or asking any questions. He allowed him to retain the name Mahādeva, and offered him instruction in the Buddhist precepts and prohibitions.

Now Mahādeva was quite brilliant and so, not long after he had entered the priesthood, he was able to recite and adhere to the text and the significance of the Buddhist canon. His words were clear and precise and he was adept at edifying others in the faith. In the city of Pāṭaliputra, there were none who did not turn to Mahādeva in reverence. The king heard of this and repeatedly invited him into the inner precincts of the palace. There he would respectfully provide for Mahādeva's needs and invite him to lecture on the Law of the Buddha.

Mahādeva subsequently went to live in the monastery. There, because of improper thoughts, he sometimes had nocturnal emissions. But he had previously declared himself an arhat and so he commanded a disciple to wash his soiled clothing. The disciple addressed Mahādeva: "The arhat is one in whom all outflows have been exhausted.[3] How, then, master, can you endure such a thing as this to persist?"

Mahādeva informed him, saying, "It was the Wicked One[4] who tempted me. You should not think this something unseemly. Outflows, however, may broadly be classified in two categories; the first results from delusions and the second from impurity. The arhat is without outflows due to delusion. But he is yet unable to avoid those due to impurity. And why is this? Although the

2. "Chicken Garden Monastery," built by Aśoka, the great king and patron of Buddhism.

3. Sanskrit *āsrava-kṣaya*. This term generally implies "outflow from the mind," hence "passion." But because of the context, we may understand it in the bare, literal meaning of the Chinese *lou* (leak, drip, effluvia, discharge, emission).

4. Sanskrit *Deva māra*. He delights in obstructing the Buddhist saints as they strive to achieve the truth by sending his daughters to seduce them.

arhat may put an end to delusion, how can he be without urine, bowels, tears, spittle, and the like? Furthermore, the Wicked Ones are ever hatefully jealous of the Buddha's Law. Whenever they see someone who is cultivating goodness, they invariably attempt to ruin him. Even the arhat is tempted by them. This was the cause of my emission. It was all their doing—you should not be skeptical in this regard." This is termed "the origin of the first false view." 5

Again, Mahādeva wished to make his disciples like him and be intimately attached to him. He cleverly created opportunities whereby he was able to note and differentiate the degree of achievement each monk had attained along the four stages of religious perfection. Whereupon one of his disciples kowtowed to him and said: "The arhat ought to have experiential knowledge. How is it that none of us have this sort of self-awareness?"

Mahādeva informed him, saying, "But arhats also have ignorance. You should not, then, lack faith in yourselves. I tell you that, of the various forms of ignorance, there are broadly two types. The first is that which is defiling; the saint is without this type. The second is that which does not defile; the saint still has this type of ignorance. On account of this, you are unable to have full awareness of yourselves." This is termed "the origin of the second false view."

At another time, his disciples said to him: "We have heard that the sages have transcended all doubts. How is it that we still harbor doubts in regard to the truth?"

Again, Mahādeva informed them, saying, "The arhat also has his doubts and suspicions. Of doubts, there are two types. The first is that of muddle-headedness; the arhat has excised this type. The second derives from mistakes in judgment; the arhat has not yet excised this type. The self-enlightened have made great accomplishments in spite of this. How, then, can you who are mere listeners be without doubt regarding the manifold truths and thereby allow yourselves to feel humbled?" This is termed "the origin of the third false view."

Later, when the disciples opened the sūtras to read, they learned that the arhat is possessed of the eye of sage wisdom. Through self-emancipation he is able to attain experiential knowledge of self. And so they spoke to their master, saying, "If we are arhats, we ought to have experiential knowledge of

5. Altogether there are five views, *pañca dṛṣṭayaḥ*: 1. The arhat may ejaculate while asleep. 2. The arhat may remain subject to certain forms of ignorance. 3. The arhat may still have doubts. 4. The arhat may be made aware of his level of enlightenment by someone other than himself. 5. The arhat shouts at the moment of enlightenment. The upshot of all this is a loss of dignity for the arhat and, conversely, a move toward equality for the laymen vis-à-vis the *religieux*. It is, in sum, the beginning of the division between so-called Hīnayāna and Mahāyāna, the Greater and Lesser vehicles of the Buddhist faith.

self. How is it, then, that we must be initiated by our master into that fact and are without the direct insights that would enable us to have experiential knowledge of the self?"

To this, Mahādeva replied: "Though one is an arhat, he must still be initiated by others. He cannot rely on self-awareness. Even for the likes of Śāriputra who was foremost in wisdom and Maudgalyāyana who was foremost in supernatural power, if the Buddha had not remarked upon their abilities, they would not have gained self-awareness. How, then, can those who are initiated by others into that fact have self-understanding of it? Therefore you should not be endlessly inquiring in regard to this." This is termed "the origin of the fourth false view."

Mahādeva had, indeed, committed a host of crimes. However, since he had not destroyed his roots of goodness, during the middle of the night he would reflect upon the seriousness of his crimes and upon where he would eventually undergo bitter sufferings. Beset by worry and fright, he would often cry out, "Oh, how painful it is!" His disciples who were dwelling nearby were startled when they heard this and, in the early morning, came to ask him whether he were out of sorts.

Mahādeva replied, "I am feeling very much at ease."

"But why," asked his disciples, "did you cry out last night, 'Oh, how painful it is!'?"

He proceeded to inform them: "I was proclaiming the holy way of the Buddha. You should not think this strange. In speaking of the holy way, if one is not utterly sincere in the anguish with which he heralds it, it will never become manifest at that moment when one's life reaches its end. Therefore, last night I cried out several times, 'Oh, how painful it is!'" This is termed "the origin of the fifth false view."

Mahādeva subsequently brought together the aforementioned five false views and made a hymn:

Enticement by others, ignorance,
Hesitation, initiation by another,
The Way is manifested because one shouts:
This is called the genuine Buddhist teaching.

With the passage of time, the Theravāda[6] monks in the Kukkuṭārāma gradually died off. Once, on the night of the fifteenth of the month when the monks were holding their regular spiritual retreat, it was Mahādeva's turn to ascend the pulpit and give the reading of the prohibitions. He then recited the hymn which he had composed. Of those in the company of monks at that time, be they learners or learned, be they of much wisdom, attentive to the precepts, or cultivators of wisdom, when they heard what Mahādeva said,

6. A purist doctrine to which elders adhere.

there was no one who refrained from reproving him: "For shame! Stupid man! How could you say such a thing? This is unheard of in the canon." Thereupon they countered his hymn, saying:

> Enticement by others, ignorance,
> Hesitation, initiation by another,
> The Way is manifested because one shouts:
> What you say is not the Buddhist teaching.

Upon this, an unruly controversy erupted that lasted the whole night long. By the next morning, the factions had become even larger. The folk of all classes, up to and including important ministers, came from the city one after another to mediate, but none of them could bring a halt to the argument.

The king heard of it, and himself went to visit the monastery. At this point, the two factions each stated their obstinate position. When the king had finished listening, he too, became filled with doubt. He inquired of Mahādeva, "Who is wrong and who is right? With which faction should we align ourselves?"

"In the *Sūtra on Regulations*," replied Mahādeva, "it is said that, if one wishes to terminate controversy, one should go along with the voice of the majority."

The king proceeded to order the two factions of monks to separate themselves. In the faction of the saints and sages, although there were many who were elders, the total number of monks was small. In Mahādeva's faction, although there were few who were elders, the total number of common monks was large. So the king followed the majority and allied himself with Mahādeva's crowd. The remainder of the common monks were reproved and made to submit. The matter concluded, the king returned to his palace.

The controversy in the Kukkuṭārāma, however, did not cease. Afterward, the monastery split into two groups in accordance with the two different views. The first was called Sarvāstivāda and the second was called Mahāsaṃghika. When the saints and sages realized that the mass of monks were going counter to their principles, they departed from the Kukkuṭārāma with the intention of going to another place.

As soon as the ministers heard of this, they rushed to the king and reported. Hearing this, the king was outraged and issued an edict to his ministers which stated: "Let them all be taken to the edge of the Ganges River. Put them in a broken boat so that they will capsize in midstream. By this means, we shall test whether this lot is made up of saints or commoners."

The ministers carried out the test as directed by the king's words. The saints and sages each brought into play his spiritual powers. They were like the Goose King[7] vaulting through space. Furthermore, using their miracu-

---

7. An epithet of the Buddha.

lous strength, they rescued from the boat those who had left the Kukkuṭārāma with them but who had not yet attained supernatural power. They manifested many miraculous transformations and assumed various shapes and forms. Next they mounted the heavens and went off to the northwest. When the king heard this, he was deeply abashed. Stifled with regret, he fell on the ground in a swoon and revived only when water was splashed on his face. He swiftly dispatched a man to find out where they had gone. Upon the return of the envoy, the king learned that they were in Kashmir. He persistently entreated them to return but the monks all refused to obey his command. The king then donated to them the whole of the land of Kashmir and constructed monasteries to accommodate the large group of saints and sages. The monasteries were given names in accordance with the various shapes the monks had assumed during their flight—for example, "Pigeon Garden." Altogether there were five hundred such monasteries. Again he dispatched envoys to contribute precious jewels and make arrangements for the articles of daily living so that the monks would be provided for. Ever after this, the land of Kashmir has had large numbers of saints and sages who have upheld the Law of the Buddha. Its transmission and reformulation there are still very much in evidence to this day.

Having lost this large group of monks, the king of Pāṭaliputra took the initiative in providing for the monks of Kukkuṭārāma. After some time, as Mahādeva was making an excursion into the city, a physiognomist chanced to see him and secretly told his fortune: "Seven days from today, the life of this disciple of Buddha will certainly come to an end."

When Mahādeva's disciples heard this, they were frightfully worried and informed him of it. He then declared to them, "I have known this for a long time already."

After they had returned to the Kukkuṭārāma, he sent his disciples to spread out over the whole of the city of Pāṭaliputra. When the king, his ministers, and the ascetics heard the words, "In seven days I shall enter Nirvāṇa," there was none but who sighed with grief.

With the arrival of the seventh day, Mahādeva died as he had predicted. The king, his ministers, and the folk of all classes from the city were saddened and filled with affectionate longing. They all undertook to provide fragrant firewood as well as ghee, floral incense, and similar materials. These were assembled in a given place where the cremation was to take place. Each time the man who held the fire to light the wood approached it, his fire would go out. All sorts of plans were devised but it simply would not light. A soothsayer who was present spoke to the crowd: "The deceased cannot consume such splendid crematory materials as those you have provided. It is fitting that the excrement of dogs be smeared on him."

They acted in accordance with his words and the fire erupted in flames.

In seconds, the blaze had burned itself out. Suddenly, there was nothing but ashes. In the end, a howling wind blew by and scattered them everywhere till nothing was left. This is due to his having been formerly the originator of the false views. All who have wisdom ought to pay heed to this example.

Translated by Victor H. Mair

Criticism and Theory

12
Literary Selections

Preface

Hsiao T'ung (501–531)

When we look to the first beginnings and scrutinize from afar those primordial conditions—in times of winter caves and summer nests when men devoured undressed game and drank blood[1]—times then were rude and

Literary Selections (Wen hsüan) is by far the most important and influential anthology of Chinese literature. Indeed, as a bisyllabic word in modern Sinitic languages, its title has come to mean simply "anthology." The preface to *Literary Selections* is included here as a relatively concise statement of the large number of genres and subgenres of elite Chinese literature that existed in the early sixth century. Hsiao T'ung (Prince Chao-ming of the Liang dynasty) and his collaborators most probably drew extensively upon the formulations established by Liu Hsieh (c. 465–c. 520) in his *The Literary Mind and the Carving of Dragons* [i.e., Ornate Rhetoric] *(Wen-hsin tiao-lung)*, the first book-length treatment in Chinese of the major issues involved in the study of literature. Whereas the latter was partially inspired by certain Buddhist ontological and epistemological concepts, Ts'ao P'i (187–226; see selection 139 [unnumbered note]), Lu Chi (261–303), and Hsiao T'ung seem to have remained more or less immune—at least consciously so in their critical formulations—to the theoretical positions of this foreign religion.

It should be noted that this preface is not simply a straightforward piece of expository prose. It is written, rather, in the mannered parallel style (see selections 163 and 164), and logical exposition frequently gives way to the demands of symmetry.

1. "Formerly the ancient kings had no houses. In winter they lived in caves, which they had excavated, and in summer in nests, which they had framed. They knew not yet the

people plain; writing had not yet appeared. Then we come to the rule of Fu-hsi, who first traced the Eight Trigrams and invented writing to take the place of government by knotted cords; from this time written records came into being.[2]

The *Classic of Changes* says, "Observe the patterns in the sky to discover the seasons' changes; observe the patterns among men to transform All-Under-Heaven"—so far-reaching are the times and meanings[3] of pattern (*wen*)![4] Now the Imperial Chariot had its origin in the oxcart, but the Imperial Chariot has none of the crudeness of the oxcart. Thick ice is composed of accumulated water, but accumulated water has not the coldness of thick ice. Why so? The original form is preserved but elaborated on, or the essential nature changed through intensification. This is true of things, and it is also true of literature (*wen*). It changes with passing time, and to describe it is no easy task. But to make the attempt:

The Preface to the *Classic of Songs* says,[5] "There are six modes of the Songs. The first is instruction (*feng*); the second is description (*fu*); the third is simile (*pi*); the fourth is metaphor (*hsing*); the fifth is ode (*ya*); the sixth is hymn (*sung*)." Later poets deviated from the ancient [practice], and of the [six modes of the] ancient poetry, the moderns took over only the term *fu*. It appeared first of all in the works of Hsün Tzu[6] and Sung Yü,[7] and was continued subsequently by Chia Yi[8] and Ssu-ma Hsiang-ju;[9] from this time

---

transforming power of fire, but ate the fruits of plants and trees, and the flesh of birds and beasts, drinking their blood, and swallowing also the hair and feathers" (from the *Record of Rites [Li chi]*, translated by James Legge).

2. This is quoted verbatim form the opening lines of the "Preface" to the *Classic of Documents (Shu-ching)* attributed to K'ung An-kuo (fl. c. 156–c. 74 B.C.E.; a descendant of Confucius in the eleventh generation). There are conflicting legends and myths concerning the invention of writing in China (compare selection 167).

3. The same encomium occurs repeatedly in the *Classic of Changes (Yi-ching)*.

4. The word for literature and writing (*wen*) originally meant "pattern."

5. It is impossible to translate the terms satisfactorily, for they have meant many things to different commentators, but at least the nature of the difficulty can be defined. Three of the six items—*feng, ya,* and *sung*—are the names of the chief divisions of the present *Classic of Odes,* (or *Classic of Songs, Shih ching*) and, while there is no general agreement about their significance there, they are certainly not the names of tropes. *Fu, pi,* and *hsing* are variously interpreted and inconsistently applied by the commentators on the *Classic of Odes.* For our present purposes, the important question is how Hsiao T'ung understood the items, and it is apparent from the rest of this paragraph that he was concerned solely with the occurrence of the word *fu* as something associated with the *Classic of Odes.* It provides his point of departure in sketching the development of the *fu* genre, though he must have been aware that the genre was not identical with the trope, as indeed his statement in the next sentence ("the moderns took over only the term *fu*") implies.

6. In spite of their shared name, the riddles in rhyme of the "Fu" chapter of the *Hsün Tzu* have nothing in common with the *fu* ("rhapsody" or "rhymeprose") of Han times.

7. Four *fu* attributed to Sung Yu (290?–222 B.C.E.) are included in the *Literary Selections.*

8. Chia Yi's "Owl *fu*" (see selection 123) is the earliest *fu* of which the text is given in a

on the ramifications were many. Descriptive of cities and sites there are [the *fu* of Chang Heng and Ssu-ma Hsiang-ju with their imaginary interlocutors His Honor] Insubstantial[10] and [Master] No-Such[-Person].[11] Directed against hunting are the "Ch'ang-yang"[12] and "Hunting with Plumes" [*fu* of Yang Hsiung]. When it comes to *fu* describing one event or celebrating a single object (such as those on Wind, Clouds, Plants, and Trees, or the ones about Fish, Insects, Birds, and Beasts), considering their range, it is quite impossible to list them all.

There was also the Ch'u poet Ch'ü Yüan, who clung to loyalty and walked unsullied; the prince would not accept it when the subject offered advice unwelcome to his ears. Though his understanding was profound and his plans far-reaching, in the end he was banished south of the Hsiang River. Injured for his unbending integrity and with no one in whom to confide his sorrow, he stood on the verge of the abyss, determined to embrace the stone; he sighed by the pool, haggard in appearance.[13] It is from him that the writings of the *sao* poets derive.

Poetry is the product of the emotions: the feelings are moved within and take form in words.[14] In "The Osprey" and "The Unicorn" appears the Way of the Correct Beginning;[15] "The Mulberry Grove" and "On the Banks of the Pu" represent the music of a defunct state.[16] Truly the way of the *feng* and the *ya* may be seen in them at its most brilliant. From the middle period of Fiery Han[17] the paths of poetry gradually diverged. The Retired Tutor (Wei Meng) wrote his "Poem in Tsou,"[18] and the surrendered general (Li Ling) wrote the poem on the bridge;[19] with them the four-word and five-word [meters] became [recognized as] distinct classes. In addition, there were

---

contemporary Former Han period source (*Records of the Grand Historian [Shih chi]* by Ssu-ma Ch'ien [145–90? B.C.E.]).

9. See selection 129.

10. A character in the "Rhapsody on the Western Capital" by Chang Heng (78–139).

11. Occurs in the rhapsody by Ssu-ma Hsiang-ju entitled "Sir Fantasy."

12. Titled after the palace of that name at Ch'ang-an where the game was brought in cages and released.

13. Paraphrased from Ch'ü Yüan's biography in the *Records of the Grand Historian*, ch. 84.

14. A famous formula expressed in the Anonymons "Great Preface' to the classic of *Odes*, which dates to the late Western Han.

15. *Classic of Odes* (see selection 16), songs 1 and 11.

16. As stated in the *Record of Rites*.

17. The Han dynasty ruled by virtue of the Fire element.

18. Wei Meng (second century B.C.E.) was tutor to three generations of princes of Ch'u, the last of whom he found intractable and against whom he "wrote a satirical poem as a remonstrance." He retired to his native Tsou, where he wrote another poem, presumably the one referred to by Hsiao T'ung.

19. Referring to his farewell poem to Su Wu (c. 143–60 B.C.E.), which begins: "We clasp hands on the river bridge / By nightfall where will the traveler have gone?" It is now generally accepted that all the Li Ling (d. 74 B.C.E.) poems in the *Literary Selections* are forgeries.

[meters] with as few as three words and as many as nine words, the several forms developing at the same time, [like horses] galloping together though on separate traces.

Eulogy (*sung*) serves to broadcast virtuous deeds; it praises accomplishment. Chi-fu made his pronouncement, "How stately!";[20] Chi-tzu exclaimed, "Oh, perfect!"[21] Elaborated as poetry it was expressed like that; composed as eulogy it is also this way.

Next are Admonition (*chen*), which arises from ameliorating defects, and Warning (*chieh*), which derives from setting to rights. Disquisition (*lun*) is subtle in making logical distinctions, and Inscription (*ming*) is generous in narrating events. When a good man dies, a Dirge (*lei*) is made; when a portrait is painted, an Appreciation (*tsan*) is supplied.

Further, there are these branches: Proclamation (*chao*), Announcement (*kao*), Instruction (*chiao*), and Command (*ling*); these types: Memorial (*piao*), Proposal (*tsou*), Report (*chien*), and Memorandum (*chi*); these categories: Letter (*shu*), Address (*shih*), Commission (*fu*),[22] and Charge (*chi*); these compositions: Condolence (*tiao*), Requiem (*chi*), Threnody (*pei*), and Lament (*ai*); these forms: Replics to Opponents (*ta k'o*) and Evinced Examples (*chih shih*); these texts: Three Word (*san yen*) and Eight Character (*pa tzu*); Song (*p'ien*), Elegy (*tz'u*), Ditty (*yin*), and Preface (*hsü*); Epitaph (*pei*) and Columnar Inscription (*chieh*); Necrology (*chih*) and Obituary (*chuang*). A multitude of forms have shot up like spear-points; diverse tributaries have joined the main stream. Yet they might be compared to musical instruments made of different materials—some of clay, some from gourds, yet all are to give pleasure to the ear; or to embroideries of different colors and designs—all are to delight the eye. This accounts for just about all that writers have written.

When not busy with my duties as Heir Apparent, I have spent many idle days looking through the garden of letters or widely surveying the forest of literature, and always I have found my mind so diverted, my eye so stimulated, that hours have passed without fatigue. Since the Chou and the Han, far off in the distant past, dynasties have changed seven times and some thousands of years have elapsed. The names of famous writers and men of

20. *Classic of Odes*, song 260: "Chi-fu has made this eulogy, / Stately its clear melody." This poem is a eulogy of Chung Shan-fu, but it is not in the "Lauds" section of the *Odes*; nor is the preceding eulogy of the prince of Shen (*Odes* song 259) with its similar concluding lines.

21. Chi-tzu is the "Duke's-son Chao of Wu," who came on a state visit to Lu. The *Chronicle of Tso* (*Tso chuan*) (see selection 159) gives a long account of his reception, particularly of the musical performance which he requested and which included selections from the major sections of the *Odes*. After each piece he made appropriate remarks. His exclamation "Oh, perfect!" came after he had heard the "Lauds" section of the *Odes* and is followed by an enthusiastic catalog of its perfections.

22. This is written with a different sinograph than that for "rhapsody" or "rhymeprose" discussed extensively above.

genius overflow the green bag;[23] the scrolls of winged words and flowing brushes fill the yellow covers. If one does not leave aside the weeds and select the flowers, it is impossible, even with the best intentions, to get through the half.

Now the writings of the Duke of Chou and the works of Confucius are on a level with sun and moon, as mysterious as ghosts and spirits. They are the models of filial and respectful conduct, guides to the basic human relationships; how can they be subjected to pruning or cutting?

The works of Chuang Tzu and Lao Tzu, of Kuan Tzu and Mencius are devoted primarily to establishing a doctrine; they are not immediately concerned with literary values. In the present anthology they, too, have been omitted.

When it comes to the excellent speeches of the sages and the straightforward remonstrances of loyal ministers, the fine talk of the politicians and the acuity of the sophists,[24] these are "ice melting[25] and the fountain leaping,[26] gold aspect and jade echo."[27] They are what are referred to as "sitting on Mount Chü and debating beneath the Chi Gate."[28] Chung-lien's making Ch'in's army withdraw,[29] Yi-ch'i's getting Ch'i to submit,[30] the Marquis of Liu's raising eight difficulties,[31] the Marquis of Ch'ü-ni's proposing the six

23. A reference to Hsün Hsü (d. 289) who devised the four bibliographic categories to include all books, which he stored in green bags and tied with yellow cords.

24. A reference to Han Ying's Illustrations of the Didactic Application of the Classic of Odes (Han shih wai chuan): "The superior man avoids the three points: he avoids the brush-point of the literary man; he avoids the spear-point of the military man; he avoids the tongue-point of the sophist."

25. Probably refers to Tao te ching (see selection 9), ch. 15: "Yielding as ice as it starts to melt," where it is used to characterize the excellent officers of antiquity.

26. This may refer to a line from the Grave Inscription for Ts'ao Ch'üan ("Plans like a spring gushing") by Tseng Chao.

27. This probably alludes directly to Wang Yi's preface to "Encountering Sorrows" (see selection 122): "The writings of Ch'ü Yüan are truly far-reaching in their influence. . . . Of them it can be said that their aspect is of gold, their substance of jade, peerless in a hundred generations."

28. A lost work, Lu Lien Tzu, is quoted by the distinguished annotator of the Literary Selections, Li Shan (630?–689): "T'ien Pa, a sophist of Ch'i, argued on Mount Chü and debated beneath the Chi-cheng Gate. He defamed the Five Emperors and incriminated the Three Kings, in one day putting down a thousand opponents."

29. In the Intrigues of the Warring States, ([Chan-kue ts'e]) see selection 200), it is told how Lu Chung-lien dissuaded Chao from recognizing the ruler of Ch'in as emperor (as advocated by the general Hsin Yüan-yen of Wei), and the report of his indictment of Ch'in led the latter state to withdraw its armies which were besieging Han-tan.

30. In the Records of the Grand Historian, it is told how Li Yi-chi persuaded Ch'i to join with Liu Pang in the wars that led to the founding of the Han dynasty.

31. Further in the Records of the Grand Historian, it is told how Chang Liang, marquis of Liu, dissuaded the Han emperor Kao Tsu from reestablishing the Six Feudal States (as Li Yi-chi had advocated) by citing eight precedents and pointing out the differences in circumstances.

strategies: [32] their accomplishments were famous in their own time and their speeches have been handed down from a thousand years. But most of them are found in the records or appear incidentally in the works of the philosophers and historians. Writings of this sort are also extremely numerous, and though they have been handed down in books, they differ from belles-lettres, so that I have not chosen them for this anthology.

As for histories and annals, they praise and blame right and wrong and discriminate between like and unlike. Clearly they are not the same as belles-lettres. But their eulogies and essays concentrate verbal splendor, their prefaces and accounts are a succession of flowers of rhetoric; their matter derives from deep thought, and their purport places them among belles-lettres. Hence I have included these with the other pieces.

From the Chou House of long ago down to this Holy Dynasty, in all it makes thirty chapters. I have named it simply the *Anthology*. The following texts are arranged by genres. Since poetry and *fu* are not homogeneous, these are further divided into categories. Within each category the sequence is chronological.

Translated by James Robert Hightower

32. Ch'en P'ing, marquis of Ch'ü-ni, became chief minister under the Han emperor Kao Tsu. According to Ssu-ma Ch'ien in his *Records of the Grand Historian*, the six strategies had been kept secret and he had no way of knowing what they were.

13
Record of the Classification of Old Painters

Preface

Hsieh Ho (fl. c. 500–535?)

Now by classification of painters is meant the relative superiority and inferiority of all painters. As for painters, there is not one who does not illustrate some exhortation or warning, or show the rise and fall in man's affairs. The

The *Record of the Classification of Old Painters (Ku-hua p'in-lu)* is a short work, but it has had a seminal impact on all later theories of art in China. In it, Hsieh Ho laid down the six fundamental principles for Chinese painting theory. Although they are extremely difficult to interpret (it would appear that Hsieh Ho himself had not fully assimilated them), it is highly probable that there is some connection with the ṣaḍaṅga (six limbs) of Indian painting theory since the two sets correspond virtually one to one. A close correspondence should also be noted between ideas expressed in this preface and in concepts common to early Chinese literary

solitudes and silences of a thousand years may be seen as in a mirror by merely opening a scroll.

Even though painting has its Six Elements,[1] few are able to combine them thoroughly; and from ancient times until now each painter has excelled in one particular branch. What are these Six Elements? First, Spirit Resonance, which means vitality; second, Bone Method, which is a way of using the brush; third, Correspondence to the Object, which means the depicting of forms; fourth, Suitability to Type, which has to do with the laying on of colors; fifth, Division and Planning, that is, placing and arrangement; and sixth, Transmission by Copying, that is, the copying of models.

Only Lu T'an-wei[2] and Wei Hsieh[3] were thoroughly proficient in all of these.

But, while works of art may be skillful or clumsy, esthetics knows no ancient and modern. Respectfully relying upon remote and recent sources and following their classifications, I have edited and completed the preface and citations. Hence what is presented is not too far-ranging. As for the origins of painting, it is merely reported that it proceeded from gods and immortals, but none was witness to such.

Translated by Susan Bush and Hsio-yen Shih,
based on the translation of William Acker

---

theory such as *The Literary Mind and the Carving of Dragons* (see unnumbered note to selection 12).

Hsieh Ho may have been related to the famous progressive poets of the Southern Dynasties, Hsieh Ling-yün (see selection 21) and Hsieh T'iao (464–499).

1. More literally, "laws."
2. Fifth century.
3. Active late third to early fourth century.

14

Ts'ang-lang's Discussions of Poetry

An Analysis of Poetry

Yen Yü (c. 1180–c. 1235)

1. For the student of poetry, judgment is the most important thing. His introduction must be correct and his ambition must be set high. He should

The *Ts'ang-lang shih-hua* is a manifold and complex text. Nonetheless, it seems to engage in essentially four different arguments:

take the Han, Wei, Chin, and High T'ang as his teachers and not wish to be someone who has lived after the K'ai-yüan (713–741) and T'ien-pao (742–755) eras. If he yields, he will have the devil of inferior poetry enter his bosom because he did not set his ambition high enough. If one has not yet reached the end of a journey, he can increase his efforts, but, as soon as he goes off the road, the more he hurries the more he will go astray because his introduction was not correct. For, as it is said: "If one studies the very best of something, he will only manage to achieve half of it, but, if one studies second-rate achievements, it will result in something truly inferior." It is also said: "If one's judgment surpasses that of his teacher, only then will it be worthy of being handed down to posterity, but, if it merely equals that of his teacher, when handed down it will consist of the teacher's virtues diluted by half!" One's efforts must proceed from the top and work down and cannot proceed from the bottom and work up. First, one must thoroughly recite the Elegies of Ch'u [1] and sing them morning and night so as to make them his basis. When he goes on to recite *The Nineteen Ancient Poems*,[2] the *Music Bureau Ballads in Four Sections*,[3] and the pentasyllabic verse of Li Ling (d. 74 B.C.E.) and Su Wu (c. 143–60 B.C.E.) and that of the Han and the Wei, he must do them all thoroughly. After that, he will take up the collected poetry of Li Po and Tu Fu [4] and read them until, lying on top of one another, they become his pillows, just as people today study the Classics. Next, he will

---

1. The Poetry of the High T'ang masters (Li Po, Tu Fu, and their contemporaries) is the perfect realization of the true law or Dharma of poetry.
2. Perfect poetry depends upon spontaneity, which Yen Yü, the author, characterizes in terms of enlightenment, a term borrowed from Ch'an/Zen Buddhism.
3. Not all T'ang poetry is worthy of emulation, however, since after the High T'ang period poetry underwent deviation, and some Middle T'ang (766–834) poetry and Late T'ang (835–907) poetry are products of what Yen calls "false enlightenment." As the High T'ang period corresponds analogously to the "orthodoxy" of the Lin-chi School of Ch'an, so does much of the poetry of the Middle and Late T'ang eras correspond to the heterodoxy of the Ts'ao-tung School and the "lesser" (and therefore "false") attainments of the Hīnayāna tradition as a whole to the *Śrāvaka* and *Pratyeka*, and so on (see notes 7 and 8 below).
4. To a considerable extent, Yen's work of criticism is a diatribe against the poetry of his own era, against Sung period poetry in general, and against the poetry of the Chiang-hsi School in particular. He condemns Sung poetry essentially on two grounds: it is not "enlightened" (i.e., spontaneous), and it does not embody the Dharma of poetry.

Little is known about the author except that he was a native of Shao-wu (in modern Fukien), that he was in touch with several prominent poets of his day, and that he left behind a small collection of poetry. His fame, however, rests securely on the insightful critical work from which the beginning is excerpted here.

1. *Ch'u tz'u* (see selection 122).
2. See selection 135.
3. An unknown collection of ballad poetry (for *yüeh-fu*, see selection 134).
4. See selections 35 and 37.

comprehensively take up the famous masters of the High T'ang. Once he allows all this to ferment in his bosom for a long time, he will be enlightened spontaneously. Although he might not attain the ultimate end of study, still he will not go off the correct road. This is nothing less than to work from the basis of the very highest attainments, and I say that it is the "one road that leads upward," that it "cuts straight to the foundation," that it is "the gateway to immediate enlightenment," and that it is "the single sword-thrust to the heart."

2. There are five aspects to the Dharma [5] of poetry: formal structure, power of formal style, personal style, inspired feeling, and intonation and rhythm.

3. There are nine modes in poetry: the lofty, the antique, the profound, the remote, the ever-flowing, the heroic-and-powerful, the elated-and-transcendent, the sad-yet-resolute, and the forlorn-yet-gracious. There are three dimensions of poetry to which one must pay special heed: to the openings and closures of poems, to syntax, and to crucial elements of diction. There are two absolutely essential characteristics of poetry: it must flow freely and not be restricted, or it must be thoroughly imbued with deeply moving expression. There is one ultimate attainment in poetry: enter the spirit. When poetry enters spirit, it is perfect and complete, and nothing more can be added to it. Only Li Po and Tu Fu managed to do this, and if others ever do they will be very few indeed!

4. In the tradition of the Ch'anists, there are the Greater and the Lesser Vehicles, the Southern and the Northern Schools, and the heterodox and orthodox Ways. There, the student must follow the Very Highest Vehicle, embody the Correct Dharma Eye, and experience enlightenment of the first order. However, if it is Lesser Vehicle Ch'an, the fruit of the Śrāvaka [6] or the Pratyeka,[7] it will never be orthodox. Discussing poetry is just like discussing Ch'an/Zen. The poetry of Han, Wei, Chin, and the High T'ang represents enlightenment of the first order. Poetry from the Ta-li era on (after 766) corresponds to the Lesser Vehicle and has fallen into enlightenment of the second order. The Poetry of the Late T'ang is Śrāvaka or Pratyeka. He who studies the poetry from the time after the Ta-li era is as if he were an adherent of the Ts'ao-tung School.[8] For the most part, the Way of Ch'an is concerned with marvelous enlightenment and the Way of Poetry is also concerned with marvelous enlightenment. Thus, Meng Hao-jan [9] was far inferior to Han

5. This might be rendered as Law or, less literally, Way.

6. "A hearer." This generally refers to a practitioner of so-called Hīnayāna (Lesser Vehicle) Buddhism.

7. One who attains enlightenment solely for himself.

8. The "orthodox" Lin-chi School regarded the Ts'ao-tung School as teaching "false" enlightenment.

9. See selection 32.

Yü [10] in knowledge, that is, in everything but poetry where he was the superior, and this was all due to its sense of marvelous enlightenment. Only when one is enlightened can he be a real expert and show his natural color. However, there are different depths and different scopes of enlightenment. There is thoroughly penetrating enlightenment, and there is enlightenment which only achieves partial understanding. The Han and the Wei are indeed supreme! They did not have to depend upon enlightenment at all! Poets beginning with Hsieh Ling-yün [11] and including the masters of the High T'ang possessed thoroughly penetrating enlightenment; although there were others who might have achieved enlightenment, it was never that of the first order. The way I have evaluated the tradition of poetry is not presumptuous and the way I have discriminated among poets and eras is not reckless. The world has always had people it could do without, but there has never been anything written it could afford to ignore. The Way of Poetry is just like this, and, if anyone believes this not to be so, then his view of poetry is not sufficiently broad and his examination of poetry is not sufficiently deep. If one tries to take up the poetry of the Chin and the Sung and thoroughly examines it, then tries to take up the poetry of the Southern and Northern dynasties and thoroughly examines it, then tries to take up the poetry of Shen Ch'üan-ch'i (d. c. 713), Sung Chih-wen (d. c. 713), Wang Po, [12] Yang Chiung (d. 692), Lu Chao-lin (c. 641–c. 680), and Lo Pin-wang [13] and thoroughly examines it, then especially tries to take up the poetry of Li Po and Tu Fu and thoroughly examines it, then tries to take up the poetry of the Ta-li era and thoroughly examines it, then tries to take up the poetry of the Yüan-ho era (806–820) and thoroughly examines it, and then finally takes up the poetry of Su Shih and Huang T'ing-chien [14] of the present dynasty and that of their respective followers and thoroughly examines it, then what is right and what is wrong will be unable to remain hidden. If there is still any poetry not listed here, it must consist of wild-fox heterodoxy and will obscure true knowledge of poetry, so that one will be unable to save himself and thus never reach enlightenment.

5. Poetry is concerned with a different kind of talent which has nothing to do with books and involves a different kind of interest which has nothing to do with Principle, but if one does not read books widely and thoroughly investigate Principle, he will never be able to attain the ultimate meaning of poetry. That which has been called "don't travel on the road of Principle and don't fall into the fish trap of words" [15] is the superior way. Poetry is the

10. See selection 42.
11. See selection 21.
12. See selection 164.
13. See selection 27.
14. See selections 56 and 57.
15. This alludes to the *Chuang Tzu*, ch. 26:

expression of one's original nature and the poets of the High T'ang were solely concerned with inspired feeling. They were like antelopes who hung by their horns, leaving no tracks by which they might be found.[16] Their poetry is utterly marvelous because it is transparent as crystal, and thus, like echoes in the air, the play of color in phenomenal appearance, like the moon reflected in water or an image seen in a mirror, their words come to an end, but their meaning is limitless. Modern writers make bizarre interpretations and so consider poetry to consist of language or of talent and learning, or think that it is a kind of reasoned discourse. They certainly are not unskillful, but their poetry will never manage to reach the attainments of that of the ancients because it always lacks the tone made by "one singing and three joining in." [17] Moreover, in composing poems, they too often spend all their attention on allusions while remaining unconcerned with inspiration. Their every word must have a precedent in the sources, and every rhyme they employ must have been used before. Even if one reads them over and over again from beginning to end, it is still impossible to grasp what they are trying to do; the worst of them actually scream and growl, a practice completely against the principle of magnanimity, and almost go so far as to make up poetry out of abusive language! When poetry has reached such a state, it can certainly be called a disaster! However, is there no poetry of modern times that can meet with our approval? Yes, there is, but I grant approval only to that which is in accord with the poetry of the ancients. Thus poetry at the beginning of our dynasty still carried on the tradition of the T'ang poets, and Wang Yü-ch'eng (954–1001) emulated Po Chü-yi,[18] Yang Yi (974–1020) and Liu Yün (fl. c. 1016) emulated Li Shang-yin,[19] Sheng Tu

---

A fish-trap is for catching fish; once you've caught the fish, you can forget about the trap. A rabbit-snare is for catching rabbits; once you've caught the rabbit, you can forget about the snare. Words are for catching ideas; once you've caught the idea, you can forget about the words. Where can I find a person who knows how to forget about words so that I can have a few words with him?

Translated by Victor H. Mair

16. The image of the antelope that hangs by its horns from a tree branch and leaves no tracks was often employed by certain Ch'an masters of the T'ang period. For instance, Master Tao-ying (d. 902) addressed his disciples: "You are like good hunting dogs who only know how to find animals that leave tracks and who now have come across an antelope that hangs by its horns; not only are there no tracks, you don't even recognize its scent!" (from the *Record of the Transmission of the Lamp [Ch'uan-teng lu]*).

17. What these Ch'an masters are saying is: "If you want to learn, you cannot get caught up in the precise, literal meaning of what we have been saying. Sense and reason are useless since we leave no tracks for you to follow." Yen Yü here implies that this is true in great poetry as well, the real significance of which lies beyond sense and reason and the literal meaning of language.

18. See selection 149.

19. See selection 51.

(d.1041) emulated Wei Ying-wu (736–c. 790), Ou-yang Hsiu[20] emulated the ancient style verse of Han Yü, and Mei Yao-ch'en[21] emulated the even-and-bland quality of certain of the T'ang poets, but when Su Shih and Huang T'ing-chien began to bring forth their own ideas in order to make up poetry, this style based on that of the T'ang poets was changed.[22] The efforts made by Huang T'ing-chien were especially intense, and later on his teaching was extremely influential and its adherents became known throughout the world as the Chiang-hsi Sect. In more recent times, poets such as Chao Shih-hsiu (fl. c. 1195–1224) and Weng Chüan (fl. c. 1195–1224) took their sole delight in the poetry of Chia Tao[23] and Yao Ho (fl. c. 831) and to some extent drew near to a pure-and-perservering style. The Poets of Rivers and Lakes[24] mostly emulated their style and called themselves for a time the T'ang School. However, not realizing that they had become the offspring of the Śrāvaka and the Pratyeka, how could they ever think that they had come to possess the True Dharma Eye of the Great Vehicle of the Masters of the High T'ang! Alas! It has been a long time since the transmission of the True Dharma Eye has been interrupted! Although no one has yet begun to chant the doctrine of T'ang poetry, the Way of T'ang poetry may yet one day become manifest, whereas they are now chanting their style, calling it "T'ang poetry," and students will consequently say that T'ang poetry is truly limited to this alone! Can it be possible that the Way of poetry must suffer this double misfortune![25] Therefore, without any particular thought to my own limitations, I always try to determine the main tenets of poetry; borrowing Ch'an as an analogy, and making a careful analysis from the Han and the Wei on, I say with complete determination that we must take that of the High T'ang as representing the Dharma of poetry, and even if I offend all good gentlemen in the world in doing so, I will not recant!

Translated by Richard John Lynn

20. See selection 174.
21. See selections 42 and 54.
22. Became deviant, heterodox.
23. See selection 46.
24. This appellation refers to "commoner poets."
25. The first misfortune was to have poetry develop a non-T'ang "heterodox" style at the hands of Su Shih and Huang T'ing-chien and their followers, and the second misfortune was this present trend to emulate the poetry of the Late T'ang.

15
Poems on Poetry, No. 30

Yüan Hao-wen (1190–1257)

I know my foolishness, a mere ant trying to shake a tree;
Such is the tyro's urge, ever to criticize.
With old age, leaving behind a thousand poems—
By whom will their strengths and weaknesses be judged?

Translated by John Timothy Wixted

Yüan Hao-wen was the most notable literary personage of the Chin (Jürchen) dynasty, under which he was also a high-ranking official. He is best known for his poems mourning the fall of the Chin dynasty to the Mongols and for his three series of poems on poetry, which constitute a rather unusual body of literary criticism. In the latter he praised the northern (more heroic, technically oriented) tradition of which he was a part and disparaged the southern (more intuitional, Zen-like) tradition, for which see selection 14.

PART II

Verse

Classical Poetry

16
Classic of Odes

Anonymous (c. 840–620 B.C.E.)

(1)

> *Kuan-kuan* call the ospreys
> perched there on a river isle.

The *Shih ching* (the *Classic of Odes, Book of Songs,* or *Poetry Classic*) is the most ancient anthology of Chinese poetry. The 305 poems—more properly, songs, since they were lyrics accompanied by tunes now lost—date approximately from the late Western Chou to the middle of the Spring and Autumn period (c. 840–620 B.C.E.), although they appear to have undergone substantial editing and regularization in the following centuries. They are divided into four parts: 160 *Kuo feng* ("Airs of the States"), 74 *Hsiao ya* ("Lesser Ya"), 31 *Ta ya* ("Greater Ya"), and 40 *Sung* ("Temple Hymns"). Of these, the oldest are the Greater and Lesser Ya, and the youngest are the Airs of the States.

The "Airs of the States" preserve an array of folk images and themes. Included in this selection are: 1, an account of the frustrated pursuit of a desirable and mysterious woman; 6, a celebration of the virtues of a new bride; 8, a brief lesson on gathering a fertility herb, punningly named "babes-in-a-pot"; 23, a glimpse at a seduction; 42, an evocation of a woman, or perhaps a goddess, of great beauty; 57, another celebration of feminine beauty; 58, a wife's bitter complaints about her husband's mistreatment of her; 64, a sketch of a courtship ritual in which fruit is exchanged for girdle pendants; 76, a girl's plea that her ardent lover restrain himself; 113, a complaint about greedy landowners; 154, a poetical almanac outlining court rituals and agrarian activities; and 158, a miniature lesson on how a marriage should be conducted.

The "Lesser Ya" and "Greater Ya"—which perhaps take their name from the *ya* or "elegant pronunciation" used in chanting them—seem more concerned with life at the royal court. Selected from the "Greater Ya" are: 245, an account of the miraculous birth and accomplishments of "Lord Millet," mythical founder of the Chou house; and 253, a plea that the king and officials be more mindful of their suffering population.

A pure maid, so alluring,
    a mate worthy of a nobleman.

5   Long and short the water fringe;
    to left and right I hunt it.
A pure maid, so alluring,
    awake and asleep I seek her.

Seeking but not finding,
10   awake and asleep with her I long to lie.
I long, oh, how I long,
    tossing and turning from side to side.

Long and short the water fringe;
    to left and right I pick it.
15   A pure maid, so alluring,
    as lute with zither, I befriend her.

Long and short the water fringe;
    to left and right I cull it.
A pure maid so alluring,
20   as bell with drum, I delight her.

6

That peachtree so frail,
    radiant are its blossoms.
That girl come to marry,
    she is right for this house-and-home.

5   That peachtree so frail,
    swollen is its fruit.

The "Temple Hymns" are represented by one poem: 280, a description of a Chou musical performance presented both to celebrate and please the royal ancestors.

Traditionally, the *Shih ching* has been regarded as a canonical collection of important moral truths and lessons. Confucius saw in its content and language a guide for moderation in speech and action. Later followers of Confucius's teachings read the poems as if they were a detailed chronicle of praise of the heroes and heroines or blame of the villains of early Chinese history. Such interpretations are codified in the official prefaces, glosses, and commentaries written during the late Chou and the Han dynasties. Much later, during the Sung dynasty, there was a reaction against such historical and political explications, especially of the "Airs of the States." There thus emerged the view that most of the pieces are folk songs devoid of political intent and historical judgment—a view of the text that remains prominent today.

The *Shih ching* established the basis for the long and glorious tradition of Chinese classical poetry *(shih)*, which was practiced continuously as the preferred form of literati verse until this century. Other genres of verse *(tz'u, ch'ü, yüeh-fu,* and so on, for which see the following sections) competed with it in succeeding centuries, but *shih* always reigned supreme.

That girl come to marry,
    she is right for this home-and-house.

That peachtree so frail,
10   its leaves are dense.
That girl come to marry,
    she is right for this whole family.

8

So plentiful, the babes-in-a-pot,
    I pick them!
So plentiful, the babes-in-a-pot,
    I hold them!

5   So plentiful, the babes-in-a-pot,
    I squeeze them!
So plentiful, the babes-in-a-pot,
    I caress them!

So plentiful, the babes-in-a-pot,
10   I press them to my blouse!
So plentiful, the babes-in-a-pot,
    I press them to my bodice!

23

On the offering mound, a dead roe,
    white floss grass wraps it up.
There is a girl who longs for spring,
    an auspicious knight leads her forward.

5   In the grove, a trembling oak,
    on the offering mound, a dead deer.
White floss grass binds and ties them.
    The girl is like jade.

"Whoa, gently, gently.
10   Do not move my apron,
    and make the shaggy dog bark."

42

The Chaste Maiden, shining scarlet,
    awaits us at Wall-Nook.
Obscure, invisible,
    scratching her head, immobile.

5   The Chaste Maiden, so clever,
        has given us the Vermilion Stalk.
    The Vermilion Stalk glows bright red
        in celebration of a maiden's beauty.

    From our shepherd we offer young floss grass,
10   sworn to be beautiful and rare.
    Made not in payment for the maiden's beauty,
        but to praise the kind one's gift.

57

    The slender beauty, so tall and alluring,
        wears embroidery neath a grasscloth cloak.
    Child of the Marquis of Ch'i,
        wife of the Marquis of Wei,
5   Sister of the Eastern Palace Heir;
    The Lord of Hsing calls her sister-in-law,
        she calls the Sire of T'an brother-in-law.

    Hands like frail reeds,
        skin like congealed fat.
10 Neck like a tree-grub,
        teeth like melon seeds.
    A cicada head, moth eyebrows.
    Her cunning smile a pale green,
        the lovely eyes so black and white.

15 The slender beauty towers proud,
        offering prayers at the farmer's altar;
    The four stallions are tall,
        their vermilion tassels bushy;
    She rides to court screened by pheasant feathers.
20 Grand officers retire early,
        lest they tire their lord.

    The water of the River swells,
        its northerly flow rushes.
    Stretched nets still the water, *gwat-gwat!*
25   sturgeons beat their tails, *pwat-pwat!*
    Rushes and sedges reach high.
    Attendant ladies, hair coiffed high,
        attendant knights, so forceful.

58

    It takes a very stupid dolt
        to bring cloth to trade for silk.

He didn't come to trade for silk,
    he came to bargain for me!
5 I'll escort you sir across the Ch'i,
    till we come to Heap Hill.
It's not that I want to prolong the date,
    but sir you have no go-between.
I beg you sir be not angry,
10   let's make it autumn that we wed.

I climb that broken-down wall
    to look for your return to the barrier;
When I do not see your approach
    my tears flow unceasingly.
15 When I've seen your return to the barrier,
    then I smile, then I chatter;
You divine with shells, divine with stalks,
    the signs contain no evil words.
You come with your cart
20   to remove me and my dowry.

Before the mulberry has shed,
    its leaves are so glossy!
Beware, oh dove!
    eat not the fruits of the mulberry!
25 Beware, oh girl!
    dally not with a knight!
A knight's dalliances are overlooked,
    but a girl's are never forgiven.

When the mulberry sheds,
30   its leaves turn yellow and fall.
Since I went with you,
    for three years I have swallowed poverty.
When the Ch'i floods,
    it wets the curtains of a carriage.
35 The girl didn't change,
    though the knight was deceiving.
The knight was inconstant,
    his favors cast this way and that.

For three years I was your wife,
40   without tiring of household chores.
Early to rise and late to bed,
    without a morning's leisure.

I have stayed on here
    only to meet with this cruelty.
45   My brothers ignore me,
    if they knew they'd jeer at me.
When I calmly ponder it,
    I see I have hurt myself.

We were to grow old together as one
50   but growing old has made me an object of scorn.
The Ch'i has its banks,
    the marsh has its sides.
During the gay times of hair tied in girlish horns,
    the chatter and laughter were so pleasant.
55   The promises and oaths were so earnest,
    I never thought it'd change.
That it would change was unthinkable to me
    and now all is ended.

64

Throw me a quince
    and I'll repay you with carnelian.
Though not a worthy repayment,
    long may you find pleasure in it.

5   Throw me a peach,
    and I'll repay you with turquoise.
Though not a worthy repayment,
    long may you find pleasure in it.

Throw me a plum
10   and I'll repay you with obsidian.
Though not a worthy repayment,
    long may you find pleasure in it.

76

Please, Sir Second-born,
    don't jump our village wall,
    don't break our planted willows.
Would I dare begrudge them?
5   I simply fear my parents.
Though you, Sir, I cherish,
    I also fear my parents' words.

Please, Sir Second-born,
    don't jump our outer wall,

10   don't break our planted mulberries.
    Would I dare begrudge them?
        I simply fear my elder brothers.
    Though you, Sir, I cherish
        I also fear my brothers' words.

15 Please, Sir Second-born,
        don't jump our garden wall,
        don't break our planted spindletrees.
    Would I dare begrudge them?
        I simply fear the gossip of other people.
20 Though you, Sir, I cherish,
        I also fear the gossip of other people.

(113)

Big rats! Big rats!
    Don't eat our millet!
For three years we've spoiled you,
    but none of you has requited us.
5   It's got to the point where we'll leave you
        and go to that happy land.
    Happy land! Happy land!
        There we'll find a place.

Big rats! Big rats!
10   Don't eat our wheat!
For three years we've spoiled you,
    but none of you has rewarded us.
It's got to the point where we'll leave you
    and go to that happy state.
15 Happy state! Happy state!
        There we'll find a proper place.

Big rats! Big rats!
    Don't eat our sprouting grain!
For three years we've spoiled you,
10   but none of you has thanked us.
It's got to the point where we'll leave you
    and go to that happy frontier.
Happy frontier! Happy frontier!
    Who moans and groans there?

(154)

In the seventh month, declining is the Fire Star;
    in the ninth month, you must distribute clothes.

If not, in the days of the first month, when the cold wind blows,
    in the days of the second month, when the chill air stirs,
5   Noblemen will lack their robes, the poor will lack their flannels.
        How then will they end the year?
    In the days of the third month, attend to the plow;
        in the days of the fourth month, raise high your heel.
    Our assembled wives and children
10   bring food offerings to those southern fields;
    The Chief of the Fields comes and enjoys the banquet.

    In the seventh month, declining is the Fire Star;
        in the ninth month, you must distribute clothes.
    When the spring days become warm
15   and singing is the oriole,
    The women grasp their deep baskets
        and follow along tiny paths,
    There to seek tender mulberry leaves.
    "As the spring days lengthen
20   we gather in crowds to pick the multiflora."
    The girl's heart is deeply pained,
        but she'll meet a young nobleman and join him in marriage.

    In the seventh month, declining is the Fire Star;
        in the eighth month, the rushes and sedges are prepared.
25   In the silkworm month, separate the branches of the mulberry;
        take those axes and hatchets,
    Use them to cut the branches that extend far and reach high,
        and bundle those mulberry shoots.
    In the seventh month, singing is the shrike;
30   when it is the eighth month, then spin,
        spin both black and yellow.
    My vermilion dye is very bright,
        I make a skirt for a young nobleman.

    In the fourth month, seeding is the *yao* grass;
35   in the fifth month, singing is the cicada.
    In the eighth month you should harvest;
        in the tenth month, the trees shed and leaves fall.
    In the days of the first month, go and hunt badgers;
        catch those foxes and raccoon-dogs
40   and make fur garments for a young nobleman.
    In the days of the second month, you should go on the joint hunt
        and thus augment your military prowess;

Keep for yourselves the year-old boars
    but present to your sire the three-year-old boars.
45   In the fifth month, the locusts shake their legs;
    in the sixth month, the grasshoppers flutter their wings.
In the seventh month, it is in the barrens;
    and in the eighth month, under the eaves.
In the ninth month, it is at the doorway;
50   and in the tenth month, the cricket enters and stays beneath the bed.
Stop up the holes and smoke out the rats;
    block the northern window and plaster the door.
Oh, wife and children!
    Because we are passing into a new year,
55   enter this shelter and stay here.

In the sixth month, eat wild plums and cherries;
    in the seventh month, boil the mallows and pulse.
In the eighth month, harvest the dates;
    in the tenth month, reap the rice.
60   Make this spring wine
    with which to increase vigorous old age.
In the seventh month, eat melons;
    in the eighth month, cut gourds.
In the ninth month, gather hemp seeds,
65   pick bitter herbs, chop ailanto into firewood,
    thus help nourish our chief husbandman.

In the ninth month, ram the earth of the threshing floor;
    and in the tenth month, bring in the harvest:
The glutinous millet and the panicled millet,
70   the late-ripening grains and those that ripen early,
    the hemp, the pulse, and the wheat.
Oh, chief husbandman!
    Our harvest is gathered together;
    enter and manage the tasks of the palace.
75   If at dawn you attend to the floss grass,
    at dusk you weave the ropes.
Quickly mend the thatch on the roof
    and start to scatter the myriad grains.

In the days of the second month,
80   cut chunks of ice, *dong-dong!*
In the days of the third month,
    store them in the ice house.

In the days of the fourth month,
    rise early to present lamb and offer onions.
85   In the ninth month, things shrivel with the frost;
    in the tenth month, clean the threshing floor.
Twin wine vessels are offered as a feast
    and then slaughter lambs and sheep.
Enter that Noble Hall
90   and lift in a toast the rhino cup:
    May you live forever and without end!

158

How do you cut an ax-handle?
    Only an ax can do it!
How do you take a bride?
    Only a go-between can succeed!

5   In cutting an ax-handle, in cutting an ax-handle,
    the model is near at hand.
I have joined with that girl;
    basket and platter are aligned.

245

The one who first gave birth to our people,
    this was Chiang Yüan.
How did she give birth to our people?
    She knew to make the Yin and Ssu offerings,
5   Thereby to eliminate her barrenness.
    She trod on the toe-print made by God.
She was the one enriched, the one on whom the blessing rested.
    She became pregnant, she refrained from sex;
She gave birth to him, she nurtured him—
10   He was Lord Millet.

Truly she went her full term;
    her first-born came forth easily like a lamb.
He did not tear, he did not rend;
    there was no injury, no harm.
15   Thus, He made evident his magic power.
    Did not God-on-High give her comfort?
Did He not enjoy her Yin and Ssu offerings?
    For tranquilly she gave birth to the child.

Truly she placed him in a narrow lane
20   where oxen and sheep protected and cherished him;

Truly she placed him in a forested plain
    where he was met with by woodcutters;
Truly she placed him on cold ice
    where birds covered him with their wings—
25 When the birds left,
        Lord Millet bawled!

He sat up, he cried out,
    and his voice was already strong;
Truly he crawled about,
30   able to raise himself up expectantly and stand resolutely erect.
And when he sought to feed himself
    he planted giant beans.
The giant beans grew tall,
    the ears of grain grew luxuriantly;
35 The hemp and wheat grew thick,
        the gourds were abundant.

Truly Lord Millet's husbandry
    was a divinely aided method.
He cleared the thick grasses,
40   and planted the fields with the yellow crop.
It grew evenly, it became luxuriant,
    it grew singly, it grew tall;
It flowered, it eared,
    it was firm, it was fine;
45 Its ears ripened, its kernels hardened.
        Accordingly he took T'ai for his house-and-home.

Truly God sent down the blessed grains:
    the black millet, the double-kerneled;
the millet vermilion-sprouted and white.
50   He spread the black millet and the double-kerneled,
these he reaped and gathered by the acre;
    He spread the vermilion and white millet,
these he carried on his shoulder and on his back.
    He brought them home and made an offering.

55 Truly, how do we make our offerings?
        Some pound the grain, others bale it out;
Some sift, some tread;
    We wash it—sop sop,
and boil it till it's steamy.
60   We plan and we ponder;

We pick southern wood and offer fat,
    take a ram to offer to the spirit of the road;
Then we roast and we broil,
    to initiate the new year.

65   High we load the footed vessels;
    we place it on the footed vessels and stands.
Its aroma starts to ascend
    and God-on-High, well pleased, savors it:
"What smell is this, so pure and good?"
    Lord Millet inaugurated the offerings,
and without our suffering any blame or regret,
    they have continued till now.

253

The common people are very weary
    and now might be allowed a little repose;
Be kind to this Central Kingdom
    and thereby comfort the four quarters.
5   Indulge not the wily and obsequious
    and so instill care in the wicked;
Crush the robbers and tyrants
    for they have not respected your brightness.
Be gentle to those far off, be good to those nearby,
    and so make our king secure.

The common people are very weary
    and now might be allowed a little rest;
Be kind to this Central Kingdom
    so that the people will gather here.
15   Indulge not the wily and obsequious
    and so instill care in the catcallers;
Crush the robbers and tyrants
    so the people will not be made to suffer.
Neglect not your labors
20   so our king will enjoy rest.

The common people are very weary
    and now might be allowed a little respite;
Be kind to this Capital City
    and thereby comfort the four states
25   Indulge not the wily and obsequious
    and so instill care in the excessive;
Crush the robbers and tyrants,
    prevent them from doing evil.

Be mindful of your awesome bearing
30   and so bring near the virtuous.

The common people are very weary
    and now might be allowed a little relief;
Be kind to this Central Kingdom
    so that the people's cares will drain away.
35 Indulge not the wily and obsequious
    and so instill care in the evil;
Crush the robbers and tyrants,
    let them not ruin the upright.
Although you are but as small children
40   your effect is vast and great.

The common people are very weary
    and now might be allowed a little peace;
Be kind to this Central Kingdom
    so that it will suffer no injury.
45 Indulge not the wily and obsequious
    and so instill care in the parasites;
Crush the robbers and tyrants,
    let them not overturn the upright.
Oh, king, I wish to make you like jade,
50   and so have resorted to this great remonstrance.

Translated by Jeffrey Riegel

17
Cockfight

Liu Chen (d. 217)

The cinnabar cockerels sport resplendent hues,
Their paired spurs like tips of blades.
Ready to parade their blazing might,
4   They join in battle on this courtyard path.

Liu Chen was an official in the service of the Ts'ao family, who, at the time this poem was written, shortly before 217, were feudal rulers with their capital in the city of Yeh in Honan. Liu Chen was a distinguished member of the Seven Masters of the Chien-an Reign, who were patronized by Ts'ao Ts'ao (see selection 139) and his two literarily minded sons, Ts'ao Chih (192–232) and Ts'ao P'i (187–226).

Sharp claws test the jade steps,
Glaring eyes are infused with fiery light;
Long tail-feathers lift in a startling wind,
8   Hackle quills spread in display.
They spring and wield bent beaks,
Strike like lightning and again fly back.

Translated by Robert Joe Cutter

18
Songs of My Soul

Juan Chi (210–263)

1

It is the middle of the night—I cannot sleep,
I sit up to pluck my dulcet lute;
Through thin curtains, I view the bright moon,
A soothing breeze blows at my lapels.

A lone goose cries in the wild beyond,
A soaring bird sings in the woods to the north;
Pacing to and fro, I wonder what my future will bring—
Anxious and alone, my poor heart is broken.

49

My steps lead me to a junction of three roads,
I ruefully recall the object of my thoughts;
Could it be that I shall see him this morning?
Verily, he would seem to appear nebulously.

In the marsh a towering pine tree grows,
I cannot hope for its span of ten thousand generations;
The high-flying birds brush against the sky,
Happily they roam together above the clouds.

Juan Chi was a member of the Seven Sages of the Bamboo Grove, a group of poet-intellectuals noted for their eccentric behavior and aloofness from official life. His most famous poems, a series of eighty-two pieces called "Songs of My Soul," evince a mood of deep pessimism and sorrow in keeping with the atmosphere of the times. He made extensive use of symbolic language, probably to avoid the suspicions of those in power. Juan Chi lamented the shortness of life as well as the stupidity and ill will of his contemporaries. He longed for liberation or, at least, a true friend to console him in his melancholy.

But here I am, a lonely man walking along the road;
Tears falling, I bemoan the days gone by.

50

The lucent dew congeals into frost,
Flowering grasses give way to mugwort and goosefoot;
Who says that the ruler's sagacity
And perspicuity can long endure?

So I'll mount a cloud and summon immortal Sung and Wang,
Who will teach me how to respire [1] and live forever!

56

Whether one is eminent or humble depends on Fate,
Success and failure each has its own season.

Genial, glib-tongued good-for-nothings
Cheat each other in pursuit of profit;
Ingrates degrade grace bestowed,
And expose it to the scorn of slanderers.

The wagtail chirrups among the clouds,
Flying continuously with nothing to hope for,
How could one expect that the man who kept aloof
One day would be unable to preserve himself?

59

An elder lives by the side of the river,
He weaves baskets of reeds and throws away pearls; [2]
He finds pigweed and pulse sweet to his taste,
And enjoys his hut of wattle and thatch.

How could he ape those fine, young dandies,
Who go riding in light chariots drawn by fine horses?
In the morning, they are born beside the best highways,
In the evening, they are buried at the edges of byways.

Before our joy and laughter have come to an end,
We find ourselves sighing and sobbing in the twinkling of an eye;

1. A reference to the yogic breathing techniques of the Taoist practitioners. Sung is Ch'ih
Sung Tzu, Master Red Pine; Wang is Wang-tzu Ch'iao. Both were Taoist transcendents.
2. An allusion to the penultimate parable in the *Chuang Tzu*, ch. 32 (see selection 8).

As I observe these flighty fellows,
I express my indignation with these words.

60

The Confucianist is versed in the Six Arts,[3]
Once his mind is made up, nothing can sway him;
He will do nothing which contravenes the Rites,
And will say nothing which is contrary to the Law.

If he is thirsty, he drinks from a pure stream,
And, even when hungry, eats but a bamboo bowl of rice in two days.
He has nothing to sacrifice at the seasons of the year;
Through his clothing he often feels the bitter cold.

Shuffling along in his sandals, he chants "South Wind,"
In his coarse gown, he laughs at the fancy chariots;
He has faith in the Way and holds fast to *Poetry* and *History*,
Righteously he will not accept a single free meal.

But his criticism is so caustic
That Lao Tzu could only heave a long sigh of despair.

71

The hibiscus grows lushly on the grave mounds,
It shines with scintillating brilliance;
But when the bright sun plummets into the forest,
Its petals flutter forlornly by the roadside.

The cricket chirrups by my windowsill,
The cicada buzzes amidst the brambles;
Ephemerids' play lasts only three mornings,
Then they die in a teeming heap of pretty wings.

For whom do they put on all their finery?
It is just self-preening as they drift with the time;
Ah! How very short is life's alloted span!
Still, impassioned, each being pours forth all of its energy.

Translated by Victor H. Mair

3. Ritual or ceremony, music, archery, charioteering, writing, numbers.

19

Poem on the Wandering Immortal [1]

Kuo P'u (276–324)

Kingfishers frolic among the orchid blossoms,
each form and hue lending freshness to the others.
Green creepers twine over the tall grove,
4   their leafy darkness shadowing the whole hill.
And in the midst, a man of quiet retirement
softly whistles, strokes the clear lute strings,
frees his thoughts to soar beyond the blue,
8   munches flower stamens, dips from a waterfall.
When Red Pine [2] appears, roaming on high,
this man rides a stork, mounting the purple mists,
his left hand holding Floating Hill's sleeve,
12   his right hand patting Vast Cliff on the shoulder.
Let me ask those short-lived mayflies,
what could they know of the years of the tortoise and the crane?

Translated by Burton Watson

The poet was a Taoist mystic, geomancer, collector of strange tales, editor of old texts, and erudite commentator. Kuo P'u was the first commentator of the *Mountains and Seas Classic* (*Shan-hai ching*) and so probably, with the noted Han bibliographer Liu Hsin (d. 23), was instrumental in preserving this valuable mythological and religious text (see second poem in selection 20).

1. The word for "immortal" *(hsien)* is elsewhere in this anthology sometimes translated as "transcendent." Neither translation is entirely satisfactory for rendering this technical term which signifies someone highly accomplished in various Taoist arts for prolonging life. Translations such as "fairy" or "god" are even less suitable.

2. Red Pine, Floating Hill, and Vast Cliff are all legendary immortals of ancient times.

20

Poems After Drinking Wine (No. 5)

T'ao Ch'ien (365–427)

I built my hut beside a traveled road
Yet hear no noise of passing carts and horses.

T'ao Ch'ien, also called T'ao Yüan-ming, lived in the Six Dynasties, a period of disunity when northern China had fallen into the hands of non-Chinese leaders. The south, where T'ao

You would like to know how it is done?
4   With the mind detached, one's place becomes remote.
Picking chrysanthemums by the eastern hedge
I catch sight of the distant southern hills:
The mountain air is lovely as the sun sets
8   And flocks of flying birds return together.
In these things is a fundamental truth
I would like to tell, but lack the words.

                    Translated by James Robert Hightower

---

lived, was ruled by a succession of weak and short-lived dynasties that had their capitals in modern Nanking.

Of Hsi ancestry (that is, of non-Han origins), the poet was born into a family of a minor official. He was proud of his distinguished great-grandfather T'ao K'an, who had been enfeoffed as Duke of Ch'ang-sha for his services to the Chin dynasty. His maternal grandfather, Meng Chia, was a close associate of Huan Wen, a powerful figure in China at the time. Feeling an obligation to continue the family tradition of government service, T'ao Ch'ien had served as secretary or adviser to various generals, but none of the positions was very satisfying to him; he continually yearned to return to the pastoral life. In the year 415, through the assistance of an uncle, he was appointed magistrate of P'eng-tse, a post he held only for eighty days before retiring from public service for good. For twenty-two years after that, T'ao Ch'ien led a farmer's life and experienced all the hardships that it entailed. He was much admired, both by his contemporaries and by succeeding generations, for never compromising his ideals. But now he is recognized even more for the greatness of his poetry and essays.

It is easy to understand why this is one of T'ao Ch'ien's most famous poems and one of the most celebrated and oft-quoted poems in the whole of the Chinese literary tradition. It conveys admirably the detachment and repose of the Great Recluse who makes his home among men yet remains uncontaminated by the world, whose communion with nature occurs as readily through the chrysanthemums by the eastern hedge as through the distant mountain scenery. A fundamental truth seems to have been communicated, even as the poet suggests, without having been formulated in words.

The first line begins with the expression *chieh lu*, which suggests "thatched hut," though the verb *chieh* is common enough in combination with words meaning "building" or "house." Actually the line says nothing about a "traveled road"; a closer translation would be "I built my hut in an inhabited area" (i.e., not off by itself in the wilds).

T'ao Ch'ien attributes his ability to ignore the world while living in it to a "mind that is far away," and the next couplet tells what his absent mind is concerned with. He is picking chrysanthemums, not to put in a vase for decoration, but to use as medicine, probably in a wine infusion. The purpose of such a concoction is to prolong life ("Chrysanthemum is tonic against growing old," as he wrote in another poem, "Living in Retirement on the Double Ninth Festival"), and the Southern Mountain which catches his eye as he is picking the petals is not an irrelevant piece of scenery but a prime symbol of the thing he has in mind. "Longevity like the Southern Mountain" is the irresistible associative link from the *Classic of Odes*, one of T'ao Ch'ien's favorite texts. It provides a touch of irony as much as of reassurance, however, for even a confirmed believer in potions and exercises (which T'ao Ch'ien was not) could hardly hope for long life of such dimensions. At the same time, this particular Southern Mountain had for T'ao Ch'ien another, not unrelated, meaning, which made the Mountain of Long Life the prospective site for his grave.

On Reading the *Mountains and Seas Classic*

T'ao Ch'ien

I

In early summer when the grasses grow
And trees surround my house with greenery,
The birds rejoice to have a refuge there
4   And I, too, love my home.
The fields are plowed and the new seed planted
And now is time again to read my books.
This out-of-the-way lane has no deep-worn ruts [1]
8   And tends to turn my friends' carts away.
With happy face I pour the spring-brewed wine
And in the garden pick some greens to cook.
A gentle shower approaches from the east
12   Accompanied by a temperate breeze.
I skim through the *Story of King Mu*
And view the pictures in the *Mountains and Seas Classic.*
A glance encompasses the ends of the universe —
16   Where is there any joy, if not in these?

Translated by James Robert Hightower

This limpid lyric introduces the series by recreating the ideal occasion for a farmer's reading, the time of leisure after the spring planting. The poet does not expect visitors and finds an excuse for his friends' neglect; philosophically he pours himself a drink and turns to his favorite books. Nothing better dramatizes the dearth of works of the imagination in early Chinese literature than the two which he seizes upon. Both the *Story of King Mu* (*Mu t'ien-tzu chuan*) and the *Mountains and Seas Classic* are the products of fantasy; they freely introduce magic and marvels, but in a form closer to Baedeker than Malory. The first pretends to be history, the second geography; only a mind starved for fiction could rejoice in either. T'ao Ch'ien's enthusiasm is contagious; and if only the books had been safely lost, we could easily share his pleasure. We still can, if we are content to do it vicariously.

1. Deep ruts are a sign of traffic, particularly of the kind of carriage driven by officials.

21

On My Way from South Mountain to North Mountain, I Glance at the Scenery from the Lake

Hsieh Ling-yün (385–433)

At dawn I set out from the sunlit cliffs,
At sunset I take my rest by the shaded peaks.
Leaving my boat, I turn my eyes upon the distant sandbars,
4   Resting my staff, I lean against the lush pines.
The small mountain paths are far and deep,
The ring-like islets are beautiful and pleasing.
I view the twigs of tall trees above,
8   I listen to the torrents in the deep valley below.
The rocks lie flat, and the river divides its flow;
The forest is dense, tracks are buried and lost.
What is the effect of Nature's "deliverance" and "becoming"?
12 All things growing are lush and thriving.
Young bamboos are wrapped in green sheaths,
Fresh rushes embrace their purple flowers;
Seagulls play by the springtime banks,
16 Wild pheasants sport in the gentle breeze.

Translated by Kang-i Sun Chang

The poet was a descendant of an illustrious and affluent northern émigré family of the Southern Dynasties. He was especially well known for his landscape poetry but was also noted as a devout Buddhist, and many of his works combine his interest in Buddhism with his attachment to the beauties of nature, especially mountains (see introductory note to selection 181). Hsieh was censured by literary critics of his own day and succeeding generations for being difficult because he made frequent use of allusion, ambiguity, and parallelism. His work is highly imaginative yet full of natural imagery. He wrote several philosophical prose pieces and was also involved in the translation of key Buddhist scriptures. A headstrong individual, Hsieh was repeatedly banished to the far south and finally executed.

22

Harmonizing with a Poem by Left Assistant Yü Kao-chih Requesting Sick Leave

Shen Yüeh (441–513)

At year's end is there anything one can depend on?
Helter-skelter, grief and sickness come by turns.
Were it not for bath-leave, who could ever find relief?
4   How to preserve oneself has surely never been transmitted.
If you clutch an orchid, it will vainly fill your grasp;
If you await the water-clock, it never flows completely out.
Tumult and uproar both are rife before our eyes,
8   While records and directives multiply upon our laps.
What use is there for eloquence that talks of heaven?
A futile exercise to dream of being given a brush to write great things.
Hang up your cap, as Feng Meng did beside the Eastern City Gate;
12   Why ever come again out of the hills and forests?

Translated by Richard Mather

Shen Yüeh was renowned as the deviser of the basic rules for regulated verse, which became the prestige form of poetry in the T'ang and later periods. He achieved this by adapting metrical Sanskrit prosody to the tonal features of Sinitic languages. Shen successfully experimented with these revolutionary ideas in his own verse. In addition, he was the editor of the *History of the [Liu] Sung*, which, as might be expected from someone of Shen Yüeh's inclinations, includes an unusually large number of literary biographies for an official dynastic history. Imbued with a transcendent Taoist sentiment, he was also deeply attracted to Buddhism for its compassion and spirituality. At the same time, he responded to the Confucian call to public service.

Listening to Gibbons at Rock-Pool Creek

Shen Yüeh

Yow! Yow! Night gibbons cry.
Soft, soft, dawn mists mesh.
Are their voices far? nearby?
Just see mountains piled up high.
Having liked the East Hill's song,
I now await West Cliff's reply.

Translated by Richard W. Bodman

23

Describing a Dream for Someone

Wang Seng-ju (465–522)

I've known fancies turn into dreaming,
but never believed a dream could be like this:
she was fair, fair, immaculate,
4   she was pure, pure perfection,
as she sat, intimate, by hibiscus cushions,
as she turned back the joy-of-love quilt,
and her elegant footsteps were so lovely,
8   her whispered words most enchanting.
What I describe didn't seem to happen fast,
but then, strangely, became a momentary thing,
and I woke to nothingness,
12   aware that all is empty illusion.

Translated by Anne Birrell

Wang Seng-ju was from a poor family, but he rose to the rank of censor under the Liang rulers. The name Seng may denote a formal connection with Buddhist religious life. The wit of his poem stems from his intelligent and lively use of well-known Buddhist concepts such as nothingness, dreams, and empty illusion.

24

Spring Day

Yü Chien-wu (487–550)

Peach blossoms are red, willow catkins white,
Shimmering in the sun and swaying in the wind;
Their shape emerges beyond the vermilion walls,
4   Their fragrance goes back to the blue hall.
Mirrored in the water, parasitic bamboos,
Lying across the hill, a half-dead paulownia tree;

One of the foremost exponents of the so-called palace-style poetry, which focused on courtly themes in the broadest sense, including the lives, emotions, and manners of the inhabitants of the women's apartments. He was the father of the poet Yü Hsin, the author of the famous "Rhapsody of Lament for the South," a history in rhymeprose of the Liang dynasty and its fall.

The list of awardees announced, I realize the great bounty;
8   Grasping my writing tablet, I am chagrined by my paltry talent.

Translated by Victor H. Mair and Tsu-Lin Mei

25
A Pheasant on His Morning Flight

Hsiao Kang (503–551)

The dawning sun shines upon the royal wheat fields,
A spring fowl crosses the deserted plain;
At times raising his plumicorns to elude the falcon,
He suddenly wheels aslant to spite the mounds.

Young men serve on distant campaigns,
Resentful, their thoughts brim with rebellion;
Better follow after a profligate courtier,
Whose silken sleeves brush the robes of ministers.

Translated by Victor H. Mair and Tsu-Lin Mei

The author was both crown prince and center of a flourishing literary salon in the Eastern Palace of the Liang royal establishment. The efforts of the circle of poets around him resulted in the development of a palace-style poetry (see selection 24). Hsiao Kang was quite likely the sponsor of the epochal collection of love poetry entitled *New Songs from Jade Terrace* (compiled c. 545 by the court poet Hsü Ling) that enshrined this style of verse. His own brother, Hsiao T'ung, was the editor of the famous *Literary Selections (Wen-hsüan,* see selection 12), the seminal anthology of traditional Chinese prose and verse that was intended to stand in opposition to the current literary fashion as exemplified by *New Songs from Jade Terrace (Yü-t'ai hsin-yung).* Curiously, however, the *Jade Terrace* collection is also noted for its preservation of a number of earlier popular songs and ballads (see, for example, selections 132–135).

26
Untitled

Brahmacārin Wang (c. 7th–8th centuries)

I have a couple acres of land
Planted on the slopes of South Mountain;

The vast majority of the poems attributed to Wang Fan-chih (=Sanskrit Brahmacārin ["Lay Buddhist devotee or ascetic with his mind set on purity"]) were recovered only in the early part

There are four or five blue pines
And two vines of green beans.

When it's hot, I bathe in the pond,
When it's cool, I sing by its banks;
Rambling about, I take my satisfaction,
Completely unaffected by others.

Translated by Victor H. Mair

---

of last century among the Tun-huang manuscripts (see selection 214). They are important for the large amount of vernacularisms they employ. Like the Cold Mountain poems (see selection 45) with which they share so many similarities, the oeuvre of Wang Fan-chih was almost certainly not written by a single individual but, rather, represents a certain type of popular poetry with proto-Zen tendencies.

27
On the Cicada: In Prison

Lo Pin-wang (before 640–684?)

The Western Course: a cicada's voice singing;
A southern cap: longing for home intrudes.
How can I bear those shadows of black locks

The poet's youth was spent in poverty. He enlisted in the army and was stationed in the Western Regions and in Szechwan. Lo is considered one of the four most important poets in the early part of the T'ang period.

Paraphrase by the translator:

When the sun moves through the Western Course of the heavens, a sign of autumn, the cicada sings. Its singing causes homesickness in me, like that once felt by Chung Yi of Ch'u, wearing his southern cap as a memento of his homeland when a prisoner in the state of Ch'in. Like him, I am a southerner imprisoned in the North. How can I bear that those wings of the cicada, so often used to describe the curls of beautiful ladies, come to listen to my "Song of White Hair," like that which Cho Wen-chün [see selection 129] sang when Ssu-ma Hsiang-ju abandoned her? Those black cicada wings like curls remind me of youth and attractive beauty, unbearable to one who is growing old and feels rejected by his ruler. Furthermore, since the singing of the cicada is a reminder of autumn, the season associated with the coming of old age, how can I bear that it come any closer to me, reminding me of my own aging? But perhaps I have misunderstood the cicada: associated with purity and old age, it may be a kindred spirit. If my ruler hears it, it may remind him of *my* purity and old age, and thus obtain my release. In this respect, its singing is like pleading my case to the throne. But it, like me, is caught up in the autumn situation that it represents: the dew is so heavy upon it that it can fly no farther and thus will not be able to get into the palace and reach the ruler's ears. Furthermore, though I might hope that its singing will be heard from outside, the autumn wind is so strong that its voice will be drowned out. Even if his singing,

4   That come here to face my "Song of White Hair"?
    Dew heavy on it, can fly no farther toward me;
    The wind strong, its echoes easily lost.
    No one believes in nobility and purity—
8   On my behalf who will explain what's in my heart?

Translated by Stephen Owen

---

or my own in this poem, were to reach near the throne, it would do no good, because no one believes any more in nobility or purity—neither mine, my innocence of crime, nor that of the cicada. Thus there is no one to state my case for me.

28

Written Impromptu upon Returning to My Hometown

Ho Chih-chang (659–744)

I left home as a youth and am returning an old man—
The sounds of my hometown have not changed,
   yet the hair on my temples is receding;
The children look at me but do not recognize me—
Laughing, they ask, "Guest, where have you come from?"

Translated by Victor H. Mair

From the lower Yangtze valley, Ho Chih-chang was a high official in the capital, Ch'ang-an, who befriended the young Li Po (see selection 35) and became a boon drinking companion of the latter.

29

Poems of Reflection on the Vicissitudes of Life

Ch'en Tzu-ang (661–702)

5

The men in the market pride themselves on their knowledge and craft,
But they are as ignorant as babes in regard to the Way;

Though he successfully passed the highest civil service examination in 684, Ch'en Tzu-ang was more than once unjustly imprisoned on various charges, and he eventually died while

Amidst the press and grab, they make boastful display of luxury—
They know not where their bodies will one day end up.

How could they ever see the Master of Dark Purity,
Who observed the world in a jade pot?
Frustrated, he left behind him heaven and earth,
And entered Infinity mounted on Transformation.

10

I dwell in seclusion and observe the creative process,
Inarticulate, my jaws quiver in an effort to speak;
Speakers of slander devour each other,
Profit and loss are fraught with deception.

Disputatious are the sycophants,
They contend with each other for glory;
Wu Kuang turned down the rule of the empire,
But a merchant will compete for a penny.

Have done with it all! Go pick the magic mushroom,
Ten thousand generations will be as a moment.

13

I dwell in the forest nursing a long illness,
The water and trees accentuate the solitude and stillness;
I lie here idly observing the changes in nature,
And meditate absentmindedly on ending rebirth.

In spring, buds are just beginning to show,
Then summer's red sun arrives in all its fullness;
But death and decline begin from that moment—
Oh, when will my sorrowful sighs come to rest?

Translated by Victor H. Mair

---

incarcerated. He was the forerunner of early T'ang literary reforms, which rejected the decadent style of the Six Dynasties period, advocating in its place the masculine style of the Han and Wei periods. There are a total of thirty-eight poems in this series.

30
Poems of Reflection on the Vicissitudes of Life

Chang Chiu-ling (673–740)

I close my door and trace the transformations of nature,
Living in the forest, I focus on the object of my thoughts;
I sigh for the tree in the winter cold,
For in days gone by it was lushly fragrant.

In the morning sun, where is the phoenix?
At sunset, the cicada is sad and alone;
My thoughts overwhelm me in the middle of the night,
Deeply I sigh, asking myself whom I await.

What I had cherished has surely gone forever,
And since it is gone, it cannot be retrieved;
Eating from bronze tripods is no affair of mine,
Life on a clouded mountain has been my hope.

The north is so very distant from the south—
And how my chariot horses do tarry!
Heaven and earth are totally alien to each other—
Silently I lie within my curtains.

Translated by Victor H. Mair

The poet became a Presented Scholar (comparable to the academic doctorate in the West) in 702 after passing the highest civil service examination. He served as an able prime minister for Emperor Hsüan Tsung. Chang Chiu-ling's poems greatly influenced the development of a type of poetry that reflects upon the landscape while revealing the inner mind. This is the last in a series of twelve poems.

31
Climbing the Stork Pavilion

Wang Chih-huan (688–742)

The white sun leaning on the mountain disappears,
The Yellow River flows on into the sea;

The author was born into a family of officials. He himself served as a county magistrate and held other minor posts. Most of his poetic works have been lost, only six quatrains surviving. These, however, have been sufficient to establish him as a significant figure in discussions of T'ang period literature.

To stretch your gaze a thousand leagues,
Climb up still another story.

Translated by Richard W. Bodman

32

Seeking Out Master Chan on Incense Mountain

Meng Hao-jan (689?–740)

On a morning ramble I visit a great mountain,
The mountain far away in the empty azure.
Billowing mist spreads over a hundred leagues;
4   As the sun goes down I reach my goal at last.
At the valley's mouth I hear a bell sound;
By the wood's edge scent a breath of incense.
Leaning on my staff, I seek an old friend;
8   Having loosened the saddle, give my mount a rest.
The stone gate is hard by a chasm's brink;
A bamboo-lined path winds through the forest depths.
I enjoy meeting with a "Companion in the Law";[1]
12   In "Pure Talk"[2] we stay up until dawn.
All my life I have respected true reclusion,
For days on end sought spiritual mysteries.
An old rustic goes to his fields at dawn;
16   A mountain monk returns to his temple in the evening.
There are many pure notes in pines and streams;
These moss-grown walls are wrapped in a feeling of antiquity.
How I would like to retire to this very mountain,
20   "Casting off both self and world alike."

Translated by Daniel Bryant

Meng Hao-jan was the oldest of the leading poets of the High T'ang period. Unlike many others, he had never passed the official examinations or obtained a position in the civil service. Despite his lack of success in official employment, he became acquainted with many highly placed men in the government. He also gained the respect of a number of outstanding younger poets. Wang Wei, Li Po, and Tu Fu all wrote moving tributes to him (see, for example, the first poem in selection 35), although Tu Fu does not seem to have met him personally.

1. Someone who pursues a religious, usually Buddhist, life.
2. Abstruse, witty discourse that is often associated with Taoists.

Spring Dawn

Meng Hao-jan

Asleep in spring unaware of dawn,
And everywhere hear the birds in song.
At night the sound of wind and rain,
You'll know how much from the flowers gone.

Translated by Elling Eide

Passing Seven-League Rapids

Meng Hao-jan

I heed the warning not to "sit beneath the eaves,"[1]
A thousand coins are not to be taken lightly.
Finding great pleasure in hills and streams,
4   I have made many journeys, drifting in boats.
On the Five Sacred Mountains I have sought Shang Tzu-p'ing.[2]
By the Three Rivers Hsiang, mourned for Ch'ü Yüan.[3]
Lakes—I have crossed the breadth of Tung-t'ing;[4]
8   Rivers—I enter the clear Hsin-an.[5]

And now I hear the rapids of Yen Kuang,
For they lie on the course of this very stream.
Through layered ridges for hundreds of leagues,
12   Back and forth with no constant direction.
Verdure and raven-black swirl and billow together,
In parted streams pouring and tumbling at random.
The fishing reef is level enough for a seat,
16   But the mossy steps are slippery and hard to walk.

1. The sort of scion who should not "sit beneath the eaves" lest something fall from the roof and injure him was one from a family that held a thousand coins (or ingots).
2. A semi-legendary recluse.
3. See selection 122.
4. A large lake in central China.
5. A tributary of the Che. Shortly below where it joins the main stream is a stretch of rough water called the Seven-league Rapids. It was here that Yen Kuang, once a youthful companion to the man who later became Emperor Kuang-wu, restorer of the Han dynasty, retired to fish from a broad boulder above the river, refusing to join the government of his erstwhile companion.

Monkeys drink from pools below the rocks,
And birds return to the sun-rimmed trees.
I gaze on this wonder and regret that I came so late,
20   Rest on my oar and lament that darkness comes.
Swirling my hands, I dally with the swift-moving waters,
Washed clean henceforth of all dusty cares.

Translated by Daniel Bryant

33
Silent at Her Window

Wang Ch'ang-ling (698–756)

Too young to have known the meaning of sorrow,
in her spring dress she climbs the tower chamber.

New leaves on all the willows wound her;
She sent him off to war for nothing but a title.

Translated by Sam Hamill

Though from humble circumstances, Wang Ch'ang-ling became a Presented Scholar in 727. He is recognized as a poet as well as an astute esthetician and prosodist.

34
Climbing Pien-chüeh Temple

Wang Wei (701–761)

A bamboo path leads through the First Stage
Where the City of Illusion appears from Lotus Peak.
Up in its windows all Ch'u [1] is encompassed,

Wang Wei was a painter, musician, and calligrapher as well as a writer. The scion of a distinguished family, he passed the highest civil service examination in 721 at an early age and entered upon a long and distinguished career in government interspersed with periods of banishment and voluntary withdrawal to the countryside. He is best remembered for his descriptions of life at his country retreat. Wang Wei was a devout Buddhist who called himself Vimalakīrti (Wei represents the first syllable of that Sanskrit name), after the saintly Indian Buddhist layman.

4   Above its forests Nine Rivers [2] lies level.
      Pliant grasses accepted for sitting in meditation,
      Tall pines echo with sūtra chanting.
      Then, dwelling in void, beyond the Clouds of Law,
8   Observe the World, attain Non-Life.

Translated by Stephen Owen

    "Climbing Pien-chüeh Temple" illustrates the progress of the soul from the illusion of the physical world to the extinction of self in Nirvāṇa. The beauty of the temple landscape serves only to draw the deluded soul along the right path: it is the "City of Illusion" of the Buddhist parable from the *Lotus Sūtra*.
    1. Included parts of the modern provinces of Kiangsi, Anhwei, Kiangsu, and Hupei.
    2. The nine affluents of the Yangtze River or a port on the Yangtze below the city of Hankow.

Second Song for the Worship of the Goddess at Yü Mountain: "Bidding the Goddess Farewell"

Wang Wei

    In a swirl they come forward and bow
        there before the hall,
    Eyes filled with love-longing
        toward the sacred mats like jade.
    She came but did not speak,
        Her will was not made known;
4   And she is the evening rain,
        makes the empty mountains somber.
    The pipes grieve in shrillness,
    Flurried strings throb with longing;
    The carriage of the goddess
        is about to turn majestically.
8   In a flash clouds draw back,
        the rain ceases;

    In this poem we encounter the theme of exile within the description of a shamanistic performance near Chi-chou. The model was the "Nine Songs" from the *Elegies of Ch'u* (see selection 122): the accepted interpretation of these poems in the T'ang period was that Ch'ü Yüan had composed them as revisions of the popular shamanistic performances that he had seen in his exile. In Wang Wei's poem, there is a silent literary-historical context, a tacit assumption of enacting the role of Ch'ü Yüan in his own unjust exile.

And green stand the mountains
    amid water's splashing flow.

Translated by Stephen Owen

Deer Enclosure

Wang Wei

On the empty mountain, seeing no one,
Only hearing the echoes of someone's voice;
Returning light enters the deep forest,
Again shining upon the green moss.

Translated by Richard W. Bodman and Victor H. Mair

35
To Meng Hao-jan

Li Po (701–762)

    I love the Master, Meng Hao-jan,
    A free spirit known the whole world through.
    In the flush of youth he spurned the cap and carriage,
4   And rests now, white-haired with age, among clouds and pines.

Li Po seems to have been born in Central Asia and might have had Turkic or other non-Han ancestors. When he was five, the family returned to China proper, settling in Mien-chou in modern Szechwan. At age twenty-five, he began to travel extensively in central and eastern China and became popular both for his abundant talent and for his eccentricity. He was recommended to the imperial court and summoned to the capital, Ch'ang-an, by Emperor Hsüan Tsung. There he became a favorite until his unconstrained behavior eventually proved offensive and he was let go. His later life was one of constant drifting and difficulty.

More than nine hundred of Li Po's poems are still extant today, and many possess an unusual combination of boldness and grace. His works are full of the romantic and the fantastic: he had a unique ability to conceive and execute grand visions. Aptly eulogized as "a transcendant banished from heaven," Li Po is universally recognized as one of the greatest Chinese poets of all time.

Li Po's poem of praise echoes Meng Hao-jan's own poetry throughout, as if to prove that the figure in the poem is indeed Meng Hao-jan (see selection 32). In line 5, "sage" is strong wine.

Drunk in moonlight, often "smitten by the sage,"
Or led astray by flowers, he does not serve his lord.
The highest mountain—how can I look to climb it?
8   I can do no more than kneel to his pure fragrance.

Translated by Stephen Owen

Late Bloomer at the Front of My Garden

Li Po

A Queen Mother of the West[1] peach tree is planted in my yard;
    After three thousand warming springs,
        it finally had a flower.
    This strain and delay producing a fruit
        was laughed at all around,
But when I climbed up to pick it, aah, aah, I sighed aloud.

Translated by Elling Eide

1. The mythical Queen Mother of the West (see selection 156, note 5), who presided over a mountain paradise in the distant west, was famous for her peaches of immortality. The trees she grew fruited only once every three thousand years.

To Send to Tu Fu[1] as a Joke

Li Po

I ran into Tu Fu by a Rice Grain Mountain,
In a bamboo hat with the sun at high noon.
Hasn't he got awfully thin since our parting?
It must be the struggle of writing his poems.

Translated by Elling Eide

1. For Li Po's great contemporary, Tu Fu, see selection 37.

Drinking Alone in the Moonlight [1]

Li Po

> Beneath the blossoms with a pot of wine,
> No friends at hand, so I poured alone;
> I raised my cup to invite the moon,
> Turned to my shadow, and we became three.
> Now the moon had never learned about my drinking,
> And my shadow had merely followed my form,
> But I quickly made friends with the moon and my shadow;
> To find pleasure in life, make the most of the spring.
>
> Whenever I sang, the moon swayed with me;
> Whenever I danced, my shadow went wild.
> Drinking, we shared our enjoyment together;
> Drunk, then each went off on his own.
> But forever agreed on dispassionate revels,
> We promised to meet in the far Milky Way.

Translated by Elling Eide

1. This is the first in a series of four poems under this title.

Still Night Thoughts

Li Po

Moonlight in front of my bed—
I took it for frost on the ground!
I lift my head, gaze at the bright moon,
lower it and dream of home.

Translated by Burton Watson

This pentasyllabic quatrain used to be known by virtually all Chinese schoolchildren.

Poems in an Old Style

Li Po

1

Ages have passed since the stately Odes flourished,
I am growing old and there is no one else to present them;
The folk songs became tangled with creeping grasses,
In the Warring Kingdoms, thorny bushes grew thickly.

Dragons and tigers devoured each other,
Armed hostilities lasted until rabid Ch'in;
How feeble had the orthodox tradition grown!
In its place arose the sad and complaining bard.

Yang and Ssu-ma revived Ch'ü Yüan's declining ripples,[1]
And opened a new current which reached a boundless swell;
Although there has been a myriad of changes in its fortune,
Ars poetica finally sank into oblivion.

Ever since the Chien-an period at the end of the Han,
Prettiness itself has not been considered fine enough;
In our own hallowed age, we have returned to antiquity,
Our majestic monarch values purity and truth.

The assembled talents are handsome and smart,
"They have mounted fate's carriage and joined the leaping dragons";
Style and substance glitter together—
A host of stars spread over the Autumn Sea.

My determination is but "to edit and transmit,"[2]
So that this brilliance may shine through a thousand springs;
If my task is accomplished, I would hope, like the sage,
To lay down my brush with the capture of the unicorn.

21

There was a sojourner in Ying who intoned "White Snows,"
The reverberations flew to the cerulean sky;
His effort was wasted in singing this tune,
In the whole world, there was no one who could follow his song.

---

1. Referring to the rhapsodic tradition (see selection 123 and following items) that is held to have begun with the southern *Elegies of Ch'u* (see selection 122).
2. What Confucius is alleged to have said of his own role in the compilation of the *Classic of Odes* (see selection 16).

But when he tried "Scamp from Szechwan,"
Those who joined him numbered in the thousands;
He swallowed his grief but what could he say?
In vain was his sorrowful sighing.

54

My sword at my waist, I climb a high tower,
Pensive, I view the springtime scenery;
Dense thickets cover the layered mounds,
Rare grasses have gone into hiding in deep valleys.

The phoenix sings by the Western Sea,
It wishes to roost but has found no suitable tree;
The jackdaw, however, has a place to dwell,
Beneath the mugwort it gathers in teeming flocks.

As when the fortunes of Chin daily diminished,
I am like Juan Chi [1] weeping bitterly at the road's end.

Translated by Victor H. Mair

1. See selection 18.

36

The Streets of Ch'ang-an

Ch'u Kuang-hsi (707–760?)

Cracking whips, off to the wine shop,
in flashy clothes heading for the whorehouse door;
a million cash spent in an hour—
expressionless, they never speak a word.

Translated by Burton Watson

From Kiangsu, the poet became a Presented Scholar in the year 726. He wrote conventional court poetry, but sometimes gave it a surprisingly ironic or reflective twist. He also wrote bucolic poems, a foil for his absorption in the courtly life of the capital.

37
Spring View

Tu Fu (712–770)

The nation is ruined,   but mountains and rivers remain.
This spring the city   is deep in weeds and brush.
Touched by the times   even flowers weep tears.
Fearing leaving   the birds tangled hearts.
Watch-tower fires   have been burning for three months
To get a note from home   would cost ten thousand gold.
Scratching my   white hair thinner
Seething hopes   all in a trembling hairpin.

Translated by Gary Snyder

Tu Fu sat for the highest civil service examinations but failed to attain the coveted rank of Presented Scholar. Only in 755 was he given a minor post as a district police commissioner (which he rejected), and he never succeeded in gaining the higher echelons of government to which he aspired. Eventually he moved his family to Ch'eng-tu, Szechwan, where he built a thatched cottage that has become a famous symbol of his poetic sensibility.

In his verse, the poet reflects poignantly on the pressing issues of his own times while grounding himself solidly in the poetic tradition that he inherited. Where Li Po (see selection 35), the other most celebrated poet of the T'ang period (the Golden Age of Chinese poetry), revealed a Taoistic predisposition, Tu Fu was more conventionally Confucian in his outlook.

A Guest Arrives

Tu Fu

North and south of my cottage, spring waters everywhere—
All I can see are a flock of terns that come day after day;
The flowery path has not been swept for any guests,
Only today do I finally open my gate for you.

The market is far, so our supper platter lacks variety,
Our family is poor, so the wine flask holds but old home-brew;
If you're willing to sing with the gaffer next door,
I'll call across the fence for him to finish the last cup.

Translated by Victor H. Mair

Recruiting Officer of Shih-hao

Tu Fu

At dusk I sought lodging at Shih-hao village,
When a recruiting officer came to seize men at night.
An old man scaled the wall and fled,
His old wife came out to answer the door.

How furious was the officer's shout!
How pitiable was the woman's cry!
I listened as she stepped forward to speak:
"All my three sons have left for garrison duty at Yeh;
From one of them a letter just arrived,
10   Saying my two sons had newly died in battle.
Survivors can manage to live on,
But the dead are gone forever.
Now there's no other man in the house,
Only a grandchild at his mother's breast.
The child's mother has not gone away;
She has only a tattered skirt for wear.
An old woman, I am feeble and weak,
But I will gladly leave with you tonight
To answer the urgent call at Ho-yang—
20   I can still cook morning gruel for your men."

The night drew on, but talking stopped;
It seemed I heard only half-concealed sobs.
As I got back on the road at daybreak,
Only the old man was there to see me off.

Translated by Irving Y. Lo

At the Sky's End, Thinking of Li Po

Tu Fu

Cold winds   rise from the edge of heaven
True Gentleman   how fares your thought

Tu Fu was forty-seven years old when he wrote this poem in the year 759. He had just quit
his disappointing career in the state bureaucracy and had begun the wanderings that would

wild geese   what hour is your arrival
4   river and lake   swell with autumn waters
   literature   is adverse to good fortune
   marsh trolls   relish the passerby
   you ought to share   a word with the slandered spirit
8   hurl a poem   to him in the Mi-lo River

Translated by David Lattimore

---

occupy the rest of his life. His first stop was Ch'in-chou on the northwestern frontier of China, at the "edge of heaven."

Writing from Ch'in-chou, Tu Fu thinks of his elderly friend and mentor, the poet Li Po (see selection 35), who has been exiled (unjustly, Tu Fu believes) to the far south, and who now lives near Lake Tung-t'ing on the middle Yangtze, that is, in the region of "river and lake" (line 4). Tu Fu would like to know what thoughts Li Po has for him. But the autumn winds and waters rise—it is not a time of easy communication. In folklore, migrating geese can carry a letter from a loved one far away; but as it is now fall, the geese are going in the wrong direction. Not until spring can they deliver a letter to Tu Fu from his friend in the south.

Tu Fu's poem contains two folkloric references: to goose-messengers and to "trolls" of marshes (such as those around Lake Tung-t'ing) and mountain pools. These references make a gesture of courteous sympathy toward Li Po's characteristic themes, which especially include folklore, fantasy, and sublime scenery peopled with legendary beings. Goose-messengers also suggest intense affection for Li Po, since geese carry news between lovers or spouses.

Two other references in the poem express an extreme respect for Li Po.

First, in line 2 Tu Fu addresses Li Po not as *chün* ("milord") but, even more deferentially, as *chün-tzu*, a term which in Confucius and Mencius signifies the True Gentlemen. We are reminded that Li Po's poetry, besides its aspect of Taoist fantasy and self-abandon, displays as well a complementary aspect of Confucian earnestness and social concern, shown especially in his series of fifty-nine poems written to ancient airs or evoking an ancient atmosphere (see selection 35, last group).

Second, Tu Fu implies a likeness between Li Po and Ch'ü Yüan (see selection 122), the earliest Chinese poet to have come down to us with a distinct persona. Ch'ü Yüan is mentioned here as the "slandered spirit" (line 7). As writers, a certain similarity exists between the often extravagant Li Po and the rhapsodic, visionary, mythopoetic Ch'ü Yüan. From the more austere viewpoint of the Central Plain, both were poets of romantic outer regions: Li Po of Shu in the west (Szechwan), Ch'ü Yüan of Ch'u in the south (Hunan). Between the two there was also a relationship of contiguity, since Li Po now lived, as had Ch'ü Yüan, in the region of Ch'u.

There is a further similarity between Ch'ü Yüan and Li Po—as slandered spirits. Ch'ü Yüan, a minister to the king of Ch'u, had been slandered to his ruler and dismissed. He eventually drowned himself in the Mi-lo River (line 8), south of Lake Tung-t'ing. More than a thousand years later, Li Po had served, perhaps under duress, in the entourage of an illegitimate claimant to the throne, for which he had been jailed and later exiled. The charge that his friend had voluntarily joined a rebellion was regarded by Tu Fu as slanderous. Unstated is the fact that Tu Fu, an unappreciated loyal critic of the ruler—in which respect he, too, resembled Ch'ü Yüan—had reason to regard himself likewise as a slandered spirit. As such, he sends a poem to his fellow-spirit Li Po, suggesting that Li in turn offer a poem to their antique fellow sufferer in his watery resting place.

Li Po was pardoned in 759 but continued to live in the Yangtze area. Tu Fu now warns his reckless old friend that what happened before can happen again. Poets are their own worst enemies; their compulsive candor makes the literary life "adverse to good fortune" (line 5). But poets have external enemies too, envious slanderers or "trolls" (line 6) always happy to pounce upon and devour the straying traveler.

For Tu Fu's posthumous readers his lines have a poignancy that Li Po, because he predeceased Tu Fu, could not have felt—if in fact he ever received the poem. Twelve years after he wrote this poem and eight years after Li Po had died, Tu Fu's late wanderings, richly chronicled in his verses, carried him at last to the region of Ch'u. There he, too, died while traveling the rivers south of Lake Tung-t'ing. Ch'ü Yüan, Li Po, and Tu Fu, who with T'ao Ch'ien (see selection 20) and Su Shih (see selection 56) rank as China's most famous poets, all concluded their lives of adversity in the land of rivers and lakes.

38
Maple Bridge Night Mooring

Chang Chi (fl. 756)

Moon set, a crow caws
           frost fills the sky
River, maple, fishing-fires
           cross my troubled sleep.
Beyond the walls of Soochow
           from Cold Mountain temple
The midnight bell sounds
           reach my boat.

Translated by Gary Snyder

The poet was a native of Hsiang-chou (present-day Hsiang-yang in Hupei). He became a Presented Scholar in 753 and assumed a series of lower and middle-level posts in government. About forty poems attributed to him are still extant. Of these, his considerable fame rests exclusively on the one selected here.

39

A Song of the Running Horse River: Presented on Saying Farewell to the Army Going on Campaign to the West

Ts'en Shen (715–770)

Don't you see how the Running Horse River flows along the edge of the Sea
of Snow,[1]
Where vast and wild the brown of level sands reaches to the sky?

The wind howls at night in the ninth month over Lun-t'ai,
And a river full of broken boulders big as bushel baskets
Covers the earth with careening stones blown before the wind.

The Hsiung-nu [2] grass turns yellow now, their horses fit and plump;
West of the Altai [3] Range we see the dust of rebellion fly;
A general of the House of Han campaigns in the distant west.

Ts'en Shen, whose father died when he was still a child, came from an impoverished family. Nonetheless, he became a Presented Scholar in the year 744 and served for many years as an official on the western frontiers of the empire. Thus he had a personal understanding of army life in remote places and under difficult conditions. He also became familiar with the customs of non-Han peoples. This experience, unusual for a reputable Chinese author, is reflected in his poems.

The district of An-hsi, where Ts'en served for some years, was located in the far west, in what is now Sinkiang or Chinese Turkestan. It has even been suggested that Ts'en may have been present at the fateful battle of Talas (751), when Arab armies defeated the Chinese still farther to the west. Ts'en's return to court and appointment as Omissioner was the result of a petition signed by a number of officials including the poet Tu Fu. This took place at a crucial juncture in T'ang history, for Ts'en joined the court in Ling-wu, where the new emperor, Su Tsung, was rallying forces for the battle against An Lu-shan, whose army had occupied the capital.

1. The geography of this poem is, if not fanciful, at least difficult of precise definition. The Running Horse River and the Sea of Snow are entirely unidentifiable. One source places them both in Russian Turkestan. More likely, they are either long forgotten local names or fictitious ones used for effect.

2. The Hsiung-nu (Huns) were the most important nomad enemies of the Chinese during the Han dynasty. Although they were ancient history by Ts'en's day, he uses the name to refer to the frontier barbarians of his own time. This practice of referring to contemporary persons and events in the guise of their Han dynasty counterparts was extremely common among T'ang poets.

3. "Altai" here translates the term "Metal Mountains." Of the various explanations offered for this name, the Altai mountain range is the closest to the general area, but it is uncertain if Ts'en is referring to this range or to any particular place at all. Context suggests that it may be equivalent to T'ien-shan (Heavenly Mountains).

The general [4] leaves his iron armor on throughout the night;
Troops move out at midnight to the sound of rattling halberds—
The wind cuts like a knifeblade, faces feel the slash.

Snow clings to the horses' coats, their sweat ascends in steam,
Only to turn to ice again on dappled and piebald backs;
Urgent dispatches are drafted in tents, the ink congeals on the stone.

When the Hunnish horsemen hear, their hearts will tremble within;
We know they will not dare to cross their swords and spears with ours:
At the west gate of Chü-shih [5] camp we await the display of your spoils.

Translated by Daniel Bryant

4. General Feng Chang-ch'ing, who appears in the titles of several of Ts'en's poems, was at the time military governor of the western frontier with the title Protector General of Pei-t'ing. His predecessor, the Korean Kao Hsien-chih, lost the battle of Talas to the Arabs in 751. While their victory at Talas was as much the extreme point of Arab expansion into central Asia as their defeat at Tours had been of their advance into western Europe a few years before, the Arabs failed to follow up their advantage. The Chinese were put on the defensive by the defeat and began losing ground to the local nomads from this time on. Ts'en Shen joined Feng's staff in 754 at the age of forty. He hoped, by doing so, to rise to a high place in the government, an ambition that had remained frustrated while he was in metropolitan China, despite his literary talents and distinguished family background. All this may help explain the respectful and laudatory tone with which Ts'en describes his commander's exploits. General Feng's career came to an unhappy end within a few years. He was defeated by the rebel An Lu-shan and subsequently put to death.
5. Chü-shih was the Han name for the area around the eastern part of the T'ien-shan in modern Dzungaria and Turfan.

40
In Illness, Dismissing My Singing Girl

Ssu-k'ung Shu (fl. 788)

Ten thousand things wound my heart when you're before my eyes,
I, lean and withered, to sleep facing such a flower!
I've used up all my yellow gold teaching you songs and dances—
go stay with someone else now, make a young man happy.

Translated by Burton Watson

Ssu-k'ung Shu attained the rank of Presented Scholar after success in the highest level of the civil service examinations. During and after the An Lu-shan rebellion (see selection 149), he was forced to move around quite a lot, including a period of banishment to Ch'ang-lin in Hupei. He was one of the "Ten Talents of the Ta-li Era" (766–779).

41
On Failing the Examination

Meng Chiao (751–814)

The dawn moon struggles to shine its light,
the man of sorrows struggles with his feelings.
Who says in spring things are bound to flourish?
4   All I see is frost on the leaves.
The eagle sickens, his power vanishes,
while little wrens soar on borrowed wings.
But leave them be, leave them be!—
8   these thoughts like wounds from a knife!

Translated by Burton Watson

The poet lost his wife fairly early in their marriage, and his three sons all died young. He became a Presented Scholar only in 796 and, because of his unsuitability for officialdom, never had a successful career in government. Consequently, his was a life of poverty and ill fate. This is reflected in the themes of his poetry: the inconsistency of human relations, the suffering of the people, and personal misfortunes. Meng Chiao was a bitter and unhappy man.

42
The Girl of Mount Hua

Han Yü (768–824)

In streets east, streets west, they expound the Buddhist canon,
clanging bells, sounding conches, till the din invades the palace;

Orphaned at an early age, Han Yü was brought up by his elder brother and sister-in-law. He became a Presented Scholar in 792 and subsequently held a number of official posts, including that of teacher at the Imperial College (see selection 173). Han Yü was twice exiled, the second time for a famous memorial submitted to the emperor reprimanding him for his devotion to Buddhism.

Han Yü was a major figure in the development of traditional Chinese literature. He proclaimed and put into practice a literary theory called *ku-wen* (the writing of antiquity or ancient-style writing) that resulted in a revitalized style of writing based on ancient ideals of clarity, conciseness, and utility. To this end, Han Yü incorporated elements of colloquial rhythm, diction, and syntax into both his prose and poetry, at the same time reaffirming the Confucian classics as the basis of education and good writing. His transformation of the contemporary literary style still based on early medieval (third- to seventh-century) models, together with his animosity toward popular Buddhism and Taoism, mark Han Yü as an important forerunner of the Neo-Confucian movement of the Sung dynasty.

This trenchant poem, written in heptasyllabic "old poetry" form, gives a good idea of Han

"sin," "blessing," wildly inflated, give force to threats and deceptions;
4   throngs of listeners elbow and shove as though through duckweed seas.
Yellow-robed Taoist priests preach their sermons, too,
but beneath their lecterns, ranks grow thinner than stars in the flush
    of dawn.
The girl of Mount Hua, child of a Taoist home,
8   longed to expel the foreign faith, win men back to the Immortals;
she washed off her powder, wiped her face, put on cap and shawl.
With white throat, crimson cheeks, long eyebrows of gray,
she came at last to ascend the chair, unfolding the secrets of Truth.
12   For anyone else the Taoist halls would hardly have opened their doors;
I do not know who first whispered the word abroad,
but all at once the very earth rocked with the roar of thunder.
Buddhist temples were swept clean, no trace of a believer,
16   while elegant teams jammed the lanes and ladies' coaches piled up.
Taoist halls were packed with people, many sat outside;
for latecomers there was no room, no way to get within hearing.
Hairpins, bracelets, girdle stones were doffed, undone, snatched off,
20   till the heaped-up gold, the mounds of jade glinted and glowed in
    the sunlight.
Eminent eunuchs from the heavenly court came with a summons
    to audience;
ladies of the six palaces longed to see the Master's face.
The Jade Countenance [1] nodded approval, granting her return;
24   dragon-drawn, mounting a crane, she came through blue-dark skies.
These youths of the great families—what do they know of the Tao,
milling about her a hundred deep, shifting from foot to foot?
Beyond cloud-barred windows, in misty towers, who knows what
    happens there
28   where kingfisher curtains hang tier on tier and golden screens are deep?

Yü's narrative style, while displaying his well-known contempt for Buddhism and Taoism. The poem begins with a description of the immense popularity of the Buddhist preachers of Ch'ang-an, who had drawn the crowds away from their Taoist rivals, and of a sudden reversal of the situation when the "girl of Mount Hua," a beautiful young Taoist priestess, appeared in the capital to attract the attention even of the emperor himself. In the closing section, the poet chides the rich young men of the capital who flock about the priestess for other than spiritual reasons and hints that her favors are reserved for more exalted personages. The bluebird in the last line, bearer of love notes, is the messenger of the immortal spirit Hsi Wang-mu, the Queen Mother of the West (see selection 156, note 5), to whom the priestess is compared. We have no way of knowing whether Han Yü's insinuations were justified, though it might be recalled that Yang Kuei-fei, the renowned favorite of Emperor Hsüan Tsung, originally entered the palace as a Taoist priestess.

    1. The emperor.

The immortal's ladder is hard to climb, your bonds with this
    world weighty;
vainly you call on the bluebird to deliver your passionate pleas!

Translated by Burton Watson

43
Two Poems by the Most Eminent Woman Poet of the T'ang Period

Hsüeh T'ao (770?–832?)

Listening to a Monk Play the Reed Pipes

Dawn cicadas choke back sobs,
Evening orioles grieve.

Lively language,
quick,
precise,
from ten fingers' tips.

He's done with reading holy texts;
He wants to play a bit.

The poet was born into a respectable family from the T'ang capital, Ch'ang-an. Her father, a minor official, died in Szechwan, leaving his family stranded with no secure source of support. The adolescent Hsüeh T'ao joined the entertainers' guild and became well known for her poetry and wit. She was summoned to serve as a courtesan-hostess for the military governor of Szechwan. Her reputation continued to spread, and she exchanged poems with some of the most famous poets of the day. Hsüeh T'ao retired to an independent life as an artisan. Her name is still associated with sheets of beautiful paper on which poems may be written. Of about five hundred poems by Hsüeh T'ao once in circulation, no more than ninety survive.

This beautifully musical poem takes on the special problem of music played by a Buddhist monk. Strictly speaking, from the Buddhist standpoint such an attractive, emotionally stirring art form ought to be shunned: it fosters attachment to the world of illusion. Yet a plaintive or ethereal melody can mingle an austere awareness with its appeal to the senses.

The opening images remind the reader of the melancholy associations of reed pipes, which came to China from the north. Though the poem moves to a less lugubrious metaphor, comparing the melody to the rise and fall of human speech, the final image points out the tension between attachment and nonattachment in this Buddhist music. The metal chimes struck to mark the sections of the day have autumnal and transcendent associations of long standing. Their notes, and those of the pipes, are depicted as scattering through the sky like precious gold leaf applied to a maṇḍala (Buddhist painting usually having a circular form) or a copy of a sūtra (Buddhist scripture). But "to gild" (*ni*) also implies "to muddy" (*ni*).

His tune floats after
temple chimes
to gild clear autumn's air.

Translated by Jeanne Larsen

Lotus-Gathering Boat

Lotus-laden,
pushing through,
a single windblown leaf

tells the news: it's fall again,
time to fish
and sport.

The moon-hare runs, the sun-crow flies,
human chatter stills.

Pink tinted sleeves fill up the brook
and poling songs
begin

Translated by Jeanne Larsen

Hsüeh T'ao describes this scene in terms that mingle the human world with the green realm of plants. The pink or red sleeves suggest both women in appealing clothing and the rosy petals of the blossoms on the stream. The single leaf blown before the wind is, of course, the lotus gatherers' skiff. The original describes the boat with an ambiguous phrase; it is simultaneously presented as "weighed down by" gathered lotuses and as pushing its way through others yet unplucked.

The amatory air of many poems on the topic invites us to read Hsüeh's verse with the old association of fishing and sexuality in mind. The movements of the mythic rabbit in the moon and the three-legged sun-crow (see selection 122, section II, line 68) remind us of time's passing.

44
River Snow

Liu Tsung-yüan (773–819)

These thousand peaks cut off the flight of birds
On all the trails, human tracks are gone.

Liu Tsung-yüan became a Presented Scholar in 793. His official career was meteoric. Joining a group of political reformers some years later, Liu gained power for a short while prior

A single boat—coat—hat—an old man!
Alone fishing chill river snow.

Translated by Gary Snyder

---

to the death of the emperor who had supported change. The new emperor distrusted the reform coterie, and Liu was demoted to a position subordinate to the prefect of Yung-chou. Still later, he was made prefect of Liu-chou, another appointment far removed from the centers of power. Liu often satirized the meanness and corruption of officialdom. One of the finest prose stylists of the T'ang period, he was a master of the ancient-style essay (see introductory note to selection 42). and a sensitive poet. Many of his most memorable pieces describe the scenes of his exile and the complicated feelings of a northerner banished to the distant south.

45
Untitled Poems

Cold Mountain (9th century)

2

whoever reads my poems
must guard his purity of heart
his greed at once be modesty
flattery suddenly honesty
banish and be rid of evil karma [1]
trust and accept his true nature
get his buddha body today
hurry as if these were orders

16

people ask the way to Cold Mountain
roads don't reach Cold Mountain

We may think of Cold Mountain as a state of mind rather than as an individual poet. The Cold Mountain collection consists of 307 poems written during the seventh through the ninth centuries. A notable feature of these poems is the relatively large proportion of vernacular elements they include, although they are by no means written in a purely vernacular style. Their Zen Buddhist orientation has made them very popular in the present century, which has experienced a worldwide resurgence of this sect of intuitive Buddhism. As such, they have attracted some of the very best translators of Chinese poetry. Red Pine's versions are unique in capturing the spirit of the originals, perhaps because he comes close to living the life espoused in these crazy, but wise, poems.

1. The word "karma" includes the act (to be banished) as well as its result (to be rid of) and is said to be evil when its result is suffering.

summer the ice never melts
sunup the fog is thick
how did someone like me arrive
our minds aren't the same
if they were
you could get there then

29

pole your three winged galleons [2]
ride your thousand-mile stallions
you still won't reach my home
it's called the darkest wild
cliff cave deep in the mountains
clouds and thunder come down all day
I'm not Master Confucius
I have nothing to offer others

173

raise girls but not too many
once born you have to train them
smack their heads and yell watch out
beat their behinds and shout shut up
and before they learn how to work a loom
they won't touch a basket or broom
Old Lady Chang advised her young jenny
you're big but no match for your Mother

183

they laugh at me hey farm boy
your cheeks are a little rough
your hat's not very high
and your belt sure is tight
it's not that I don't catch the trends
no money I can't catch up
but one day I'll be rich
and stick a stupa [3] on my head

201

reading won't save us from death
and reading won't free us from want

2. The Chinese had three sizes of a large yet fast, and hence winged, warship that used oars
and poles.
    3. A stupa is a conical structure erected over the relics of a Buddha.

then why do we like to be literate
the literate lord it over others
if a grown man can't read
where can he live in peace
squeeze garlic juice in your crowfoot[4]
and you'll forget it's bitter

228

his mind is as high as a mountain
his ego doesn't yield to others
he can preach the Vedic Canon[5]
or discuss the Three Religions[6]
in his heart no shame
he breaks precepts and flouts the Vinaya[7]
boasts a law for superior men
and claims to be the first
fools all praise and sigh
wise men clap and laugh
a mirage of flower in the sky
how can he avoid growing old
better to know nothing at all
to sit quiet and have no cares

246

yesterday I went to a cloud observatory[8]
and met some Taoist priests
star caps and moon capes askew
they said we inhabit hill and stream
I asked them the art of immortality
they said how could we presume
for what's called the spirit sublime
the elixir must be the secret of the gods
till death we wait for a crane
and they said we'll ride off on a fish[9]
later I thought this through

4. *Coptis chinensis*, a very bitter medicinal herb.
5. The *Vedas* include the sacred literature of Hinduism.
6. Confucianism, Taoism, and Buddhism.
7. That portion of the Buddhist canon dealing with regulation of moral behavior by precept.
8. Taoists indicated their hermitages by the word "observatory."
9. The immortal Wang Tzu-ch'iao (see selection 171, note 7) rode off on a crane to the land of immortals, while Ch'in Kao rode off on a carp.

and concluded they were crazy
just look at an arrow shot into space
in a moment it falls back down
even if they do become immortals
they'll just be corpse-haunting ghosts
the moon of the mind is so perfectly clear
how can phenomena compare
if you want to know the art of immortals
within yourself is the first of spirits
don't follow Masters of the Yellow Turban [10]
holding onto idiocy maintaining doubt

267

ever since I left home
I've developed an interest in yoga
contracting and stretching the four-limbed Whole
attending intently the six-sensed All
wearing rough clothes all year
eating coarse food morning and night
hard on the trail even now
I'm hoping to meet the Buddha

283

one Budding-Talent Wang [11]
laughs at my prosody [12]
he says I don't know a wasp's waist
much less a stork's knee [13]
I can't control my flats and leans [14]
all my words come helter-skelter
I laugh at the poems he writes
a blind man's songs of the sun

10. The Yellow Turbans were a Taoist sect of the Han dynasty whose name later became associated with those Taoists whose practice emphasized alchemy and magic.

11. A Budding Talent was roughly equivalent to our Bachelor of Arts. Although the designation as an official degree ceased to be employed as of 651, it continued to be used with reference to men-of-letters throughout the T'ang.

12. In his *Poetics*, Shen Yüeh (see selection 22) set forth a number of prosodic tonal errors.

13. When the second and fifth syllables in a pentasyllabic line have the same tone, it is called a "wasp's waist." When the fifth and fifteenth syllables of the poem have the same tone, it is called a "stork's knee."

14. Referring to tones that are level/even and slanted/contoured.

307

whoever has Cold Mountain's poems
is better off than reading sūtras [15]
paste them up on your screen [16]
and read them from time to time

Translated by Red Pine

15. Buddhist scriptures.
16. The Chinese used to place inside their rooms folding frames inset with paper or silk
backed with wood to protect them from drafts.

46

Looking for a Recluse but Failing to Find Him

Chia Tao (779–843)

Under the pines I questioned the boy.
"My master's off gathering herbs.
All I know is he's here on the mountain—
    clouds are so deep, I don't know where. . . ."

Translated by Burton Watson

The poet came from a humble family. He stayed for a while in a Buddhist temple and
became a monk. Later, he gave up monkhood to make several attempts at the civil service
examinations. Having failed them all, he continued to live a life of constant frustration and
misfortune. Chia's poetry, mostly in the form of presentations and responses to Buddhist and
Taoist monks or recluses, is full of understated oddities and mysteries.

47

Pitying the Farmer

Li Shen (780–846)

He hoes the grain under a midday sun,
sweat dripping down on the soil beneath the grain.

Li Shen was one of the initiators of the new ballad movement.

Who realizes that the food in the food bowl,
every last morsel of it, is bought with such toil?

Translated by Burton Watson

48

To Patriarch Sun at Hua-yang [1] Grotto

Li Te-yü (787–849)

I

In what place is one most free of bonds?
At Hua-yang, eighth of the Heavens.
The wind in the pines carries dew in all its clarity;
The moon, through the bearded lichen, is cleansed of mist.
Suddenly startled—a crane at the gemmy altar;
Humming in season—cicadas on the jeweled tree.
I long to post my thoughts from a thousand tricents:
"My only love is the spring at Phoenix Gate."

II

The torrent-iris on the stone puts out purple floss;
The dark blue hills clumped in seclusion—the waters swollen full.
Sweetflag flowers are fixed there, where no men are;
On such a day in spring one must meet only a "feathered visitor." [2]

III

Searching alone on the sand-bar with its orchids, diverted by dilatory beams
    of light;
Leaning at ease on the window with its pines, gazing off at blue-misted hills;
Imagining afar the spring mountains in the pale glow of the luminous moon,
And the clear lithophones at a jadestone altar—where you return from
    "Pacing the Void." [3]

Translated by Edward H. Schafer

A noted parallel prose stylist, Li Te-yü became a leader of an important court faction to
which many excellent writers were attached. These included authors of some of the most
memorable classical language short stories, for instance, Li Kung-tso (see selection 208). Like
many politicians of his day, Li Te-yü had Taoist predilections.

1. "Golden-altared" Hua-yang is a grotto-heaven hidden at the roots of Mao Shan, a
mountain sacred to Taoists.

2. A Taoist divinity or, by courtesy, a priest or mature initiate.

3. A traditional chant about the transit of space by a Taoist adept.

49

At Ch'ang-ku,[1] Reading: To Show to My Man Pa

Li Ho (790–816)

Echo of insects where the lamplight thins;
the cold night heavy with medicine fumes:
because you pity a broken-winged wanderer,
through bitterest toil you follow me still.

Translated by Burton Watson

Li Ho came from a good family and enjoyed the patronage of Han Yü (see selection 42), but was disappointed in his aspirations to forge a career in government service. As his dates indicate, he died at a young age. The works of the youthful genius, written in an old style, seek to recapture some of the mysteries and myths of the shamanic songs in *The Elegies of Ch'u* (see selection 122). A general aura of eeriness and allusiveness informs much of his imagery, which he uses to criticize the ills of his own times.

1. Ch'ang-ku, the poet's country home, was west of Loyang. This poem was probably written shortly before his death.

My Man Pa Replies

Li Ho

Big-nose looks best in mountain-coarse clothes;
bushy-brows should stick to his poetry toils!
Were it not for the songs you sing,
who would know the depths of autumn sorrow?

Translated by Burton Watson

In this poem, Li Ho imagines how his servant might answer the previous quatrain. It picks up the heavy melancholic tone of the first poem and gently mocks it.

Ravine on a Cold Evening

Li Ho

White foxes[1] howl at mountain wind beneath the moon;
Its autumn cold sweeps up clouds and leaves a sapphire void.

1. White animals, especially foxes, often appear as manifestations of the supernatural in Chinese lore.

Jade mists shimmering wet are white as curtains;
The Silver Channel's [2] arcing swell flows to the eastern sky.
By the stream a sleeping egret dreams of migrating geese;
Faint ripples, without a murmur, drift slowly by.
Twisting cliffs of layered hills, dragons coil on coil;
Bitter bamboo [3] sound for a stranger their sighing flutes.

Translated by Maureen Robertson

2. The River of Heaven or Milky Way.
3. A variety of bamboo used in the manufacture of song-flutes.

50
The Robe of Golden Thread

Autumn Maid Tu (T'ang)

I urge you, milord, not to cherish your robe of golden thread;[1]
Rather, milord, I urge you to cherish the time of your youth.
When the flower is open and pluckable, you simply must pluck it;
Don't wait till there are no flowers, vainly to break branches.

Translated by Victor H. Mair

The poet was a celebrated beauty of Chin-ling (present-day Nanking) who became the concubine of Li Ch'i, the military commissioner of Chen-hai (present-day Chekiang province). Li was executed for treason about the year 807, whereupon Tu Ch'iu-niang (Autumn Maid) became a favorite in the imperial palace. The poet Tu Mu (803–852), in a biography of her, relates how she became intoxicated after drinking wine from a jade cup and wrote this poem to encourage Li Ch'i to relax and enjoy himself. Li was reported to have been quite fond of the song and sang it often.

1. Your official career and dignity.

51
Master Chia [1]

Li Shang-yin (c. 813–c. 858)

To the audience hall [2] the worthy banished minister was recalled;
Master Chia's talents were matchless in the world.

The poet lost his father at age nine and had an unsettled early life. He became a Presented Scholar in 837, but he never attained high rank and died out of office. Li Shang-yin's poems

Alas, in vain did the Emperor move his seat forward at midnight—
Instead of asking about the people, he asked about the gods!

Translated by James J. Y. Liu

---

are full of bizarre fantasy and evoke a mood of subtle sentimentality that is highly symbolic yet romantic. This strange and obscure quality is enhanced by a language that is both archaic and colloquial. Also a master of parallel prose, Li is said to be the author of an extremely earthy and witty *Miscellany* (see selection 187).

The poem is a satire on the superstitions of the T'ang emperors, many of whom tried to obtain the elixir of life. The poet shows his disapproval by deploring the fact that when Emperor Wen of Han recalled the banished Chia Yi to court, all he wanted to learn from Chia was the nature of spirits and gods instead of the life of the people.

1. Chia Yi (201–169 B.C.E.) was a famous scholar and statesman who was banished from the court of Emperor Wen of Han but later recalled. When the emperor asked him about the gods, Chia embarked on a discourse on the subject. It so interested the emperor that he moved his sitting mat forward and listened until midnight (see selection 123).

2. The main hall of the Wei-yang Palace in Han times, where the emperor summoned Chia Yi.

52
Impromptu on a Hangover

P'i Jih-hsiu (c. 833–883)

I block out the midday brightness with a screen depicting dark woods,
burn a stick of heavy incense, nursing my hangover.
What's this? As evening comes I'm ready for a drink again!
Beyond the wall I hear the cry of someone selling clams.

Translated by Burton Watson

P'i Jih-hsiu became a Presented Scholar in 867 but was a recluse before embarking upon an official career. Much of his early prose and poetry is concerned with social injustice (see, for example, selection 195) and advocates the moral philosophy of Mencius (see selection 7) and Han Yü (see selection 42). But during a sojourn in Soochow as a virtual guest of Lu Kuei-meng (?–c. 881, see selection 199), a fellow bard, he indulged himself in pleasure and the study of Taoism. He made a return to his early social commitment by joining a rebel group, but was executed by its leader for his forthright criticism.

53

On a Visit to Ch'ung-chen Taoist Temple I See in the South Hall the List of Successful Candidates in the Imperial Examinations

Yü Hsüan-chi (c. 844–c. 868)

Cloud-capped peaks fill the eyes
In the spring sunshine.
Their names are written in beautiful characters
And posted in order of merit.
How I hate this silk dress
That conceals a poet.
I lift my head and read their names
In powerless envy.

Translated by Kenneth Rexroth and Ling Chung

Yü Hsüan-chi is the most celebrated woman poet of the T'ang period after Hsüeh T'ao (see selection 43). She had been a courtesan and the concubine of a government official, but later took up residence in a Taoist convent. She is said to have been executed for murdering a maid of hers who had become intimate with one of her gentlemen callers.

Exceedingly few women gained literacy in traditional China and, of those who did, virtually none of them took part in the vaunted civil service examinations. The ability to write passable poetry was considered to be a requisite for becoming a successful bureaucrat in old China. Yü Hsüan-chi was a poet, but her gender disqualified her from becoming an official.

54

Sharing Lodging with Hsieh Shih-hou [1] in the Library of the Hsü Family and Being Much Bothered by the Noise of Rats

Mei Yao-ch'en (1002–1060)

The lamp burns blue, everyone asleep;
from their holes the hungry rats steal out:

The author, one of the best-known early Sung poets, held a series of minor government posts. He wrote in a simple, unpretentious style about the details of daily life and about various social ills. An admirer of Han Yü (see selection 42), he participated with Ou-yang Hsiu (see

flip-flop—a rattle of plates and saucers;
clatter-crash!—the end of my dream.
I fret—will they knock off the inkslab on the desk?
worry—are they gnawing those shelves of books?
My little son mimics a cat's miaowing,
and that's a silly solution for sure!

Translated by Burton Watson

---

selection 174) and others in the revival of Confucianism. The poet and critic Liu K'e-chuang
(1187–1269) characterized him with a technical term for the founder of a Buddhist sect as "the
Mountain-opening Patriarch of the poetry of this dynasty." The tragic deaths of his first wife
and two young children led Mei to write poems of great pathos. He stressed the "flat and bland"
(*p'ing-tan*) and wrote about reality as opposed to Buddhist and Taoist mysticism and enlightenment.

1. Hsieh was a nephew of the poet's wife, who had died earlier in the year this poem was
written (1044) in K'aifeng. He was married to a daughter of the Hsü family. The poet and his
two little children were spending the night at the Hsü home.

Shih-hou Pointed Out to Me That from Ancient Times There Had Never Been a Poem on the Subject of Lice, and Urged Me to Try Writing One

Mei Yao-ch'en

A poor man's clothes—ragged and easy to get dirty,
easy to get dirty and hard to keep free of lice.
Between the belt and the lower robe is where they swarm,
ascending in files to the fur collar's margin.
They hide so cleverly—How can I ferret them out?—
dining on blood, making themselves at home.
My world, too, has its sallies and withdrawals;
why should I bother to pry into yours?

Translated by Burton Watson

55

Bald Mountain

Wang An-shih (1021–1086)

My duties took me to a spot by the sea—
there to gaze upon a mountain isle I stopped my boat
as I wondered who had denuded it so;
4   a villager explained it to me and I quote:

"One monkey on the mountain did chatter,
another followed in playful pursuit;
they mated and gave birth to a son—
8   a host of sons—and still more grandsons to boot.

Lush vegetation covered the mountain,
roots and berries, at first, they easily took;
they clambered up to the highest places
12   and, crouching, ferreted out every nook.

Each in this host of monkeys made himself sleek and fat,
while the mountain was utterly ravished;
wrangling with each other to fill their stomachs,
16   on talk of conservation no leisure was lavished.

The big monkeys found the going tough,
the small monkeys were, of course, all the more constrained;
little by little, they nipped and they nibbled,
20   till not a single blade of grass remained."

Though the monkey possesses superhuman craft,
he isn't adept at wielding hoe and plow himself;
the craving he has for fruit and grain
24   is invariably satisfied through pelf.

Alas for this mountain encircled by sea!
On all four sides they spy, but there's nowhere to flee;

Wang An-shih was famous for the enormously controversial reforms in all spheres of government that he instituted during his period in power at the Sung court. He was intent on rectifying social mores, the deterioration of which he believed had led to the imminent disintegration of the state. The measures that he advocated, however, were too harsh and their implementation was too rapid, causing a strong reaction even from those, such as Su Shih (see selection 56), who sympathized with his aims.

In his earlier poetry, Wang focused on social and political problems and stressed Confucian ideals. After retirement, his works became more intimate and reflective. He is also considered to be one of the eight prose masters of the T'ang-Sung period.

while the progression of life goes on without cease
28   and the year draws to a close, what plan will there be?

Translated by Victor H. Mair

56
When Yü-k'o Painted Bamboo

Su Shih (1037–1101)

Written on paintings of bamboo by Wen Yü-k'o in Ch'ao Pu-chih's collection: three poems.

When Yü-k'o painted bamboo,
He saw bamboo only, never people.
Did I say he saw no people?
So rapt he forgot even himself—
He himself became bamboo,
Putting out fresh growth endlessly.
Chuang Tzu ¹ no longer with us,
Who can fathom this uncanny power?

Translated by Burton Watson

For a note on Su Shih, see selection 127.
Written in 1087 when the poet was in the capital serving as a member of the imperial Han-lin Academy, which drafted government documents, and acting as tutor to the young ruler, Emperor Che Tsung. Wen Yü-k'o or Wen T'ung (1018–1079) was a cousin of the poet's from Szechwan and a painter noted for his works of bamboos. Ch'ao Pu-chih (1053–1110) was one of the poet's leading disciples. This is the first poem of the series.
1. See selection 8.

Reading the Poetry of Meng Chiao

Su Shih

Night: reading Meng Chiao's poems,
Characters fine as cow's hair.

Written in 1078 when Su Shih was governor of Hsü-chou in the northwest corner of Kiangsu. Meng Chiao (see selection 41), a well-known T'ang poet, was a disciple of the even

By the cold lamp, my eyes blur and swim.
4   Good passages I rarely find—
Lone flowers poking up from the mud—
But more hard words than the *Odes*[1] or "Li sao"[2]
Jumbled rocks clogging the clear stream,
8   Making rapids too swift for poling.
My first impression is of eating little fishes—
What you get's not worth the trouble;
Or of boiling tiny mud crabs
12   And ending up with some empty claws.
For refinement he might compete with monks
But he'd never match his master Han Yü.
Man's life is like morning dew,
16   A flame eating up the oil night by night.
Why should I strain my ears
Listening to the squeaks of this cold cicada?
Better lay aside the book
20   And drink my cup of jade-white wine.

Translated by Burton Watson

---

better known poet and statesman Han Yü (see selection 42). Su was probably reading a printed edition of the so-called small-character variety. This is the first of two pentasyllabic poems with the same title.
  1. See selection 16.
  2. See selection 122.

Lament of the Farm Wife of Wu[1]

Su Shih

Rice this year ripens so late!
We watch, but when will frost winds come?
They come—with rain in bucketfuls;
4   the harrow sprouts mold, the sickle rusts.
My tears are all cried out, but rain never ends;
it hurts to see yellow stalks flattened in the mud.
We camped in a grass shelter for a month by the fields;
8   then it cleared and we reaped the grain, followed the wagon home,

  1. Wu is the region around the mouth of the Yangtze River.

sweaty, shoulders sore, carting it to town—
the price it fetched, you'd think we came with chaff.
We sold the ox to pay taxes, broke up the roof for kindling;
12   we'll get by for the time, but what of next year's hunger?
Officials demand cash now—they won't take grain;
the long northwest border tempts invaders.
Wise men[2] fill the court—why do things get worse?
16   I'd be better off bride to the River Lord![3]

Translated by Burton Watson

2. "Wise men" is literally Kung (Sui) and Huang (Pa), two officials of Han times who worked for the welfare of the peasants.
3. This line refers to the ancient custom of sacrificing a young girl each year as a "bride" to the River Lord, the god of the Yellow River.

57

To Go with Shih K'o's[1] Painting of an Old Man Tasting Vinegar

Huang T'ing-chien (1045–1105)

Old lady Shih, braving acerbity, pokes in her three-foot beak;
old man Shih, vinegar-tasting, face in a hundred wrinkles:
who knows how it feels to scrunch up your shoulders, shivering clear to the
    bone?
A painting not to be surpassed even by the brush of Master Wu![2]

Translated by Burton Watson

Huang T'ing-chien, who became a Presented Scholar in 1067, was a disciple of Su Shih (see selection 56) and shared his interest in Zen Buddhism. Huang, fastidious in his use of language, was accomplished both as a poet and lyricist (see selection 97). He was also one of the most eminent Sung period calligraphers.
1. A tenth-century painter noted for his treatment of humorous and supernatural subjects. The painting, as we know from other sources, actually depicted an elderly couple.
2. The famous T'ang painter Wu Tao-tzu.

58

Watching a Village Festival

Yang Wan-li (1127–1206)

The village festival is really worth seeing—
mountain farmers praying for a good harvest.

Flute players, drummers burst forth from nowhere;
laughing children race after them.
Tiger masks, leopard heads swing from side to side.
Country singers, village dancers perform for the crowd.

I'd rather have one minute of this wild show
than all the nobility of kings and generals.

Translated by Jonathan Chaves

The poet was born shortly after the Jürchen established the Chin dynasty in the north of China. He became a Presented Scholar in 1154. Yang's emphasis on the development of a personal style was undoubtedly influenced by Zen Buddhism, which advocates enlightenment attained through individual insight and effort. Often called "the colloquial poet" for the rough quality of his diction, he paid great attention to the small details of everyday life.

Songs of Depression

Yang Wan-li

1

I don't feel like reading another book,
and I'm tired of poetry—that's not what I want to do.
But my mind is restless, unsettled—
I'll try counting raindrop stains on the oilcloth window.

2

I finish chanting my new poems and fall asleep—
I am a butterfly journeying to the eight corners of the universe.
Outside the boat, waves crash like thunder,
but it is silent in the world of sleep.

Translated by Jonathan Chaves

59

The Merchant's Joy

Lu Yu (1125–1210)

The wide wide Yangtze, dragons in deep pools;
wave blossoms, purest white, leap to the sky.
The great ship, tall-towered, far off no bigger than a bean;
4   my wondering eyes have not come to rest when it's here before me.
Matted sails: clouds that hang beyond the embankment;
lines and hawsers: their thunder echoes from high town walls.
Rumble rumble of oxcarts to haul the priceless cargo;
8   heaps, hordes to dazzle the market—men race with the news.
In singing-girl towers to play at dice, a million on one throw;
by flag-flown pavilions calling for wine, ten thousand a cask;
the Mayor? the Governor? we don't even know their names;
12   what's it to us who wields power in the palace?
Confucian scholar, hard up, dreaming of one square meal;
a limp, a stumble, prayers for pity at His Excellency's gate;
teeth rot, hair falls out—no one looks your way;
16   belly crammed with classical texts, body lean with care—
See what Heaven gives me—luck thin as paper!
Now I know that merchants are the happiest of men.

Translated by Burton Watson

As Su Shih (see selection 56) was the most important poet of the Northern Sung period, so was Lu Yu the most important poet of the Southern Sung period. Lu, noted for his passionate patriotism, made repeated calls for mounting military strikes against the Tungusic Jürchen who had occupied the northern Chinese heartland in the middle of the 1120s. Many of his poems were written explicitly in this very public vein, but a wholly different mood prevails in his other poems, which describe the quiet joys and experiences of quotidian existence.

Lu Yu was extraordinarily prolific, having left behind close to ten thousand poems in his collection. There is also good evidence that he had destroyed thousands of others. This stupendous figure owed partly to his longevity but mostly to his huge reservoir of determination and energy. Arranged chronologically, Lu Yu's poems constitute a virtual poetic biography.

This poem was written in 1187.

Written in a Carefree Mood

Lu Yu

Old man pushing seventy,
in truth he acts like a little boy,
whooping with delight when he spies some mountain fruits,
laughing with joy, tagging after village mummers;[1]
with the others having fun stacking tiles to make a pagoda,
standing alone staring at his image in the jardiniere pool.
Tucked under his arm, a battered book to read,
just like the time he first set off for school.

Translated by Burton Watson

Written in 1192 in Shao-hsing (Chekiang), this is the first of two poems with the same title.
1. Villagers dressed up in costume who go from house to house at the beginning of spring to drive out evil spirits.

To Show to My Sons

Lu Yu

In death I know well enough all things end in emptiness;
still I grieve that I never saw the Nine Provinces[1] made one.
On the day the king's armies march north to take the heartland,
at the family sacrifice don't forget to let your father know.

Translated by Burton Watson

This is Lu Yu's deathbed poem, written in 1209, when he was eighty-four years old.
1. The divisions of China in ancient times.

60
Chin-ling Post Station

Wen T'ien-hsiang (1236–1282)

Grasses enclose the old palaces as waning sunlight shifts.[1]
A lone wind-tossed cloud stops briefly: on what can it depend?
The view here, mountains and rivers, has never changed,
Yet the people within the city walls already are half gone.[2]
The reed flowers that fill the land have grown old with me,
But into whose eaves have the swallows of my former home flown?[3]
Now I depart on the road out of Chiang-nan;[4]
Transformed into a weeping cuckoo, reeking of blood, I shall return.[5]

Translated by Michael A. Fuller

Wen T'ien-hsiang was a great statesman and general who fought a losing war to defend the Southern Sung emperor from the invading Mongol (Yüan) armies. This poem was probably written when the poet was captured and being taken north to the Yüan capital.

1. Chin-ling (modern Nanking) was a secondary capital during the Southern Sung.

2. This relates to a story about a Taoist adept, Ting Ling-wei, who turned himself into a crane and returned to his home town after being away for ten years. While he perched on a roost, a youth of the town shot an arrow at him. As he flew away, he sighed, "The town is as of old, but the people are not."

3. This bird imagery—part of a series in the poem—alludes to a famous couplet by the T'ang poet Liu Yü-hsi (see selection 87): "The swallows that in former day flew before the courtyards of the great Wang and Hsieh clans/Have flown into the houses of common folk."

4. That is, he is about to head north, across the Yangtze.

5. There is much lore on the cuckoo. In one story, Tu Yü, a king of Shu (part of the modern province of Szechwan), ceded his throne to his very able minister and then left the country. Later he regretted this noble deed, and after his death his soul transformed into a cuckoo that returned to Shu. Its plaintive cry was said to sound like spitting blood as well as the words "It's best to return."

61
To a Pyrotechnist

Chao Meng-fu (1254–1322)

This wondrous art in the human realm
      rivals nature's skill:

A master poet, painter, and calligrapher, Chao Meng-fu set new standards in all these fields. He was a descendant of the Sung imperial family. His willingness to serve the Yüan government

concocting formulas, igniting lanterns,
                    turning night to day!
Willow catkins flutter downwards,
                    carpeting earth in white;
peach blossom petals drop and scatter,
                    covering courtyards with red.
Bursting, spreading, scintillating—
                    just like stars that fall;
bubbling, boiling, roaring, blasting—
                    like warfare by fire!
Some other night, again you will unfurl brocade of flowers:
no need to grieve that they have scattered in the eastern wind.
                                    Translated by Jonathan Chaves

---

and subsequent rise to eminence led to an uncertainty about his reputation in later Chinese historiography.

62

Mating

Yang Wei-chen (1296–1370)

Eyebrow mounds dark, facing the spluttering lamp,
Her billowy half chignon spills over pillow's edge.
Arms and legs joined with another's, fetchingly about to sob,
She grasps the fine silk, nearly kneading it to pieces.
                                    Translated by John Timothy Wixted

The poet became a Presented Scholar in 1327, after which he held several minor positions under the Yüan dynasty. As the foremost figure in classical poetry of his time, Yang Wei-chen represents a break from the stiffness and rationality of much Northern Sung poetry. This poem is about the pleasures of the night.

63
Inscribed on a Painting by Myself

Ni Tsan (1301–1374)

On the eastern seacoast lives a sick man
who calls himself mad and deluded.
He writes on walls and paints silk and paper:
surely he is more than insane.

Translated by Jonathan Chaves

One of the most innovative painters in the history of Chinese art, Ni Tsan was also an excellent poet. The understated, spare diction of his verse may be linked with the same qualities in his painting.

64
Saying Goodbye to a Monk from Japan

Hsü Pen (1335–1380)

Thousands of miles away—the Fu-sang Tree,[1]
            among the faint colors of dawn!
Vast ocean sky, seen by few travelers.
No need to follow the tides with your wooden bowl:
you can fly toward the sun on your golden staff!
You'll go on eating Chinese food as you travel back east,
but you'll put on native clothes again after you reach home.
Your countrymen are sure to ask: "How's the Dharma[2] doing there?"
Just show them the palm-leaf manuscripts[3] you're bringing back
            with you.

Translated by Jonathan Chaves

Hsü Pen was among a number of great poets and artists who hailed from Soochow. Hsü led a checkered political life but conjured up a world of serene detachment in his simple, profound poems.
    1. In Chinese mythology, a tree at the easternmost point of the sky, from which the sun rises.
    2. The Buddhist law or doctrine.
    3. Buddhism originally came to China from India. The presence in China of Sanskrit palm-leaf manuscripts of the original Buddhist scriptures seems to indicate that China was still in touch with the motherland of Buddhism. The Japanese monk may, however, have been given some manuscripts that had already been in China for centuries.

65

Written on Seeing the Flowers, and Remembering My Daughter

Kao Ch'i (1336–1374)

I grieve for my second daughter.
Six years I carried her about,
Held her against my breast and helped her eat,
4   Taught her rhymes as she sat on my knee.
She would arise early and copy her elder sister's dress,
Struggling to see herself in the dressing-table mirror.
She had begun to delight in pretty silks and lace,
8   But in a poor family she could have none of these.
I would sigh over my own recurring frustrations,
Treading the byways through the rain and snow.
But evenings when I returned to receive her greeting
12   My sad cares would be transformed into contentment.
What were we to do, that day when illness struck?
The worse because it was during the crisis;
Frightened by the alarming sounds, she sank quickly into death.
16   There was no time even to fix medicines for her.
Distraught, I prepared her poor little coffin;
Weeping, accompanied it to that distant hillside.[1]
It is already lost in the vast void.
20   Inconsolate, I still grieve deeply for her.
I think how last year, in the spring,
When the flowers bloomed by the pond in our old garden
She led me by the hand along under the trees
24   And asked me to break off a pretty branch for her.
This year again the flowers bloom.
Now I live far from home, here by this river's edge.
All the household are here, only she is gone.
28   I look at the flowers, and my tears fall in vain.

Kao Ch'i is still another of the fine poets produced by the Yangtze Valley city of Soochow. Executed on the dubious grounds that he was peripherally involved in a rebellion, Kao was one of the many victims of the repressive atmosphere fostered by the uncouth founder of the Ming dynasty, Chu Yüan-chang, who distrusted even his closest associates.

The poet spent several months during the spring and early summer of 1367 in a city under siege. His five-year-old daughter died during that difficult period. The following spring, seeing the flowers bloom again reminded him of an incident that called her to mind. This prompted him to write the above poem.

1. This probably took place some months after both her death and the end of the siege.

A cup of wine brings me no comfort.
The wind makes desolate sounds in the night curtains.

Translated by F. W. Mote

Silkworm Song of Torchlit Fields

Kao Ch'i

In eastern village and western village
        they celebrate New Year's Eve:
towering torches, a thousand of them,
        light the fields all red!
The old people pray with smiles,
        the young folk sing songs:
"We wish for a year good for silkworms
        and also good for wheat."
In bright starlight strange shadows are cast,
        startling the perched crows;
flames from torches burn off the cold,
        giving birth to spring.
Late at night, torches all burned out,
        the people return to their homes;
they all say prognostications
        show a prosperous year ahead.

Translated by Jonathan Chaves

66

Night Rain: A Wall Collapses

—*Sent to My Neighbors*

Yang Shih-ch'i (1365–1444)

A heavy rain crumbles a wall of my house;
I rise at night, grab my clothes, and run!

The holder of the exalted position of Grand Secretary under four emperors, Yang Shih-ch'i was a brilliant political tactician. Few officials in Chinese history who rose to such prominence also achieved such a high degree of authority as poets.

The wind enters the room, flapping the curtains;
water pours in a stream down the stairs.
The pots beneath the stove still not inundated;
quickly, I run to save the books on my desk.
If only I could be like my eastern and western neighbors:
calmly sleeping, not a thing to worry about.

Translated by Jonathan Chaves

67

The Taoist Huang Has Died of Alcoholism

Shen Chou (1427–1509)

Your master died from drinking too much;
now you have followed in his steps.
A mound of dregs will be your grave,
your tombstone inscribed with the "Ode in Praise of Wine."

Unsteady on your feet, you tripped and stumbled,
your face flushed, your liver wasted.
Now you are gone, not even your shadow remains;
there is only your portrait, drawn in my poem.

Translated by Jonathan Chaves

Another Ming notable who hailed from Soochow (compare selections 64 and 65), Shen Chou was one of the greatest painters in the history of Chinese art. He was also a poet of significance who lived an uneventful life devoted to painting and literature.

68

Inscribed on the Doors of My Bookshelves

Yang Hsün-chi (1456–1544)

Mine was a trading family
Living in Nan-hao district for a hundred years.

In Soochow and its environs there were probably several thousand people writing poetry in the second half of the fifteenth century, and their activities revolved around Shen Chou (see selection 67) and his disciples. Among them was Yang Hsün-chi. Born into a trading family without a single volume in the house, he turned into a true bibliophile. He became a Presented Scholar in 1484. A few years later, rather than continuing to serve as an official, he feigned

I was the first to become a scholar,
4   Our house being without a single book.
Applying myself for a full decade,
I set my heart on building a collection.
Though not fully stocked with minor writings,
8   Of major works, I have nearly everything:
Classics, history, philosophy, belles-lettres—
Nothing lacking from the heritage of the past.
Binding up the volumes one by one in red covers,
12   I painstakingly sew them by hand.
When angry, I read and become happy;
When sick, I read and am cured.
Piled helter-skelter in front of me,
16   Books have become my life.
The people of the past who wrote these tomes,
If not sages, were certainly men of great wisdom.
Even without opening their pages,
20   Joy comes to me just fondling them.
As for my foolish family, they can't be helped;
Their hearts are set on money alone.
If a book falls on the floor, they don't pick it up;
24   What do they care if they get dirty or tattered?
I'll do my best by these books all my days,
And die not leaving a single one behind.
There are some readers among my friends—
28   To them I'll give them all away.
Better that than have my unworthy sons
Haul them off to turn into cash.

Translated by John Timothy Wixted

---

illness and returned to Soochow to devote himself to his books. In this pentasyllabic old-style poem, he relates his progress from bookless son to literary scholar.

69

A Fan from Korea

Chu Yün-ming (1460–1526)

This oriental country, year after year,
    sends its long-journeying ships;

Chu Yün-ming is recognized as the most important calligrapher of the Ming period. His verse owes much to the expressive diction of T'ang poetry, but possibly even more to the unostentatious depiction of everyday life characteristic of Sung poetry.

presenting a tribute of wind and moonlight,
     they come to China.
I trust you will not view this as some trifling affair:
the world now is a single family.

Translated by Jonathan Chaves

70

Ballad of Selling a Child

Wang Chiu-ssu (1468–1551)

    The village woman brings her five-year-old son
    to sell to our household for four and a half measures of grain.
    I ask her, "Why do you wish to sell your son?"
4   And she answers me, with repeated sighs:
    "My husband is old, sick in bed, and blind in both eyes;
    from morning to evening, there's no telling if he'll live or die.
    Our five acres near the village are only poor land.
8   and our two rooms, circled by a wall, are falling apart.
    My eldest son is thirteen, and he can push a plow,
    but our fields are few, our profit meager, so we don't have enough
       to eat.
    Last winter we were late with our tax payments:
12 the officials came knocking at our door, pressuring us to pay.
    Only when a rich family made us a loan did we manage to get through,
    but thinking back, that only made our life more difficult than before.
    My second son, eight years old, knows oxen and sheep,
16 so the eastern neighbor bought him to care for his herds.
    Meanwhile, the rich people demand payment of our debt, as if they
       expected us to pay with our lives,
    and my sick husband coughs and wheezes, his stomach completely
       empty.
    Come to such a pass, we realized we had no choice at all,
20 and so I've brought my youngest son here to exchange for grain.
    Half this grain will be used to repay the rich folks' loan,
    half will be used to make some gruel to feed my poor husband."
    When the village woman stopped speaking, she prepared to leave,

Wang Chiu-ssu was a master of long narrative poems with a moralizing tendency. At the same time, he was interested in the eccentric T'ang Buddhist poet Han Shan (see selection 45). This indicates how difficult it is to establish a simple dichotomy of stuffy orthodoxy versus eccentric individualism in Ming poetry.

24 but her son tugged at her clothes, crying his mother's name.
The woman, miserable, lingered for a while,
and borrowed the use of a spare bed, so she could pass the night with
her son.
When the morning drums beat solemnly, and the roosters cried their
wild cry,
28 the woman rose, and hesitated as she watched her son in his
sound sleep.
Then, stifling her sobs, holding back the tears, she left the city walls
with the grain that would at least alleviate her terrible suffering.
When the boy woke up, he called for his mother, but she was nowhere
to be seen,
32 so he walked around the house, crying out loud, unsteady on his feet.
Everyone who saw him wept tears at the sight,
everyone who heard him knit his brow.
Alas! The wild tiger does not eat its cub,
36 and the old ox will lick the calf.
How can we throw away this pearl we hold in the palm of our hand,
cutting away this flesh from our heart!

Please realize:
The rich grow crueler as their fields increase,
40 and they buy servants and slaves with their wealth.
Then, one day, they curse them in anger,
whipping them unfeelingly until their blood flows!
Don't they know that all flesh and bone comes from the same womb,
44 that another's son and my son are of one form?
Alas! Will the four seas and the nine continents ever share the same
springtime,
so there will be no more people who must sell their daughters and sons?

Translated by Jonathan Chaves

71

Ballad of the Government Granary Clerk

Ho Ching-ming (1483–1521)

Spiked thorns all over, and a thirty-foot wall;
towering entrance with iron bolts

A leader of the archaist movement of the mid-Ming period, Ho Ching-ming particularly excelled in long, expansive poems about paintings. At his best, Ho could infuse his poems, founded though they were on High T'ang models, with dynamic energy and life.

double doors sealed shut.
The minor clerk of the granary
                with gray whiskers and green shirt
writes out ten columns of vermilion characters
                on the wood-plank board.
Standing in front of an official banner,
                all day he reads out loud;
with clipped tallies, people form lines,
                and listen to the numbers being called.
The rich families get plenty of grain,
                piles of it like hills;
their big carriages go creaking off,
                taking two oxen to pull;
A hungry man from the countryside
                stands beneath the wall:
he too wants to come forward for grain,
                but the clerk just curses at him.

Translated by Jonathan Chaves

72
[Title Lost]

Huang Ě (1498–1569)

Pearl-teardrops roll and gather,
        water in the inkstone;
broken-hearted, how can I write
        broken-hearted poems?
Ever since that distant day
        when we last held hands
right to this time I've been too lazy
        to paint in my eyebrows.

There is no medicine that can cure
        my grief through the long nights;
I do have money, but can't buy back
        the time when we were young!

This poem is by Huang Ě, the second wife of Yang Shen (see selection 117). From a respectable family, she was well educated.

Earnestly I entrust my message to the mountain birds:
soon, fly down, south of the river,
      urge him to return!

Translated by Jonathan Chaves

73

A Parable

Li K'ai-hsien (1501–1568)

There was a man who studied the art of disappearing.
Before he had mastered the technique, he boasted to his wife:
"Tell me, can you see my body now?"
4   The wife laughed: "My eyes have not been taken by a ghost!
Your face is right in front of mine, just inches away;
it's not as though you're at the neighbor's or behind a fence!
Since you have a body, why shouldn't I be able to see it,
8   unless you were clever enough to pull off some trick!"
The man was outraged at his wife's frank words;
he kicked her, slapped her, and cursed her out.
Then he asked the same thing of his concubine, and she pretended to
    be amazed:
12   she looked all around behind her, then stared straight ahead.
Lying, she said, "Master, what art is this!
Your body is hidden away—I only hear your voice!"
The man, delighted, went to town, and stole something from a shop.
16   At first the shopkeeper was too startled to move—then he became
    furious,
and gave the man a worse beating than the man had given his wife,
screaming and cursing with a voice like a thunderclap.
As for the "master of invisibility," he yelled too: "Go ahead, beat me up,
20   but if you want to *see* my body, you'll have a hard time!"
Now I once lived in the capital, where I became stuck-in-the-mud.

From a family of officials in Shantung, Li K'ai-hsien became a Presented Scholar in 1529. Like Yang Shen (see selection 117), he was an individualist writer difficult to categorize. Li was friendly with a number of orthodox poets but was far more innovative and idiosyncratic. He was instrumental in the revival of Yüan drama in the later Ming period. A playwright of romances (*ch'uan-ch'i*), Li also wrote suites of arias and a variety of prose works.

In his ability to turn defeat into apparent victory, Li's "master of invisibility" in this parable foreshadows the main character of Lu Hsun's "The True Story of Ah Q," written in 1921.

I was afraid to visit the ministers and high officials.
I was rejected, sent away—but still I didn't change . . . ,
24   Until I escaped, and held my old fishing rod again.

Translated by Jonathan Chaves

Earthquake

Li K'ai-hsien

The earthquake covered Shansi and Shensi;
millions of people died or were hurt.
Homes were flattened to the ground,
and skeletons could be seen lying everywhere.
The prognostication? "Too much Yin." [1]
Perhaps this is an omen of some fault in government. [2]
Three lifelong friends of mine
in one night fell to the dust. [3]

Translated by Jonathan Chaves

One poem from a group of ten, all to the same rhymes.
Poet's notes:

1. "The prognostication says, 'An earthquake occurs when there is an excess of yin.' "
2. "Local officials submitted a memorial, saying, 'The land here is usually quiet, but now it has moved: this is because we officials have not been doing our duty.' "
3. "Yang Shou-li, the Secretary, Han Pang-ch'i, the Investigator, and Ma Li, the Lord of the Imperial Banquets: taken by surprise, they were all crushed to death."

Yang Shou-li (1484–1555), Han Pang-ch'i (1479–1555), and Ma Li (1474–1555) all died in the quake. Han Pang-ch'i had earlier memorialized to the effect that another earthquake was a sign of inadequacy in government, which is in accordance with the Confucian idea that the moral state of human society exerts an influence upon nature. Note that Yin (line 5) is the female cosmic principle.

74

A Buddhist Monk Cut and Burned His Own Flesh to Make the Rains Stop—a Man from His Native Place Asked Me to Write a Poem to Send to Him

Hsü Wei (1521–1593)

The sky extends upward for ninety thousand miles.
When it wants to be clear it is clear,
      when it wants to rain it rains.
For the rain god and the sun god
      it's as easy as herding sheep:
they receive their orders and carry them out;
      who would presume to complain?
So what kind of man is this Buddhist monk,
daring to set up an altar with banners and drums?
With his cracking whip he stands up to Heaven
and cries out to Hsi-ho [1] to bring back the chariot of the sun!
The immortal Chang in broad daylight flew up into the sky—
now this monk has a chance to do even better than that!
All he does is to burn a bit of incense on an inch of his flesh
and the ocean calls the clouds back to the kingdom of water.
The local alchemists are all impressed by what the monk has done,
and the magistrate gives him a piece of red silk.
But still, this man, virtuous as King Aśoka, [2]
      must bear the pain with his own body
while the farmers all bow down to the Inspector of Fields.

Translated by Jonathan Chaves

Hsü Wei was one of the most original painters and calligraphers of the Ming period. His poetry provided inspiration for the burgeoning of poetic creativity in the late Ming period, and he was also noted for his plays. Hsü was a most unstable individual; having attempted suicide by smashing his testicles (pretending insanity at the time), he murdered his third wife, was put in prison, and was sentenced to death. After seven years, however, he was released.

This poem provides a rare example of a member of the scholar-official class taking interest in the practices of folk religion.

1. The mythical charioteer of the sun.

2. King Aśoka (reigned c. 268–232 B.C.E.) was an Indian king who united most of the South Asian subcontinent and converted the region to Buddhism, becoming its first important royal patron. he is believed to have encouraged missionary work throughout much of Asia, including to the borders of China.

A Kite

Hsü Wei

A man who lives by the sea tells of a young boy who, preparing to eat some candy, tied the string of his kite around his waist. Suddenly, a great wind started to blow, sweeping the kite off toward the sea. The boy fell to his death. When his body was recovered, the candy was found still clutched in his hand.

(The kite speaks:)

When the wind is gentle
     and I want to rise
          I cannot rise.

When the wind is strong
     and I want to land
          I cannot land.

Can I cross the ocean?—Depend on me
     to make it by myself;

What a shame that I have carried a boy—
     as he ate some candy—
          to his death.

Translated by Jonathan Chaves

One poem from a group of twenty-five.

75

Song of Selling Flowers

Tsung Ch'en (1525–1560)

People who buy flowers in Ch'ang-an [1]
pay millions for just a few stems.
Beside the road there is a hungry man:
they don't give him a single cent.

Translated by Jonathan Chaves

Tsung Ch'en's poetry is consistent with the orthodox program of writing in emulation of High T'ang models, although he brings in effective references to contemporary events and has a refreshingly direct touch in his shorter poems (see also selection 166).

1. Present-day Sian, Ch'ang-an served as the capital for many dynasties.

76

Saying Good-bye to a Singing Girl Who Has Decided to Become a Nun

Mo Shih-lung (c. 1539–1587)

You have called at the gate of the True Vehicle,
                    your worldly self is no more.
You have said farewell forever
                    to the golden chambers,
                              the wind and the dust.
Lightly you wield the yak-tail whisk;
                    your singing fan lies on the floor.
You learn to adjust your meditation cushion,
                    and laugh at the dancer's mat.
No more resentment when rouge fades
                    like red flowers;
no longer will the feathered hairdo appear in your mirror.
Mist, light, water—quiet Zen mind:
I know a new springtime
                    will bloom
                              in the Realm of Emptiness.

Translated by Jonathan Chaves

Famous as a painter and a theoretician of art, as a poet Mo Shih-lung demonstrates a delicate lyricism of considerable evocative power.

77

Twenty-Two Quatrains on Receiving the Obituary Notice for My Son Shih-ch'ü [1]

T'ang Hsien-tsu (1550–1617)

My son, you loved telling the story of Prince Naṭa [2]
who stripped off his own flesh, returned it to his mother,

Possibly the greatest dramatist of the Ming dynasty, T'ang Hsien-tsu is especially well known for his masterpiece, *The Peony Pavilion (Mu-tan t'ing)* (see selection 217). He was a friend of Yüan Hung-tao (see selection 78) and other figures in the late Ming individualist movement and shared with them an appreciation for romantic love. Somewhat surprisingly, however, the arias in *The Peony Pavilion* are, if anything, more erudite and even bookish than the writings

and gave his father his bones!
Now your flesh has gone to the Ninefold Springs [3]
　　　—does your mother understand?
and your father must gather your bones
　　　and bring them home.

Translated by Jonathan Chaves

------

of the orthodox masters themselves—virtually every line has embedded in it a literary allusion, and the play is therefore a kind of scholarly *tour de force*. T'ang's poetry, far less familiar, is beautifully crafted and shares with his arias an interesting fusion of lyrical tone and density of diction.

One poem from the group of twenty-two.

1. The poet's son died in 1600 in Nanking, where he had gone to take the official examinations.

2. According to a Buddhist text of the Sung dynasty, *Combined Essentials of the Five Lamps* (*Wu-teng hui-yüan*) (ch. 2), "Prince Naṭa [the son of the guardian king of the north, Vaiśravaṇa] stripped off his own flesh and returned it to his mother, and took out his bones and returned them to his father. Only then did he manifest his True Body, wield his great spiritual power, and expound the dharma [law/doctrine] to his parents."

3. The underworld.

78

The "Slowly, Slowly" Poem

—*Playfully inscribed on the wall*

Yüan Hung-tao (1568–1610)

The bright moon slowly, slowly rises,
the green mountains slowly, slowly descend.
The flowering branches slowly, slowly redden,
4　the spring colors slowly, slowly fade.
My salary slowly, slowly increases,
my teeth slowly, slowly fall out,
my lover's waist slowly, slowly expands,
8　my complexion slowly, slowly ages.

Yüan Hung-tao was the leader of the late Ming Kung-an School of literature, so named for the subprefecture in Hupei province where he was born. Tsung-tao (1560–1600) and Chung-tao (1570–1624), his elder and younger brothers, were also important members of this influential literary circle. Known as an individualist, Yüan is a highly eccentric figure within the context of Ming literature. But his eccentricity falls well within the parameters of Chinese tradition and can even be seen as weighing the balance back toward moderation after decades of domination of the cultural scene by the extreme archaism of the orthodox masters.

We are low in society
            in the days of our greatest health,
our pleasure comes when we are no longer young.
The Goddess of Good Luck
            and the Dark Lady of Bad Luck
12   are with us every step we take.
Even heaven and earth are imperfect
and human society is full of ups and downs.
Where do we look for real happiness?
16   —Bow humbly, and ask
            the Masters of Taoist Arts.

Translated by Jonathan Chaves

On Receiving My Letter of Termination

Yüan Hung-tao

The time has come to devote myself to my hiker's stick:
I must have been a Buddhist monk in a former life!
Sick, I see returning home as a kind of pardon.
A stranger here—being fired is like being promoted.
In my cup, thick wine; I get crazy-drunk,
eat my fill, then stagger up the green mountain.
The southern sect, the northern sect, I've tried them all:
this hermit has his own school of Zen philosophy.

Translated by Jonathan Chaves

79

The Grain-Barge Wife

Wu Chia-chi (1618–1684)

Autumn winds blow along the river,
blow upon a man in hunger;

Disillusioned with the moral failure of the Ming leadership, Wu Chia-chi turned to the common people around him for exemplars of loyalty and filial piety, key Confucian virtues, and recorded acts of such people, which he believed bore testimony to the ongoing vitality of

he has a wife lovely as a flower,
4   but no means to put food on her plate!
Toward sunset with great clamor
a grain barge moors in the harbor.
The officer in charge sits at the prow;
8   gazing about, he sees the lovely face.
He sends a man with an urgent message:
"I have plenty of clothes and food.
You are going to starve to death—
12   why not join me, and we'll work together.
Work with me for one year,
and I'll send you home for a fee.
Work with me for three years,
16   and I'll send you home for free!"
The husband pleads with his wife:
"I urge you to do what he asks.
If you don't, we will starve to death,
20   and then we'll be parted forever."
He lifts his wife—lifelong companion—to her feet;
her tears fall like drops of rain.
One day a wife in her bedchamber,
24   the next, a boatman's mistress!
When the man's cronies hear he may have a son,
they prepare a feast, the fatted calf and wine.
They come in boats from south of the river;
28   they come in boats from north of the river.
The boatman is delighted in his heart;
with his own hand he pours out goblets of wine.
He tells himself that lovely piece of goods
32   is like a bird, caught within his nets.
But the netted sparrow has a mate,
the woman has a husband.
How could they know this woman's will
36   could never be bent or broken?
Her husband, weeping, clings to her:
"Follow what he says, lower your eyes!
Work for him for three years' time,
40   and he'll let you return for free."
The woman remains silent, not a word;
as people sleep, the moon sinks at the window.

---

these virtues. His medium-length narrative poems are distinguished by a stark, uncompromising
power.

Quickly she leaves the boatman's place,
44 determined to seek ghostly companions.
Clutching a rock, she jumps into the Grand Canal:
the waves stop flowing for her.
Passersby wipe their tears and stare
48 at her body floating in the water.

Translated by Jonathan Chaves

80

Singing of the Source of Holy Church

Wu Li (1632–1718)

Before the firmament was ever formed,
   or any foundation laid,
high there hovered the Judge of the World,
   prepared for the last days!
This single Man from His five wounds
   poured every drop of blood;
a myriad nations gave their hearts
   to the wonder of the Cross!
The heavenly gates now have a ladder
   leading to their peace;
demonic spirits lack any art
   to insinuate deception.
Take up the burden, joyfully
   fall in behind Jesus,
look up with reverence towards the top of that mountain,
   follow His every step.

Translated by Jonathan Chaves

This is among the earliest known Chinese poems that deal explicitly with Christian themes. The poet, Wu Li, is famous as one of the Six Orthodox Masters of painting in the early Ch'ing period. His works hang in such major American museums as the Freer Gallery, Metropolitan Museum of Art, Cleveland Museum of Art, and William Rockhill Nelson Gallery of Art. His poems, though little known, are worthy of attention for his bold experiment in creating virtually from scratch a Chinese Christian poetry. Having converted to Catholicism and entered the Society of Jesus in 1682, Wu Li was one of the first Chinese to be ordained a priest, in 1688.

81

Medicine

Wang Shih-chen (1634–1711)

What do we know about the efficacy of medicine?
Full of worries, one's easy prey to sickness and old age.
Now, my eyes are cried dry weeping for my children [1]
And heart broken by chanting poignant ballads.
Who knows when letters from home might arrive,
As autumn waves run deep both day and night.
While here, the apes of Pa [2] are most inconsiderate,
For crying so sadly in the maple forest.

Translated by Richard John Lynn

Wang Shih-chen was a native of Hsin-ch'eng, Shantung. He had a long, successful career in the state bureaucracy, in which he rose to become president both of the Censorate and the Board of Punishments. His literary career was equally illustrious, and he was one of the most prominent writers of the Ch'ing era. His poetry, essays, works of literary criticism and theory, and literary anthologies made an enormous impact then and continue to be widely studied and admired today.

1. By this time (1672) the poet had lost two children to illness.
2. Pa is an old name for Szechwan.

82

Lines in Praise of a Self-Chiming Clock

K'ang-hsi (1654–1722)

The skill originated in the West,
But, by learning, we can achieve the artifice:
Wheels move and time turns round,
Hands show the minutes as they change.

Red-capped watchmen, there's no need to announce dawn's coming.
My golden clock has warned me of the time.
By first light I am hard at work,
And keep on asking, "Why are the memorials late?"

Translated by Jonathan Spence

This poem was written by the Manchu emperor K'ang-hsi about 1710. He was an ardent supporter of scholarship, literature, and the arts in general throughout his six-decade reign (1661–1722).

83

Song of Surfing on the Bore [1]

Cheng Hsieh (1693–1765)

The boys of Ch'ien-t'ang practice riding the bore:
with firm poles and long oars they stroke and plunge!
One boy, alone, stands on each deck as if cast in iron,
face the color of ashes, his eyes unblinking, fixed.
The bore rolls in like a mountain—they shoot their boats ahead;
masts and sculls flip over sideways
        as the boats stand up on end!
Then—suddenly, they all disappear, without a trace . . .
then reappear on the slow after-waves, a fleet of boats again.
Now the bore has gone down, the waves flow softly,
        the boats follow the gulls.
The boys sing and laugh, the mountains are green,
        the blue water laps the shore.
This is the way we all should go through the troubles of life:
put up with them while they last—calm waters lie ahead.

Translated by Jonathan Chaves

One of the Eight Eccentrics of Yang-chou, Cheng Hsieh had a highly distinctive style both as a painter and a calligrapher. His poetry is full of humor and has a bold search for unusual subject matter, though not without a noticeable moralizing tendency.

1. "An abrupt rise of the tide which breaks in an estuary, rushing violently up the channel" (*The American College Dictionary*). In China, the mouth of the Che River at Hangchow (also known as the Ch'ien-t'ang River at this location) is famous for this phenomenon (see selection 184).

84

On the Way to Pa-ling

Yüan Mei (1716–1797)

From Lake Tung-t'ing we travel west
        to the Shrine of the Goddess;

Yüan Mei became a Presented Scholar in 1739 when he was only twenty-three years old. He was appointed to the imperial academy and instructed to learn the Manchu language, but failed the Manchu examinations miserably. After other minor appointments, he resigned from public life and devoted himself to writing and teaching.

One of the most attractive of the later poets and essayists, Yüan Mei combines humor with

here to comfort weary travelers
>   are women with painted brows.
The mountain town is desolate,
>   shops close at early hours;
the fortress tower's light still far,
>   we're late to moor our boat.
The dialect here I do not speak—
>   I'll hire interpreters;
such strange birds—I don't know their names,
>   ashamed as a scholar of the *Odes*.[1]
How rare to find a boatman
>   who understands my heart:
each time I open the cabin window
>   there's a branch of blossom on shore.

>   *Translated by Jonathan Chaves*

---

affection for mundane detail. His *Poetry Talks from the Sui Garden (Sui yüan shih-hua)* is one of the best compilations of poetic criticism from the later period and a veritable treasure-trove of insightful discussions of poems and poets.

Yüan Mei had an extremely broad range of interests. For example, he wrote several fine essays on the culinary arts. He also advocated education for young women and even served as the director of a school for female poets whose works he published, for which he was sternly rebuked by many of his more orthodox contemporaries.

Although critical of Li Yü (see selection 179) for being effete and ill-considered, Yüan Mei sponsored a traveling troupe of actors and had extraordinarily close relationships with the more handsome among them.

Last, but not least, Yüan Mei was an ardent fan of strange tales in the tradition of P'u Sung-ling (see selection 205) and Chi Yün (see selection 206). He collected and published several volumes of these, the most famous being *What the Master* [i.e., Confucius] *Would Not Discuss (Tzu pu yü).*

1. One of the benefits to be derived from studying the *Classic of Odes (Shih ching,* see selection 16), according to instructions by Confucius to his disciples, is that the reader learns the names of animals and birds.

Lyrics and Arias

85

A Suite in the *Ch'ing-p'ing* Mode [1]

Attributed to Li Po (701–762)

Part One

> As clouds think of her clothing, as blossoms think of her face,
> Spring wind caresses the railings
> and dew is thick on the flowers.
> [Stanza continues.]

This is one of the earliest sets of lyrics, "lyric" (also called "lyric meter" or "song lyric" in English) here being used as a technical term equivalent to the Chinese literary genre *tz'u*. All the poetry in the previous section of the anthology belongs to the genre known as *shih* and is of quite a different nature from that of *tz'u*. *Shih* normally consist of lines of equal length, usually pentasyllabic or heptasyllabic, and may be thought of as prosodically "square" in shape. One of the most common words for "character" in Mandarin is *fang-k'uai-tzu* (square graph or tetragraph). The square shape of a regular number of graphs in the lines of a poem results in a square or rectangular shape for the poem as a whole. It also invites abundant use of such literary devices as parallelism and antithesis in matching lines and couplets. Traditionally, however, Chinese texts—whether poetry or prose—were written out in continuous strings of sinographs without any indication of line length or punctuation, these being determined during the act of reading.

Tz'u, or lyrics, usually consist of lines of unequal length. Originally, the length of each line was determined by the music to which these lyrics were sung. Such tunes frequently entered the repertoire from Central Asia and other surrounding regions or from the popular culture, especially the entertainment world, of various localities within China. A suite of matching or grouped tunes was said to belong to a given "mode" *(tiao)*, which may be regarded as analogous to a musical "key" (i.e., several related *tz'u*-tunes were "in the mode/key of . . ."). The system of Chinese lyrical tunes and modes bears certain resemblances to Indian ragas and, indirectly

> If you do not find her by the Mountain of Numerous Jewels,[2]
> You may head for the Jasper Terrace [3]
> to meet her beneath the moon.

Part Two

> A branch of red voluptuousness, the dew congealed perfume,
> For clouds and rain on Sorceress Mountain,[4]
> why go breaking your heart?

—————————   [Stanza continues.]

through Indianized Central Asian and South Asian musical sources, may have been influenced by them and by other Indian musical and prosodic conventions. With the passage of time, the musical quality of the tunes and modes in China was forgotten, but the syllabic lengths and prosodic quality of the lines became fixed, arbitrary patterns to which new lyrics could be fitted. Thus lyrics may be said to be "to the tune of . . . ," even though the actual tunes were lost while only the line lengths and certain tonic, syntactic, grammatical, and other characteristics were retained.

The subject matter of the earliest lyrics was often related to the titles of the tunes to which they were written. Before very long in the evolution of the genre, however, there developed a complete divorce between the meaning of tune title and the content of a given lyric. Indeed, a separate title apart from the tune title was often provided for each new lyric. Many translators simply transcribe the tune titles because of their irrelevance to content and because they are often extremely difficult to understand. This is particularly the case for the later stages in the development of the tradition where the relationship between the tune title and the content of a lyric or aria is usually meaningless.

It is not just the structure of the *tz'u*-lyric that is so different from that of the *shih*-poem. The themes and diction are also distinctive. The lyric, for example, is typically far less allusive than a classical poem. In contrast, the language of the lyric may often be more effusive. Where the classical poem is largely governed by the quasi-monosyllabic nature of the literary (written) language, the lyric is full of polysyllabic words from the vernacular (oral) language. It is commonplace for the lyric, furthermore, to be spoken in the persona of a woman, even though most lyrics, like the vast majority of all Chinese verse, were written by men. A constant theme of the lyric is love, normally considered an unworthy or trivial subject in the tradition of classical poetry.

The lyric had its precursors in the T'ang period and its heyday in the Five Dynasties and Sung periods but was replaced by the aria (see selections 105 ff.) during the Yüan period. The genre continued to be practiced by scattered authors during the Ming and Ch'ing periods. Mao Tse-tung, the founder of the People's Republic of China, was an avid practitioner of *tz'u*-lyrics.

The question of the authorship of "A Suite in the *Ch'ing-p'ing* Mode" is a thorny one. One problem with the set is that each of the three parts is actually written as though it were a regular heptasyllabic poem. Yet this is in keeping with the early involvement of literati poets with the lyric. Often their regular verse would be adapted to the irregular line lengths of lyric meters by the addition of filler words and syllables.

For a note on the poet, see selection 35.

1. These lyrics are believed to have been written at imperial command on an occasion in 743 or 744 when Emperor Hsüan Tsung and Precious Consort Yang (Yang Kuei-fei) were enjoying the tree peonies in the imperial gardens.

2. In the wonderful realm of the mythical Queen Mother of the West, who is attended by beautiful immortals.

3. The palace of the Queen Mother of the West.

4. "Clouds and rain" are the usual figure for delicately suggesting sexual intimacy. The

I wonder who could be compared in the palaces of the Han?
Would it be dear Flying Swallow [5]
trying new powder and rouge?

Part Three

Beauty to topple a nation in the company of famous flowers,
They always succeed with His Majesty
making him turn with a smile.
Knowing that the spring wind may bring regrets unending,
North of the Aloeswood Pavilion
they lean on the balustrade.

Translated by Elling Eide

---

original dalliance that resulted in sex being associated with clouds and rain took place on Sorceress Mountain (Wu Shan) in southwest China.

5. Chao Fei-yen. A beautiful Han dynasty dancer who caught the eye of Emperor Ch'eng and ultimately became his empress in 16 B.C.E. It is said that Li Po was banished from court when the eunuch Kao Li-shih called it slanderous to compare Precious Consort Yang with Flying Swallow.

86
A Lyric from Tun-huang

Anonymous (8th–9th century)

Tune: "Magpie on the Branch"

I can't stand the wily magpie and all his extravagant stories!
He brings me good news, but what proof does he ever have?
One of these times when he flies by, I'll grab him, capture him live,
shut him up in a golden cage to put a stop to his chatter!

With the best of intentions I went to her, delivered my good news—
who'd have thought she'd shut me up in a golden cage?

Approximately five hundred lyrics, mostly dating to the tenth century or somewhat earlier, were discovered at Tun-huang (see selection 214). Except for three or four known T'ang poets, all are anonymous, but in some cases the names of the singers were given. The Tun-huang lyrics include a total of sixty-nine different tune titles. They are extremely important for understanding the early history of lyric meters.

I only hope her soldiering husband comes home soon
so she'll lift me up, turn me loose to head for the blue clouds!

Translated by Burton Watson

87
Tune: "Memories of the South"
A Spring Lyric After Po Chü-yi

Liu Yü-hsi (772–842)

Spring is going, gone!
Having thankfully bid adieu
To the people of Loyang.
Willow tendrils quivering in the breeze
Wave good-bye;
Clustered orchids drip dew
To wet their handkerchiefs.
And she sits alone,
Knitting her moth-eyebrows.

Translated by Jiaosheng Wang

Imbued with Confucianism through his family tradition and upbringing, Liu Yü-hsi became a Presented Scholar in 793 at the age of twenty. However, a setback in his official career occurred when he wrote a number of poems thought to be politically offensive. Liu was one of the earliest literati poets to experiment with the prosodic arrangements of popular songs. He was also influenced by non-Sinitic folk songs with which he came to be familiar during two periods of banishment.

88
Tune: "Deva-Like Barbarian"

Wen T'ing-yün (?–866)

The mountains on the screen shimmer in the golden dawn;
A cloud of hair brushes the fragrant snow of her cheek.

A native of T'ai-yüan in Shansi, Wen T'ing-yün failed the highest civil service examination many times. An accomplished musician on the flute and zither, he was able to create new

Lazily, she rises and paints mothlike brows;
Slowly, tardily, she gets ready for the day.

Mirrors, front and behind, reflect a flower,
Face and flower shining each upon the other.
Stitched in the silk of her bright new coat,
Golden-threaded partridges fly pair by pair.

Translated by Lois Fusek

---

tunes of his own. Most lyrics attributed to earlier literati poets are barely distinguishable from "square" or "rectangular" classical poetry in form. Performers relied heavily on so-called padding words to flesh them out so that they would fit the irregular contours of popular tunes. Wen's lyrics, in contrast, are full-fledged with a sprightly rhythm unlike that of classical poetry. The first major poet to produce unabashedly a substantial number of genuine lyrics, Wen did the most to legitimize the lyric as an appropriate genre for literati. Sixty-six of his seventy extant lyrics are preserved in the *Among the Flowers Collection (Hua chien chi)*, the famous anthology of lyrics about love and separation compiled by Chao Ch'ung-tso (fl. 934–965). This is by far the largest number of poems by which any author is represented in this highly significant collection. Ou-yang Chiung, who (like most of the poets included in the collection) was from Shu (present-day Szechwan), wrote a preface dated 940 that attempted to justify this new effete and ornate style of verse as an appropriate vehicle for the expression of literati sentiment.

The lyric selected here is from a group of fourteen by Wen to the same tune title. Although the sinographs usually used to write the tune title *P'u-sa man* seem to mean "Bodhisattva Southwesterners," there is much controversy over their correct interpretation. One modern literary historian, Elling Eide, gives evidence that they should be rendered as "Strings of Jewels for Bodhisattvas," and that the lyrics to this tune were originally all strings of couplets about beautiful women. A Bodhisattva is a savior figure in Mahāyāna (Great Vehicle) Buddhism and "deva" (the translation given for the same word by the translator of Wen T'ing-yün's lyric) is simply a Sanskrit word for "deity." The same tune title *(P'u-sa man)* is rendered as "The Bodhisattva Foreigner" in selection 89.

89

Tune: "The Bodhisattva Foreigner"

Wei Chuang (836–910)

Recalling now the pleasures of the South,
When I was young in light spring tunic —

Wei Chuang hailed from Tu-ling in Shensi. He was the great-great-grandson of the poet Wei Ying-wu (fl. 765–785). His parents, however, passed away when he was but a child, and he grew up in reduced circumstances. By 894, when he became a Presented Scholar, the T'ang dynasty was already in serious decline, so there was little hope of a meaningful career in officialdom. For this and for other personal reasons, his verses are filled with melancholy. Forty-

Astride my horse by the sloping bridge,
Red-sleeved ones beckoned from every storied house.

By gilt-hinged kingfisher screens,
Drunk, I'd enter the flower groves to spend the night.
Seeing such flower twigs now,
Though gray-haired, I swear I'd not go home.

Translated by John Timothy Wixted

---

eight of his lyrics are included in the *Among the Flowers Collection*, which shows that he was one of the more active literati practitioners of the new genre. He was also the author of the celebrated poem "Lament of the Lady of Ch'in," an account of the sacking of Ch'ang-an by the rebel Huang Ch'ao. This long, dramatic piece, which was phenomenally popular shortly after its composition, was lost for over a thousand years and recovered only in this century among the Tun-huang manuscripts (see selections 86 and 214). While living in Szechwan, Wei purchased and lived in the former residence of the great poet Tu Fu (see selection 37).

90

Tune: "Offering Congratulations to the Enlightened Reign"

Ou-yang Chiung (896–971)

I remember the day when we first met among the flowers.
I lifted my red sleeve to hide my face,
And so frivolously turned my head away.
I played with the sash on my red skirt,
And quite deliberately with my slender,
Jadelike fingers, I began to pick away,
A pair of phoenixes stitched with gold.

The green *wu-t'ung* [1] trees are locked deep in the garden.
Who could know how much we would love one another?

A native of the culturally and historically important town of Hua-yang in Szechwan, Ou-yang Chiung served as a high-ranking official under both the Earlier Shu (907–925) and Later Shu (934–965) dynasties, as well as under the Sung government which reunified China after the Five Dynasties. He was the author of a noteworthy preface to the *Among the Flowers Collection* (see selection 88), from which this lyric is taken. It is the first of two by him to the same tune title.

1. The scientific name for the *wu-t'ung* is *Sterculia platanifolia* or *Firmiana platanifolia*. In

Will there be a time when we can be forever close?
I envy the mated swallows that come in the spring.
Flying, they descend to the jade tower,
Where day and night, they are together!

Translated by Lois Fusek

English, it is called the kolanut or Chinese parasol tree. An ornamental tree frequently found growing in the courtyards of Chinese temples and houses, it has large leaves that afford excellent shade. As a literary trope, it occurs constantly in poems and plays to evoke feelings of sadness experienced by someone who hears raindrops lugubriously falling upon its broad leaves. Here, we may also interpret its name as a homophone for "we-together."

91

Tune: "The Crow's Nocturnal Cry"

Li Yü (937–978)

Last night there was rain with a soughing wind.
In the air was the sound of autumn,
And the screens and curtains rustled.
Again and again I turned on my pillow,
As the candlelight waned, and the clepsydra stopped dripping.
Nor could I compose myself when I sat up.

Worldly affairs simply drift away
In the wake of the running stream:
Methinks my life is but a floating dream.
Fittest to frequent—
The calm Land of Drunkenness.
Other than it, there's no path
I can bear to travel.

Translated by Jiaosheng Wang

Li Yü was the last emperor of the Southern T'ang dynasty. Apparently ineffective as a ruler, he was a true esthete. A painter, calligrapher, and lyricist, he favored Buddhism and tried his best to avoid war. But his dynasty was quickly conquered and replaced by the Sung, with the result that much of his later verse dwells upon lost glory. Li Yü enlarged the scope of writing in lyric meters beyond the previously normal confines of the teahouse and women's apartments. With him, it became possible to use the lyric as a vehicle for writing about such subjects as the downfall of his own dynasty, the shortness of life, and the futility of human endeavor.

Tune: "New Bounty of Royalty" [1]

Li Yü

There's no helping
Autumn colors slipping imperceptibly by.
Dusk descends on courtyard steps
Strewn with fallen petals and leaves.
Once more the Double Ninth Festival [2] returns,
And I ascend the terrace pavilion
Letting fade the fragrance of dogwood.

Aroma of chrysanthemum wine
Wafting by the hall entrance;
Drizzling rain robed in evening mist.
Wild geese just come back
Honking drearily in the chill air.
Regrets untold—from year to year unchanging.

Translated by Jiaosheng Wang

1. After the loss of his empire to the Sung dynasty, Li Yü was imprisoned in the Sung capital. Later, the Sung Emperor T'ai Tsung granted him a pardon, and he was allowed to live in a separate residence. This lyric was presumably written during that period of comparative ease. In some later poems, however, he expressed the strong nostalgic feelings of a deposed monarch. This enraged the Sung emperor, who not long afterward ordered him to be poisoned.

2. The ninth day of the ninth lunar month, a festival celebrated by climbing a hill and drinking wine. It is also associated with longevity and thus becomes an appropriate occasion for drinking an infusion of chrysanthemum petals in wine, a concoction thought to confer long life.

Tune: "Pure Serene Music"

Li Yü

Spring is half gone since we parted.
My heart breaks when I see
Snowy plum petals at the foot of the stairs in disarray
That all but cover my body
For all my brushing.

Wild geese come back—can I trust the message they bring?
The way so long—no use to dream of returning.

The pain of separation is just like the spring grass:
The more it grows, the farther away you are.

Translated by Jiaosheng Wang

Tune: "Memories of the South"
A Reminiscence

Li Yü

Regrets untold!
In a dream last night
I was again out touring High Park
As in days of old:
Luxurious coaches in streams,
Fine steeds soaring like dragons—
A blaze of moonlight and flowers
In the balmy breezes of spring.

Translated by Jiaosheng Wang

92
Tune: "Bells Ringing in the Rain"
Sadness of Parting

Liu Yung (987?–1053)

It was at the roadside pavilion that we were to bid adieu.
A sudden evening rain had just come to a lull,
Lugubrious the chirp of cicadas in the chill air.

Liu Yung came from the southeastern coastal region of Fukien. He achieved the rank of Presented Scholar in 1034 at the relatively late age of forty-seven but never energetically embarked upon an official career. Liu spent a lot of his early years frequenting the demimonde of Pien-ching (modern K'aifeng), the Northern Sung capital, where he became well known among the courtesans for whom he wrote new lyrics. He is noted for creating the subgenre of long lyrics *(man-tz'u)*. Liu's works depict urban life and make free use of colloquial language. He was considered by other lyricists to be unconventional and even vulgar, but was also capable of employing highly refined literary language when he felt it appropriate.

At the farewell dinner outside the city gate,
We drank in low spirits,
Unable to tear ourselves away at the boatman's summons.
Hand in hand we gazed at each other's tear-stained eyes,
Words choked on the verge of utterance,
As we brooded over the misty waves
That swept a thousand tricents away,
And a dusky haze silhouetted against
A wide southern sky.

Parting with a loved one has ever been painful since days of old,
Let alone in the season of bleak autumn.
Where shall I be this evening when I sober up?
On a bank o'ergrown with willows—
The moon waning, the wind of dawn blowing.[1]
Once parted, year after year must elapse
When to relive pleasant hours and gay scenes
Will be but an illusion,
And even though I have a thousand delicate sentiments,
To whom can I bare my aching heart?

Translated by Jiaosheng Wang

1. In the original Chinese, this line is traditionally considered famous for its poignant picturesqueness.

93

Tune: "Sumuche [1] Dancers"

Fan Chung-yen (989–1052)

Blue cloud sky
Yellow leaf ground

Fan Chung-yen's father died when he was still very young and he took the surname Chu when his mother remarried. He studied in a rural Buddhist temple and received the assistance of a number of generous patrons, with the result that he was able to pass the examinations for Presented Scholar in 1015. He became the leader of an initial reform of Northern Sung institutions and thus prepared the way for the major reforms of Ou-yang Hsiu (see selection 174) and Wang An-shih (see selection 55). Although he was not a prolific author, his poems, prose pieces, and lyrics (especially his short lyrics) are nonetheless highly appreciated.

1. The name is probably the transcription of some Central Asian word, whence the tune originally came.

Autumnal waves
Under cold blue mist.
Hills catch the setting sun, sky and water merge.
Unfeeling, fragrant grasses grow
On and on past the setting sun.

Unhappy homesick soul
Obsessed with travel cares—
Night brings no relief
Except when pleasant dreams prolong the sleep.
Don't look out the high window when the moon shines—
The wine in your melancholy heart
Will turn to tears of longing.

Translated by James Robert Hightower

94

Tune: "Spring in the Jade House"

Yen Shu (991–1055)

Green willows and fragrant grass by the posthouse road
Where the young man left me without a pang.
An unfinished dream at the fifth watch bell
The sorrow of parting under the blossoms in a third month rain.

Insensitive misses susceptible's bitterness,
Whose every inch turns into a thousand myriad strands.
The sky's edge, earth's corner—sometime they come to an end;
It's just this longing that is never done.

Translated by James Robert Hightower

The lyricist, who was from Lin-ch'uan in Kiangsi, passed the Presented Scholar examination at the incredibly young age of fourteen and soon thereafter received an official appointment. By the age of forty-four, he had become Grand Councilor and was one of the few southerners to achieve such a high rank at the Northern Sung court. A true statesman-poet, Yen sponsored a literary salon in his own home. He was particularly skilled in composing short lyrics and followed the tradition of the Southern T'ang lyricists.

95

Tune: "Drunk in Fairyland"

Ou-yang Hsiu (1007–1072)

Shyly she knits her brows
And shows a face delicately rouged:
Supple waist in white silk
Beside the peony balustrade.
Vexed, she won't let him approach—
Half hiding her coy face,
Her voice low and shaking,
She asks, "Does anyone know?"
Smoothing her silk skirt,
She steals an upward glance
And takes a step or two away.

Then she asks,
"If I do it and then
My hair comes all undone
And mother guesses what's up?
No, I am going home—
You leave me alone for now.
Besides, I've needlework to do for mother;
She'll scold me if I don't get it done.
Wait until late tonight,
And come again
Under the shadows of the courtyard trees, okay?"

Translated by James Robert Hightower

For a note on Ou-yang Hsiu, see selection 174.

96

Tune: "Partridge Sky"
Written While Banished to Huang-chou

Su Shih (1037–1101)

Where the forest breaks,
Hills emerge into view;

For a note on Su Shih, see selection 127.

Where the walled courtyard is hidden in bamboo,
Obstreperous cicadas riot over a small pond o'ergrown with withered grass.
Frequent is the appearance of white birds looping in the air,
Delicate the fragrance of pink lotus blooms mirrored in water.

Beyond the village houses,
Beside the ancient town,
Cane in hand, a leisurely stroll I take
In the wake of the slanting sun.
Thanks to last midnight's bounteous rain,
My floating life[1] now enjoys one more day of delicious cool.

Translated by Jiaosheng Wang

1. An expression meaning "precarious life" which originates from the *Chuang Tzu* (see selection 8).

Tune: "Fragrance Fills the Courtyard"

Su Shih

Vainglory in Snailhorn,
Petty profit on Flyshead:
It all adds up to effort wasted.
If everything is determined in advance,
Then who is weak, who is strong?
With what time I have left before I am old,
Let me be irresponsible for a little bit.
In my hundred years,
I'd still like to be drunk
Thirty-six thousand times.

Reckon it up—
How much can you have,
With worry and grief, wind and rain
Taking away a good half?
But why
Go on till you die, talking about the short end and the big deal?
Here we have a fresh breeze and a bright moon,
The moss-mat spread,
The cloud-curtain drawn—
It's good here in the south:

A thousand measures of fine wine
And "Fragrance Fills the Courtyard"[1] for a song.

Translated by James Robert Hightower

1. The tune title of this lyric. Compare selection 97, the first lyric.

Tune: "Immortal by the River"

Su Shih

I drank at night on East Slope, sobered up, got drunk again.
When I came home it was sometime past midnight,
The houseboy was already snoring like thunder.
I pounded on the gate and got no response,
Then leaned on my staff and listened to the river noises.

I have long deplored that this body is not one's own.
When can I forget the restless striving?
The night is late, the wind still, the ripples smooth.
In a little boat I shall put out from here,
Entrusting my remaining days to river and sea.

Translated by James Robert Hightower

97
Tune: "The Courtyard Full of Fragrance"
Tea

Huang T'ing-chien (1045–1105)

Spring wind in North Park—
Square tablet, round disk of jade,

For information on Huang T'ing-chien, see selection 57.

A panegyric on tea. North Park in Fukien produces a famous tea, pressed into round or square cakes for transport, as was the Sung custom. To prepare an infusion, the cake had to be broken and ground to powder: this is the sacrifice that makes the tea deserve at least a commemorative tablet. It wins at the banquet for being the last comestible consumed. It banishes fatigue and the necessity of a springtime nap, and for the Chinese, too, it was the cup

Fame that stirs capital and frontier a myriad miles away;
Shattered body, powdered bones—
Achievements worthy of the Ling-yen Hall of Heroes.
At the banquet it wins the palm of refinement,
Downs spring sleep,
Pushes back the boundary of grief.
Offered by slender hands,
Rubbed to paste and whipped to milky froth.
Golden thread, partridge-striped.

Ssu-ma Hsiang-ju, though sick of thirst,
Produced a song for every flask—
We have poets here,
And it will support them by the lamp—
Drunken jade, toppling mountain.
Rummage through your memory of a thousand volumes,
And pour forth your inexhaustible spring of poetry;
When I go home at last,
Wen-chün is waiting up
By the little window, to sit with me.

Translated by James Robert Hightower

---

that cheers. It should be served by a pretty maid who prepared the brew by whipping up the powder into a frothy, creamy beverage familiar today only in the Japanese ceremonial tea.

Ssu-ma Hsiang-ju was said to suffer from an ailment—possibly diabetes—that made him thirsty. In spite of his disability, he could still drink enough wine to be inspired to write poems. The same is expected of the talented guests at the banquet, who, supported by a drink of the sobering tea, are exhorted to write poetry though so drunk they are ready to collapse, like Hsi K'ang (223–362; see selection 171), a crumbling mountain of jade. Back home the poet will find his faithful wife, like Hsiang-ju's Cho Wen-chün (see selection 129), waiting for him, so that they can have a cup of tea together before retiring.

Tune: "A Thousand Autumns"

Huang T'ing-chien

The best thing in the world
Is precisely being together like this;
The nights getting longer,
The weather cool,
The rain dripping a bit outside the curtain,

The molded incense in the burner—
I've long dreamed about it
And now it's really happening.

Our joy reached its peak and she turned lovely limp;
The jade was soft, the flower drooped and fell,
Her hairpin dangling on my sleeve,
Her hair piled on my arm.
The lamp lights her ravishing eyes,
Wet with perspiration, intoxicated—
Sleep, sweetheart, sleep;
Sweetheart, sleep.

Translated by James Robert Hightower

98

Tune: "Sand of Silk-Washing Brook"
A Spring Morning [1]

Ch'in Kuan (1049–1100)

A suggestion of chill pervades the little bower,
The haze of dawn sulky as though it were deep autumn.
On the painted screen, thin mist hovering over a running brook—
A scene tranquil and serene.

Fallen petals flying at ease—ethereal like dreams;
Mizzling rain in an endless stream—fine as sorrow.
The jeweled curtain hung up idly on a little hook of silver.

Translated by Jiaosheng Wang

Ch'in Kuan became a Presented Scholar in 1085. He served as an editor in the imperial library and an officer of the bureau of compilation. He was demoted when his sponsor, Su Shih (see selection 127), fell from power in 1095. Ch'in is especially noted for perfecting the poetic language of the lyric without disregarding its musical requirements.

1. In the opinion of the critic Wang Kuo-wei (see selection 121), this is one of the most noteworthy of Ch'in Kuan's short lyrics.

Tune: "Perfumed Garden"
Bidding Adieu

Ch'in Kuan

Mountains wreathed in wisps of light cloud;
Withered grass stretches to meet the far horizon.[1]
Muted the sound of bugles on the gate tower;
Ready to depart, a boat moored at the river's edge.
How many things bygone at the Fairy Pavilion
Return to mind in a misty haze,
As listlessly we drain our cups to bid adieu!
Beyond the setting sun, a scattering of crows in the cold air
Are winging above a stream
That winds round a solitary village.[2]

Heart-rending this moment of separation
When the scented bag is tenderly given away as a memento,
And the silk girdle untied in token of farewell.[3]
All this, however, has but earned me the name of a fickle lover,
A drifter in the Green Mansions.[4]
Once parted, who can say when we'll meet again?
On my coat and sleeves are stains of tears shed in vain.
It grieves me to see the lofty city-walls
Receding from view in the lurid lights of evening.

Translated by Jiaosheng Wang

1,2. These lines in the original Chinese are widely recited.
3. The scented bag was worn at his waist by a man as a mark of affection for the girl he loved, and the silk girdle worn by the girl had a knot which she would cut should the romantic relation come to an end.
4. A euphemism for brothels.

99
Tune: "The Diviner"

Li Chih-yi (fl. 1071)

I live at the head of the Long River,[1]
You live along its lower reaches;

The poet, a successful scholar-official, was a follower of Su Shih (see selection 56).
1. The Yangtze.

Day after day I think of you but cannot see you,
Yet we both drink the waters of the Long River.

When will these waters ever cease?
When will this yearning ever end?
I wish only that your heart will be like my heart,
And that you will never repudiate our mutual affection.

Translated by Victor H. Mair

100

Tune: "Nien-nu Is Charming"

Chu Tun-ju (1080?–1175?)

Old age has come and I am glad;
I've experienced what the world holds
And know too well the way things are,
Have seen through the shams.
The sea of sorrow, the mount of pain,
All shattered in a trice.
No longer misled by flowers
Or led into trouble by wine,
I know all the scores now.
When full I look to take a nap;
Awake again, I play the role called for.

Don't talk of time a-passing!
In this old man's heart
Is no wish to meddle much in affairs.
I don't try to become a Taoist immortal
Or flatter the Buddha
Or imitate the busy Confucius.
I have no wish to compete with worthy men;
Let them laugh —
This is just the way I am.

A reclusive poet and painter of the Southern Sung period, Chu Tun-ju was born into a family of bureaucrats from Loyang. He attained the rank of Presented Scholar in 1135 but declined several appointments offered to him. He settled in Canton after the Jürchen took control of the north of China and established the Chin dynasty, displacing the Sung to the south. Chu Tun-ju's works are filled with nature imagery and nostalgia for the north.

When the play is over,
I will leave my costume for the dumb actors.

Translated by James Robert Hightower

101
Tune: "Rouged Lips"
Naïveté

Li Ch'ing-chao (1084–c. 1151)

Stepping down from the swing,
Languidly she smooths her soft, slender hands,
Her flimsy dress wet with light perspiration—
A slim flower trembling with heavy dew.

Spying a stranger, she walks hastily away in shyness:
Her feet in bare socks,
Her gold hairpin fallen.
Then she stops to lean against a gate,
And looking back,
Makes as if sniffing a green plum.

Translated by Jiaosheng Wang

Li Ch'ing-chao is universally recognized as China's greatest woman poet and one of the foremost lyricists in her own right. She was born in Li-ch'eng (modern Tsinan in Shantung province) of an outstanding literary family. Her father was a noted writer of prose and a literary associate of Su Shih (see selection 127). Her mother, also a poet, was descended from a distinguished family. Li Ch'ing-chao was already recognized as a talented voice in her adolescence. In 1101 she married Chao Ming-ch'eng, a student in the imperial academy. The couple shared compatible tastes in literature, painting, and calligraphy, and she wrote warmly of their mutual joys. Later, however, she experienced the traumatic events surrounding the fall of the Northern Sung to the Jürchen and the transfer of the dynasty to the Southern Sung. This dislocation was attended by much personal loss (see selection 170), and she wrote sensitively of her suffering and sadness during this period.

Tune: "Magnolia Flowers" (short version)

Li Ch'ing-chao

From the flower vendor I bought
A sprig of spring just bursting into bloom—
Sprinkled all over with teardrops
Still tinged with traces of
Roseate clouds and morning dew.

Lest my beloved should think
I'm not so fair as the flower,
I pin it slanting in my cloud hair,
And ask him to see
Which of us is the lovelier:
The flower or I.

Translated by Jiaosheng Wang

Tune: "Fisherman's Pride" [1]
A Dream

Li Ch'ing-chao

Billowing clouds surging across the heavens
Merge into dawn's hazy mist.
Sails in their thousands toss and dance
As the Milky Way recedes.
In a vision I find myself before the Heavenly Ruler,
Who asks solicitously
Where I wish to be off to.

"My journey is a long one," I reply.
"The sun is setting all too soon.
And my brilliant poetic attempts, alas!

1. Among Li Ch'ing-chao's lyric poems, this one is unique in style and content. Written probably after the fall of the Northern Sung dynasty, when she found herself an exile in South China with all her hopes and aspirations frustrated, it is a work of pure romance, conceived in a trance, and worthy of the greatest masters of romantic lyric poetry. It shows the versatility of her genius in producing a masterpiece in a style other than that of the elegantly restrained lyric of which she was generally recognized as the foremost exponent. Among its most enthusiastic admirers was Liang Ch'i-ch'ao, a great essayist and critic in the last years of the Ch'ing dynasty.

Have come to no purpose."
Presently a whirlwind rises, and lo!
The Mighty Roc[2] is winging to the Empyrean
On a flight of ninety thousand tricents.
Blow, O Whirlwind! Blow on without cease.
Blow my tiny craft to the three far-off isles[3]
Where the Immortals dwell.

Translated by Jiaosheng Wang

2. A fabulous bird first described in the works of Chuang Tzu (see selection 8). When migrating to the South Seas it is said to strike the waters for three thousand tricents before soaring to a height of ninety thousand tricents on a whirlwind. Hence the popular saying "Roc's Journey" used by Chinese to this day to congratulate someone embarking on a career of lofty aspirations.

3. The three legendary isles, P'eng-lai, Fang-chang, and Ying-chou in the Po-hai Sea.

A Long Melancholy Tune (Autumn Sorrow)[1]
Despair

Li Ch'ing-chao

Searching, seeking,[2]
    Seeking, searching:
What comes of it but
    Coldness and desolation,
A world of dreariness and misery
And stabbing pain!
As soon as one feels a bit of warmth
A sense of chill returns:
A time so hard to have a quiet rest.
What avail two or three cups of tasteless wine
Against a violent evening wind?
Wild geese wing past at this of all hours,

1. In this poem, Li Ch'ing-chao expresses her sentiments with rapidity and abandon but none of the characteristics of the elegant, restrained style in which most of her lyrics are written. The poem is in fact rather like a rhapsody that recalls to mind Ou-yang Hsiu's famous prose-poem "Autumn Sounds" (see selection 174).

2. This masterpiece of Li Ch'ing-chao's is admired, among other things, for the three groups of reiterated characters at the beginning of the poem. The three groups are ingeniously interrelated, with the second group being the result of the first, and the third the result of the second. This arrangement heightens the pathos.

And it suddenly dawns on me
That I've met them before.

Golden chrysanthemums in drifts—
How I'd have loved to pick them,
But now, for whom? On the ground they lie strewn,
Faded, neglected.[3]
There's nothing for it but to stay at the window,
Motionless, alone.
How the day drags before dusk descends!
Fine rain falling on the leaves of parasol-trees—
Drip, drip, drop, drop, in the deepening twilight.
To convey all the melancholy feelings
Born of these scenes
Can the one word "sorrow" suffice?[4]

Translated by Jiaosheng Wang

3. Some commentators interpret the above lines as follows:

"Golden chrysanthemums in full bloom,
Their fallen petals in drifts—
Who would pick them
Now I'm withered and worn?
On the ground they lie strewn, neglected."

4. Instead of using hyperboles in the conventional way, Li Ch'ing-chao shows great creativity in saying that the word "sorrow" is inadequate to convey a multitude of melancholy feelings.

Tune: "Spring at Wu Ling"[1]
Spring Ends

Li Ch'ing-chao

The wind has subsided,
Faded all the flowers:
In the muddy earth
A lingering fragrance of petals.
Dusk falls. I'm in no mood to comb my hair.
Things remain, but all is lost
Now he's no more.
Tears choke my words.

1. Written in 1135, six years after her husband's death, when the poet was living at Chinhua in today's Chekiang province as a temporary refuge from the Jürchen invasion.

I hear Twin Brooks[2] is still sweet
With the breath of spring.
How I'd, too, love to go for a row,
On a light skiff.
I only fear at Twin Brooks my grasshopper of a boat
Wouldn't be able to bear
Such a load of grief.[3]

Translated by Jiaosheng Wang

2. A stream in the southeast of Chin-hua often visited by poets in T'ang and Sung times as a scenic resort.

3. A line (three lines in the format presented here) famed for the beauty and freshness of its imagery.

102

Tune: "Spring in the Ch'in Garden" (About to swear off drinking, he warns the wine cup to go away)

Hsin Ch'i-chi (1140–1207)

Cup, you come here!
Your old man has been
Looking himself over today.
For years on end he's had a thirst
With a throat like a scorched pot.
But now he's ready to go to sleep and snore like thunder.

Like Li Ch'ing-chao (see selection 101), Hsin Ch'i-chi was born in Li-ch'eng (modern-day Tsinan, Shantung). He was passionate and insistent in his patriotic advocacy of a more determined effort to recapture the north of China from the Jürchen, who had established the Chin dynasty there. Hsin was a friend of the renowned Neo-Confucian scholar Chu Hsi (1130–1200) and entertained at his villa near the Fukien-Kiangsi border many of the greatest thinkers and statesmen of his day. His youthful espousal of Confucian virtues gave way to a more Taoist view in later life, and he held great store by the writings of Chuang Tzu (see selection 8). Hsin was primarily responsible for developing the lyric as a more erudite, expansive, and allusive genre than it had been. The most prolific Sung period author of lyrics, of which 626 by him survive, he also played a large role in the ultimate divorce of the metrical patterns of the genre from their once musical background. After Hsin, the lyric became a vehicle for the display of technical virtuosity, where it had once been the voice of popular songs.

You say, "Liu Ling [1]
Was the great philosopher of all time.
Once drunk, what did it matter if he died and was buried on the spot."
A shame you're so ruthless
With your very best friend.

Worse, you're in league with song and dance.
I reckon you are man's worst poison.
What's more, the thing we hate, a lot or a little,
Is what we once loved.
Nothing itself is good or bad,
It's excess makes the trouble.
Here's my ultimatum:
Don't stay, go away fast.
I have the strength to dispose of you.
The cup bowed and said,
"If you say so, I'll leave;
I'll come again when you call me."

Translated by James Robert Hightower

1. Liu Ling (c. 221–300) was one of the seven bohemian sages of the Bamboo Grove. A famous toper and author of "Hymn to the Virtue of Wine," Liu declared that he would not mind being buried so long as he died drunk. His abstinence-advocating wife once compelled him to renounce wine before the gods, but he tricked her by persuading her to prepare an offering of meat and wine for the celestial spirits and then guzzling down the alcoholic beverage by himself.

Tune: "Pure Serene Music"
Rural Life

Hsin Ch'i-chi

Low hang the eaves of the thatched hut,
Green, green grows the grass beside the brook.
To whose family belongs that tipsy white-haired couple,
Chatting and merry-making in the dulcet accents of the south?

Their eldest son is hoeing the bean-field east of the brook,
The second is busy weaving a hen-coop;
But the one they think most lovable is the youngest, that scamp of a boy:
Lo! he is sprawled on the bank peeling lotus pods!

Translated by Jiaosheng Wang

103

Tune: "Rouged Lips"
Rain Just Over on the
Night of the Lantern Preview

Wu Wen-ying (c. 1200–c. 1260)

Dark clouds have rolled clean away.
Goddess of the Moon looks down after her evening toilet,
Laying the dust and moistening the ground
That Fairy Maidens tread.

Back again in the bustling thoroughfare,
I feel myself reliving
Scenes of jolly lantern shows of other days.
With nostalgic feelings tender as water,
What can I do but retrace my steps to the small chamber,
Where under heated quilts
I'm soon lost in spring dreams,
Still haunted by the din of music and song.

Translated by Jiaosheng Wang

Only scanty biographical information is available about the poet. Wu Wen-ying lived during the period when the Southern Sung was about to collapse before the Mongols. Oddly, most of his works seem to deal with his own concerns, especially his affection for two favorite concubines. A different reading of his subtly stated works, however, reveals a concern for his country and his people. After Hsin Ch'i-chi (see selection 102), Wu was the second most prolific Sung period author of lyrics with approximately 350 known pieces to his credit.

104

Tune: "Pure Serene Music"

Chang Yen (1248–c. 1320)

All of a sudden my delight in sightseeing wanes,
Now the maidens gathering flowers

Chang Yen was a native of Hangchow. Though descended from a Southern Sung nobleman, he experienced so many misfortunes in life that at one time he had to support himself as a fortune-teller in the marketplace of the city of Ningpo. Chang spent forty years studying music and wrote an important work on the theory and history of lyric meters entitled *Sources of the Lyric (Tz'u yüan)*. His summation of the genre in this work also represents its culmination. After him, the waning lyric gave way to the newly exuberant aria and was only revived sporadically much later during the Ming and Ch'ing periods.

Are nowhere to be found.
Away from home one cares little
For spring outings,
Distracted by composing mournful verses.

Under whose roof are the swallows
That last year were roaming the ends of the earth?
I'd rather not listen to the patter of evening rain:
Late spring is no time to speed
The blossoming of flowers.

Translated by Jiaosheng Wang

105

In the Southern Mode,
to the Tune of "A Sprig of Flowers"
The Refusal to Get Old

Kuan Han-ch'ing (c. 1220–c. 1307)

I've plucked every flower that grows over the wall,
And gathered every willow overhanging the road;[1]
The tenderest buds were the flowers I picked,
And the willows I gathered, of the supplest green fronds;
A wastrel, gay and dashing,
Trusting to my willow gathering, flower plucking hand,
I kept at it till the flowers fell and the willows withered;
Half my life I've been willow gathering and flower plucking
And for a whole generation slept with flowers and lain among the willows.

Like the majority of the better-known Yüan dramatists, Kuan Han-ch'ing hailed from Ta-tu (modern-day Peking). A professional actor himself, Kuan is regarded as the greatest playwright of the Yüan period and the virtual creator of the genre generally referred to as Yüan drama (*tsa-chü*, literally "variety show"; see selection 216). Kuan was not only the best but also the most productive Yüan playwright, there being sixty titles associated with his name, eighteen of which are extant. His main characters are mostly female, which is atypical of Yüan drama. Kuan's arias employ highly colloquial language and deal primarily with romantic themes, often in a humorous vein, as is the case here.

For a note on the new genre of verse called the aria (*ch'ü*), which became popular during the Yüan period, see selection 107.

1. Throughout the poem flowers and willows refer to courtesans.

Yellow Bell Coda

But I am an
Un-steam-soft-able, un-boil-through-able,
Un-pound-flat-able, un-bake-dry-able
Rattling plunkety-plunk coppery old bean.[2]
Who said you young gentlemen could intrude upon her
Un-hoe-up-able, un-cut-down-able,
Un-disentwine-able, un-cast-off-able,
Intricate, thousand-fold brocade snare?[3]
As for me, I can take pleasure in the Liang-yüan[4] moon,
Drink no less than East Capital[5] wine,
Enjoy the flowers of Loyang,
And pluck the willow of Chang-t'ai.[6]
Besides, I can compose poems, write ancient script,
Play the lute and play the flute;
I know how to sing the Che-ku, dance the Ch'ui-shou,[7]
Drive game for the hunt, kick the football,
Play chess and roll dice;
Even if you knock out my teeth, stretch my mouth out of shape,
Lame my legs, break my arms,
Even if heaven afflicted me with these several ills and disabilities,
I'd still not give up;
Not unless Yama[8] himself gives the order
And the evil spirits themselves come to hook out
My three souls and return them to hell,
My seven shades and consign them to oblivion,[9]
Only then
Will I retire from the path of mist and flowers.[10]

Translated by Wayne Schlepp

2. Literally, "copper garden pea"—Yüan slang for a libertine who is somewhat past his prime.

3. A courtesan's methods of getting a man into her clutches.

4. Liang-yüan was a vast park built in Han times by Prince Hsiao of Liang, here suggesting sophisticated tastes.

5. The Eastern Capital, i.e., Loyang, was noted for its luxuriance and beauty. See also note 1 on flowers and willows.

6. A district of Ch'ang-an, the Western Capital, where a famous T'ang courtesan named Liu (i.e., "willow") lived. *Chang-t'ai liu* is often used in reference to courtesans generally.

7. *Che-ku* (Partridge) or *Che-ku t'ien* (Partridge Sky) is the name of a lyric verse form. *Ch'ui-shou* (Hanging Hands) is the name of a song to which one danced, hands hanging down the while.

8. King of the underworld.

9. The belief that one dies only after the evil spirits have hooked out of one's body all ten of its souls.

10. The gay life among courtesans.

106

Tune: "Shua Hai-erh"
Country Cousin at the Theater

Tu Shan-fu (fl. 1230)

When the rains are in season and the wind sets fair
Nothing is better than the farmer's share.
Our silkworms had mulberries to spare.
Our grains had been reaped to the final stook
And the tax men had left us more than they took.
Since my village had a vow at the temple to pay,
They sent me to redeem it on market day.
As I reached the high road by the top of the town
I saw a paper banner they had just hung down.
On it was writing with designs in between
And below it the biggest gaggle I had ever seen.

(Liu-sha)

Among 'em was the one who was working a door,
Yelling, "This way, this way, pay your fee before
The whole place is full and you can't find a bench!
Our first act's a *yüan-pen* [1] called *Seductive Wench*,
This is followed by a short *yao-mo*, [2]
It's easy on the stage to make time go
But hard to get applause for doing so."

(Wu-sha)

Then, without a pause in his hullabaloo,
He snapped up my coppers and shoved me through.
Now inside the door was a cliff made of wood
Where layers of people sat around or stood.
Like inside a bell-tower I would have said
When I stood at the bottom and lifted up my head.
But looking the other way it seemed as though
I was watching a whirlpool down below
Of people sitting everywhere.

Little is known of the author of this folksy set of arias.
1. A type of variety play or skit; forerunner of the full-fledged Yüan drama.
2. Reprise.

And a bunch of women sitting there
Watching a platform—it was not a god's day,
But the drums and the cymbals were a-crashing away!

(Ssu-sha)

On the floor came a girl who capered, and then
Went off and led on a bunch of her men.
One of that gang you could tell right away
Spelled trouble if you met him whatever the day.
His head was wrapped in a jet-black cloth
With some kind of brush-pen stuck in the swath.
(One look at him and you couldn't go wrong,
You knew right away how *he* got along)
His whole face was limed an ashy white
With some black streaks on top of that—
Now there was a sight!
He wore on his body one of those kinds
Of tunics covered with big designs.

(San-sha)

Well, he
Recited some verses and one or two rhymes,
Then he spoke a kind of *fu* [3] and sang a few times.
His mouth kept on goin' right through every verse!
He wasn't *real* good, but I've heard a lot worse.
And the memory he'd got I wish I had—
To tell all those jokes and japes wouldn't be bad.
Then he came to the end:
"That's all," he said.
Then he slapped his feet around a bit and bowed his head.
And that was all for one part, so the music played.

(Erh-sha)

Now in comes "Little Brother" and "Squire Chang,"
The last tellin' the first one just where he's wrong.
They cross the stage and go round and roun'
All the time sayin' they're walking into town.
Then they say they're in town (though they went nowhere!)

3. Rhapsody or rhyme-prose (see selections 123 ff.).

And they spy a young girl under the awning there.
Old Chang's got to have her if it costs him his life.
And he sets right out tryin' to get her to wife.
He's sure in a hurry and just that keen
That he teaches Little Brother how to be go-between.
But she wants silk and satin, millet and rice,
And ol' Squire Chang?—she won't look at him twice.

(Yi-sha)

Squire Chang backs up 'cause forward won't do
And with his right foot in the air he hoists his left one too!
Poor Chang is whipsawed fro and to
Till he's so hotted up he don't know what to do,
So he
Bangs his meat-club on the ground and snaps it right in half
And I nearly bust my side while I double up and laugh.

(Wei) [4]

Now the lawsuits would start just as sure as there's rain,
But I got such a bladderful I'm dyin' in pain,
I keep hangin' on and hangin' around to see the thing through.
Just to listen to them talk and to see what they would do,
But my bladder is achin' so I can't catch my breath—
Those crazy pizzles made me leave—
Else I'd have laughed myself to death!

Translated by James I. Crump

4. The section titles signify "six" through "one" and "coda," the last.

107
Tune: "Heaven-Cleansed Sands"
Autumn Thoughts

Ma Chih-yüan (1250?–1323?)

Withered wisteria, old tree, darkling crows—
Little bridge over flowing water by someone's house—

With this epochally memorable piece (note that it lacks a single verb), we can mark the shift from the lyric (tz'u) to the aria (ch'ü). Although other poets were writing arias before him

Emaciated horse on an ancient road in the western wind—
Evening sun setting in the west—
Broken-hearted man on the horizon.

Translated by Victor H. Mair

(see selections 105 and 106), it was from Ma Chih-yüan that dominance of the new genre began.

The aria in many respects is similar to the lyric but employs a separate corpus of tunes and is used to express different sentiments. As with the lyric, aria verses are written to song music. Distinctively a product of the period of Mongol rule in China, the aria undoubtedly owes much to the specific political and cultural configuration of that era. The aria, for example, typically employs more colloquial expressions than even the most earthy of the lyrics, yet the form remains hospitable to both literary and vernacular phrase and structure. The subject matter of the aria is diverse, but lovesongs probably preponderate, as with the lyric. The full range of the arias contain nearly every literary device found in the historical arsenal of Chinese verse.

Several arias are sometimes grouped together in sets or suites, with all the tunes in a given suite belonging to the same mode or key. Altogether, there are some five hundred known tune titles which were part of the public domain and to which arias were composed. Arias range in length from pithy twenty-character gems to long, narrative confections of ten or twelve songs in a suite. They were the favored form of entertainment for the age, whether sung by themselves or incorporated into the flourishing musical dramas (see selection 216). Perhaps because of their show-business history, however, they were much underrated by Chinese literary scholars until the beginning of the twentieth century.

Ma Chih-yüan, a native of Ta-tu (modern-day Peking), is generally recognized as the most distinguished author of arias and aria sequences and an outstanding playwright. His most famous dramatic work, *Autumn in the Han Palace (Han kung ch'iu)*, tells of the forced marriage of a Han dynasty court beauty to a Tatar chieftain as part of a diplomatic maneuver. His other plays are mostly about Taoism and reclusion.

108
[Untitled]

Chang Yang-hao (1269–1329)

Ch'ü Yüan's "sorrow" [1]
none can explain
yet its meaning is
clear as the sun and the moon.
the sorrow remains

A native of Tsinan, Shantung, Chang Yang-hao was an official who held several important positions. He wrote most of his arias after retirement.

1. See selection 122.

the man is gone
to feed
      the shrimp and crabs of the river Hsiang.
that gentleman was silly
I'll stay in this green mountain shade
singing wild
      and drinking till it hurts
here's *joy*
    that's boundless.

Translated by Jerome P. Seaton

109

Tune: "Rapt with Wine, Loudly Singing— Joy in Spring's Coming" My Love

Kuan Yün-shih (1286–1324)

Natural demeanor warm and soft,
Winsome face demure.
When we chance to meet, her sidelong glances encourage me,
Kindling the pangs of my lovesickness.

Matchmaker bees and go-between butterflies fail to coax her:
Swallows or orioles can't do as they please.
Just like a sprig of red almond blossoms peeping over a wall
She lies beyond the reach of plucking hand.
How I feel, in vain, that for those blossoms' sake the wind
    and rain bear shame!

Translated by Richard John Lynn

Kuan Yün-shih was a Sinicized Uighur (a Central Asian Turkic people) whose original name was Sävinč Qaya. He was an excellent horseman, hunter, and warrior. After serving briefly in the Mongol military establishment, he became a student of the leading Confucian scholar of his time, Yao Sui (1239–1314). Significantly, he wrote a *Vernacular Exegesis on the Classic of Filial Piety* and served as tutor to the heir apparent. Toward the end of his life he developed an interest in Zen and alchemy.

110
Tune: "Tsui-chung T'ien"
To the Giant Butterfly

Wang Ho-ch'ing (Yüan)

This butterfly escaped, it seems,
From the chrysalis of Chuang Tzu's dreams,[1]
Spread two great wings upon the spring air,
Then sucked three hundred gardens bare!
Might not elegant creatures such as these
Shame to death our simple honeybees?
Or, giving their wings a tiny shake,
Blow our flower vendors in the lake?!

Translated by James I. Crump

The wag of his times, Wang Ho-ch'ing composed occasional—and probably impromptu—pieces. This song is said to have been written in response to the sudden appearance of a species of large butterfly in the environs of the capital.

1. See selection 8.

Tune: "Po Pu-tuan"
Long-Haired Little Dog

Wang Ho-ch'ing

Ugly as a jackass
But the size of a pig.
This curious thing
Is nowhere to be found
In the *Shan-hai Ching*.[1]
Head to toe and everywhere—
Body completely covered with hair.
I believe you're a wicked household sprite—
The Malevolent Dustmop with a bite!

Translated by James I. Crump

1. *The Mountains and Seas Classic*, an ancient work that includes descriptions of fantastic and faraway people, places, and creatures (see selection 20, second poem).

Tune: "Po Pu-tuan"
Fat Couple

Wang Ho-ch'ing

A rather obese Master Shuang[1]
Bore off an overweight Su Niang.[2]
(Each one of that pair
Was the size of a bear.)

On the wings of romance, off they sped,
But paused a while at Yü-chang[3] to pant—
These lovebirds the size of an elephant—
And bang their bellyskins in bed!

Translated by James I. Crump

1. His name means "double" or "pair."
2. Miss Su.
3. A name for Kiangsi.

111
Tune: "San-fan Yü-lou Jen"

Anonymous (Yüan)

Wind disturbing the eave-chimes again.
Cloth at the window rustles with rain.
That empty pillow,
Cold counterpane
All tangled up with me,
I curse with fine particularity.
My emotions are confused and dim
But the darker thoughts are reserved for him!
Oh, wait until he comes back here,
Then won't I pick a fight!
And scratch his face!
And twist his ear!
"And where did *you* sleep all last night!"

Translated by James I. Crump

112
Tune: "Hung Hsiu-hsieh"
To a Flea

Yang Na (Yüan)

Small as he is he can nimbly dance
From fold of collar to waist of pants.
The prick of a lance
Is this creature's bite,
And he can elude the keenest sight.
How can one capture a creature who
With a somersault can vanish from view?!

Translated by James I. Crump

A dramatist and poet of Mongol extraction, Yang Na was an excellent lutanist and bon vivant.

113
Tune: "Wu Yeh-erh"
Twitting the Teller of Tall Tales

Anonymous (Yüan)

In Easton a certain citizen
Had a Phoenix born to his hen!
In Southville there was a paradox,
Someone's horse turned into an ox!
August is the month for fur coats,
On a pile of tile you can plant a tree,
A dry-gulch [1] is good for sailing boats.
Our dumplings are bigger than soup-tureens;
We grow barrel-sized aubergines.

Translated by James I. Crump

1. *Yang-kou* (open ditch) was also the name of a famous fighting cock (cf. selection 17).

114

In the Chung Mode, to the Tune of "P'u T'ien Lo"

Anonymous (early 14th century?)

I thought when he hadn't been there for two or three days—
When he walks in the door I'll really bawl him out!
He'll come over to me, full of excuses,
Spluttering, making no sense, stuttering;
The slippery devil will try to worm out of it, how can anyone trap him!
I can't describe how I long for him to ask for my favors;
But I'll put him out of mind, and when I've got over it, I'll tell him we're
    through.
If we're through, we're through, but even if he's sorry I won't be able to tell
    whether he really means it.
But then he boldly came up and asked me how I'd been,
And all I could do was smile back, keep in my temper for fear he'd get
    angry,
So when he leaves and doesn't come back again for a couple of days, I'll be
    looking for someone to go and hunt him up.

Translated by Wayne Schlepp

115

[Untitled]

Yün-k'an Tzu (late Yüan)

out of chaos,
        Chang Kuo-lao [1] popped
riding his white ass backwards
through illusion
born in purple clouds
coiled in ruby mist
every night he folded that old ass up
swallowed it
        to sleep in bliss.

Translated by Jerome P. Seaton

The poet's name is obviously a pseudonym, but nothing else is known about him.
    1. One of the eight immortals of Taoism. This is part of a series of poems by the same poet
about these legendary individuals.

116
Lazy Cloud's Nest 1

Ali Hsiying (late Yüan)

write poems when I'm sober, and sing when I'm drunk
I leave my fancy lute untuned,
throw down my book, and sleep.
I don't dream dreams of empire
to have a little idle time is good enough
the sun and moon race like the weaver's shuttle
wealth and rank are blossoms, bloom and fall
spring goes
why not enjoy it?

Translated by Jerome P. Seaton

Ali Hsiying was a Moslem, the son of Ali Haiyai.

Lazy Cloud's Nest 2

Ali Hsiying

If someone came what would I do
dozing here with my clothes on
completely at ease, feeling frisky
human life? What can you say
rank is above me a bit
wealth, I don't need it
haha, you laugh
I laugh, haha.

Translated by Jerome P. Seaton

117

Tune: "Moon Over West River"

Yang Shen (1488–1559)

I've brewed myself a whole bunch of trouble,
and all because of feelings of love!
The spring dream in this house of passion
　　　　　never really formed:
I wasted days and evenings
　　　　　of "rain-and-cloud." [1]

The swallow—what does he know
　　　　　of my feelings?
It's the oriole who seems to call her name!
To get rid of this passion ·
　　　　　I can talk about the Void—
or turn within to look at my own heart.

Translated by Jonathan Chaves

Yang Shen wrote poetry in all the major genres, but his lyrics, including the one chosen
here, are among the most expressive examples after the Sung period.

1. A traditional euphemism for sexual intercourse.

118

Tune: "Dreaming of Southland"
Thinking of Someone

Liu Shih (1618–1664)

1

He is gone,
Gone somewhere west of Feng-ch'eng. [1]

Liu Shih's beginnings are obscure. What we know for sure is that she became an accomplished courtesan and poet-painter while still in her teens, and many literati in the Chiang-nan
area (south of the Yangtze) came to admire her literary achievements. That several portraits of
her were made by Ming-Ch'ing literati painters is proof of her standing among her male
contemporaries. She published her first collection of poems at the age of twenty and enjoyed
the reputation of being a courtesan of superb talent and beauty. Her intense love relationship
with the young poet Ch'en Tzu-lung (1608–1647) and her later marriage to the literary giant
Ch'ien Ch'ien-yi (1582–1664) made her a legendary figure in the field of literature. Most

A thin rain dampens my red sleeves,
New weeds lie as deep as my jade brows are low,
The butterfly is most bewildered.[2]

2

He is gone,
Gone from the Isle of Egrets.
Lotus blossoms turn to emerald remorse,
Willow catkins rise to join the zither's grief,
Behind the brocade curtain—the early autumn startles.

3

He is gone,
Gone from the painted chamber tower.
No longer lustrous and beautiful, I sit idle,
Why bother about rouge powder and jade hairpin?
Only the wind coming at night.[3]

4

He is gone,
Gone from the small water pavilion.
Would you say we "have not loved enough"?
Or that we "have little to regret"?
All I see is trodden moss.

5

He is gone,
Gone from the green window gauze.
All I gain is frail sickness. Lighter than a swallow,

---

important, her numerous love poems to Ch'en Tzu-lung—and for that matter, Ch'en's to her—
engendered a whole new interest in the lyric, a genre characterized by the intensity of emotion.
Since traditionally a proficiency in song lyrics was closely associated with the courtesan culture,
Liu Shih, as might be expected, greatly influenced the late Ming revival of the lyric genre.

Liu Shih and Ch'en Tzu-lung's lyric poetics was clearly patterned on the late Ming notion
of reciprocal love. Her numerous poetic exchanges with Ch'en—in some cases her poems are
more elaborate in scope and length than Ch'en's—are framed as personal letters, telling the
secrets of a passion felt by two equally talented poets. She was no longer a mere singer like the
earlier courtesans, whose prime duty was to perform song lyrics for men. As a poet herself, she
has acquired a personal voice. In her perhaps most brilliant song-series, "Dreaming of Southland" (subtitled "Thinking of Someone," twenty poems), she tells a moving story of her
relationship with Ch'en, narrating her struggles with love's agonized passion.

1. Most likely refers to the hometown of the late Ming scholar-official and loyalist Ch'en
Tzu-lung, with whom the poet was closely associated over a long period of time.

2. A reference to Chuang Tzu's famous dream experience (see selection 8).

3. This song alludes to one of Li Shang-yin's (see selection 51) love poems: "Last night's
stars, last night's winds / By the wall of the painted chamber tower, east of the hall of cassia."

Pitiful is my lone self, now that we are far apart.
Secretly we hide sweet memories in our hearts.

6

He is gone,
Gone, leaving the jade pipe cold.[4]
Phoenix pecked at the scattered tiny red beans,
Pheasants, joyfully embracing the censer, gazed at us,[5]
Apricot was the color of my spring dress.

7

He is gone,
Gone from the shadow of the green *wu-t'ung*[6] tree.
I can't believe this has earned us a heartbreaking tune,
Still I wonder why our love has failed.
Whence this brooding grief? No need to look.

8

He is gone,
Gone from the small Crab-apple Hall.
I force myself to rise; the fallen petals are quivering,
A few red parting tears still remain,
Outside the door, willows leaning against one another.

9

He is gone,
Gone, yet dreams of him come even more often.
Recalling the past: our shared moments were mostly wordless,
But now I secretly regret the growing distance.
Only in dreams can I find self-indulgence.

10

He is gone,
Gone, and the nights are longer.
How can this jeweled belt warm my thoughts about the black steed?[7]

---

4. This line alludes to Li Ching's (916–961) line: "In the small chamber the song of the jade flute has become cold." By this allusion, Liu Shih's line is a subtle reference to the chamber in the Southern Villa where she lived with Ch'en Tzu-lung during the spring and summer of 1635.

5. The pheasant designs of the incense-burner.

6. For a note on the *wu-t'ung* ("we-together") tree, see selection 90.

7. The "jeweled belt" might be a gift from Ch'en Tzu-lung. The "black steed," a symbol of the male lover, is metaphorically connected with Ch'en here.

Gently putting on the silk robe in chill jade moonlight,
Behind the rosy curtain, a single wisp of incense.

11

Where was he?
On the Isle of Smartweed.
The duck-censer burning low, the fragrant smoke warm,
Spring mountains winding deeply in the painted screen,
The golden sparrow ceased to weep.

12

Where was he?
At the middle pavilion.
Recall once after washing his face,
His carefree laughter seemed so unconcerned—
Who knows for whom he smiled?

13

Where was he?
In the moonlight.
In the middle of the night, I clutched his priceless arm,
Lethargic, I looked at the lotus flowers again and again,
My inner sentiments, how hazy!

14

Where was he?
In the magnolia boat.
Often talking to herself when receiving guests,
Feeling more lost while combing her hair,
This beauty still broods over his charms.

15

Where was he?
At the magnificent banquet.
My perfumed arms fluttered up and down,
Words issued in song, like profound thoughts,
Chiefly from my faintly glossed lips.

16

Where was he?
At the Autumn Crab-apple Hall.
Fun was playing hide-and-seek,

Round after round, no need to linger for long.
Again, how many sunsets have gone by!

17

Where was he?
On the Lake of Misty Rain.
Water rippled by the bamboo oar, the moon shining bright in the lustrous
    and gentle spring,
Our storied boat filled with wind and daphne fragrance,
Willows caressing the delicate waves.

18

Where was he?
At the jade steps.
No fool for love, yet I wanted to stay,
Overly sensitive to any sign of indifference,
It must be that I feared love would run too deep.

19

Where was he?
Behind the curtain patterned with thrushes.
A parrot dream ends in a black otter's tail,
Incense smoke lingers on the tip of the green spiral censer,
Delicate were the pink jade fingers.

20

Where was he?
By my pillow side.
Nothing but endless tears at the quilt edge —
Wiping off secretly, but only inducing more,
How I yearn for his pity and love.

Translated by Kang-i Sun Chang

119

Tune: "Happily Flitting Oriole"

From Music of Harmonious Heaven in Reverent Thanks to the Lord of Heaven

Wu Li (1632–1718)

Late in Han
God's Son came down from Heaven
to save us people
and turn us toward the good.
His grace goes wide!
Taking flesh through the virginity
            of the Holy Mother,
                    in a stable He was born.
Joseph too came to present Him in the temple:
there to offer praise was
Simeon.
They say He can
save our souls from their destructiveness
and sweep away the devil's wantonness.

Translated by Jonathan Chaves

For information on the poet and his creation of a Chinese Christian poetry, see selection 80. This particular poem is in the aria *(ch'ü)* form.

120

Tune: "As If in a Dream"

Nara Singde (1655–1685)

In a myriad arched yurts, the men are drunk.
Stars' reflections quiver, about to drop.

Nara Singde was a thoroughly Sinicized Manchu of aristocratic birth. He accompanied the K'ang-hsi emperor (see selection 82) in his travels to distant parts of the empire, including his ancestral homeland in Inner Asia. Nara's finely crafted verse is filled with inexplicit Buddhist sentiments and melancholy thoughts. He lived a tragically short but highly productive and

My homing dream, sundered by Wolf River,[1]
Is then shaken to bits by the river's roar.
        Back to sleep!
        Back to sleep!
Well I know that in waking there's no savor.

Translated by David McCraw

---

active life. Nara may well be regarded as the most significant writer of lyrics after the Sung period and was certainly a major figure in the revival of the genre.

"As If in a Dream" is famous for its opening strophe.

1. The White Wolf River flows east from White Wolf Mountain (near Ling-yüan, Liaoning) into the Pohai Sea.

121
Tune: "Sand of Silk-Washing Brook"

Wang Kuo-wei (1877–1927)

Faded hibiscus and its leaves
Wilt side by side
Artemisia that stood high above the wall
Now half-decayed
Under the slanting sun's gaze
Someone in a lonely lodge
Is prone to heart-rending sorrow.

Sit and you sense the broad sweep

Wang Kuo-wei was a wondrously learned philosopher and literary critic-historian of the late Ch'ing and early Republican period. Possessing a magnificent blend of traditional Chinese scholarship and modern Western theories (Nietzsche and Kant were two of his favorite thinkers from youth), Wang made startlingly fresh and fundamental contributions to research on such difficult and varied subjects as the origins of Chinese drama, the decipherment of oracle shell and bone inscriptions, and the essence and development of lyric meters, and carried out a profoundly creative analysis of the novel *Dream of Red Towers* (see selection 213) in which he applied the concept of the will put forward by Schopenhauer. Wang, however, was deeply exasperated by Chinese reformers who attempted to use Western ideas merely as expedient tools without attempting to comprehend their universal value. A political conservative, Wang was loyal to the Ch'ing royal family long after the dynasty had collapsed in the 1911 revolution. Whether his suicide by drowning on June 2, 1927 is related to his disappointment with political events or personal crises (of which there were indeed many) remains a mystery. As a lyricist, he is considered the finest exponent of the genre after Nara Singde (see selection 120).

Of clear returning autumn;
Watch and you are dazzled by
The brilliance of the departing sun
How can the human world ever
Live out these lengthening nocturnal hours?

Translated by Jiaosheng Wang

Elegies and Rhapsodies

122
Heavenly Questions

Attributed to Ch'ü Yüan (340?–278 B.C.E.)

I

'Tis said:

At the beginning of remote antiquity,
Who was there to transmit the tale?
When above and below had not yet taken shape,
5   By what means could they be examined?

Ch'ü Yüan is the first Chinese poet known by name and about whom a modicum of biographical information is available. A member of the royal family of the southern kingdom of Ch'u, he was a loyal official to two of its rulers. But the intrigues and slanders of other courtiers who were jealous of him led to his banishment to the even more distant south. There he eventually committed suicide by drowning himself in the Mi-lo river out of despair over the capture of the capital of Ch'u by armies of the state of Ch'in.

The "Heavenly Questions" (T'ien wen—this title might also be rendered as "Celestial Riddles" or "Divine Conundrums"), like "Encountering Sorrows" (Li sao—the title may also be interpreted as "Departing Sorrows"), Ch'ü Yüan's anguished poem of longing for his idealized ruler, forms a part of the collection of early southern verse known as the Elegies of Ch'u (Ch'u tz'u). Edited by Wang Yi (d.158 C.E.), who was also its first and most influential commentator, Elegies includes works written by and attributed to Ch'ü Yüan as well as works from the Han period composed in imitation of his style.

Upon first encounter, "Heavenly Questions" is one of the most unusual and baffling texts in all of Chinese literature. It consists entirely of a long series of mysterious and essentially unanswered queries concerning the origin and nature of the universe, the founding of civilization by various semidivine beings, and the complicated affairs of the rulers of the legendary and

When darkness and light were obscured,
Who could fathom them?
When primal matter was the only form,
How could it be recognized?

---

historical kingdoms right up to the time of the poet himself. Most of the questions are of such maddening obscurity that they are extremely difficult to interpret, let alone answer.

Aside from merely being puzzled or flabbergasted by the "Heavenly Questions," the reader might take a number of productive approaches to this intriguing text. One can view it as offering guideposts to a fragmentary mythology, as evidence for a lost religiosity, as a matrix for comprehending archeological discoveries, and so forth. There have also been several traditional explanations of the text, such as that it represents an expression of personal frustration or that it constitutes a key to early narrative wall paintings. This type of explanation is hard to sustain, however, for it is usually based on sheer conjecture or misinterpretation of the text.

The seeming impenetrability of the "Heavenly Questions" has by no means prevented commentators and annotators from attempting to provide a complete set of answers to them. Unfortunately, these answers are almost invariably based on Han period and later legends, so they lack validity and the power to convince. Indeed, many of the explications in Han and later works were created at least partly with the intention of making sense of the "Heavenly Questions," so naturally they cannot serve as reliable explanatory devices for the very text upon which they are premised.

In recent decades, a completely new strategy for comprehending the "Heavenly Questions" has been applied with increasing success. Both the context and the content of the text can be partially reconstructed through the use of comparative mythology. For this interpretive scheme to function successfully, however, it is necessary to abandon the notion that early Chinese civilization developed entirely in isolation from the rest of the world. There are, for example, such obvious indications of linkages with other civilizations as the rabbit in the moon or the tortoise bearing blissful isles on its back, both of which betray Indian parallels. Even more striking is the very form of the genre itself. The "Heavenly Questions" shares a whole set of resemblances to the Indo-European wisdom texts commonly known as "riddles."

The authors of the ancient Vedic hymns, the earliest of which date to roughly the beginning of the first millennium B.C.E., were often deliberately cryptic (e.g., *Ṛg Veda*, I.164). The subject matter of their riddles is, furthermore, virtually the same as that of the "Heavenly Questions" (e.g., *Atharva Veda*, X.7–8). The *Upaniṣads*, which followed the *Vedas*, are even more similar to the "Heavenly Questions." The *Śvetāśvatara Upaniṣad* begins with a series of comparable questions and the *Praśna Upaniṣad* (literally, the "*Upaniṣad* [Secret Session] of Questions") consists entirely of all sorts of difficult and profound questions that are put to a *ṛṣi* (seer). Elsewhere in the *Upaniṣads* and in the *Brāhmanas* as well, there are series of questions concerning cosmology and mythology that are quite like the "Heavenly Questions."

In the ancient Iranian *Zend-Avesta*, doctrine is presented in a series of questions and answers between Zarathustra and Ahura Mazda. In "Yasna" 44, for example, the questions posed by Zarathustra are astonishingly reminiscent of those in the opening portion of the "Heavenly Questions": "Who is it that supported the earth below and the sky above so that they do not fall?" "Who is it that joined speed with wind and welkin?" "Who is it that created blessed light and the darkness?" Even at the far northwestern end of the Indo-European range, the same types of riddles persist in some of the earliest of the poetic *Edda*. In "Vafthrudnismāl," questions between Gangrath (Wodan) and Wabedrut focus on the origins of heaven and earth. Similar questions abound in "Fiölvinnsmāl," "Alvissmāl," and other songs in the *Edda*.

J. Huizinga, in chapter VI ("Playing and Knowing"), pp. 105–118, of his classic *Homo Ludens: A Study of the Play-Element in Culture* (Boston: Beacon, 1955; tr. from the German

10   Brightness became bright and darkness dark;
      What has caused them to be like this?
      Yin and yang commingle;
      What was basic, what transformed?

---

ed. of 1944), has analyzed such question series as related to cult indoctrination and sacrifices. In this sense, they function as a sort of catechism. The tradition of imparting and testing knowledge through a series of riddles is prominent throughout the ancient Indo-European tradition, especially its Indo-Iranian and Germanic branches. The texts consisting of questions cited above (and many others like them) may thus be viewed as vestiges of ancient riddle-solving contests, the contestants in which were rewarded or punished (sometimes with their lives), depending upon their performance in responding to the questions. The emphasis on cattle in the "Heavenly Questions" also indicates an Indo-European connection.

But the pan-Eurasian quality of the "Heavenly Questions" would appear not to be limited solely to their increasingly obvious Indo-European affinities. Within the past couple of decades, Chinese scholars have written enormous studies detailing numerous other apparently foreign elements in the *Elegies of Ch'u* in general and in the "Heavenly Questions" in particular. Especially to be noted are Su Hsüeh-lin, *T'ien wen cheng chien (The Authentic Text of "T'ien Wen")* (Taipei: Kuang-tung, 1974), who occasionally overstates her case, and Hsiao Ping, *Ch'u tz'u hsin t'an [New Investigations on the Elegies of Ch'u]* (Tientsin: T'ien-chin ku-chi, 1988), pp. 43–49, 56–74, and 503–805, who is an extremely careful and thorough scholar. Su, Hsiao, and others have pointed out many close parallels between the "Heavenly Questions," on the one hand, and West Asian, North African, and European mythologies and symbol system, on the other. Another outstanding study of this type is Joseph Fontenrose's masterful *Python: A Study of Delphic Myth and Its Origins* (Berkeley and Los Angeles: University of California Press, 1959), especially appendix 3. Although *Python* is by no means specifically devoted to the "Heavenly Questions" or even to the Chinese tradition at all, it provides an extraordinarily well documented and extremely revealing comparison of the combat and flood myths in China and elsewhere in the Eurasian ecumene.

The only old literary text in Chinese that is remotely comparable to the "Heavenly Questions" is found at the beginning of the thirteenth chapter of the *Chuang Tzu*, "Heavenly Revolutions." Not only is the title manifestly similar to that of the "Heavenly Questions," but the reader is actually met with a barrage of questions remarkably like those of the "Heavenly Questions" in asking about the origins and nature of the universe. It is significant that, after the presentation of the riddles at the opening of "Heavenly Revolutions," a magus proceeds to answer them. There is solid evidence that Iranian magi were at the Chou court by 800 B.C.E. and quite possibly were also active in Shang ruling circles by around 1200 B.C.E. See Victor H. Mair, "Old Sinitic *$m^{\gamma}ag$, Old Persian *maguš*, and English 'Magician,' " *Early China* 15 (1990): 27–47. We should also note that, like the "Heavenly Questions," the *Chuang Tzu* had close associations with Ch'u culture.

The reader will observe that few notes have been provided for the first parts of the "Heavenly Questions" but that more of them are given for the later parts of the text. The reason for this is simple, namely, there are more accurate historical sources available for the Chou dynasty and Warring States periods than for the beginning of the world and the invention of civilization. "Heavenly Questions" is the *locus classicus* for much of the lore that it mentions. Rather than speculate on unanswered questions concerning cosmology and mythology, it is better to let the text speak for itself unless there are other trustworthy materials available. As we get closer to the time when the piece was written down, it becomes progressively easier to fill in the answers.

"Heavenly Questions" is divided into eleven main sections according to their subject matter. Within each section, stanzas are determined by rhyme breaks. Some of the main mythological

Round heaven with its nine layers,
15 Who managed and measured it?
What sort of achievement was this?
Who was the first to make it?

How was the Cord tied to the Hub?
How was the Heavenly Pole added to them?
20 What did the Eight Pillars hold up?
Why was there a gap in the southeast?

The borders of the ninefold heavens —
Where do they stretch: where do they join?
Many are their corners and angles —
25 Who knows their number?

Upon what are the heavens folded?
Where are the twelve stages divided?
How are the sun and moon attached?
How are the constellations arrayed?

30 The sun emerges from the morning vale,
It comes to rest on the crepuscular horizon.
From dawn until dusk,
How many miles does it travel?

What virtue hath the moon,
35 That it dies and then is reborn again?
What benefit is there
To harbor a bunny in its belly?

The goddess of fertility had no mate;
How did she get nine sons?
40 Where does the god of pestilence dwell?
Where does the benign wind breathe?

What closes and brings darkness?
What opens and brings light?

---

themes of the various sections are as follows: I. The origin of the world (cosmogony and cosmology); II. the flood myth of Kun and Yü, the marplot myth of Kung-kung (not explicitly named), the solar myth of the sun goddess Hsi-ho; III. the foundation of the Hsia dynasty, miraculous birth, the metamorphoses of Kun; IV. Nüwa, creatrix of humankind, the moral leader Shun; V. the sacrificial tripod; VI. miraculous birth, foundation of the Shang dynasty, cattle raids (a typical Indo-European theme), birth from a tree (the same would later be said of Confucius, Brahmacārin Wang [see selection 26], and others); VII. [historical themes]; VIII. miraculous birth of child hero and founder of the Chou dynasty; IX. external youth; X. cattle, dogs, and kurgans (Indo-European themes); XI. [rise of the south].

Before the Horn rises in the east,
45   Where does the numinous sunlight hide?

II

Kun was incapable of controlling the flood;
Why did the masses esteem him?
Everyone said, "There's no need to worry.
Why not let him try to carry it out?"

5   The linked hawk-turtles dragged along;
What did Kun learn from them?
He completed the work in accord with the will of the people;
Why did Deus punish him?

Eternally imprisoned at Feather Mountain,
10   Why did Kun's corpse not disintegrate after three years?
Lord Yü was born from the belly of Kun;
How did this transformation occur?

Taking up the thread of his predecessor,
Yü thereupon completed the dead father's work;
15   How did he continue the original enterprise,
Even though his plan was different?

The floody abyss was extremely deep—
How did he fill it in?
Nine were the regions of square earth—
20   How did he pile them up?

What did the respondent dragon draw on the ground?
Where were the lakes and rivers channeled off?

What was it that Kun had managed?
What was it that Yü completed?
25   When the tumultuous thunder rumbled,
Why did the earth tilt toward the southeast?

How were the nine continents laid out?
Where were the stream beds sunk?
They flow to the east but never fill the sea—
30   Who knows the reason why?

From east to west or from north to south,
Which length is greater?
The earth is elliptical from north to south—
What is its breadth?

35 The hanging gardens of K'un-lun,
    Where does their base lie?
    With nine layers of tiered walls,
    How many tricents is its heights?

    The gates of the four directions—
40 Who is it that passes through them?
    When the northeast gate opens,
    What air breezes through it?

    Where does the sun not reach?
    Where does the incandescent dragon not shine?

45 Before Hsi-ho, the solar charioteer, has risen,
    Whence cometh the light of the Jo flower?

    In what place is the winter warm?
    In what place is the summer cold?
    Where is the forest of stones?
50 What beast can speak?

    Where is there a hornless dragonet,
    That roams about carrying a bear on its back?

    The horrible hydra with nine heads—
    Where does it flit about so swiftly?
55 Where is the place of immortality?
    What do the giants guard?

    The spreading nine-stemmed nuphar,
    And the cannabis flowers, where do they grow?
    The snake that can swallow elephants—
60 How big must it be?

    Black Waters, Dark Toes,
    And Three Dangers—where are they?
    The years extend without death;
    What is the limit of longevity?

65 Where does the merman live?
    Where does the monster bird dwell?
    Why did Yi shoot down the suns?
    Why did crow feathers fall from them? [1]

    1. A mythological explanation of maculae (sunspots). The great archer-prince Yi, hero of
the Chuang people (Moz Yiz Daihvuengz), shot down nine extra suns that once appeared in
the sky and scorched the earth.

III

Yü's energy was devoted to his work,[2]
Having descended to inspect the land below.
How did he get that T'u mountain maid,
And unite with her midst the terraced mulberries?

5   Yearning for a consort, he mated with her,
From whose body was born a successor.
Why did he crave different tastes,
And feel satisfied with a morning's delight?

Ch'i[3] replaced Yih[4] as the lord,
10   But suddenly encountered troubles.
How did Ch'i suffer from sorrow,
And yet avert his predicament?

All returned to hunting and husbandry,
So that no harm came to his[5] person.
15   Even though Yih made these reforms,
Why was it Yü's line that was passed down?

Ch'i paid court to Deus with lance dance and damsels,
Receiving from him the "Nine Disputations" and the "Nine Songs."
Why did the diligent son slay his mother,
20   So that her stone corpse split upon the ground?

Deus sent down Yi of the East
To remove the troubles of the Hsia people;
Why did Yi shoot the god of the Yellow River
And take for wife the goddess of the Lo River?

25   With full-drawn pearl-inlaid bow and nimble thimble,
Yi shot the great wild boar;
When he presented the fat of the sacrificial meat,
Why was Lord Deus not pleased?

Cho[6] married Sable Fox;
30   Deluded by his wife, he plotted against Yi.
How is it that Yi could shoot through leather,
Yet he was swallowed up by conspiracy?

2. Draining the land (see above, line II.14).
3. Son of Yü.
4. A high official of Yü, who had been chosen to succeed him as ruler of the Hsia dynasty.
5. Yih's, that is.
6. Minister of Yi.

Traveling westward on a perilous journey,
How did he [7] cross the mountain cliffs?
35 When he [8] was transformed into a yellow bear,
How did the magus bring him back to life?

Everyone sowed black millet,
And exploited the rushes and reeds;
For what reason did they scatter in all directions,
40 And why was the enmity against Kun so long-lasting?

With white rainbow skirts and cloudlike adornments,
What is she doing in this hall?
Where did he get the excellent medicine
That he could not hide securely?

45 Heaven's framework spans the vertical and the horizontal;
When the vital yang breath dissipates, death will ensue.
Why did the great bird call?
How did it lose its body?

The pluvial sprite causes rain to fall;
50 How does he bring it about?
The god of wind has a deer's head and a bird's body;
How did he receive it?

When giant turtles bearing islands on their backs stir,
How do they keep them steady?
55 If one launches a boat to cross the land,
By what means does it move?

When Ao [9] stood before his sister-in-law's door,
What was he seeking from her?
Why did Shao-k'ang [10] go in pursuit of him with hounds,
60 But end up decapitating her?

The woman Ch'i sewed his lower garment,
And he rested with her in the same house;
How did the wrong head fall by mistake,
When she herself met disaster?

65 Ao planned to reorganize his troops;
How did he strengthen them?

7. This may refer to Yi.
8. Kun.
9. Son of Cho.
10. A ruler of the mid-Hsia dynasty.

After he capsized the boats of Chen-hsün,[11]
By what method was he taken?

IV

There were portents at the beginning;
By whom were they predicted?
A jade terrace ten stories tall;
By whom was it erected?

5   Fu-hsi[12] was established as Deus;
By what principle was he raised up?
Woman Wa[13] was embodied with a serpent's tail;
Who was it that created her?

Shun was tormented at home;
10   Why did his father let him remain a bachelor?
If Yao did not inform Shun's father,
How could he marry his two daughters to him?

Shun deferred to his younger stepbrother,
Who harmed him nonetheless.
15   How could the stepbrother unleash his brutish instincts,
But never be endangered himself?

Ngwa's heritage reaches into the past,
Having been founded among the southern peaks;
Who would have expected that, fleeing to this place,
20   Two princes[14] Ngwa would gain?

V

When Chieh attacked Meng-shan,
What did he get thereby?[15]
How was Mo-hsi dissipated?
Why did T'ang kill her?

11. A feudal state of the Hsia royal family.
12. The first ancient sage-king, he is almost certainly related to the flood-hero, Phu-Hay, of the Hmong (i.e., Miao) people.
13. She shares a number of similarities with Eve, the first woman of the Judaeo-Christian tradition.
14. Chung-yung and T'ai-po of the Chou royal house. They had ceded their rights to the throne in favor of a younger half-brother. The name of the southern kingdom transcribed here as Ngwa would be transcribed as Wu in Modern Standard Mandarin.
15. The answer is two beautiful women presented to him by the conquered state of Meng-shan as a form of appeasement. Chieh was the last king of the Hsia dynasty. After he returned with the two concubines, his deserted queen, Mo-hsi, had a conspiratorial affair with his servant, Yi Yin, and assisted T'ang, the first ruler of the Shang dynasty, to overthrow the Hsia.

5   From a tripod trimmed with swans and ornamented with jade,
Lord Deus was feted;
How did he receive the plans against Chieh of Hsia,
Who was finally destroyed?

When Deus descended to survey the world,
10   There below he encountered Yi Yin;
When Chieh was banished to Ming-t'iao for his crimes,
Why did the black-hairs [16] rejoice so greatly?

VI

Chien Ti [17] was on a tall terrace;
Why did K'u think that she was suitable?
A dark bird made a gift to her;
Why was the woman happy?

5   Hai [18] inherited Chi's virtues,
For his father was a good man;
Why was he finally murdered in the freehold of Yee,
Where he pastured his cattle and sheep? [19]

When he danced for her with his shield,
10   Why did she cherish him?
With his smooth loins and sleek skin,
How did he seduce her?

In the freehold of Yee there were herdsmen;
How did they encounter him?
15   They struck the bed, but he went out first;
Whose command were they following?

Heng inherited Chi's virtues;
How could he have retrieved their docile cattle?

16. From West Asia to East Asia, this was a standard way of referring to the commoners during antiquity. Some modern languages, such as Russian, still retain this expression.

17. Deus K'u, divine ancestor of the Yin (Shang) rulers, presented her with an egg brought to her nine-storied terrace by a dark bird. She swallowed the egg and became pregnant. The son she gave birth to was Hsieh, Minister of Education for Shun, who helped Yü control the floods and who was the founder of the house that later established the Yin dynasty.

18. Said to be the first herdsman, he was the brother of Heng and the father of Wei, through whom the Yin line was passed on.

19. The answer is that he apparently developed a licentious relationship with the wife of the ruler of this freehold. One version of the story says that his own brother, Heng, was also having an affair with the same woman and so killed Hai out of jealousy. In any event, with the death of Hai, the family lost their cattle in the freehold of Yee until Hai's son, Wei, recovered them. In the following stanzas, there is an undercurrent of censure against Heng for not taking action to retain the cattle himself.

Why was he concerned only with position and pay,
20   And did not even come back for them?

Meritorious Wei traced his father's footsteps,
And the freehold at Yee had no peace;
How numerous were his soldiers, like birds flocking to brambles,
When the responsible son gave vent to his emotions?

25   The deluded younger brothers were all profligate,
And threatened the older brother;
How did he transform them through deception,
So that their descendants met with lasting success?

T'ang [20] the Achiever toured the east,
30   And reached the freehold at Hsin;
How is it that he requested a servant,
But instead got an auspicious wife? [21]

From a tree by the water's edge,
They got the little boy, [22]
35   Why, then, did they hate him,
And send him away as an escort for the lady from Shen?

T'ang was released from the Double Springs prison;
Now what was his crime?
He overcame his inhibitions and attacked the monarch; [23]
40   Now who was it that incited him?

At first, Yi Yin was T'ang's servant,
But afterwards was accepted as councilor;
How was he T'ang's minister to the very end,
Later receiving offerings along with the ancestors of the Shang?

VII

To Yin was given all under heaven;
How was the throne bestowed upon Chou?

20. Seven generations after Wei, he was the founder of the Yin (Shang) dynasty.
21. T'ang requested from the freeholder of Hsin the talented Yi Yin who was later instrumental in helping him overthrow the Hsia dynasty. Although his request was not granted, he married the freeholder's daughter and Yi Yin came along as part of her entourage.
22. Legend holds that Yi Yin's mother turned into a mulberry tree when she was fleeing from a flood that engulfed her village. The night before, she had been warned in her dream by a god not to look back, but she could not keep herself from doing so.
23. Here referring to Chieh, who had imprisoned him.

Yin had prospered but then was lost;
What was Chow's crime? [24]

5   Though Chow was of kingly stature,
Who caused him to be foolish and deluded?
Why did he hate his close councilors,
While trusting in slanderers and flatterers?

How did Pi Kan [25] offend,
10   So that he was suppressed?
How did Lei K'ai truckle,
So that he was enfeoffed?

How can sages who are of equal virtue
End up behaving so differently?
15   Chow made mincemeat of Mei Po for his directness,
Master Chi feigned madness to preserve his life.

They convened at dawn and swore fealty;
How was this face-to-face appointment actualized? [26]
Like flocks of gray hawks they came flying;
20   Who was it that caused them to assemble?

They vied to mobilize their offensive weaponry;
How was this carried out?
They rushed forward together with their wings of attack,
How were the troops led?

25   When Chow's body was mutilated,
Why was Uncle Tan unhappy? [27]
When Wu personally directed the operations,
Why were there sighs of admiration?

24. This section deals with the toppling of the last ruler of the Shang, Chow.

25. Pi Kan was the loyal uncle of King Chow. The latter was much annoyed by the frequent admonitions of his uncle. When someone told him that a sage's heart has seven openings, he had Pi Kan's heart cut out so that he could see for himself.

26. King Wu, who became the first king of the Chou dynasty, was joined by eight hundred feudal lords whom he convened at a great meeting. The character *wu*, which many commentators interpret as a first-person pronoun indicating King Wu, actually stands for a homonymous cognate meaning "meet face to face." The only first-person reference in the "Heavenly Questions," quite properly, comes in the section dealing with Ch'u (see line XI.12), the home state of the presumed author. The "Wu" of the king's title is a separate sinograph meaning "martial."

27. "Uncle Tan" is an appellation of the Duke of Chou, who was so important in helping to establish the Chou dynasty. His name was Tan and he was the younger brother of King Wu. From the viewpoint of the succeeding generation, then, he was "Uncle Tan." The Duke of Chou was upset at King Wu's treatment of Chow's corpse because the Shang dynasty had been sanctioned by Heaven. Even though Chow was a tyrant, as an incarnation of Deus, he should have been treated with due respect.

VIII

Lord Millet[28] was the firstborn son;
Why did Deus[29] detest him?
Thrown out upon the ice,
How did the birds keep him warm?

5   How was it that he, drawing his bow full and grasping his arrows,
Had the unique ability to be a general?
Since he had startled Deus and made him agitated,
Why did he encounter lasting success?

The Earl of the West[30] gave orders while Yin declined;
10   He grasped a whip and acted as herdsman.
Who ordered the transfer of the altar to the earth to Ch'i,[31]
To take over the mandate of the Yin state?

When the tribal elders moved to Ch'i,
What made the people willing to follow them?
15   In Yin there was a bewitching woman;
How did she cause him to be censured?[32]

When Chow bestowed upon him the mincemeat of a vassal,[33]
The Earl of the West reported it to Heaven above.
How did he personally deliver the punishment of Exalted Deus,
20   So that the mandate of Yin could not be saved?

When Preceptor Wang was in the butchery,
How did the Earl of the West recognize him?
He drummed with his knife and raised his voice in song;
Why was his lord so happy?

25   When King Wu set forth to kill Chow of the Yin,
What was it that made him so grieved?
Carrying a corpse,[34] he assembled his warriors;
What was it that made him so hasty?

28. Hou Chi, the first ancestor of the clan that later established the Chou dynasty.
29. See line VI.1 and the note there.
30. Po Ch'ang, the future King Wen, who laid the groundwork for the Chou state.
31. The cradle of Chou culture, whence Hou Chi's descendants moved to escape annihilation by the Dik tribesmen. This move was suggested by the "Old Duke, Father T'an," also known as King T'ai, who was the grandfather of King Wen.
32. The beguiling woman of Yin was Ta-chi, King Chow's concubine. Chow was so infatuated by her that his ears were deaf to all protests.
33. See line VII.15.
34. That of the Earl of the West, his father, who was posthumously canonized as King Wen after the founding of the Chou.

Kuan Shu [35] hung himself in the arbor vitae grove;
30 What was the reason for that?
How was Heaven moved and the earth agitated?
Who was frightened by this?

When August Heaven bestowed the mandate,
What warning was given?
35 One may receive control of all under heaven,
Until another is caused to replace one.

Lord Chao [36] embarked on a royal tour,
Journeying all the way to the southern land.
What benefit did he receive
40 By meeting that white pheasant?

King Mu [37] was cunningly covetous;
What was his purpose in traveling all around?
When he made a circuit of all under heaven,
For what was he seeking?

45 A strange couple dragged along their wares;
What were they hawking in the market? [38]
Who executed King Yu? [39]
How did he obtain Pao Ssu?

IX

The mandate of Heaven shifts from side to side;
Whom does it punish, whom protect?

35. After the overthrow of Chow, Kuan Shu was one of the representatives of the Chou dynasty established in the eastern part of the kingdom to oversee the remnants of the Shang aristocracy. Implicated in a plot to cause dissension among the new rulers by casting aspersions on the loyalty of the Duke of Chou, he was forced to commit suicide.

36. Fourth of the Chou kings. He traveled to Ch'u in pursuit of southern rareties, but drowned while crossing a river.

37. Fifth king of the Chou, he was celebrated in legend for his love of horses and for his many long journeys, especially to the distant west.

38. During the reign of King Hsüan, the eleventh of the Chou rulers, a prophecy was heard in a children's song that the dynasty would fall because of a wild mulberry bow and a wicker quiver. A peasant couple were caught selling these items in the market, but they made good their escape. As they were fleeing, they rescued a baby who had been abandoned by an unmarried palace maid. The little girl grew up to be Pao Ssu, the demanding queen of King Yu, who was the twelfth and last ruler of the Western Chou.

39. The answer is the so-called Dog Barbarians, who were able to penetrate the neglected defenses of the capital because of King Yu's preoccupation with Pao Ssu.

Duke Huan of Ch'i [40] nine times convened his vassals,
Yet even he was murdered in the end.

5   Ho the Valiant [41] was the grandson of Meng; [42]
As a youth, he met with rejection.[43]
How did he gain military might in his prime,[44]
So that he could spread his prowess across the land? [45]

Progenitor P'eng [46] cooked a pheasant;
10 How did Deus partake of it?
He received lasting longevity;
How could he exist so long?

X

They pastured their livestock together in the center; [47]
Why was the lord [48] angry?
Their lives were slight as those of bees and ants;
How could their power persist?

5   The goddess was startled to see them picking ferns; [49]
How did a deer [50] protect them?
North they traveled to the bend in the river;
Why were they happy to congregate there?

40. During the Eastern Chou period, when the dynasty was in decline, numerous city-states contested for power. The strongest of these during the seventh century B.C.E. was Ch'i, whose duke was nine times chosen to be leader of the feudal lords.

41. Ho Lü, king of Ngwa (r. 514–496 B.C.E.).

42. King of the powerful southern state of Ngwa.

43. Ho Lü was the legitimate heir to the Ngwa throne, but was passed over in a complicated, irregular succession. After a period of exile when he was young, Ho Lü had his cousin, who occupied the throne, assassinated and finally became king himself.

44. Through the assistance of the talented minister, Wu Tzu-hsü.

45. Like Duke Huan of Ch'i, King Ho Lü of Ngwa acted as one of the five hegemons during the Spring and Autumn period.

46. P'eng Keng or P'eng Tsu, the Chinese counterpart of Methuselah, was a practitioner of yogic breath control and an excellent chef.

47. At the beginning of the Chou dynasty, the Ch'in tribe, which would ultimately supplant it roughly a thousand years later, was still a small group that shared the pastures of the Chou heartland.

48. King Wu of the Chou dynasty.

49. King Wu pushed the Ch'in northward out of the center of the Chou kingdom into less hospitable territory. There they were for a time forced to subsist by foraging off the sparsely vegetated land.

50. Fei-lien, the antlered god of the wind (see line III.51), who was also thought of as the first ancestor of the Ch'in people. Fei-lien (*piwər-gliam) may merely be the binomial spelling of the Sinitic word for "wind" (MSM feng, ancient reconstruction *pium).

The elder brother [51] possessed Dog Mound;
10   Why did the younger brother [52] desire it?
In exchange, he was offered a hundred chariots,[53]
And ended up losing his entitlements.

XI

Midst evening thunder and lightning,
Why was he [54] afraid to return?
His majesty could not be maintained;
What was Deus seeking?

5   He [55] hid away in caves;
How can his predicament be described?
Illustrious Ch'u raised armies;
How did it take the lead? [56]

Recognizing the errors of his predecessor,[57] he [58] corrected them;
10   What more can be said?
Ho Lü vied to conquer our state;
Long was he victorious over us.

She circled round the village gates and passed through the altars to the
   earth,
Till she reached the burial mounds.

51. Master Fei, an important ancestral figure of the Ch'in house. He was responsible for reestablishing the Ch'in at Dog Mound after they had wandered in the inhospitable wilds of the north.

52. Master Fei's stepbrother, Ch'eng, whose mother was the daughter of the powerful Marquis of Shen.

53. King Hsiao, the eighth ruler of the Chou dynasty, refused to enfeoff Ch'eng as lord of Dog Mound. Instead, he presented him with a hundred chariots and appointed him as ambassador to the distant Western Jung tribe. This move was designed to defuse the conflict between the two brothers and resulted in Ch'eng's losing his regular feudal entitlements.

54. This refers to King Ling of the southern state of Ch'u, the home of the author of "Encountering Sorrow" and "Heavenly Questions." Once when the king went on an excursion, his younger brother took advantage of the situation to usurp the throne and install himself as King P'ing. The latter was an evil despot who, among other dastardly deeds, killed his loyal adviser Wu She, father of Wu Tzu-hsü (see note 44), and relied upon the unscrupulous Fei Wu-chi instead.

55. King P'ing's son and successor, King Chao, was forced to flee when the armies of the state of Ngwa entered the Ch'u capital.

56. King Chuang, grandson of King Ch'eng (see notes 60 and 61) brought his state to eminence and served as hegemon.

57. King P'ing.

58. King Chao.

15   She was licentious, she was wanton,
     And consequently gave birth to Tzu-wen.[59]

It was reported that Hsiung[60] would not reign long;
How did Tzu-wen chasten his superior[61] and renounce himself,
Thereby making his loyal name all the more illustrious?

Translated by Victor H. Mair

59. The result of an illicit union, Tzu-wen was abandoned in the wilds. There a tigress suckled him and he grew up to be the able minister of King Ch'eng of Ch'u.

60. The text has *tu-ao*, a transcription of the Ch'u word for a monarch who rules but a short time. Hsiung (Bear) was both the surname and the totem of the Ch'u royal family. Hsiung Chien was the son of King Wen of Ch'u and the older brother of King Ch'eng.

61. Hsiung Yün (later King Ch'eng) who was in conflict with his brother, Hsiung Chien, over the succession. Since Hsiung Yün was privy to the excellent advice of Tzu-wen, he emerged the victor and led Ch'u to glory.

123
The Owl

Chia Yi (201–169 B.C.E.)

Chia Yi had been Tutor to the Prince of Ch'ang-sha[1] for three years when one day an owl flew into his house and perched in a corner of his room. (In

The *fu* (rhapsody, rhymeprose, or prose-poem) stands at the very beginning of the most important anthology of traditional Chinese literature, *Literary Selections* (see selection 12) and fully one-quarter of the large volume is devoted to this genre. The prominence awarded to *fu* by the editor of *Literary Selections* is not accidental, for this is the first genre to have afforded Chinese authors broad scope in which to display their narrative, descriptive, and lyrical talents. It is highly significant that both the elegy (see selection 122) and the rhapsody, which constitute the earliest forms of imaginative and expressive belles-lettres in China, were invented and matured in the peripheral southern state of Ch'u, which was fundamentally of non-Sinitic origins and, in any event, culturally and ecologically quite dissimilar from the northern homeland of the Chinese people.

"The Owl" by Chia Yi is the earliest work in the rhapsody form whose authorship and date of composition are reasonably certain. The text is recorded in the biography of the poet in chapter 84 of the *Records of the Grand Historian* by Ssu-ma Ch'ien, compiled around 100 B.C.E. The prefatory note accompanying "The Owl" is based upon Ssu-ma Ch'ien's description of the circumstances under which the work was composed. The position of tutor to the Prince of Ch'ang-sha, in a remote region (modern Hunan) of the Yangtze Valley, was actually a form of banishment. This fact, along with the poet's failing health, accounts for the air of gloom that pervades the work. Using the owl as his mouthpiece, Chia Yi preaches himself a fervently Taoist sermon on the equality of life and death. His poem, far more personal and overtly

Ch'u the word for owl is *fu*; it is a bird of ill omen.) [2] This was after he had
been banished to Ch'ang-sha (Ch'ang-sha is a low, damp place), and he was
greatly depressed at what he took to be a sign that he had not much longer
to live. On this occasion he wrote a rhapsody to console himself. It reads as
follows:

> The year was *tan-wo*, [3] it was the fourth month, summer's first,
> The thirty-seventh day of the cycle, [4] at sunset, when an owl alighted in
>   my house.
> On the corner of my seat it perched, completely at ease.
> I marveled at the reason for this uncanny visitation
> 5   And opened a book to discover the omen. The oracle yielded the
>   maxim:
> "When a wild bird enters a house, the master is about to leave."
> I should have liked to ask the owl: Where am I to go?
> If lucky, let me know; if bad, tell me the worst.
> Be it swift or slow, tell me when it is to be.
> 10   The owl sighed; it raised its head and flapped its wings
> But could not speak.—Let me say what it might reply:
> All things are a flux, with never any rest
> Whirling, rising, advancing, retreating;
> Body and breath do a turn together—change form and slough off,
> 15   Infinitely subtle, beyond words to express.
> From disaster fortune comes, in fortune lurks disaster [5]
> Grief and joy gather at the same gate, good luck and bad share the
>   same abode.
> Though Wu was great and strong, Fu-ch'ai met with defeat;
> Yüeh was driven to refuge on K'uai-chi, but Kou-chien became
>   hegemon. [6]

philosophical than most of the other early rhapsodies, stands apart from the mainstream of
literary development, its tone too somber for the social uses to which the rhapsody form was
customarily put, its intense conviction inimitable by anyone not afflicted as its author was. One
of the most intriguing aspects of this rhapsody on "The Owl" is its uncanny resemblance to
Edgar Allan Poe's "The Raven," a work which it predates by more than two millennia.

1. In Hunan.

2. This is quite obviously an aside which introduces both a linguistic fact and a relevant
custom from the far southern setting of the work. The following parenthetical sentence is of a
similar nature.

3. There are varying opinions—175, 174, and 173 B.C.E.—as to which year this is meant to
indicate.

4. This corresponds to the twenty-eighth day of the fourth lunar month, 173 B.C.E., and to
the twenty-third day of the fourth lunar month, 174 B.C.E. The fourth lunar month of 175
B.C.E. had no such cyclical date.

5. Shortened from *Tao te ching* (selection 9), chapter 58.

6. The rivalry between Wu (Ngwa) and Yüeh (Viet) provides one of the most dramatic

20 Li Ssu emigrated to become minister, but in the end he suffered the
    Five Punishments.[7]

Fu Yüeh was once in bonds, before he was minister to Wu-ting.[8]

So

Disaster is to fortune as strands of a single rope,
Fate is past understanding—who comprehends its bounds?[9]
Force water and it spurts, force an arrow and it goes far.[10]

25 All things are propelled in circles, undulating and revolving—
Clouds rise and rain falls, tangled in contingent alternation.
On the Great Potter's wheel creatures are shaped in all their infinite
    variety.
Heaven cannot be predicted, the Way cannot be foretold,
Late or early, it is predetermined; who knows when his time will be?
Consider then:

30 Heaven and Earth are a crucible, the Creator is the smith;[11]
Yin and yang are the charcoal, living creatures are the bronze:
Combining, scattering, waning, waxing—where is any pattern?
A thousand changes, a myriad transformations with never any end.
If by chance one becomes a man, it is not a state to cling to.

35 If one be instead another creature, what cause is that for regret?
A merely clever man is partial to self, despising other, vaunting ego;
The man of understanding adopts the larger view: nothing exists to
    take exception to.
The miser will do anything for his hoard, the hero for his repute;

---

examples of the reversals of fortune that Chia Yi is illustrating. Fu-ch'ai, the last ruler of Wu,
failed to take advantage of his opportunity to destroy Yüeh when Kou-chien's army was surrounded on top of Mount K'uai-chi (or Kuei-chi). Years later the situation was reversed and
Yüeh destroyed Wu. Under King Kou-chien, Yüeh became the leading state among those
contending for supremacy during the breakup of the Eastern Chou dynasty.

7. Li Ssu was instrumental in preparing the way for the establishment of the Ch'in dynasty
which succeeded in establishing a unified state.

8. Fu Yüeh spent time as a convict, but he became a star in the sky after being adviser to
the Shang ruler Wu-ting.

9. In the *Tao te ching*, this question follows immediately after the line about fortune and
calamity (compare with note 5).

10. This proverbial expression occurs in the *Huai-nan Tzu* and in *The Springs and Autumns
of Mr. Lü (Lü shih ch'un-ch'iu)*. In the former it is used to emphasize the need for effort at the
right time: the best arrow needs a bow to send it far, etc. In the latter it is a warning against
attempting to cope with that which is "stirred up," in particular a ruler. In the present context
the arrow and water are examples of things at the mercy of an outside force: even so all of
creation, man included, is driven by the impersonal workings of the Way.

11. This line and lines 33, 34, 36, 37, 38, 39, 50, and 51 are all based on sentences from
the *Chuang Tzu*. It is clear that Chia Yi was inspired by the ideas and images of Master Chuang
in creating this rhapsody.

The vainglorious is ready to die for power, the common man clings to
    life.
40   Driven by aversions and lured by desires, men dash madly west or east;
The Great Man is not biased, the million changes are all one to him.
The stupid man is bound by custom, confined as though in fetters;
The Perfect Man is above circumstance, Tao is his only friend.
The mass man vacillates, his mind replete with likes and dislikes;
45   The True Man is tranquil, he takes his stand with Tao.
Divest yourself of knowledge and ignore your body, until, transported,
    you lose self;
Be detached, remote, and soar with Tao.
Float with the flowing stream, or rest against the isle,
Surrender to the workings of fate, unconcerned for self,
50   Let your life be like a floating, your death like a rest.
Placid as the peaceful waters of a deep pool, buoyant as an unfastened
    boat,
Find no cause for complacency in life, but cultivate emptiness and
    drift.
The Man of Virtue is unattached; recognizing fate, he does not worry.
Be not dismayed by petty pricks and checks!

Translated by James Robert Hightower

124
Seven Stimuli

Mei Ch'eng (d. 140 B.C.E.)

The Crown Prince of Ch'u having fallen ill, a guest from Wu [1] went to ask
after his health.

"I have heard," said the guest, "of Your Highness's discomfort, and was
wondering whether you might have improved somewhat?"

This prose-poem occupies an important place in the early development of the *fu* (rhapsody
or rhymeprose), which established itself as a genre of lush verbiage and elaborate description.
The rhapsody enabled Chinese writers to expand the scope of their literary creativity far beyond
the limits of the traditional short, lyrical verse and usually utilitarian prose. As such, it is a key
genre in the history of imaginative belles-lettres in China. Still, like virtually all the other major
fu, "Seven Stimuli" makes a perfunctory nod toward didacticism at the end to justify its
existence in the highly moralistic Confucianism of its day.

    1. The author himself was from the Wu (Ngwa) area (Huai-yin).

"I am exhausted," said the Prince. "Thank you ever so much for your concern." The guest, accordingly, seized this opportunity to offer his advice:

"Presently,
      The kingdom is at peace;
      everywhere, there is harmony.
And you are,
      at this moment, in the prime of your life.
Yet, I should imagine that
      you have long been besotted with pleasures,
      day and night indulging yourself without limit.
      An irruption of noxious humors
      has balled up inside of you.
      Distracted you are and listless;
      distraught and crapulous,
      fearful and timorous,
      you lie in bed but cannot sleep.
      Debilitated and dull of ear,
      you detest hearing the sound of another's voice.
      Your vitality dissipated,
      a hundred illnesses befall you at the same time;
      your senses confused,
      joy and anger become imbalanced.
      If you persist much longer this way,
      your life itself may be imperiled.

Could it be, Crown Prince, that this is your plight?"

"Thank you ever so much for your concern," said the Prince. "Relying on my father's royal grace, I do, from time to time, enjoy such pleasures, but not to the degree which you have described."

"Nowadays,"
    said the guest,
      "The sons of good families
    are sure
      to hide away
        in the inner recesses of palaces.
      Within, they have governesses to look after them,
      without, they have preceptors to instruct them;
      though they wish to make friends, they have not the
        wherewithal.
Their food and drink
      are smooth, savory, sweet, and crisp;
      their meat is fat, their wine is thick.

Their clothing
          is endlessly varied, light but warm;
          they swelter and suffocate in it as in the heat of summer.
     Even something
          as durable as metal or stone,
     would soon
          fuse and dissolve
               in the face of such
                    heat:
need
     I say
          what becomes of flesh
               and bone?
Therefore, it is said:
     he who
          gives free rein
               to his sensual desires
          and dissipates
               himself in physical pleasures
          will damage
               the equilibrium of his circulatory system.

     What's more,
          riding a chariot or carriage no matter where one goes
     is called
          a 'paralytic portent.'
          Cave-like winter rooms and airy summer palaces
     are called,
          likewise, 'aguish agents.'
          Pearly teeth and moth-eyebrows
     are called
          'hatchets to trim the tree of life.'
          Things sweet, crisp, oily, and syrupy
     are called,
          likewise, 'rot-gut reagents.'

Now
     you, Crown Prince,
          have a pallid, pasty complexion.
          Your arms and legs move sluggishly,
          your muscles and bones have lost tone and fiber,
          your blood pressure is much too high,
          your hands and feet are infirm.
          Yüeh lasses wait upon you in front,

Ch'i maidens attend you behind;
you are forever engaged in dalliance or banqueting.
You dissipate yourself
in
hidden rooms and private
parlors,
All this
is willingly to dine on poison;
playing
with the claws and teeth
of savage
beasts.
But the effects
of your past activities
are very deep-seated,
and you have postponed,
for such a long time,
the abandonment of these ways.
Thus, though one should command
Pien-ch'üeh [2] to treat you internally
and Shaman [3] Hsien to treat you externally,
what good would it do?

Now,
an illness such as Your
Excellency's
surely calls for
the superior men of our age—
men of broad learning and strong memory.
They should, when occasion allows, offer their opinions,
thus changing your habits and altering your ideas.
They should never leave your side,
and should serve as your assistants.
These pleasures in which you wallow,
the intemperance which holds your mind,
the apathy which stifles your will—
how could they then
arise?"

"Very well," said the Crown Prince. "When I am over my illness, I shall
carry out these instructions of yours."

2. A famous physician of old.
3. Recent research has shown that it may be more accurate to identify him as a magus.

"But your illness," said the guest, "has now reached the point that neither plant nor mineral medicines, acupuncture nor cauterization can cure you. Only through the exposition of essential apothegms and marvelous maxims may you be rid of it. Wouldn't you like to hear them?"

"Yes," said the Crown Prince, "I am desirous of hearing your exposition."

The guest spake:

> "The paulownia of Dragon Gate Mountain
> reaches
>   a height of one hundred feet
>   before it branches.
>   Its center
>   has a tightly packed mass
>   of concentric rings;
>   its roots
>   spread out
>   in all directions.
> Above it,
>   there are thousand-meter peaks;
> below,
>   it looks over hundred-fathom canyons.
>   The backwash from the rising current
>   swashes and swirls against it.
>   Its roots
>   are half-dead, half-alive.
>
> In winter,
> sleet and snow driven by fierce winds
>   assail
>
>   it;
>
> in summer,
>   resounding peals of thunder and lightning
>   shake
>
>   it.
> Mornings,
>   the yellow oriole and the bulbul sing
>   there;
> evenings,
>   the mateless hen and birds which have gone astray roost
>   there.
>
>   The solitary snow-goose calls out at daybreak
>   above it;
>   the heath-cock

sadly chirps as it flutters about
beneath it.

Then,

with autumn behind and winter coming on,

send
the Lutemaster Chih to chop it down and make it into a lute.
Filaments from the cocoons of wild silkworms are used for its strings,
the buckle of an orphan child is used as an ornamental inlay,
the pearl eardrops of the widowed mother of nine are used for its frets.

Command
Master T'ang to play on it 'All Things Pleaseth,'
Po-ya[4]
to accompany him with a song.

The words of the song are:
'The bearded spikes of the wheat do ripen, the pheasant flies up in the
morn—
heading for a desolate valley, it sets its back to the withered locust tree;
it skirts along deserted lands, peers down upon twisting mountain
streams.'

Hearing this song, flying birds
fold their wings—they cannot go on;
hearing this song, wild beasts
droop their ears—they can proceed no farther;
hearing this song, daddy longlegs, caterpillars, crickets
and ants
prop their proboscises—they cannot advance.

This, indeed, is the most lugubrious music in the world! Could you force yourself to rise and listen to it?"

"I am still ill," replied the Crown Prince, "and am, as yet, unable to get up."

The guest spake:

"A fatty stomach-cut of veal
with bamboo shoots and rush stems to go with it;
a blended mixture of plump dog
and edible lichens for a potage.
Whether rice from Miao Mountain in Ch'u
or wild rice of the zizania grass,

4. A distinguished lutanist of ancient times.

> > it is so sticky it can be patted into balls,
> > so slippery it dissolves upon touching your tongue.

Then,

> > call upon
> > > Yi Yin to sauté and simmer,
> > > Yi-ya to season and spice.[5]
> > > There will be well-stewed bear's paw
> > > prepared with a finely flavored sauce.
> > > You shall have thinly sliced sections of roast loin
> > > and fresh strips of minced carp,
> > > perilla plucked in autumn when it is yellow,
> > > vegetables succulent from the white dews of late
> > > > summer.
> > > This will be followed by wine made fragrant with orchid
> > > > petals
> > > which you may pour for a mouthwash.
> > > At last, you will dine on hen pheasant
> > > and fetus of domesticated panther.
> > > Whether you eat but little or sup a lot,
> > > it will digest as quickly as hot water poured upon snow.

These, indeed, are the most delectable dishes in the world! Could you force yourself to rise and partake of them?"

"I am still ill," replied the Crown Prince, "and am, as yet, unable to get up."

The guest spake:

> > > "You shall have stallions from Chung and Tai,[6]
> > > chosen at the prime age, they will pull your chariot.
> > > From the front, they seem like Flying Duck coursers,
> > > behind, they appear to be mythical mules.
> > > Panic-grass and wheat their provender,
> > > they are restless within and chafe without.
> > > > They are harnessed with strong reins
> > > > and stick to the good roads.

Thereupon,

> > Po-le [7] examines the steeds front to back,
> > Wang Liang and Tsao-fu [8]

5. These lines mention two famous cooks from the past.
6. Two small states noted for producing excellent horses.
7. A celebrated horse-trainer of antiquity.
8. Two famous charioteers.

serve as the charioteers,

Ch'in Ch'üeh[9] and Lou Chi[10]

ride on the right as guards.

These two

can stop runaway

horses,

can raise overturned

chariots.

Therefore,

you could make

a bet

of one thousand pounds

on a race

of a thousand miles.

These, indeed, are the finest steeds in the world! Can you force yourself to rise and ride in the chariot they pull?"

"I am still ill," replied the Crown Prince, "and am, as yet, unable to get up."

The guest spake:

"Or you could mount

the Ching-yi observation tower,

gaze south to Thorn Mountain,

gaze north across the Ju River.

On the left, the Yangtze, on the right, Tung-t'ing Lake —

the pleasures such a view affords are unexcelled.

Thereupon,

you should call

elocutionists with broad learning

to expound on the origins of the rivers and mountains

and to name all of the grasses and trees,

finding analogies and making allusions,

categorizing and classifying.

Let your eye roam and your gaze drift,

then come down from the tower and have wine prepared

in

Heart's Pleasure Palace,

9. A fleet warrior in ancient times.
10. A great jumper.

with its corridors leading in all four directions,
its terraced walls and storied structures,
all decorated with variegated colors;
with its crisscross carriageways,
its winding lakes and pools.
There are dabchicks and egrets,
precious peacocks and sylvan swans,
birds of paradise and flamingoes—
a riot of bluish-green crowns and purple necks.
Hens and cocks, stipple-crested and speckle-breasted,
warble harmoniously in flocks.
Sunfish jump and leap,
fins flapping and scales skittering.
Beside still waters grow scizanthus and smartweed,
creeping grasses and aromatic licorice,
supple mulberries and riverside tamarisks—
a profusion of silken-white leaves and purple stems.
The ginkgo and the camphor
have branches which reach to the very heavens;
firmiana and coir palm
make forests which stretch as far as the eye can see.
An almost palpable assembly of fragrant aromas
mingles with the breezes which come from all
    directions.
The trees sway lazily with the wind,
their leaves showing, by turns, light bottoms and dark
    tops.
As we take our places on the banquet mats, let wine
    flow freely
and lilting strains bring joy to our hearts!
Let Ching Ch'un [11] assist with the wine,
Tu Lien [12] be in charge of the music,
Let all sorts of gustful flavors be spread before us,
an assortment of cooked meats, fish, and cereals be
    prepared.
Refined hues will delight our eyes,
lilting strains give pleasure to our ears.

Thereafter,
    the orchestra strikes up

11. Mentioned in the *Mencius* (see selection 7).
12. A famous lutanist.

the dance tune
for the Whirling Ch'u,[13]
wafts aloft
the dazzling songs
of Cheng and Wei.[14]
Send for
Hsi-shih
Cheng Shu,
Yang Wen,
Tuan-kan,
Wu-wa
Lü-chü
Fu Yü,[15]
such handsome lads and lovely ladies as these.
In their kaleidoscopic skirts and trailing swallow-tails,
they cast flirtatious glances which show their hearts have
already given in.
The luster of their eyes flows in ripples,
they are imbued with the scent of turmeric;
they are as though covered with stardust,
and have anointed themselves with orchid pomade.
Having changed into something comfortable,
they come to wait on you.
These, indeed, are the world's most
luxurious, extravagant,
and sumptuous delights!

Can you force yourself to rise and enjoy them?"
"I am still ill," said the Crown Prince, "and am, as yet, unable to get up."

The guest spake:

"For you, Crown Prince,
I should like
to train
prancing piebald horses,
harness them
to a chariot with streamers flying from the hubs,
or have you ride
in a fine carriage and four.
In your right hand

13. A regional style of dance.
14. Two kingdoms noted for their talented female singers.
15. All seven names refer to legendary beauties or attractive men.

are sharp-pointed arrows from
Emperor Hou's [16] quiver,
in your left hand,
the decorated bow known as
'Crow Call.'
You wend your way through
the Dream-cloud Forest,
make a quick circuit around
moors where orchids grow,
slow your pace when you come to
the Yangtze's banks.

Bending the sedge as you pass,
you head into the soothing breezes;
drunk on the sunny air,
you revel in the ardor of spring.
You chase down crafty beasts,
gather in fleet-winged fowl.

Then,
you give full play
to the ability of your dogs and horses.
Weary
are the legs of the wild animals,
as full scope is given
to the knowledge and skill
of the guides and charioteers.
They strike terror in the tiger and leopard,
cause birds of prey to cower in fright.
The bells on the bits of the pursuing horses tinkle,
causing fish to leap in nooks along the river's edge.
They trod upon roe and rabbit,
trample over elk and deer.
Sweat dripping, froth dropping,
the quarry succumbs to the relentless pressure.
Those which die without even being
wounded
are quite
enough to fill the carts in the
rear.

This is the grandest sort of martial hunt. Could you force yourself to rise and join the chase?"

16. Great Yü, queller of the flood.

"I am ill," said the Crown Prince, "and am, as yet, unable to get up."

But this time a sunny sparkle appeared in the space between his brows and gradually spread till it almost covered his entire face. The guest saw that the Crown Prince had a happy look and so pressed forward:

> "The fire in the dark of night lights the skies,
> the army-carts trundle thunderously;
> banners and pennants flutter aloft,
> an imposing array of feathers and fur.
> Galloping, racing, they contend for the lead;
> caught in their zest for the hunt, each strives to be first.
> Vast stretches are scorched to intercept the game;
> as one gazes across it,
> > the land stands out in relief.
> Immaculate, intact sacrificial animals
> are presented at the gates of the feudal princes."

"Excellent!" exclaimed the Crown Prince. "I'd like to hear more."

"I'm not finished yet," said the guest.
> "Then,

> in dense forests and deep marshes,
> 'neath a murky layer of mists and clouds—
> aurochs and tigers sally forth together.
> But the gladiators are ferocious—
> bodies bared to the waist, they grapple with the beasts.
> Naked swords gleam and glitter,
> spears and lances cross in a tangle.
> The game is collected and achievements noted,
> rewards of gold and silk are presented.
> Sedge is pressed down and turmeric spread over it
> as a mat to be used by the Breeder for State Sacrifices.
> There are excellent wines and delectable dishes,
> savory meats barbecued and roasted,
> to entertain the honored guests.
> Brimming beakers are raised together,
> pledges rouse the heart and excite the ear.
> Sincere and honorable, they have no regrets;
> whether in consent or refusal, they are decisive.
> The cast of genuine trust on their faces
> is embodied in the music of metal bells and stone
> > chimes.
> Loudly they sing, clearly they shout:
> 'Long live the Crown Prince!' and never weary of it.

This, Crown Prince, is what you really delight in! Can you force yourself to rise and join us?"

"I should very much like to take part," said the Crown Prince. "It is just that I am afraid I would be a great burden to the high officials." But it looked as though he were about to get up.

The guest spake:

"On the fifteenth of the eighth month, together with the nobles and your acquaintances and brothers who come from afar, we shall go to view the tidal bore [17] at Winding River in Kuang-ling. When we first get there, we won't be able to see the shape of the tidal flood itself. But simply viewing the force of the water which precedes it is startling enough to terrify the beholder.

> Viewing
>> the way it
>>> o'erleaps
>>>> itself,
>> the way it
>>> plucks itself
>>>> up,
>> the way it
>>> flaunts its
>>>> turbulence,
>> the way it
>>> whirls and
>>>> swirls,
>> the way it
>>> washes and
>>>> swishes,
> though one have
>> a clear impression in his mind of what it is and be gifted
>> with words,

he still could not describe in detail its intrinsic quality.

>> Blurred—vague—
>> frightful—terrifying—
>> a confused rumble;
>> hazy—fuzzy—
>> swelling—cresting—
>> vast and extensive—
>> o'erstepping into the boundless.

17. A rare phenomenon that occurs in certain rivers where a wall of water moves inland at times of high tide (see selection 184).

The beholder fixes his mind
            on South Mountain,
from there, gazes all the way
            to the Eastern Sea;
The waters conjoin
            with the azure sky,
imagination is exhausted in trying to distinguish
            where the horizon ends.

After scanning this limitlessness,
turn your attention to Aurora's bed.

Rushing waves
        borne by the counter-current
            come bearing down—
one hardly knows
        where they will halt.
Or perhaps,
        in a tumultuous tangle,
            the waves break.
Suddenly,
        resolved, they go off,
            never to return.
As the water approaches
        Crimson Creek on the southern bank
            and then flows into the distance,
inside,
        one feels empty, troubled,
            and rather enervated.
From evening,
        when the tide recedes
            until it rises again in the
                        morning,
in his mind's eye,
        he retains an impression of it
            without even trying.
And then,
        having experienced this catharsis of the spirit
        and purgation of his internal organs,
        his hands are laved, his feet are bathed,
        his hair shampooed, his teeth brushed.
        He renounces indolence, relinquishes sloth,
        discards impurity, divests filth,
        sunders suspicion, dispatches doubt,

opens ear, illumines eye.

At the time of the bore,
even though
one's illness be chronic, his infirmity protracted,
be he
hunchbacked, he would straighten himself, crippled, he
would rise and walk,
blind, his eyes would open, deaf, his ears would hear,
so as to behold this
spectacle.
This is all the more true of those who merely
have traces of melancholy and trivial ennui,
suffer from crapulence or oenomania
and the like!
Therefore, I say that
relief from stupor and deliverance from torpor
are not even worthy of
mention."

"Splendid," exclaimed the Crown Prince. "But just what is the essence of this bore?"

"There are no records in the ancient books," the guest replied, "but I have heard from my teacher that there are three aspects wherein it seems almost as though it were divine:

Its urgent
thunder can be heard hundreds of furlongs away;
the river's waters flow in reverse,
the ocean's waters go upstream with the tide;
the mountains exhale and inhale vapors
all day and all night without cease.

Welling and swelling, the tidal race picks up speed,
its waves surge
and its billows rise.
At the very beginning,
it is a cascading
torrent,
like
the downward swoop
of white egrets.
After it has progressed
a short while,
it becomes a vast expanse of dazzling whiteness,

like
        a silk-white chariot drawn by white horses,
                        curtains and canopy unfurled.

                The bore's
                        waves surge
                                in nebulous confusion,
                                        tumultu-
                                                ous
                as though
                        the three regiments were
                                plunging into preparedness.
        It
                spreads out to the sides
                        and suddenly rears
                                up,
                        airily and graceful-
                                        ly
        as
                the light chariot
                        of a commander marshalling his troops.

                The bore is harnessed to six flood-dragons,
                and follows close upon Great White, the god of the river.
                It is high and mighty, whether resting or racing,
                continuous and unbroken from front to back.
                The waves are enormous, towering,
                consecutive and recurring—
                jos-jostling, ca-capering.
                Row after row of stout bulwarks and ramparts,
                multitudinous
                        as the ranks of an army.
                with the stentorian and cacophonous roar,
                they surge uncurbed across the breadths;
                the fount of this flood is not to be stayed!

                Observing both banks of the river,
        we see there a
                        convulsive, boiling, brooding, seething,
                        troublous, roiling, jolting, heaving;
                        it smashes upward, flings boulders below.
        There is, about it, something which resembles
                        a valiant, mighty warrior

bursting with rage
and completely undaunted.
It tramples revetments, bursts through ferry-crossings,
inundates inlets and courses coves,
then leaps its banks, spills over its dikes.

He who encounters it perishes;
that which blocks it is destroyed.

The bore has its beginning
along the shore of
Surrounding Site.
Diverted by foothills, dividing in valleys,
it swirls past Green Splint,
is muzzled at Sandalwood Signpost.
It slackens its pace
at sacred-to-the-son Wu Tzu-hsü [18] Mountain,
marches on past
mother of Tzu-hsü Arena.
It shoots beyond Red Bank,
Sweeps by Mulberry Brushwood.

It runs amok
like stalking thunder.
Truly aroused is its warlike energy,
as though it were moved with anger!
Rumble, rumble, grumble, grumble,
it has the appearance of galloping horses;
grumble, grumble, rumble, rumble,
its sound is like thundering drums.
Enraged when checked, it boils over,
clear waves arch up and leap across;
river-spirit Yang-hou's billows stir and shake.
They all join battle at
the gorge known as Clashcrash.
Birds are unable to fly away in time,
fish are unable to turn back in time,
animals are unable to flee in time.
There is a flurry of fins, feathers, and fur
amidst the surging waves and chaotic clouds.

18. The bore was considered to be a manifestation of Wu Tzu-hsü's spirit, which was outraged at his dead body having been disrespectfully thrown into the river in a leather sack (see selection 151).

The bore takes the southern hills by storm,
then attacks the northern bank at its back;
it overturns hillocks and mounds,
levels flat the western riverside.

Perilous!   Precipitous!
Storage basins collapse, reservoirs break—
only with decisive victory does it leave off.

Yet it gurgles, bubbles, murmurs, ruffles;
displaying its spray, flaunting its splash,
it is the extreme of perversity.
Fish and turtles lose their bearings in it—
they are tossed and turned topsy-turvy;
disoriented and bewildered,
they stumble, tumble, fumble, bumble.
Since even sprites are left spellbound,
there is no way adequately to describe it.

It is quite simply enough to bowl a person
                              over,
         reeling in the gloom of
                              consternation,

    This is the world's most
              extraordinary and wondrous
                              spectacle!
Can you force yourself to rise and enjoy it?"
    "I am ill," said the Crown Prince, "and am, as yet, unable to get up."

The guest spake:

    "I should like to introduce to you men who are practitioners of the occult,
who are capable and learned,
              such as
                         Chuang Chou [19]
                         Wei Mou [20]
                         Yang Chu [21]
         Mo Ti [22]
              P'ien Chüan [23]

19. See selection 8.
20. A Warring States thinker.
21. An egoist thinker, foil for the pragmatist Mo Tzu.
22. Mo Tzu.
23. This and the following figure, Chan He, were apparently comparable to Izaak Walton.

Chan He

and the like.

I would have them
    expound upon
        the mystic profundity of
            the world,
    argue about
        the morality of
            all creation.

        Confucius and Lao Tzu will be moderators and
            observers;
Mencius
        will verify by manipulating
            tallies;
        not once in ten thousand times will a mistake be made.

Theirs, indeed, are the most essential apothegms and most marvelous maxims in the world. Wouldn't you like to hear them?"

Thereupon, the Crown Prince, supporting himself on a small table, rose and declared: "I feel enlightened as though I had already heard the words of the sages and dialecticians." Then he broke out in great beads of sweat and, all of a sudden, his illness was ended.

Translated by Victor H. Mair

125
Rhapsody on Whistling

Ch'eng-kung Sui (231–273)

I

The secluded gentleman,
1   In sympathy with the extraordinary,
    And in love with the strange,
2   Scorns the world and is unmindful of prestige.

The technique of transcendental whistling in old China (also in Turkey, where it was still extant in the 1960s, and some other countries) was a kind of nonverbal language with affinities to the spiritual aspects of meditation. There were many famous whistlers in Chinese history before the composition of this definitive rhapsody on the subject. Among them were Liu Ken (first or second century) and Sun Teng and Juan Chi (both third century c.e.).

The notes for this selection are keyed to the numbered verses.

He breaks away from human endeavor and leaves it behind.
3   He gazes up at the lofty, longing for the days of old;
He ponders lengthily, his thoughts wandering afar.
He would
4   Climb Mount Chi in order to maintain his moral integrity;
Or float on the blue sea to amble with his ambition.

II

5   So he invites his trusted friends,
Gathering about himself a group of like-minded.
6   He gets at the essence of the ultimate secret of life;
He researches the subtle mysteries of Tao and Te.
7   He regrets that the common people are not yet enlightened;
He alone, transcending all, has prior awakening.
8   He finds constraining the narrow road of the world—
He gazes up at the concourse of heaven, and treads the high vastness.
9   Distancing himself from the exquisite and the common, he abandons
         his personal concerns;
Then, filled with noble emotion, he gives a long-drawn whistle.

III

Thereupon,
10   The dazzling spirit inclines its luminous form,
Pouring its brilliance into Vesper's Vale.
11   And his friends rambling hand in hand,
Stumble to a halt, stepping on their toes.
12   He sends forth marvelous tones from his red lips,
And stimulates mournful sounds from his gleaming teeth.
13   The sound rises and falls, rolling in his throat;
The breath rushes out and is repressed, then flies up like sparks.
14   He harmonizes 'golden *kung*' with 'sharp *chiao*,'
Blending *shang* and *yü* into 'flowing *chih*.'
15   The whistle floats like a wandering cloud in the grand empyrean,
And gathers a great wind for a myriad miles.
16   When the song is finished, and the echoes die out,

4. A mountain in Honan where Ch'ao-fu and Hsü Yu retired when Yao offered them the empire. Po Yi also went there to avoid Yü's son.

6. This verse touches on the very essence of the theory of whistling as a process of self-cultivation. The two key texts alluded to are the *Tao te ching*, especially chapter 1, and several critical passages in the appendices to the *The Classic of Changes* (see selections 3, 4, and 9).

14. The notes of the Chinese pentatonic scale (*fa, sol, la, do, re*).

15. The grand empyrean is another word for the transcendental void. The wandering is a metaphor for the illusory individual self.

It leaves behind a pleasure that lingers on in the mind.
17   Indeed, whistling is the most perfect natural music,
Which cannot be imitated by strings or woodwinds.

IV

Thus, the Whistler
18   Uses no instrument to play his music,
Nor any material borrowed from things.
19   He chooses it from the near-at-hand—his own Self,
And with his mind he controls his breath.

V

20   By moving his lips, there is a melody;
By pursing his mouth, he makes the sounds.
21   For every category he has a song;
To each thing he perceives, he tunes a melody.
The Music is
22   Loud, but not raucous,
Tenuous, but not terminated.
23   Pure, surpassing both reed and mouth-organ,
Richly harmonious with lute and harp.
24   Its mystery is subtle enough to unfold fully pure consciousness and
enlighten creative intelligence;
Its essence is refined enough to explore completely the hidden and
plumb the depths.
25   It holds back the distressing abandon of a Whirling Ch'u melody;
It regulates the extravagant dissipation of a Northern Ward song.

19. The text comes from *The Classic of Changes*, appendix 2.2. The word *shen* (Self) here is more than just "body" or "person." The whistler finds the music and the means of producing it within himself; this refers to meditation. The sages of *The Classic of Changes* and the Taoist adepts could cognize anything and achieve anything from within themselves without leaving their seat or going out of their "room." Everything is available within the Self. The breath and the mind are closely linked. By cultivating the flow of his attention, he simultaneously gains control over the flow of his breath.

21. The key principle here is found in the continuation of *The Classic of Changes*, appendix 2.2: "The sages make the eight trigrams to comprehend the power of pure consciousness and to categorize the conditions of all things." From any given point of view, each object or situation fits into a category for which there is a corresponding hexagram. Each hexagram consists of yin and yang lines, which may be interpreted as patterns of sound. These are the "songs." So, whenever the whistler perceives something, he immediately transposes it into a "melody." With his control of the vital breath (*ch'i*), he can manipulate these sounds and thereby control any phenomena.

24. "Mystery" and "subtle" recall the first chapter of the *Tao te ching*. In the remainder of this verse, the author weaves in the vocabulary of *The Classic of Changes*, appendix 2.5.

25. Two celebrated dance tunes from antiquity.

26   It turns floods into drought,
      And turns Pure Creativity into Solid Intelligence.

      VI

27   Since the cantos induce all possible transformations,
      The applications of the tunes are unbounded.
28   The harmonious and happy are made joyful and satisfied;
      The grieved and wounded are torn within.
29   At times it is deep and dispersed—about to break off;
      At other times it is strong and harsh—filled with high spirits.
30   It wanders slowly to and fro, persuasive and clear;
      It rises swiftly in a crescendo, complex and intricate.
31   Though you be lost in thoughts, it can bring you back to your Mind;
      Though you be distressed, it will never break your Heart.
32   Whistling combines the eight sounds into perfect harmony;
      Indeed, it stabilizes extreme pleasure without going to excess.

      VII

Now, if
33   You climb your lofty terrace to look out at the view;
      You open your study door and let your gaze roam the distances;
34   With a gasp you raise your head to look up and tap the rhythms;
      With a din your long-drawn canto resonates with reverberations.
35   Sometimes the melody rolls out easily and turns back by itself;
      Sometimes it hesitates, and then lets loose again.
36   Sometimes it is soft and yielding, tender and pliant;
      Sometimes it is rushing and vigorous, like the sound of waves and
          gushing water.
37   Unexpectedly, the echo is suppressed and the torrent dries up;
      Then a pure note floats out, limpid and bright.

      VIII

38   Now excessive vitality stirs up an effusion,
      A confusing mixture, interchanging and intertwining,

   26. "Solid" may more literally be rendered as "redoubled." It refers to the second hexagram (*K'un*) of *The Classic of Changes*, which is made of the *K'un* trigram redoubled. The phrase "Pure Creativity" (more literally, "indomitable or excessive yang") refers to the sixth line of the first hexagram (*Ch'ien*). The sense here is that yang has reached its maximum when we have six solid yang lines forming *Ch'ien*. The power of the whistle can turn the pure yang hexagram, *Ch'ien*, inside out to form the pure yin hexagram, *K'un*. This shows the capacity of whistling to take us from one pole of creation to the opposite pole.
   32. Eight kinds of musical sounds—produced from the calabash (gourd), earthenware, stretched hides, wood, stone, metal, silk strings, and bamboo.
   38. The expression rendered as "interchanging and intertwining" also happens to be a technical term for the way the hexagrams of *The Classic of Changes* interrelate.

39   Like a rising whirlwind, *lieh-lieh*,
      Tracing echoes, *chiu-chiu*;
40   Or like the long-drawn neighing of a Tatar horse,
      Facing into the cold wind of the northern steppes.
Or also like
41   The wild goose leading her little ones;
      The flock cries out as it flies over the desert wastes.

       IX

Thus, the Whistler can
42   Create tones based on the forms,
      Compose melodies in accordance with affairs;
43   Respond without limit to the things of Nature,
      Trigger his inspiration, sending echoes rushing off,
44   Like a turbulent torrent bursting forth,
      Or clouds piling up endlessly,
45   Now breaking up, now running together,
      About to die out—and then continuing.

       X

46   Fei Lien, the Wind God, swells out of his deep cavern,
      And a fierce tiger replies with a howl in the central valley.
47   The Southern Sieve moves in the vaulted sky,
      And a bright whirlwind quivers in the lofty trees.
48   It shatters our crammed-up cares and scatters them,
      Purging the turbid constipations of life's dusty cloud.
49   It works the changes of yin and yang in perfect harmony,
      And transforms the base vulgarity of lewd customs.

       XI

Now if the Whistler
50   Wanders over lofty ridges and crags,
      crossing a huge mountain,
51   And, at the edge of a gorge,
      overlooking a purling stream,
52   Sits down on a massive rock,
      And rinses his mouth with the sparkling spring;

   39. The italicized bisyllabic words in this line, here somewhat anachronistically given in their MSM pronunciation, are onomatopoeic descriptions of how the whirlwind rose and the echoes were traced. A fairly common device in ancient Chinese poetry, it probably derives from the vernacular realm. Especially in highly colloquial or topolectal speech, many Chinese are still fond of employing such expressions.
   46. For the Wind God, compare selection 122, line III.51 and note 50.
   47. The Southern Sieve is a constellation.

53   Or leans into a luxuriant profusion of marsh-orchids,
     In the shade of the elegant charm of tall bamboos—
54   Then his warble pours forth,
     An endless succession of echoing reverberations.
55   He unfolds the melancholic thoughts harbored mutely in his mind;
     And arouses his most intimate feelings, which have long been knotted
        up.
56   His heart, cleansed and purified, is carefree;
     His mind, detached from the mundane, is sylphlike.

     XII

Should he then
57   Imitate gong and drum,
     Or mime clay vessels and gourds;
58   There is a mass of sound like many instruments playing—
     Like reed pipe and flute of bamboo—
59   Bumping boulders trembling,
     An horrendous crashing, smashing, rumbling.
Or should he
60   Sound the tone chih, then severe winter becomes steaming hot;
     Give free play to yü, then a sharp frost makes summer fade;
61   Move into shang, then an autumn drizzle falls in springtime;
     Strike up the tone chiao, then a vernal breeze soughs in the bare
        branches.

     XIII

62   The eight sounds and five harmonies constantly fluctuate;
     The melody follows no strict beat.
63   It runs, but does not run off;
     It stops, but does not stop up.
64   Following his mouth and lips, it expands forth;
     Floating on his fragrant breath, it travels afar.
65   The music is terse and exquisite, with flowing echoes;
     The sound stimulates brilliance, with its clear staccatos.
66   Indeed, with its supreme natural beauty,
     It is quite distinguished and incomparable!
67   It transcends the music of Shao Hsia and Hsien Ch'ih;
     Why vainly find the exotic in Cheng and Wei?

     60–61. See note to verse 14 for the identification of these four musical tones.
     67. Whistling is more sublime than the music of Shao Hsia and Hsien Ch'ih, two musicians
of the mythical Yellow Emperor. It is more wild and exotic than the music of Cheng and Wei,
two states known for the dissipation of their music.

XIV

For when the Whistler performs,
68   Mien Chü holds his tongue and is distraught;
      Wang Pao silences his mouth and turns pale.
69   Duke Yü stops singing in the middle of a song;
      Master Ning restrains his hands from tapping and sighs deeply.
70   Chung Ch'i abandons his lute and listens instead;
      Confucius forgets the taste of meat and stops eating.
71   The various animals all dance and stomp their feet;
      The paired phoenixes come with stately mien and flap their wings.
72   They understand the magnificent beauty of the long-drawn Whistle;
      Indeed, this is the most perfect of sounds!

Translated by Douglass A. White

68. Mien Chü was famous for singing in a prolonged manner whereas Wang Pao was noted for singing in an abrupt manner.

69. Duke Yü was a great singer of the Han period whose voice shook the rafters and raised the dust. Master Ning was remembered for singing a deeply moving, sad song.

70. Chung Ch'i was a celebrated lutanist. It is said that Confucius forgot the taste of meat for three months after hearing the music of Shao.

126
The Return

T'ao Ch'ien (365–427)

I was poor, and what I got from farming was not enough to support my family. The house was full of children, the rice-jar was empty, and I could not see any way to supply the necessities of life. Friends and relatives kept urging me to become a magistrate, and I had at last come to think I should do it, but there was no way for me to get such a position. At the time I happened to have business abroad and made a good impression on the grandees as a conciliatory and humane sort of person. Because of my poverty an uncle offered me a job in a small town, but the region was still unquiet and I trembled at the thought of going away from home. However, P'eng-tse[1] was only thirty miles from my native place, and the yield of the fields assigned the magistrate was sufficient to keep me in wine, so I applied for the office.

For information on the author, see selection 20.

1. Just southeast of the present-day town of the same name and ten miles east of the present-day town of Hu-k'ou in Kiangsi.

Before many days had passed, I longed to give it up and go back home. Why, you may ask. Because my instinct is all for freedom, and will not brook discipline or restraint. Hunger and cold may be sharp, but this going against myself really sickens me. Whenever I have been involved in official life I was mortgaging myself to my mouth and belly, and the realization of this greatly upset me. I was deeply ashamed that I had so compromised my principles, but I was still going to wait out the year, after which I might pack up my clothes and slip away at night. Then my sister who had married into the Ch'eng family died in Wu-ch'ang,[2] and my only desire was to go there as quickly as possible. I gave up my office and left of my own accord. From mid-autumn to winter I was altogether some eighty days in office, when events made it possible for me to do what I wished. I have entitled my piece "The Return"; my preface is dated the eleventh moon of the year Yi-ssu (405).

> To get out of this and go back home!
> My fields and garden will be overgrown with weeds—
>   I must go back.
> It was my own doing that made my mind my body's slave
> Why should I go on in melancholy and lonely grief?
> 5   I realize that there's no remedying the past
> But I know that there's hope in the future.
> After all I have not gone far on the wrong road
> And I am aware that what I do today is right, yesterday wrong.
> My boat rocks in the gentle breeze
> 10   Flap, flap, the wind blows my gown;
> I ask a passerby about the road ahead,
> Grudging the dimness of the light at dawn.
> Then I catch sight of my cottage—
>   Filled with joy I run.
> 15   The servant boy comes to welcome me
>   My little son waits at the door.
> The three paths[3] are almost obliterated
>   But pines and chrysanthemums are still here.
> Leading the children by the hand, I enter my house
> 20   Where there is a bottle filled with wine.
> I draw the bottle to me and pour myself a cup;
> Seeing the trees in the courtyard brings joy to my face.

2. In modern Hopei.

3. An allusion to Chiang Yü, an official who became a recluse rather than serve Wang Mang (usurper of the Han dynasty). Chiang had a hut in a bamboo grove, to which he cleared three paths. He sought only the company of two bosom friends; both were men of principle who renounced fame and refused to come out of retirement.

I lean on the south window and let my pride expand,
I consider how easy it is to be content with a little space.
25 Every day I stroll in the garden for pleasure,
Although there is a gate, it is always shut.
Cane in hand I walk and rest,
Occasionally raising my head to gaze into the distance.
The clouds aimlessly rise from the peaks,
30 The birds, weary of flying, know it is time to come home.
As the sun's rays grow dim and disappear from view
I walk around a lonely pine tree, stroking it.

Back home again!
May my friendships be broken off and my wanderings come to an end.
35 The world and I shall have nothing more to do with one another.
If I were again to go abroad, what should I seek?
Here I enjoy honest conversation with my family
And take pleasure in books and cither to dispel my worries.
The farmers tell me that now spring is here
40 There will be work to do in the west fields.
Sometimes I call for a covered cart,
Sometimes I row a lonely boat,
Following a deep gully through the still water
Or crossing the hill on a rugged path.
45 The trees put forth luxuriant foliage,
The spring begins to flow in a trickle.
I admire the seasonableness of nature
And am moved to think that my life will come to its close.
     It is all over—
50 So little time are we granted human form in the world!
Let us then follow the inclinations of the heart:
Where would we go that we are so agitated?
I have no desire for riches
And no expectation of Heaven.
55 Rather on some fine morning to walk alone
Now planting my staff to take up a hoe,
Or climbing the east hill and whistling long[4]
Or composing verses beside the clear stream:
So I manage to accept my lot until the ultimate homecoming.
60 Rejoicing in Heaven's command, what is there to doubt?

Translated by James Robert Hightower

4. For the type of "long whistling" that the author probably engaged in, see selection 125.

127
Red Cliff Rhapsody

Su Shih (1037–1101)

In the fall of the year *jen-hsü* in the seventh month on the day after the full moon,[1] I traveled in a boat with some guests to the foot of Red Cliff.[2] A light wind wafted by, and not a ripple was stirred. I poured wine for my guests as we chanted the poem about the bright moon and sang the song about the graceful maiden.[3] Before long, the moon appeared over East Mountain and

Su Shih or Su Tung-p'o ("Eastern Slope" Su) was one of the dominant figures in Chinese literati culture, influencing not only prose and poetry but also esthetic theory, painting, and calligraphy as well. He was born into a gentry family of limited means and educated primarily by his father, Su Hsün (1009–1066), later famous as a political essayist, and also by his mother, née Ch'eng. He and his younger brother, Su Ch'e (1039–1112), were regarded as newly discovered talents after passing the Presented Scholar examination in 1057 under Ou-yang Hsiu (see selection 174). In 1061, Su Shih passed the special examination held to recruit new officials and began his career as a Case Reviewer at the Court of Judicial Review. During these early years, he wrote numerous memorials identifying critical national problems in areas of finance and military defense. Although supportive of reform, he opposed the overly rapid implementation and Legalist approach of the statesman Wang An-shih's (see selection 55) New Policies. Between 1079 and 1100, depending upon which ruler was on the throne and which faction was in power, Su Shih experienced a series of exiles and pardons.

Though an activist Confucian official, Su Shih was eclectic in his intellectual interests. He was deeply influenced by Zen Buddhist ideals of enlightenment, yet searched for transcendence through engagement with social reality and the natural environment. Such themes as the equivalence of objective and subjective viewpoints, the Tao as a ceaseless alternation between change and constancy, the affirmation of happiness in this life, equanimity toward fate, and endless curiosity about the natural world pervade his prolific writings. His classical poems (*shih*) alone number almost 2,800, of which those containing perceptions of nature and his philosophical views are the most widely read. His lyrics (*tz'u*), numbering about 350, expanded the range of content in this genre and are considered innovative examples of an attitude of "heroic abandon." One of the "Eight Masters of T'ang and Sung Prose," Su was further canonized by the literary tradition as the personification of the Northern Sung *Zeitgeist*—an expansive, optimistic personality who later was celebrated in drama, painting, and the decorative arts.

This is the first of two rhaspsodies by Su Shih bearing the same title. The two pieces on Red Cliff were written during his exile in Huang prefecture. They soon became monuments of Chinese literature and calligraphy, and established the place as a literary shrine.

1. The date is equivalent to August 12, 1082, in the Western calendar.

2. Located in modern-day Huang-kang, Hupei. Su Shih noted elsewhere that Red Cliff was located several hundred paces from his residence in Huang prefecture, but he was unsure whether it was the same Red Cliff where the famous naval battle in 208 occurred between the forces of Wei under Ts'ao Ts'ao (155–220) and those of Wu under the general Chou Yü (175–210). In fact, the battle site was located elsewhere along the Long River (Yangtze), in modern P'u-chi, Hupei. According to some sources, Su Shih's Red Cliff was originally named "Red Nose" because of its color and shape; the names were thought to have been confused because of their similar pronunciation.

3. The poem about the bright moon is traditionally identified as "The Moon Appears" from

lingered by the constellations Dipper and Ox.[4] White dew extended over the Long River; the water's gleam mingled with the sky. We let our reed of a boat follow its course as it traversed myriad acres [5] of expanse. I felt boundless, as if gliding through the void, not knowing where I might land; I felt as if I were soaring about, having left the world behind to stand alone as I sprouted wings to become a transcendent.

Then we drank more wine and reached the height of joy. I beat out a rhythm against the side of the boat and sang:

> Cassia-wood oars,
> Magnolia-wood rudder,
> Stroke the moon's pure reflection
> As we glide upstream on its shimmering light.
> Ever distant, the object of my longings.
> I gaze at the beautiful one
> In a faraway corner of heaven. [6]

One of the guests could play the flute and accompanied my song.[7] Yet his sounds—*wu-wu*—were plaintive, yearning, weeping, accusing. The lingering notes meandered through the air, drawn out like silken threads. They would have aroused a submerged dragon to whirl around in the cavernous depths, and caused a widow to weep in her lonely boat.

I was saddened. Straightening my clothes, I sat up and asked my guest, "Why are you playing this way?" He replied,

> "The moon is bright, stars are few,
> Crows and magpies are flying south.[8]

"Isn't this from the poem by Ts'ao Meng-te? Look westward and there is Hsia-k'ou. Look east and there lies Wu-ch'ang.[9] The mountains and the river

---

the *Classic of Odes,* in which the moon is a beautiful woman whose unattainability provokes longing and anxiety. The poem about the graceful maiden is " '*Kuan-kuan'* Cry the Ospreys," also from the *Classic of Odes,* in which a nobleman courts a virtuous lady for his palace. See selection 16 (poem 1).

4. These constellations lie above the northern horizon, indicating that Su was looking toward the northeast.

5. The Chinese word used is actually a unit of measure equal to approximately sixteen acres.

6. In the traditional Confucian interpretation of poetry, such imagery of the distant beauty personified as the moon can be read as the exile's longing for the imperial court. Naturally, other more erotic and metaphysical interpretations are also possible.

7. Later commentators have identified this guest as Yang Shih-ch'ang, a Taoist known for his expert playing of the *hsiao* (vertical bamboo flute).

8. A quote from a poem by Ts'ao Ts'ao, courtesy name Meng-te. Ts'ao wrote two ballads entitled "Short Song" (Tuan-ko hsing) sometime after the Battle of Red Cliff in 208. The first, from which these lines are taken, begins with melancholy observations about the futility of human ambition and the shortness of life but ends with a renewed determination to unify the country.

9. The city of Hsia-k'ou, built by the Wu emperor Sun Ch'üan (reigned 222–252) in 223,

encircle one another; how dense the viridian growth! Yet is this not the place where Meng-te was trapped by Chou Yü? [10] He had just conquered Ching-chou and sailed down to Chiang-ling [11] as he followed the course of the river eastward. His fleet stretched bow to stern for a thousand tricents; his banners and flags blotted out the sky. As he drank wine by the bank of the river, he lay down his lance crosswise and composed this poem. Indeed, he dominated his age, yet where is he now? And what about you and me conversing here by the riverbank like a fisherman and a woodcutter, joined by fish and shrimp with the deer as our companions? We ride on a boat no bigger than a leaf as we drink to each other out of simple gourds. We exist no longer than mayflies between heaven and earth, and are of no more consequence than a kernel in the vast ocean. I grieve that my life is but a moment and envy the Long River's endless flow. If only I could grasp hold of a flying transcendent and wander with him through the heavens to embrace the bright moon and live forever. But, I realize this cannot be attained so I confide these lingering sounds to the sad autumn wind."

I said, "Do you really understand the water and the moon? Here, it flows by yet never leaves us; over there, it waxes and wanes without growing or shrinking. If you look at things as changing, then heaven and earth do not last for even the blink of an eye. If you look at them as unchanging, then I along with everything am eternal. So why be envious? Moreover, each thing within heaven and earth has its master. If I did not possess it, then I would not take even a hair of it. However, the pure wind over the river becomes sound when our ears capture it, and the bright moon between the mountains takes on form when our eyes encounter it. There is no prohibition against our acquiring them, and we can use them without ever consuming them. They are from the inexhaustible treasury of the Creator of Things, which you and I can enjoy together."

My guest became happy and laughed. We washed out the cups and drank again. Soon the food was gone, and the cups and plates were strewn about. We lay down in the boat, leaning against each other for pillows, unaware that it was becoming light in the east.

Translated by Richard Strassberg

---

was located in modern-day Wu-ch'ang, Hupei; ancient Wu-ch'ang was located in modern Ŏ-ch'eng district, Hupei, and was not the modern city of the same name.

10. A reference to the Battle of Red Cliff in 208.

11. Ching-chou refers to a city, now Hsiang-yang, Hupei, which administered a region in the Later Han covering much of modern Hupei and Hunan provinces. Ts'ao Ts'ao was able to obtain this strategic place by the surrender of the commander without a fight. Chiang-ling was located in modern-day Chiang-ling, Hupei.

Folk and Folklike Songs, Ballads, and Narrative Verse

128
Song of the Great Wind

Liu Pang (256–195 B.C.E.)

A great wind arises—billowing clouds fly;
His majesty dominating all within the seas, he returns to his old hometown.
Where can he find brave warriors to guard the four directions?

Translated by Victor H. Mair

The poet was founder of the Han dynasty.

129
Cock-Phoenix, Hen-Phoenix

Ssu-ma Hsiang-ju (c. 179–118 B.C.E.)

Preface

While Ssu-ma Hsiang-ju was traveling through Lin-ch'iung, a rich man there named Cho Wang-sun had a daughter, Wen-chün, who had recently been

Two songs set to the accompaniment of the lute.

The author hailed from Chengtu, the old capital of Shu in modern-day Szechwan. Very poor until his literary talent was finally recognized by the Han emperor Wu, he was the author

widowed. She hid behind a screen and peeped through. Hsiang-ju won her heart with these songs:

Cock-Phoenix

Cock-phoenix, cock-phoenix goes back to his hometown
From roaming the four seas in search of his hen.
Unlucky days—he found no way to meet her.
What a surprise! Tonight up in this hall,
In this very place is a girl sweet and pretty.
My bedroom so near, she so far—it pains my heart.
How can we be mandarin ducks caressing neck to neck?

Hen-Phoenix

Hen-phoenix, oh hen-phoenix, come nest with me!
Tail to tail we'll breed, be my bride forever!
Passionately entwined, bodies ones, hearts united,
At midnight come with me! Who will ever know?
Let's rise together wing to wing and fly on high.
Unmoved by my love she makes me pine.

Translated by Anne Birrell

---

of several famous rhapsodies, a genre popular in the Han era, the best known of these being "Sir Fantasy" and "Shang-lin Park."

130

Ground-Thumping Song

Anonymous (Western Han?)

When the sun comes up we work,
when the sun goes down we rest.
We dig a well to drink,
plow the fields to eat—
the Emperor and his might—what are they to us!

Translated by Burton Watson

Reputed to be a song of very early times sung by peasant elders as they beat on the ground to keep time. In irregular meter.

131

A Song

Li Yen-nien (c. 140–87 B.C.E.)

In the north there is a lovely woman,
Beyond compare, unique.
One glance destroys a man's city,
A second glance destroys a man's kingdom.
Would you rather not know a city and kingdom destroyer?
Such beauty you won't find twice!

Translated by Anne Birrell

Li Yen-nien was a court musician and entertainer in the reign of the Han emperor Wu. He had a beautiful sister whose praises he sang before the emperor in this poem. The emperor was introduced to her, and she became his favorite concubine. She received the title of *Fu-jen*, translated as "Lady," and Li Yen-nien was promoted to the rank of Harmonizer of the Tones. His poem, considered to be the earliest example of the pentasyllabic meter, belongs to the *ko-shih* (song-poem) category. It alludes in lines 3–4 to song 264 of the *Classic of Odes*, and itself became a much quoted verse.

132

Lost Horizon

Attributed to Hsi-chün (fl. 110 B.C.E.)

Preface

In the reign of Emperor Wu of the Han dynasty during the years 110–104 B.C.E., the emperor made Hsi-chün, daughter of the king of Chiangtu,[1] a princess and married her off to Kunmi, the ruler of the Wusun tribe.[2] When she reached their land, she settled in Kunmi's palace. Through all those years she only met him once or twice, but did not speak to him. The princess became melancholy and composed a song[3] that went like this:

My family married me to a lost horizon,
Sent me far away to the Wusun king's strange land.

1. Liu Chien. Since she was the daughter of the prince of Chiangtu, this made her a relative of Emperor Wu.
2. The apparently Indo-European Wusun people lived in the region of modern-day Lake Balkash and northwestern Sinkiang province.
3. This poem features the caesural sound-carrier particle *hsi* (ancient pronunciation *gig*) in each line, reminiscent of the *sao*-song style of *The Elegies of Ch'u* (see selection 122).

A canvas hut is my mansion, of felt its walls,
Flesh for food, mare's milk to drink.
Longing ever for my homeland, my heart's inner wound.
I wish I were the brown goose going to its old home.

Translated by Anne Birrell

133
Song of the Viet Boatman

Anonymous (1st century B.C.E.)

Preface

The ruler of Ngo kingdom in the state of Ch'u, Tzu-hsi, was traveling in a blue-plumed boat with a kingfisher awning. The Viet oarsman fell in love with Tzu-hsi, and sang a Viet song as he plied the oars. The ruler of Ngo was touched. Full of desire, he raised his embroidered quilt and covered the boatman. His song went like this:

Tonight, what sort of night?
I tug my boat midstream.
Today, what sort of day?
I share my boat with my lord.
Though ashamed, I am loved.
Don't think of slander or disgrace!
My heart will never fail,
For I have known my lord.
On a hill is a tree, on the tree is a bough.
My heart delights in my lord, though he will never know.

Translated by Anne Birrell

Initially recorded in the first century B.C.E. by Liu Hsiang, this poem apparently derives from an earlier oral tradition of the southern state of Viet (pronounced Yüeh in Modern Standard Mandarin) and was then rendered in the Ch'u language (another southern tongue), whence it seems to have been translated into Sinitic, i.e., Chinese. It has in its present form elements of the *sao*-song style, similar to some poems in *The Elegies of Ch'u* (see selection 122). This poem is thought by many critics to offer evidence of homosexuality in ancient China.

134
Mulberry Up the Lane

Anonymous (c. 100 C.E.)

Sunrise at the southeast corner
Shines on our Ch'in [1] clan house.
The Ch'in clan has a fair daughter,
She is called Lofu.

Lofu is good at silkworm mulberry,
She picks mulberry at the wall's south corner.
Green silk is her basket strap,
Cassia her basket and pole.

On her head a twisting-fall hairdo,
At her ears bright moon pearls.
Green silk is her lower skirt,
Purple silk is her upper shirt.

Passersby see Lofu,
Drop their load, stroke their beard.
Young men see Lofu,
Take off caps, put on headbands.
The plowman forgets his plow,

The first of six old folk-songs preserved in the *Jade Terrace* anthology (see selection 25), this is the famous narrative poem concerning Ch'in Lofu, about whom refrains occur in many later love poems. It goes by several other titles, including "The Sun Rises from the Southeast Corner Suite" and "The Lofu Love-Song Suite." A "suite" is a series of related stanzas linked to make one long poem. Ch'in Lofu is also mentioned as a model of feminine decorum in the still longer and more famous narrative poem entitled "A Peacock Southeast Flew" (see selection 142).

"Folk-song" is used as a general reference for the poetic form called *yüeh-fu*. Often translated simply as "ballad," this term originally signified the Bureau of Music re-established by the Han emperor Wu about 120 B.C.E. on the model of an earlier office set up by the Ch'in dynasty. It then came to mean those anonymous folk-songs collected by officials attached to this bureau. Still later, the term indicated folk-songs in general, whether they were genuine folk pieces or polished imitations by named poets. They are characterized by narrative, formulaic, and musical elements, as well as by simple diction, bold imagery, and punning devices. The earlier type of *yüeh-fu* was metrically irregular, while the later version was metrically inseparable from the old poem (*ku-shih*).

1. Ch'in Lofu, the daughter of the Ch'in clan from Hantan, capital of the Chao state. She married a man called Wang Jen. One day the king of Chao caught sight of her from the pillars and parapet of his palace terrace when she was picking mulberry up the lanes. He was so attracted to her that he asked her to drink with him. She eluded his advances by composing a song for the lute, "Mulberry up the Lane," in which she praised her husband and rejected the casual love of a passing official. The king then desisted from his efforts to seduce her.

The hoer forgets his hoe.
They come home cross and happy—
All from seeing Lofu.

A prefect from the south is here,
His five horses stand pawing the ground.
The prefect sends his servant forward
To ask, "Whose is the pretty girl?"
"The Ch'in clan has a fair daughter,
Her name is Lofu."
"Lofu, how old is she?"
"Not yet quite twenty,
A bit more than fifteen."

The prefect invites Lofu,
"Wouldn't you like a ride with me?"
Lofu steps forward and refuses:
"You are so silly, Prefect!
You have your own wife, Prefect,
Lofu has her own husband!
In the east more than a thousand horsemen,
My husband is in the lead.
How would you recognize my husband?
His white horse follows black colts,
Green silk plaits his horse's tail,
Yellow gold braids his horse's head.
At his waist a Lulu dagger [2]—
Worth maybe more than ten million cash.

"At fifteen he was a county clerk,
At twenty a court official,
At thirty a chancellor,
At forty lord of his own city.

"As a man he has a pure white complexion,
Bushy whiskers on both cheeks.
Majestic he steps into his office,
Dignified he strides to the courtroom,
Where several thousand in audience
All say my husband has no rival!"

Translated by Anne Birrell

---

2. A dagger with a hilt shaped like the pulley of a well. The word for the ring of the pulley, a pun for return or reunion, naturally evoked romantic associations for lovers who were separated.

135
From the "Nineteen Old Poems"
Green, Green Riverside Grass

Anonymous (Han)

Green, green riverside grass,
Lush, lush willow in the garden,
Sleek, sleek a girl upstairs,
White, white faces her window.
Fair, fair her rouge and powder face,
Slim, slim she shows her white hand.

Once I was a singing-house girl,
Now I am a playboy's wife.
A playboy roves, never comes home,
My empty bed is hard to keep alone.

Translated by Anne Birrell

This is the second of the celebrated "Nineteen Old Poems," an anonymous set of fine poems in the new pentasyllabic form evidently dating from the Eastern Han period, although eight of them have been attributed to Mei Ch'eng of the Western Han period (see selection 124). It was imitated numerous times by later poets in succeeding centuries.

136
They Fought South of the Wall

Anonymous (Han?)

They fought south of the wall,
died north of the outworks,
lie dead in the fields unburied,
4 fine food for the crows.
Tell the crows for me,
weep for these strangers!
Dead in the field, if no one buries them,
8 how can their rotting flesh hope to escape you?
Waters are deep, swift and strong,

A music bureau ballad in irregular meter.

rushes and reed banks cluster darkly;
the brave horsemen have fought and died,
12   their weary mounts wander here and there, neighing.
On the bridge they built sentry huts—
how could we go south? how could we go north?
And if we do not gather in the grain and millet,
16   what will our lord have to eat?
We want to be loyal subjects, but what can we do?
I think of you, good subjects,
good subjects, how I remember—
20   at dawn you set off to battle;
night fell, but you never came back.

Translated by Burton Watson

137

Crows on City Walls
A Children's Ditty from the Early Years
of the Reign of the Later Han Emperor Huan

Anonymous (Eastern Han)

Crows on city walls,
Tails down in retreat.
Father became an officer,

Ssu-ma Piao (240–306) included this song in his "Treatise on the Five Elements." He dated the origin of the ditty at around 150 C.E. and the events it "foretold" at around c. 167 C.E. He attached this interpretation to it:

This is a children's ditty circulating in the capital in the early part of Emperor Huan's reign. It refers to government greed. "Crows on city walls,/ Tails down in retreat" means to occupy a position of great advantage and eat on one's own, refusing to share with those beneath one, which refers to those in authority who amass a great fortune. "Father became an officer,/ Son became a conscript" says that when the Man and Yi tribes rebelled, a father had to become an officer in the army, while his son became a conscript and went out to attack them. "One soldier dies,/ One hundred chariots" says that when one man dies in the punitive expedition against the Huns, behind him are another hundred war chariots. "Chariots clatter, clatter/ As they enter Ho-chien" says that when Emperor Huan was about to die, chariots clattered into Ho-chien to welcome Emperor Ling. "At Ho-chien a pretty girl is skilled at counting cash,/ With her cash she makes a mansion, with gold she makes a hall" means that when Emperor Ling ascended the throne his mother, the Yung-lo Dowager Empress, loved to amass gold to make a hall. "On the stone-mill, greedy, greedy, she pounds yellow millet" says that although the Yung-lo Dowager Empress piled up gold and cash, she

Son became a conscript.
One soldier dies,
One hundred chariots.
Chariots clatter, clatter
As they enter Ho-chien.[1]
At Ho-chien a pretty girl is skilled at counting cash,
With her cash she makes a mansion, with gold she makes a hall.
On the stone-mill, greedy, greedy, she pounds yellow millet.
Under the rafter there is a hanging drum.
I want to strike it, but the minister will be angry.

Translated by Anne Birrell

was so greedy she never had enough and she made the people pound yellow millet for her own use. "Under the rafter there is a hanging drum./ I want to strike it, but the minister will be angry" says that the Yung-lo Dowager Empress ordered Emperor Ling to sell offices as a source of cash, and that those who received official emoluments were not the right people. It says that we are loyal and sincere; we are men of honor who look on all this with resentment and want to strike the hanging drum in order to seek an audience. But the chief minister is the one who controls the drum, and he for his part is a flatterer and toady. He is angry and stops me from striking the drum in protest.

1. The place name Ho-chien is the only detail that permits a link beteen the song and historical events. Ssu-ma Piao's interpretation focuses on two targets in the late Later Han: social upheaval caused by war and the greed of the emperor's mother. Ho-chien was an ancient province in the state of Chao, modern-day Hopei. It became a kingdom in the Han and was ruled by members of the royal family.

138

Watering Horses at a Long Wall[1] Hole

Anonymous or Attributed to Ts'ai Yung (133–192)

Green, green riverside grass.[2]
Skeins, skeins of longing for the far road,

Ts'ai Yung, from Honan, was a well-known poet, musician, and calligrapher. He was well versed in astronomy and musical theory, and redacted the authorized version of the six Confucian classics. Later he incurred the displeasure of the authorities and was condemned to death, the sentence commuted to having his hair pulled out. Eventually Ts'ai became a recluse. When the warlord Tung Cho challenged the Han dynasty he summoned Ts'ai to court, inviting him to take office and ennobling him as a marquis. At Tung's defeat, Ts'ai was again imprisoned for an indiscreet remark, and he died in jail. He was known by the colorful nickname "Drunken

The far road I cannot bear to long for.
In bed at night I see him in dreams,
Dream I see him by my side.
Suddenly I wake in another town,
Another town, each in different parts.
I toss and turn, see him no more.

Withered mulberry knows wind from the skies,
Ocean waters know chill from the skies.
I go indoors, everyone self-absorbed,
Who wants to speak for me?

A traveler came from far away,
He brought me a double-carp.[3]
I call my children and cook the carp.
Inside there is a white silk letter.
I kneel down and read the white silk letter.
What does it say in the letter, then?
Above it has "Try and eat!"
Below it has "I'll always love you."

Translated by Anne Birrell

Dragon" for his drinking bouts. Ts'ai was the subject of a play by the fourteenth-century playwright Kao Ming, who portrayed him in less than flattering terms. The title of the play is "The Lute."

1. The "long wall" was part of a system of defensive fortifications that was built starting from the Chou period and was linked up more closely during the Ch'in period. It ultimately came to be part of the group of fortified barriers now known collectively as the Great Wall.

2. Compare the first line of selection 135.

3. In the old poems a letter was sometimes carried in a container shaped like a fish, which was said to be "cooked" when opened. The carp is a prolific fish, and the double carp was probably an emblem of fertility or wedded bliss.

139

Song on Enduring the Cold

Ts'ao Ts'ao (155–220)

North we climb the T'ai-hang Mountains;[1]
the going's hard on these steep heights!

This poem was probably written early in 206, when Ts'ao Ts'ao was crossing the T'ai-hang Mountains between Shansi and Hopei to attack a rival. The author was the founder of the Wei

Sheep Gut Slope dips and doubles,
enough to make the cartwheels crack.

Stark and stiff the forest trees,
the voice of the north wind sad;
crouching bears, black and brown, watch us pass;
tigers and leopards howl beside the trail.

Few men live in these valleys and ravines
where snow falls thick and blinding.
With a long sigh I stretch my neck;
a distant campaign gives you much to think of.

Why is my heart so downcast and sad?
All I want is to go back east,
but waters are deep and bridges broken;
halfway up, I stumble to a halt.

Dazed and uncertain, I've lost the old road,
night bearing down but nowhere to shelter;
on and on, each day farther,
men and horses starving as one.

Shouldering packs, we snatch firewood as we go,
chop ice to use in boiling our gruel—
That song of the Eastern Hills [2] is sad,
a troubled tale that fills me with grief.

Translated by Burton Watson

---

dynasty and father of the noted poets Ts'ao Chih (192–232) and Ts'ao P'i (187–226). Ts'ao P'i was also the first critic in China to treat literature as a medium of esthetic expression rather than as a mere vehicle for political propaganda and didactic instruction. Ts'ao Ts'ao is the antihero of the famous historical novel entitled *Romance of the Three Kingdoms* (*San-kuo chih yen-yi*).

1. A large mountain system stretching through several of China's northern provinces.
2. *Odes* 156, a song describing the hardships of a military campaign.

140
Pity Me!

Fu Hsüan (217–278)

Pity me! my body is female,
My lowly state is hard to describe.

Born in Shensi, the poet rose from poverty and obscurity to wealth and fame through his literary talent. He served as censor and lord chamberlain under the Chin emperor Wu.

A boy faces door and gate,
Comes down on earth with a natural birthright,
His manly heart burns for the four seas,
Ten thousand leagues he yearns for windy dust.

A girl is born, there is no celebration,
She is not her family's prized jewel.
Grown up she is hidden in private rooms,
Veils her head, too shy to look on others.

Shedding tears she marries in another village,
Sudden like a cloudburst of rain.
With bowed head she calms her features,
White teeth clenched beneath red lips.
She kneels down countless times
To maids and concubines like grim guests.
Happy love is like Cloudy Han,[1]
Like mallow or bean that leans toward spring sun.
Loving hearts in conflict are worse than water on fire,
One hundred wrongs are heaped upon the girl.

Her jade face with the years alters,
Her husband takes many new loves.
Once they were form and shadow,
Now they are Hun and Chinese.
Hun and Chinese sometimes see each other.
Love once severed is remote as Antares and Orion.[2]

Translated by Anne Birrell

1. The celestial river, counterpart of the Milky Way in the West. It is also called Starry River, Long River, Long Han, Sky River, or River of Heaven. It was believed that the Yellow River on earth flowed from the Han River in the sky. This reference usually conjures up ideas of the amorous legend of the Weaver Girl and Herdboy stars. The Han River is seen as an obstacle between the stellar lovers as it is in full flood every night of the year except the seventh night of the seventh month. On that night the waters ebb, allowing the lovers to meet. Weaver Girl is sometimes called the Girl of the Han River.

2. In Chinese lore, these two astronomical bodies are believed to be quareling brothers who never meet. In equinoctial opposition, they symbolize estranged lovers or friends.

141
Midnight Songs

Anonymous (late 4th century)

1

The sun sinks low. I
go to my front gate,
and look long, and see
you passing by.

Seductive face,
so many charms,
such hair!

Tradition has it that these untitled poems were written by a woman known as Tzu-yeh (Midnight). She lived sometime before the end of the fourth century and evidently made her living as a professional singer. Her dialect was of southeast China, a region known for its women poets.

The originals of these translations appear in a group of forty-two poems attributed to Midnight. The number for each poem here simply reflects its position in the collection. These lyrics might actually be the work of more than one person; and probably many female entertainers composed such popular poems using the sad melody—now lost—to which the words were originally sung.

Other sequences, such as the seventy-five "Midnight Songs on the Four Seasons," testify to the continuing popularity of poetry in this voice. Later poets—including men of the educated class—found the poems moving, artistically satisfying, and well worth imitating. As witty, fluent examples of the five-syllable quatrain form, they had a significant influence on the poetry of ensuing centuries.

The poems display a range of attitudes toward love and desire. Sometimes the speaker expresses heartbreak, and other times, intense physical longing. At times she is playful, cynical, or wry. Often the original texts can as easily be read in the third person as in the first. However, they do use personal pronouns—such as a colloquial word for "I" or for "you, my love"—more than the poetry of elite writers generally does.

The Midnight songs employ a folksong-like—usually female—voice: they are rich in puns on words related to love and passion. The best example in this selection is poem number 7, which uses "silk" as a traditional pun on "thoughts [of love]," along with a word that can be understood as either "a mate" or "a length of cloth." The translation here is necessarily much freer than in the other poems: the last line of the original simultaneously says, "How could I have known [those threads] wouldn't become a length of cloth?" and ". . . [we] wouldn't become mates?"

Certain phrases recur in the poems. This may be evidence that the lyrics were created, and circulated, orally. At any rate, in the first two poems, repeated phrases make it possible to read poem number 2 as an answer to number 1.

After the Midnight songs, the next significant source for poems by women is the mid-sixth-century anthology entitled *New Songs from a Jade Terrace* (*Yü-t'ai hsin-yung*; see selection 25) edited by the court poet Hsü Ling. Out of the one hundred and five poets represented in this celebrated anthology, thirteen are women. See selection 144 for an erotic poem by one of them.

—and sweet perfume
that spills
in from the road.

2

My perfume?
No more
than incense leaves.
Seductive face?
You really think I'd dare?

But heaven doesn't rob us
of desires:
that's why it's sent me
here, why I've
seen you.

3

Night after night, I do not
comb my hair. Silky
tangles hang
across my shoulders.

I stretch my limbs
around that young man's
hips. Is there any
place on him
I could not
love?

7

When I started wanting
to know that man,
I hoped our coupled hearts
would be like one.

Silk thoughts threaded
on a broken loom—
who'd have known
the tangled snarls to come?

9

So soon. Today, love, we
part. And our re-
union—when
will that time come?

A bright lamp
shines on an empty place,
in sorrow and longing:
not yet, not yet, not
yet.

    12

Through the front gate,
my morning thoughts
take off; from river-
isles out back,
at twilight, they return.

Talk and
laughter—who
shall I share them with?
Deep in my belly, dark and
damp, I think of you.

    16

Seize the moment!—
while you're still young.
Miss your chance—
one day, and you've grown old.

If you don't
believe my words, just look
out at those grasses
underneath the frost.

Translated by Jeanne Larsen

142

A Peacock Southeast Flew

Anonymous (5th century)

Preface

At the close of the Han Dynasty, during the years of 196–220 C.E., the
wife of Chiao Chung-ch'ing, the magistrate of Luchiang prefecture, whose

This is a long narrative poem—rare in Chinese literature (it is unique for this early period).
Though it is usually assigned to the third or fourth century, linguistic evidence points to a

maiden name was Liu, was dismissed from home by her husband's mother. She swore to herself that she would never remarry, but her own parents and family brought a great deal of pressure to bear on her. So she committed suicide by drowning herself. When her husband, Chung-ch'ing, learned of this, he also committed suicide by hanging himself from a tree in the garden. A contemporary poet felt deep sympathy for these two and composed a poem about them. It goes as follows:

A peacock southeast flew,
After five leagues it faltered.

"At thirteen I could weave white silk,
At fourteen I learned to make clothes.
At fifteen I played the many-stringed lute,
At sixteen recited *Odes* and *History*.[1]
At seventeen I became your wife
And my heart was full of constant pain and sorrow.

"You became a government clerk,
I kept chaste, my love never straying.
At cockcrow I went in to weave at the loom,
Night after night found no rest.
In three days I cut five lengths of cloth,
Mother-in-law still nagged at my sloth.
It wasn't my weaving that was too slow,
But it's hard to be a wife in your home.
I don't want to be driven out,
But there's no way I can stay on here.

---

somewhat later origin. The extreme length and narrative properties of the poem, as opposed to the brief lyrical and descriptive quality of typical Chinese verse, have prompted some historians to posit Indian influence. Kan Pao (fl. 317 C.E.), however, records in scroll 11 of *Search for the Supernatural* (see selection 204) a story of marital fidelity that contains numerous parallels: a devoted couple, the wife torn from her husband, vows of eternal love despite separation, separate suicides, graves joined by overarching trees, sad chorus of mandarin ducks, and the sympathy of the public for the dead couple. The content of the narrative therefore appears to be Chinese, unless Kan Pao's tale (like many others in his collection) was also influenced by a foreign source. Indeed, many of the themes and features in this extraordinary poem, including the regal bird mentioned in the title and first line, seem to indicate some sort of connection with India.

The poem also goes by another, more Chinese-sounding, title: "An Old Poem Written for Chiao Chung-ch'ing's Wife." The formulaic opening of the narrative contains an image popularly used in the folksong tradition—a bird which becomes separated from its mate or its flock. The theme of separation is echoed toward the end of the story, when Chiao Chung-ch'ing commits suicide on a "southeast" bough of a garden tree.

The preface, of unknown date, appears to have been composed separately. The Luchiang prefecture mentioned in the preface was located in what is now Anhwei province.

1. Two of the Confucian classics.

So please speak with your mother
To let me be sent home in good time."

The clerk heard these words
And up in the hall spoke with his mother.
"As a boy my physiognomy chart was unlucky,
I was fortunate to get such a wife as she.
We bound our hair,[2] shared pillow and mat,
Vowed to be lovers till Yellow Springs.[3]
We both have served you two years or three,
From the start not so long a time,
Yet the girl's conduct is not remiss,
Why do you treat her so unkindly?"

His mother said to the clerk,
"How can you be so soft!
This wife has no sense of decorum,
Whatever she does she goes her own way.
I've borne my anger for a long time now,
You must not just suit yourself!
Our east neighbors have a good daughter,
Her name is Ch'in Lofu.[4]
So pretty her body, beyond compare,

Your mother will seek her for your wife.
It's best to dismiss this one as soon as we can,
Dismiss her, we won't let her stay!"

The government clerk knelt down in reply,
"Now I only have this to say, Mother.
If you dismiss this wife today,
For the rest of my life I will not remarry!"
His mother heard these words,
Thumped her bed, then in a fierce rage:
"My son, have you no respect?
How dare you speak in your wife's defense!
I have lost all feeling for you,
On no account will I let you disobey me!"

The government clerk silent, without a word,
Bowed twice and went back within their doors.
He started to speak to his new wife,

2. At the age of puberty, boys and girls bound their hair. The phrase comes to mean marriage. It is sometimes used with another ritual, the first wine of marriage.
3. The land of the deceased that lies beneath the earth.
4. See selection 134.

Stammered, unable to talk.
"I myself would not drive you away,
But there's my mother, scolding and nagging.
You just go home for a little while,
Today I must report to the office.
It won't be for long, I'll soon be coming home,
And when I come back I'll be sure to fetch you.
So let this put your mind at rest.
Please don't contradict me!"

His new wife said to the clerk:
"No more of this nonsense!
Long ago in early springtime
I left home to come to your gates.
Whatever I did I obeyed your mother,
In my behavior never dared do as I pleased.
Day and night I tried hard at my work.
Brought low I am caught in a vice of misery.
My words have been blameless,
I fulfilled my duties diligently.
Why then, as I'm being summarily dismissed,
Do you still talk of my coming back here?
I have embroidered tunics,
Gorgeous they shine with a light of their own;
Red silk funnel bedcurtains,
At the four corners hang scent sachets;
Dressing cases sixty or seventy,
Green jasper, green silk cord;
Many, many things, each of them different,
All sorts of things in these boxes.
I am despised, and my things also worthless,
Not worth offering your next wife,
But I'll leave them here as gifts.
From now on we'll never meet again,
But it will be a constant comfort for me,
If you never, never forget me!"

The cock crew, outside it was getting light.
The new wife got up and carefully dressed.
She puts on her broidered lined gown
And four or five different things.
On her feet she slips silk shoes;
On her head tortoise-shell combs gleam;
Round her waist she wears flowing silk white,

On her ears wears bright moon pendants.
Her hands are like pared onion stems,
Her mouth seems rich scarlet cinnabar.
Svelte, svelte she walks with tiny steps,
Perfect, matchless in all the world.

She went up the high hall, bowed to Mother.
The mother heard she was leaving, didn't stop her.
"Long ago when I was a child,
I grew up in the countryside.
I had no schooling from the start,
On both counts would shame the man of a great house.
I received from you, Mother, much money and silk,
I do not want to be summarily dismissed;
Today, though, I am going back home.
I am afraid I have brought trouble to your house."

She withdrew and took leave of her sister-in-law.
Tears fell, beads of pearl.
"When I first came as a bride
You were beginning to lean on the bed.
Now as I am being dismissed,
You are as tall as I, sister.
Care for Mother with all your heart,
Be nice and help all you can.
On the first, seventh, and last ninth [5] of the month,
When you're enjoying yourself, don't forget me!"

She left the gates, climbed the coach, departed,
Tears fell in more than a hundred streams.
The clerk's horse was in front,
The new wife's coach behind.
Clatter-clatter, how it rumbled, rumbled!
They met at the mouth of the main road,
He dismounted, got into her coach.
With bowed head he whispered these words in her ear:
"I swear I won't be parted from you,
Just go home for a little while.
Today I am going to the office,
But I'll return before long.
I swear by Heaven I'll not betray you!"

5. On the seventh and twenty-ninth days of each lunar month, women were permitted to rest from their work.

His new wife said to the clerk:
"I feel you love me fondly,
And you seem to hold me in high esteem.
Before long I hope you will come for me.
You must be rock firm,
I must be a pliant reed.
The pliant reed is supple as silk,
The firm rock will not be rolled away.
I have my father and brothers,
Their temper is wild as thunder;
I fear they will not abide by my wishes,
But oppose me, destroy my hopes."
They raised their hands in a long, long farewell,
For both loves the same wistful longing.

She entered the gates, went up the family hall,
Approaching, withdrawing with expressionless face.
Her mother beat her fist loud:
"We didn't plan for you to return on your own!
At thirteen I taught you to weave,
At fourteen you could make clothes,
At fifteen you played the many-stringed lute,
At sixteen you knew ceremonial rites,
At seventeen I sent you off in marriage,
Telling you to swear not to give offense.
What have you done wrong now that
Uninvited you come home yourself!"
"I, Lanchih, have brought shame on my mother,
But your child has truly done no wrong."
Her mother's heart was broken with deep sorrow.

She had been home more than ten days
When the district magistrate sent a matchmaker.
He said, "We have a third young master,
Charming beyond compare in all the world!
He is barely eighteen or nineteen,
Eloquent, very talented he is!"

Mother said to daughter:
"Go, you may answer 'yes.' "
Her daughter choked back the tears:
"When I, Lanchih, first came home,
The clerk showed me great kindness,

Swore on oath he'd never desert me.
If I were now to betray our love,
I fear this act would be wrong.
Let's break off the betrothal talks.
In good time we'll discuss the matter again."

Her mother explained to the matchmaker:
"In all humility, I do have such a daughter,
She went away in marriage, but is returned to our gates.
She was reluctant to be an official's wife,
How would she please a fine gentleman's son?
I hope you will be successful with other inquiries.
We cannot at present give permission."

The matchmaker was gone many days,
Then a deputy was sent for, asked to reconsider.
"They say they have a daughter, Lanchih,
Whose forefathers for generations have held office.
Say, 'My master says he has a fifth son,
Elegant, refined, not yet married.
My deputy I've sent as matchmaker,
And a secretary to bring his message.' "

Immediately they put their case: "The prefect's family
Has such a fine son,
He wishes to take solemn vows of marriage
And so we are sent to your house."

The mother refused the matchmaker:
"My daughter has already sworn an oath.
What dare a mother say?"
When her brother learned of this
He was disappointed and furious in his heart.
He broached the matter, telling his sister:
"In these arrangements, why are you so unreasonable?
First you married a government clerk,
Later you might marry a squire.
Fortune is like Heaven and Earth,
It can bring glory to your person.
Not to wed this lord now,
What will happen in the future?"

Lanchih looked up and replied:
"In fact what my brother says is right.

I left home to serve my bridegroom.
Midway I returned to my brother's gates.
It's my place to follow my brother's wishes,
Why would I do as I please?
Though I made a vow with the government clerk,
I may never chance to meet him again.
Tell them straight away I agree to marry,
They may arrange a betrothal."

The matchmaker got down from the ritual couch:
"Yes, yes!" and "Quite, quite!"
He went back to the office and explained to the prefect:
"Your servant has carried out your command.
Our discussion has met with great success!"
When the prefect heard this
He rejoiced in his heart.
He scanned the calendar, opened the almanac:
"It will be auspicious this month,
The Six Cardinal Points are in conjunction.
The luckiest day is the thirtieth,
Today it's now the twenty-seventh,
You may go and conclude the nuptials."

Discussions on both sides hastened the wedding gifts,
In succession like floating clouds.
A green sparrow and white swan boat,
At the four corners were dragon banners
Softly curling in the wind.
A gold coach of jade its wheels,
Prancing piebald horses,
Colored silk threads and gold stitched saddles.
A wedding gift of three million cash,
All strung on green cord.
Assorted silks, three hundred bolts,
From Chiaokuang [6] a purchase of fine fish.
A retinue of four or five hundred men
Densely massed set out to the palace.

Mother said to daughter:
"I have just received a letter from the prefect,
Tomorrow he will come to invite you in marriage.
Why aren't you making your clothes?
Don't fail to start now!"

6. Chiao-chou and Kwangchow on the far southern seacoast.

Her daughter, silent, without a word,
Sobbed with her kerchief stifling her mouth.
Tears fell as if poured.
She moved her seat of lapis lazuli,
Set it near the window.
Her left hand held shears and rule,
Her right hand took the sheer silk.
By morning she finished an embroidered robe,
Later she finished an unlined dress of silk.
Dim, dim, the sun was about to darken,
With sad thoughts she left the gates and wept.

When the government clerk heard of this affair
He asked for furlough to go home a while.
Before he had come two or three leagues
His wearisome horse sadly whinnied.
His new wife recognized his horse's whinny,
Slipped on her shoes and met him.
Sadly from a distance they gazed at each other,
She knew it was her long lost one coming.
She raised her hand, patted his horse's saddle,
Her loud sighs tore his heart.
"Since you parted from me
Unimaginable things have happened!
Things have turned out not as we once wished,
Nor could I make you understand.
I have had my parents—father and mother,
Bringing pressure to bear joined by my brother,
To make me consent to marry another man.
You have come back, what do you hope for?"

The government clerk said to his new wife:
"Congratulations for winning such high promotion!
The firm rock square and strong
Could have endured a thousand years.
The pliant reed, once so supple,
Is reduced to this in the space of dawn to dusk!
You may reign supreme like the sun,
I will face Yellow Springs alone."

His new wife said to the government clerk:
"What do you mean by such words?
Together we have suffered this great crisis,
First you, and then your wife.

Down in Yellow Springs we will meet,
Don't betray our vow made this day!"
They held hands, then went their separate ways,
Each returning to their different gates.
For the living to make a parting unto death
Is more hateful than words can tell.
They think of their farewell from this world,
Never in a million years to be brought back to life.

The government clerk went back home,
Up in the hall he bowed to his mother:
"Today the great wind is cold,
Cold winds have crushed a tree,
Harsh frosts grip the garden orchid.
Your son today goes to darkness,
Leaving Mother to survive alone.
For I must carry out a most unhappy plan;
Torment our souls no more!
May your life be like South Mountain's [7] rock,
Your four limbs healthy and strong!"

When his mother heard these words
Teardrops fell with each word:
"You are the son of a great family,
With official position at galleried courts.
Don't die for the sake of that wife!
About noble and base are you so naive?
Our east neighbor has a good daughter,
Meek and mild, the loveliest in town.
Your mother will seek her for your wife,
All will be arranged between dawn and dusk."

The government clerk bowed twice and went back
Sighing long sighs in his empty rooms.
The plan he made was fixed as ever.
He turned his head toward the door,
Slowly he watched, grief's oppressive rage.

That day horses and cattle lowed,
His new wife goes into her green hut.
After dusk had fallen
A quiet hush, people start to settle down.

---

7. Occurs early on in the *Classic of Odes*, song 172, where the blessings of long life and happiness are invoked. A symbol of longevity, the mountain stood south of Ch'ang-an.

"My life will end today,
My soul will vanish, my corpse will linger a while."
She lifts her skirt, removes her silk shoes,
Stands up and goes toward the clear lake.

When the government clerk hears of this act,
His heart knows it is the long separation.
He hesitates under a garden tree,
Hangs himself from a southeast branch.

The two families asked for a joint burial,
A joint burial on the side of Mount Hua.[8]
East and west were planted pine and cypress,
Left and right catalpa were set.
Branch with branch joins to form a canopy,
Leaf with leaf meets in wedlock.
Among them is a pair of flying birds,
Called mandarin ducks, drake and hen,
Lifting their heads they call to each other,
Night after night until the fifth watch.[9]
Passersby stay their steps to listen,
Widows get out of bed and pace to and fro.
Be warned, men of the future,
Learn this lesson and never forget!

Translated by Anne Birrell

8. A sacred mountain in Shensi (see selection 42).
9. Just before dawn (3–5 A.M.).

143
Magic Cinnabar[1]

Pao Chao (415–466)

The king of Huainan[2]
Craving immortality

From Kiangsu, Pao Chao served in several posts under the Liu-Sung emperor Hsiao-wu, the poet Liu Chün. His ambitions were frustrated by the rigid class distinctions of his day, which barred him from the high places that his genius might otherwise have earned him. Compelled to spend his life as a staff writer and administrator for various aristocrats, he was eventually assassinated by rioting soldiers when one of his patrons was forced to commit suicide

Drank potions, ate health foods, read arcane tomes.
Of lapis lazuli his drug bowls, of ivory his plates;
Gold cauldron, jade ladle, he mixed magic cinnabar,
Mixed magic cinnabar,
Pleasured in purple rooms,
In purple rooms where exotic girls fondle bright earrings.
Paradise birdsong, phoenix dance broke his heart.

Translated by Anne Birrell

---

for rebellion. He is generally regarded as a major poet of the Southern Dynasties, especially for his ballads and his innovative developments in the folksong genre.

1. A red mineral used in preparing elixirs of immortality.

2. "South of the Huai [River]"; an area that lies mostly within the modern province of Anhwei. A brilliant group of scholars assembled there by the king of Huainan, Liu An (d. 122 B.C.E.), a member of the royal family of the Han dynasty who upheld Taoism, wrote some of the earliest Chinese texts on cosmology.

144

Added to a Letter Sent to a Traveler

Pao Ling-hui (fl. c. 464)

Since you went away, oh,
I lean on the porch-rail, my face tense.
Nights, no block and pounder sound;
Noontimes, my high gate stays closed.
Within the curtains of my bed, a stream of fireflies;

The female poet Pao Ling-hui was the younger sister of the poet Pao Chao and, like her brother, wrote in the style of refined imitation of Han dynasty folksongs and ballads (see selection 143).

As its opening line, this poem borrows from "Bedroom Longing" by Hsü Kan (171–218 C.E.), a poem of sixty lines by a member of the literary circle under the patronage of the Ts'ao royal family in the Wei dynasty (see selection 139). Pao Ling-hui's poem develops in a very different way from her predecessor's—where he is meditative, she is observant; where he is verbose, she is succinct. The images of the silent block and pounder in line 3 function as surprisingly coarse puns, given the generally decorous eroticism of *New Songs from a Jade Terrace* (*Yü-t'ai hsin-yung*), the mid-sixth-century anthology in which this poem is preserved (see selection 25). The block (*chen*) was a heavy stone on which wet clothes were beaten by a wooden pounder (*ch'u*) to clean and thicken the cloth. Another name for the block was *kao-chen*, also called a *fu*, which is a pun for a man, lover, or husband (*fu*). The tactile, auditory, and visual imagery of the two objects combines to simulate lovemaking.

Out front in the courtyard, a bloom of purple orchids.
Nature's things dry up: they sense the season's changed—
Wild geese arrive: they know a traveler's chill.
Your journey may end at winter's close—
Though spring wears on, I'll wait for your return.

Translated by Jeanne Larsen and Anne Birrell

145
The Ballad of Mulan

Anonymous (5th–6th century)

Click, click, forever click, click;
Mulan sits at the door and weaves.
Listen, and you will not hear the shuttle's sound,
4 But only hear a girl's sobs and sighs.
"Oh tell me, lady, are you thinking of your love,
Oh tell me, lady, are you longing for your dear?"
"Oh no, oh no, I am not thinking of my love,
8 Oh no, oh no, I am not longing for my dear.
But last night I read the battle-roll;
The Khan has ordered a great levy of men.
The battle-roll was written in twelve books,
12 And in each book stood my father's name.
My father's sons are not grown men,
And of all my brothers, none is older than me.
Oh let me to the market to buy saddle and horse,
16 And ride with the soldiers to take my father's place."
In the eastern market she's bought a gallant horse,
In the western market she's bought saddle and cloth.
In the southern market she's bought snaffle and reins,
20 In the northern market she's bought a tall whip.
In the morning she stole from her father's and mother's house;

Mulan (old pronunciation Muklan) was a member of the Šärbi (Hsien-pei) people. This celebrated ballad tells of her resolve to take her father's place in fending off the encroaching Jou-jan nomads. She is often compared with Joan of Arc, although the two do not share much more in common than the fact that they were both women warriors. The people and places in the ballad are all from the far northern borderlands of China, and it is likely that this remarkable work was first conceived in one of the languages of that land of nomads.

At night she was camping by the Yellow River's side.
She could not hear her father and mother calling to her by her name,
24   But only the song of the Yellow River as its hurrying waters hissed and
        swirled through the night.
At dawn they left the River and went on their way;
At dusk they came to the Black Water's side.
She could not hear her father and mother calling to her by her name,
28   She could only hear the muffled voices of Scythian horsemen riding
        on the hills of Yen.
A thousand leagues she tramped on the errands of war,
Frontiers and hills she crossed like a bird in flight.
Through the northern air echoed the watchman's tap;
32   The wintry light gleamed on coats of mail.
The captain had fought a hundred fights, and died;
The warriors in ten years had won their rest.
They went home; they saw the Emperor's face;
36   The Son of Heaven was seated in the Hall of Light.
To the strong in battle lordships and lands he gave;
And of prize money a hundred thousand strings.
Then spoke the Khan and asked her what she would take.
40   "Oh, Mulan asks not to be made
      A Counsellor at the Khan's court;
She only begs for a camel that can march
      A thousand leagues a day,
44   To take her back to her home."

When her father and mother heard that she had come,
They went out to the wall and led her back to the house.
When her little sister heard that she had come,
48   She went to the door and rouged her face afresh.
When her little brother heard that his sister had come,
He sharpened his knife and darted like a flash
51   Toward the pigs and sheep.

She opened the gate that leads to the eastern tower,
She sat on her bed that stood in the western tower.
She cast aside her heavy soldier's cloak,
55   And wore again her old-time dress.
She stood at the window and bound her cloudy hair;
She went to the mirror and fastened her yellow combs.
She left the house and met her messmates in the road;
59   Her messmates were startled out of their wits.
They had marched with her for twelve years of war
And never known that Mulan was a girl.

For the male hare has a lilting, lolloping gait,
63   And the female hare has a wild and roving eye;
But set them both scampering side by side,
And who so wise could tell you "This is he"?

Translated by Arthur Waley

146
Song of the Tölös

Hulü Chin (fl. mid-6th century)

Along the Tölös River,
Beneath the Shady Mountain,
The sky seems like a vaulted yurt,
Covering the wilderness all around.

The sky is azure,
The wilderness is vast,
And when the wind blows, the grasses bend to reveal cattle and goats.

Translated by Victor H. Mair

Hulü Chin, the chieftain of a northern Turkic tribe known as the Tchirek, was attached to the courts of Eastern Wei (534–550) and Northern Ch'i (550–557). His song was said to have originally been sung in the Särbi (Hsien-pei) language current in those courts and subsequently translated into Chinese. Compare the introductory notes to selections 133, 145, and 147.

147
Song of the Breaking of the Willow

Anonymous (6th century?)

Far off I see the River [1] at Meng Ford,
willows thick and leafy there.

Written from the point of view of a non-Han prisoner in the north, this song must have originally been sung in a non-Sinitic language, as is obvious from the last line.

1. The Yellow River.

I am the son of a captive family
and cannot understand the Han man's[2] song.

Translated by Burton Watson

2. "Han" is a term for the largest ethnic group among the Chinese.

148
Army Ballad

Wang Wei (701–761)

The bugle blows, setting the marchers moving,
A grumbling hubbub as the soldiers rise.
Fifes screech, a tumult of neighing horses
As they struggle to ford the Golden River.[1]
Sunset at the edge of a great desert,
Sounds of battle within the dust and mist.
Having bound up the necks of all the famous chieftains,
They return to report to the emperor.

Translated by Stephen Owen

For a note on Wang Wei, see selection 34.
1. This geographical feature fixes the setting of the ballad along the northern borderlands.
Unlike the previous three selections, however, it is clearly written from a Chinese point of view.

149
The Song of Lasting Regret

Po Chü-yi (772–846)

Monarch of Han,[1] he doted on beauty, yearned for a bewitching
temptress;[2]

"The Song of Lasting Regret" is the romanticized retelling of the love affair between the
great Emperor Li Lung-chi (reigned 712–756, posthumously known as Hsüan Tsung) and Yang
Yü-huan, the lady raised by him in 742 to the high rank of "Precious Consort" (*kuei-fei*).
The emperor's infatuation with Lady Yang and his virtual abandonment of government

Through the dominions of his sway, for many years he sought but did
   not find her.
There was in the family of Yang a maiden just then reaching fullness,
4   Raised in the women's quarters protected, unacquainted yet with others.

---

affairs (first to the dictatorial Li Lin-fu, who held sway as Minister of State until 752, and then
to the equally grasping Yang Kuo-chung, a distant cousin of Lady Yang) have long been
regarded in both official and popular history as the main factors leading to the ruin of Hsüan
Tsung's long reign and the near-destruction of the dynasty itself. The effective instrument of
overthrow was a Sogdian-Turkic general with the sinicized name An Lu-shan, who, as a
personal favorite of both the emperor and his consort, gradually accumulated supreme military
power in the northeast border region (near modern-day Peking) and, in December 755, turned
his troops against the government. By July 756 the rebel forces were in position to overrun the
capital city, Ch'ang-an. In the face of this imminent threat, the emperor and his immediate
entourage and military guard fled the capital in the early morning of July 14, intending to take
refuge in Shu (present-day Szechwan) in the southwest, where Yang Kuo-chung had built up a
private stronghold and sphere of influence. The next day, at the Ma-wei post-station (located
some thirty miles west of the capital), the imperial troops killed Yang Kuo-chung and refused
to move on unless the emperor put Lady Yang to death as well. Hsüan Tsung was compelled
to appease the soldiers, and Lady Yang submitted to being strangled to death with a cord
wielded by Kao Li-shih, chief eunuch and the emperor's oldest confidant. After this event the
emperor moved on to sanctuary in Shu, while the heir-apparent Li Heng (posthumously known
as Su Tsung, reigned 756–62) broke off from the main party with a contingent of soldiers to
progress northwest and organize a base of loyalist resistance to the rebels. Shortly thereafter, Li
Heng proclaimed himself emperor; Hsüan Tsung had no choice but to acknowledge his now
emeritus status. About a year and a half later, Ch'ang-an was retaken by T'ang forces, and Su
Tsung invited the old emperor to return to the capital, where he would live out his remaining
years in sad remembrance of earlier glories. But it was not until 763 that the rebellion begun
by An Lu-shan would be fully quelled. When the state was finally reunified, and the forty-four-
year reign of Hsüan Tsung—unprecedented in its splendor—was but a memory, it seemed to
most that a great turning point in history had been passed. Notwithstanding more serious
political and military causes for the disaster, that a reign of such magnificence could end with
such a crash confirmed most members of the traditionally misogynist mandarinate in the view
that the root cause of the debacle was lodged in the emperor's allegedly shameful relationship
with Precious Consort Yang.

This is the view adopted by Po Chü-yi in his poem. But Po is as interested in the sentimental
aspects of the tale as he is in its political implications. Indeed, it is primarily, in his telling, a
love story—one which he allows himself license to embroider at times with incidents contrary
to fact (such as the trampling of Lady Yang under the army's horses and the emperor's reduced
entourage passing by Mount Omei) as well as the insertion of scenes of pure fantasy (such as
the Taoist adept's visit to Lady Yang's ethereal essence in the isles of the immortals and his
conversation with her there).

The latter part of the poem describes Lady Yang's visit to Hsüan Tsung as a ghost. Their
deeply emotional encounter, as indeed their entire relationship, became the theme of many
later poems, stories, and plays (e.g., Ma Chih-yüan's [see selection 107] popular Yüan drama
entitled *Autumn in the Han Palace* [*Han kung ch'iu*]).

The poem was written early in 807 c.e. and was originally supplemented with a more
historically accurate prose recitation of events, "Tale of the Song of Lasting Regret" by Po's
friend, Ch'en Hung. Composed in 120 heptasyllabic lines, the poem is organized in a series of
vignettes set forth in rhyming couplets and in quatrains. These short, lilting units are framed by

Heaven had given her a ravishing form, impossible for her to hide,
And one morning she was chosen for placement at the side of the
    sovereign king.
When she glanced behind with a single smile, a hundred seductions
    were quickened;
8   All the powdered and painted ones in the Six Palaces[3] now seemed
    without beauty of face.

In the coolness of springtime, she was permitted to bathe in the Hua-
    ch'ing[4] pools,
Where the slickening waters of the hot springs washed over her firm
    flesh.
Supported as she rose by a waiting-maid, she was so delicate, listless:
12 This was the moment when first she acceded to His favor and
    beneficence.

Cloud-swept tresses, flowery features, quivering hair-pendants of gold,
And behind the warmth of lotus-bloom drapings, they passed the
    springtime nights—
Springtime nights so grievously brief, as the sun rose again high!
16 From this time onward the sovereign king no longer held early court.

Taken with pleasure, she attended on the feasts, continuing without let;
Springtime followed springtime outing, evening after evening she
    controlled.

---

octets at the beginning and the end of the poem. Rhyme changes in the original are indicated
as stanza-breaks in the translation.

    Po Chü-yi became a Presented Scholar in 799 but, because of his uncompromising honesty
and forthrightness, his official career was not smooth. In his later years, he settled in Loyang
where he formed a society with some Buddhist monks of Fragrant Hill temple and styled
himself "Lay Buddhist of Fragrant Hill." Po left behind more than three thousand poetic works,
making him the most prolific of all T'ang poets. His language was plain and relatively easy to
understand, a cause for scorn by literary critics inclined to more mannered and pretentious
styles. A story about Po tells of how he would not consider a poem finished if it could not be
understood when read aloud to a washerwoman. Perhaps it is his comprehensibility and
naturalness that contribute to making him by far the best-known Chinese poet in Japan.

    1. Po Chü-yi here adopts the convention—often used by T'ang poets when writing of
contemporary political matters—that he is speaking of the first great Chinese imperium, the
Han.

    2. "Bewitching temptress" is literally "state-toppler," i.e., a beauty for whom one would lose
everything.

    3. The dwellings of the imperial concubines.

    4. The Hua-ch'ing (Floriate Clear) Palace on Mount Li, some fifteen miles east of Ch'ang-
an, included several hot springs. Hsüan Tsung was particularly fond of this imperial retreat. He
had the buildings, grounds, and pools refurbished, and removed there with Lady Yang and
necessary court officials at increasingly frequent intervals during the later years of his reign (see
also lines 28–29).

Of the comely beauties of the rear palace,[5] there were three thousand
    persons,
20   And preferments and affection for all three thousand were placed on
    her alone.
In her golden room, with makeup perfect, the Delicate One[6] serves
    for the night;
In a tower of jade, with the feast concluded, drunkenness befits love in
    spring.

Her sisters and brothers, older or younger, all were enfeoffed with land;[7]
24   The most enviable brilliance and glory quickened their doorways and
    gates.
Then it came to pass, throughout the empire, that the hearts of fathers
    and mothers
No longer valued the birth of a son but valued the birth of daughters.

The high sites of Mount Li's palace reached into clouds in the blue,
28   And transcendent music, wafted on the wind, was heard there
    everywhere.

Measured songs, languorous dancing merged with sound of strings and
    bamboo,
As the sovereign king looked on all day long, never getting enough . . .
Until, out of Yü-yang,[8] horse-borne war-drums came, shaking the
    earth,
32   To dismay and smash the melody of "Rainbow Skirts and Feathered
    Vestments."[9]

                       ✳   ✳   ✳

By the nine-layered walls and watchtowers, dust and smoke arose,
And a thousand chariots, ten thousand riders moved off to the
    southwest.[10]

The halcyon-plumed banners jounced and joggled along, moving and
    stopping again,

    5. The women's quarters, whose numerous maidens are now wholly neglected by the
emperor, for whom Lady Yang is the only woman that exists.
    6. The "Delicate One" (*chiao*) figures Lady Yang in the person of Ah-chiao, beloved of
Emperor Wu of Han (Han Wu Ti) in his youth and about whom he once said, "If I could
have Ah-chiao, I should have a room of gold made in which to treasure her."
    7. Besides Yang Kuo-chung, other relatives of Lady Yang, including most conspicuously
three of her sisters, received lavish conferments and marks of favor from the emperor.
    8. An Lu-shan's headquarters, about seventy miles east of present-day Peking.
    9. The new name given by Hsüan Tsung to an exotic Indo-Iranian melody that he rescored
and to which Lady Yang danced in a costume made to resemble the fairy garments of moon
maidens. According to one tradition, the emperor brought the melody back with him from a
mystical voyage to the moon.
    10. The emperor and his personal retinue are fleeing the capital.

36   As they went forth westward from the metropolis' gates, something
    more than a hundred tricents.
And then the Six Armies would go no farther—there was no other
    recourse,
But the fluently curved moth-eyebrows [11] must die before the horses.

Floriform filigrees were strewn on the ground, to be retrieved by no
    one,
40   Halcyon tailfeathers, an aigrette of gold, and hairpins made of jade.
The sovereign king covered his face—he could not save her;
When he looked back, it was with tears of blood that mingled in their
    flow.

                    *   *   *

Yellowish grit spreads and scatters, as the wind blows drear and doleful;
44   Cloudy walkways turn and twist, climbing Saber Gallery's [12] heights.
Below Mount Omei [13] there are very few men who pass by;
Lightless now are the pennons and flags in the sun's dimmer aura.

Waters of Shu's streams deepest blue, the mountains of Shu are
    green—
48   For the Paragon, the Ruler, dawn to dawn, night upon night, his
    feelings:
Seeing the moon from his transient palace—a sight that tears at his
    heart;
Hearing small bells in the evening rain—a sound that stabs his
    insides. [14]

                    *   *   *

Heaven revolves, the days roll on, and the dragon carriage was turned
    around;
52   Having reached the spot, faltering he halted, unable to leave it again.
But amidst that muddy earth, below Ma-wei Slope,
Her jade countenance was not to be seen—just a place of empty
    death.

Sovereign and servants beheld each other, cloaks wet from weeping;
56   And, looking east, to the metropolis' gates, let their horses take them
    homeward.

    11. Those of Lady Yang.
    12. The lofty pass that connects the territory of Ch'in (in which Ch'ang-an is located) with
that of Shu.
    13. About one hundred miles southwest of Chengtu, this is the most important mountain
in Szechwan. It was officially ennobled in T'ang times for its supernatural potency (see selection
183).
    14. The sight of the moon pains him because he remembers other nights when he and
Lady Yang enjoyed it together, just as he recalls the music she used to play as he hears the
plaintive sound of little bells tinkling in the rain under the eaves of a roof.

*   *   *

Returned home now, and the ponds, the pools, all were as before—
The lotuses of Grand Ichor Pool, the willows by the Night-Is-Young
    Palace.[15]

The lotus blossoms resemble her face, the willow branches her
    eyebrows;
60   Confronted with this, would it be possible that his tears should not fall?
From the day that peach and plum flowers open, in the springtime
    breezes,
Until the leaves of the "we-together"[16] tree are shed in the autumn
    rain. . . .

The West Palace and the Southern Interior[17] were rife with autumn
    grasses,
64   And fallen leaves covered the steps, their red not swept away.
The artistes, once young, of the Pear Garden[18] have hair gone newly
    white;
The Pepper Room[19] attendants and their budding nymphs are become
    aged now.

Fireflies flit through the hall-room at dusk, as he yearns in desolation;
68   When all the wick of his lone lamp is used, sleep still fails to come.
Ever later, more dilatory, sound the watch-drum and bell in the
    lengthening nights;
Fitfully sparkling, the River of Stars[20] streams onward to the dawn-
    flushed sky.

The roof-tiles, paired as love-ducks, grow chilled, and flowers of frost
    grow thick;
72   The halcyon-plumed coverlet is cold—whom would he share it with?
Dim-distanced, far-faded, are the living from the dead, parted more
    than a year ago;
Neither her soul nor her spirit have ever yet come into his dreams.

15. Both were famous Han-time sites. The House of T'ang had its own pool of this name within the grounds of the emperor's Palace of Great Light.

16. The *Wu-t'ung* (*Sterculia platanifolia*). Its name is homophonous with the phrase "we together" (*wu t'ung*), and the falling of its leaves in the autumn rain suggests to Hsüan Tsung the extinction of the love he once shared with Lady Yang.

17. Referring respectively to the Sweet Springs Hall in the "palace city" and the Palace of Ascendant Felicity near Ch'ang-an's east market-ward. Both were the residences assigned by Su Tsung to the retired emperor, who was not permitted to live in the grander compound of the Palace of Great Light again.

18. This garden had housed Hsüan Tsung's group of private musicians in the years of his glory and pleasure.

19. The dwelling of the chief consort.

20. The Milky Way.

*   *   *

A Taoist adept from Lin-ch'iung,[21] a visitor to the Hung-tu Gate,[22]
76   Could use the perfection of his essential being to contact souls and
         spirits.
      Because of his broodings the sovereign king, tossing and turning, still
         yearned;
      So he set to task this adept of formulas, to search for her sedulously.

      Cleaving the clouds, driving the ethers, fleeting as a lightning-flash,
80   Ascending the heavens, entering into the earth, he sought her out
         everywhere.
      On high he traversed the sky's cyan drop-off,[23] and below to the Yellow
         Springs;[24]
      In both places, to the limits of vision, she was nowhere to be seen.

      Of a sudden he heard rumor then of a transcendent mountain in the
         sea,
84   A mountain resting in void and nullity, amidst the vaporous seemings.

      High buildings and galleries shimmer there brightly, and five-colored
         clouds mount up;
      In the midst of this, relaxed and unhurried, were hosts of tender
         sylphs.
      And in *their* midst was one, known as Greatest Perfection,[25]
88   Whose snow-white skin and flower-like features appeared to resemble
         hers.

      In the western wing of the gatehouse of gold, he knocked at the jade
         bolting,
      In turn setting in motion Little Jade who made report to Doubly
         Completed.[26]

21. In modern-day Szechwan.
22. A Han dynasty designation for one of the capital portals.
23. The distant deep-blue reaches of the sky, and more specifically—to Taoist initiates—
the region bearing that name in the Heaven of Nascent Azure.
24. The traditional Chinese underworld destination of one's *p'o* or carnal (earth-bound)
souls.
25. "Greatest Perfection" (T'ai-chen) was the religious name adopted by Lady Yang when
she briefly took orders as a Taoist priestess, prior to being recognized with a formal title as
sharer of Hsüan Tsung's bed. Yang Yü-huan had originally been the wife of Hsüan Tsung's
eighteenth son, Li Mao (Prince Shou). Her short period as a Taoist priestess, while not entirely
a sham (Hsüan Tsung was intimately interested in Taoist teachings), served to "purify" her for
attachment to the emperor.
26. "Little Jade" (Hsiao-yü) and "Doubly Completed" (Shuang-ch'eng) are T'ai-chen's
maids. The latter was known in Taoist tradition as an attendant of the goddess Hsi Wang-mu
("Queen Mother of the West," see selection 156, note 5); the former was the beautiful daughter
of King Fu-ch'ai (reigned 495–473 B.C.E.) of the ancient state of Wu.

When word was told of the Son of Heaven's envoy, from the House of
    Han,
92   Then, within the nine-flowered drapings, her dreaming spirit startled.

She searched for her cloak, pushed pillow aside, arose, walked forth
    distractedly;
Door-screens of pearl, partitions of silver, she opened out one after
    another.
With her cloud-chignon half-mussed to one side, newly awakened
    from sleep,
96   With flowered cap[27] set awry, down she came to the ceremonial hall.

Her sylphine sleeves, puffed by a breeze, were lifted, flared and
    fluttering,
Just the same as in the dance of "Rainbow Skirts and Feathered
    Vestments."
But her jade countenance looked bleak, forlorn, crisscrossed with
    tears—
100 A single branch of pear blossom, in springtime laden with rain.

Restraining her feelings, focusing her gaze, she asked her sovereign
    king's indulgence:
"Once we were parted, both voice and face were lost to limitless
    vagueness.
There, within Chao-yang Basilica,[28] affection and favor were cut short,
104 While here in P'eng-lai's[29] palaces, the days and months have
    lengthened.

"Turning my head and looking down to the sites of the mortal sphere,
I can no longer see Ch'ang-an, what I see is dust and fog.
Let me take up these familiar old objects to attest to my deep love:
108 The filigree case, the two-pronged hairpin of gold, I entrust to you to
    take back.

"Of the hairpin but one leg remains, and one leaf-fold of the case;
The hairpin is broken in its yellow gold, and the case's filigree halved.
But if only his heart is as enduring as the filigree and the gold,
112 Above in heaven, or amidst men, we shall surely see each other."

As the envoy was to depart, she entrusted poignantly to him words as
    well,
Words in which there was a vow that only two hearts would know:

27. That worn by Taoist priests and priestesses.
28. The Chao-yang (Splendid Sunshine) Basilica was one of the halls occupied by imperial
consorts during the Han.
29. Named after the Taoist isles of immortality in the eastern ocean.

"On the seventh day of the seventh month, in the Hall of Protracted
  Life,[30]
116 At the night's mid-point, when we spoke alone, with no one else
  around—
  'In heaven, would that we might become birds of coupled wings!
  On earth, would that we might be trees of intertwining limbs! . . .' "
  Heaven is lasting, earth long-standing, but there is a season for their
  end;
120 *This* regret stretches on and farther, with no ending time.

Translated by Paul W. Kroll

30. The Hall of Protracted Life (Ch'ang-sheng tien) was part of the Hua-ch'ing complex on
Mount Li. Its name was used as the title of a famous early Ch'ing drama about the ill-fated
love affair between Hsüan Tsung and "Precious Consort" Yang, ten years and three drafts in
the writing by Hung Sheng (1650?–1704).

150
Iranian Whirling Girls

Po Chü-yi and Yüan Chen

I

Presented by the kingdom of Sogdiana at the end of the Heavenly Jewel
  reign period.[1]

An admonition against contemporary morals.

Iranian whirling girl, Iranian whirling girl—
  Her heart answers to the strings,
  Her hands answer to the drums.

The poets Po Chü-yi (see selection 149) and Yüan Chen (see selection 207) did not simply
fabricate these happenings. Records exist in the official *T'ang History* (*T'ang shu*) of the
presentation of whirling dancers at court as tribute in 718, 719, 727, and 729. They came from
Keš (near Tashkent), Samarkand, Maimargh, and Khumdeh, all of which lay within Sogdiana,
hence we are justified in referring to them as Sogdian or northeast Iranian whirlers. Such
vigorous, rapidly twirling dances were common among the Iranian peoples. Compare, for
example, the sacred whirling dance of the Sufi dervishes, most of whom were Iranians or who
modeled themselves after Iranian styles. As for the pseudo-Iranian whirlers at the T'ang court,
the history of the intrigues surrounding them is described in the introductory note to selection
149.

1. 742–755.

At the sound of the strings and drums, she raises her arms,
5   Like swirling snowflakes tossed about, she turns in her twirling dance.
Whirling to the left, turning to the right, she never feels exhausted,
A thousand rounds, ten thousand circuits—it never seems to end.
Among men and living creatures, she is peerless;
Compared to her, the wheels of a racing chariot revolve slowly and a
   whirlwind is sluggish.

10   When the tune is over she bows twice in gratitude to the Son of
   Heaven,
And the Son of Heaven smiles a bit of a toothsome smile for her.

Iranian whirling girl,
You came from Sogdiana.
In vain did you labor to come east more than ten thousand tricents.
15   For in the central plains there were already some who could do the
   Iranian whirl,
And in a contest of wonderful abilities, you would not be their equal.

In the closing years of the Heavenly Jewel reign period, the times were
   about to change,
Officials and concubines all learned how to circle and turn:
Within the palace was the favorite Precious Consort Yang, without was
   Roxshan,[2]
20   The two were most highly acclaimed for being able to do the Iranian
   Whirl.
She was registered as a consort in the Pear Garden for entertainment,
He was treated as a son in the intimacy of the Golden Pheasant
   Screen.
Roxshan entranced the ruler with his Iranian Whirl,
His soldiers had crossed the Yellow River before the emperor
   suspected him of rebellion.
25   The Precious Consort stole the ruler's heart with her Iranian Whirl,
And when she was murdered by mutinous troops at Ma-wei, he
   thought of her all the more.
From then on, heaven and earth have been out of kilter,
And for fifty years it has been impossible to suppress the dissolution.

Iranian Whirling girl,
30   Don't dance to no purpose;
Sing this song several times to enlighten our illustrious sovereign.

Translated by Victor H. Mair

---

2. Referring to the rebellious general An Lu-shan (Chinese transcription for Roxshan the
Arsacid [i.e., Persian/Iranian]), who was of mixed Sogdian and Turkic ancestry.

II

Yüan Chen (779–831)

When the Heavenly Jewel reign period was about to end and the
    Iranian [3] wished to rebel,
Iranians presented to the emperor a girl who could do the Iranian
    Whirl.
She whirled so well that, before he knew what was happening, the
    illustrious monarch was captivated by her,
And, before long, the bewitching Iranian had moved in with him in
    the Palace of Long Life.

5   The world does not know the meaning of the Iranian Whirl,
But I can tell you what the appearance of the Iranian Whirl is like:

A tumbleweed nipped from its root by the frost and blown wildly by a
    twister,
A red platter balanced at the top of a pole and dazzling as a wheel of
    fire.
Black-dragon pearl earrings fly out like shooting stars,
10   Rainbow halo of a light scarf fast as a flash of lightning.

A submerged whale inhales in the dark, causing the ocean waves to
    dip inward,
A wildly dancing whirlwind, sleet in space.

After ten thousand passes, who can distinguish beginning from end?
Among those seated around her in the audience, who can discern
    back from front?

15   The lower-ranked concubines who look on say to one another:
"The way to win our lord's favor is through circular transformations."
Right and wrong, good and bad—they all depend on what the lord
    says,
North, south, east, west follow upon the lord's glance.

Supplely do her sashes cling to her body,
20   Flying to and fro, they wrap around her like so many bracelets.

Hearing of this, deceitful officials turn over schemes in their hearts,
They confuse the mind of the lord with smooth talk while the lord's
    eyes are bedazzled.

If the lord's words seem to bend, then she crouches like a hook,
If the lord's words favor the straight, she releases as an arrow.

---

3. An Lu-shan (see note 2).

25 Nimbly she pursues the shadows of the moonlight everywhere they
  wend,
  Skillfully she mimics the manifold warblings of the oriole in
  springtime.

Using the lord's power, they overthrow heaven and subvert earth,
Fearful the lord might discover them, they are busily concerned with
  covering up.

The imperial banners travel south to Ten Thousand Mile Bridge,[4]
30 Finally Emperor Hsüan Tsung realizes that things have gone awry.
  This holds a message for those who whirl the eye and whirl the heart:
  Everyone in the nation ought to join in rebuking them!

Translated by Victor H. Mair

4. On his flight to Szechwan.

151
Poem of Medicine Puns

Anonymous (9th century?)

His wife then composed a poem with the names of medicines its theme and,
by means of it, asked him a series of questions:

"I, Belladonna, am the wife of a man named Wahoo,
Who early became a mandrake in Liang.

This *tour de force* of punning is taken from the Tun-huang (see selection 214) story of Wu
Tzu-hsü. The hero was a fugitive from his home state of Ch'u to the state of Wu (Ngwa) during
the latter part of the sixth century B.C.E. The king of Ch'u executed his father and brother
because they had remonstrated with him over his disreputable conduct. On his flight, Wu Tzu-
hsü happens to stop where his wife was living at the time. We should note that Wu Tzu-hsü
has been separated from her for a long time because of his official duties. Although he is in
need of food and shelter, as soon as Wu realizes that it is his wife's house that he has come to,
he wishes to hurry on without being recognized by her, for fear that any knowledge of his
identity might lead to apprehension by the authorities. Wu, however, has prominent front teeth,
and his wife is more than suspicious about who this visitor really is.

Each line of the poem bears at least one pun on the name of a medicine, most of which
are herbs. During the Sung period, there was a category of storytelling which consisted entirely
of such puns. The present text is the earliest and most elaborate example known of this genre.
All of the medicines mentioned in these lines are identified in Victor H. Mair, *Tun-huang
Popular Narratives* (Cambridge: Cambridge University Press, 1983), pp. 275–279.

The Tun-huang story of Wu Tzu-hsü was probably originally composed around the first
quarter of the eighth century, but the actual copy that has been miraculously preserved for us
dates from the late ninth or early tenth century.

Before our matrimonyvine could be consomméted, he had to go back,
Leaving me, his wife, to dwell here ruefully alone.
5   The mustard has not been cut, the flaxseed bed remains unvisited—
Hemlocked in here without any neighbors, I raised my head and
     sighed for my Traveler's Joy:
'Parsley, sage, rosemary, and thyme—
I pray that he'll forget me not!'
Gingerly, I hoped, but I recently heard that the King of Ch'u,
10   Acting without principle and unleashing a bitterroot heart,
Slaughtered my pawpaw and brother-in-law with a jalap! jalap!
Clovered with shame, weak as a wisp of straw,
And arrowhead-swift, my husband fled with fear as a dog would.
Quick as a periwinkle, he became a fungative,
15   And hid amongst the stinkbushes;
But hiding became a hell-of-a-bore.
He seemed like a jackal pursued by horehounds;
Laudanum almighty, how he hopsed and hyssopped like a
     jack-in-the-pulpit!
When I think of it, bittersweet tears stain my bleedingheart;
20   I am arti-choked with antimony.
At nightshade when I sleep, it's hard to endure till the morning's glory;
I recite his name all day until my tongue curls up like a sliver of
     cypress.
His voice, begging balm, so ingenuous entered my ears;
Drawn by aniseedent causes, I dillied up to the visitor,
25   And, seeing it was my long orrised honeysuckle whom I mint at the
     gate,
Sloed down my steps to a hibiscus pace.
And then I saw your toothwort smile;
It reminded me of my husband's dog's tooth violets.
Borax you don't remember me but, no madder what caper you're up
     to,
30   I'm willing to lay out my scurvy Butter and Eggs."

Tzu-hsü answered in the same cryptic vein:

"Potash! Nitre am I this fellow Wahoo whom you speak of,
Nor am I a fungative from injustice.
Listen while I tell you the currant of my travels.
I was born in Castoria and grew up in Betony Wood;
5   My father was a Scorpio, my mother a true Lily-of-the-valley.
Gathering up all of my goldenrod and silverweed,
This son of theirs became a Robin-Run-Around.
Rose Hips was my low-class companion,
Nelson Rockyfeldspar my uppercrust chum.

10   Together with them, I waded Wild Ginger Creek,
      And caught cold in its squilling, wintergreen waters;
      Saffronly, of the three of us, I found myself alone.
      Day after day, my lotus-thread hopes dangled tenuously;
      My thoughts were willows waving in the wind.
15   All alone, I climbed Witch Hazel Mountain;
      How hard it was to cross the slippery elms and stone roots!
      Cliffs towering above me, I clambered over stoneworts and rockweeds;
      Often did I encounter wolfsbanes and tiger thistles.
      Sometimes I would be thinking of soft spring beauties,
20   But suddenly would meet up with a bunch of pigsheads;
      My thoughts would linger over midsummer vetches,
      Yet I could never see an end to my tormentils.
      So I reversed my steps, feeling compelled to spurry back;
      Fennelly, I arrived here.
25   I grow goatsbeard,
      Not dog's tooth violets.
      Methinks you've scratched a fenugreek but found no tartar,
      So furze tell me what you mean and don't make such a rhubarb."

Translated by Victor H. Mair

152

Ballad on the Investigation of a Disaster

Yao Chen (1448–1478)

Having heard that an official was coming to investigate the disaster,
The starving people stood near the head of his horse.
"Are you starving?" asked the official.
"This is a rich village," replied his clerk.
"Our food is already exhausted," said the people.
"There is some extra grain," said the lictor.

Hearing the words of his assistants,
He turned away, unwilling to enter the village.
Starvation and repletion depend upon clerks and lictors;
The official merely holds on to the register in his hand.

Before the investigation, in some cases the people had enough to eat,
Having stored up extra rice during the twelfth month of the previous year;
After the investigation, all the people were starving.

When an official passes by, tax money must be handed over completely;
When he leaves, he will report on his diligent labors—
While the starving people will be weeping together in the night.

Translated by Victor H. Mair

153
The Half-and-Half Song

Li Mi-an (16th century?)

By far the greater half have I seen through
This floating life—ah, there's the magic word—
This "half"—so rich in implications.
It bids us taste the joy of more than we
Can ever own. Halfway in life is man's
Best state, when slackened pace allows him ease.

A wide world lies halfway 'twixt heaven and earth;
To live halfway between the town and land,
Have farms halfway between the streams and hills;
Be half-a-scholar, and half-a-squire, and half
In business; half as gentry live,
And half related to the common folk;
And have a house that's half genteel, half plain,
Half elegantly furnished and half bare;
Dresses and gowns that are half old, half new,
And food half epicure's, half simple fare;
Have servants not too clever, nor too dull;
A wife who is not too ugly, nor too fair.

—So then, at heart, I feel I'm half a Buddha,
And almost half a Taoist fairy blest.
One half myself to Father Heaven I
Return; the other half to children leave—
Half thinking how for my posterity
To plan and provide, and yet minding how
To answer God when the body's laid at rest.

"This is the soundest and most mature philosophy of living comprised in a single poem that I know, although I know, too, that it is one of the most exasperating to the hundred-percenters" (Lin Yutang).

He is most wisely drunk who is half drunk;
And flowers in half-bloom look their prettiest;
As boats at half-sail sail the steadiest,
And horses held at half-slack reins trot best.

Who half too much has, adds anxiety,
But half too little, adds possession's zest.
Since life's of sweet and bitter compounded,
Who tastes but half is wise and cleverest.

Translated by Lin Yutang

154
Mountain Songs

Feng Meng-lung (1574–1645)

My Old Man's Small

1

My old man's small, shriveled and shrunk;
When a crummy horse has no bridle, who enjoys the ride?
The river swells, the boat rides high,
Too bad his pole is short.
How will he ever touch bottom?

2

My old man's small and unromantic;
We share the same bedcurtains but not the same pillow.
I joined to your household a fine patch of land;

The modern literary historian Y.W. Ma has called Feng Meng-lung "the personification of popular Chinese literature," who did more to champion and preserve this sorely neglected field than any other individual in premodern times. A native of the Soochow area in the lower Yangtze basin, he was devoted to the collection and publication of the literature of the people, something otherwise almost unheard of for a Chinese scholar until the 1920s and 1930s. It is indicative of the culturally subversive nature of his enterprise that Feng Meng-lung felt compelled to do his writing, compiling, and editing under dozens of different pseudonyms.

Feng is best known for the three highly acclaimed volumes of vernacular fiction, each including forty short stories, that he collected (see selection 210). He was also involved in the authorship of several historical novels and of a still larger number of plays. Feng's eclectic interests extended to the compilation of joke books (see selection 190) and the writing of rule books for cards and other games. The folksongs presented here were originally sung in the Wu topolect and are of great linguistic importance even in Feng's imprecise sinographic transcriptions (compare the unnumbered first note to selection 161).

Too bad you don't know how to plant it.
Every year the harvest of its flowers will be reaped by others.

No Old Lady

People laugh at me for having no old lady.
But they don't know that "when you scrub rice in a busted sieve, you get a
    lot outside."
Just like a wild mountain cock that spends the night along the road,
The old bird without a nook always manages to squeeze in somewhere.

Fooling Mom

Last night I spent beside my lover
While Mom slept by my feet.
I said, "Lover, when boating on the Yangtze, to get rice from the pot,
Lightly, lightly slip the scoop in.
The iron shovel's rough and bulky,
So slowly, slowly, draw it out."

Smart

Mom is smart,
But her daughter's smart too.
Mom sifted ashes all across the floor,
But I rashly carried my lover into bed and out again,
The two of us sharing a single pair of shoes.

Feeling the Itch

I itched inside and caught my lover's eye,
But once he came to me he wouldn't leave me alone.
From the prow down to the cabin, the deck began to burn;
Luckily my lover put out the fire in my stern.

Translated by Richard W. Bodman

155

A Lament for Fortune's Frailty

from *Cantonese Love-Songs*

Chiu Tsz-yung (fl. 1820–1830)

Man is lonely: the moon shines all the brighter.
Those sinful debts of the sea of lust and of the heaven of love are still
  unpaid.
Since parting and meeting, sorrow and gladness, have their season:
Why is there at all times a blight on famous flowers?
5   Look you! Yöng Fê's [1] jade bones were buried beside the mountain
  track.

The Cantonese love-song was in essence created single-handedly by the poet-official Chiu Tsz-yung (Chao Tzu-yung in Modern Standard Mandarin [MSM] pronunciation). The genre was written in a mixture of three languages: vernacular Cantonese (the poet's native language), classical Chinese (an archaic book language), and Mandarin (the artificial language of the officials [i.e., the Mandarins] based on the speech of the capital [Peking at the time Chiu's book was written, probably around 1828]).

The proper names in the extensive notes are rendered in Cantonese pronunciation to show that the various regions of China had their own greatly different ways of reading the sinographs. Mandarin equivalents are provided in parentheses for those who are not familiar with Cantonese.

1. Yöng Kwai-fê (MSM Yang Kuei-fei), celebrated as the all-powerful favorite of the Emperor Thong Yün Tsung (T'ang Hsüan-tsung, reigned 713–756 C.E.). She was the daughter of Yöng Yün-yím (Yang Hsüan-yen), a petty functionary of Shukchau (Shu-chou) in western China, and bore the childhood name Yuk Wán (Yü-huan, Jade Bracelet/Ring), to which there is no doubt an allusion in the "jade bones" of the text. Having attracted notice by her surpassing beauty, she became in 735 one of the concubines of Prince Shau (Shou Wang), the emperor's eighteenth son. Three years later, on the death of the then imperial favorite, the ministers of Yün Tsung cast their eyes upon the lovely Princess Yöng. No sooner had the emperor obtained a sight of his daughter-in-law than he became violently enamored of her and caused her to be enrolled among the ladies of his seraglio, bestowing in exchange another consort on his son. In 745, she was raised to the rank of Kwai-fê (Kuei-fei), a title second in dignity to that of the empress. Year after year the emperor abandoned himself more completely to amorous dalliance with his concubine, ransacking tributary kingdoms for gems to enhance her beauty and sparing no extravagance to gratify her caprices. These days of licentious enjoyment terminated in the rebellion of Oan Luk-shán (An Lu-shan), the emperor's unworthy minion. During the hurried flight of the court before the advancing insurgents in 756, the imperial cortège halted at the entrenched position of Má Ngai (Ma-wei). The beaten and famished soldiery rose in revolt, and satiated their vengeance in the blood of the imperial consort. With unutterable anguish, the still fondly enamored monarch was constrained to order his faithful attendant, the eunuch Kô Lek-sz (Kao Li-shih) to strangle Yöng Fê (some say she was hanged on a pear tree) and bury her by the roadside (compare with selections 149 and 150).

The grass remained green above Chhîû-kwan's [2] tomb.
In fallen fortune Sîû Tsheng [3] sadly mourns o'er her likeness.
Shap Nöng [4] drank of misery abundant as water.

2. Wong Chhîû-kwan (Wang Chao-chün), a famous heroine of romance. She was said to have been taken into the harem of Hoan Yün Tai (Han Yüan-ti) in 48 B.C.E., where, however, she was hidden from the notice of her imperial lord through the malice of his treacherous minister Mô Yín-shau (Mao Yen-shou). On a report of her beauty reaching the court, Mô was commissioned to bring her to the palace, and she was found by him to be of surpassing loveliness, the daughter of poor but worthy parents. Her father refused to pay a bribe demanded by Mô Yín-shau, who in revenge presented to Hoan Yün Tai a portrait so little like the original that the emperor conceived no wish to see the new addition to his seraglio. She thereby languished in oblivion for years, until chance threw the emperor across her path, and he at once became enamored of her beauty. The faithless minister, his wiles discovered, fled the court and took refuge with the khan of the Hung Nô (Hsiung-nu; Huns), to whom he showed the real portrait of Chhîû-kwan. The khan, fired by the hope of obtaining possession of so peerless a beauty, invaded China in irresistible force and only consented to retire beyond the Great Wall when the lady was surrendered to him. She accompanied her savage captor, bathed in tears, until the banks of the Amur were reached, when, rather than go beyond the fatal boundary, she plunged into the waters of the stream and was drowned. Her corpse was interred on the banks of the river, and it is related that the tumulus raised above her grave remained covered with undying verdure, whence the tomb is called "Green Mound." Another version, perhaps nearer to the truth, has her bearing the khan children and staying with him until old age. This pair of versions constitutes but one of countless examples in Chinese literature of the constant interplay between self/center/Han and other/periphery/"barbarian."

3. The tragedy of this brilliant heroine has been recorded in a book of popular love stories as follows: "Sîû Tsheng was the concubine of a certain graduate of Fúlam: her home was in Kwongleng. Because her surname was the same as that of her lover, it has been suppressed. The girl is only known as Sîû Tsheng [Hsiao Ch'ing, 'Little Green'], and her second names were Wan Nöng [Yün-niang, 'Cloud Lass']. Unusually intelligent, when ten years of age she met an old woman who taught her the *Prajñâpâramitâ-hṛdaya-sûtra* (*Heart Sūtra*). After reading it once, she was word-perfect. The old woman said: 'This girl is precocious in learning, but her fortune will be fragile.'" This prophecy came true, for Sîû Tsheng and her lover's wife became bitter enemies. One day, after a passionate quarrel, in which the wife carried the day, the story continues: "Sîû Tsheng said to her maids: 'Bid the artists' studios send me a good portrait painter.' The painter came, and she bade him paint her portrait. When he had finished it, she took a mirror, and, gazing long into it, she said: 'The likeness is there, but not the expression.' So she set it aside. When a second portrait had been painted, she said: 'The expression is there, yet it lacks vivacity. Perhaps it is because the melancholy of my face deceives you.' So she again set it aside, and bade him take his brush and stand beside her, while she spoke to her maids, looked at them, talked and laughed, or fanned the tea-stove, or chose a book, or plucked at her clothes, or ground paints for the artist. Soon the portrait was painted, surpassing in grace and loveliness. She smiled and said: 'That will do.' When the painter left, she took the picture and made obeisance to it at her bedside, burning joss-sticks and pouring a libation of pear-wine before it. Then with a cry—'Sîû Tsheng! Sîû Tsheng! Was this your fate?'—she fell back upon a chair, weeping like rain, and with the cry she died."

4. Tô Mê (Tu Mei) was the tenth among her brothers and sisters and so was called Tô Shap Nöng (Tu Shih-niang, "Daughter [Who Is] Tenth [Among the] Tô [Children]"). She lived during the years 1573–1620. At the age of thirteen she became a courtesan and at the age of nineteen, when already rich with her earnings, she met in Peking a certain Leï Yü-sìn (Li

In fine, from birth to womanhood more than the half among rosy girls
    are ill-fated:

10   How much the more are we, flowers and paint of love's arbor, injured
    by lustful passions.

Since we are willow blossoms, more than the half of us are weak as
    water:

How can we learn to start stainless from the mire, ever displaying
    ourselves strong and pure?

I fear, I do but fear, that sad autumn will whirl the elm leaves into the
    golden well: [5]

Therefore I must ever be as the winter plum tree which steadfastly
    endures the spite of snow and frost.

15   Methinks in all four seasons flowers and trees are as a happy land.

Only sad men, in face of one another, gulp down their grief and stifle
    their words.

Ah! needs must I myself be wakeful.

Who can bear witness to fortune's frailty?

I were best recount my way of life o'er the Tomb of a Hundred
    Flowers.[6]

Translated by Cecil Clementi

Yü-hsin), whose father, the lieutenant-governor of Chekiang, had sent him there to advance his studies for the civil service examinations. Leï and Shap Nöng fell deeply in love. After a year in Peking, the student had spent all his money, and his father, hearing of his son's doings, ordered him to return home. Shap Nöng went with her lover, and on their way they met a wealthy acquaintance of Leï Yü-sín named Sün Fû (Sun Fu), who, availing himself of the poverty of Leï and his fear of his father's anger, induced the lover to sell his mistress for the sum of a thousand dollars. Shap Nöng, learning of the bargain, brought with her a casket when she was passed from the ship of her lover to that of Sün Fû the next morning. Before the eyes of both Leï and Sün, she opened the casket, showing them its contents of priceless jewels. Then, reproaching her lover for his cruelty and avarice, she held the casket in her arms, sprang into the river, and drowned.

5. Compare the line of Wang Ch'ang-ling (see selection 33): "Yellow in autumn are the elm leaves over the golden well." The story is told of a certain Portuguese astronomer at the imperial Chinese court, who, when asked by a rival astronomer about the day on which summer changed to autumn, replied: "In Hok-kung [Hsüeh-kung, the Palace of Learning] is a well: beside this well is an elm, which, if autumn has not yet come, does not lose its leaves. Take a golden bowl and place it at the edge of the well: then, when the exact day comes, an elm-leaf will fall into the bowl. That is the day!"

6. In a book of Cantonese legends, we read the following: "In the time of Shung Chen [Ch'ung-chen, 1628 C.E.], there was a famous courtesan named Chöng Khîû [Chang Ch'iao]. Upon her death, each of her lovers planted a flower on her tomb. In all there were some hundred flowers. The colors of the flowers were variegated and beautiful. It was within sight of the Jasmine Hill and was called the Tomb of Flowers."

156
Ballad of the Maiden of Lan-ling [1]

Chin Ho (1818–1885)

After the general had broken the blockade at Hsüan-chou,[2]
'Midst triumphal songs he sped along the road;
Marching eastward until he reached the Lai river,[3]
He constructed an opulent encampment.
Portable screens ten layers deep were arrayed with fine silks,
Feathery tassels by the hundreds were hung with strings of pearls;
Carpets with mythical creatures were spread on the ground,
Trees of coral and jade reflected brilliantly in the lamplight.
There were bowls made of tortoise shell and cups fashioned from mollusks,
Pepper flower wine was brewed and lambkins were fatted;
Seated in their furs and embroidery were the toast of the time,
The assembled grandeur of those present was rare for that age.
'Twas said that the general would conclude a wedding ceremony,
The damsel whose betrothal was arranged long ago would join him today;
A matchmaker sent to distant Lan-ling to fetch her
Directed the Soochow boatmen along the rivers swollen with spring rain.

This ballad is unusual for its expansive narrative quality and great length (compare the introductory notes to selections 142 and 145). The combination of folkish diction and high literary flavor in this rhymed work of uneven line lengths is also uncommon, if not altogether unprecedented, in the Chinese literary tradition. Chin Ho was, indeed, one of the most original and forward-looking poets of the nineteenth century. He foreshadowed many of the developments that took place around the end of the Ch'ing dynasty and the beginning of the Republican period, when innovative writers strove to break free from the constraints of traditional norms for versification.

This long verse tale describes the chaotic conditions in the Yangtze valley during its occupation by the revolutionary armies of the T'ai-p'ing T'ien-kuo (Heavenly Kingdom of Great Peace), a massive convulsion which shook central China to its foundations during the middle of the nineteenth century, in the course of which millions of people died. The efforts of the Ch'ing government to retake the area were not without their own ill effects. Like the opium wars which followed it, the T'ai-p'ing rebellion was a major contributing factor in the final collapse of the imperial system. The author of this ballad himself lost over half his family in the depradations of the long struggle between the Manchu government and the T'ai-p'ing rulers. Many of his works severely criticize both the rebels and the imperial forces sent to quash them. Aside from its scathing denunciation of the military leaders, this particular poem is also distinguished by the vivid depiction of the heroine who may in one sense be said to foreshadow the phenomenally popular characters in Chinese novels of knight errantry still being turned out in large quantities today.

1. In Kiangsu province, about thirty miles northwest of Wu district.
2. Modern-day Hsüan-cheng district in Anhwei province.
3. The modern-day Li River in Kiangsu province.

On a beautiful morning with a bright sun and a gentle breeze,
The snow had melted on the warm sandbanks and the waves shone
    aquamarine;
The children at Twin Bridges [4] vied in their cries of joy,
The new year's plum and willow were suffused with spring.
At the stroke of noon, from afar were heard the sounds of bugle and drum,
The vanguard announced that the lady would soon arrive;
Smiling, the general came down the terrace steps to meet her,
Silent, the guests waited in a walled circle around him.
No sooner had her gaily decorated boats docked at the general's gate,
Than a maiden debarked with simian swiftness and hawkish determination.
She was dressed plainly yet elegantly, eschewing ornamentation,
Her expression was as ingenuous as that of a divine being;
If she were not a princess in the retinue of the Queen Mother of the West, [5]
She surely was the Weaving Maid [6] come down from her heavenly palace.
Her tall, slender body standing erect,
A look of troubled apprehension on her face,
She smoothed her dress politely and spoke to the assembled guests:
"You who have come to this hall are all from high-ranking families,
And I am not without my own upbringing;
Allow me to explain clearly from the very beginning.
I am the daughter of an official from Lan-ling,
Whose family encountered many difficulties in these troubled times;
Now I have just my mother and two brothers,
Trying to make do in an out-of-the-way place.
A while back, as I was watering the vegetables on our meager plot,
The general fixed his gaze upon me as he was passing by;
Carrying my buckets, I returned home quickly and closed the door,
Not having exchanged a single word with him.
Yesterday, two officers came to our house,
Bearing coffers overflowing with gold and other presents;
They said that we were already engaged,
And that my mother had previously given her consent.
Today they came a-rowing to bring me here,
Saying that the wedding would be soon and that I should take care not to
    resist.
When my brother merely asked what was going on,
They rebuffed him with loud voices that shook the foundations;

4. A place approximately three miles south of Ch'un district in Kiangsu.
5. A mythical matriarch who was said to live in splendor by a jadelike pool in the far-off K'un-lun Mountains.
6. Vega in the constellation of Lyra, around whom many touching legends grew up.

Several dozen soldiers brandished their swords,
Then milled about menacingly like wolves and tigers.
A command was barked and they swiftly regrouped,
Frightening the travelers on the road outside our door;
The situation was so intimidating that,
Even if I had wings, I would not have been able to get very far.
Had I not agreed to come with them,
The startled souls of our whole family would not have died in peace;
Now that I have come with them,
I wish to ask the general what this is all about."

Seething with anger as she unleashed this torrent of words,
The maiden suddenly reached out with one hand and grabbed the general;
With her other hand resting on a sword that she was about to draw, she
    continued:[7]
"Have I spoken the truth or not?
Have your ears heard me or not?
I want to take you to Soochow,[8]
To accuse you point by point before the governor's tribunal,
Entreating him to inform our sage ruler on behalf of a commoner.
From old, how many famous generals have had their glorious deeds
    inscribed in bronze?
Aside from all of the feudal titles, estates, and rewards of money and silk
    presented by the nation to show its gratitude,
Have they ever been permitted to ravish innocent, defenseless women in
    recognition of their achievements?
When an imperial proclamation comes from the capital, which seems far
    but is actually quite near,
Supposing that it instructs me to marry you,
Wouldn't you be content?
Without the mandate of the Son of Heaven,
There's absolutely no way to solve this dispute.
In your rage you may kill me,
Like a wee, tiny flea or mosquito that has landed on a pile of manure;
Or perhaps I shall take your life with my sword,
And before I have gone five steps, the blood gushing from your neck will
    instantly splatter my homespun skirt.
On the long embankment outside the gate, there are countless wild crab-
    apple trees,

---

7. The maiden's impassioned speech is delivered in a plainer style than that of the rather
florid language which precedes it.
   8. The capital of Kiangsu province.

Beneath them there's lots of empty land for us to build you a lecherous
    general's grave;
Make up your mind fast whether you want to live or die,
What's the point of hanging your head in abject silence as though you were
    shy?"

The general, who usually shouted thundrously,
And who could casually toss a stone weighing hundreds of pounds,
At this moment wore a deathly, ashen pallor,
Then flushed red like a man in a drunken stupor.
His subordinates and bodyguards boiled with fury,
Clenched their fists, bared their claws, and gnashed their teeth;
But the general was in the maiden's hands,
And they could not be separated rashly.
"When throwing something at a mouse, watch out for the plates and
    saucers" —
It was impossible for them to unleash their spears and lances.
Flailing his arms left and right, the general directed his men to back off,
And looked beseechingly at the assembled guests as though pleading with
    them to intervene.

After their initial shock, the guests regained composure
And went forward to bow before the maiden, saying,
"Listening to your ladyship's words,
We were so outraged that our hair stood on end;
In the end, we can only hope
That this was originally not the general's intention.
To seek your hand in marriage is one thing,
But would he dare be so unprincipled as to take you by force?
Because of their ineptness and lack of understanding,
The fault lies with the people he employed;
Those two officers, for example,
Will certainly be severely bastinadoed for feigning orders.
Now there's nothing else to say,
But that you should be sent back to your village.
The general will himself go to your gate,
Where, baring his shoulders, he will beg a thousand pardons;
He will present some humble gifts,
Delicacies to offer your mother.
The matter will pass over like the misty clouds
That leave no stain upon the sky;
Please return to the boat at once,
And then it will be plain as day if he goes back on his word."

The maiden frowned at the assembled guests and said with a laugh,
"Sirs, do you take me for a child?
I've lost all confidence in him now;
How could anyone with such a wild nature become gentle?
Even mountain spooks always search for their enemies,
So it's unlikely that someone who harbors evil thoughts will turn humane.
How painful to think that, since the armed uprisings,
Troops have been killing the people everywhere;
They consider that killing the people is like killing thieves,
And this poisonous attitude has spread across the land.
On the highway to Lan-ling,
They come and go in droves;
If it's not on a frosty evening,
Then it's on a rainy morning.
Our house is but a few rooms,
A pile of kindling buffeted by the barren winds;
Our family is but a few kin,
Pitiful fish confined to a cauldron.
At a snap of the fingers, turmoil arises,
In the blink of an eye, all becomes dust and ashes.
Would one rather that the seeds of disaster be sown,
To end up a grieving will-o'-the-wisp?
Who knows whether Yama [9] exists,
And who can you complain to in the tomb of endless night?
Better to cry out before the ninefold empyrean, [10]
Heaven will certainly not make a partial judgment;
Perhaps if I take decisive action,
Public opinion will naturally prove true.
I knew clearly when I came here,
That I was like a mantis trying to block a huge chariot with its forelegs; [11]
Do you think that I would seek to preserve my life at the expense of my
    honor,
Or that I cherish this insignificant, little body?
Your efforts to mediate, sirs,
Are but so much verbiage that I cannot go along with."

The assembled guests again went forward and bowed, saying,
"Please do not be so angry.
The general has a worthy name

---

9. The Buddhist king of the underworld, who is supposed to judge the souls sent there.
10. In the *Elegies of Ch'u* (see selection 122), it was thought that heaven was nine layers deep. Here heaven stands for the emperor.
11. From a parable in the twelfth chapter of the *Chuang Tzu* (see selection 8).

And has all along treasured his plumage;
His every thought is to emulate the Confucian literati,
His broadminded character is particularly sincere.
This affair was most improper;
Once news of it gets out,
Ten thousand mouths will proclaim the injustice,
And will surely rebuke him endlessly.
A bad reputation will come of its own accord—
He may wish to defend himself, but he'll scarcely be able to open his mouth;
A piece of white jade that has sullied itself
Is not worth a string of cash.
Realizing that there may be no time to regret his error,
He laments the fact that he has nothing to cover his face with.
The elders of the lower Yangtze
Will be too ashamed to recognize him when they meet,
How much less would he be willing to confront the anger of the masses,
And raise troops because of a marriage!
His crime would be so great that it obliterates the teaching of the sages—
He would no longer be counted a human being.
This man is by no means ordinary,
He fights the bandits tirelessly in all directions;
Though his great talent may not be equal to that of Kuan Chung and Yüeh
    Yi,[12]
His heroism is a match for Chao She and Lien P'o.[13]
Since your ladyship comes from an old family of officials,
Be so kind as to pardon a brave servant of the court.
As to the affairs of another day, we can assure you with one voice,
That so-and-so will be appointed to government office and so-and-so will be
    made a member of the gentry.
Together we kneel before you and beg for the general's life,
May your ladyship be forgiving as a transcendent, a Buddha, or a heavenly
    spirit."

The maiden realized that it would be difficult to ignore the sentiments of
    the guests, so she said,
"For you, sirs, I will yield.
For the moment, let us set aside all that you have just said,
I ask only to borrow one thing from you, sirs.
I have heard that the general owns an excellent steed named 'White Fish,'

12. Two famous generals of the Spring and Autumn and the Warring States periods,
respectively, to whom the celebrated strategist of the Three Kingdoms, Chu-ke Liang, often
compared himself.
13. Two outstanding generals of the Warring States period.

Who can travel a thousand tricents per day with ease.
From the time I left Lan-ling
And said goodbye to my family, it has already been more than four days;
My old mother must be leaning against the village gate crying bitterly,
My two brothers must be clasping their arms in our courtyard sighing vainly.
If I ride this horse back to my home,
I can reach there by early nightfall.
Henceforth, we will abandon our humble hut,
And take up residence in a Peach Blossom Spring not of this world;[14]
There I shall wait upon my mother attentively,
And read Yellow Stone's [15] book on strategy with my brothers—
No foolish fisherman from Wu-ling [16] will be able to find us.
Three or four days later,
After we have moved,
From the shrine of Chiang Tzu-wen,[17]
I'll send you back the horse, all right?"

The general seldom rode this horse,
But now his only fear was that she would not leave on it;
Hurriedly, he called out to his attendants to bring the horse forward,
Its four legs white as snow and flossy hair dangling from its ears.
Verily, not in vain was it a Soochow stepper,[18]
'Twas descended from the wind that Master Lieh [19] used to ride.
As soon as the maiden took one look at this horse,
Her brows unfurled with a touch of joy;
Finally releasing the general's clothes from her grasp,
She was already in the saddle before anyone saw her leap.
With a long, drawn-out "Thanks!" she burst through space and was gone,
Like a flash of lightning or a shooting star, she left not a trace.

For several days after the girl had gone, the army did not stir,
Because the general displayed courage and prowess in restoring them to
     order.
His encampment encircled the sides of Mount Chung;

14. A utopian refuge (see selection 172).

15. A hermit who lived during the Ch'in and Han dynasties, he bequeathed his book to Chang Liang, who in turn used the teachings in it to help Liu Pang found the Han dynasty.

16. Another reference to T'ao Ch'ien's utopian essay about the Peach Blossom Spring (see note 14).

17. Located in modern-day Nanking, the shrine commemorates a high-ranking officer of the ancient kingdom of Wu (Ngwa).

18. An allusion to a fleet steed of antiquity.

19. The Taoist Master Lieh was thought to be able to ride on the wind (see selection 10). This allusion and the one mentioned in note 18 are missing in some editions of the text, an indication that their scholarly quality makes them suspect in such a popular ballad.

There guests and advisers came to pay their respects to the general,
Encouraging him to quaff the new vintage,
While gongs and pipes continuously blared forth a medley.
Out of the cloudy distance appeared a lone horse in a dusty clatter,
Glistening and without blemish it came onrushing;
Her word was as good as gold, the contract was redeemed,
The general went forward to take the reins and led the horse back to its
    stable.
Covered with bloodlike sweat, it gave a long whinny;
On its back was bound crosswise a bulging, twisted object three feet high,
'Twas the bundle of betrothal presents brought that day by the two officers,
Returned with its seal unbroken and not the slightest thing missing.
When the bundle of betrothal presents was unloaded, beneath it there lay
In addition, like the single slip of a shallot, a knife,
Light flashing from its razor-sharp blade.
Transfixed by the sight, for many nights the general did not sleep soundly.

Translated by Victor H. Mair

PART III

Prose

Documents

157
The Great Announcement

from the *Classic of Documents*

Anonymous (early Chou period?)

I

The king speaks to the following effect:—"Ho! I make a great announcement to you, the princes of the many States, and to you, the managers of my affairs.—Unpitied am I, and Heaven sends down calamities on my House, without exercising the least delay. It greatly occupies my thoughts, that I, so very young, have inherited this illimitable patrimony, with its destinies and domains. I have not displayed wisdom, and led the people to tranquility, and

This selection is taken from the *Classic of Documents* or *Book of History (Shu ching)*, one of the main Confucian classics. It is a collection of documents, mainly speeches, attributed to various rulers and ministers of high antiquity. The documents, however, contain almost no information concerning the circumstances under which they were composed, nor is there any historical narrative relating one document to another. The work is thus more an archive of source materials—some of dubious derivation—than a connected history. "The Great Announcement" is considered by scholars to be one of the more authentic items in this collection of materials from diverse origins and periods.

The prefatory note states, "When King Wu died, the three overseers and the wild tribes of the Huai rebelled. The Duke of Chou acted as prime minister to King Ch'eng and, having proposed to make an end of the house of Yin [i.e., the Shang dynasty], composed 'The Great Announcement.'"

how much less should I be able to reach the knowledge of the decree of Heaven!

"Yes, I who am but a little child am in the position of one who has to cross a deep water;—it must be mine to go and seek how to cross over. I must diffuse the elegant institutions of my predecessor, and augment the appointment which he received from Heaven;—so shall I be not forgetful of his great work. Nor shall I dare to restrain the majesty of Heaven seen in the inflictions it sends down.

II

"The Tranquilizing king[1] left to me the great precious tortoise,[2] to bring into connection with me the intelligence of Heaven. I consulted it, and it told me that there would be great trouble in the region of the west, and that the western people would not be still. Accordingly we have the present senseless movements.

"Little as the present prosperity of Yin is, its prince greatly dares to take in hand its broken line. Though Heaven sent down its terrors on his House, yet knowing of the evils in our kingdom, and that the people are not tranquil, he says—'I will recover my patrimony'; and so he wishes to make our State of Chou a border territory again.

"One day there was a senseless movement, and the day after, ten men of worth among the people appeared to help me to go forward to restore tranquility and to perpetuate the plans of my father. The great business I am engaging in will have a successful issue, for I have divined and always got a favorable intimation. Therefore I tell you, the princes of my friendly States, and you, the directors of departments, my officers, and the managers of my affairs,—I have obtained a favorable reply to my divinations. I will now go forward with you from all the States, and punish those vagabond and transported ministers of Yin.

III

"And now, you the princes of the various States, and you the various officers and managers of my affairs, all retort on me, saying, 'The hardships will be great, and that the people are not still has its source really in the king's palace, and in the mansions of those princes of the troubled State. We, little ones, and the old reverent men as well, think the expedition ill-advised. Why does your majesty not go contrary to the divination?'

"I, in my youth, think also continually of the hardships, and say, Alas! these senseless movements will deplorably afflict widowers and widows! But

---

1. This presumably refers to King Wu, father of King Ch'eng, who is ostensibly the speaker of the announcement.
2. Signifying the rights and ability to consult the oracle (see selection 1).

I am the servant of Heaven, which has assigned me this great task, and laid this hard duty on my person. I therefore, the young one, do not pity myself, and it would be right in you, the princes of the States, and in you, the many officers, the directors of departments, and the managers of my affairs, to soothe me, saying, 'Do not be distressed with sorrow. We shall surely complete the plans of your Tranquilizing father.'

"Yes, I, the little one, dare not disregard the charge of God. Heaven, favorable to the Tranquilizing king, gave such prosperity to our small State of Chou. The Tranquilizing king divined and acted accordingly, and so he calmly received his great appointment. Now Heaven is helping the people; — how much more must I follow the divinations! Oh! the clearly intimated will of Heaven is to be feared: — it is to help my great inheritance."

IV

The king says, "You, who are the old ministers, are fully able to examine the long-distant affairs; — you know how great was the toil of the Tranquilizing king. Now where Heaven shuts up and distresses us is the place where I must accomplish my work; — I dare not but do my utmost to complete the plans of the Tranquilizing king. It is on this account that I use such efforts to remove the doubts and carry forward the inclinations of the princes of my friendly States. Heaven also assists me with sincere expressions of attachment, which I have ascertained among the people; — how dare I but aim at the completion of the work formerly begun by the Tranquilizer? Heaven moreover is thus toiling and distressing my people, so that it is as if they were suffering from disease; — how dare I allow the appointment which the Tranquilizer, my predecessor, received, to be without its happy fulfillment?"

The king says, "Formerly, at the initiation of this expedition, I spoke of its difficulties, and revolved them in my mind daily. But when a deceased father, wishing to build a house, had laid out the plan, if his son be unwilling to raise up the hall, how much less will he be willing to complete the roof! Or if the father had broken up the ground, and his son is unwilling to sow the seed, how much less will he be willing to reap the grain! In such a case will the father, who had himself been so reverently attentive to his objects, be willing to say, 'I have an heir who will not abandon the patrimony'? — How dare I, therefore, but use all my powers to give a happy settlement to the great charge entrusted to the Tranquilizing king?

"If a father have those among his friends who attack his child, will the elders of his people encourage the attack, and not come to the rescue?"

V

The king says, "Oh! Take heart, ye princes of the various States, and ye managers of my affairs. The enlightening of the country was from the wise, even from the ten men who obeyed and knew the decree of God, and the sincere assistance given by Heaven. At that time none of you presumed to change the royal appointments. And now, when Heaven is sending down, calamity on the State of Chou, and the authors of these great distresses appear as if the inmates of a house were mutually to attack one another, you are without any knowledge that the decree of Heaven is not to be changed!

"I ever think and say, Heaven in destroying Yin is doing husbandman's work;—how dare I but complete the business of my fields! Heaven will thereby show its favor to the former Tranquilizer.

"How should I be all for the oracle of divination, and presume not to follow your advice? I am following the Tranquilizer, whose purpose embraced all the limits of the land. How much more must I proceed, when the divinations are all favorable! It is on these accounts that I make this expedition in force to the east. There is no mistake about the decree of Heaven. The indications of the divinations are all to the same effect."

Translated by James Legge

158
The Contract for a Youth

Wang Pao (fl. 61–54 B.C.E.)

Wang Tzu-yüan of Shu Commandery[1] went to the Chien River on business, and went up to the home of the widow Yang Hui, who had a male slave named Pien-liao. Wang Tzu-yüan requested him to go and buy some wine. Picking up a big stick, Pien-liao climbed to the top of the grave mound and said: "When my master bought me, Pien-liao, he only contracted for me to care for the grave and did not contract for me to buy wine for some other gentleman."

Wang Tzu-yüan was furious and said to the widow: "Wouldn't you prefer to sell this slave?"

Dating to 59 B.C.E., this powerfully written and at times funny text must have been meant as a parody. The author was a literatus who served in the imperial court. A native of Yi-chou in the present-day province of Szechwan, Wang Pao (styled Tzu-yüan) became prominent for three panegyrics celebrating the virtues and accomplishments of the emperor and his ministers, which he wrote at the request of the governor of the region. He also wrote a fourth panegyric as an exegesis of the first three. These compositions much ingratiated him with the emperor. The simple, slightly vernacular style of "The Contract for a Youth," however, stands in striking contrast to his other, more florid compositions.

1. Szechwan. All of the place names in the text are located in this province, except for Yi-chou, which is in Yunnan.

Yang Hui said: "The slave's father offered him to people, but no one wanted him."

Wang Tzu-yüan immediately settled on the sale contract, etc.

The slave again said: "Enter in the contract everything you wish to order me to do. I, Pien-liao, will not do anything not in the contract."

Wang Tzu-yüan said: "Agreed!"

The text of the contract said:

Third year of Shen-chiao, the first month, the fifteenth day,[2] the gentleman Wang Tzu-yüan, of Tzu-chung, purchases from the lady Yang Hui of An-chih village in Chengtu, the bearded[3] male slave, Pien-liao, of her husband's household. The fixed sale price is 15,000 cash. The slave shall obey orders about all kinds of work and may not argue.

He shall rise at dawn and do an early sweeping. After eating he shall wash up. Ordinarily he should pound the grain mortar, tie up broom straws, carve bowls and bore wells, scoop out ditches, tie up fallen fences, hoe the garden, trim up paths and dike up plats of land, cut big flails, bend bamboos to make rakes, and scrape and fix the well pulley. In going and coming he may not ride horseback or in the cart, nor may he sit crosslegged or make a hubbub. When he gets out of bed he shall shake his head to wake up, fish, cut forage, plait reeds and card hemp, draw water for gruel, and help in making *tsu-mo* drink.[4] He shall weave shoes and make other coarse things, catch birds on a gummed pole, knot nets and catch fish, shoot wild geese with arrows on a string, and shoot wild ducks with a pellet bow. He shall ascend the mountains to shoot deer, and go into the waters to catch turtles. He shall dig a pond in the garden to raise fish and a hundred or so geese and ducks; and shall drive away owls and hawks. Holding a stick, he shall herd the pigs. He shall plant ginger and rear sheep; rear the shotes and colts; remove manure and always keep things clean; and feed the horses and cattle. When the drum sounds four he shall arise and give them a midnight addition of fodder.

In the second month at the vernal equinox he shall bank the dikes and repair the boundary walls of the fields; prune the mulberry trees, skin the palm trees, plant melons to make gourd utensils, select eggplant seeds for planting, and transplant onion sets; burn plant remains to generate the fields, pile up refuse, and break up lumps in the soil. At midday he shall dry out things in the sun. At cockcrow he shall rise and pound grain in the mortar, exercise and curry the horses, the donkeys, and likewise the mules—three classes.

When there are guests in the house he shall carry a kettle and go after

2. February 18, 59 B.C.E.
3. The word used here seems to indicate that the slave was of non-Han extraction.
4. Apparently a fine brew made from the skimmings of boiled butter.

wine; draw water and prepare the evening meal; wash bowls and arrange food trays; pluck garlic from the garden; chop vegetables and slice meat; pound meat and make soup of tubers; stew fish and roast turtle; boil tea [5] and fill the utensils. When the dinner is over he shall cover and put away leftovers; shut the gates and close up the passageways for dogs; feed the pigs and air the dogs.

He shall not argue or fight with the neighbors. The slave should only drink bean-water and may not be greedy for wine. If he wishes to drink good wine he may only wet the lips and rinse the mouth; he may not empty the dipper or drain the cup. He may not go out at dawn and return at night, or have dealings with close chums.

Behind the house there are trees. He should hew them and make a boat, going downriver as far as Chiang-chou and up to Chien-chu. On behalf of the storehouse assistants he shall seek spending money, rejecting the strings of cash which are defective. He shall buy mats at Mien-t'ing, and when traveling between Tu and Lo he should trade in the small markets to get powder for the ladies. When he returns to Tu he shall carry hemp about on his pole, transporting it out to the side markets. He shall lead dogs for sale and peddle geese. At Wu-yang he shall buy tea, and he shall carry lotus on his pole from the Yang family pool. When he travels to market assemblies he shall carefully guard against the practice of theft. When he enters the market he may not squat like a barbarian, loll about, or indulge in evil talk and cursing. He shall make many knives and bows, and take them into Yi-chou to barter for oxen and sheep. The slave shall teach himself to be smart and clever, and may not be silly and stupid.

He shall take an axe and go into the mountains; cut memorandum tablets and hew cart shafts; if there are leftovers he should make sacrificial stands, benches, and wooden shoes, as well as food pans for pigs. He shall burn wood to make charcoal; collect stones and heap them into retaining walls, make huts and roof houses; and whittle books to take the place of commercially prepared writing tablets. On his return at dusk he should bring two or three bundles of dry wood.

In the fourth month he should transplant; in the ninth month he should reap; and in the tenth month gather in the beans. He shall gather quantities of hemp and rushes and stretch them into rope.

When it rains and there is nothing to do, he should plait grass and weave reeds. He shall plant and cultivate peach, plum, pear, and persimmon trees. He shall set out mulberry trees, one every thirty feet in rows eight feet apart, and fruit trees in corresponding sequence with the rows

5. There is some doubt whether the Chinese knew tea this early. The graph used to write the word is ambiguous and may simply mean "bitter [sauce]." Tea did not become a popular drink in China—certainly not in the heartland—until the T'ang period (see selections 97 and especially 193).

and intervals matching. When the fruit is ripe and is being picked or stored he may not suck or taste it.

At night if the dogs bark he should arise and warn the neighbors, block the gate and bar the doors, mount the tower and beat the drum, don his shield and grasp his spear. Returning down he shall make three circuits of inspection.

He shall be industrious and quick-working, and he may not idle and loaf. When the slave is old and his strength spent, he shall plant marsh grass and weave mats. When his work is over and he wishes to rest he should pound a picul of grain. Late at night when there is no work he shall wash clothes really white. If he has private savings they shall be the master's gift or from guests. The slave may not have evil secrets; affairs should be open and reported. If the slave does not heed instructions, he shall be bastinadoed a hundred strokes.

The reading of the text of the contract came to an end. The slave was speechless and his lips were tied. Wildly he beat his head on the ground, and beat himself with his hands; from his eyes the tears streamed down, and the drivel from his nose hung a foot long.

He said: "If it is to be exactly as master Wang says, I would rather return soon along the yellow-soil road,[6] with the grave worms boring through my head. Had I known before I would have bought the wine for master Wang. I would not have dared to do that wrong."

Translated by C. Martin Wilbur

6. In the underworld.

History

159

Two Brothers of Cheng and the Mother Who Doted on the Younger

from *The Commentary of Mr. Tso*

Attributed to Tso Ch'iu-ming (3d century B.C.E.?)

Duke Yin First Year (722 B.C.E.)

sister

mother

In the past, Duke Wu of Cheng had taken a bride from the state of Shen, known as Lady Chiang of Duke Wu.[1] Lady Chiang gave birth to the future

The putative author of the *Tso chuan* or *Tso shih chuan* (*The Chronicle* or, more accurately, *Tradition* or *Commentary of Mr. Tso*) is Tso Ch'iu-ming. No biographical information exists concerning him, however, and his relationship to the work that bears his name remains unknown. The word *chuan* in the title implies that the work was considered a commentary on the *Spring and Autumn Annals* (*Ch'un-ch'iu*), but it is uncertain whether the *Tso chuan* was originally compiled for that purpose. Nonetheless, because the period of time that it covers (722–468 B.C.E.) is almost the same as that of the *Annals* (722–481 B.C.E.) and it contains detailed accounts of events referred to in the latter, the *Tso chuan* can conveniently serve as a commentary on the *Annals*—even though the entries do not always match.

The *Annals*, one of the five main classics of the Confucian tradition, provides a bare record of the events in the various feudal states. The entries are extremely brief, consisting mostly of notices of accessions to rule, marriages, deaths, diplomatic meetings, wars, and other events in the lives of the ruling dukes of the state of Lu and the other feudal states with whom they interacted, along with notations on unusual occurrences in the natural world such as earthquakes, comets, droughts, insect plagues, and so forth, all of which were thought to reflect the political condition of the realm. The *Tso chuan*, on the other hand, consists of thirty densely

Duke Chuang and to his brother, Tuan of Kung. Duke Chuang was born wide awake and consequently greatly startled Lady Chiang.[2] Therefore she named him Born Awake and came to hate him. But she loved his younger brother Tuan and wished to have him declared heir to the throne of Cheng. Repeatedly she begged Duke Wu to do so, but he would not agree.

Later, when Duke Chuang became ruler of Cheng (743 B.C.E.), Lady Chiang asked him to assign the city of Chih to his younger brother Tuan. But the duke replied, "Chih is a strategic city, the place where Kuo Shu[3] met his death. Any other city you have only to ask for."

She then requested that Tuan be given the city of Ching, and he was accordingly sent to reside there. He came to be called the T'ai-shu or Grand Younger Brother of Ching City.

Chai Chung, a high official of Cheng, said to the duke, "If any of the major cities have walls exceeding a hundred *chih* in length, they pose a danger to the capital.[4] According to the regulations of the former kings, even the largest cities should not exceed one third the size of the capital, while middle-sized cities should be one fifth and small cities one ninth. Now the city of Ching does not fit these dimensions and violates the regulations. You may find yourself unable to endure the consequences!"

---

written chapters and is China's oldest work of narrative history. Its entries provide a year-by-year—often month-by-month—account of happenings only mentioned in the *Annals*. The narratives focus primarily on political, diplomatic, and military affairs, but also contain considerable information on economic and cultural developments.

The original form of the *Tso chuan* is unknown. The narratives may initially have been grouped under the various states but later broken up and appended to the year-by-year entries of the *Annals* that focused on the reigns of the dukes of Lu. This rearrangement may have been made in the latter part of the third century C.E. Linguistic and philological evidence, however, indicates that the text was originally composed sometime during the third century B.C.E., considerably later than the date of 463 B.C.E. when it was supposed to have been completed. In spite of the mysteries surrounding its composition, the *Tso chuan* is a masterpiece of the early prose tradition and has had an immense influence on later Chinese literature and historiography. From the first century on, it was numbered among the texts of the enlarged Confucian canon.

The present selection is the first extended narrative from the *Tso chuan* and deals with the aftermath of a difficult breech delivery.

1. Shen was ruled by a branch of the Chiang family, hence the bride was referred to as Lady Chiang.

2. The phrase *wu-sheng*, translated here as "born wide awake," is also interpreted to mean born just as his mother was waking up, or born feet first. To help explain the mother's loathing for the child, Ssu-ma Ch'ien in *Records of the Grand Historian* (Shih chi), ch. 42, the account of the state of Cheng, adds that the birth was a difficult one.

3. An evil ruler of the nearby state of Kuo who made his capital at Chih and behaved evilly until overthrown by Cheng. Duke Chuang fears his younger brother will do likewise.

4. According to commentators, one *chih* represents a section of city wall one *chang* in height and three *chang* (or, according to another theory, five *chang*) in length. One *chang* is said to equal ten feet.

The duke said, "Lady Chiang would have it that way—how can I avoid the danger?"

"There is no end to what Lady Chiang would have!" replied Chai Chung. "Better tend to the matter at once and not let it grow and put out runners, for runners can be hard to control. If even plants that have put out runners cannot be rooted out, how much more so the favored younger brother of a ruler!"

The duke said, "If he does too many things that are not right, he is bound to bring ruin on himself. I suggest you wait a while."

After some time the T'ai-shu ordered that the western and northern border regions acknowledge fealty to him as well as to the duke. The ducal son Lü,[5] an official of Cheng, said to the duke, "The state cannot tolerate a system of double fealty! What do you intend to do? If you sanction what the T'ai-shu has done, then I beg leave to serve him rather than you. If you do not intend to sanction it, then I urge you to do away with him before he stirs up the hearts of the people!"

"No need," said the duke. "He will bring on his own downfall."

The T'ai-shu proceeded to take over the cities that had previously acknowledged double fealty and make them his own, extending his control as far as Lin-yen. The ducal son Lü said, "Now is the time to act! If he expands his territory, the people will go over to his side."

The duke replied, "If he acts wrongly, no one will side with him.[6] Though he expands his territory, he will face ruin."

The T'ai-shu completed the building of his walls, called together his men, mended his armor and weapons, equipped his foot soldiers and chariots, and prepared for a surprise attack on the capital of Cheng. Lady Chiang was to open the city to him. When the duke learned the date planned for the attack, he said, "Now is the time!" He ordered the ducal son Lü to lead a force of two thousand chariots and attack Ching. Ching turned against the T'ai-shu Tuan, who took refuge in Yen. The duke attacked him at Yen, and on the day *hsin-ch'ou* of the fifth month, the T'ai-shu fled the state and went to Kung.[7]

In the end the duke confined his mother, Lady Chiang, in Ch'eng-ying and took a vow, saying, "Not until we reach the Yellow Springs[8] shall we meet again!"

5. *Kung-tzu*, "ducal son," is a designation used for sons of feudal rulers; *kung-sun*, "ducal grandson," is used for grandsons; descendents in the next generation were given a surname of their own. Both Kung-tzu and Kung-sun later became surnames.

6. Or, following Tu Yü's (222–284) interpretation, "He is acting wrongly and in an unbrotherly manner."

7. At this point there appears a passage explaining the wording of the *Spring and Autumn Annals* entry pertaining to these events. In the present translation passages of this type have been omitted.

8. The springs within the yellow earth, a term for the land of the dead.

Later he regretted the vow. Ying K'ao-shu, a border guard of Ying Valley, hearing of this, presented gifts to the duke, and the duke in turn had a meal served to him. He ate the meal but set aside the meat broth. When the duke asked him why, he replied, "Your servant has a mother who shares whatever food he eats, but she has never tasted your lordship's broth. I beg permission to take her some."

"You have a mother to take things to. Alas, I alone have none!" said the duke.

"May I venture to ask the meaning of that?" said Ying K'ao-shu.

The duke explained why he had made the remark and confessed that he regretted his vow.

"Why should your lordship worry?" said the other. "If you dig into the earth until you reach the springs, and fashion a tunnel where the two of you can meet, then who is to say you have not kept your vow?"

The duke did as he suggested. As the duke entered the tunnel he intoned this verse:

> Within the great tunnel,
> genial, genial is my joy!

When Lady Chiang emerged from the tunnel she intoned this verse:

> Outside the great tunnel,
> fai-flung, fai-flung is my joy!

So in the end mother and son became as they had been before.

The gentleman remarks:[9] Ying K'ao-shu was a man of utmost filial piety. He loved his mother, and succeeded in inspiring a similar feeling in Duke Chuang. Is this not what the *Book of Odes* means when it says:

> While filial sons are unslacking,
> forever shall be given you good things.[10]

Translated by Burton Watson

9. The *Tso chuan* frequently introduces didactic comments on the events of its narrative in this fashion. Though it has been asserted that "the gentleman" refers to Confucius, this is clearly impossible in many cases. These remarks are presumably judgments made by the author or authors of the *Tso chuan*, though some may have been added by later hands. There are eighty-four such passages in the *Tso chuan*.

10. This is from song 247 of the *Classic of Odes* (see selection 16).

160

The Passing of Kung Sheng

from *History of the Han*

Pan Ku (32–92)

When Wang Mang took control of the government, Kung Sheng and Ping Han together petitioned to resign from office on account of their age and health. Earlier, during the time of Emperor Chao,[1] when Han Fu of Cho commandery came to the capital having been summoned for audience on account of his virtuous conduct, he was presented with an imperial document of entitlement and rolls of bundled silk, and was dispatched to return home. The emperor issued an edict saying: "We feel compunction about burdening him with the affairs of official duties. Let him endeavor to cultivate filial devotion and brotherly respectfulness, and so edify his district and town. On his journey home, he shall stay at the government relay lodges, and the local hostels will provide him with wine and meat, and feed his entourage and horses. The Senior Subaltern shall seasonally pay him visits, and shall present him one head of sheep and two *hu*[2] of wine yearly in the eighth month. In

Wang Mang's founding of a new dynasty has been condemned throughout Chinese history as an unrightful act of usurpation. The portrayal of Kung Sheng's conduct evinces the general commendation of acts against "usurpers" and the specific disparagement of Wang Mang that was common throughout all periods of imperial China, especially during the Later Han. The account of Kung Sheng was composed during the second half of the first century C.E. and thus merely some fifty years after Wang Mang's "usurpation" and his subsequent overthrow resulting in the reinstitution of "legitimate" rule. The construction of Kung Sheng's life and career, and the approbatory portrayal of Kung's righteous self-sacrifice, reflect the sentiments of a historiography wherein praise and blame are accorded retrospectively in compliance with the dominant values of the historian and his time. Thus, Kung Sheng is portrayed as a humble savant, who, especially later in his career, accepted appointments with great reluctance and, even then, only until such time as he was able to retire on the excuse—or pretext—of age and health. At the advent of "illegitimate" rule, Kung Sheng withdrew in moral protest.

The *History of the Former Han* was started by Pan Piao (3–54), largely written by his son Pan Ku, and completed by the latter's sister Pan Chao (see selection 162). It deals with the period from 206 B.C.E. to 23 C.E. and is one of the most renowned and influential of all Chinese historical works. Admired for the rich detail of its narrative and the purity and economy of its style, along with the *Records of the Grand Historian* which was completed by Ssu-ma Ch'ien around the year 90 B.C.E. (see selection 173, note 10), the *History of the Former Han* served as a model for the official histories compiled in later centuries to cover all the Chinese imperial dynasties. From the time they were written until the end of period of traditional culture, no one in China could consider himself truly educated who was not thoroughly familiar with their pages.

1. In 80 B.C.E.
2. Approximately 40 liters.

the case of something untoward,[3] he shall be presented with one set of burial shroud and coverlet, and sacrificed to with the medium offering."[4]

Wang Mang then, in accordance with the precedent, announced he would dismiss Sheng and Han. The imperial document read: "Today, the fourth day of the sixth month of the second year of the Yüan-shih reign,[5] the two elders, Imperial Household Grandee[6] and Grand Palace Grandee,[7] shall cease their duties due to age and illness." The Grand Empress Dowager sent the Supervisor of the Receptionists to issue an imperial edict to them, which said: "It is heard that of old, when those holding office came to advanced age, they retired from office; in this way their resignation was respected and their energies not exhausted. At the present, the Grandees' years have advanced, and We would feel compunction at troubling them with the affairs of official duties. Let them present their sons, as well as one each of grandchildren, brothers, and sons of brothers. Let the Grandees cultivate their persons and cleave to the Way, and thus finish their long years. They shall be granted bundled silk and the privilege of lodging in the official guesthouses while on their journey, and at the new year be granted a sheep, wine, a tunic, and a cloak, all in accordance with the Han Fu precedent. The male progeny they present all shall be selected for the office of Gentleman." Thereupon, Sheng and Han returned to grow old in their native districts. . . .[8]

When Wang Mang usurped the rule of the country,[9] he dispatched the Commanding General of the Five Awesome Armies to conduct the conventional observances throughout the empire. The Commanding General personally paid respects to Sheng, offering him a sheep and wine. On the New Year,[10] Mang sent an emissary to go to Sheng and confer upon him the appointment of Chancellor of Academicians. On the pretext of illness, Sheng did not comply to the summons to audience.

Two years later, Mang again dispatched emissaries to present a document bearing the imperial seal, and the seal and seal-cord of the office of Academic Chancellor for the Preceptors and Companions of the Heir Designate, and he sent a comfortable quadriga[11] to receive Sheng. They went forward to accord respect and to confer the rank of Superior Chancellor, presenting in advance the amount of six months' emolument to facilitate his transfer to the

3. I.e., death.
4. Of a sheep and a pig.
5. Equivalent to the first of July, 2 C.E.
6. Kung Sheng.
7. Ping Han.
8. The text here breaks to discuss an unrelated matter.
9. On January 10, 9 C.E.
10. Five days later.
11. Outfitted with rush-padded wheels so as to ride smoothly.

capital. The emissaries along with the Grand Administrator of the commandery, the Senior Subaltern of the prefecture, the district elders, the sundry
officials and those known for their conduct and fealty, as well as their students, in all amounting to a thousand men and more, entered Sheng's hamlet
to present the edict.

The emissaries wished to induce Sheng to come forward and greet them,
and so stood long outside the gate. Sheng claimed aggravated illness and
prepared a bed in his quarters, below the southern window in the room west
of the entry. He lay his head to the east, neatly spread his court attire and
drew up his sash.[12] The emissaries passed through the entry, filed west and
stood facing south. They presented the edict to which was attached the
document with the imperial seal, removed to the courtyard, twice did obeisance and offered up the seal and seal-cord of office. They brought in the
comfortable quadriga and went forward to address Sheng, saying, "The sage
court has never been neglectful of you, lord; when the codes and regulations
were not yet established at the advent of the new dynasty, we waited for you
to formulate the government, hoping to hear that what we had wished for
could come to be realized, and thus bring peace to all between the seas."

Sheng responded, "I have always been unclever, and adding to that being
advanced in years and afflicted with illness, liable to expire at any moment.
Were I to follow your lordships the emissaries and take to the road, I would
be certain to die during the journey. This would be without benefit, to the
greatest degree." The emissaries sought to persuade him of the importance of
this appointment, going so far as advancing to place the seal and seal-cord
upon Sheng's body. But Sheng pushed the articles aside and would not
accept them.

The emissaries then memorialized: "We are just in full summer's torrid
heat, and Sheng ails from asthenia; possibly he could be allowed to wait for
autumn's coolness before setting out." This was approved by imperial edict.
Once each five days, one of the emissaries went together with the Grand
Administrator to inquire as to his daily welfare. They said to Sheng's two sons
and his disciple Kao Hui and others, "The court humbly wishes to accord
your lordship ceremonial entitlement. Though he be afflicted with illness, it
would be better to set out and move to the official relay lodge, to demonstrate
his intention to go. This would assure for his sons and grandsons a legacy of
great endeavors." Hui and the others related the words of the emissaries.

Sheng realized that he would never be listened to, and addressed Hui and
the others: "I was the recipient of great favor from the House of Han, but
there was nothing with which I could repay it. Now I am old in years, and
imminently will be put into the earth. In my opinion, how could I with my

---

12. This description alludes to the way in which an ill Confucius insisted on correct posture
and dress; it is taken from *Analects* 10.13.

single life serve two ruling houses, and face my former rulers below?" Sheng then gave instructions on the matter of mourning, and on restraint in terms of the coffin: "The shroud surrounds the body; the coffin surrounds the shroud. You are not to follow vulgar custom and stir up my grave, nor plant cypresses, nor erect a memorial hall." When he had finished speaking, he did not again open his mouth to drink or eat. When fourteen days had passed he died; he was seventy-eight years[13] old at death.

The emissaries and the Grand Administrator oversaw the restraint in funeral matters, and presented the double burial coverlet and sacrificial memorial services according to the law. Disciples, hemp-clad mourners, and funeral participants were counted by the hundreds. An elderly fellow came to mourn, whose wailing was extremely grave. Presently he said, "Alas, incense burns itself up on account of its fragrance; oil depletes itself on account of its brightness. Master Kung in the end cut off prematurely his appointed years—he was no cohort of mine." He then left in a hurry; nobody knew his identity.

Sheng's residence was at Lien hamlet[14] in P'eng-ch'eng.[15] Those of later ages engraved stone tablets to mark the gates of his hamlet.

Translated by Alan J. Berkowitz

13. The text has "seventy-nine *sui*."
14. Hamlet of the Incorrupt.
15. Modern-day Hsü-chou in Kiangsu province.

Moral Lessons

161
Exemplary Sayings

Chapter 2

Yang Hsiung (53 B.C.E.–18 C.E.)

Someone asked, "Sir, when young, were you fond of the rhapsody?" I answered, "Yes, young lads carve worm characters and engrave seal script." [1] After a moment I said, "But a grown man does not engage in such activities."

Someone asked, "Can a rhapsody be used for admonition?" I answered, "Admonish? If it admonishes, it should stop there. If not, I am afraid it cannot avoid being anything but an encouragement."

Someone asked, "But does it not have the elegant beauty of misty gauze?" I responded, "It is only a defect in a seamstress' work."

The author was born in Chengtu (in present-day Szechwan). A great admirer of Ch'ü Yüan (see selection 122) and Ssu-ma Hsiang-ju (see selection 129), Yang Hsiung mined their works for fine phrases and stylistic devices. Yang was himself one of the most distinguished practitioners of the rhapsody, so it is ironic that he is at pains to disparage the genre so thoroughly in this piece. He was a major thinker and had composed his own transformed version of the *Classic of Changes*, entitled *Classic of the Grand Mystery* (*T'ai-hsüan ching*). His deep interest in the languages and topolects of the various regions of China was hampered by the lack of a phonetic script with which to record them accurately and unambiguously.

1. Yang Hsiung is saying here that the writing of *fu* or rhapsody (see selections 122–127) is a puerile exercise comparable to the calligraphic exercises of young boys, who were expected to master six types of script, including the worm and seal script.

The *Swordsman's Disquisition* says, "A sword can be used to protect the body." I responded, "Does prison make a person more mannerly?"

Someone asked, "Were the rhapsodies of Ching Ts'o, T'ang Le, and Mei Ch'eng beneficial?"[2] I answered, "What is certain is that their writing was immoderate." "What do you mean by immoderate?" "The rhapsodies of the *Songs* poets were beautiful but regulated. The rhapsodies of the epideictic writers are beautiful but immoderate. If the school of Confucius had used the rhapsody, Chia Yi would have mounted the hall and Ssu-ma Hsiang-ju would have entered the inner compartments. But they did not use the rhapsody, so what of it?"

Someone asked, "What about flies, red, and purple?"[3] I said, "Look sharply." Someone asked, "What about such semblances as the music of Cheng and Wei?"[4] I said, "Listen carefully." Someone asked, "When the five tones and the twelve pitches are combined, why is it that sometimes one hears classical music, and sometimes the music of Cheng?" I responded, "When the sounds are moderate and proper, one produces classical music. When the sounds are lewd and lascivious, we have the music of Cheng." "I beg to ask about the basis of classical music." I responded, "It begins with the Yellow Bell,[5] and is harmonized with moderation and propriety. Thus, we can be certain that the music of Cheng and Wei does not intrude."

Someone asked, "Women have a physical attraction. Does writing also have a similar attraction?" I responded, "Yes. But, in women one detests the powder and rouge spoiling their modesty and grace, and in writing, one detests extravagant verbiage that detracts from the moral code."

Someone asked, "Was Ch'ü Yüan wise?" I said, "At first he was like jade, like a lustrous gem, but then he changed to vermeil and green pigment. Such was his wisdom! Such was his wisdom!"

Someone asked, "Does a gentleman admire rhetoric?" I responded, "What a gentleman admires are the facts. But when factual detail overpowers style and rhetoric, one has a dry discourse. When rhetoric and style overpower a factual presentation, one has a rhapsody. When facts and rhetoric are in balance, one has a classic. Verbosity and excessive posturing are mere ornaments on virtue."

2. Ching Ts'o and T'ang Le (both late third century b.c.e.) were poets from the Ch'u region. Except for a few pieces of dubious authenticity, none of their writings survive. Mei Ch'eng (or Sheng) was a prominent rhapsody writer of the Former Han.

3. Blue flies, thought to contaminate the pure colors of black and white, are the traditional symbol of petty men and slanderers. Red and purple are the impure "intermediate" colors that detract from the "proper" pure colors of vermilion and black respectively.

4. Confucius reputedly said that he "detested things that seemed to be proper but were not." One of the semblances he detested was the "licentious" music of Cheng and Wei, which could be confused with the proper, orthodox music.

5. The fundamental pitch of the five-tone scale.

Someone asked, "Kung-sun Lung thought his ten thousand paradoxes could serve as standards. Are they standards?" I responded. "There are standards to be followed even in cutting wood to make a game board or to turn leather into a ball. But whatever does not conform to the standards of the former kings a gentleman will not follow.

"Reading books is like viewing mountains and rivers. By climbing the Eastern Peak one may understand the smallness of other mountains, not to mention the tiny hillocks. Having floated the azure sea, one may understand the shallowness of the Yangtze and the Yellow River, not to mention a dried-up swamp. Abandoning the Five Classics and trying to reach the Way—it simply cannot be done. He who abandons common fare and craves strange delicacies—how can one say he has good taste? He who abandons the great sage and shows a preference for other philosophers—how can one say he knows the Way?"

A path leading into mountain defiles cannot be followed. A door that leads into a wall cannot be entered. Someone said, "By what means does one enter?" My response: "Through Confucius. Confucius is the door." He asked, "Have you entered his door?" I responded, "I have indeed entered his door! Indeed I have! How could I have not entered his door?"

Someone wished to study the *Ts'ang Chieh* and *Shih p'ien.*[6] I said,"What fine scribal works! What fine scribal works! Studying them is preferable to making reckless guesses or leaving lacunae in the text."

Someone asked, "Suppose there were a man who said his surname was K'ung and his sobriquet was Chung-ni, that he entered Confucius' door, mounted his hall, leaned on his armrest, and wore his clothes. Could one call him Confucius?" I responded, "His outer form is that of Confucius, but his essence is not." "I venture to ask what you mean by essence." I responded, "Suppose there is an animal with the essence of a goat dressed in a tiger skin. Upon seeing grass it would rejoice, but if it saw a dhole, it would tremble. This is because it would forget it was dressed in a tiger's skin. A sage has the distinction of a tiger: his outer adornment is brilliant. A gentleman has the distinction of a leopard: his outer adornment is elegant. A sophist has the distinction of a racoon-dog: his outer adornment is thick. If a racoon-dog changes, it can become a leopard; if a leopard changes, it can become a tiger."[7]

To be fond of books but not seek the essentials in Confucius is to be a book-stall. To be fond of disquisition but not seek the essentials in Confucius is to be storyteller's clapper. There is nothing hurtful in a gentleman's speech,

6. Early dictionaries that contained standard forms for the lesser and greater seal script respectively.

7. That is to say, with effort, a sophist can become a gentleman, and a gentleman can become a sage.

and nothing immoderate in what he hears. Hurtfulness leads to disorder, and immoderation leads to depravity. There are cases of those who followed the proper way yet had a little iniquity, but there has never been a man of iniquity who even slightly followed the proper way.

The way of Confucius is clear and easy! Someone asked, "Although one practices it from his youth, he is still befuddled when he becomes old and gray. How can it be clear and easy?" I responded, "This means that he did not treat the wicked as wicked and did not treat falsehood with falsehood. If he had treated the wicked as wicked and falsehood with falsehood, even if they saw him with their own eyes and heard him with their ears, how could he have rectified them?"

When one hears many things, he holds only to the essentials; when one sees many things, he holds only to the distinctive. If one hears little, he has no essentials; if he hears little, he has nothing distinctive.[8]

Three hundred green robes—but what about the color?[9] Three thousand grass-cloth remnants—but what about the cold?[10]

There are four easy aspects to the way of the gentleman: it is simple and easy to use, it is focused on the essentials and is easy to grasp, it is brilliant and easy to see, and it follows the norms and is easy to speak about.

It is only after a raging wind and a pounding rain that we begin to appreciate the cover provided by a great house; it is only after a cruel government has oppressed the age that we begin to appreciate the protection provided by a sage.

In ancient times Yang Chu and Mo Ti blocked the road, but Mencius opened it with his eloquent speech, and all was clear and open again. In later times there were others who have blocked the road. I compare myself with Mencius.

Someone asked, "Each person approves of what he considers right and condemns what he considers wrong. Who can determine what is correct?" I answered, "The myriad things are manifoldly complex and thus their disposition depends upon Heaven. The words of the many thinkers are confused and chaotic, and must be judged by a sage." Someone asked, "But how can

8. Partly following Mencius, Yang Hsiung is saying here that a man may acquire broad learning, but the most important thing is to discern what is essential among the many things he has learned.

9. Green is one of the intermediate or impure colors. Yang Hsiung is probably alluding to the following lines from the *Classic of Odes* (song 27): "Green is the robe, /A green robe with yellow lining." Yellow is one of the five correct colors. According to the Confucian interpretation current in Yang's time, using an intermediate color such as green for the outer part of the garment and a correct color for the lining shows a reversal of what is proper. Yang Hsiung is saying here that anything improper, regardless of number, cannot be used.

10. Yang Hsiung is saying here that anything of inferior quality, even in great numbers, is of no use.

one find a sage to evaluate them?" I answered, "When he is living, one may consult the man; after his death, one may consult his books. The principle to be obtained in either case is the same."

Translated by David Knechtges

162
Lessons for Women

Instructions in Seven Chapters for a Woman's Ordinary Way of Life in the First Century C.E.

Pan Chao (45–120?)

Introduction

I, the unworthy writer, am unsophisticated, unenlightened, and by nature unintelligent, but I am fortunate both to have received not a little favor from my scholarly father, and to have had a cultured mother and instructresses upon whom to rely for a literary education as well as for training in good manners. More than forty years have passed since at the age of fourteen I took up the dustpan and the broom [1] in the Ts'ao family. During this time with trembling heart I feared constantly that I might disgrace my parents, and that I might multiply difficulties for both the women and the men of my husband's family. Day and night I was distressed in heart, but I labored without confessing weariness. Now and hereafter, however, I know how to escape from such faults.

Being careless, and by nature stupid, I taught and trained my children without system. Consequently I fear that my son Ku may bring disgrace upon the Imperial Dynasty by whose Holy Grace he has unprecedentedly received the extraordinary privilege of wearing the Gold and the Purple,[2] a privilege for the attainment of which by my son, I a humble subject never even hoped. Nevertheless, now that he is a man and able to plan his own life, I need not

These admonitions for women, particularly as reformulated and popularized by later writers, had a tremendous impact on the way women were expected to behave in ancient China. The author was undoubtedly the most celebrated female writer of early China. She was the sister of Pan Ku (32–92), whose *History of the Han Dynasty (Han shu)* she completed (see selection 160), the daughter of Pan Piao (3–54), a famous poet who had begun the compilation of the *History of the Han Dynasty*, and grandniece of Pan Chieh-yü (c. 45–5 B.C.E.), who also had a great literary reputation.

1. A conventional expression for the inferior position of the daughter-in-law in relation to her parents-in-law.

2. Gold seal and purple robe (symbols of high nobility).

again have concern for him. But I do grieve that you, my daughters,[3] just now at the age for marriage, have not at this time had gradual training and advice; that you still have not learned the proper customs for married women. I fear that by failure in good manners in other families you will humiliate both your ancestors and your clan. I am now seriously ill, life is uncertain. As I have thought of you all in so untrained a state, I have been uneasy many a time for you. At hours of leisure I have composed in seven chapters these instructions under the title *Lessons for Women*. In order that you may have something wherewith to benefit your persons, I wish every one of you, my daughters, each to write out a copy for yourself.

From this time on, every one of you strive to practice these lessons.

Chapter 1: Humility

On the third day after the birth of a girl the ancients observed three customs: first to place the baby below[4] the bed; second to give her a potsherd with which to play;[5] and third to announce her birth to her ancestors by an offering. Now to lay the baby below the bed plainly indicated that she is lowly and weak, and should regard it as her primary duty to humble herself before others. To give her potsherds with which to play indubitably signified that she should practice labor and consider it her primary duty to be industrious. To announce her birth before her ancestors clearly meant that she ought to esteem as her primary duty the continuation of the observance of worship in the home.

These three ancient customs epitomize a woman's ordinary way of life and the teachings of the traditional ceremonial rites and regulations. Let a woman modestly yield to others; let her respect others; let her put others first, herself last. Should she do something good, let her not mention it; should she do something bad, let her not deny it. Let her bear disgrace; let her even endure[6] when others speak or do evil to her. Always let her seem to tremble and to fear. When a woman follows such maxims as these, then she may be said to humble herself before others.

Let a woman retire late to bed, but rise early to duties; let her not dread tasks by day or by night. Let her not refuse to perform domestic duties whether easy or difficult. That which must be done, let her finish completely, tidily, and systematically. When a woman follows such rules as these, then she may be said to be industrious.

3. Not necessarily her own daughters only, but girls of her family as a whole.
4. On the floor or the ground.
5. In the *Classic of Odes*, it is written that "daughters . . . shall have tiles to play with." Since potsherds were used as spindle weights, they served both as toys for little girls and as an early introduction to domesticity.
6. Literally, "let her hold filth in her mouth," i.e., let her swallow insult.

Let a woman be correct in manner and upright in character in order to serve her husband. Let her live in purity and quietness of spirit, and attend to her own affairs. Let her love not gossip and silly laughter. Let her cleanse and purify and arrange in order the wine and the food for the offerings to the ancestors. When a woman observes such principles as these, then she may be said to continue ancestral worship.

No woman who observes these three fundamentals of life has ever had a bad reputation or has fallen into disgrace. If a woman fail to observe them, how can her name be honored; how can she but bring disgrace upon herself?

Chapter 2: Husband and Wife

The Way of husband and wife is intimately connected with yin and yang, and relates the individual to gods and ancestors. Truly it is the great principle of Heaven and Earth, and the great basis of human relationships. Therefore the *Rites* honor union of man and woman; and in the *Classic Book of Poetry*, the "First Ode" manifests the principle of marriage. For these reasons the relationship cannot but be an important one.

If a husband be unworthy, then he possesses nothing by which to control his wife. If a wife be unworthy, then she possesses nothing with which to serve her husband. If a husband does not control his wife, then the rules of conduct manifesting his authority are abandoned and broken. If a wife does not serve her husband, then the proper relationship between men and women and the natural order of things are neglected and destroyed. As a matter of fact, the purpose of these two, the controlling of women by men and the serving of men by women, is the same.

Now examine the gentlemen of the present age. They only know that wives must be controlled and that the husband's rules of conduct manifesting his authority must be established. They therefore teach their boys to read books and study histories. But they do not in the least understand that husbands and masters must also be served, and that the proper relationship and the rites should be maintained.

Yet only to teach men and not to teach women—is that not ignoring the essential relation between them? According to the *Rites*, it is the rule to begin to teach children to read at the age of eight years, and by the age of fifteen years they ought then to be ready for cultural training.[7] Only why should it not be that girls' education as well as boys' be according to this principle?

Chapter 3: Respect and Caution

As yin and yang are not of the same nature, so man and woman have different characteristics. The distinctive quality of the yang is rigidity; the function of

---

7. Not merely literary studies, but all the accomplishments of a gentleman: ceremonies, music, archery, horsemanship, writing, and numbers.

the yin is yielding. Man is honored for strength; a woman is beautiful on account of her gentleness. Hence there arose the common saying: "A man though born like a wolf may, it is feared, become a weak monstrosity; a woman though born like a mouse may, it is feared, become a tiger."

Now for self-culture nothing equals respect for others. To counteract firmness nothing equals compliance. Consequently it can be said that the Way of respect and acquiescence is woman's most important principle of conduct. So respect may be defined as nothing other than holding on to that which is permanent; and acquiescence nothing other than being liberal and generous. Those who are steadfast in devotion know that they should stay in their proper places; those who are liberal and generous esteem others, and honor and serve them.

If husband and wife have the habit of staying together, never leaving one another, and following each other around within the limited space of their own rooms, then they will lust after and take liberties with one another. From such action improper language will arise between the two. This kind of discussion may lead to licentiousness. Out of licentiousness will be born a heart of disrespect to the husband. Such a result comes from not knowing that one should stay in one's proper place.

Furthermore, affairs may be either crooked or straight; words may be either right or wrong. Straighforwardness cannot but lead to quarreling; crookedness cannot but lead to accusation. If there are really accusations and quarrels, then undoubtedly there will be angry affairs. Such a result comes from not esteeming others, and not honoring and serving them.

If wives suppress not contempt for husbands, then it follows that such wives rebuke and scold their husbands. If husbands stop not short of anger, then they are certain to beat their wives. The correct relationship between husband and wife is based upon harmony and intimacy, and conjugal love is grounded in proper union. Should actual blows be dealt, how could matrimonial relationship be preserved? Should sharp words be spoken, how could conjugal love exist? If love and proper relationship both be destroyed, then husband and wife are divided.

Chapter 4: Womanly Qualifications

A woman ought to have four qualifications: 1. womanly virtue, 2. womanly words, 3. womanly bearing, and 4. womanly work. Now what is called womanly virtue need not be brilliant ability, exceptionally different from others. Womanly words need be neither clever in debate nor keen in conversation. Womanly appearance requires neither a pretty nor a perfect face and form. Womanly work need not be work done more skillfully than that of others.

To guard carefully her chastity, to control circumspectly her behavior, in every motion to exhibit modesty, and to model each act on the best usage — this is womanly virtue.

To choose her words with care, to avoid vulgar language, to speak at appropriate times, and not to weary others with much conversation may be called the characteristics of womanly words.

To wash and scrub filth away, to keep clothes and ornaments fresh and clean, to wash the head and bathe the body regularly, and to keep the person free from disgraceful filth may be called the characteristics of womanly bearing.

With wholehearted devotion to sew and to weave, to love not gossip and silly laughter, in cleanliness and order to prepare the wine and food for serving guests may be called the characteristics of womanly work.

These four qualifications characterize the greatest virtue of a woman. No woman can afford to be without them. In fact they are very easy to possess if a woman only treasure them in her heart. The ancients had a saying: "Is Love far off? If I desire love, then love is at hand!" [8] So can it be said of these qualifications.

Chapter 5: Wholehearted Devotion

Now in the *Rites* is written the principle that a husband may marry again, but there is no canon that authorizes a woman to be married the second time. Therefore it is said of husbands as of Heaven, that as certainly as people cannot run away from Heaven, so surely a wife cannot leave a husband's home.[9]

If people in action or character disobey the spirits of Heaven and of Earth, then Heaven punishes them. Likewise if a woman errs in the rites and in the proper mode of conduct, then her husband esteems her lightly. The ancient book, *A Pattern for Women*, says: "To obtain the love of one man is the crown of a woman's life; to lose the love of one man is to miss the aim in woman's life." [10] For these reasons a woman cannot but seek to win her husband's heart. Nevertheless, the beseeching wife need not use flattery, coaxing words, and cheap methods to gain intimacy.

Decidedly nothing is better to gain the heart of a husband than wholehearted devotion and correct manners. In accordance with the rites and the proper mode of conduct, let a woman live a pure life. Let her have ears that hear not licentiousness and eyes that see not depravity. When she goes

8. This is a direct quotation from the *Analects* (7.29) of Confucius. The word translated here as "love" is usually rendered as "benevolence" but is more accurately represented by "humaneness."

9. Even after the death of her husband, the worthy wife does not leave the home of his extended family.

10. More literally, this may be rendered as: "To become of like mind with one man may be said to be the final end; to fail to become of like mind with one man may be said to be the eternal end."

outside her own home, let her not be conspicuous in dress and manners. When at home let her not neglect her dress. Women should not assemble in groups, not gather together, for gossip and silly laughter. They should not stand watching in the gateways. If a woman follows these rules, she may be said to have wholehearted devotion and correct manners.

If, in all her actions, she is frivolous, she sees and hears only that which pleases herself. At home her hair is disheveled and her dress is slovenly. Outside the home she emphasizes her femininity to attract attention; she says what ought not to be said; and she looks at what ought not to be seen. If a woman does such as these, she may be said to be without wholehearted devotion and correct manners.

Chapter 6: Implicit Obedience

Now "to win the love of one man is the crown of a woman's life; to lose the love of one man is her eternal disgrace." This saying advises a fixed will and a wholehearted devotion for a woman. Ought she then to lose the hearts of her father- and mother-in-law?

There are times when love may lead to differences of opinion between individuals; there are times when duty may lead to disagreement. Even should the husband say that he loves something, when the parents-in-law say "no," this is called a case of duty leading to disagreement. This being so, then what about the hearts of the parents-in-law? Nothing is better than an obedience that sacrifices personal opinion.

Whenever the mother-in-law says, "Do not do that," and if what she says is right, unquestionably the daughter-in-law obeys. Whenever the mother-in-law says, "Do that," even if what she says is wrong, still the daughter-in-law submits unfailingly to the command.

Let a woman not act contrary to the wishes and opinions of parents-in-law about right and wrong; let her not dispute with them what is straight and what is crooked. Such docility may be called obedience that sacrifices personal opinion. Therefore the ancient book, *A Pattern for Women*, says: "If a daughter-in-law who follows the wishes of her parents-in-law is like an echo and a shadow, how could she not be praised?"

Chapter 7: Harmony with Younger Brothers- and Sisters-in-Law

In order for a wife to gain the love of her husband, she must win for herself the love of her parents-in-law. To win for herself the love of her parents-in-law, she must secure for herself the good will of younger brothers- and sisters-in-law. For these reasons the right and the wrong, the praise and the blame of a woman alike depend upon younger brothers- and sisters-in-law. Consequently it will not do for a woman to lose their affection.

They are stupid both who know not that they must not lose the hearts of younger brothers- and sisters-in-law, and who cannot be in harmony with them in order to be intimate with them. Excepting only the Holy Men, few are able to be faultless. Now Yen Tzu's [11] greatest virtue was that he was able to reform. Confucius praised him for not committing a misdeed the second time. In comparison with him a woman is the more likely to make mistakes.

Although a woman possesses a worthy woman's qualifications and is wise and discerning by nature, is she able to be perfect? Yet if a woman lives in harmony with her immediate family, unfavorable criticism will be silenced within the home. But if a man and woman disagree, then this evil will be noised abroad. Such consequences are inevitable. The *Classic of Changes* says:

> Should two hearts harmonize,
> The united strength can cut gold.
> Words from hearts which agree,
> Give forth fragrance like the orchid.

This saying may be applied to harmony in the home.

Though a daughter-in-law and her younger sisters-in-law are equal in rank, nevertheless they should respect each other; though love between them may be sparse, their proper relationship should be intimate. Only the virtuous, the beautiful, the modest, and the respectful young women can accordingly rely upon the sense of duty to make their affection sincere, and magnify love to bind their relationships firmly.

Then the excellence and the beauty of such a daughter-in-law becomes generally known. Moreover, any flaws and mistakes are hidden and unrevealed. Parents-in-law boast of her good deeds; her husband is satisfied with her. Praise of her radiates, making her illustrious in district and in neighborhood; and her brightness reaches to her own father and mother.

But a stupid and foolish person as an elder sister-in-law uses her rank [12] to exalt herself; as a younger sister-in-law, because of parents' favor, she becomes filled with arrogance. If arrogant, how can a woman live in harmony with others? If love and proper relationships be perverted, how can praise be secured? In such instances the wife's good is hidden and her faults are declared. The mother-in-law will be angry, and the husband will be indignant. Blame will reverberate and spread in and outside the home. Disgrace will gather upon the daughter-in-law's person, on the one hand to add hu-

---

11. Yen Hui, the favorite disciple of Confucius.

12. In the *Record of Rites* (*Li chi*), the power of control over the other sons' wives is accorded to the eldest daughter-in-law.

miliation to her own father and mother, and on the other to increase the difficulties of her husband.

Such then is the basis for both honor and disgrace, the foundation for reputation or for ill-repute. Can a woman be too cautious? Consequently, to seek the hearts of young brothers- and sisters-in-law decidedly nothing can be esteemed better than modesty and acquiescence.

Modesty is virtue's handle; acquiescence is the wife's most refined characteristic. All who possess these two have sufficiency for harmony with others. In the *Classic of Poetry* it is written that "Here is no evil; there is no dart." So it may be said of these two, modesty and acquiescence.

Translated by Nancy Lee Swann

Parallel Prose

163
Memorial of Indictment Against Liu Cheng

Jen Fang (460–508)

As Palace Aide to the Censor-in Chief, your subject, Jen Fang, bows his head to the ground and declares:

> Your subject has heard that
> Ma Yüan [1] honored his widowed sister-in-law;
> Unless he were wearing official garb, he would never approach her.
> Fan Yü [2] was kind to the orphans of his clan;

This text is a literary curiosity. The basic structure is that of highly mannered parallel prose. However, the euphuistic, allusive quality of this genre contrasts sharply with the quoted depositions of the witnesses, which contain a number of vernacular elements. These extremely rare passages constitute one of the earliest examples of written vernacular in China outside a Buddhist context. It is interesting to observe that Hsiao T'ung (501–531), the compiler of the *Literary Selections (Wen hsüan)*, in which this text was first anthologized, removed the vernacular passages, probably because of his belief that, while "content should derive from deep thought, form should be expressed in an elegant style." We must be grateful to Li Shan, the early T'ang commentator of the *Literary Selections*, who restored the vernacular passages to their rightful place.

The author was an official who served ably under three of the southern dynasties—Sung, Ch'i, and Liang—during the division between the north and south. Toward the end of his career, he was viewed as the chief arbiter in matters of prose writing.

For another example of parallel prose, see selection 12.

1. A general of the early Eastern Han period.

2. A man from the early Western Chin period who refused office and was content to live in poverty.

He treated them no differently from his own children.
Thus,
> The righteous sire and the man of mettle,
> Hearing these examples, strive to emulate them.
> As felicitous accounts of the last millennium,
> These two must be placed at the forefront.

Your subject, Jen Fang, kowtows repeatedly and begs your mercy over and over. Respectfully do I submit that the widow Fan of the last Chamberlain Administrator of Hsi-yang under the Ch'i dynasty, Liu Yin, came before the censorate to make a complaint. Her testimony was as follows:

> "I was married to Liu Yin for twenty some years. After his death, the care and upbringing of his orphaned children fell to me. Liu Yin's younger brother, Cheng, was constantly trying to do me harm. Before the division of the family property, he snatched away the slaves Docile Lad and Nunky, making them part of the clan's common holdings. Then he proceeded to compensate his sisters and younger brother Wen with cash, but kept the two slaves for his personal use. He then appropriated the maid, Green Grass, who belonged to Yin's son, Chün, and surreptitiously sold her for cash without even sharing any of it with Chün. Last year in the tenth month, Śrī (Good Fortune), Yin's second son by a concubine, betook himself to Cheng's fields where he stayed for twelve days, whereupon Cheng charged me six pecks of rice for feeding him. Before I had sent him the rice, he suddenly appeared at my door, shaking his fist at me through the curtain and cursing mightily. Abruptly, he barged into the room and seized the canopy for our cart that was hanging on the movable door-screen, taking it away as surety for the rice.
>
> "On the night of the ninth day of the second month, his maid Pretty Voice stole the railings, shafts, and harness for our cart. When I asked about the missing objects, Cheng gave my son Chün a beating. Cheng, his mother, and four servants came into my room and began cursing mightily with loud voices. The maid Pretty Voice raised her hand and grabbed me by the arm. I request that you apprehend them and investigate the matter in accordance with the complaint I have made."

I forthwith had the old slave, Ocean Frog, who had been owned by Liu Cheng's deceased father, apprehended and brought before the bench for interrogation. His testimony was as follows:

> "Cheng's deceased father Hsing-tao, who was the former general of Ling-ling commandery, had acquired four male and female slaves. When his property was divided up, the slave Docile Lad was given to his eldest son, Yin. After Yin died, his second son, Cheng, appropriated Docile Lad, saying: 'He should become part of the clan's common holdings.' Yet he

kept him for his personal use, compensating his sisters and younger brother to the amount of five thousand cash,[3] without sharing any of it with Chün. As for Yin's slave, Nunky, he had formerly been part of the clan's common holdings. Before Cheng and his brothers divided up the family property,[4] Cheng's older brother Yin mortgaged him for seven thousand cash so that he could work in the clan's fields.[5] When Yin gave up his position in Hsi-yang and returned, although the brothers had not yet broken up their households into separate eating units, he redeemed Nunky for seven thousand cash from his private funds and took him along to serve him in his new post at Canton. Later, when Yin died, Cheng divided up the male and female slaves with his brother and sisters, leaving only the maid Green Grass to become part of the clan's common holdings. Moreover, Cheng said that Yin had never paid for the redemption of Nunky, so he should revert to the clan's common holdings. Cheng's greedy intention was to get Nunky for himself and push Green Grass off on Chün. Cheng reckoned that when Nunky returned from Canton he would take him for his own purposes. Seven years passed, however, and Nunky did not come back, so Cheng thought he had already died and would never be back again. Consequently, he appropriated the maid Green Grass and sold her for seven thousand cash. Cheng divided up this money with his brother and sisters, once more not sharing any of it with Chün. Yin's wife Fan said, 'Nunky was privately redeemed by my late husband, so he should belong to our son Chün.' In the sixth month of the second year of the Heavenly Supervision reign period [503], Nunky returned from Canton. When he arrived, Cheng appropriated the slave for himself, saying, 'He should become part of the clan's common holdings as recompense for four years of wages[6] when he was employed by Yin in Canton.' Nunky is now working at Cheng's place."

I then had Cheng's maid Pretty Voice brought in for questioning. Her testimony was as follows.

"Last year on the twelfth day of the tenth month, Liu Cheng's older brother Yin's second son, Śrī, suddenly went off to the cottage of Cheng's where he stayed for twelve days. Cheng requested six pecks of rice from

3. A "cash" (< Portuguese *caixa* < Tamil *kācu* < Sanskrit *karṣa*) is a coin of small denomination, especially one with a perforated center through which a string may be passed for ease of carrying.

4. After their father's death.

5. It would have been Cheng's right to take Nunky with him when he assumed his position in Hsi-yang.

6. Since he was a slave, the value of Nunky's labor belonged to the clan as a whole, not to himself. Cheng refused to admit that Yin had ever paid the clan for the right to use Nunky for his own purposes in Canton.

his brother's wife, Fan, for feeding him. Before Fan was able to return the rice, Cheng got angry and barged into Fan's dwelling place, taking away a cart canopy that was hanging on her movable door-screen as security. Fan then sent Cheng the six pecks of rice, which he accepted at once.[7] This year on the night of the ninth of the second month, Fan lost the railings, shafts, harness, and so forth for her cart. She and her son Chün thought that they must have been stolen by me. When Cheng heard about their suspicions, he gave Chün a beating. Fan called out to him, asking, 'What do you mean by beating my son?' At that moment, Cheng and his mother came out from the central courtyard and argued with Fan through the curtain. I and the slaves Docile Boy, Ch'u Jade, and Dharmacārin, four of us all together, were standing to the left and right of Cheng and his mother at the time. Cheng told me, 'She said that you stole her cart furnishings. Why don't you go inside and bawl her out?', upon which I went in and wrangled with Fan. As I was raising my hand, I grabbed Fan by mistake. The cart railings, shafts, and harness were not stolen by me."

I then had Slovenly Slave, the slave of Yin's wife Fan, brought in for questioning. His testimony was as follows:

"The mistress said that on the night of the ninth of the second month, she lost the railings, shafts, and harness for her cart. She suspected that they were stolen by Cheng's maid Pretty Voice. The young master Chün and I went to the Chin-yang gate to sell rice and happened to see Pretty Voice there selling the railings and shafts for a cart. I wanted to catch her right away and take back the cart furnishings, but Chün said to me, 'Let it be! Don't try to take them back!' I lingered there stealthily for a little while and observed someone buy the harness for a price of five thousand cash. As I had to follow Chün home, I didn't see the money being handed over."

The testimonies of Pretty Voice, Slovenly Slave, and the others roughly corresponded with Fan's complaint. I then reexamined Nunky and Docile Lad, who testified: "We were appropriated from the mistress and are now working at Cheng's place." Since this was completely in agreement with the testimony of Ocean Frog, I turned the case over to the law. The director of the court, P'an Seng-shang (Saṃgha-Respecter), deliberated as follows:

"For summarily snatching away the maid of his brother's son Chün and selling her off before the division of the family property, and for using the slave Docile Lad and others for his own purposes, as if there were no official regulations, he should be forthwith detained in a nearby prison while his punishment is being determined. All those who have been

7. The implication being that Cheng never thought of returning the cart canopy.

implicated should be handed over to the penal officials while they are being cleared of the responsibility for what happened. Everything should be carried out in accordance with the institutions of the law. It is the opinion of the court that Cheng is the chief culprit."

Your servant respectfully states:

The recently appointed Adjutant of the Middle Army, Liu Cheng,

> Is nothing but a vulgar villain,
> Who flouts the doctrine of the sages.

Simply because

> He married the descendant of an erstwhile empress,
> He associated in office with the silk-stocking crowd.
> His evil deeds and violent offenses have long accumulated,
> So that even his family and friends look at him askance.
> In defiance of principle he directly confronted his sister-in-law,

And

> Recklessly gave vent to the most vile expressions.
> For his own child he would stay awake the whole night,

But

> He wantonly gave his nephew a sound thrashing.

> When Hsüeh Pao[8] divided up his property,
> He kept the old and weak slaves for himself;
> Kao Feng[9] besmirched himself to keep out of office,
> Fraudulently brought suit against his widowed sister-in-law.

Cheng did not observe

> The profound generosity of Hsüeh Pao;

He only emulated

> The mendacious precedent of Kao Feng.

> The ancient paragons regarded their relatives so magnanimously
> That not even clothing was considered a constant possession;
> While Cheng's niggardly treatment of his nephew
> Was like Kung-sun Hung's[10] feeding an old friend brown rice.[11]

Why could he not

> Tear up the debts for the bushels his sister-in-law owed,

8. A man of the Eastern Han period who, when faced with the demands of the younger members of his family to live separately, kept the worst of slaves, maids, fields, utensils, clothes, and so forth, for himself.

9. Another man of the Eastern Han period who, desperately desirous of keeping out of officialdom, defamed himself by claiming that he was originally a wizard and by pretending that he was engaged in a suit brought against the widow of his older brother.

10. A typical tightwad.

11. To serve someone imperfectly hulled rice was regarded as an insult in old China.

But instead
    Seized her fringed cart canopy for security?

    To think that human unkindness
    Could reach such a degree as this!
Truly, this is
    Something that cannot be tolerated by the doctrine of righteousness,
    Something that all men of stature must unanimously reject!

After consultation and deliberation, we request that Cheng be removed from office for his role in the present affair and that instructions forthwith be used for him to be detained externally [12] by the Chamberlain for Law Enforcement who will administer punishment according to legal and penal regulations. All those who have been involved should be handed over to the penal authorities while they are being cleared of responsibility for what happened. Everything should be carried out in accord with the institutions of the law. The maid Pretty Voice does not admit that she stole the cart railings, shafts, and harness, so we request that she be detained by the penal authorities while the truth is being determined. As for the clan elders and local authorities who did not intercede at the beginning and all others who are involved, we request that further investigation be suspended on the grounds of insufficient evidence. In sincere fear and trembling, your subject kowtows repeatedly and begs your mercy over and over. I bow my head to the ground as I inform you.

Translated by Victor H. Mair

12. That is to say, Liu Cheng is now to be tried and sentenced in the criminal courts, *outside* the special disciplinary proceedings reserved for officials.

164

Preface to "Ascending the Pavilion of King T'eng in Hung-chou on an Autumn Day for a Parting Feast"

Wang Po (648–675)

The pavilion is in the ancient prefecture of Yü-chang
Which is now the administrative center of Hung-chou.[1]

Li Yuan-ying (enfeoffed as King T'eng in 639) was the twenty-second son of the first T'ang emperor, Kao Tsu. He built the celebrated pavilion in 659 after he was appointed Military

> Its astronomical field is determined by Wing and Axletree;
> The land it is on adjoins the mountains Heng[2] and Lu.[3]

Governor of Hung-chou. It was a very fancy specimen of architecture and was considered to be the tourist spot *par excellence* in the south. After Li left this post, the pavilion seems to have fallen into disrepair, but it was renovated by 675, when Wang Po passed through Hung-chou on the way to see his father in distant Vietnam.

On the day of the Double Ninth Festival, Wang ascended the pavilion of King T'eng with the current Military Governor, Yen, and other guests for a farewell feast. Legend has it that the Military Governor first requested his son-in-law to compose a suitable piece in commemoration of the event and that he had a rough draft already prepared on the day of the feast. Out of courtesy, paper and brush were passed around to the guests, but they politely and sensibly declined to write the proposed commemorative piece. When the materials reached Wang, however, he impulsively accepted. The Military Governor brushed his clothes in indignation, stood up, and stepped outside to relieve himself. During his absence, his underlings were ordered to watch Wang closely as the latter wrote. As the preface came from Wang's brush, it was reported to the Military Governor line by line. The first report was:

> The pavilion is in the ancient prefecture of Yü-chang
> Which is now the administrative center of Hung-chou.

Upon hearing this, the Military Governor smiled and said, "This is the commonplace talk of old pedants." The next report was:

> Its astronomical field is determined by Wing and Axletree;
> The land it is on adjoins the mountains Heng and Lu.

To which His Honor commented, "Old hat!" A further report came:

> It is girdled by the three rivers and belted by the five lakes,
> Controls the way to barbarous Ch'u, is the gateway to the southeast.

The Military Governor muttered to himself but said nothing. Then, in rapid succession, a number of underlings came to announce what Wang Po had written. He could do no more than flap his jowls in grudging approval. When these famous lines (lines 41–42) were reported,

> Evening clouds descend and fly along together with a lonely wild duck;
> Autumn's waters coalesce in a single shade with the outstretched heavens.

the Military Governor, completely taken aback, was forced to admit: "This is true genius! It will last through the ages without tarnishing." In no time at all, the preface was completed and the Military Governor was greatly pleased with it. The feast was a joyous event, and Wang was presented with five hundred pieces of silk. Unfortunately, the poet died at the tender age of twenty-eight of complications from a near-drowning while on his journey to the remote south.

The Preface to "Ascending the Pavilion of King T'eng . . . ," deemed more important than the poem that it was ostensibly meant to accompany, is a fine model of parallel prose. Like nearly all such pieces, it is ornately euphuistic and highly mannered. Wang Po, recognized as one of the "Four Distinguished Poets of the Early T'ang," was about twenty-five years old when he wrote this enduring work of art.

1. Yü-chang and Hung-chou are two different names for the same place, located in north central Kiangsi, not far south of P'o-yang Lake.

2. Southernmost of the five sacred mountains of China, it would have been to the southwest of the pavilion in Hunan.

3. South of Chiu-chiang in Kiangsi, it would have been to the north of the pavilion.

5   It is girdled by the three rivers and belted by the five lakes,
    Controls the way to barbarous Ch'u,[4] is the gateway to the southeast.

The richness of its material culture is a heavenly treasure—
    the aura of swords transformed into dragons shoots up into
        space between the Dipper and the Herdboy;[5]
The excellence of its human resources is an earthly wonder—
    the Prefect, Ch'en Fan, put down a couch for a commoner, Hsü Ju-
    tzu.[6]

Grand cities spread out in a misty blur;
10 Brilliant men rush about like shooting stars.

Its walls and dry moats are a buffer at the nexus between central
    China and the southern barbarians;
The host and his guests are one and all the finest people of the
    southeast.

His Honor the Military Governor Yen has a reputation for
    refinement—
    preceded by a silk-covered spear for an insignia, he has made the
        long journey hither;
The Governor of Hsin-chou, Yü-wen, is a model of perfection—
    he has stopped his curtained carriage here to join us for a while.
15 The Military Governor is enjoying his fortnightly vacation—
    his bosom friends gather like clouds;
From hundreds of miles away they arrive to be welcomed—
    his illustrious companions fill all of the places.

Their writing is replete with dragon flourishes and phoenix flights—
    'tis the skill of the literatus Meng;[7]
Electric blue lightning and steely frost—
    here is an arsenal of military sagacity to match that of General
        Wang.

My father is now a district magistrate—
    on my way to see him, I have come to this famous place;
20 I am but a young man and have little knowledge—
    yet I have been fortunate enough to attend this sumptuous feast.

            ~   ~   ~

    4. A powerful southern kingdom during the Warring States period.
    5. Constellations.
    6. Ch'en (?–168 c.e.) was serving as Prefect of Yü-chang when this incident supposedly
occurred.
    7. Literatus Meng and General Wang are contrasting paradigms of talent.

Today is the ninth of the month;
The season is late autumn.[8]

Summer's rain puddles have all dried up, the water in the ponds is cold
    and clear;
A misty glimmer precipitates in a purple glow over the sunset hills.

25   Three abreast and heads held high, my chariot horses race along the
        high road,
There I visit scenic spots on lofty crests;
I look down on the long island of the imperial son, King T'eng,
And attain at last the venerable hall of that ethereal being.

Storied terraces raise their halcyon-colored roofs—
    above, the pavilion penetrates the layered clouds;
30   Soaring balconies seem a whirl of scarlet—
    below, they are suspended over empty space.

Spits for cranes and islets for wild ducks
    extend the length of the sinuous and islanded shores;
Cassia courts and magnolia mansions
    match the topography of the ridges and peaks.

           ~   ~   ~

The embroidered door-screens are thrown open;
We look down upon sculptured ridge-poles.

35   The vast breadth of the mountains and plains fills one's vision;
The tortuous turnings of the streams and marshes startles the eye.

Village gates and ward gates cover the ground—
    inside them are families that ring gongs for dinner and cook in
        huge bronze tripods;
Junks and barges obscure the ferry-crossings—
    their sterns are decorated with blue birds and yellow dragons.

The clouds clear, the rain stops;
40   The setting sun cuts a swath of light across the land.

Evening clouds descend and fly along together with a lonely wild duck;
Autumn's waters coalesce in a single shade with the outstretched
    heavens.

On the fishing boats, they are singing songs of evening—
    the echoes carry to the shores of P'o-yang Lake;

8. This would date the farewell feast on the ninth of the ninth month, which would be the
Double Ninth Festival.

A formation of wild geese is startled by the cold—
    their cries cut across the banks of Heng-yang[9]

~   ~   ~

45   Distant thoughts begin to unfurl;
    Surpassing fancies begin to take flight.

Nature's brisk pipes are vented, causing a soothing breeze to spring up;
Lilting songs linger in the air, bringing the white clouds to a halt.

As it did 'neath the green bamboos of King Hsiao's park by the Sui
    River,[10]
    the convivial atmosphere here, too, exceeds that of T'ao Ch'ien's
        solitary cup.[11]
As it did by the pink lotuses in the ponds of Ts'ao P'i's garden at Yeh,[12]
    the literary brilliance here, too, could illuminate Hsieh Ling-yün's[13]
        talented brush.

50   Here we have complete the four fortunes—a nice day, beautiful
        scenery,
                    appreciative hearts, and pleasant entertainment;
And, equally difficult to come by, both excellent guests and a worthy
    host.

They give full scope to the play of their vision which scans the mid-
    heavens;
Allow free rein to the pursuit of pleasure on this, their day of leisure.
The skies are high, the land is broad—
    one is made aware of the boundlessness of the universe;
55   Pleasure passes and sadness arrives—
    one is made to recognize that waxing and waning are fated.

I gaze toward Ch'ang-an[14] which seems to be beyond the sun,
Then point at Kuei-chi Mountain[15] amidst the clouds;

9. Southwest of Hung-chou in Hunan.

10. King Hsiao of Liang, the second son of Emperor Wen of the Han dynasty, built a pleasure garden at Sui-yang in Honan, where a coterie of the most famous rhapsody writers of the day gathered. One of them was Mei Ch'eng (see selection 124).

11. T'ao Ch'ien (see selection 20) was magistrate of P'eng-tse in Kiangsi and a famous toper.

12. The famous general Ts'ao Ts'ao (see selection 139) was enfeoffed here. Toward the end of the Chien-an reign period (196–219) of the Han dynasty, his sons, Ts'ao P'i and Ts'ao Chih, and other illustrious poets of the age would enjoy themselves in the Yen-hsi garden there.

13. See selection 21.

14. The capital of the T'ang dynasty, which was far to the north.

15. A reference to Shao-hsing, the intellectual and political seat of power in the south.

The latter's lay of land runs far—far to the deep South Sea,
Above the former, the Pillar of Heaven towers high—high as the
distant North Star.

60   Frontier passes and mountain peaks are difficult to cross—
who mourns for the man who loses his way?
Duckweed drifting on the water's surface, we meet—
we are one and all sojourners from another land.

I yearn for My Lord's gate but it is lost to my view;
When will I ever be summoned to his hall of audience?

~   ~   ~

Alas!

65   Fortunes differ,
Fate is often perverse;
Feng T'ang grew old without recognition,[16]
Li Kuang fought valiantly sans reward.[17]

Chia Yi was sent to Ch'ang-sha under duress, [18]
yet the reigning emperor was not unenlightened;
70   Liang Hung felt compelled to scurry away to a corner of the sea,[19]
but can one say that the age was lacking in sagacity?

Depend upon it:

The gentleman is unruffled by poverty;
The man of intelligence understands fate.

As we grow old, we ought to become stronger—
shall our hearts waver simply because our heads turn white?
75   In extremity, we should remain firm
and not allow our high and noble ambitions to flag.

Even when we drink from the fountain of avarice, we may still feel
generous;
Even if we be as fish in a dried-up rut[20] we may yet remain joyful.

16. Feng T'ang's true virtue and ability were recognized only very late in his life, at an age
when such recognition was of little practical value to him.
17. Li Kuang (?–119 B.C.E.) was an illustrious general who, through ill fortune, did not
receive the recognition he deserved.
18. A brilliant scholar who was slandered by jealous officials and banished to the south as
tutor of the king of Ch'ang-sha (see selection 123).
19. A farmer-recluse and poet sought by Emperor Chang (r. 76–88) who preferred to hire
himself out as a huller of rice rather than enter public life.
20. A reference to a well-known parable in the Chuang Tzu (see selection 8) about the
immediate urgency of a desperate request.

Though the North Sea is far away,
  one could reach it by riding a cyclone;
The sun may leave its bed in the east,
  but it is not too late even when it is resting in the treetops of the
    west.

80 Meng Ch'ang was a man of lofty ideals [21] —
  in vain did he cherish the desire to exert himself for the empire;
Juan Chi was wildly unrestrained [22] —
  one should not emulate him by crying when the road comes to an
    end.

~ ~ ~

I, Wang Po,

Am but a minor official who wears a short sash;
A mere student and a rather bookish one at that.

~ ~ ~

85 The way is not open for me to request the tokens of an important
    mission
  as Chung Chün [23] did, though I am still in my twenties as he
    was;
I yearn to throw aside my writing-brush
  in admiration of Tsung Ch'üeh's far-ranging aspiration. [24]

I renounce official hatpin and tablet for the rest of my life,
So that I may wait on my father, morning and night, in a distant
  place;
I am not so praiseworthy a son as the "jade trees" of the Hsieh
  family, [25]
90 But am pleased to find myself in virtuous company that Mencius'
    mother [26] would have approved of.

21. An upright official of the later Han dynasty.
22. Juan Chi (see selection 18) was a man given to strange behavior. Among other eccentricities, he would get in a chariot and drive off by himself when the urge took him. Leaving the beaten track, he would go on and on until he could go no farther, upon which he would cry pitifully.
23. Chung Chün (140–113 B.C.E.) was a precocious official who volunteered to go on a difficult mission to Annam.
24. As a youth, Tsung Ch'üeh was asked by his uncle what his ambition was. He replied that he wanted to mount a far-ranging wind to subdue a thousand miles of waves.
25. Hsieh Hsüan (343–388) declared as a youth that people desire worthy descendants because they are like "iris and orchid or a jade tree" growing in one's courtyard.
26. An allusion to the oft-repeated story of Mencius' mother moving thrice in order to find the ideal neighborhood for the benefit of her son.

Before long, I shall be hurrying across my father's courtyard
  respectfully to attend him and comply with his instructions as
    Confucius' son did;[27]
Today, however, I present myself to Your Lordship here,
  happy for this chance to entrust myself to your good graces.

Not having met a Yang Te-yi[28] who could introduce my work to an
    appreciative audience,
  I can but coddle my cloud-transcending artistry in self-
    commiseration:
Since I have already chanced upon an auditor as discerning as
    Chung Tzu-ch'i,
  why should I blush to perform my rills and trills?

~   ~   ~

95   Alack!

Places of scenic beauty do not last long,
Sumptuous feasts such as this are seldom repeated;
The Orchid Pavilion[29] is, alas, no more,
The Catalpa Marsh[30] has become a wasteland.

100   It is customary, on the eve of departure, to make a gift of words,
  Fortunate are we for having received from the Military Governor
                  this splendid farewell dinner;
To climb to a height and compose poetry
  is what he hopes from you, honorable gentlemen.

I have been so bold as to exert myself in all humility and sincerity
By respectfully inditing this brief introduction.
One word shall be assigned as the rhyme for all,

27. "Once Confucius was standing alone when his son, Li, came hurrying across the courtyard. Confucius asked him: 'Have you learned *The Classic of Odes* yet?' Li replied that he had not. 'If you do not study *The Classic of Odes*, you'll have nothing to talk about.' Li withdrew to study *The Classic of Odes*. Sometime later, Confucius was again standing alone when Li came hurrying across the courtyard. Confucius asked him: 'Have you learned the *Rites*?' Li replied that he had not. 'If you do not study the *Rites*, you will have nothing to stand on.' Li withdrew to study the *Rites*" (from the *Analects*).

28. Emperor Wu of the Han dynasty, on reading Ssu-ma Hsiang-ju's "Mr. Nonentity Rhapsody," lamented that he had not been fortunate enough to live at the same time as the author of such a marvelous piece of writing. Yang Te-yi, director of the palace kennels, informed him that the author was a native of his hometown in Szechwan and still quite alive. The emperor, of course, made much of Ssu-ma Hsiang-ju. The name Yang Te-yi, as an allusion, thus came to stand for an individual who could introduce a talented young writer to an appreciative and influential audience, particularly the emperor himself.

29. Site of the famous drinking party celebrated in selection 168.

30. A fabulous park owned by the inordinately wealthy Shih Ch'ung (249–300).

105   And four couplets will be required to complete the stanza;
       Be so kind as to let your rivers of poetic talent flow freely like that
           of P'an Yüeh,
       Each of you, pour out your oceans of genius as Lu Chi [31] did,
                                                               if you please. [32]

    ~ ~ ~   ~ ~ ~

   The high pavilion of King T'eng looks down upon the islets in the
       river,
   The jade pendants and tinkling carriage bells of visiting officials, the
       songs and dances of old are all silent now;

   In the morning, painted beams soar like the clouds over South Bank,
IV In the evening, beaded curtains are rolled up like the rain above West
       Mountain.

   Lazy clouds are reflected in deep pools, the days pass leisurely by,
   The landscape changes, the stars shift—how many autumns have there
       been?

   Inside the pavilion, where is the royal scion today?
VIII Outside the balustrade, the long river flows on—expressionless and
       unheeding.

Translated by Victor H. Mair

31. P'an and Lu, often linked together, were poets of the Western Chin period.
32. The parallel prose preface ends here with an invitation to the assembled worthies jointly to compose the poem which follows.

Letters

165
Letter to Han Ching-chou

Li Po (701–762)

I have heard that, when the empire's chatty scholars gather together, they say to each other, "During one's lifetime, it is not necessary to be a marquis with the income from ten thousand households, if one could hope but once to make the acquaintance of Han, the Governor of Ching-chou." [1] How is it that you have caused men to lionize you to such a degree? Is it not because you have the spirit of the Duke of Chou, who, in his anxiety not to miss any callers, would interrupt his meals by spitting out his food and his bath by wringing his half-washed hair? [2] The result is that all the elite within the realm rush to you and give you their allegiance. Once having passed the hurdle of gaining your recommendation, [3] their credit increases tenfold. Thus, those gentlemen who are hidden away in retirement like coiled dragons and reclusive phoenixes are all desirous of receiving a good name and establishing their worth with Your Honor. I pray that Your Honor does not pride yourself

This is one of a series of letters which the famous T'ang poet Li Po (see selection 35) wrote in search of political patronage. It has been dated to the year 734.

1. Han Ch'ao-tsung's (686–750) checkered official career included a drastic demotion late in life for cowardice in the face of rumors that rebels were on the verge of insurrection.

2. The mention of the Duke of Chou seems to have been a common technique in letters such as these.

3. The famous "dragon gate" through which aspiring candidates for preferment had to pass in order to become transformed from small fry into adult fish (i.e., officials).

on association with the rich and noble,[4] nor scorn the poor and lowly. Then, if among your many guests there would be a Mao Sui,[5] should I but get a chance to show the tip of my head, I shall be that man.

I am a commoner from Lung-hsi[6] and have drifted here to Ching-chou.[7] At fifteen, I was fond of swordsmanship and ranged broadly in search of employment with various lords. At thirty, I became an accomplished litterateur and contacted successively a number of high officers. Although I am not quite a six-footer,[8] I am braver than ten thousand men. Princes, dukes, and high ministers admit that I have moral courage and high principles. This, then, has been my past spiritual biography. How could I venture not to explain it fully to Your Lordship?

Your writings are worthy of the gods and your virtuous conduct moves Heaven and Earth. Your pen is imbued with creative energy and your scholarship plumbs heavenly principles and human affairs. I hope, because of your open-mindedness and good nature, that I shall have the good fortune not to meet with a refusal in making this low bow before you.[9] If you receive me with grand feasts, give free rein to my untrammeled discourse,[10] and then request that I attempt to indite ten thousand words a day, just wait! I'll dash

---

4. "Not to pride yourself on the rich and noble" is from the ninth chapter of the *Tao te ching* (see selection 9).

5. Li Po, in asking for a chance to show his talents, cannot avoid comparing himself to Mao Sui, a follower of the Lord of P'ing-yüan of the Chao kingdom during the Warring States period. Mao, though occupying an obscure position in his lord's entourage, volunteered to go to Ch'u in search of aid for the relief of the Chao capital, Han-tan, which had been surrounded by Ch'in. The Lord of P'ing-yüan was at first reluctant to allow Mao the privilege of the mission because he had not distinguished himself in the three years he had dwelt with his lord. The situation, said the lord, was similar to an awl being placed in a bag. If it were at all sharp, surely it would show its tip at once. To this Mao replied that were he really placed in the bag of opportunity, his sharpness would allow him to come completely out. The expression "Mao Sui introduces himself" has come to be used as an epithet to describe one who volunteers for a task that others may have thought him less than qualified to perform. We may note that, although Mao Sui did indeed "introduce himself," the metaphor of an awl in a bag was originally suggested by the Lord of P'ing-yüan. Mao but elaborated upon it.

6. Not so. For Li Po to say that he was from Lung-hsi (the southeast corner of Kansu) is to make the same sort of claim of aristocratic connections that someone with the surname Wang makes when he says that he comes from Lang-yeh (the eastern portion of Shantung). Li is known to have spent his early years at Ch'ing-lien village of Ch'ang-ming district in Szechwan, but his ancestry is also generally acknowledged to include certain Central Asian connections. The scholarly consensus now would appear to be that Li Po was of at least partially Turkic extraction.

7. Li Po uses the ancient appellation, Ch'u Han.

8. A rough approximation from the "seven (Chinese) feet" in the text.

9. That is, "in paying this formal call."

10. The "untrammeled discourse" ("pure talk" or "unsullied discourse") is a carryover from the epoch of division between the north and the south.

them off on the spur of the moment.[11] Today, the whole empire holds you to be the life-and-death arbiter in literary matters and the scales upon which men are weighed. Once having been adjudged worthy by you, one can then be a superb scholar. So why should you begrudge me a modest space before your stairs, thus neither allowing me a feeling of pride and self-fulfillment nor stimulating me to rise up to the cloudy blue?[12]

Of old, when Wang Tzu-shih[13] was serving as Governor of Yü-chou, he summoned Hsün Tz'u-ming[14] even before he had assumed office.[15] And, when he did assume office, he summoned K'ung Wen-chü.[16] When Shan T'ao was acting as Governor of Chi-chou, he picked out more than thirty individuals who became either court attendants or state secretaries, for which he was admired by previous generations.[17] Your Lordship, as well, had but to recommend Harmonizer of the Scales Yen and he was admitted to the court as Secretary in the Imperial Library. Among others, there are people like Ts'ui Tsung-chih,[18] Fang Hsi-tsu, Li Hsin, and Hsü Jung, some of whom made your acquaintance because of their reputation for brilliance and some of whom were appreciated by you because of their unimpeachable character. I have often observed their introspective devotion and the way they exert themselves in acts of loyalty. As a result, I am deeply impressed and realize the empathy which you extend to worthy individuals. Therefore, I shall not give my allegiance to anyone else but willingly entrust myself to you who are without peer in our land. Should you ever get into difficulty such that I might be of use to you, may I be so bold as to offer, in gratitude, my humble services? Yet none of us is a Yao or a Shun.[19] Who can be perfect? How

11. This allusion is from A New Account of Tales of the World (see selection 202): "Huan Hsüan-wu (312–373) was engaged in a northward expedition. Yüan Hu (328–376), at this time, was in attendance. He was reprimanded and relieved of his office. But when there was a necessity for spreading abroad a proclamation, Yüan was called forward and ordered to write while leaning against his horse. The pen in his hand did not stop once and, before long, seven pages were produced. It was decidedly something worth seeing. Wang Tung-t'ing (350–401) was standing nearby and exclaimed at length on Yüan's genius, to which Yüan Hu replied, 'It ought to gain some advantage for us in a war of words.' "

12. A euphemism for "official employment."

13. Wang Yün (137–192), a precocious official of the Later Han period.

14. Hsün Shuang (128–190), another noted official from the latter part of the Later Han.

15. Literally, "even before he had descended from his carriage."

16. K'ung Jung (153–208), a twentieth-generation descendant of Confucius and an active proponent of the sage's teaching.

17. Shan T'ao (205–283). In his biography in the Chin History, we read, "When Shan T'ao was serving as the governor of Chi-chou, he discerned and elevated men who dwelt in obscurity or who had been wronged. He sought out and visited men of virtue and talent."

18. His name was Ch'eng-fu, but he went by his style. Ts'ui held the hereditary title of Duke of Ch'i as well as several posts in the T'ang government. He was also a drinking companion of Li Po. Little is known of the following three individuals.

19. Two legendary emperors.

could I be so presumptuous as to boast of my counsels and plans? As for my own writings, I have accumulated a large number of scrolls. Although I flatter myself that you will deign to look at them, I fear that these "insect carvings" and trivial exercises will not suit Your Honor's taste. If you would do me the favor of reading my rustic pieces, please provide me with paper and ink along with a copyist. Then I shall retreat to a vacant room and, having tidied it up, will have a copy of them made to present to you. This is similar to the increased value which would accrue to the sword, Cyan Duckweed, by placing it at the door of Hsüeh Chu and to the gem, Congealed Greenness, by placing it at the door of Pien Ho.[20]

May you extend your blessings to me in my lowly station, greatly encouraging and rewarding me. It all depends on how Your Lordship views[21] the matter.

Translated by Victor H. Mair

20. Hsüeh Chu, an expert at identifying swords, was from Viet, and Pien Ho was a man who knew the value of gems—one in particular (see selection 14, note 4). Both men lived during the Spring and Autumn period of antiquity. The translation assumes a pair of hypothetical situations—not that Hsüeh Chu actually saw Cyan Duckweed or that Pien Ho really knew of Congealed Greenness. Li Po does not associate the two connoisseurs with the objects normally linked with them (namely, the swords Ch'un-kou and Chan-lu, on the one hand, and the gem Ho-shih Pi, on the other), probably because he thought it would leave a flat taste and because of the faint, but pleasant, echo between the two types of greenness in the names that he does use.

21. To be more blunt, how you "plan" for me, i.e., "the matter is now in your hands—it's up to you!"

166
Letter in Reply to Liu Yi-chang

Tsung Ch'en (1525–1560)

From several thousand tricents away, I occasionally receive a letter from you, which satisfies my constant sense of yearning. This, indeed, makes me feel already very fortunate. Why need you have further troubled yourself by favoring me with gifts? This leaves me wondering all the more how I shall

In this well-known description of literati toadying during the Ming dynasty, the sycophant is mercilessly satirized. The blatant ills of parasitism described here were fostered by the ruthlessness and corruption of the prime minister, Yen Sung (d. 1562), and his son, Yen Shih-fan.

Tsung Ch'en was a member of a group of writers and critics active during the mid-sixteenth century who were known as the later Seven Masters and who were advocates of archaism.

repay you. The cordiality of your letter is evidence of your not forgetting my father and your awareness that his regard for you is profound. And, when you speak to me of "superior and inferior persons having mutual trust" and "ability and good character corresponding to position," I am deeply moved.

That my ability and character are not in keeping with my position is something of which I am keenly aware; and I am especially to be faulted when it comes to the question of trust. But nowadays when we speak of mutual trust what do we mean? Here is one who whips up his horse day and night to wait at the gates of the powerful. The gatekeeper, on purpose, does not admit him. Then, with sweet words and seductive phrases, and putting on the airs of a woman, he takes some money from his sleeve and presses it upon the gateman. Even if the gateman does take in his calling card, the host does not come out to see him at once. Standing in the stable amidst the grooms, noxious fumes permeating his clothing, even if the hunger and cold or the cruel summer heat are unbearable, he does not leave.

When evening comes, the one who had earlier received the money comes out and announces to the guest, "His Lordship is weary and cannot see any more guests. You are requested to come back tomorrow." So the next day, he dares not refrain from coming. At night, he sits up with a robe thrown over his shoulders. As soon as he hears the cock crow, he rises and performs his morning toilet. As he races his horse up to the gate, the gatekeeper angrily asks, "Who are you?," to which he responds, "The guest who came yesterday." Whereupon the gatekeeper angrily counters, "You're very persistent, aren't you? Do you think that His Lordship receives guests at such an hour?"

The guest feels shamed yet forces himself to forbear.

"But I'm desperate! You'll just have to let me in."

The gatekeeper again collects his gift of money, gets up, and goes in. Again, the guest stands in the stable where he previously stood.

Fortunately, the host comes out and, facing the south, beckons him. Whereupon he runs timorously and crawls on hands and knees to the foot of the steps.

"Enter!" the host says. He prostrates himself twice and purposely is slow about rising. When he does rise, he offers up his gifts of gold and silk. The host purposely refuses them but the guest is firm in insisting that he take them. The host purposely persists in his refusal and the guest persists with his offer. At last, the host orders an underling to take them for him, upon which the guest again prostrates himself twice and is again purposely slow about rising. When he does rise, he bows five or six times before finally going out. As he leaves, he bows to the gatekeeper and says, "It was so kind of you to be considerate of me. When I come again some day, I hope that you'll not hinder me." The gatekeeper bows in reply.

Overjoyed, he goes rushing off. Riding along on his horse, when he meets someone he knows, he at once flourishes his whip and informs him, "I'm just coming from His Lordship's house. His Lordship is so good to me! Oh, he's so good to me!" And he makes up a lot of stories describing his visit. Even those with whom he is well acquainted are awed by His Lordship's liberal reception. His Lordship, too, voices it about here and there, "So-and-so is a man of virtue. He really is!" And those who hear this approve and praise him to one another. This, then, is what people call "the superior and the inferior having mutual trust." Do you believe that I am capable of this?

As for the powerful families mentioned, I never visit them the whole year long except to hand in a calling card at New Year's and on the summer and winter holidays. If, on occasion, my path takes me by one of their gates, then I stop up my ears, close my eyes, and gallop away on my horse as fast as though there were someone in pursuit. It is on account of this narrow-mindedness of mine that I have never been liked by the senior officials. But, increasingly, I pay no heed to all this and am always making such grandiose statements as: "Human life is fated; the only thing for me to do is to be content with my own lot." When you hear this, can you not but be exasperated by my nonconformity?

Translated by Victor H. Mair

Prefaces and Postfaces

167

Postface to *Explanation of Simple and Compound Graphs*

Hsü Shen (fl. 100–121)

In ancient times, P'ao-hsi[1] came to rule the world. Looking up, he contemplated the phenomena in the sky, and looking down, the markings on the

The *Explanation of Simple and Compound Graphs* (*Shuo wen chieh tzu*) is the oldest extant comprehensive dictionary of the sinographs or Chinese characters. The *Shuo wen* (as it is usually styled for short) was preceded—probably by a couple of centuries—by a small lexicon entitled *Elegance* (*Erh-ya*), which was a listing of synonyms arranged according to categories together with occasional short definitions. It cannot be emphasized too strongly, however, that the *Shuo wen* itself is not a true dictionary of words but rather one of graphs. That is to say, the *Shuo wen* does not explain either the semantic or the true etymological properties of words in the spoken language. Rather, it analyzes the forms, sounds, and meanings of the graphs used to write individual syllables, which are usually—but by no means always—equivalent to monosyllabic words. Recent phonological and etymological researches have shown that the explanations of the graphs in the *Shuo wen* are often mistaken or irrelevant for an understanding of the words of the living language that they are meant to represent, a significant proportion of which were bisyllabic even at the time of the writing of the *Shuo wen*. It is essential, when conceptualizing the nature of the sinographs and trying to comprehend how they function, that a clear distinction be made between a given language and a particular script (which is one possible vehicle among many that might be used to record the language).

Regardless of its classification, the *Shuo wen* has been enormously influential in shaping Chinese conceptions of the nature of writing. The opening and closing sections of its postface are included here to afford the reader some idea of how sinographs are constructed and,

earth. He observed the patterns on birds and animals and their adaptations to the earth. From nearby, he took some hints from his own body, and elsewhere from other things. Then he began to make the eight trigrams of the *Changes*,[2] to pass on to others the regular patterns in the world.

Later, when the Divine Farmer[3] made knots in rope[4] to direct and regularize activities, all kinds of trades and professions were multiplied, and then artificial and refined things sprouted and grew.

Ts'ang Chieh, scribe for the Yellow Emperor, on looking at the tracks of the feet of birds and animals, realizing that the principles and forms were distinguishable, started to create graphs,[5] so that all kinds of professions could be regulated, and all categories of people could be kept under scrutiny. This he probably took from the hexagram *Kuai*. "*Kuai*: exhibit in the royal court" — means the patterns show education and enlightenment to the king's court. "Thus the ideal man bestows benefits on his subordinates. If one is virtuous, one is cautious."[6]

When Ts'ang Chieh first created writing (*shu*), he probably imitated the forms according to their categories; so the figures were called "patterns" (*wen*). Later, when the writings were increased by combining the forms and phonetics, the results were called "compound graphs" (*tzu*). "Compound graph" means reproduction and gradual increase. When they are written on bamboo and silk, they are called "records" (*shu*). "Records" means likeness.

During the time of the Five Emperors and Three Kings,[7] the writing

moreover, to provide a sense of the mythological awe in which writing was held by the early Chinese.

The compiler of the *Shuo wen* was Hsü Shen, who came from the present-day Yen-ch'eng district, Honan province. His activities were centered on the study of the Five Classics: *Changes, Documents, Odes, Rites,* and *Spring and Autumn Annals*. Hsü belonged to the ancient text school of textual critics, who often differed on points of interpretation with the modern text school (it is actually ancient now, of course, but was considered "modern" to Hsü Shen and his contemporaries). According to the biographical information in the *History of the Han Dynasty*, Hsü was considered to be without peer in the study of the Five Classics. Indeed, his motivation in compiling the *Shuo wen* was to counter the ideas on the interpretations of the Classics espoused by a rival school of textual critics.

Hsü held several official posts, but retired to carry on his studies. He probably finished the *Shuo wen* in 100 c.e., but it was not until 121 that Hsü's son presented it to the throne, while the compiler was ill.

1. Alternate name Fu-hsi, the mythological emperor and first man.

2. See selection 3.

3. The mythological emperor and supposed inventor of agriculture.

4. Compare with the Peruvian quipu.

5. This could be interpreted as "graphs" or "carving of graphs."

6. With minor differences, these quotations can be found in the *Classic of Changes* (see selection 3).

7. Mythological rulers of hoary antiquity.

changed into various styles. Of the seventy-two[8] eras in which altars were made on Mount T'ai, all used different styles.

In the *Rites of Chou* it says:[9] "When children reached the age of eight *sui*,[10] they began the study of language arts under the Protector, who started teaching the children of the nobles the six types of graphs."

The first is called "indicate-things." When one sees a graph of this type it may be understood on seeing it; by inspection one sees the meaning.[11] The graphs "up" (*shang* 上) and "down" (*hsia* 下) are of this sort.

The second is called "imitate-form." For this type one draws a picture of an object; thus the lines follow the natural shape. "Sun" (*jih* 日) and "moon" (*yüeh* 月) are of this sort.

The third is called "form-and-sound." For this type, a name is made after considering a relation of things, i.e., a comparison is made by combination of phonetic and classifier. "Stream" (*chiang* 江) and "river" (*ho* 河) are of this sort.

The fourth is called "join-meaning." For this type, suitable figures are compared and suitably combined, whereby appears what is indicated. "Warrior" (*wu* 武) and "trust" (*hsin* 信) are of this sort.

The fifth is called "interchangeable notation." For this type, one establishes a category, then puts other graphs with similar meanings under that category. The two graphs for "aged" (*k'ao* 考 and *lao* 老) are of this sort.

The sixth is called "loan-borrowing." These are for words which originally had no graph of their own and depend on the sounds to stand for something else. "Command" and "honorable" (*ling* 令) and "grow" or "long" (*chǎng* and *ch'áng* 長) are of this sort.[12]

~   ~   ~   ~   ~   ~

The *Documents* says: "I wish to contemplate the designs of the ancients."[13] This means one must follow the old writings and not make distortions.[14] Confucius said: "I can remember when a scribe left a blank in his text. Now this is no longer done, alas."[15] It is not because men do not know and do not ask, but because if they all used their own private judgment, right and wrong would have had no standard, and clever opinions and heterodox

8. Eurasian mystical number not to be taken literally.

9. There is no such statement in the *Rites of Chou (Chou li)* as the text now exists, although it mentions the six types of graphs taught by the Protector.

10. I.e., having passed the seventh lunar new year after birth.

11. These characterizations of the six types of graphs are all in the form of two rhymed lines of four syllables each, as though a mnemonic device. The meanings are subject to speculation.

12. Here the translation skips from the opening section of the postface to its final section.

13. Quoted from the *Classic of Documents* (see selection 157).

14. Literally, "to bore through," hence "to give a farfetched or strained interpretation," "to read too much into something," "to overinterpret."

15. Quoted from the *Analects* (see selection 6).

pronouncements would have caused confusion among all the scholars under heaven.

Now the written language is the foundation of classical learning, the source of kingly government. It is what the former generations relied on to transmit culture to later ages and what men of later times rely on to understand antiquity. Therefore it is said: "When the foundation is established, the Way grows";[16] and "When you know all under heaven that is extremely obscure, you cannot be confused." [17]

Now I have arranged the small seal graphs together with ancient Chou graphs. I have broadly adopted from those who understand the small and the great, from those who are believable and have proof, and I preserve and explain their opinions.

In order to classify all kinds of things and correct mistakes, and to state clearly to wise scholars the subtle meanings, I have divided the graphs into groups, so as not to confuse them with each other. The myriad things can be found here, and nothing has been omitted. If some meanings are not clear, then I explain with examples.

I follow the interpretations in the text of the *Changes* preserved by Meng Hsi, the *Documents* by K'ung An-kuo, and the *Odes* by Mao Kung. As to texts on ritual, I have used that of the Chou officials, and I took Tso's commentary on the *Spring and Autumn Annals*. I also used the *Analects* and the *Classic of Filial Piety*. In each case I used the ancient text.[18] That with which I am not familiar I omitted.

Translated by K. L. Thern

16. Quoted from the *Analects*.
17. A similar line occurs in the *Classic of Changes*.
18. However, in the dictionary Hsü actually cites texts from both ancient and modern texts.

168
Preface to *Collected Poems from the Orchid Pavilion*

Wang Hsi-chih (c. 303–c. 361)

In the ninth year of the Eternal Harmony era in the beginning of the last month of spring when the calendar was in *kuei-ch'ou*,[1] we met at the Orchid

Wang Hsi-chih, from Kuei-chi (modern-day Shao-hsing, Chekiang), was an influential official, writer, and, above all, calligrapher during the Eastern Chin dynasty. He wrote this

Pavilion in Shan-yin, Kuei-chi, to celebrate the Bathing Festival.[2] All the worthy men assembled; the young and the senior gathered together. Here were lofty mountains and towering hills, thick groves and tall bamboo. And, there was a clear, rapid stream reflecting everything around that had been diverted to play the game of floating wine-cups along a winding course. We sat down in order of precedence. Though we had none of the magnificent sounds of strings and flutes, a cup of wine and then a poem was enough to stir our innermost feelings.

This was a day when the sky was bright and the air was pure. A gentle breeze warmed us. Upwards we gazed to contemplate the immensity of the universe; downwards we peered to scrutinize the abundance of living things. In this way, we let our eyes roam and our emotions become aroused so that we enjoyed to the fullest these sights and sounds. This was happiness, indeed!

Men associate with each other but for the brief span of their lives. Some are content to control their innermost feelings as they converse inside a room. Some are prompted to give rein to their ambitions and lead wild, unfettered lives. There is all the difference between controlled and abandoned natures, just as the quiescent and the frenzied are unalike. Yet, both take pleasure from whatever they encounter, possessing it but for a while. Happy and content, they remain unaware that old age is fast approaching. And, when they tire of something, they let their feelings change along with events as they experience a deep melancholy. What they had taken pleasure in has now passed away in an instant, so how could their hearts not give rise to longing? Furthermore, a long or short life depends on the transformation of

---

preface to commemorate a festive springtime gathering of forty-one notable figures, who made an excursion outside Kuei-chi to a spot about ten miles southwest of modern-day Shao-hsing on April 22, 353. As part of the entertainment, wine-cups were floated down a winding stream, and the guests were asked to write a poem before the cups passed their seats or else drink a forfeit. Only twenty-six guests were able to comply, and their efforts were gathered in a volume to which Wang wrote this short introduction. Despite its brevity, few examples of Chinese prose have had such widespread influence on subsequent literati culture. Wang was canonized as the "sage" of calligraphy, and the original text in his hand became a model of the "running script." The image of the gathering generated a veritable cult of the Orchid Pavilion celebrated in poetry, painting, and the decorative arts while the area of the original event became a literary shrine.

The preface was an important place for a Chinese author to make a statement about the purpose of his own literary work or about the nature of literature in general. Beyond that, however, the prefaces themselves often have literary significance. Other prefaces collected in this anthology are found in selections 12 and 164.

1. April 22, 353.

2. The Bathing Festival was originally an ancient festival of purification held in the first ten days of the third lunar month when the people would go to sacrifice and bathe in a nearby river or lake. During the Six Dynasties period, its early religious significance was lost, and it became a social occasion for the literati to gather and write poetry.

all things: everything must come to an end. An ancient said, "Life and death are the greatest of matters, indeed!" [3] Isn't this reason enough to be sad?

Whenever I read of the causes of melancholy felt by men of the past, it is like joining together two halves of a tally. I always feel sad when I read them, yet I cannot quite understand why. But I know that it is meaningless to say life and death are the same; and to equate the longevity of P'eng-tsu with that of Shang-tzu is simply wrong.[4] Future readers will look back upon today just as we look back at the past. How sad it all is! Therefore, I have recorded my contemporaries and transcribed what they have written. Over distant generations and changing events, what gives rise to melancholy will be the same. Future readers will also feel moved by these writings.

Translated by Richard Strassberg

3. See *Chuang Tzu* (see selection 8), chapter 12: "Confucius said, 'Life and death are the greatest of matters, indeed, but he [Wang T'ai] is unaffected by them. Although Heaven may overturn and the Earth might sink, it is no loss to him. He carefully observes whatever is pure and does not let things influence him. He recognizes as fate the transformation of things and holds fast to their guiding principles.' " Here, Confucius is ironically made to espouse Chuang Tzu's philosophy by praising a cripple, Wang T'ai, who had his foot cut off as a penalty yet gathered as many disciples as Confucius himself.

4. See *Chuang Tzu*, chapter 5: "No one has lived longer than Shang-tzu and P'eng-tsu died young." Chuang Tzu paradoxically reverses the common belief that P'eng-tsu lived for eight hundred years, longer than any other man, and that Shang-tzu died in his youth.

169
Preface to the "Foolish Brook Poems"

Liu Tsung-yüan (773–819)

To the north of the Kuan River, there is a brook. It flows eastward into the Hsiao River. Some say that a Mr. Jan once lived there and hence named it Jan Brook. Some say that the water in the brook can be used for dye [*jan*]

This preface, written in 810, also functions as a landscape essay. The author, Liu Tsung-yüan (see selection 44), was one of the most brilliant practitioners of that genre. In this very peculiar landscape essay, Liu dwells on the theme of "foolishness" (*yü*) and expresses not so much his love of nature, but his obsession with the recent change in his fortunes and his own role in his disgrace. Because of his association with the Wang Shu-wen faction at court, he lost favor after Emperor Shun Tsung (reigned 805) was forced to abdicate on account of severe illness. It was during his banishment to a minor post in remote Yung-chou (Hunan province) that he wrote the "Foolish Brook Poems" and their preface.

and that it was named "Dye Brook" because of this property. I have transgressed through my foolishness and consequently have been banished to the bank of the Hsiao River. I am fond of this brook. I went upstream one day for two or three tricents and came upon an especially exquisite place, and I made my home there. In ancient times, there was a Valley of the Foolish Old Man.[1] Now, having made the brook the site of my home, I could not decide on a name for it. Every day, people passing by argued continually over its name, so that the name could not remain unchanged. Therefore I changed its name to Foolish Brook.

Along Foolish Brook I purchased a small hill and called it Foolish Hill. Sixty paces to the northeast of Foolish Hill, there is a spring. I purchased it for my dwelling place and called it Foolish Spring. The spring has six mouths out of which water gushes up from under the hill. Flowing together, the water from the six openings meanders southward to form Foolish Ditch. I had earth carried there and stones piled up to dam the water where the passage is narrow, and thereby made Foolish Pond. East of Foolish Pond, I built Foolish Hall, and south of the hall, I built Foolish Pavilion. In the pond is Foolish Island. Beautiful trees and rare stones are placed there. They are all remarkable sights in this landscape, but because of me, they suffer the mortification of carrying the name "foolish." Water is a substance in which the wise man takes delight. Why must this brook alone suffer the mortifying name "foolish"?

Its water level is so low that it cannot be used for irrigation. Moreover, its currents are too rapid, and there are too many islets and rocks in it, so large boats cannot enter it. Besides, it is too secluded and too recessed, too shallow and too narrow; no dragon would ever deign to live in it because there is not enough water with which to make clouds and rain. It has nothing to offer to the world. In that respect it is exactly like me. This being the case, it might as well tolerate the humiliation of being called "foolish."

Ning-wu Tzu acted as if he were foolish when his country was in disorder.[2] He was a wise man, but he acted in an apparently foolish way. Master Yen Hui never disagreed with any of Confucius' teachings as if he were a foolish man.[3] He was someone who was intelligent but appeared to be foolish. In my case, I live under an orderly government, but I have gone against the

1. Lin-chih district in Shantung.
2. An allusion to *Analects*, 5.20: "The Master said, 'When good order prevailed in his country, Ning Wu acted the part of a wise man. When his country was in disorder, he acted the part of a stupid man. Others may equal his wisdom, but they cannot equal his stupidity'" (translated by James Legge).
3. *Analects*, 2.9: "I have talked with Hui for a whole day and he has not made any objection to anything I said; as if he were stupid. He was retired, and I have examined his conduct when away from me and found him able to illustrate my teachings. Hui! He is not stupid" (translated by James Legge).

inherent principle of things and mishandled state affairs. Hence no one who has acted foolishly is as foolish as I am. This being so, then no one in the world can rival my claim to this brook. I have the sole right to name it "foolish."

The brook has nothing to offer to the world, but it serves well as a mirror to all creation. It is limpid, lustrous, graceful, and pure. It jingles like the ancient bells and lithostones. It delights the foolish one so much that he, laughing merrily, is totally infatuated with it and cannot bear to leave.

Although I am out of tune with the times, yet I still take considerable comfort in writing. I can immerse the myriad creatures in my works and capture all their forms and poses, letting nothing escape. I sing about Foolish Brook with my foolish verses; they go surprisingly well together in their common obscurity. Overtaking the undifferentiated state of the primordial world, and submerging myself in its insentience, vacuous and inane, I will thus be recognized by no one. Therefore, I have written eight foolish poems and have recorded them on rocks by Foolish Brook.

Translated by Yu-shih Chen

170

Postface to a Catalog on a Collection of Bronze and Stone Inscriptions

Li Ch'ing-chao (1084–c.1151)

I married into the Chao family in 1101. My father-in-law [1] was the minister of civil service, but the family did not live extravagantly. Te-fu (my husband) was at that time a student at the Imperial University. On the first and fifteenth of every month, he could leave college. He would pawn his clothing and with 500 cash [2] in his pocket go to Hsiang-kuo Temple in search of old prints and come home with some fruit. We would enjoy examining what he had bought while munching fruit together. Two years later, when he got a post in the government, he started to make as complete as possible a collection of rubbings or prints from bronze or stone inscriptions and other ancient scripts. When a print was not available, he would have a copy made and thus our

The famous poet Li Ch'ing-chao (Li Yi-an, see selection 101) and her husband fled south during the fall of the Northern Sung dynasty to the Chin (Jürchen) invaders in 1126. She survived her collector-husband and had an unhappy second marriage.

1. A former premier.
2. One thousand cash equals one "dollar."

collection of famous calligraphy and antiques began. Once a man tried to sell us Hsü Hsi's painting of "Peony" for 200,000 cash, and Te-fu asked permission to take it home and keep it for a few days and consider. We found no means to buy it and reluctantly returned it to the owner. Te-fu and I were upset about it for days. When he served as magistrate at two posts, he spent his entire salary over the care and preservation of rare editions. Every time we obtained a rare book, we would examine it critically and see about its repair and rebinding, or if it was a painting or antique vessel, we would spend the evening pawing over it and looking for imperfections. Because of this, our collection was considered the best among all the collectors in regard to mounting and care and condition of the scripts. Whenever we found in bookstalls a volume which was complete and had no bad errors, we would purchase it for the purpose of comparison with other texts.

I have a power for memory, and sometimes after supper, sitting quietly in the Homecoming Hall, we would boil a pot of tea and, pointing to the piles of books on the shelves, make a guess as to which line of which page in which volume of a book contained a certain passage and see who was right, the one making the correct guess having the privilege of drinking his cup of tea first. When a guess was correct, we would lift up the cup and break out into a loud laughter, so much so that sometimes the tea was spilled on our dress and we were not able to drink at all. We were then content to live and grow old in the world. Therefore, we held our heads high, although we were living in poverty and sorrow. . . .[3] In time our collection grew bigger and bigger and the books and art objects were piled up on tables and desks and beds, and we enjoyed them with our eyes and with our minds and planned and discussed the collection, tasting a happiness above those enjoying the horse races and music and dance.

In the year 1126, Te-fu was magistrate at Tsechuan[4] when the northern invaders threatened the national capital.[5] He had a presentiment that we were not going to be able to keep the collection intact during the ensuing chaos. The following year, we came down south on the occasion of the funeral for his mother.[6] We realized that a part of the collection had to be

---

3. The translator has omitted a passage of more than a hundred sinographs giving details of how Li Ch'ing-chao economized on food and jewelry, etc., to get their treasured volumes into fine shape on the shelves of the Homecoming Hall. He has also omitted a brief introduction of approximately the same length and simplified the ending. In general, Lin Yutang's translations, tremendously popular in the United States about half a century ago, are much freer and looser than the standard required by sinological scholarship today. Still, his renderings have a flair and charm all their own.

4. Or Tzu-ch'uan, in Shantung province.

5. Kaifeng.

6. Of course they fled for another more imperious reason, the fall of North China. But to ascribe it to the occasion of a mother's funeral is accepted as the correct way of saying it. Likewise, it is highly improbable that her husband, the son of a minister, had to "pawn clothing"

sacrificed. First we discarded the heavy, bulky volumes, the less important works of a painter, and vessels that bore no inscriptions. Next we threw out books of which standard editions existed, paintings of no extraordinary merit, and bronze that was too heavy for transportation. Even then, the collection filled fifteen cartloads and was carried in a fleet of boats when we came down the Huai River. We had planned on moving things kept at our old house at Chingchow[7] the following year, but the house, we found later, was burned down with its dozen roomfuls of objects.

In 1129,[8] we were living at Chihyang.[9] Te-fu had to go to the temporary capital.[10] As he stood on the bank to say good-bye, I felt sick at heart and asked, "What shall I do in case of trouble?" He replied from the bank, "Do as the others. If necessary, abandon the food supplies first, then the clothing; books next, the scrolls after that, and the bronze last of all. But never part with the Sung ware no matter what happens. And take good care of it!" Then he left on horseback.

In August, Te-fu died of an illness. At that time, the imperial court was fleeing to Kiangsi. I asked two employees to bring more than 20,000 volumes of books and over 2,000 prints of inscriptions to Hungchow[11] first. In winter of that year, the town fell and all was lost. What we had brought down the river in a fleet of boats was all gone. What was saved were a few small scrolls, the works of Li Po, Tu Fu, Han Yü, and Liu Tsung-yüan,[12] the *Shih Shuo*,[13] the *Debate on Iron and Salt*,[14] several dozens of rubbings, over a dozen pieces of bronze, and several boxes of *Southern T'ang History*, which happened to be with me in my personal luggage. As I could not have gone upriver, I came down south and moved from Taichow, to Wenchow, to Chuchow, to Yueh-chow, finally to Hangchow, and had the collection stored at Cheng-hsien.[15] In 1130, rebel troops came to the town and raided it, and all that passed into the ownership of old General Li. About 50 or 60 per cent of what had been saved was again gone. I had still six or seven baskets which I brought with me when I moved to Yüehcheng.[16] One night, a burglar came and got away

to buy odd curios, as said at the beginning, but this is the generally accepted euphemism. It has become the tradition for scholars to say that one's wife took off a gold bodkin from her hair to sell for money with which to buy wine to entertain a friend for the night.

7. In Shantung province.

8. When the enemy came down to Nanking.

9. In Anhwei province.

10. Then at Nanking.

11. Present-day Nan-ch'ang city in Kiangsi province.

12. Famous T'ang authors, all of whom are represented in this volume.

13. See selection 202.

14. A book by Huan Kuan (fl. 73 B.C.E.) about an important government monopoly.

15. All of these cities are located in Chekiang province. Hangchow was where the Southern Sung capital was finally established.

16. Modern-day Kuei-chi in Chekiang province.

with five baskets. What I have left now are only a few odd volumes of several incomplete books.

I suddenly came upon this Catalog (compiled by my husband) and the feeling was like that of meeting an old friend. I remember when we were living at Tunglai [17] at our house called "Tsingchiht'ang," [18] Te-fu was working every day on the volumes, giving each ten volumes a protecting cloth case with silk fastenings. Usually, he checked over two volumes per day and wrote a postscript note on one volume. Among the 2,000 volumes of prints from stone and bronze, only 502 now bear his signature and notes. The ink is as fresh as the day he wrote them, but the tree over his grave has shot up to a considerable height already. I realize that this is the common fate of things: they come and go, or change ownership or are destroyed. There is nothing surprising in it. I merely write this story down, that collectors may take warning from it.

The fourth year of Shaohsing (1134)
Translated by Lin Yutang

17. In Shantung.
18. Hall of Quiet Governance.

Discourses, Essays, and Sketches

171
Discourse on Nourishing Life

Hsi K'ang (223–262)

There are people nowadays who say that immortal sagehood can be attained though study, that immortality can with effort be reached. There are also those who put the longest life at one hundred and twenty years and claim it has always been so. They say all accounts of people living longer than this are nothing but lies. Both of these positions miss the way things are, so permit me to try, in my coarse way, to explain.

It is true that immortals cannot be seen with your eyes, but if we examine clearly and weigh all that has been written in the records and documents and all that has been transmitted by the former historians, their true existence is a certainty. They seem to be the special recipients of a unique *ch'i* (vital

Hsi (or Chi) K'ang was one of the celebrated Seven Worthies (or Sages) of the Bamboo Grove, a group of literati who chose to avoid the normal course of government service during politically troubled times and retire to a life of estheticism and indulgence (compare with selection 18). Though admired in a caricatured form for their antiestablishment stand, self-indulgences, humor, and explorations of intoxication by alcohol and other drugs, Hsi and his colleagues contributed a wealth of serious prose and poetry to subsequent ages.

Hsi was an acknowledged master of the *lun* (essay), and the "Essay on Nourishing Life" was one of nine he wrote on themes of personal cultivation, longevity, feelings, and the arts. This essay illustrates the tide of interest in practices associated with Taoism, artistic expression and individual emotions, and the obligations of the individual to himself and society that typified Hsi's era, one that witnessed a basic shift in views on life and art after the collapse of the Han dynasty.

breath), the receiving of which comes about spontaneously. It is not something one can reach with an accumulation of learning. But if we talk about the proper care of oneself, according to the principles, in order to maximize one's allotted span of life, then it is certainly possible for a person to get, at the best, more than a thousand years, at the very least, several hundred. Nowadays, no one is skilled in this care, and therefore no one can achieve such longevity. How can I explain this?

If you take some drug to make yourself perspire, it will perhaps in some cases have no effect. But should you suffer some terrible embarrassment, sweat will literally pour forth. If you skip eating all morning, your mouth will water and you'll dream of eating. Yet Tseng Tzu,[1] choked with grief, went seven foodless days without feeling hunger. If you sit up half the night, you'll begin to nod off and dream of bed. But if inside you're stirred with a great anxiety, the dawn will come before you fall asleep. You can brush energetically to get your hair to stand up or drink a strong wine to redden your face, but the results will only be marginal. Yet a young fellow when angry will redden with a fearsome face and his hair will push up against his hat. From these examples, I assert that the relationship of a person's spirit to his body is like that of a country and its ruler. When the spirit is rash within, the body decays without, just as when the ruler on top is muddled, the country below falls to chaos.

Now, for those growing grain during the drought of Emperor T'ang,[2] there was from time to time the contribution of an isolated rainfall. When that was over, things returned to being parched and dried, and what depended on that single rain would later wither up; nonetheless, the benefits of that single rainfall can certainly not be gainsaid. Nowadays people often say that a single burst of rage is not sufficient to do violence to one's innate nature or that a single bout of grief to harm one's body. Treating these things lightly, they indulge themselves often, as if they did not recognize the benefits of a single rainfall, but looked forward to getting good grain from desiccated sprouts.

By this, the gentleman knows that form can stand only by relying on spirit, and that spirit in turn needs form for its existence. When one grasps how easily the system of life is unbalanced, one realizes the harm to life of even one such excess. Therefore, one's innate nature is cultivated in order to preserve the spirit, and the mind is kept peaceful to keep whole the body. Love and hate must not come to rest in one's feelings, nor must grief and joy

---

1. Also called Tseng San, he was a disciple of Confucius renowned for his filiality and extreme attendance on his parents. Upon their death, Tseng Tzu did not even taste water for seven days.

2. King T'ang, also called Ch'eng T'ang, is credited in traditional accounts with defeating the Hsia dynasty and founding the Shang dynasty in 1766 B.C.E. A ruler of great virtue, he expanded a small, seventy-tricent state to one that stretched across the Yellow River plain through a series of eleven conquests.

be harbored in one's thoughts. Drifting, insensate, the bodily *ch'i* is level and quiet. Then inhale and exhale in a rigorously controlled manner, and ingest the things which will nourish your body. This will bring form and spirit closer together, and will benefit you inside and out.

Now, if a field when planted yields ten measures of grain, it's called a "prime" field, and it will be so named throughout the underheaven. No one realizes that under close and intense cultivation, it could yield more than one hundred measures. Planting a field is one thing, and arboriculture is quite another. With trees, successful planting lies in spreading them apart. It is said that a merchant can never make a thousand percent profit, and a farmer has no prospects for a hundred measure yield. These are cases of clinging to the status quo and not changing. Beans make a person gain weight; elm seeds make one sleepy. The acacia relieves anger; the day-lily helps one forget sorrow. The wise and the foolish alike know these things.

Garlic and onion harm the eyes, and pork and fish are not life-prolonging foods. These facts too are common knowledge today. If lice live in your hair, they absorb the black, and a musk-deer that eats cypress leaves becomes cedar fragrant. The necks of people who live in high places develop goiters, and the people of Chin[3] have yellow teeth. Deducing from this, it is clear that the *ch'i* of everything you eat permeates the innate nature and pervades the body. There is nothing that does not elicit some reaction. Is it possible there is only steaming to make things heavy but none to make them light, injury to make things dark but none to make them bright, smoking to make things yellow but none to make things firm, perfuming to make things fragrant but none to make things endure? Thus Shen Nung's[4] maxim, "Superior medicines nourish one's life; middle medicines nourish one's nature," truly recognizes the interrelation of innate nature and life, perfected through a course of support and nourishment.

But people nowadays do not look into these things. Nothing more than the five grains is seen, blinded as people are by addiction to glaring sights and sounds. Their eyes are blunted by deep red and yellow, and their ears are enslaved to raucous music. The spicy flavors they consume fry their vital organs; the wines stew their stomachs and entrails; the spices and aromatics rot their bones and marrow; and alternating passions of joy and anger pervert their proper *ch'i*; dwelling on worries dissipates their spirit essence; suffering and pleasures wreak havoc on their equilibrium. The attacks on their petty persons come from all sides. The body so easily exhausted must meet enemies from inside and out. Not being made of wood or stone, can we last long under these conditions?

3. Shansi.

4. The Divine Farmer was one of China's cultural heroes of high antiquity to whom is credited the organization and presentation of agricultural and herbal skills to the Chinese people.

People today both laugh at and pity those who go to extremes with themselves, those who eat and drink without measure and then fall victim to a myriad of illnesses, those who indulge tirelessly in sex until their vitality comes to a weary end. The banes of the wind and the cold, the injuries of the hundred toxins will plague them with a host of obstacles only halfway along life's allotted span.

We say they are not skilled at maintaining life. Where do they lose touch with the basic principles in caring for themselves? They perish by the most subtle points. The subtle points compound to become harm, and the compounding of harm adds up to decline. From decline comes whiteness, and from whiteness comes agedness, and agedness brings on the end. Enclosed in this syndrome, a person has no way out. People of only average understanding or less refer to this as "natural." Even though victims come to a minor realization of things, it is invariably expressed as remorse as soon as the disaster is actually encountered. Never are people aware and cautious about the many dangers before symptoms manifest themselves. For this reason, Lord Huan was already gripped by fatal illness before he realized it, and yet he cursed the physician Pien Ch'üeh's early diagnosis.[5] He mistakenly thought that the day one first feels the pain is the day an illness begins. What harmed him had its trivial origins, but he sought help only after the ailment was obvious, and the cure, therefore, was unsuccessful.

Travel around the world of ordinary men and you will find they all have the same slice of longevity. Look up, look down; there are no exceptions. This span of life is said to be all that nature's principles allow. The numbers alone make it self-evident, and the company makes for each one's solace. Even when someone has heard stories about "nourishing life," he will say they're untrue, basing his judgment on what he can see around him. Slightly better than this person is someone who approaches, wary as a fox, and although he gets a wee bit closer, does not know where to begin. Slightly better than this is someone who energetically consumes elixirs, then decides after six months or a year that there is no visible effect and he is wasting his efforts, and thus gives up along the way. Perhaps such people feel their attempts are like a trickle into the oceans, while water leaks in torrents out the other side. They want to sit down and watch for obvious rewards. Perhaps they are people who have suppressed their feelings or held their desires in check, lopped off and discarded their worldly ambitions. But the objects of temptations are always directly before their eyes and ears, and the goal of their nobler aspirations lies several dozen years away. So, fearing that they'll lose both, they lack inner resolve; inside the heart is fighting with itself and

5. The story is told by the philosopher Han Fei Tzu. Lord Huan refers to Duke Huan of Chin. The physician Pien Ch'üeh (see selection 192, note 3) visited Duke Huan several times, at ten-day intervals, charting the course of Huan's illness at its early stages. Feeling no symptoms, Huan refused to listen until he was beyond curing.

outside things are luring them from the path. The forces combine to drag them from the Way, and they too fall in defeat.

Only by reason can we know the subtlety of esoteric things, not by perception with our eyes. This may be likened to the Yü-chang tree, growing for seven years before it is recognizable. Now with hasty and tempestuous hearts, we climb on the path of stillness and quietude. Our idea is for hasty progress, but events come slowly; our expectations focus on the near future, but responses to our efforts are far-off, and thus no one is able to reach to the end. Those who push anxiously do not seek on, because they see no immediate results, and those who do seek on fail in the endeavor for lack of concentration. Those who incline toward one side or the other achieve nothing for lack of breadth, and those who pursue occult practices become quagmired in the byways. In all efforts of this sort, of ten thousand people who seek long life, not a single one can succeed.

Those truly skilled at nourishing life are not at all this way. Clear, empty, quiet, expansive, they reduce the selfish and minimize desires. Knowing the harm that fame and status do to virtue, they simply ignore them, leave them beyond the confines of their lives. It is not a case of wanting these things and forcibly forestalling them. They recognize the harm that the rich-flavored does one's innate nature and discard it, pay it no heed. It is not that they hunger for such things and then control themselves. External things entangle the heart, so they have no presence. Spirit *ch'i* alone is manifest, by virtue of its purity. Those skilled at nourishing life are open wide, without worry or grief, at peace without thoughts and ponderings. They preserve this state with oneness, nourish it with harmony. Harmony with the principles brings daily advance, becoming one with the great flow. Afterward one is infused with the numinous nutrient, imbued with the ambrosial spring waters, basked in the dawning sun, and made tranquil with the *ch'in* zither's five strings. So with nonaction, it comes in and of itself, the body subtle and the heart profound, forgetting pleasure so that joy is complete, abandoning the trappings of life so that the person may be preserved. Proceeding in this manner, one's life span could compare with Hsien Men's;[6] one could compete in years with Wang Ch'iao.[7] How could anyone think that such people do not exist!

Translated by Kenneth J. DeWoskin

6. An ancient who achieved transcendence and longevity. Living atop the remote Mount Chieh-shih, he was pursued for his secrets of long life by China's first emperor, Ch'in Shih-huang.

7. Also called Wang-tzu Ch'iao, he was an immortal transcendent who lived atop Mount Sung-kao during the time of the Chou king Ling (571–544 B.C.E.).

172

The Peach Blossom Spring

T'ao Ch'ien (365–427)

During the T'ai-yüan period[1] of the Chin dynasty, a fisherman of Wu-ling[2] once rowed upstream, unmindful of the distance he had gone, when he suddenly came to a grove of peach trees in bloom. For several hundred paces on both banks of the steam there was no other kind of tree. The wild flowers growing under them were fresh and lovely, and fallen petals covered the ground—it made a great impression on the fisherman. He went on for a way with the idea of finding out how far the grove extended. It came to an end at the foot of a mountain whence issued the spring that supplied the stream. There was a small opening in the mountain and it seemed as though light was coming through it. The fisherman left his boat and entered the cave, which at first was extremely narrow, barely admitting his body; after a few dozen steps it suddenly opened out onto a broad and level plain where well-built houses were surrounded by rich fields and pretty ponds. Mulberry, bamboo, and other trees and plants grew there, and crisscross paths skirted the fields. The sounds of cocks crowing and dogs barking could be heard from one courtyard to the next. Men and women were coming and going about their work in the fields. The clothes they wore were like those of ordinary people.[3] Old men and boys were carefree and happy.

When they caught sight of the fisherman, they asked in surprise how he had got there. The fisherman told the whole story, and was invited to go to their house, where he was served wine while they killed a chicken for a feast. When the other villagers heard about the fisherman's arrival, they all came to pay him a visit. They told him that their ancestors had fled the disorders of Ch'in times and, having taken refuge here with wives and children and neighbors, had never ventured out again; consequently they had lost all

---

This is the most important and most quoted description of a utopia in the whole of Chinese literature. Note that the prose preface is actually far more famous than the poem to which it is attached. The poem, indeed, is usually taken to be little more than a perfunctory versification of the story.

For information on T'ao Ch'ien, see selection 20.

1. 376–396.

2. Modern-day Ch'eng-te in Hunan. It is not far from the town of T'ao-yüan ("Peach Spring") on the Yüan river.

3. This line is probably intended to convey the idea that these were not immortals or other-worldly beings clad in shining raiment or covered with feathers, but people just like any other. The term translated here by "ordinary people" (literally, "outside people") occurs later as "outsiders," those who live outside this hidden retreat. This second occurrence makes it unlikely that it means "foreigners" here—that they were wearing a garb not familiar in fourth-century China, as might be the case if they were actually dressed in the style of the Ch'in dynasty.

contact with the outside world. They asked what the present ruling dynasty was, for they had never heard of the Han, let alone the Wei and the Chin. They sighed unhappily as the fisherman enumerated the dynasties one by one and recounted the vicissitudes of each. The visitors all asked him to come to their houses in turn, and at every house he had wine and food. He stayed several days. As he was about to go away, the people said, "There's no need to mention our existence to outsiders."

After the fisherman had gone out and recovered his boat, he carefully marked the route. On reaching the city, he reported what he had found to the magistrate, who at once sent a man to follow him back to the place. They proceeded according to the marks he had made, but went astray and were unable to find the cave again.

A high-minded gentleman of Nan-yang named Liu Tzu-chi[4] heard the story and happily made preparations to go there, but before he could leave he fell sick and died. Since then there has been no one interested in trying to find such a place.[5]

> The Ying[6] clan disrupted Heaven's ordinance[7]
> And good men withdrew from such a world.[8]
> Huang and Ch'i went off to Shang Mountain[9]
> And these people too fled into hiding.
> 5   Little by little their tracks were obliterated,
> The paths they followed overgrown at last.
> By agreement they set about farming the land
> When the sun went down each rested from his toil.
> Bamboo and mulberry provided shade enough,
> 10 They planted beans and millet, each in season.[10]
> From spring silkworms came the long silk thread,
> On the fall harvest no king's tax was paid.

4. An individual whose devotion to principle and whose refusal to accept office must have excited T'ao Ch'ien's admiration. He surely would have been one to appreciate the advantages of such a retreat.

5. The concluding line of the story more literally reads, "Since then no one has asked about the ford," an allusion to the *Analects* (selection 6, passage 18.6) upon which T'ao Ch'ien so often drew.

6. The first emperor of the Ch'in is here referred to by his clan name.

7. This refers to a passage in the *Classic of Documents* (selection 157) where Hsi and Ho are blamed for throwing heaven into disorder. There it is the regular progression of the heavenly bodies; here it is the order of nature generally that has been upset by bad rule.

8. This line versifies a phrase from the *Analects* (14.37): "The worthy man withdraws from the world."

9. Hsia Huang-kung and Ch'i Li-chi, two of the Four White-head recluses who withdrew from society to the isolation of Shang Mountain.

10. This line is constructed with components from two songs in the *Classic of Odes* (selection 16).

No sign of traffic on overgrown roads,
Cockcrow and dogsbark within each other's earshot.
15 Their ritual vessels were of old design,
And no new fashions in the clothes they wore.
Children wandered about singing songs,
Graybeards went paying one another calls.
When grass grew thick they saw the time was mild,
20 As trees went bare they knew the wind was sharp.
Although they had no calendar to tell,
The four seasons still filled out a year.
Joyous in their ample happiness
They had no need of clever contrivance.[11]
25 Five hundred years [12] this rare deed stayed hid,
Then one fine day the fay retreat [13] was found.
The pure and the shallow belong to separate worlds:
In a little while they were hidden again.
Let me ask you who are convention-bound,
30 Can you fathom those outside the dirt and noise?
I want to tread upon the thin, thin air
And rise up high to find my own kind.

Translated by James Robert Hightower

11. Based on *Tao te ching* (selection 9), chapter 18: "When cleverness appears, then we have the Great Imposture."
12. It was more like six hundred years from 220 B.C.E. to 380 C.E., but "five hundred" is a good, round number.
13. The retreat is hyperbolically called "spiritual" in the sense of "not of this world."

173
An Explication of "Progress in Learning"

Han Yü (768–824)

One morning a professor at the Imperial University entered his college and called all the students to line up in front of the school. He then instructed them as follows:

"Progress in Learning" is defined by the following paragraph from the "Record of Studies" chapter of the *Record of Rites* (*Li chi*):

A good student, even though his teacher be lax, will outperform others, but ultimately attribute the merit to his teacher. The bad student, even though his teacher be strict, will do only half as well as others, and in the end will ultimately put the blame on his teacher.

"Hard work will perfect your studies,
    which can be lost through play;
hard thought will achieve right conduct,
    which sloth may then undo.
5 At this moment,
    our Sage-king[1] has met
    his men of worth,[2]
    and tools of good rule
    have covered the earth.
10 They have rooted up, destroyed
    the evil and cruel,
    have raised and honored
    the perfect and true.
    Even those with the smallest skill
15   are all enrolled,
    those known for a single art
    are all employed.
    They dig, they unearth, they comb, they screen,[3]
    they rub out blemishes, they polish to a sheen.
20 Some, indeed, are perhaps
    by chance selected,
    but none can say he was
    worthy and unaccepted.
    So all you students—
25 beware lest your studies
    go unperfected,
    and worry not that our officials
    may be unaware;

Those who are good at asking questions are like a woodsman who trims a great tree: first he cuts the easy parts, then later the joints and knots. After a long while, teacher and student enjoy solving problems through mutual discussion. Those who are not good at asking questions are the opposite of this. Those who are good at being questioned are like a bell when struck: when that which strikes it is small, the sound is small; when that which strikes it is large, the sound is large. When the bell is struck consistently and with force, then it gives forth its full sound. Those who are not good at answering questions are the opposite of this. And this is the way of making progress in learning.

It is important to observe that this inimitable piece is a comic attempt at the "explication" (a genre of commentary) of the classical idea of "progress in learning." In other words, this is a mimicry of commentarial writing at the same time that it is a self-satire of intellectuals like the author himself.

For Han Yü, see selection 42.

1. "Sage-king" refers to Emperor Hsien Tsung of the T'ang period, who was on the throne during Han Yü's active years.

2. The sage-king's prime ministers.

3. Describing the work of the prime ministers.

           beware your conduct
30   is not yet true,
       and worry not that our officials
               may be unfair."

Before this lecture was over, someone in the ranks laughed and said,

           "You would deceive us, Sir!
       We pupils have served you now
35   these many years,
       and your mouth has not ceased
               to intone the texts
               of the Six Classics,
       and your hands not ceased
40   to unroll the scrolls
               of the hundred persuasions;
       you have extracted the essence
               of historical accounts
       and plumbed the mysteries
45   of abstruse compilations.
       Yet still you strove
               and worked for more,
       and big or small
               did all belong;
50   you burned your oil
               to stretch the sun's shadow,
       tired and weary
               year after year.
       Truly, Sir, of your own studies,
55   it must be said,
               you've worked hard and long.

       "You refute, resist
               false doctrines,
       repel, reject
60   Buddhist and Taoist,
       you patch and mortar
               crack and leak,
       fill out and expand
               the dark and oblique.
65   Alone you search the far
               maze of fallen threads,
       and everywhere seek to join them
               across time's gap.

You have channeled and brought home
70   the hundred streams,
have turned back a raging wave,
     already crested.
Truly, Sir, it must be said,
     your labors for Confucian teaching
75   are uncontested.

"You have immersed, submerged
     yourself in ambrosial essence,
taking flowers to your mouth
     to savor their blooms;
80 and these you have worked
     to your own literary art,
these writings that now
     fill your rooms.
Your earliest models
85 are the 'Books of Yüh'[4]
and the 'Books of Hsia,'[5]
     without end vast and profound;
the 'Pronouncements of Chou,'[6]
the 'Proclamations of Yin,'[7]
90   tortuous and hard to construe;
the *Spring and Autumn,*
     strict and severe;
the *Chronicle of Tso,*
     verbose and inflated;
95 the *Changes,*
     prodigious yet ordered;
the *Odes,*
     refined yet true.
Your later models
100   are *Chuang Tzu*[8]
and 'Encountering Sorrows'[9]

---

4. "Books of Yüh" refers to the early chapters of the *Classic of Documents* (see selection 157), traditionally ascribed to Emperor Shun, whose dynastic name was Yüh.

5. "Books of Hsia" refers to the following chapters of the *Classic of Documents* attributed to Yü the Great, founder of the Hsia dynasty.

6. "Pronouncements of Chou" refers loosely to the latter chapters of the *Classic of Documents,* supposedly dating from the Chou dynasty, such as the "Grand Pronouncement."

7. "Proclamations of Yin" refers to the *P'an keng* chapters of the *Classic of Documents,* allegedly dating from Shang times.

8. See selection 8.

9. See selection 122.

and what the Grand
    Historian [10] recorded;
then Yang Hsiung [11]
105   and Ssu-ma Hsiang-ju,[12]
all skilled alike, yet
    each in a separate norm.
Truly, Sir, it can be said,
    your labors at literature
110 have enlarged its core,
    set free its form.

"Ever since you were young
    and began to study,
you've been strong in
115   your courage to act.
Now grown, and versed
    in the social arts,
you've made all around you
    into what it should be.
120 Truly, Sir, it can be said,
    your behavior as a man
is perfect in all its parts.

"Yet in spite of all this
    in public no one
125   will trust you;
    in private no one
    will help you.
Stumbling ahead,
    falling behind,
130 whenever you move
    there's ruin anew.
For a short time, you
    served as censor,
but then were exiled

10. Ssu-ma Ch'ien (145–90? B.C.E.)., whose place in the development of Chinese historiography is comparable to that of Herodotus in the Western tradition. His *Records of the Grand Historian* (*Shih chi*, also rendered in English as *Records of the Scribe*) provided the pattern for all later official dynastic histories of China. Begun by his father Ssu-ma T'an, Grand Astrologer of the Han court during the early years of Emperor Wu's reign, the bulk of the *Records of the Grand Historian* was researched and written by Ssu-ma Ch'ien himself. Much of the finest writing in this enormous work occurs in the "Memoirs" (sometimes referred to as "Biographies of Hereditary Houses") section.

11. See selection 161.

12. See selection 129.

135   to the southern wilds.
          For three years, you
              held the doctorate,[13]
          a useless post, no merits
              at all to come by.
140   You are fated always
              to fight with your foes,
          and another reverse could
              come at any time.
          Even in a warm winter,
145   *your* children cry of cold;
          even after a good harvest,
              your wife weeps in hunger.
          Your head's gone bald,
              your teeth are gapped;
150   and things'll never get better
              till the day you die.
          But you yourself refuse to reflect
              on any of this,
          Preferring instead to teach
155   to others what you deem apt."

The master replied,[14]

          "You, there, stand to the front!
          Great timber is
              turned into beams,
          the smaller logs
160   become rafters,
          columns, batten,
              and shorter stays,[15]

---

13. This actually happened to Han Yü (806–809).

14. The metaphors in the ensuing lines derive from the following passage in the *Huai-nan Tzu*:

> A wise lord uses men like a skilled craftsman works his lumber. The large pieces he uses for boats and barges, for beams and rafters; the smaller ones he uses for poles and wedges. Long ones become planks and eaves; short ones become stays and cornices. Thus for him no piece is too large, small, long, or short; but each functions as best it will. He measures their shapes, and so each is used and placed.
>
> No substance under Heaven is more lethal than wolf's-bane; and yet a good physician collects and stores it, for it does have some use. Therefore no tree or shrub from the forest should be discarded. How much truer is this of men!

15. "Shorter stays" may also be translated as "dwarf, a man of small stature." This and most of the other architectural terms in this passage derive from the *Record of Rites*.

doorjambs, pivots,
    posts and seams;
165 that each of these
    works as it will
and is used and placed
    to complete a house
is all the master
170   craftsman's skill.

    "Shavings of jade,[16]
    red cinnabar,
'Scarlet arrow,'[17]
    brown mushrooms,
175 bull's urine,
    and puffballs,
and old leather
    drum skins,
all these he searches out
180   then stores apart,
awaiting the time
    and use for each—
such is the master
    physician's art.

185 "With wise promotions
    and fair selections,
he uses alike
    both able and inept,
so the devious are refined,
190   the outstanding enshrined:
he examines for failings,
    weighs for strengths
so that each to his measure
    is staffed—
195 such is the prime
    minister's craft.

    "In ancient times,
because Mencius was fond of dispute,
    the way of Confucius was brought to light:

16. The substances in this and the following lines are all important in traditional Chinese medicine.

17. "Scarlet arrow" is the root of *Gastrodia elata*, a plant belonging to the orchid family, used as a restorative.

200 but the tracks of his wagon
    encircled the world,
and he ended
    old in his travels.
Hsün Tzu embraced
205   what was right,
his great teachings
    towered over everything,
yet he fled to Ch'u
    to escape slander
210 and died an exile
    in Lan-ling.
These were two scholars
    who brought forth words
    that became our classics,
215   who trod the steps
    that became our models.
They surpassed by far
    the ranks of their peers
and entered deep
220   in the realm of the Sage.
Yet how were they
    met by their age?

"Now although your professor has worked hard at his studies,
    he could not trace their lineage;
225 although he has spoken much,
    he could not strike their heart;
his literary style is outstanding,
    but could not succeed at real use;
his conduct has been exemplary
230   but has not marked him as one apart.
And yet in spite of all this,
    every month [18] he
    receives a salary,
    and every year
235   consumes his rice and wheat;
his children do not hoe,
his wife does not sew;
he travels by horse,
    is attended by pages,

18. T'ang officials received a monthly salary in cash and a yearly allotment of grain.

240   and sits in comfort
          and ease to eat;
      he earnestly treads the narrow,
          common lanes,
      pores over old pages
245   to rob and to plunder.
      And yet our Sagacious Lord
          imposes no wrath upon him,
      nor have ministers rebuked
          him for blunder.
250   How fortunate indeed has he been!

      "If his every action
          has drawn slander,
      so renown too
          has followed him.
255   To be thrown this idle
          empty post
      is thus for him
          a proper fate.
      And so, were he now
260   to argue the extent
          or not of his wealth,
      to reckon the status
          of his rank and estate,
      to forget what best befits
265   his own gifts,
      and to mark his elders
          as evils incarnate,
      all such were to query a master craftsman
          who would not use a pear-tree stake
270   for a column head,
      or to malign a master physician
          who prescribed sweet flag for long life
          and then take chinaroot instead." [19]

Translated by Charles Hartman

19. The root of "sweet flag" or calamus (*Acorus calamus*) was commonly ingested for longevity. Chinaroot, on the other hand, a variety of tuckahoe, was an ancient purgative.

174
The Three Zithers

Ou-yang Hsiu (1007–1072)

My family owns three zithers, one of which is said to have been made by Chang Yüeh, one by Lou Tse, and one by the Lei clan. They all show exquisite craftsmanship and are constructed in accordance with ancient standards. Still, it is impossible to be sure about their provenance. But the important thing about a zither, after all, is how it sounds, not who made it. The upper boards of these instruments have transverse cracks like the markings on a snake's belly, and those who know zithers tell me that these are antique instruments. It seems that the lacquer used on zithers only develops such cracks after a hundred years, hence they are generally considered proof of an instrument's age.

One of the zithers has gold studs, one has stone studs, and one has jade studs. The one with gold studs is the Chang Yüeh zither, the one with stone studs is the Lou Tse zither, and the one with jade studs is the Lei clan zither. The tone of the one with gold studs is rich and penetrating, that of the one with stone studs is pure and gentle, and that of the one with jade studs is harmonious and resonant. At the present, anybody who possessed a single one of these would treasure it, and now I own all three.

However, it is really only the zither with stone studs that is suitable for an old man like me. Contemporaries like to play zithers with studs of gold, jade, pearl-mussel shell, or lapis-lazuli, because when such instruments are placed beside a candle at night, the studs shimmer in the light. But it is hard for an old man whose eyesight is failing to place his fingers squarely on those studs. It is only the stone studs that do not reflect light, and so even when they are placed beside a candle, the white studs can be readily distinguished from the dark wood. That is why stone-studded zithers are best for old men.

Ever since I was young I never liked popular music. Zither music is the only kind I like, and I am particularly fond of the zither piece "Flowing Waters." During my many difficult years, when duties kept me running north

The author was one of the dominant figures of Northern Sung literature and politics. He was noted as a leader of a group of literary stylists who revived the ideals of ancient-style writing. Later recognized as one of the "Eight Masters of T'ang and Sung Prose," Ou-yang Hsiu was a prolific author in a number of genres. As editor of the *New T'ang History*, he ensured that it was compiled on the model of ancient-style prose and, as Chief Examiner in 1057, required the use of the ancient style in essays, failing those who used a more elaborate and florid style. It was through this examination that he discovered Su Shih (see selection 127) and his brother Su Ch'e (1039–1112). Twice falsely accused of incest, he experienced several setbacks to his political career. He had a fondness for singers and was given to writing romantic poetry. Unlike Su Shih, he was not very interested in metaphysics, but was more concerned with the practical questions of quotidian life.

and south, I forgot all the zither pieces I once learned. But "Flowing Waters," that one piece, never went out of my head, even in my dreams. Nowadays, although I have already grown old, I can play it from time to time. Otherwise, all I can play are a few short melodies, yet these too suffice to give me pleasure.

One need not learn many zither pieces. The important thing is to enjoy playing. Likewise, one need not own many zithers. But since I have already come into possession of this many, it would be foolish for me now to start worrying about having a surplus and to get rid of some. On the day after the Double Third Festival in the seventh year of the Chia-yu period (1062), having asked for a leave of absence because of illness, I was practicing calligraphy and, letting my brush write what it would, I composed this account of the three zithers of the Ou-yang family.

Translated by Ronald Egan

A Record of the Pavilion of an Intoxicated Old Man

Ou-yang Hsiu

All around Ch'u [1] there are mountains, but the forests and valleys of that assemblage of peaks to the southwest are the finest. There is one that appears from afar most luxuriant and deepest in verdure—that is Lang-ya. After you have walked six or seven tricents into the mountains, there you will gradually notice the sound of water gurgling. Where it drains out between the two peaks, this is Brewer's Spring. Rounding the peak the road winds; there a pavilion hangs, like a wing, out over the spring. This is the Intoxicated Old Man's pavilion. Who was it that built this pavilion? A monk of these mountains, Chih-hsien. And who named it? The prefect, who called it after himself. When prefect and guests come to drink here, because he becomes intoxicated after only drinking a little and because he is the oldest in years, that is why he nicknamed himself the Intoxicated Old Man. But what he means by Intoxicated Old Man has nothing to do with the wine; it has to do instead with being in the mountains by the water. This joy from the mountains and the water he feels within his mind; he merely ascribes it to the wine.

Now the sun rises and the forest mists dissipate, the clouds return and the caves in ravines grow gloomy—these alternations of dusk and light mark mornings and evenings amid the mountains. Wild flowers bloom with their hidden scents, beautiful trees leaf out with deepening shade, then winds rise

This playful self-portrait is the most celebrated of Ou-yang Hsiu's many fine essays.
1. Ch'u prefecture was located in modern-day Ch'u district of Anhwei province.

and pure frost appears, the water level drops and the rocks protrude—such
are the four seasons amid the mountains. In the morning he goes there, in
the evening he returns; the scenery of the four seasons is never the same,
hence his joy knows no bounds.

Those who carry loads on their backs sing along the path; sojourners rest
beneath the trees. The ones in front call out and those behind respond. Some
are bent over with age and others so young that they must be led by the
hand. They come and go without cease—such are the travelers around Ch'u.
One may lean over this stream and fish; the stream being deep, the fish are
fat. Or one may brew wine with the spring water; the spring being fragrant,
the wine is crystal clear. Sliced meats from the mountains and wild vegetables
arrayed in profusion before the guests—such are the prefect's banquets. The
joys of the feast are not from strings or winds; they are from winning at pitch-
pot, from victory in chess. Passing goblets and mugs back and forth, shouting
with abandon, now sitting, now on their feet—such is the happy abandon of
the guests. And the one who, ruddy-faced and white of hair, lies sprawled in
their midst—that is the prefect intoxicated.

When the merriment is over and the evening sun sets among the mountains, the prefect goes home with his guests in tow, their shadows jumbled
together. The forest gloom deepens; birds call high and low. The revelers all
gone, the birds are joyful. Yet, though birds may know the joy of mountain
forests, they know not the joy of mankind; men may know the joy of revels
with the prefect and yet never know the prefect's enjoyment of their joy.

Intoxicated yet able to share their joy, able when sober to describe it in
writing—such is the prefect. And what is this prefect's name? Ou-yang Hsiu
of Lu-ling.

Translated by Robert E. Hegel

175
Brush Talks from Dream Brook

Shen Kua (1030–1094)

[On a UFO] [1]

In the Chia-yu period,[2] a "pearl"[3] appeared in Yang-chou. It was very large
and frequently appeared at night. At first it emerged from the swamps of
T'ien-ch'ang county; later it moved to Pi-she Lake; and finally it was at Hsin-

Shen Kua served in a number of governmental positions in the capital and in the provinces.
His duties concerned river control, compilation of the imperial diary, border fortifications
against the Tanguts (Hsi-hsia), and diplomatic missions to the Khitans (Liao). Wherever he

k'ai Lake. For more than ten years, residents and travelers would constantly see it.

My friend had a study by the lakeside and one night saw that the "pearl" was very near. At first it opened its door very slightly, and light shot out from the crack like a golden ray. After a moment, it opened wider to the space of half a mat; within there was white light like silver. The "pearl" was as big as a fist and so bright you couldn't look at it directly. For over ten tricents, the trees cast shadows, exactly as when the sun has just come up. In the distance you saw only a sky reddened as if by a forest fire. All of a sudden it went far off, moving as if in flight, floating over the waves, shining like the sun.

In the past there was a "moongem," but its color was unlike the moon; shimmering with sharp flames, it rather resembled the sun. Ts'ui Po-yi once wrote a "Rhapsody on the Bright Gem." Ts'ui was from Kao-yin [4] and so must have seen it often.

In recent years, it hasn't appeared again; no one knows where it has gone. Fan-liang-chen is where the "pearl" used to appear, and when travelers reach there, they usually tie up their boats for a few nights to watch for its appearance. The pavilion there is called "The Playful Pearl."

Translated by Richard W. Bodman

---

went, he was always a keen observer and wrote voluminously about all manner of things that he encountered. Possessed of a polymathic mind, Shen jotted down his diverse data and thoughts in the form of random notes—*pi-chi*, "brush talks." His extremely broad interests in science, technology, language, and literature are evident in the celebrated collection known as *Sketches from Dream Brook* (*Meng hsi pi-t'an*, named after the place where his estate was located), from which the present selection has been taken.

1. Section title provided by the translator.

2. 1056–1063.

3. In Chinese folklore, pearls are endowed with the magic power to give off their own light, to protect their owner from sickness, and to repel water (when their owner is swimming).

4. Kao-yin is in Kiangsu province near Yangchow.

176
Liu Ching-t'ing [1] the Storyteller

Chang Tai (1597–1679)

Pockmarked Liu from Nanking had a swarthy face that was covered all over with bumpy scars. He was relaxed and at ease, but his body looked as though

Chang Tai was the scion of a prominent family of Shan-yin (modern-day Shao-hsing, Chekiang). Like a number of wealthy literati during the late Ming, he did not pursue an official career. Instead, during the first half of his life, he led an idyllic existence as a talented esthete

it were made out of wood or clay. Liu was good at telling stories.[2] Each day he would tell one chapter of a story, for which he charged an ounce of silver. Whoever wanted to invite Liu for a storytelling session had to send him the program and earnest money ten days in advance. Even then he was often too busy to come. In those days there were two extremely popular performers in Nanking; one was the songstress, Moonbeam Wang, and the other was Pockmarked Liu.

I once heard Liu tell the plain text[3] of "Wu Sung Beats the Tiger on Ching-yang Ridge."[4] It was quite different from what was written in the book.[5] His descriptions were graphic and went into the tiniest details, yet he was very clear-cut about when to be expansive and when to stop short and was by no means garrulous. Liu's full voice was like a giant bell and, as the story reached a climax, his stentorian exclamations were so awesome that they shook the house. When Liu told how Wu Sung went into the wine-shop to order a drink and found no one there, he gave a mighty roar that made all of the empty jugs and jars in the shop reverberate. Even when there was a lull in the plot, he would spruce it up, so particular was he about minutiae.

The sponsors of a performance by Liu had to sit quietly with bated breath and listen attentively before he would begin to wag his tongue. If he saw anybody in the audience murmuring or whispering, or if one of the auditors yawned or stretched, he would stop speaking immediately and no one could force him to continue. Often it would be the middle of the night, when his table had been wiped clean, the lampwick trimmed, and he was sipping tea from a white porcelain cup, before Liu would begin slowly to tell his story. The pace and emphasis of Liu's narrative, the quality and amplitude of his delivery—all were perfectly in accord with sentiment and reason, and all struck a deep chord in the fiber of every listener's being. If you could grab all of the storytellers in the world by the ear and make them listen carefully to him, rest assured that even they would gasp in wonderment.

Pockmarked Liu's face was unusually ugly, but his enunciation was pre-

---

and socialite. During the final four decades of the Ming, he was able to travel extensively in comfort and observe many of the fashionable scenes of the time. At some point, he took the artistic name "Studio of Contentment (T'ao-an)." After the collapse of the dynasty in 1644, his fortunes declined and he withdrew from society. During the remaining forty years or so of his life, he lived in reduced circumstances as a recluse, writing his memoirs in the form of miscellanies. *Dreamy Memories from the Studio of Contentment (T'ao-an meng-yi)*, his best-known collection, contains short, epigraphic narratives of the travels of his youth as well as vignettes of personalities, customs, and various cultural pursuits.

1. Born in 1587.

2. The word used here is *shuo-shu* (literally, "say/explain book"), which refers to a specific genre of Chinese oral performing arts.

3. "Plain" refers to the spoken language as opposed to singing. In other contexts, it refers to the classical book language (in which verse was most likely to be composed).

4. See selection 212.

5. *River Banks (Shui-hu chuan*, also translated as *Water Margin* and *All Men Are Brothers*).

cise, his eyes were expressive, and his clothes were spotless. Thus he was as handsome as Moonbeam Wang was beautiful, and his standing in the entertainment world was equally high.

Translated by Victor H. Mair

Professional Matchmakers

from *Dream Memories of West Lake*

Chang Tai

At Yangchow, there were hundreds of people making a living from activities connected with the "lean horses." One should never let it be known that one was looking for a concubine. Once this leaked out, the professional agents and go-betweens, both men and women, would swarm about his house or hotel like flies, and there was no way of keeping them off. The next morning, he would find many of them waiting for him, and the matchmaker who arrived first would hustle him off, while the rest followed behind and waited for their chance.

Arriving at the house of the "lean horse," the person would be served tea as soon as he was seated. At once the woman agent would come out with a girl and announce, "*Ku-niang,*[1] curtsy!" The girl curtsied. Next was said, "*Ku-niang*, walk forward!" She walked forward. "*Ku-niang*, turn around!" She turned around, facing the light, and her face was shown. "Pardon, can we have a look at your hand?" The woman rolled up her sleeve and exposed her entire arm. Her skin was shown. "*Ku-niang*, look at the gentleman." She looked from the corner of her eyes. Her eyes were shown. "How old is *Ku-niang?*" She replied. Her voice was shown. "Please walk again a bit." This time the woman lifted her skirts. Her feet were shown. There is a secret about judging women's feet. When you hear the rustle of her skirts when she comes out, you may guess that she has big feet, but if she wears her skirts relatively high and reveals her feet as she takes a step forward, you already

---

The original title is "Lean Horses," a local name for matchmakers. The author describes the practice of Yangchow, nationally famed as the center of luxury and the place where regular houses trained girls to be singsong artists or concubines. The time was the early seventeenth century.

This piece describes what may be called the "concubine market" and its efficiency. It is the most unromantic way of securing a mistress; only coarse businessmen would buy a concubine this way.

1. Mademoiselle.

know that she has a pair of small feet that she is proud of. "*Ku-niang,* you can go back."

As soon as the girl went in, another came out, and the same thing was repeated. Usually there were five or six girls in a house. If the gentleman decided he would take a certain girl, he would put a gold hairpin or ornament on her hair; this was called *tsatai.* If no one was satisfactory, a tip of several hundred cash was given the woman agent or the maids of the house, and one was shown another house. When one woman agent had completed the round of the houses she operated with, other women agents came around. Thus it continued for one, two, perhaps four or five days. There was no end to it and the agents were never tired. But after one had seen fifty or sixty of them, they were all just about alike, with a painted face and a red dress. It is like writing characters; by the time you have made the same sign a hundred times or a thousand times, you cannot recognize it any more. One does not know what to decide or which one to take, and eventually makes his choice on one of them.

After the choice was made, signaled by *tsatai,* the owner came out with a red sheet of paper and a writing brush. On the paper were written the items: silks, gold flowers, cash present, and pieces of cloth. The owner would dip the brush in ink and hold it ready for the customer to fill in the number of pieces and the cash present he was prepared to give for the girl. If this was satisfactory, the deal was concluded and the customer took his leave.

Before he arrived at his own place, drummers and musicians and carrier-loads of lamb and red and green wines were already there. In a moment, ceremonial papers, fruit, and pastry also arrived, and the senders went back accompanied by the musicians. Before they had gone a quarter mile, there came back with the band floral sedan chairs, floral lanterns, torches, handled torches, sedan chair carriers, bridesmaids, candles, more fruit, and roasts. The cook arrived with a carrier-load of vegetables and meats, sweets, followed by awnings, tablecloths, chair cushions, table service, longevity stars, bed curtains and stringed instruments. Without notice and even without asking for approval, the floral sedan chair and another chair supposed to accompany the bride started off to welcome the bride with a procession of bridal lanterns and handled torches. Before you knew it, the bride had arrived. The bride came up and performed the wedding ceremony,[2] and she was ushered to take her place at the dinner table already laid. Music and song began, and there was much ado about the house. Everything was efficient and fast. Before noon, the agent asked for her tip, said good-bye, and rushed off to look for other customers.

Translated by Lin Yutang

2. By bowing to the groom and guests.

177

Account of a Peach-Stone Boat

Wei Hsüeh-yi (c. 1606–c. 1625)

During the Ming period there was an ingeniously skilled craftsman named Wang Shu-yüan who could make houses, implements, human figures, and even birds, beasts, trees, and rocks from a piece of wood an inch in diameter. He never failed to image the shape of an object in accord with the configuration of his raw material, and each of his creations possessed its own sentiment and mood.

Wang bequeathed to me a peach-stone boat that might well be entitled "The Elder Su Drifting on the River at Red Cliff." From stem to stern the boat was approximately eight tenths plus a fraction of an inch long, and its height was roughly that of a bit more than two millet grains. In the center was a lofty, spacious part which served as the cabin. This was covered by a mat made of broad-leaved bamboo. Small windows were inserted on the sides, four each to the left and the right for a total of eight shutters. When the windows were thrown open and you looked in, you could see across to the carved railings on the opposite side. If you closed them, on the right was engraved "MOUNTAINS HIGH MOON SMALL; WATER RECEDES STONES EMERGE," and on the left was engraved "PURE WIND SLOWLY COMES; WATERY WAVES NOT RISE." The characters were filled in with azurite pigment.

Seated in the prow were three men. In the center, with a high-peaked cap, was East Slope (Su Tung-p'o).[1] To his right was Buddha Imprint[2] and to his left was Simple Straight (Huang T'ing-chien).[3] Su and Huang were reading a handscroll together. East Slope held the beginning of the scroll with his right hand and was patting Simple Straight's back with his left hand. Simple Straight held the end of the scroll with his left hand and was pointing

Late Ming society displayed a particular fondness for such minor arts as inside-painted snuff bottles, decorated incense burners, detailed ivory figurines, elaborately carved buckles, and engraved seals. This sort of kitschy craftsmanship, which fueled European chinoiserie in the following centuries, was mirrored in literature by a taste for intricately descriptive essays. Art and literature come together in this famous piece inspired by an actual object, the likes of which may still be seen—with the aid of a magnifying glass—in the National Palace Museum (Taipei, Taiwan). The boat made of a kernel was, in turn, inspired by Su Shih's celebrated "Red Cliff Rhapsody" (selection 127 in this volume), which is quoted directly by Wei Hsüeh-yi.

The author, a brilliant young student, died of grief over the death of his father at the hands of the notorious eunuch faction of the Ming court.

1. Su Shih, the famous Sung period scholar-official and author of the "Red Cliff Rhapsody."

2. Fo-yin, a monkish friend of Su Tung-p'o.

3. A celebrated calligrapher and poet who was also a close associate of Su Tung-p'o (see selection 57).

to the scroll with his right hand, as though he were saying something. East Slope's right foot was showing and Simple Straight's left foot was showing. Both of their bodies were leaning slightly. Their two knees that were next to each other were hidden beneath the bottom of the scroll and in the folds of their clothing. Buddha Imprint bore an extremely close resemblance to Maitreya.[4] His chest was bare and his breasts were revealed. Head raised, he was looking upward in a spirit quite unlike that of Su and Huang. His right knee was stretched out horizontally, and his bent right arm was supported by the boat while he dangled a rosary from his left arm, which rested on his perpendicular left knee. The rosary beads could be counted one by one.

A scull was lying horizontally across the stern. To the left and right of the scull there were two boatmen. The one on the right side had his hair tied up in the shape of a mallet. His left hand was braced against a horizontal board and his right hand was grabbing his right toes. He looked as though he were shouting. The one on the left held a fan made of palm leaves in his right hand and was touching a stove with his left hand. On top of the stove was a kettle. The man had a fixed gaze and a quiet expression, as though he were listening to the tea-water.

The back of the boat was rather even and the craftsman had written an inscription on its surface. The inscription read: "Carved by Wang Yi, styled Shu-yüan, of Yü-shan,[5] on an autumn day in the *jen-hsü* year[6] of the Heavenly Revelation." The characters, black in color, were fine as the legs of a spider, yet each of the strokes was clearly distinct. There was also a seal, red in color, written in an archaic script. It read: "Hermit of Ch'u-p'ing."[7]

If we calculate for the whole boat, there were five men, eight windows, one broad-leaved bamboo mat, one scull, one stove, one kettle, one handscroll, and one rosary. All together, there were thirty-four characters in the matching couplets, the inscription, and seal. Yet, when we calculate the length of the boat, it was not even a full inch. As a matter of fact, the craftsman had made it from a long, narrow peach-stone that he had selected. After I had finished scrutinizing the boat in detail, I marveled, "Ah! that skill could be so preternatural! There are a good many stories recorded in the *Chuang Tzu*[8] and the *Lieh Tzu*[9] in which beholders are startled by those who possess supernatural skills, yet who among them could let a knife play

---

4. The Buddha of the future. Popularly referred to as the "Laughing Buddha," he is usually depicted with an exposed fat belly.

5. In the province of Kiangsu.

6. I.e., 1622.

7. Ch'u-p'ing is the soubriquet of Wang Yi (Shu-yüan). It is likely that he adopted this fancy name from the legend of Huang Ch'u-p'ing, a Taoist recluse for more than forty years who was said to have been able to metamorphose rocks into goats.

8. See selection 8.

9. See selection 10.

freely in a piece of material less than an inch in size while producing figures with beards and eyebrows that are clearly visible? If someone were to repeat my own words to me, I would certainly suspect that they were exaggerating. But now I have seen the peach-stone boat with my own eyes. Judging from what I have observed, it is not necessarily impossible to carve a female monkey on the tip of a jujube thorn.[10] Ah! that skill could be so preternatural!"

Translated by Victor H. Mair

10. A feat falsely claimed by a couple of tricksters in the book attributed to Master Han Fei (d. 233 B.C.E).

178
The Vocal Mimic

Lin Ssu-huan (fl. c. 1644–1661)

In the capital,[1] there was a man who was good at vocal mimicry. On the occasion of a great banquet to which many guests were invited, a screen eight feet in height was set up in the northeast corner of the hall. The vocal mimic was seated behind the screen. His only properties were a table, a chair, a fan, and a ruler that he used as a clapper. The assembled guests were seated around the front of the screen. After a short while, they heard from behind the screen the sound of the ruler being struck against the table once, whereupon the entire audience grew quiet. No one dared to make any more noise.

Far off, they heard a dog barking in a deep alley, then a woman who was startled awake stretched and yawned while her husband mumbled in his sleep. Before long, her baby woke up and started bawling loudly, causing the husband to wake up too. He told the woman to soothe the baby by letting it nurse, but the baby continued to cry while sucking on her teat, so she patted it and cooed to it. The husband got up to urinate, and the wife got up to urinate while still holding the baby. Then an older child who was on the bed also woke up and began to jabber unceasingly. By this time, the sounds of the wife patting her baby and cooing to it, the baby sucking on her teat, the older child as he was waking up, and the husband scolding the older child

Next to nothing is known of the author other than that he hailed from Chin-chiang in Fukien province and that he passed the Presented Scholar examination sometime between 1644 and 1661.

1. Peking.

were all issuing simultaneously, and each sound was performed to marvelous perfection. All of the guests who were seated in the audience craned their necks, strained their eyes sideways, smiled, and sighed in silent admiration, thinking to themselves how utterly wonderful it all was.

Before long, the husband got back in bed and went to sleep. The wife told the older child to go pee and, when he had finished, they got back in bed and went to sleep too. Gradually, even the baby began to fall asleep. As the husband started to snore, the sounds of the wife patting her baby gradually became intermittent. Then there were the faint sounds of a rat scrabbling about, a bowl being knocked over, and the woman coughing while she dreamed. The guests felt a bit more relaxed and sat up a little more straight.

Suddenly, somebody loudly shouted, "Fire!" The husband got up and started shouting loudly too and the wife did likewise. Both of the children were crying and soon there was a multitude of people shouting, children crying, and dogs barking. Amidst this commotion were the multitudinous sounds of houses collapsing with a thud, fire crackling, and wind howling all at once. And interspersed among all the rest were the multitudinous sounds of people calling for help or coming to the rescue, of people pulling down houses² with a heave and a ho, of saving things from the fire, and of splashing water. Whatever sounds would be expected of a conflagration were all to be heard. Even if you had a hundred hands and every hand had a hundred fingers, you wouldn't be able to point out each of them. And if you had a hundred mouths and every mouth had a hundred tongues, you wouldn't be able to name each of them.

The result was that all of the guests got up from their seats with ashen faces, rolled-up sleeves, and wobbly legs. Just as they were on the verge of scrambling to get out ahead of the others, the ruler struck against the table once and the myriad echoing sounds came to a halt. When the screen was removed, all that could be seen were a man, a table, a chair, a fan, and a ruler.

Translated by Victor H. Mair

2. This would have been done for one of two reasons: to stop the path of the fire or for safety's sake if a building was already tottering.

179

The Arts of Sleeping, Walking, Sitting, and Standing

from *The Arts of Living*

Li Yü (1610/11–1680)

There are many ways of enjoying life that are hard to hold down to any one theory. There are the joys of sleeping, of sitting, of walking, and of standing up. There is the pleasure in eating, washing up, hairdressing, and even in such lowly activities as going about naked and barefooted, or going to the toilet. In its proper place, each can be enjoyable. If one can enter into the spirit of fun and take things in his stride anywhere any time, one can enjoy some things over which others may weep. On the other hand, if one is a crude person and awkward in meeting life or taking care of one's health, he can be the saddest person amidst song and dance. I speak here only of the joys of daily living and of the ways in which advantage may be taken of the commonest occupations.

1. The Art of Sleeping

There was a yogi who traveled about, teaching the secrets of conservation of life force and of prolonging life, and he wanted me to be his pupil. I asked him what he could do to attain longevity and where such blessings were to be found. I thought it would be fine if his methods agreed with my way of thinking, and if not, I could at least befriend him.

This man told me that the secret of longevity lay in controlled breathing, and peace of mind was to be sought through séance. I said to him, "Your

Li Yú was a most original and versatile writer who was not so much a scholar as an artist of living. Aside from writing the preface for the well-known *Guide to Painting from the Mustard Seed Garden*, he was also the author of a number of popular works, including one on making couplets. The book entitled *The Arts of Living* or *Sketches of Idle Pleasure* gives his always original thoughts on musical plays, acting, houses and their interiors, food and drink, horticulture, and sundry other subjects.

Li Yú is the comic specialist of Chinese literature—in drama, fiction, and the essay. To an unprecedented degree, he emphasized originality and invention in literature; he usually presents himself in his work as challenging some accepted belief. His plays were written throughout the 1650s and 1660s, but his fiction was confined to a brief period from about 1655 to 1658. *Silent Operas* (*Wu-sheng hsi*), his first collection of stories, appeared probably in 1655 or 1656. It was soon followed by *Silent Operas, Second Collection,* by a novel, *The Carnal Prayer Mat* (*Jou-p'u t'uan*), which is a sexual comedy, and by a third collection of stories, *Twelve Towers* (*Shih-erh lou*).

ways are hard and forced, and only people like you can practice it. I am lazy and like motion. I seek joy in everything. I am afraid it is not for me."

"What is your way then?" he asked. "I should like to hear it, and we can compare notes."

And this is what I said to him:

In the natural scheme of things, it is meant for man to spend half his time in activity and half at rest. In the day, he sits, moves, or stands, and at night, he rests. If a man labors by day and does not rest by night and continues this day after day, you can get ready and wait for his funeral to pass by. I try to keep my health by dividing half my time in rest and half my time in activity. If something troubles me and prevents me from sleep, there's the danger signal! I should count my remaining years on my fingers!

In other words, the secret of good health lies in a good and restful sleep. One who sleeps well restores his energy, revitalizes his inner system, and tones up his muscles. If you do not believe me, compare a sick man with a healthy person. A man who is not permitted to rest will get sick; his eyes become sunken, and all kinds of symptoms appear. A sick man becomes worse without sleep. But after a good sleep, he wakes up full of eagerness for life again. Is not sleep the infallible miracle drug, not just a cure for one illness but for a hundred, a cure that saves a thousand lives? To seek health by controlled breathing and the hard exercises of sitting in meditation would only involve great concentration and effort to keep awake instead! Would I throw away the best medicine in the world for an untested formula?

The man left abruptly, considering me not worth his time. And, indeed, I am not worth his teaching: I merely presented what I myself had achieved, sincerely for the sake of discussion, to see clearly which way is better.

An ancient poem goes, "After a long, sound sleep in bamboo-shaded quiet, I feel so far removed from the day's turmoil. If the hermit of Huashan comes to visit me, I shall not ask for the secret of becoming an immortal, but of sleeping well." A modern saying goes, "First rest your mind, then rest your eyes."

There is a proper time and a proper place for sleep, and there are certain sleeping habits which should be avoided. To be specific, one should rest between 9 P.M. and 8 A.M. To go to bed before nine is too early; it is a bad sign to be craving for sleep like a sick person. To sleep after eight in the morning is bad for health, like all oversleeping. Where would be the time left for other pleasures?

I know a friend who never gets up before noon, and anyone visiting him before noon is kept waiting. One day I sat miserably in his parlor waiting, and with ink and brush ready, I playfully parodied an ancient poem and wrote as follows:

I am busy sleeping,
Throughout the whole morn.
If I live to seventy,
Five and thirty are gone.

Although it was done in fun, it is close to the truth. One should only sleep at night as a rule. The pleasure of an afternoon nap is understandable, but it should be reserved only for summer when the day is long and the night is short. It is natural that one tires easily in the heat, and it is as good for a man to sleep when tired as to drink when thirsty. This is common sense. The best time is after lunch. One should wait a while until the food is partly digested and then leisurely stroll toward the couch. Do not tell yourself that you are determined to get a nap. In that way, the mind is tense and the sleep will not be sound. Occupy yourself with something first and before it is finished, you are overcome with a sense of fatigue and the sandman calls. The never-never land cannot be chased down. I love that line in a poem which says, "Dozing off, the book slips out of my hand." Thus sleep comes without his artifice or knowledge. This is the secret of the art of sleeping.

Next, one must consider the place, which should be cool and quiet. If it is not quiet, the eyes rest but not the ears. If it is too hot, the soul rests but not the body, and body and soul are at loggerheads. This goes against the principle of good health.

Lastly, we will consider the sleeper himself. Some people are busy, and others have plenty of time. Logically, the man of leisure needs little sleep; it is the busy man who needs it most of all. But often the busy man cannot sleep well. He rests his eyes in sleep but not his mind. In fact, he gets no rest from sleep at all. The worst of it is to think of something during the half-awake hours of the morning and suddenly remember something he hasn't done or someone he hasn't seen. It is very, very important! He must not sleep another wink or something will be spoiled! That very thought drives away all sleep. He becomes tense and gets up more keyed up than before. Such is the rest of the busy man. The man of leisure rests his mind before his eyes are shut, and his mind wakes up refreshed before his eyes are open, happy to slumber and happier to wake up. Such is the sleep of the man of leisure.

Yet in this world how many such idle men are there? All men cannot lead a life with nothing to do. Therefore a method must be found. It is best to dispose of the urgent business of the day in the morning, and delegate to others those things that are not finished. Then one knows that everything is in order and under control. He can afford to seek the pillow and go for that slumber which is described as the "dark, sweet village." He will then sleep as well as the man of leisure.

Another thing: to enjoy a perfect sleep requires a peaceful conscience. Such a man will not be "frightened when there is a knock on the door at midnight," as the saying goes. He will not mistake the peckings of chickens in the barnyard for policemen's footsteps!

2. The Art of Walking

The rich man will go out only in a horse and carriage. It may be called a comfort and a luxury, but it can hardly be said that it fulfills the intention of the Creator in giving man a pair of legs. He who does not use his legs is by that very fact deprived of the use of his legs. On the other hand, a man who uses his legs is giving exercise to his entire body. That is why an ancient poor scholar [1] boasted that "a leisurely stroll is as good as a drive." Now to drive or to go on foot are both methods of transportation or locomotion. A man who is used to driving or riding on horseback can learn to enjoy the pleasures of a walk. Perhaps he comes upon a beautiful view or beautiful flowers on the way, or stops to talk with a peasant in his palm hat or meets a recluse philosopher-turned-woodcutter in the deep mountains. Sometimes one might enjoy a drive, and sometimes a walk. Surely this is better than the obstinacy of that proud scholar of ancient days!

What the poor man can be truly proud of is not the fact that he uses his legs, but that he does not depend on others for going anywhere. If he is not in a hurry, he can go slowly, and if he is, he breaks into a run. He does not have to wait for someone else, and he is not dependent on the carriage, unlike the rich man who is helpless when the driver is not there. The poor man has fulfilled the intentions of the Creator in giving him legs to walk with. It makes me happy just to think of this.

3. The Art of Sitting

No one knew the art of living better than Confucius. I know this from the statement that he "did not sleep like a corpse [2] and did not sit like a statue." If the Master had been completely absorbed in keeping decorum, intent on appearing like a gentleman at all hours and being seen as a sage at all times, then he would have had to lie down like a corpse and sit like a statue. His four limbs and his internal system would never have been able to relax. How could such a stiff wooden statue expect to live a long life? Because Confucius did not do this, the statement describes the ease of the Master in his private life, which makes him worthy of worship as the father of all cultured gentlemen. We should follow Confucius' example when at home. Do not sit erect and look severe as if you were chained or glued to the chair. Hug your knee

1. Yen Cho, of the third century B.C.E., was a Diogenes who refused gifts of money and power from a king.
2. With straight legs.

and sing, or sit chin in hand, without honoring it with the phrase of "losing oneself in thought."[3] On the other hand, if a person sits stiffly for a long time, head high and chest out, this is a premonition that he is heading for the grave. He is sitting for his memorial portrait!

4. The Art of Standing

Stand straight, but do not do it for long. Otherwise, all leg muscles will become stiff and circulation will be blocked up. Lean on something!—on an old pine or a quaint rock, or on a balcony or on a bamboo cane. It makes one look like one is in a painting. But do *not* lean on a lady! The foundation is not solid and the roof may come down!

Translated by Lin Yutang

3. As Chuang Tzu said (see selection 8).

180

Thoughts upon Student Huang's Borrowing of Books

Yüan Mei (1716–1797)

The student, Huang Yün-hsiu, asked to borrow some books from me and I, the master of Sui Garden,[1] gave them to him with the following admonition:

If you don't borrow books, you can't read them. Have you not heard about those who collect books? The "Seven Categories"[2] and the "Four Divisions"[3] were imperial collections, but how many emperors actually read them? Books fill the homes of the rich and the honored to the very rafters, but how many of the rich and the honored actually read them? As for all the fathers and

For information on the author, see selection 84.

1. The name of Yüan Mei's estate north of Nanking, the ostensible meaning of which is "Follow Garden."

2. Divisions of the Imperial Library assembled by Liu Hsiang (77–6 B.C.E.) and his son, Liu Hsin (c. 50 B.C.E.–23 C.E.), for the Han emperor Ch'eng Ti. Compare selections 200, 203, and especially 204, note 4.

3. Probably short for "Complete Library in Four Divisions" (*Ssu-k'u ch'üan-shu*), an enormous project initiated by the Ch'ien-lung emperor in 1772, although the bibliographical term "Four Divisions" goes back well over a thousand years before that time (see selection 206, introductory note).

grandfathers who have amassed books only to see their sons and grandsons throw them away, there's no need to discuss it.

But it's not just books that are treated like this; everything under heaven is treated the same way. If we manage to borrow something that is not our own, we worry that someone will force us to give it back and so we fondle it fearfully without end, saying, "Today I have it; tomorrow it may be gone and then I won't see it any more!" If it's something that already belongs to us, then we wrap it up and put it on a high shelf, storing it away and saying, "I'll leave it there for the time being and take a peek at it later on."

When I was young, I loved books but my father was poor, so it was hard to get hold of them. There was a Mr. Chang who had a rich collection of books; I went to borrow some from him but he wouldn't give me any. When I returned home, I had a dream about my unsuccessful attempt to borrow books, which shows how eager my desire was. Thus, when I did get to read something, I invariably remembered it. After I became an official and was established in my own residence, as I spent out my salary the books came pouring in till they were piled up everywhere in great profusion and the scrolls and tomes were covered with silverfish and cobwebs. Later I would sigh with admiration at the attentiveness with which those who borrowed books read them and think how precious the months and years of one's youth are.

Now, Student Huang, you are poor like I used to be and you borrow books like I used to. It would seem that the only difference is that I share my books with you whereas Mr. Chang was stingy with his books to me. But was I unfortunate to have encountered Mr. Chang? And are you fortunate to have encountered me? To know whether someone is fortunate or not, it depends on how diligently he reads the books he has borrowed and how swiftly he returns them. To explain my thoughts on borrowing, I am sending this note [4] along with the books.

Translated by Victor H. Mair

---

4. Here and in the title, this piece is actually called a *shuo* (explanation) by the author.

Travelogues and Scenic Descriptions

181
A Poem on Wandering at the Stone Gate, with Introduction

Laymen of Mount Lu Associated with Hui-yüan (344–416/17)

The Stone Gate is over ten tricents south of the *vihāra*,[1] and is also known as Screen Mountain. Its base joins the great range of Mount Lu, and its form

The preface and accompanying poem on wandering at the Stone Gate Gorge of Mount Lu in 400 C.E. have long been associated with the charismatic Buddhist monk Hui-yüan and his community of monks and laymen who studied and practiced Buddhism on Mount Lu (Kiangsi province). Hui-yüan himself is referred to in the preface as "the Master of the Doctrine" and hence is unlikely to be the author. Among his influential literary lay disciples were two avid mountain-climbers who mention in their writings a Stone Gate that may be the Mount Lu Gorge. One was Tsung Ping (375–443), a Buddhist apologist, musician, and landscapist, who defended Hui-yüan's doctrine of the immortal spirit and believed in the direct experience of a limitless universe newly conceived from the reading of Buddhist texts. The other was the poet Hsieh Ling-yün (385–433, see selection 21), a rugged individualist who nonetheless felt the need of an understanding mind with which to share his "landscape Buddhism," a mystical insight into the natural order.

Like other sacred sites where spectacular scenery and fantastic rock formations were taken as a sign of the supernatural, Mount Lu had been hallowed by popular Taoism before it became a center of Buddhist learning, and appreciations of its views were already being written in Han times. Although the preface on the Stone Gate expedition offers an explicit definition of the experience of nature in a Buddhist context, it was evidently influenced by the famous "Preface to the Festival at the Orchid Pavilion," written by Wang Hsi-chih (303–379) at the gathering of 353 C.E. in the Kuei-chi district (Chekiang province) (see selection 168). Like the poetry-writing contest during the spring purification festival at the Orchid Pavilion, the "land-

rises above the clustered hills. It constitutes the juncture of three streams; standing close together, it initiates their currents. The inclining cliffs darkly gleam from above; they receive their external shapes from Nature. On this account it was named the Stone Gate. Although this spot is but one corner of the Lu range, nonetheless it is the most extraordinary view of the region. All this was known through earlier accounts, but there were many who had never seen it themselves. This was perhaps due to the fact that the waterfall was so precipitous that trails for men and beasts were cut off, and, since paths wind about twisting hills, access was blocked and walking difficult. Hence few people have visited it.

In the second month of spring in the fourth year of Lung-an (400 C.E.), Shih Hui-yüan, the Master of the Doctrine, who had been hymning the landscape, accordingly took up his ringed abbot's staff and wandered off. On this occasion there were some thirty men of like mind among his companions. Together we donned our robes and set off at dawn in low spirits but felt increasingly exhilarated. Although the forests were gloomy and valleys deep, we still broke a path through and vied to push forward. And ascending the heights and treading on rock we were wholly at ease through what gave us pleasure. On reaching the gorge, we pulled ourselves up by trees and grasped

---

scape Buddhism" of Mount Lu was a communal experience of emotional release in a setting of great natural beauty. Esthetic impressions served to stimulate meditation or focus the mind in a manner similar to Hui-yüan's devotional practice of visualizing the Buddha's body. Hui-yüan also fostered a strong feeling of community among his lay disciples. In a collective vow made during the year 402 for rebirth in the Western Paradise, all present were to help one another ascend to the supernatural realm of the mountain paradise, "mindful of the principle of marching together!" The smaller group of men who climbed the Stone Gate two years earlier were moved to express their shared joy in a communal hymn.

The occasion described in the introduction to "A Poem on Wandering at the Stone Gate" requires little explanation. Interestingly enough, Hui-yüan and his companions are inspired to climb by poems on landscape. Through their efforts they gain a view, which is initially characterized in general terms; then they note the layout of mountain and rock formations that seem to indicate the palace grounds of the immortals. Illusory qualities of shapes are underlined by shifting light and atmospheric effects, and a feeling of spatial disorientation is given by the blurring of sense impressions. These accidental perceptions arouse a selfless delight, which is then analyzed by the group as the correct response to phenomena. At sunset the view from on high suggests the vast scale of the universe; in turn this stimulates thoughts of eternal time and the remoteness of the Buddha. After meditating on him for a while, the group is moved by a shared emotion to compose a poem on their experience. Despite a few Taoist references, it treats the climb up the cliffs of the Stone Gate as a stage in a spiritual ascent that leads through meditation to nirvana. In the preface, purification of the mind through the perception of emptiness allows it to respond correctly without emotion and to seek the merging with the universal spirit that was the aim of Hui-yüan's teaching. A gradual detachment from illusory forms and an enlarging perspective that diminishes personal concerns are the qualities valued in the landscape experience.

1. The Tung-lin monastery. The Stone Gate Gorge is "the ravine with the waterfall" located on the western side of Mount Lu near the Tung-lin monastery.

for creepers, traversing the perilous and plumbing the precipitous; only when arms, stretched apelike, were extended to each other did we advance to a summit. Thereupon, leaning against the cliff, we seized the view and clearly saw what was below, experiencing for the first time the beauty of the seven ridges and the gathering of exceptional sights in the spot.

The twin gate-towers soared up in opposition before us, while layered precipices gleamed about behind; peaks and hills twisted and turned to form a screen, and high cliffs built up on all sides to support the roof of heaven. Within there was a stone tower and a rocky pond, semblances of palace halls and representational shapes; it was all most pleasing.

Limpid brooks ran separately and poured together; pellucid depths were of a mirrorlike translucency in the Heavenly Pond. Patterned rocks displayed their colors, tangibly present in their glory, while tamarisks, pines, plants, and herbs dazzled the eyes with their luxuriance; all that constitutes spirited beauty was present.

On this day, various emotions hastened our enjoyment and we gazed at length without tiring. We had not looked about for long before the weather changed several times. In the dusty gathering of mist and fog, all things concealed their forms; in the reflected illumination of radiating light, the myriad peaks were inverted as mirrored scenery. At intervals of clearing, appearances had a numinous quality yet could not be fathomed.

When we went on to climb, hovering birds fluttered pinions and crying apes harshly clamored. Homing clouds, driving back, called to mind the visitations of feathered men;[2] mournful cries blended in harmony like the lodging of mysterious tones. Even though they were heard only faintly, one's spirit felt expansive. And, although in enjoying one did not expect delight, nonetheless happiness lasted throughout the day. At that time, this experience of empty pleasure truly had subtleness yet was not easy to define.

We then withdrew to seek an explanation. For, as the assembled beings in these cliffs and valleys lacked conscious selves, response was not through emotions. Yet they awakened an exhilaration that drew us onward to such an extent. Could it not be that emptiness and luminosity clarify reflections, and quietness and distance solidify the emotions? Altogether we repeated this discussion several times, and its subtlety was still inexhaustible.

Suddenly the sun announced evening, and this world was gone. We then became aware of the mysterious perception of world-renouncers and comprehended the true nature of enduring things: could it be merely the landscape that caused such divine pleasure? Thereupon, as we roamed on cliffs and precipices, shifting our gaze to scan all sides, the nine rivers[3] were like a belt

2. The "feathered men" are Taoist transcendents.
3. Of Kiukiang, i.e., Chiu-chiang.

and foothills formed low mounds. From this one could deduce that as in forms there are large and small, so knowledge is also proportionate.

We then sighed deeply, lamenting that though the universe is of long duration, ancient and modern are of a piece. The Vulture Peak is far away, and the overgrown path is daily more impassable. Without the Sage,[4] even though His influence and traces of His teaching still remain, His profound enlightenment must necessarily be remote. With feeling we reflected for a long while. As each of us was enjoying the shared happiness of a rare time, moved by an auspicious moment that would be hard to recreate, emotions burst forth from our midst, and we accordingly hymned them together:

> Supermundane exhilaration is without root cause;
> When one is moved by insight, exhilaration comes of itself.
> Suddenly, as we heard of roaming at the Stone Gate,
> These unusual lays brought forth our hidden feelings.
> Plucking up our robes, we thought of cloud-charioteering immortals;
> And gazing at precipices, we envisaged the tiered city of K'un-lun.
> Spurring forward, we climbed up the great cliffs
> Without perceiving the diminishing of substantial being.
> Lifting up our heads, we ascended the cloudy gate-tower
> As remote as if it reached to the Great Purity of heaven.
> Seated upright, we turned the empty wheel of the mind,
> Setting in motion the Norm from within Profundity.
> Spirits and immortals share in the changes of all beings;
> It is better that both self and others be altogether darkened in oblivion.

> *Translated by Susan Bush*

4. Śākyamuni Buddha.

182

The Establishment of the White Horse Temple

from *The Record of the Monasteries of Loyang*

Yang Hsüan-chih (fl. 555)

The establishment of the Pai-ma Temple (Temple of the White Horse) by Emperor Ming[1] of the Han marked the introduction of Buddhism into

This is the "official" version of the introduction of Buddhism to China. In all likelihood, the powerful Indian religion must have begun to filter into China in an unrecognized and inchoate fashion long before Emperor Ming's dream, although the early history of the religion

China. The temple was located on the south side of the Imperial Drive, three tricents outside the Hsi-yang Gate.

The emperor dreamed of the golden man sixteen Chinese feet tall, with the aureole of sun and moon radiating from his head and his neck. A "golden god," he was known as Buddha. The emperor dispatched envoys to the Western Regions in search of the god, and, as a result, acquired Buddhist scriptures and images. At the time, because the scriptures were carried into China on the backs of white horses, White Horse was adopted as the name of the temple.

After the emperor's death, a hall for meditation[2] was built on his tomb. Thereafter stūpas were sometimes constructed even on the graves of the common people.

The scripture cases housed in the temple have survived until this day; to them incense was often burned and good care was given. At times, the scripture cases gave off light that illuminated the room and hall. As a result, both laymen and Buddhist devotees reverently worshiped as if they were facing the real Buddha.

In front of the stūpa were pomegranate trees and grapevines that were different from those grown elsewhere: they had luxuriant foliage and huge fruits. The pomegranates each weighed seven catties, and the grapes were bigger than dates. The taste of both was especially delicious, superior to all others in the capital.[3] At harvest time the emperor often came in person to pick them. Sometimes he would give some to ladies in the harem, who in turn would present them as gifts to their relatives. They were considered rare delicacies. The recipients often hesitated to eat them; instead, the fruits would be passed on and on to several households. In the capital there was a saying:

> Sweet pomegranates of the White Horse,
> Each fruit is as valuable as an ox.

Translated by Yi-t'ung Wang

---

is very difficult to document. This account of the White Horse Temple, the title of which has been supplied by the editor, is taken from a book dedicated to the description of the Buddhist monasteries of Loyang in the early sixth century. The city, with all its grandeur, was destroyed in 534. Noted for its superb literary quality as well as for the wealth of valuable historical, social, and cultural data that it preserves, *The Record of the Monasteries of Loyang* (*Loyang ch'ieh-lan chi*) was written by Yang Hsüan-chih, an official of the Northern Wei (Tabgatch) dynasty.

1. Reigned 58–75 C.E.

2. *Jetavana*—a term that derives from a garden donated by Prince Jeta for the orphaned and helpless, literally "Jeta's Grove."

3. Loyang.

183
A Climb Up Mount Omei

from *Diary of a Boat Trip to Wu*

Fan Ch'eng-ta (1126–1193)

[*Sixth lunar month*] *twenty-fifth day* (22 July 1177): Set out from Omei town. Leaving by the West Gate, we began climbing the mountain and passed the two monasteries of Benevolent Fortune and Universal Security, White River Manor, and Shu Village Way-Stop. After twelve tricents came to Dragon Spirit Hall. From here on, mountain torrents ripped and roared; shady forests stood mighty and deep. Took a brief rest at Avataṁsaka Monastery. Then crossed Green Bamboo Bridge, Omei's New Abbey Crossroad, Plum Tree Bank, West Dragon Hall, and reached Central Peak Monastery. The monastery has a Samantabhadra Gallery wreathed by a circle of seventeen peaks. It nestles against White Cliff Peak. The highest of the peaks rising prominently on the right is called Shout-and-Response Peak. Below is the retreat of Mao Chen the Venerated One—a place rarely visited by man.[1] Sun Ssu-miao lived in seclusion on Mount Omei. When Mao Chen was here he often

This selection is an excerpt from a well-known travel diary titled *Wu-ch'uan lu* (*Diary of a Boat Trip to Wu*). Written in 1177 by the famous Sung dynasty statesman and poet Fan Ch'eng-ta, this text describes a boat journey from Ch'eng-tu (in modern-day Szechwan), where the author had just finished serving as governor, to his home in Wu township (near modern-day Soochow, Kiangsu). After an initial sightseeing trip that took Fan to several scenic and historic sites situated to the north and west of Ch'eng-tu, his custom-made riverboat carried him, his family, and attendants down the Yangtze River all the way to Chen-chiang (modern-day Kiangsu). From there they proceeded south on the Grand Canal directly to Soochow. In all, the trip took 122 days (from 27 June to 26 October) and covered a distance of almost two thousand English miles.

During the journey, Fan Ch'eng-ta kept detailed records in the *Wu-ch'uan lu* of his many visits to local places of interest. Among these, his account of a ten-day trip to Mount Omei (Omei shan) in Szechwan is the most widely acclaimed, not only because it is the earliest detailed account of the mountain known, but also because of Fan's lively prose style and eye for fascinating details. The excerpts translated here describe his ascent to the mountain's summit. Without a doubt, his observation of the "Buddha Light" (Fo-kuang), an optical phenomenon that the devout believed to be a manifestation of Omei's "resident" Bodhisattva, P'u-hsien (Samantabhadra in Sanskrit), is the highlight of Fan's experience on Mount Omei. We join Fan and his traveling party (which did not include his family; they were sent earlier to a town downriver to wait for him) just as they are departing from the town at the base of the mountain and begin their ascent into the clouds.

1. Mao Chen was a Taoist adept of the Sui dynasty who supposedly gained immortality during his stay on Mount Omei. Sun Ssu-miao, mentioned in the next sentence, is also reported to have sought eternal life during his residence on Omei in the Sui and T'ang periods. He had a strong interest in alchemy and is well known for having authored several important medical treatises.

shouted and responded back and forth with Sun Ssu-miao from this spot, or so it is said.

Left the monastery and passed the two precipices of Camphor-Wood and the Ox Heart Monastery Crossroad. Then we reached the Twin Stream Bridges. The jumbled mountains hereabout huddle together like standing screens. There are two mountains opposite one another, each of which produces a stream. Side by side they flow to the base of the bridge. Their rocky channels are several tens of fathoms deep. With dark waters of deep green hue, the soaring torrents spurt foamy snowcaps as they race beyond the bridges and then pass into a high thicket. Several tens of paces from there the two streams form into one and then plunge into a great ravine. The waters in the abyss, still and deep, clear and pure, disperse to form stream rapids. All the small stones in the rapids are either multicolored or have patterns of green on a white background. The pale yellow hue of the water complements the colors of the stones, making the rapids look like an out-stretched piece of emerald-colored brocade. This scene is not something that could be captured in a sketch. When the sunlight of dawn shines on the water and rocks, a shimmering brilliance emits from the surface of the stream that reflects off the cliffs and ravines. Tradition says this is a "Minor Manifes-tation" of the Noble Master (or Samantabhadra). As for Ox Heart Monastery, when Chi-yeh,[2] Master of the Tripiṭaka, was returning home from the West-ern Regions he was going to found a sect here. He came upon two rocks poised against one another on the bank of the stream. He picked up one of them, in which there was an eyelike hole that ran straight through to its base. Chi-yeh regarded it as something precious and auspicious. To this day it still is housed in the monastery. The river here is thus named "Precious Manifes-tation Stream."

From here we climbed some precipitous stone steps and passed the Bo-dhisattva Gallery. On the road there was a sign that read: "The Empire's Great Mount Omei." Then we reached the White River Samantabhadra Monastery. Every step along the way from the town to here is nothing but steep hillsides for more than forty tricents. Only now are we beginning to climb the foothills of the crested peaks.

Twenty-sixth day (23 July): Spent the night at White River Monastery. It was raining heavily, so we could not ascend the mountain. Paid a visit to the bronze statue of the Noble Master Samantabhadra. It was cast in Ch'eng-tu by imperial decree at the beginning of the dynasty. Among the gifts conferred on the statue by the courts of the emperors T'ai-tsung,[3] Chen-tsung,[4] and Jen-

2. Chi-yeh was a famous Buddhist monk from Kaifeng who, under imperial auspices, traveled with three hundred other monks to India in 964 in order to get copies of various sūtras. He did not return to China until 976.

3. Reigned 976–997.

4. Reigned 997–1022.

tsung [5] are more than one hundred scrolls of texts of imperial authorship, a seven-jeweled headdress, a gemmy necklace of gold and pearls, a Buddhist's cassock, a gold and silver urn, an alms bowl, a makeup case, a censer, an incense spoon, joss sticks, a fruit plate, a bronze bell, a drum, a gong, a stone chime, "foamy" tea,[6] a pagoda, and a *chih*-mushroom.[7] There are also many other items conferred on the state by the Empress during the Ch'ung-ning reign,[8] such as pennants embroidered with gold coins and pennants woven with red silk. Among these treasures is a Buddhist cassock of red silk with purple embroidery conferred by the emperor Jen-tsung. On it are proclamations written in the emperor's own hand that read: "'Buddha's Dharma is enduring and exalted'; 'The Dharma Wheel is forever turning'; 'May the Empire be mighty, the people secure, winds favorable, and rains opportune'; 'May spears and pikes be forever at rest'; 'May the people know peace and joy'; 'May sons and grandsons be abundant'; 'May all living beings reach to the opposite shore of salvation.' Recorded and signed by the emperor in the Hall of Prosperity and Peace on the seventh day of the tenth month in the seventh year of the Chia-yu reign (20 November 1062)."

Next we reached the monastery's Sūtra Depository, which is a treasure-depository built by artisans from the Directorate of Manufacturing dispatched here by the Imperial Court. The front of the depository is a gate-tower. Smaller towers flank it on both sides. The gate-tower's nails and hinges are all made of jade-stone, and are extremely well crafted and amazingly extravagant. Tradition says they are modeled exactly after the style of the main gate in the National Capital.[9] The sūtras here were produced in Ch'eng-tu. They use blue, weighty paper with characters written in liquid silver. At the head of each scroll is a picture painted in liquid gold. Each picture covers the events in one scroll. A wheel sign [10] and objects such as small bells and pestles are embroidered on the outside covers of the sūtras, as well as expressions such as "Peace in the Empire!" and "Long Live the Emperor!" which are placed amid patterns of dense flowers and elaborate foliage. Today one no longer sees this type of embroidery pattern.

Next we reached the Hall of the Three Thousand Iron Buddhas. We were told that Samantabhadra resides on this mountain, and that a company of three thousand disciples live with him. Thus, they built these Buddhas. The

5. Reigned 1022–1063.

6. Fan is probably referring to a special variety of tea from Fukien which, when brought to a boil, produces a waxlike film on the surface of the water. It is also possible, however, to read this as "candles, tea. . . ."

7. A *chih* is a wood-fungus believed by some to confer longevity.

8. 1102–1107.

9. That is to say, the gate is styled after the main access gate to the Forbidden City in Kaifeng (Honan), the capital of the Northern Sung dynasty.

10. Referring to the nine-leveled wheel or karma sign placed on top of a pagoda.

casting is very plain and simple. On this day we set out offerings and prayed to the Noble Master (or Samantabhadra), begging for three days of fine, clear skies so we could climb the mountain.

Twenty-seventh day (24 July): It was a clear, beautiful day and so we began our ascent to the upper peak. From here to the Luminous Form Monastery and Seven Treasure Cliff on the peak's crest is another sixty tricents. The distance there from the level terrain in the town is probably no less than one hundred tricents. Moreover, no longer do we find any stone-step paths. Timbers have been cut and made into a long ladder, which is fastened into the cliff wall. One ascends the mountain by crawling up it. I submit that of all the mountains to climb in the empire, none matches this one in danger and height. As strong yeomen supported my sedan-chair in its forced ascent, thirty mountain lads drew it upward while they advanced pulling on a huge rope. My fellow travelers made use of the "ladder sedan-chairs" on the mountain.[11]

We left the White River Monastery through a side gate and then ascended to Touching Heart Mountain. It is said to be so steep that it makes climbers' feet and knees touch their hearts and bosoms. Passed Thatch Pavilion Point, Small Stone Thunder, the Greater and Lesser Deep Gullies, Camel Precipice, and the Clustered Bamboo Way-stop. Generally, when one speaks of a way-stop, they mean a one-room wooden structure facing the road. If there are travelers about to climb the mountain, monks at the monastery first dispatch men ahead to boil water at a way-stop so that a hot, steamy meal will await the travelers.

Next we passed Peak Gate, Arhat Way-stop, the Greater and Lesser Supports and Lifts, Illusory Joy and Delight, Tree Bark Village, Monkey's Ladder, and Thunder Cavern Flat. Generally, when one speaks of a flat, one means a place where one can more or less find a foothold. As for Thunder Cavern, the path here is on a steep cliff ten thousand rods high. There is a breach in the stone steps. If you spy down through it into the murky, black depths, it seems like a cavern. Tradition says that a divine dragon lives in a deep pool down there. In all, there are seventy-two caverns here. If there is a drought, people pray for rain at the third cavern. At first, they cast down perfumes and silks. If the dragon does not respond with rain, they then cast down dead swine and worn-out women's shoes, which are meant to excite and arouse him. Often, thunder and wind then suddenly burst forth. Most of the so-called fleecy clouds above the Luminous and Bright Cliff on the peak's summit are produced in this cavern.

Passed New Way-stop, Eighty-Four Switchbacks, and Teak Tree Flat. As

---

11. The term "ladder sedan-chairs" probably refers to wooden litters for one person that are tied on a bearer's back.

for the teak tree, its frame and leaves are similar to those of the *tobira* shrub. They also resemble the red bayberry tree. Their blossoms are red and white, and they bloom between spring and summer. Teak trees are found only on this mountain. I first saw them when we had reached halfway up the mountain. But when you get here, they are everywhere. For the most part, the plants, trees, birds, and insects on Mount Omei are not found anywhere else in the world. I certainly heard about this long ago. Today I personally verified it.

I came here during the last month of summer. A few days ago there was a heavy snowfall. The tree leaves were still marked with mottled patterns of snow. As for the extraordinary vegetation, examples would be the eight immortals, which here is deep purple, the herdboy, which here is several times the usual size, and the knotweed, which here is pale green. I heard that in springtime the extraordinary flowers are especially numerous. But in that season the mountain is cold, so few people are able to become acquainted with them. As for the extraordinary plants and leaves, their numbers are also beyond calculation. The mountain is high and windy. Trees do not grow well here. Their branches all droop down. Ancient mosses, like disheveled hair, hang loosely and laxly from treetops, drooping to the ground, several yards long. There are, as well, pagoda pines that resemble conifers in shape, but their needles are round and slender. They are also unable to grow tall. Layer upon layer, they turn and twist upward like a pagoda. When you get to the mountain's summit they are especially numerous. Furthermore, there are absolutely no birds here, probably because the mountain is so lofty that they cannot fly up this high.

From Teak Tree Flat we went on to pass Longing-for-the-Buddha Pavilion, Tender Grass Flat, and Foot-washing Stream. Then we reached our destination, the Luminous Form Monastery on the peak's summit. This monastery is also a wooden structure with several tens of rooms. No one was staying there. Inside there is a Minor Hall of Samantabhadra. We had begun our ascent in the *mao* double-hour (5:00–7:00 A.M.). When we reached here it was already past the *shen* double-hour (3:00–5:00 P.M.). At first, I wore my summer garments, but it gradually got colder as we climbed higher. When we reached the Eighty-Four Switchbacks, it quickly turned cold. By the time we got to the summit of the mountain, I hastily put on two layers of wadded jackets, over which I added a fur cloak and a fur robe. This exhausted all the clothes stored in my trunk. I wrapped my head with a double-layered scarf and put on some felt boots. Still, I couldn't stop shivering and trembling. Then we burned some coals and sat stiffly as we pressed against the brazier.

On the summit of the mountain there is a spring. If you boil rice in the spring water it will not cook. It just disintegrates into something like fine sand. One cannot cook things in the icy, snowy juices of ten thousand antiquities! I knew about this before. I had some water in an earthenware pot brought up from the lower reaches of the mountain, which was barely enough for myself.

A short time later we braved the cold and climbed to the Heavenly Immortal Bridge. Reached the Luminous and Bright Cliff. We burned incense in a small hall covered with a roof made of tree bark. Wang Chanshu,[12] the Vice Grand Councilor, once put tiles on the roof but they were worn away by snow and frost. Without fail, the tiles crumble to pieces within a year. Later he changed the roof back to tree bark, which on the contrary can last two or three years.

Someone told us that "Buddha's Manifestation" (or "Buddha Light") only comes out during the *wu* double-hour (11:00 A.M.–1:00 P.M.). Since it was already past the *shen* double-hour, we thought it might be best to return to our lodgings and come back the next day. Just as we pondered our decision, clouds suddenly emerged from the gorge to the side and below the cliff, which is Thunder Cavern Mountain. The clouds marched in columns like the Imperial Honor Guard. When they met with the cliff, the clouds halted for a short while. On top of the clouds there appeared a great globe of light with concentric coronas of various colors in several layers positioned opposite one another. In the middle was a watery, inky reflection that looked like the Immortal Sage (or Samantabhadra) riding an elephant. After the time it takes to drink a cup of tea, the light disappeared. But off to the side appeared yet another light just like the first one. In an instant it too disappeared. In the clouds there were two shafts of golden light that shot across into the belly of the cliff. People also call this a "Minor Manifestation." At sunset all the cloud forms scattered. The mountains in the four directions fell silent. At the *yi* night-watch (9:00–11:00 P.M.) the lamps came out.[13] They teemed everywhere below the cliff — tens of thousands of them filling our gaze. The night was so cold that we couldn't stay outside for too long.

Twenty-eighth day (25 July): Again we climbed up to the cliff to view and

---

12. Or Wang Chih-wang (1103–1170).

13. Earlier in his journey Fan Ch'eng-ta had observed similar "lamps" on Mount Green Wall in Szechwan and commented on their possible origins: "Some people say they are the glow of cinnabar drugs hidden away by the ancients. Others say they are the essence of plants and trees, which has a glow. And still others say they are made by dragon spirits and mountain demons. The explanation most people believe is that they have been devised by immortals and sages." Others in traditional China identify these same lights as "flitting fires," which, they explain, emit from long-standing concentrations of blood found in places such as old battlefields. Western scholars have also offered possible explanations of these "lamps." Some equate them with *ignis fatuus* (or "will-o'-the-wisp"), the spontaneous combustion of an inflammable gas derived from decaying organic matter. Others say they might be the result of sparks of static electricity or a kind of electroluminescence known as *ignis lambens*. All these explanations, however, are tentative at best. For now at least, the precise origin of Mount Omei's "lamps" remains a mystery.

gaze at the sights. Behind the cliff are the ten thousand folds of the Min Mountains. Not far to the north is [Little] Tile-roof Mountain, which is in Ya county. Not far to the south is Big Tile-roof Mountain, which is near Nan-chao.[14] In shape it looks just like a single tile-roofed house. On Little Tile-roof Mountain there is also a luminous form called the Pratyeka-Buddha Manifestation. Behind all these mountains are the Snow Mountains [15] of the Western Regions. Their jagged and cragged peaks, which seem carved and pared, in all number in the tens and hundreds. When the first light of day shines on them, their snowy hue is piercing and bright, like glistening silver amid the dazzling and resplendent light of dawn. From ancient times down to today, these snows have never melted. The mountains stretch and sweep into India and other alien lands, for who knows how many thousands of tricents. Gazing at them now, they seem spread out on a little tea-table right before my eyes. This magnificent, surpassing view tops everything I have seen in my life.

We paid a second visit to the hall on the cliff and offered prayers. Suddenly a dense fog arose in the four directions, turning everything completely white. A monk said: "This is the Silver World." A short time later, there was a heavy downpour and the dense fog retreated. The monk said: "This is the rain that cleanses the cliff. Buddha is about to make a Great Manifestation." The fleecy clouds again spread out below the cliff, gathered thickly, and mounted upward to within a few yards of the cliff edge, where they abruptly halted. The cloud tops were as smooth as a jade floor. From time to time raindrops flew by. I looked down into the cliff's belly, and there was a great globe of light lying outstretched on a flat cloud. The outer corona was in three layers, each of which had blue, yellow, red, and green hues. In the very center of the globe was a hollow of concentrated brightness. Each of us onlookers saw our forms in the hollow and bright spot, without the slightest detail hidden, just as if we were looking in a mirror. If you raise a hand or move a foot, the reflection does likewise. And yet you will not see the reflection of the person standing right next to you. The monk said: "This is the Body-absorbing Light." When the light disappeared, winds arose from the mountains in front and the clouds scurried about. In the wind and clouds there again appeared a huge, globular form of light. It spanned several mountains, exhausting every possible color and blending them into a beautiful array. The plants and trees on the peaks and ridges were so fresh and alluring, so gorgeous and striking, that you could not look at them directly.

When the clouds and fogs have scattered and only this light remains shining, people call it a "Clear-Sky Manifestation." Generally, when the Buddha Light is about to appear it must first spread out some clouds—this

14. An ancient Buddhist kingdom situated in what is now Yunnan province.
15. The Himalayas and their associated ranges.

is the so-called Fleecy-Cotton World. The light-form depends on the clouds to make its appearance. If it does not depend on the clouds, it is called a "Clear-Sky Manifestation," which is extremely rare. After the time it takes to eat a meal, the light gradually moves off, traversing the mountains and heading off westward. If you look back to the left, on Thunder Cavern Mountain another light appears like the first one but a little smaller. After a short while, it too flies off and beyond the mountains. When the light reaches the level countryside, it makes a special point of circling back into direct alignment with the cliff. Its color and shape change completely, turning into a golden bridge that somewhat resembles Suspended Rainbow Bridge on the Wu River.[16] But the ends of this bridge have purple clouds holding them up. In general, the cloud forms clear away between the *wu* and *wei* double-hours (11:00 A.M.–3:00 P.M.). This is called "Closing the Cliff." Only the "Golden Bridge Manifestation" waits until after the *yu* double-hour before it disappears.

Those accompanying me to the peak's summit included the Aide-de-Camp Chien Shih-chieh, style Po-chün; Yang Kuang, style Shang-ch'ing; Chou Chieh-te, style Chün-wan; the Presented Scholar Yü Chih, style Tzu-chien; as well as my younger brother Fan Ch'eng-chi. Today we were also joined by my fellow graduate Yang Sun, style Po-mien, and the Aide-de-Camp Li Chia-mou, style Liang-chung, both of whom had come from Chia-chiang town to join us. The light appeared just when they arrived.

Twenty-ninth day (26 July): Started down the mountain. When we first made our ascent, although we clambered upward with difficulty and had ropes pulling us in front, it was dangerous but not perilous. When we started down the mountain, although ropes were again tied to our sedan-chairs to lower us down the rungs of the ladder, the bearers found it difficult to keep their footing, and it was both dangerous and perilous. As we went down the mountain, gradually I began to feel the hot summer air, and so I peeled off my heavy winter garments one by one. During the *wu* double-hour, when we reached the White Water Monastery, I put on the light summer linens I had on before. . . .

Translated by James M. Hargett

16. This famous bridge was near Fan Ch'eng-ta's home in Kiangsu.

184

Observing the Tidal Bore

from *Reminiscences of Wu-lin*

Chou Mi (1232–1298)

The tidal bore on the Che River[1] is one of the great sights of the world. It reaches its full force from the sixteenth to the eighteenth of the month. When it begins to arise far away at Ocean Gate,[2] it appears but a silver thread; but, as it gradually approaches, it becomes a wall of jade, a snow-laden ridge, bordering the sky on its way. Its gigantic roar is like thunder as it convulses, shakes, dashes, and shoots forth, swallowing up the sky and inundating the sun, for its force is supremely vigorous. Yang Wan-li described this in a poem:

> The ocean surges silver to form a wall;
> The river spreads jade to gird the waist.[3]

Many writers and poets since the T'ang period have mentioned the tidal bore along the Ch'ien-t'ang River as an awesome phenomenon. Known to foreigners during the last century and a half as the "Hangchow Bore," it is a series of high waves which occurs near the first and middle of each month and crests at a height of five to six feet. The two occurrences nearest the spring and autumn equinoxes, however, often reached a height of eighteen to twenty-five feet. These used to be occasions for festivities and Chou Mi vividly recalled the autumnal one in the eighth lunar month around 1280.

Following the establishment of the Yüan dynasty in 1279, Chou Mi remained a Sung loyalist and moved to Hangchow when his family business burned down in Wu-hsing (in modern-day Chekiang). His later years were spent preserving Sung literature and culture, and he wrote several unofficial histories including *Reminiscences of Wu-lin*, completed c. 1280. The latter is one of the most extensive and detailed records of life in the Southern Sung capital. It contains a variety of short descriptions such as this one, in addition to poems, lists of things, and selections from other sources covering not only court life, but popular culture, scenic places, and daily life of the common people.

Today, the height of the tidal bore along the Ch'ien-t'ang River, diminished because of modern dams, can no longer be seen from the city as in the past. One must travel forty miles away to Hai-ning on Hangchow Bay for the best view, where the sixty-mile-wide bay narrows to two miles and the incoming tide confronts the outgoing flow of the Ch'ien-t'ang River.

This prose description of a tidal bore may be compared with the rhapsodic treatment of another one from a much earlier period by Mei Ch'eng in selection 124, pages 223–28, and a later poetic description by Cheng Hsieh in selection 83.

1. The Che River (Che-chiang) is another name for the Ch'ien-t'ang River.

2. Ocean Gate (Hai-men) is located on the northeast coast at the juncture of the Che River and Hangchow Bay.

3. Yang Wan-li (1127–1206) was considered one of the major poets of the early Southern Sung (see selection 58). The author of over 4,200 poems, he espoused a literary theory influenced by Zen Buddhist ideals of enlightenment and often employed illusionistic imagery. These lines, however, do not appear in his collected works.

As in every year, the governor of the capital appeared at the Che River Pavilion [4] to inspect the navy. Warships in the hundreds were arrayed along both banks. Suddenly, they all rushed to divide into "quintuple formation." Moreover, there was equitation, banner waving, spear juggling, and sword dancing while afloat, just as on land. In an instant, yellow smoke arose on all sides, and people could barely see each other. The explosions on the water were deafening and earth-shaking; the sounds were like those of mountains collapsing. When the smoke dispersed and the waves calmed, there was not a trace of a hull: all the "enemy ships" had been burned by fire and had disappeared under the waves.

There were several hundred youths of Wu who were expert at swimming. They had loosened their hair and had tatoos on their bodies. In their hands, they held ten colored banners some twenty feet long and raced each other with the utmost exertion, swimming against the current, floating and sinking in the leviathan waves a myriad yards [5] high. Their leaping bodies executed a hundred different movements without getting the tail of the banners even slightly wet— this was how they showed off their skill. Prominent commoners and high officials competed to bestow silver prizes.

Up and down along the river banks for more than ten tricents, pearls, jade, gauze, and silk flooded the eyes; horses and carriages clogged the roads. Every kind of food and drink cost double the normal price and yet, where viewing tents were rented out, not a bit of ground was left for even a mat. The palace viewed the scene, as customary, from Nature's Picture.[6] From this high terrace, the bird's-eye view made it all appear as if in the palm of one's hand. The people of the capital gazed up at the yellow canopies and feathery fans above the empyrean, just as if it were the Flute Terrace or the Island of P'eng-lai.[7]

Translated by Richard Strassberg

4. The Southern Sung capital of Lin-an (modern-day Hangchow). The Che River Pavilion was located south of the city on the northern bank of the river.

5. The word translated as "yards" actually signifies a measurement eight feet in length. The description, in any event, is hyperbolic.

6. A terrace located within the imperial palace at Lin-an.

7. According to legend, the Flute Terrace was built by Duke Mu of Ch'in (reigned 659–621 B.C.E.) for his daughter Nung-yü and her husband, Hsiao-shih, an excellent flutist. Hsiao-shih summoned phoenixes with his flute, and he and Nung-yü flew off to become transcendents. P'eng-lai was one of the mythological islands where transcendents were said to dwell, located in the sea off the northeastern coast.

Miscellanea

185
Fan Sheng-chih's Book

Chapter 1: Basic Principles of Farming

Fan Sheng-chih (1st century B.C.E.)

The basic principles of farming are: choose the right time, break up the soil, see to its fertility and moisture, hoe early, and harvest early.

With the choice of appropriate time and favorable conditions of the soil, a harvest of ten piculs per sixth-acre [1] is obtainable even from very poor land.

This selection shows that even something so seemingly mundane as a treatise on farming might be written in an expressive, almost lyrical fashion. The original text, an agricultural treatise of the first century B.C.E., was lost long ago, but portions of it were preserved in *Essential Arts for the Common People (Ch'i min yao shu)*, a comprehensive and authoritative handbook completed about 535 by Chia Ssu-hsieh, who was a government official in Shantung. *Fan Sheng-chih's Book* is the earliest Chinese book of individual authorship devoted wholly to agriculture to which we still have access.

1. The approximate equivalents of measures used in Fan's book are as follows:

Length

one *ts'un* (inch) = 22 millimeters
one *ch'ih* (foot) = ten *ts'un* = 22 centimeters
one *chang* (decafoot) = ten *ch'ih* = one hundred *ts'un* = 2.2 meters

Volume

one *sheng* (pint) = 167 millimeters

In springtime, after thawing, the breath of the earth [2] comes through, so the soil breaks up for the first time. With the summer solstice, the weather begins to become hot and the yin breath strengthens, so the soil breaks up again. Ninety days after the summer solstice, the duration of the day equals to that of the night, and the breath of heaven harmonizes with that of the earth. To plow in these proper seasons, one operation is worth five. Such conditions are denoted as "fecund moisture"; therein lies the benefit of appropriate timing.

In the spring, when the breath of the earth comes through, hard heavy lands and black soils may be plowed first. Then harrow to level down the clods, and let the grasses sprout. After the sprouting of the grasses, plow again. Then plow again after a drizzle. Always break up any clod, and wait for the proper time to sow. This is what is denoted by "making the heavy soils light."

In the springtime, watch for the coming through of the breath of the earth: sharpen a wooden stake one foot and two inches long, bury one foot of it below and let the remaining two inches appear above the ground level. After "Setting of Spring," [3] the clods begin to disintegrate, hence the soil will heap up and cover the top of the stake, then old stumps of the previous year can be lightly pulled out. This is the proper time to plow.

Twenty days later, the mellow breath of the earth is gone and the soil hardens. One plowing in proper time is worth four, but four plowings will not be equal to one after the mellow breath is gone.

Light soils are to be plowed when apricot trees come in blossom.[4] Plow again when the blossoms fade, and roll down [5] every time after plowing. After the grasses sprout, plow and roll down again when it rains and the soil is moist. With soils which are too light, drive cattle over them to tread them

---

one *tou* (peck) = ten *sheng* = 1.67 liters
one *tan* (picul) = one *hu* = ten *tou* = one hundred *sheng* = 16.7 liters

Area

one *mou* (sixth-acre) = 5.078 ars [one ar = one hundred square meters]

Weight

one *chin* (catty) = 177.8 grams
one *tan* (picul) = 120 *chin* = 21.336 kilograms

This is basically a decimal system already in use in China over two thousand years ago.

2. "Breath of the earth" or "yin breath" means the complex conditions of low temperature and high humidity of the soil and the reverse conditions of the air. "Breath of heaven," on the other hand, indicates warm and dry conditions prevailing under sunshine (yang).

3. The first of the twenty-four subseasons of a year.

4. About the time of the first ten days in April.

5. This calls for pulling a weighted roller across the field.

down. The soils will then become hard. This is what is denoted by "to make the light soils heavier."

In the spring, when the breath of the earth has not come through, the soil will be lumpy when plowed, it will be unable to retain moisture, and thus will not support the growth of crop plants for the whole year to come unless heavily manured.

Never plow too early. Wait till the grasses sprout. Plow only when the time for sowing comes and it rains, so that the seeds and the soil will be in good contact; seedlings alone grow well, while sprouted weeds now rot beneath the clods and a good field results. This is what "one plowing worth five" means.

If a field is plowed too early, the clods will be hard, and seedlings will come out of the same crevices with weeds. No hoeing can be done and a bad field will result.

If one plows in the autumn when it does not rain, the breath of the earth is cut off and the soil will be hard and cloddy. This is called "bacony field." If one plows in a severe winter, the yin breath of the earth is broached and the soil will be dry and parched. This is called "jerked [6] field." Both bacony and jerked fields are damaged.

If a field gives a poor crop in the second year, fallow it for one year.

Fields intended for wheat should always be plowed in the fifth month. Plow again in the sixth month. Don't plow in the seventh month, but diligently harrow it level and wait for sowing. One plowing in the fifth month is worth three; one in the sixth month, two; but five in the seventh is not worth one.

Upon every pause of snowfall, roll down so as to catch any snow on the ground surface and stop its drifting away by wind. Roll down the later snowfalls in the same way. The moisture of the soil is thus secured for the spring to come, insects will be killed by the freezing of the soil water, and good crops for the harvest will thus be warranted.

Translated by Shih Sheng-Han

6. From the verb "to jerk" (to cut meat into long strips and dry in the sun or cure by exposing to smoke).

186

Miscellanies, Secret H

A Fragment

Anonymous (2nd century C.E.)

In the first year of Chien-ho (147 C.E.), the fourth moon, the *ting-hai* day, Maid Wu of the Court of Serving Women went with the edict of the *ping-shu* day [1] to the house of Chamberlain Chao. The edict says, "We hear that the first poem of the *Classic of Odes* celebrated a royal marriage, and that the choice of a good royal spouse has ever been the concern of good rulers of the past. The chaste reputation of the bereaved young daughter of the late General Cheng Shang has reached our ears. Let the Chamberlain go with Maid Wu to the late general's house, and examine her deportment and all intimate details and report faithfully. We intend to select her for the palace."

Bringing the letter of authorization, I [Maid Wu] and Chao went to the house of the late General Shang and found the family just having dinner. Our arrival created a great excitement in the house. The girl, named Nu-ying, left the hall and went to her inside quarters. Chao and I followed the instructions of the edict and studied her deportment carefully and were satisfied. Chao then went out and I went with Ying [the girl] to her private room, where I sent away all attendants and closed the door. At that time, the sunlight came through the shell windows and shone upon Ying's face, which radiated a brightness like the morning cloud or snow, so that I instinctively avoided looking at her directly. Ripples of light came from her eyes and her eyebrows were curved. She had red lips and white teeth, a long pair of ears, and a pointed nose. Her cheeks were full and her chin well-formed, all in proper proportion. I then took off her long, bending hair

This is one of the most curious fragments to have survived the ages. The title of the document, "Miscellanies, Secret H" (*Tsa-shih mi hsin*), seems to indicate that it came from the secret archives of the Han palace, the word *hsin* having no meaning unless it serves as a symbol in the Chinese cycle for labeling a series, like the letter H in the alphabet standing for "Number 8." This is a court record of the queen of Emperor Huan (reigned 147–167 C.E.) of the Later Han dynasty, beginning with a report of the physical examination of her when she was a girl of sixteen, given by a woman servant of the palace. The rest deals with the formal six ceremonies of engagement (first set of presents; asking for the name of the girl, her age, and her ancestors; divination; second set of formal gifts, which signified the formal engagement; asking for the date of the marriage; and finally the wedding itself), and ends with her "coronation" as empress. The woman's report is full of realistic details. The phrases she used, not found in literary language, are part of her spoken language. Here only the woman's report is given.

1. The day before. The designations *ting-hai* and *ping-shu* are based on a cycle of sixty.

ornament[2] and let down her hair, which was jet-black. I felt it in the palm of my hand, and it reached the ground, with more to spare.

This done, I asked her to loosen her underclothes. Ying blushed all over and refused, and I said to Ying, "It is a palace rule, which must be complied with. Please let a poor old woman see it. Loosen the belt knot and I shall be very careful." Ying's tears came to her eyes and she turned her face away and closed her eyes. I then loosened her belt knot, and turned her toward the light. I smelled an exquisite smell. Her skin was white and fine and so smooth that my hand slipped as it touched it. Her belly was round and her hips square. Her body was like congealed lard[3] and carved jade. Her breasts bulged out, and her navel had enough depth to permit a half-inch pearl to go in. Her *mons veneris* rose gently. I opened her thighs and saw that the vulva was bright red, while the labia minora slightly protruded. I was satisfied that she was a chaste virgin. In general about Ying's body, her blood well nourished her skin, her skin well covered her muscles, and her muscles well concealed her bones. Her dimensions were right. She stood seven feet one inch,[4] her shoulders were one foot six wide, her hips three inches less [sic] than her shoulders. She measured two feet seven inches from her shoulders to the tips of her fingers, and her fingers were four inches from the tips to the palm, looking like ten pointed bamboo sticks. The length of her legs from the thighs to the feet was three feet two inches, and her feet measured eight inches. Her ankles and arches were round and full, her soles smooth, and her toes small.[5] The tight silk and close-fitting socks were gathered in as with ladies in the palace. For a long time she stood speechless. I urged her quickly to thank His Imperial Majesty, and she bowed and said, "Long Live[6] the Emperor!" Her voice was like a wind moving through a bamboo grove, very pleasant to the ear. She had no piles, no bad marks, no moles, and no sores, or defects in the mouth, the nose, the armpit, the private parts, or the feet.

I am a stupid humble woman and cannot express properly what I saw or felt. I make this secret report, properly sealed, knowing that my life depends upon Your Imperial pleasure.

Translated by Lin Yutang

---

2. A hairpin several inches long, made of light, soft metal so that it bobbed as the girl walked. Hence the name used here, *pu-yao*, which means "shaking at every step."

3. Literally, "constructed fat." Such phrases are evidently from the woman's patois.

4. The foot in Han days was probably about seven-tenths of a modern English foot, which means that the girl was just under five feet tall.

5. This line contains evidence that her feet were not bound. Bound feet cannot have smooth soles, for the soles are bent and folded over. Footbinding did not become a custom in China until nearly a thousand years later.

6. Literally, *wan-sui* (= Japanese *banzai*), which means "ten thousand years."

187

Li Shang-yin's Miscellany

Li Shang-yin (c. 813–c. 858)

1. Definitely Won't Come!

1. An intoxicated guest deserting the feast (won't come to take farewell).
2. A guest making off with the spoons.
3. Noblemen's servants when sent for.
4. A dog whistled by one holding a stick.
5. Singing-girls invited by a hard-up scholar.

2. Incongruities

1. A poor Persian.
2. A sick physician.
3. A (Buddhist) disciple not addicted to drink.
4. Keepers of granaries coming to blows.[1]
5. A great fat bride.
6. An illiterate teacher.
7. A pork-butcher reciting sūtras.
8. A village elder riding in an open chair.
9. A grandfather visiting courtesans.

3. Shameful

1. A new wife careless of the proprieties.
2. A pregnant nun.
3. Wrestlers with swollen faces.
4. A rich man suddenly poor.[2]
5. A maid offending public opinion.
6. A son in mourning getting drunk.

Li Shang-yin is best known for his imagistic, recondite poetry (see selection 51). This *Miscellany* (*Yi-shan tsa tsuan*), which is not included in his collected works, reveals Li as capable of writing blunt, earthy prose as well (if, indeed, he is the actual author; the attribution is doubtful). The four hundred sayings are grouped under forty-two heads. Although they vividly reflect the manners and morals of the period in which the book was written, many of them are still applicable to life in all Chinese communities today. The language, too, is astonishingly modern.

1. Too well fed to fight. Another version is "Lean men fighting," Chinese wrestlers and boxers being always fat and heavy.
2. The wealthy are respected and loss of wealth involves loss of respect.

4. *Guilty Secrets*

1. Kidnapping another's children.
2. Seducing another's concubine.
3. Dodging the Customs.
4. A robber's cache.

5. *Not to Be Despised*

1. Coarse food when hungry.
2. A poor steed when traveling afoot.
3. A second-class seat after a long walk.
4. Cold broth to drink when thirsty.
5. A small boat when traveling in haste.
6. A small house in a storm.

6. *Reluctant*

1. A new wife to see strangers.
2. A poor devil to contribute to a feast.
3. A poor family to make marriages.
4. To visit retired officials.
5. A pregnant woman to go afoot.

7. *No Alternative* [3]

1. Drinking wine when ill.
2. Attending meetings in hot weather.
3. Beating children without explanation.
4. Being ceremonious when sweating.
5. Being cauterized when in pain.
6. Abusing one's concubine at the behest of one's wife.
7. Receiving visitors in hot weather.
8. Applying to resign on account of old age.
9. Entertaining guests in a miserable temple.

8. *Resemblances*

1. A metropolitan official, like a winter melon, grows in the dark.
2. A raven, like a hard-up scholar, croaks [4] when hungry and cold.

3. I.e., things done only if there is no alternative.
4. *Yin*, to croak, also to hum over verses when composing.

3. A seal, like an infant, always hangs about one.
4. A magistrate, like a tiger, is vicious when disturbed.
5. Nuns, like rats, go into deep holes.
6. Swallows, like nuns, always go in pairs.
7. A slave, like a cat, finding any warm corner, stays.

9. "'Tis Folly to Be Wise"

1. A hard-up scholar who knows about music spoils his career.
2. A woman who knows about poetry gets herself talked about.
3. A priest who knows about drink breaks his vows.
4. A wretched slave who knows about reading makes mistakes.
5. A young man who knows about alchemy invites poverty.
6. A scholar who knows about manual work demeans himself.

10. Passing Hates

1. Squabbles between man and wife.
2. Finding fault with a concubine.
3. Bad temper shown by underlings of a high official.
4. Abuse of his staff by a corrupt official.
5. Debauched monks and nuns maligning a novice.

11. Vexations

1. Happening upon a tasty dish when one's liver is out of order.
2. Making a night of it and the drinks giving out.
3. For one's back to itch when calling upon a superior.
4. For the lights to fail just when the luck begins to favor one at cards.
5. Inability to get rid of a worthless poor relation.
6. A man cleaning out a well who has to go to the toilet in a hurry.

12. The Name Without the Reality

1. A student who does not study the appointed themes is not a real student.
2. A mourner who feels no grief when condoling with the bereaved is not a real mourner.
3. An old servant who neither tidies things away nor chatters about family affairs is not a real old servant.
4. A host who escorts a guest no farther than the door is not a real host.

5. A cook without an apron or a knife and chopping-block is not a real cook.
6. A teacher who does not correct his pupil's exercises and studies is not a real teacher.
7. Underlings who do not squabble and curse are not real underlings.
8. A head of a family who does not check his possessions regularly is not a real head.
9. A servant who is slovenly in his dress is not a real servant.
10. A guest who sends his host no word of thanks after a feast is not a real guest.
11. An officer who mutters replies and marches lazily is not a real officer.

13. Ambiguity

1. Only of a poor gift does one say, "Can it be repaid?"
2. Only of an ugly bride does one say, "She is my fate!"
3. Only of a nobody does one say, "T'ai Kung met King Wen at eighty." [5]
4. Only of a poor appointment does one say, "It's a place to make a living."
5. Only to be rude to a guest does one say, "Make yourself at home."
6. Only of a poor dwelling does one say, "It's quite all right to live in."
7. Only those incapable of making a living for themselves rail at their ancestors.

14. Indications of Prosperity

1. Horses neighing.
2. Candles guttering.
3. Chestnut husks.
4. Lichee shells. [6]
5. Flower petals flying about.
6. The twittering of orioles and swallows. [7]
7. The sound of reading aloud. [8]
8. Dropped hair ornaments.

---

5. T'ai Kung ("Grand Duke"), a high state official, retired into exile to avoid the tyranny of Chow Hsin, last ruler of the Yin (i.e., Shang) dynasty. Years later King Wen, founder of the Chou dynasty, which overthrew the Yin in 1122 B.C.E., saw T'ai Kung (who was then eighty years old) fishing and invited him to become his chief adviser.
6. Chestnuts and lichees are luxuries.
7. This refers to the birdlike sound of women's voices.
8. Leisure to enjoy literature and music.

9. A flute being played in a lofty belvedere.
10. The sound of pounding drugs and rolling tea.

15. Misleading Statements

1. To say that a courtesan feels affection.
2. To say that alchemy brings wealth.
3. To say that official work gets its reward.
4. To say that one is on intimate terms with one's master.
5. To say what income one derives from one's land.
6. To say that one's concubine is young.
7. A needy magistrate prating about official probity.
8. To say of oneself that one studies hard.
9. To boast of the cost of one's possessions.[9]

16. Humors of Low Life

1. A rural magistrate transferred to the city.
2. The way being cleared for a village magistrate.[10]
3. A village magistrate entertaining guests.
4. A mule braying in the village.
5. A country lout calling chickens.
6. A rustic with new clothes.
7. Playing the flute on cowback.
8. A beggar driving out the demon of pestilence.
9. Unofficial performers on the "single-stick" drum.

17. Disheartening

1. Cutting with a blunt knife.
2. Catching the wind in a torn sail.
3. Trees shutting out the view.
4. Building a wall that hides the mountains.
5. No wine at blossom time.
6. A summer feast spread out of the breeze.

18. Dismaying

1. To infringe on another's taboo.
2. To meet an enemy.

9. Literally, "vessels, dishes."

10. It is not a prerogative of the village magistrate to have the road cleared for his sedan-chair, as it is for higher-ranking officials.

3. To meet a creditor.
4. To blunder at a reception.
5. To hear one's drunken remarks when sober.

19. *Desecration (spoiling the scenery)*

1. To be "moved on" when enjoying flowers.
2. To weep when looking at flowers.
3. To spread a mat on moss.
4. To cut down a weeping poplar.
5. To dry small clothes amid flowers.
6. To carry a load on a spring jaunt.
7. To tether a horse to a decorative stone pillar.
8. To bring a lamp into moonlight.
9. To talk banalities at a musical banquet.
10. To plant cabbages in a fruit garden.
11. To build a pavilion that shuts out the mountains.
12. To keep poultry under a flower-stand.

20. *Unbearable*

1. A lonely house and gibbons crying.
2. The coarse talk of the marketplace.
3. Sounds from the threshing floor at a wayside inn in autumn.
4. A young wife mourning her husband.
5. An old man mourning his son.
6. A magpie [11] after "flunking."
7. Beggars calling at night.
8. The sound of music when in mourning.
9. To hear one has graduated among the first three and die forthwith.

21. *A Waste*

1. Being ill at blossom time.
2. Being harassed in fine weather.
3. A eunuch with a handsome wife.
4. A festival day in a poor home.
5. A well-to-do family at loggerheads.
6. A poverty-stricken family with a taste for flowers.
7. Seeing a beautiful view and not making a poem.
8. A fine house and no entertaining.

11. The call of the magpie denotes good luck.

22. Unendurable

1. The hot season by a fat man.
2. To go home to an ill-tempered wife.
3. To come across greedy and tyrannical superiors.
4. Colleagues with bad habits.
5. A long journey in the hot season.
6. Long contact with a coarse person.
7. A wet day in a boat with leaky awnings.
8. Dirt and damp in a poor cottage.
9. An officious official.

23. Hard to Bear

1. Priests joking with courtesans.
2. Servants imitating the behavior of scholars.
3. Juniors behaving arrogantly to their betters.
4. Servants and concubines cutting into the conversation.
5. Soldiers and rustics trying to talk like scholars.

24. The Power of Suggestion

1. Wearing green in winter makes one feel cold.
2. Seeing red in summer makes one feel hot.
3. Entering the shrine of a good spirit suggests seeing a bad one.
4. A nun with a big belly makes one think of pregnancy.
5. Heavy curtains suggest someone lurking.
6. Passing a butcher's gives a frowzy feeling.
7. Seeing water cools one.
8. Seeing plum trees makes one's mouth water.

25. Bad Form

1. To wrangle with one's fellow guests.
2. To fall from one's polo pony.
3. To smoke in the presence of superiors.
4. Priests and nuns lately returned to ordinary life.
5. To vociferate orders at a banquet.
6. To cut into the conversation.
7. To fall asleep in somebody's bed with one's boots on.
8. To preface remarks with a giggle.
9. To kick over the table when a guest.

10. To sing love songs in the presence of one's father- or mother-in-law.
11. To reject distasteful food and put it back on the dish.
12. To lay chopsticks across a soup-bowl.

26. Inopportune

1. To talk books in the presence of a nobody.
2. To recite poems to a courtesan.
3. To claim relationship with an exalted person.
4. To be hospitable at the expense of one's master.
5. To return half-eaten food to the host.
6. To take children to a banquet.
7. To boast of the cleverness of one's children.
8. To encourage children to be silly and spoiled.
9. To find fault with the dishes at a banquet.
10. To insist upon the latest fashion.
11. To hinder one's host by sitting on after a meal.
12. To ask one's host the price of his food.
13. To be on friendly terms with a widow.
14. To eat another's food and not defer to him.
15. To make the lender come for a borrowed article.
16. To pick up things and examine them in another person's rooms.
17. To be ungrateful to a benefactor.
18. To pick fruit in another's garden.
19. To talk big when hard up.
20. To play the rich man when poor.
21. To be a visitor and call oneself a guest.[12]
22. To stay overly long when invited to a summer banquet.

27. Mortifications

1. Failure of an honored guest to accept one's invitation.
2. The arrival of a hated person [13] uninvited.
3. To be unable to rid oneself of a drunken man.
4. To be penniless when things are cheap.
5. To go for a stroll and run across a creditor.
6. To find oneself seated next to an enemy.
7. To meet a disliked person on a hot day.
8. To have a lovely concubine and a jealous wife.

12. I.e., claim the privileges of a guest.
13. Literally, "a bad guest."

28. *Stupidities*

1. To have money and not pay off debts.
2. To recognize one's faults and be unable to reform.
3. To listen to another's conversation and contradict him sharply.
4. To read another's essay and assail it violently.
5. To be blind to one's own failings but violently disapprove of another's.
6. To guess wrongly in a drinking game but refuse to pay the forfeit.[14]
7. Trying hard to pose as wealthy when poor.

29. *Foolishness*

1. To discuss a man's faults behind his back.
2. To love betraying secrets.
3. To destroy one's family for love of wine.
4. To be a suborned witness.
5. Deceitfully to hasten to flatter.
6. To blab abroad the shortcomings of one's relatives.
7. To demand division of property while parents are alive.
8. To be ignorant of the order of precedence in an assembly or a wedding.
9. To cherish resentment and yet expect forgiveness.
10. To be kind to a man and expect gratitude.

30. *Contemporary Crazes*

1. Unreasoning jealousy.
2. Invoking the Spirits in one's cups.
3. A son in mourning reciting ditties.
4. A son in mourning for his parents going to cock-fights and dog-races.
5. Enemies remembering those who were kind.
6. Adults flying kites.
7. Supporting idlers.
8. Women cursing in public.
9. Selling property to defray wedding or funeral expenses.
10. Mortgaging one's house and lands.

31. *Improper*

1. To call upon sons and grandsons to testify to one's virtue.
2. To hail a maternal uncle as an "unc" during one's mother's lifetime.

14. Guessing games to encourage drinking were (and are) common in many forms, the penalty for an error being to drink a cup of wine.

3. To call wife or younger brother in the presence of one's parents.
4. To uphold one's wife and blame one's elders.
5. To sacrifice to the dead and yet play music.
6. To walk straight into another's private rooms.

32. *Things Gone Awry*

1. Good parents lacking good sons.
2. A good son lacking a good wife.
3. A good daughter lacking a good husband.
4. Having money and not being able to use it.
5. Having fine clothes and not being able to wear them.
6. A fine dwelling left unswept.
7. Having silk and not making clothes.
8. Having a beautiful color and not knowing how to match it.
9. Being obliged to set a beloved concubine to do menial tasks.
10. Grudging the money to get treatment when sick.
11. Letting children grow up untaught.
12. Having a library and not knowing how to read.
13. Going to bed early on moonlit nights.
14. Looking at beautiful flowers and neither reciting poetry nor drinking wine.
15. Failing to enjoy fine scenery when near it.
16. Having delicately flavored food and yet being stingy enough to hoard rancid bean-curd.
17. An official demanding probity in others and himself breaking the law against bribes.
18. Wasting one's talents in idling.
19. Having power and not using it to do good.
20. In youth loving ease and learning nothing.

33. *Unlucky*

1. To eat lying down.
2. To sigh for nothing.
3. To sing in bed.
4. To eat bareheaded.
5. To write bareheaded.
6. To swear an oath involving one's parents.
7. To beat one's breast while cursing another.[15]

15. Curses are apt to light upon the person pointed at, and an angry man beating his own breast inadvertently indicates himself as the object of his curses.

8. To sit on matting on which a corpse has lain.
9. To go to the toilet or let down one's hair in the light of the sun or moon.
10. To dip spoon or chopsticks in the bowl before the meal begins.

34. *Poverty Is Inevitable When One—*

1. Has a lazy wife.
2. Lies long abed.
3. Brings up a boy to be inferior to his father.
4. Runs into debt.
5. Does not check storehouse lists.
6. Neglects one's farm.
7. Throws away food or wine.
8. Likes gambling or drinking.
9. Fills storerooms with useless objects.
10. Is careless about grain.
11. Wastes one's estate in the pursuit of pleasure.
12. Is not thrifty.
13. Maintains many concubines.
14. Is always changing one's residence.
15. Frequents the company of the powerful and rich.
16. Is economical to the point of meanness.
17. Insists on buying when things are dear.
18. Does not buy when things are cheap.
19. Tries too many smart tricks.
20. Screens the members of one's family when they do wrong.

35. *Wealth Is Assured When One—*

1. Seeks diligently and uses sparingly.
2. Widens knowledge by practical experience.
3. Frequently takes stock of family affairs.
4. Is not infatuated with wine and women.
5. Does not fail to collect debts.
6. Has slaves who understand plowing and maids who understand weaving.
7. Sleeps by night and rises early.
8. Rears stock.
9. Tills in proper season.
10. Stores up when the season arrives.
11. Has apprentices who work in harmony.
12. Has a wife who does not believe in Buddha.

13. Has womenfolk who all agree.
14. Can put up with hardships.
15. Keeps an inventory of one's valuables.
16. Gathers the "mites" that make the "muckle."
17. Catches the market.
18. Does not damage his possessions.

36. *They Are Wise and Capable Who—*

1. Keep their natures within moderate bounds.
2. Are discreet in secret matters.
3. Associate with the wise.
4. Are wide awake in a crisis.
5. Do not babble in their cups.
6. Respect other people's taboos.
7. Are acquainted with things ancient and modern.
8. Do not practice meannesses.
9. Boast not unbecomingly.
10. Esteem the virtuous.
11. Join not themselves to the meaner sort.
12. Credit not blindly the words of servants.
13. When they enter a house inquire its tabooed words.
14. Inquire about the customs of any state they enter.
15. Are on the alert at night.
16. Ask when in doubt.
17. Do not argue with fools.
18. Do not speak much after drinking.

37. *Train a Son to—*

1. Learn the ancestral business.
2. Keep faith.
3. Be ceremonious, just, moderate, modest.
4. Be thoroughly versed in the six arts.[16]
5. Converse intelligently.
6. Be dignified in social intercourse.
7. Be loyal, true, respectful, economical.
8. Be filial, reverent, kindly, gracious.
9. Read widely and hold liberal views.
10. Make friends with the worthy.

16. Propriety, music, archery, charioteering, writing, and mathematics, i.e., the sum of education.

11. Avoid becoming a slave to amusement.
12. Practice restraint.
13. Be resourceful.

38. Train a Daughter to—

1. Learn women's duties.
2. Discuss food and drink.
3. Be meek, true, respectful, thrifty.
4. Be attractive in person and manner.
5. Learn writing and reckoning.
6. Be careful to speak softly.
7. Remain pure and chaste in the inner apartments.
8. Sing no ditties.
9. Avoid gossip.
10. Serve her elders well.

39. Lapses

1. Talking to people with one's hat off.
2. Scolding another's servants.
3. Boring a hole in the wall to spy upon neighbors.
4. Entering a house without knocking.
5. Being careless about dripping snot or spitting on the mat.
6. Going into the room and sitting down uninvited.
7. Opening other people's boxes and letters.
8. Lifting chopsticks before the host's signal.
9. Laying down chopsticks before all have finished eating.
10. Stretching across the table to reach things.

40. Presumption

1. Seeing another man's dispatches and insisting on opening and reading them.
2. Seeing another man's saddled horse and insisting on riding it.
3. Seeing another man's bow and arrows and insisting on trying them.
4. Seeing another man's possessions and insisting on appraising them.
5. Criticizing another's composition.
6. Settling another's domestic affairs.
7. Taking part in another's quarrel.
8. Deciding in a dispute.

41. *Want of Judgment*

1. To abuse another without saying why.
2. To join in a scheme without investigation.
3. For a layman to imitate the ways of the priesthood.
4. Not to discriminate between right and wrong in a matter.
5. To allow a son to take up music.
6. To allow a son to cage animals.
7. For a man to learn women's work.
8. To be on the lookout for petty advantages.

42. *Some Don'ts*

1. Don't drink to intoxication.
2. Don't enter a widow's house alone.
3. Don't go alone in the dark.
4. Don't consort with rogues.
5. Don't take things for fun and say nothing about it.
6. Don't open another's private letters.
7. Don't borrow without returning promptly.

Translated by E. D. Edwards

188
Lay Student Notations from Tun-huang

Anonymous (third quarter of the 9th century)

Pitee the poor lay stoodent
Whose horse has gone up to the stebul in haven.
[Which] family haz a nice girl
That can be married off to a lay student?

When copying, do not drink wine,
Lest the whole day, the tip of your brush be drie;

These random jottings appear in the margins and in the unused spaces of a scroll from Tun-huang (see selection 214) that consists of a commentary on chapter 5 of the Confucian *Analects* (see selection 6). They were written by two or three lay students enrolled in a school attached to one of the Buddhist monasteries at Tun-huang. Although such lay students obviously did not possess full literacy, they were of enormous importance in the creation of written vernacular narrative in China. The overwhelming majority of the earliest written vernacular texts in China, dating to approximately a thousand years ago, were copied by just such lay students. This translation attempts to replicate in English the orthographically erroneous quality of their writing, here apparently exacerbated by drunkenness.

Just doo what seems appropriate.
This morning I was at a boring meeting,
It brought my worries home to me all the more;
I bought five pints of good wine,
And sent my worries a thousand miles away.

One scroll of corrected copying by two students Li.

The smoke which has been spit out settles to form a vapor.
At the tip of the mountain, the fifth month's moon is bright;
Having received a summons, I anchor my boat 'midst the islets at night,
The peach trees come out to pay their respects to the wal sity.

When copying, do not drink wine,
Lest the whole day the tip of your brush be drae;
Just doo what seems appropriate,
If there are mistakes, later people will see them.

If there are mistakes, people will. . . .

Pity the poor lay stodent
Whose horse has gone up to haven;
Which family has a nice girl
To marry off to a lay stodent?
Which family have a Lady's Finger
To marry of too thish bu givup two mush. . . .
Pity the poor lay student
Whose horse has gone up to haven.
Whose family has a nice girl
To merry off to a stud-. . . ?

Translated by Victor H. Mair

189

That Which Is Mandated by Heaven Is Called Nature

Ch'ü Ching-ch'un (d. 1569)

A. Breaking Open the Topic
  1. It has been said: "Heaven is the origin of the Way,"

The practice of selecting topics for civil service examinations from one of the four Confucian classics (the *Analects*, the *Mencius*, the *Great Learning*, or the *Doctrine of the Mean*)

2. And: "The Superior Man embodies It and thereby provides Heaven with assistance."

3. By following the Way, the singularity of the principles of things can be seen.

B. Carrying the Topic Forward

1. The principles of Heaven and Man are one and the same, not two.

2. In the beginning the Way is mandated by Heaven.

3. In the end It becomes an ability of one's own.

4. Such being the case, how could it be permissible for the Superior Man

5. To excuse himself from making an effort to embody the Way?

C. Opening Statement

1. Formerly, Tzu-ssu [1] worried about the Way not being clear,

2. And about many people burdening their minds with selfishness.

3. Thus, he discussed these matters in order to instruct people, saying that

4. Originally our human mind circulates through Heaven, Earth, and the Ten Thousand Things.

5. When trying to embody the Way,

6. If our minds are not used to exhaust completely the measure of Heaven, Earth, and the Ten Thousand Things,

7. But are instead shackled by their appearance,

8. Then we split Heaven and Man into two things.

D. Taking up the Topic

1. Do we not see the source from which the Way arises, and the end toward which It is heading?

2. Now, just what is the action of the Way?

E. Opening Limb

a   1. The Way guides our human Nature which is mandated by Heaven;

---

began during the Yüan dynasty and continued into the Ming and Ch'ing. The topic of Ch'ü Ching-ch'un's essay is the opening line of Tzu-ssu's *Doctrine of the Mean*. To be successful, a candidate had to develop philosophical themes according to Chu Hsi's Neo-Confucian commentaries. The essay had to follow rigid rules of composition requiring grammatical as well as thematic parallelism developed in specific rhetorical segments. Skill in this so-called eight-legged essay composition remained a prescription for success in the civil service examinations until their abolition early in the last century.

Many scholars were hesitant to accept the eight-legged essay, a product of the examination hall, as a genre of prose literature. Others distinguished themselves as eight-legged essay stylists. During the late Ming and early Ch'ing, exemplary essays were anthologized, widely discussed, and evaluated. By the end of the Ch'ing, however, the eight-legged essay had become a fashionable target of criticism and a scapegoat for the ills of a declining empire.

1. Confucius' grandson (483–402 B.C.E.?), to whom the *Doctrine of the Mean* has traditionally been attributed.

    b 2. It is not an embellishment external to ourselves.

    a 3. The Way is practiced in accord with Teachings which are culti-
vated through the Way;

    b 4. The self originally possesses It.

    c 5. Since nothing under Heaven is not the Way,

    c 6. There is nothing which is not also the self.

       7. The Way truly should not be left even for a moment.

       8. For can one leave the Way yet suppose that one is studying It?

       9. Hence, one who enters the Way out of instruction never relaxes
his effort.

F. Empty Limb

    a 1. Sometimes the Way is invisible and inaudible,

    b 2. As though one could get away from it.

    c 3. But, whether one is active or at rest, there is no departing from
the Heavenly Principle.

    d 4. Therefore, how should the Superior Man be wary and vigilant in
order to preserve the Nature mandated by Heaven?

    e 5. Must he wait to verify Its color and sound?

    a 6. Sometimes the Way is neither evident nor manifest,

    b 7. As though one could get away from It.

    c 8. But, with regard to the minute and the obscure, the human mind
should allow no lacunae.

    d 9. Therefore, how should the Superior Man be careful when alone
to practice the Way of following his Nature?

    e 10. Must he wait for what is most evident and most manifest?

     11. It is not that the Way originally is separate from man,

     12. And that the merit of the Superior Man therefore consists in
making It inseparable.

     13. Rather, it is that the spirit of the Way permeates Heaven, Earth,
and the Ten Thousand Things,

     14. And actually fills our single mind.

G. Middle Parallel

    a 1. That is to say, the mind that is not yet aroused

    b 2. Is at rest and simply unmoved.

    c 3. Thus, when our mind breaks away from the prejudices of bias and
inclination,

    d 4. One word, "impartiality," suffices to characterize the Way of all
under Heaven.

    e 5. The embodiment of the Way is within our mind;

    f 6. Can we stop at being watchful and wary?

    a 7. That is to say, the mind that is already aroused

    b 8. Responds simply by opening to the Way.

    c 9. Thus, by following guidelines of appropriate cooperation,

d   8. A single word, "harmony," suffices to encompass the situation of the Ten Thousand Things.

e   9. The function of the Way is within our mind;

f   10. Can we stop at being cautious when alone?

    11. Although some people have not yet completely embodied It,

    12. That

g   13. Has nothing to do with Heaven and Earth

g   14. And is unrelated to the Ten Thousand Things.

H. Back Parallel

    1. If one really can,

a   2. By being watchful and wary, achieve impartiality,

b   3. Thereby daily strengthening one's preservation of the heavenly mandate;

a   4. And, by being cautious when alone, achieve harmony,

b   5. Thereby daily broadening behavior which follows our Nature,

    6. Then

c   7. Heaven, Earth, and oneself will all have the same body,

d   8. So that by using mind to respond to mind,

e   9. Heaven and Earth will not be destroyed

f   10. But will stay fixed,

c   11. And moreover, the Ten Thousand Things will function like oneself,

d   12. So that compliance will attract compliance;

e   13. All categories of being will prosper,

f   14. And will fulfill their lives.

I. Concluding Parallel

    1. Hence,

a   2. In the beginning Heaven endowed us with this principle;

a   3. In the end we use this principle to assist Heaven and Earth.

b   4. The Way does not exceed the capacity of our mind.

b   5. The mind is not inadequate for conforming to the Way.

J. Postlude

    1. If someone cannot fully actualize the Way with his mind,

    2. Just because his mind is small,

    3. That is not the fault of the Way.

    4. Tzu-ssu, being the first to speak of this,

    5. Revealed his concern for the Way.

Translated by Wayne Alt

190
Jokes

The Man Who Bit Off His Own Nose
from *Grove of Laughter (Hsiao-lin)* [1]

Han-tan Ch'un [2] (fl. early 3rd century).

While A and B were having a fight, A bit off B's nose. When a government official wished to prosecute him, A claimed that B had bitten off his own nose. "A person's nose is higher than his mouth," said the official, "so how could he have reached his nose to bite it off?" "He stepped up on a bed and bit it off" was A's reply.

The Frog That Was Afraid of Being Executed
from *Master Mugwort's Miscellany (Ai Tzu tsa-shuo)*

Compiled by Su Tung-p'o (1037–1101)

Master Mugwort was floating his boat on a lake and stopped one evening to moor it on an islet. At night, he heard the sound of crying beneath the water. Since it also seemed as though someone were talking, he listened more closely. This is what he heard: "Yesterday the dragon king issued an order that all members of the watery tribe who have tails should be beheaded. I'm a water-lizard, so I'm crying because I'm afraid of being executed. But you're a frog who has no tail. Why should you cry?" Then he heard another voice say, "I'm lucky that I don't have any tail now, but I'm worried that I'll be treated for what I was as a tadpole."

Contrary to the view of China as a humorless country devoid of wit, the Middle Kingdom has a long and rich heritage of jokes and funny stories, some of them by well-known authors. The usual subjects of Chinese humor are physical deformities, bodily functions, stupidity, sons-in-law, blindness, illiteracy, misreading characters (i.e., sinographs), greedy officials, rich land-lords, poverty, and other conditions that are highly revealing of social mores and customs. There are also more subtle types of humor, examples of which are included in this selection of jokes from collections made throughout the centuries.

1. The original work is lost, but twenty items from it are preserved in *Extensive Records from the Reign of Great Peace (T'ai-p'ing kuang-chi)*.

2. The compiler had another name, Chu, which usually means "India."

Flattery Will Get You Everywhere
from *A Collection of Witticisms*

Liu Yüan-ch'ing (Ming period)

The magistrate of Canton, by nature, enjoyed being flattered. Whenever he issued a directive, his underlings would join in unanimous praise, which would make the magistrate happy. A retainer who wished to curry favor with him calculatingly said to the person standing next to him, "Almost everyone who occupies a position of power over the people enjoys being flattered by others. Only our host is different—he despises those who praise him." When the magistrate heard these words, he immediately called the retainer forward. Patting his chest with satisfaction and prancing with glee, he commended the retainer endlessly, saying, "Splendid! You're the only one who understands my heart! What an excellent retainer!" From that time on, the magistrate increased his intimacy with the retainer.

Monkey Business
from *Grove of Laughter (Hsiao-lin)*

Master Bottoms Up (Fu-pai Chu-jen) (Ming period)

A monkey who had died went before the king of the underworld and requested that he be reborn as a human being. "If you want to be a human being," said the king, "then you must pull out all of the hairs on your body." Whereupon he called his *yakṣa*[3]-guards to start pulling out the monkey's hairs. The monkey, unable to endure the pain, cried out. "You're not even willing to part with a single hair," said the king with a laugh. "How could you be a man?"

A Quick Bow
from *Grove of Laughter*

Master Bottoms Up

A man who performed his bows much too quickly often offended other people. Someone instructed him, saying, "When you bow, recite the names of the months from the first to the second and all the way to the twelfth before you finish. That way you will naturally bow slowly."

One day, the man met a friend of his on the street and bowed to him very

3. Demons who torment the occupants of hell.

slowly as he had been told. By the time he finished his bow, the friend had already gone off. Whereupon the man asked a bystander, "Which month did he leave?"

Tofu
from Grove of Laughter

Master Bottoms Up

A man who had a guest for dinner served him only various dishes made with tofu. As he did so, he said out loud to himself, "Tofu is my life! In my estimation, no other flavor can match it."

On another day, the man went to the home of his former guest and the latter, remembering his culinary preferences, added tofu to the meat and fish dishes. But the man picked out only the meat and fish, gorging himself on them.

"I once heard you say, 'Tofu is my life!' How come you're not eating any of it today?" asked the former guest.

"When I get a glimpse of meat and fish," replied the man, "I'd even give up my life!"

Geomancy
from Grove of Laughter

Master Bottoms Up

There was a firm believer in geomancy who would always consult a yin-yang diviner before he made the slightest move. One day, just as he happened to be seated at the base of an earthen wall, the wall toppled over upon him. Pinned beneath it, the man frantically called out for someone to come save his life.

When his family heard him crying out and saw him pinned beneath the wall, they wanted to rescue him. At the same time, however, they immediately remembered that he was ordinarily such an ardent believer in geomancy, so they dared not act rashly. Instead, they consoled him, saying, "Just be patient for a while until we can go ask the yin-yang master whether today's a good day for moving earth."

Borrowing an Ox
from *Grove of Laughter*

Master Bottoms Up

A person came bearing a note asking to borrow a plow-ox from a rich old man. The rich man was just at that moment entertaining guests and didn't want to let them know that he was illiterate. So he opened the seal on the note and, pretending to read it, said,"I understand. I'll come over in a few minutes and do it myself."

A Seven for Elocution
from *Jests* (*T'iao-nüeh*)

compiled by Wang Shih-chen (1526–1590)

The following story was told by Li Hsiao-chang.

When Kuo Kung-fu was passing through Hangchow, he brought out a scroll of his poems which he showed to Su Tung-p'o and then proceeded to recite them himself. The sound of his voice reverberated in every corner of the room.

When he was finished, he said to Tung-p'o, "How would you rate my poems?"

"I'd give 'em a ten," said Tung-p'o.

Delighted, Kung-fu asked, "On what basis did you rate them?"

"I gave them a seven for elocution," said Tung-p'o, "and a three for the poetry. Doesn't that add up to a ten?"

The Wife Who Was Born Under the Sign of the Ox
from *Treasury of Laughs* (*Hsiao-fu*)

Master of the Ink Idiot's Studio (Mo-han-chai chu-jen),
Feng Meng-lung (1574–1645)

The subordinates of a prefect who was having a birthday heard that he was born under the sign of the rat, so they each contributed some gold from which a full-scale rat was cast to celebrate his longevity. Much pleased, the prefect said, "Did you know that my bosom mate's birthday is coming up soon? She was born under the sign of the ox."

Dreaming of the Duke of Chou[4]
from *Treasury of Laughs*

Feng Meng-lung

A teacher who had fallen asleep during the daytime woke up and fibbed, saying, "I was dreaming of the Duke of Chou." The next day, his pupil emulated him, but the teacher woke him up with the swat of a paddle and said, "How could you do such a thing?" "I, too, dreamed that I went to see the Duke of Chou," said the pupil. "What did the Duke of Chou say to you?" asked the teacher. The pupil answered, "The Duke of Chou said, 'I did *not* see your respected teacher yesterday.'"

The God of the Archery Target Helps Win the War
from *Expanded Treasury of Laughs* (*Kuang hsiao-fu*)

Feng Meng-lung

A military officer engaged in a campaign was on the verge of being defeated when suddenly a superhuman warrior joined his formation so that he ended up achieving a great victory instead. The officer kowtowed before the warrior and asked to know his name. "I am the spirit of the archery target," said the superhuman warrior. "What virtue does a humble general like me have that would induce you, O honored spirit, to trouble yourself to come to my aid?" To which the spirit replied, "I was moved by the fact that, in the past, when you practiced on the archery range, you never once wounded me with an arrow."

Vegetables, Wine, et nihil alter[5]
from *Expanded Treasury of Laughs*

Feng Meng-lung

A Confucian official who had to go to meet a superior of his had just gotten on his horse and was ready to leave when a fellow villager dropped in for a

---

4. An important figure in the founding and early rule of the Chou dynasty. "Dreaming of the Duke of Chou" is a conventional expression in Chinese that means approximately the same as "went to the Land of Nod," except that it sounds as though something more important than mere sleep were taking place.

5. The proper Latin should be *et nihil aliud* or, better still, *et neque aliud*. But since the Confucian official who is the main character in this joke displays a rather shaky command of the classical language, it is not inappropriate to use a bit of inferior Latin to convey his errant pedantry.

visit. Not having leisure to give detailed instructions to his wife, he told her curtly, "Offer him vegetables, wine, *et nihil alter.*"

His wife, who couldn't understand literary language, had no idea that *et nihil alter* meant "and nothing else." After consulting with the maids and servants, she believed that when her husband said **alter,** he must have meant **tail.** By "tail," she guessed that he must have been referring to the long-tailed goat that they kept, so she butchered the goat and prepared a rich feast for the visitor who ate it and then left.

The Confucian official returned and asked his wife why she had butchered the goat. When he found out, he sighed and lamented that she had been needlessly extravagant. His chagrin over the loss of the goat was endless. Later on, whenever the official would go out, he would invariably order his wife, saying, "From now on, if guests come when I'm away, just give them 'vegetables and wine.' Be sure not to give them any '*et nihil alter.*' "

Comparing Ages
from *Expanded Treasury of Laughs*

Feng Meng-lung

A man with a newborn daughter was visited by another man who had a boy two years old and who wished to make a match between the two children.[6] The first man was indignant, saying, "My daughter's in her first year[7] and your son's in his second year. When my daughter turns ten, your son will be twenty. It wouldn't be right for her to be married to such an old husband!"

When the first man's wife heard what had happened, she said, "You fool! Our daughter's one now, but next year she'll be as old as their boy. What's wrong with a match like that?"

That's Preposterous!
from *In Praise of Laughter (Hsiao tsan)*

Chao Nan-hsing (Ming period)

A man who was trying to improve his vocabulary heard someone say "That's preposterous!"[8] and, falling in love with the expression, he practiced using it from time to time. It so happened, however, that once when he was busily

---

6. Marriage alliances in traditional China were often contracted by parents while children were still in their infancy.

7. A Chinese baby was considered to be one *sui* (year) old at birth.

8. The original text has *ch'i yu tz'u li,* a Classical Chinese expression borrowed into Mandarin. Since this expression is actually a whole question sentence in Classical Chinese ("How can there be such a principle?") and is completely based on Classical Chinese vocabulary and grammar, it can be learned by Mandarin speakers only through rote memory.

concerned with crossing a river in a ferryboat he suddenly forgot it, so he kept walking around the boat trying to recover it. A boatman asked whether he had lost something, to which he replied, "Yes, a sentence."

"Whoever heard of losing a sentence?" said the boatman. "That's preposterous!"

"You found it for me," said the man. "Why didn't you say so earlier?"

Severe Amnesia
from *Further Tales of Master Mugwort (Ai Tzu hou yü)*

Lu Shao (Ming period)

There was a man from Ch'i who suffered from amnesia. If he were walking, he would forget to stop, and if he lay down, he would forget to get up. His wife was worried about him and so she said, "I've heard that Master Mugwort is a humorous and wise man and that he can cure diseases that other doctors consider to be hopeless. Why don't you go and make him your teacher?" "All right," said the man, whereupon he got on his horse and went off with his bow and arrow tucked under his arm. Before he had completed the first stage[9] of his journey, his bowels felt distended so he got off his horse to relieve himself. He stuck his arrow in the ground and tied his horse to a tree. After hc had finished his bowel movement, he turned to the left and saw his arrow. "Boy, was that close!" he said. "I wonder where that came from? It almost struck me!" Then he turned to the right and exclaimed with delight, "Although that whizzing arrow gave me quite a fright, I've found myself a horse!" As he grabbed the reins and started to turn the horse around, he stepped in his own mess. Stomping his foot, he said, "Drat! I would have to step in a pile of dog-do and get my shoe all dirty!"

He whipped up the horse and headed it for home. When he reached there, he paced back and forth outside the gate, saying, "Whose place is this? Could it be Master Mugwort's residence?" Just at that moment, his wife caught sight of him and, realizing that he was experiencing another bout of forgetfulness, she scolded him. Annoyed, the man said to his wife, "Look, lady, I've never met you before. So why are you chewing me out?"

Dying for Money
from *Sequel to Ticklish Tales (Hsi-t'an hsü lu)*

Man of the Way from Smallstone (Ch'ing period)

A traveler who was returning to his village with all of his luggage passed through Shantung on his way home. The province was experiencing a great

9. Thirty tricents (about ten miles).

famine and the number of poor people who had died was incalculable. All the inns had been deserted and were no longer accepting guests. The traveler was forced to put up in a temple. In the east wing of the temple he saw several dozen coffins, but in the western wing there was only one coffin that stood all alone in magnificent isolation. After the third watch, around midnight, a hand extended from each of the coffins. The hands were all sallow and skinny, except for the hand that reached out of the coffin in the western wing, which was fat and fair. The traveler, being a bold fellow by nature, looked about him to the left and the right, then said with a laugh, "I suppose you bunch of poor ghosts are all dead broke and want some money from me, right?"

Thereupon he opened his purse and put a big coin in each of the extended hands. All of the ghosts' hands in the eastern wing withdrew into their coffins, but the hand of the ghost in the western wing remained extended as before.

"It looks like a single coin won't satisfy you," said the traveler, "so I'd better give you some more."

The traveler added an additional hundred coins for the ghost in the western wing, but its hand still did not move. Becoming angry, the traveler said, "What an insolent wretch! Your greed is insatiable!" In the end, however, he took out two strings of cash with a thousand coins in each which he placed in the outstretched palm, whereupon the ghost withdrew its hand instantly.

Surprised by what happened, the traveler picked up a lamp and shone it around on all sides of the temple. What he discovered was that all of the coffins in the eastern wing had written on them "So-and-so Who Died of Starvation." Only the single coffin in the western wing had written on it "Casket of His Honor So-and-So, the Jailor of Such-and-Such a District."

Conversation Between a Senior Official and His Subordinate
from *Sequel to Ticklish Tales*

Man of the Way from Smallstone

A district duty officer who had obtained his position through purchase did not understand Mandarin.[10] After he took office, he paid a courtesy call upon

---

10. Mandarin (< Sanskrit *mantrin* ["counselor"]) quite literally means "language of the officials." The Mandarin equivalent of this word is *kuan-hua* (official speech). Mandarin was the vernacular language employed by members of the Chinese bureaucracy who hailed from different parts of the country and, as such, spoke a variety of more or less mutually unintelligible native languages and topolects. Mandarin was based upon—but not entirely equivalent to—the language of the capital, being a somewhat refined version of the latter. This joke, which is challenging to render in English, reveals the difficulties inherent in forging a national bureaucracy from a multilingual constituency.

a regional official who asked him, "What are the **customs** like in your honorable district?"

"People don't **cuss** much there and there aren't many **toms** either."

"How are the **fingerlings** this year?"

"**Finger rings** cost two hundred and eighty cash."

"Are there many contributions of **gentry grain?**"

"Your servant's teeth **gently gleam.**"

"How are the **commoners** getting on?"

"We only have a couple of **cum**min bushes, but there are lots of cinna**mon** trees."

"I was asking about the **populace.**"

"We've got lots of **poplars,** but they don't produce much timber."

"I wasn't asking you about trees and such. What I am trying to find out about is the condition of the **citizens.**"

Standing up hurriedly, the duty officer replied, "I regret to inform you, sir, that I have a face full of **zits** and an arse full of **wens.**"

How to Get Rid of Robbers
from *Bowled Over with Laughter* (Hsiao-tao)

Ch'en Kao-mo (Ch'ing period)

A fool who heard that robbers had entered his courtyard gate quickly wrote the four words "Off Limits, Keep Out" on a piece of paper and stuck it on the door to the main hall of his house. When he heard that the robbers had already stepped into his main hall, he wrote "Road Closed" on another piece of paper and stuck it on the door to his inner chambers. When he heard that the robbers had already reached his inner chambers, he fled to the toilet. The robbers, hot on his trail, pursued him to the toilet, so he closed the door and coughed, saying, "Occupied."

Moving the Statues of Lao Tzu and the Buddha
from *Have a Good Laugh* (Hsiao te hao)

Stone Becomes Gold (Shih Ch'eng-chin) (Ch'ing period)

There was a certain temple that had a clay image of Lao Tzu on the left side and a clay image of the Buddha on the right side. Upon seeing this arrangement, a Buddhist monk said, "The dharma of our Buddha is profound. How can he be placed to the right of Lao Tzu?" So he moved the statue of the Buddha to the left of Lao Tzu.

Some later time, upon seeing this new arrangement, a Taoist priest said, "The Taoist doctrine deserves the utmost respect. How can Lao Tzu be placed to the right of the Buddha?" So he moved the statue of Lao Tzu to the left of the Buddha.

This moving back and forth went on relentlessly until, before they knew what had happened, the monk and the priest has caused the statues made of mud to crumble.

"You and I were getting along all right," said Lao Tzu with a laugh to the Buddha, "until those two scoundrels destroyed us with their constant moving."

Blaming the Farter
from *Have a Good Laugh*

Shih Ch'eng-chin

Somebody farted in a group of people who were sitting around. Although they didn't know for sure who it was, they all suspected a certain person, so they pointed at him and started to blame him. As a matter of fact, it wasn't he who had left the fart. Instead of defending himself, however, the accused began to laugh.

"What's so funny?" asked all the others.

To which he replied, "I'm having a good laugh at the guy who really left the fart but who is blaming me for it along with all the others."

A Method for Taking a Nap
from *Have a Good Laugh*

Shih Ch'eng-chin

A nursemaid became exasperated when the little child she had just finished feeding kept crying and wouldn't be quiet and go to sleep. All of a sudden, she called out to the child's father to bring her a book quickly. When the father asked what for, she replied, "I've noticed that you always fall asleep when you start to read a book."

The Odor's Even Worse over Here
from *Have a Good Laugh*

Shih Ch'eng-chin

There was a wealthy old man who would from time to time leave an occasional fart in the presence of his guests. Once when he did so, two guests were sitting right next to him.

"Although your fart was loud," said the first guest, "I can't smell the slightest odor."

"Not only is there no bad odor," said the second guest, "on the contrary, there is a sort of extraordinary fragrance."

Knitting his brows, the wealthy old man said, "I've heard that if someone's farts don't stink, his five viscera are internally damaged and that the time of his death is not far off. Do you suppose I'm about to die?"

The first guest fanned the air with his hand and went sniffing about with his nose. "Phew!" he said. "The odor's finally hit me."

The second guest wrinkled his nose and inhaled deeply through it. Then, covering his nose with his hands and furrowing his forehead, he said, "The odor's even worse over here where I am!"

Goldfinger
from *Have a Good Laugh*

Shih Ch'eng-chin

A transcendent spirit who could transmute stone into gold appeared among mankind. He went about testing people, trying to find someone whose heart was not avaricious so that he could convert that person into a transcendent like himself. Though he searched the whole land over and transformed big rocks into gold at the touch of his finger, all whom he encountered complained that they were too tiny.

Finally, the transcendent met a person to whom he said as he pointed at a stone, "How would you like it if I touched this stone and turned it into gold for you?" The man shook his head to indicate that he didn't want it. The transcendent suspected that the man had rejected the offer because the stone was too small, so he pointed at a big rock and said, "How would you like it if I touched this great big rock and turned it into gold for you?" Again the man shook his head to indicate that he didn't want it. The old transcendent began to think that this man was completely without avariciousness, a rare person indeed, and someone who ought to be converted to transcendenthood. Consequently, he asked the man, "Since you want neither big nor little pieces of gold, what is it you'd like?"

The man extended his finger and said, "I don't want anything at all. Just exchange for mine the tip of your finger which can transmute stone into gold at a touch, oh old transcendent. That way I can go about everywhere transmuting gold as I please and won't even have to keep track of the amount."

Translated by Victor H. Mair

Biographies, Autobiographies, and Memoirs

191

The Biography of Hua-t'o [1]

from *History of the Three Kingdoms*

Ch'en Shou (233–297)

Hua-t'o, whose style was Yüan-hua ("Primal Evolution"), was a man of the district of Ch'iao [2] in the kingdom of P'ei. Another name of his was Fu. As a peripatetic student in the area of Hsü-chou,[3] he became familiar with a number of the classics. The senior administrator of P'ei, Ch'en Kuei, recommended him as a high-level candidate for appointment and the defender-in-

---

The *History of the Three Kingdoms* is the official history of the three states—Wei, Shu, and Wu—that resulted from the breakup of the Later Han dynasty and that jockeyed for power in the perennial quest to [re]unite China. Among its biographies is to be found some of the most interesting writing in the dynastic histories. The material of the *History of the Three Kingdoms* was fictionalized in the popular novel *Romance of the Three Kingdoms*.

1. The reconstructed ancient Sinitic pronunciation of this phenomenal physician's name was roughly *ghwa-thā*. It is quite likely that this name derives from an Indian source (Sanskrit *agada* [with the initial syllable lopped off] = "medicine"), as do a number of the stories recounted in this biography which have a suspiciously Ayurvedic character to them. Hua-t'o was many hundreds of years ahead of his time in medical knowledge and practice. The precise sources of his remarkable expertise remain to be investigated. It is perhaps significant, however, that the cities and towns in which Hua-t'o was active lay precisely in the area where the first Buddhist communities were established in China. Hua-t'o's dates are traditionally given as 110–207. These, too, are compatible with the period of early Buddhist activity in China.

2. Corresponding to the modern-day district of Po in Anhwei province.

3. The area in Kiangsu north of the Yangtze and the southeast part of Shantung.

chief, Huang Wan, offered him employment, but he did not accept either position. Hua-t'o had mastered the technique for nourishing one's nature. Although his contemporaries thought that he must have been a hundred years old, he still looked hale and hardy.

Hua-t'o was also highly skilled in prescribing medicines. In curing illnesses, the decoctions that he prepared required only a few ingredients. His mind was so adept at dividing up and compounding according to the right proportions that he did not have to weigh the different components of his medicines with a balance. Once the decoction was boiled thoroughly it could be drunk. Hua-t'o would tell the patient how to take the medicine and then he would go away, after which the patient's condition would promptly improve.

If Hua-t'o employed moxibustion, he would only burn punk in one or two places and in each place he only made seven or eight separate cauterizations, to which the disease would rapidly respond during the course of its elimination. If he employed acupuncture, it was also only in one or two places. As he inserted the needle, he would instruct the patient, "I am going to guide the point to such-and-such a spot. When you feel it reach there, tell me." As soon as the patient told him that the point had already reached the designated spot, he would withdraw the needle and the sickness would likewise be virtually alleviated.

If a sickness were concentrated internally where the effect of acupuncture needles and medicines could not reach it, Hua-t'o would recognize that it was necessary to operate. In such cases, he would have his patients drink a solution of morphean[4] powder[5] whereupon they would immediately become intoxicated as though dead and completely insensate. Then he could make an incision and remove the diseased tissues. If the disease were in the intestines, he would sever them and wash them out, after which he would stitch the abdomen together and rub on an ointment.[6] After a period of about

4. The Chinese text has *ma-fei* (literally, "hemp-boil," hitherto unidentified), which appears to be a transcription of some Indo-European word related to "morphine," which in turn is derived from Morpheus, the name of the god of sleep. Although morphine was not chemically isolated and identified until about 1805 by the German scientist Friedrich W. A. Sertürner, it is a naturally occurring substance, being the principal alkaloid of opium. It is conceivable that some such name as morphine was already in use before Sertürner as a designation for the anesthetic properties of this opium derivative or some other naturally occurring substance. If this is so, it would have enormous implications not only for the history of Chinese medicine, but also for the history of Indian and Western medicine. There are ancient Indian records which describe doctors traveling to the area of Bactria, where they learned acupuncture, cauterization, surgery, and external medicine.

5. The corresponding passage of Hua-t'o's biography in the *History of the Later Han*, written over a hundred years after that by Ch'en Shou translated here, states that *ma-fei* powder was administered in an alcohol solution.

6. The corresponding passage in the *History of the Later Han* reads: "He would sever them

four or five days, there would be no more pain. The patient would gradually regain full consciousness and within a month he would return to normal.

When the late wife of the senior administrator of Kan-ling[7] was six months pregnant, a pain in her abdomen caused her disquietude. Hua-t'o examined her pulse and said, "The fetus is already dead." He had someone[8] manipulate her abdomen to discover the position of the fetus, saying that it would be a boy if it were on the left and a girl if it were on the right. The person reported that it was on the left. Thereupon a solution was used to cause an abortion and, indeed, the dead fetus was a male. After that, the lady swiftly recovered.

The district subofficial functionary Yin Shih was tormented by discomfort in his limbs. His mouth was parched, he could not abide the sound of other people's voices, and it was not easy for him to pass urine. "Let us try giving him hot food," said Hua-t'o. "If we can get him to break into a sweat, he'll recover. If he does not sweat, he'll die after three days." So hot food was prepared for him to eat but he did not produce any sweat. "The vital breath of his viscera has already been extinguished within." Indeed, the result was as Hua-t'o predicted.

The commandery subofficial functionaries Ni Hsün and Li Yen came together to see Hua-t'o. Both had headaches and felt feverish; their complaints were exactly the same. Hua-t'o declared, "Hsün should receive a purgative and Yen should receive a febrifacient." Someone called Hua-t'o's prescription into question, to which he responded, "Hsün's firmness is external and Yen's firmness is internal, so it is fitting that their treatment should be dissimilar." Whereupon he gave each of them the appropriate medicine. By dawn the next day they had both improved.

Yen Hsin of Salt Sluice[9] and several others were waiting for Hua-t'o. No sooner had he arrived than he said to Hsin, "Are you feeling all right?"

"Just as usual," replied Hsin.

---

and wash them out. Then he would remove the diseased portion[s] and, after that, he would sew [them/it] back up and apply a miraculous ointment."

7. Modern-day Lin-ch'ing in Shantung.

8. Note that, due to strict rules of decorum, Hua-t'o took the woman's pulse but could not touch her abdomen. Chinese physicians even later in history would "examine" female patients by pointing to a model rather than by actual contact with their bodies.

9. Yen-tu, the equivalent of modern-day Yen-ch'eng ("Salt City") in Kiangsu.

"You have a severe illness which I can see in your face," said Hua-t'o. "You had better not drink so much wine."

After they had sat together for a while, everybody returned to their own places. When he had gone several tricents, Hsin suddenly became dizzy and fell out of his cart. Someone helped him get up and took him back to his home. He died that night.

The late local inspector, Tun Tzu-hsien, had been ill but was already convalescing. He paid a visit to Hua-t'o, who felt his pulse and said, "You're still depleted and won't be able to recover. Don't overexert yourself. If you engage in intercourse, you will die soon and, at the moment of death, your tongue will hang out several inches."

When Tun's wife heard that he had gotten over his illness, she came from a distance of more than a hundred tricents to look in on him. That night they had sex and, within three days, Tun suffered a relapse that was in all particulars just as Hua-t'o had said it would be.

The local inspector, Hsü Yi, fell ill and Hua-t'o went to look in on him. "Last night, after I had the subaltern in the medical section treat me by the insertion of acupuncture needles in the stomachic duct,[10] I suffered a bitter fit of coughing. I felt as though I wanted to go to sleep, but couldn't relax."

"The needles should not have been inserted in the stomachic duct because they have mistakenly affected the liver. Your appetite will decrease from today and within five days you will be beyond saving."

The illness progressed as Hua-t'o had said it would.

The two-year-old baby boy of Ch'en Shu-shan, who was from Tung-yang,[11] became ill and was experiencing diarrhea. At first he cried a lot but, with each day, the baby was becoming thinner and more listless. Ch'en asked Hua-t'o what the problem was and Hua-t'o replied, "His mother is pregnant and her vital yang breath is being directed inward toward the nourishment of the fetus, leaving her milk coldly devoid. Since the baby acquired this coldness from his mother, it will be impossible to cure him right away." Hua-t'o gave him a pill made of *Aster fastigiatus* and three other ingredients. After ten days, the child's illness was eliminated.

10. An acupuncture point located four inches above the navel.
11. Northwest of modern-day T'ien-ch'ang district in Anhwei province.

A woman of P'eng-ch'eng [12] went to the toilet in the middle of the night and was stung on the hand by a scorpion. The pain was so unbearable that all she could do was groan. Hua-t'o had the woman soak her hand in a tepid decoction with the result that she was finally able to fall asleep, but several attendants had to keep changing the decoction to ensure that a constant warmth was maintained. She recovered completely by dawn.

The army subaltern, Mei P'ing, having fallen ill, disenrolled and returned home, which was in Kuang-ling. [13] While he was still two hundred tricents away, he stopped off at the home of a relative. Before long, Hua-t'o also happened to visit the owner of the house who requested that he examine P'ing. Hua-t'o did so and told him, "If you had seen me earlier, sir, you could have avoided coming here. Your sickness has already solidified, so you had better go home quickly to see your family, for in five days it will all be finished." P'ing went back to his home immediately and everything transpired as Hua-t'o had predicted.

Hua-t'o was walking along the road when he saw someone suffering from a blocked pharynx. He was fond of eating, but could not get anything down. The members of his family had put him in a cart with the intention of taking him to a doctor. When Hua-t'o heard the man's moaning, he stopped the cart and went over to examine him, saying, "Just now I passed a biscuit seller by the side of the road who had some vinegar with mashed garlic. If you procure three pints from him and drink it, the sickness will go away of its own."

They proceeded to do as Hua-t'o had directed and the man immediately vomited a snakelike parasite. He hung it from the side of his cart and went off to visit Hua-t'o to thank him. Hua-t'o had not yet returned, but his children who were playing outside the gate saw the man coming toward them and said to each other, "He must have met our old man. You can tell by the sickness-causing thing that is hanging from the side of his cart." The patient went inside to sit down and saw hanging on the north wall of Hua-t'o's house some ten-odd snakelike parasites the same as his own.

Then there was a commandery governor who was sick. Hua-t'o suspected that the man would be healed if he really got angry, so he accepted many payments-in-kind from the man but did nothing to cure him. Before long,

12. Modern-day Hsü-chou in Kiangsu province.
13. The area around the modern-day city of Yangchow in Kiangsu province.

Hua-t'o abandoned the man and went away, leaving behind a letter in which he cursed the man. As expected, the governor flew into a great rage and ordered his men to catch up with Hua-t'o and kill him. The governor's son understood what was going on and told the functionaries not to pursue Hua-t'o. Because the governor became so tremendously angry, he vomited several pints of black blood, upon which he recovered.

Then there was a high official who was feeling uncomfortable and to whom Hua-t'o said, "Your sickness is deep-rooted, sir, so I would have to cut open your abdomen to remove it. But you won't live more than ten years longer in any event and the sickness will not kill you. If you can endure the sickness for ten more years, by that time you will also have achieved the peak of your longevity, so it's not worth undergoing an operation on account of this sickness." But the official could not bear the pain, so he insisted that it be removed, whereupon Hua-t'o did the operation. The official's complaints were promptly alleviated, but he died in ten years after all.

The governor of Kuang-ling, Li Teng, had an illness which caused him to be distressed by a feeling of stuffiness in his chest. He also had a red face and no desire for food. Hua-t'o took his pulse and said, "Your honor, there are several pints of parasitic bugs in your stomach and you are on the verge of developing an ulcer. This was caused by eating raw fish." Whereupon he prepared two pints of a decoction for the governor. Hua-t'o had him drink one pint first and then after a little while had him finish the remainder. In the space of time that it takes to eat a meal, the governor vomited up three pints or so of parasites. They had red heads and were all wriggling; half of their bodies looked like sashimi.[14] The discomfort that he had experienced was immediately relieved. "This sickness will erupt after three years. If you are attended by a good doctor, he will be able to save you." The sickness did indeed erupt after the specified period. At the time, Hua-t'o was not in the area and the governor died as Hua-t'o had said he would if he did not have a good doctor.

Ts'ao Ts'ao[15] heard about Hua-t'o and summoned him to court where he henceforth was often in attendance. Ts'ao Ts'ao suffered from blustery head-aches. Whenever an attack came on, he would become dizzy and confused.

14. Raw fish strips.
15. The text here and below has T'ai Tsu ("Grand Progenitor"), a posthumous title conferred upon Ts'ao Ts'ao (155–220, the tyrannical founder of the Wei dynasty) for use in sacrificial ceremonies held in the ancestral temple.

Hua-t'o would employ acupuncture treatment at the diaphragmatic transport insertion point and the condition would be alleviated as soon as the procedure was carried out.

The wife of General Li was quite sick and Hua-t'o was called to examine her pulse. "She was injured during pregnancy," said Hua-t'o, "but the fetus did not miscarry."

"I was informed not only that she had truly been injured during pregnancy," said the general, "but that the fetus had also miscarried."

"My reading of her pulse is that the fetus has not yet miscarried," said Hua-t'o.

The general believed that Hua-t'o's diagnosis was incorrect. After Hua-t'o went away, the lady improved slightly. A hundred days later, however, she was again beset by sickness. When they called Hua-t'o once more, he said, "The indications of her pulse are that there is still a fetus. Initially, she had conceived twins, but one of them came out first during the miscarriage. She must have lost a lot of blood then, so that the second child was not born on time. The mother herself was unaware of this and other people did not realize it either. Since there was no longer any movement toward parturition, the child could not be born. The fetus then died, but the pulse did not return to normalcy because the dead fetus desiccated and stuck to the mother's spinal column and it is this which caused her much pain along the spine. Now she ought to be given a decoction and I will insert acupuncture needles in one spot, then the dead fetus will come out." After the decoction was given and the acupuncture treatment carried out, the woman experienced sharp pain as though she were going into labor. "This dead fetus has already been dried up for a long time and cannot come out by itself. It is necessary for someone to probe for it and pull it out." And, indeed, they found a dead baby boy with hands and feet that were completely formed. Its color was blackish and it was about a foot or so in length.

Examples of Hua-t'o's superlative skills are in general of this sort. However, since he was originally a scholar, he often regretted that he was looked upon as a physician by profession. Later, when Ts'ao Ts'ao took personal control of the affairs of state, his sickness intensified and he had Hua-t'o attend him exclusively. "It will be difficult to heal you in the near term, but if we maintain a program of treatment over a longer period, it will be possible to extend your life-span."

Hua-t'o had been far away from home for a long time and wished to return, so he said, "I just received a letter from home and would like to go back temporarily." After he reached home, excusing himself on the grounds of his wife's illness, he requested several extensions of his leave and did not come back. Ts'ao Ts'ao repeatedly wrote letters to Hua-t'o calling him back, and he issued imperial orders to the commandery and district authorities to send Hua-t'o back. Proud of his ability and finding it distasteful to wait upon others for a living, Hua-t'o continued to procrastinate in setting off on the journey.

Ts'ao Ts'ao became very angry and dispatched men to go and investigate. If Hua-t'o's wife were really sick, Ts'ao Ts'ao would present him with forty bushels of lentils and be lenient in setting a date when his leave would expire. But if Hua-t'o were prevaricating, then he was to be apprehended and escorted back. Consequently, Hua-t'o was handed over to the prison at Hsü,[16] where, after interrogation, he confessed his guilt. Interceding on behalf of Hua-t'o, Hsün Yü [17] said, "Hua-t'o's techniques are truly effective and people's lives are dependent upon them. It is fitting that you be clement toward him."

"Don't worry," said Ts'ao Ts'ao. "Do you think there aren't any other rats like him under heaven?"

Whereupon the investigation against Hua-t'o was concluded with the announcement of the death penalty. When Hua-t'o was about to be executed, he brought out a scroll with writing on it and handed it over to the jailer, saying, "This can preserve people's lives." Fearful of the law, the prison subaltern would not accept it, nor did Hua-t'o force it upon him. Instead, he asked for a fire in which he burned the scroll.

After Hua-t'o's death, Ts'ao Ts'ao's blustery headaches did not go away. "Hua-t'o could have cured me," said Ts'ao Ts'ao, "but the scoundrel prolonged my illness, wishing thereby to enhance his own position. Thus, even if I hadn't put the knave to death, he never would have eradicated the source of my sickness." Later on, when his beloved son Ts'ang-shu was critically ill, Ts'ao Ts'ao said with a sigh, "I regret having put Hua-t'o to death and causing my son to die in vain."

Formerly, the army subaltern Li Ch'eng suffered from a cough that prevented him from sleeping day and night. Occasionally he would vomit bloody pus. When he asked Hua-t'o about this, Hua-t'o said, "Your illness is an intestinal ulcer. What you're spitting up when you cough does not come from the lungs. I will give you two-tenths of an ounce of a powder that should make you vomit a little over two pints of bloody pus. When that's over, you'll feel better and, if you nurse yourself, in a month there will be some small improvement. If you take good care of yourself for a year, you'll return to full health. After eighteen years, you'll have a minor recurrence, but if you take

16. Modern-day Hsü-chang in Honan.
17. Ts'ao Ts'ao's adviser.

this powder it will be alleviated again. If you cannot obtain this medicine, you'll surely die." Hua-t'o gave Ch'eng an additional two-tenths of an ounce of the powder and he went away with the medicine.

Five or six years later, one of Ch'eng's relatives developed the same sickness that he had. "You're strong and healthy now," he said to Ch'eng. "I'm on the verge of death. How can you bear to hide your medicine away, waiting for something unfortunate to happen, when your situation is not critical? Lend me the medicine now and when I get better I'll ask Hua-t'o for some more for you." Ch'eng gave the medicine to his relative and made a special trip to Ch'iao, but by that time Hua-t'o was already incarcerated and Ch'eng was so flustered that he could not bear to request the medicine. After the eighteen years were up, Ch'eng's sickness did flare up and, since there was no medicine for him to take, it progressed till he died.

Wu P'u of Kuang-ling and Fan Ah [18] of P'eng-ch'eng [19] both studied with Hua-t'o. Using Hua-t'o's methods of treatment, many people were completely cured by Wu P'u. "The human body needs exertion," Hua-t'o told Wu P'u, "but it shouldn't be pushed to the limit. Movement of the limbs facilitates the absorption of nutrients in food and enables the blood in the arteries to flow freely, preventing sickness from occurring. It's like a door-pivot that never decays from bugs or worms because of the constant opening and closing. That's why, when the ancient transcendents [20] practiced duction,[21] they strode like a bear and turned their head backward like an owl. They elongated their waist and limbs and moved all of their joints, seeking to stave off old age. I have a technique called 'the exercise of the five animals.' [22] The first is the tiger, the second is the deer, the third is the bear, the fourth is the ape, the fifth is the bird.[23] They may also be used to get rid of illness and are beneficial for the legs and feet because they are a type of duction. If there is discomfort somewhere in your body, get up and do one of my animal exercises until you're soaking with sweat, then sprinkle powder on yourself. Your body will feel relaxed and you'll have a good appetite."

Wu P'u followed this regimen and lived to be more than ninety. His sight

18. This is an unusual name and may indicate that the individual in question was a foreigner.

19. The area around modern-day T'ung-shan ("Copper Mountain") in Kiangsu, location of the first known Buddhist community in China.

20. The word used here may refer to ancient Indian rishis ("holy men").

21. Guiding of the vital breath through the channels of the body.

22. These postures are clearly related to the *āsanas* that are well known from yoga.

23. This passage is extremely important for understanding the yogic basis of Taoist physical regimens. It is discussed in detail in Victor H. Mair, "[The] **File** [on the Cosmic] **Track** [and Individual] **Dough**[tiness]: Introduction and Notes for a Translation of the Ma-wang-tui Manuscripts of the *Lao Tzu* [Old Master]," *Sino-Platonic Papers* (October 1990), 20: 38.

and hearing were still sharp and all of his teeth remained solidly in place. Fan Ah was good at acupuncture. Whereas ordinary doctors would say that on the back and in the area between the chest and the viscera one should not carelessly insert acupuncture needles, and that if one did insert them they should not go in more than four-tenths of an inch, Fan Ah would insert needles in the back up to one or two inches and, in the area of the solar plexus, the chest, and the viscera, he would insert them up to five or six inches, bringing about an immediate cure of the patient's ailment. Fan Ah requested from Hua-t'o the recipe for an orally ingested medicine that would be beneficial to one's health, and Hua-t'o instructed him how to make a powder of varnish tree leaves and herbe de flacq. The proportions are four-teen ounces of shredded herbe de flacq for each pint of shredded varnish tree leaves. Hua-t'o said that if one takes a long course of this medicine, it will get rid of the three worms,[24] benefit the five viscera, make the body feel nimble, and prevent your hair from turning white. Fan Ah followed his words and lived to be more than a hundred years old. Varnish tree leaves are available everywhere, and herbe de flacq grows in Feng, P'ei, P'eng-ch'eng,[25] and Ch'ao-ko.[26]

Translated by Victor H. Mair

24. Different types of parasites that can eat away the five viscera.
25. Places around Hsü-chou in modern-day Kiangsu.
26. Southwest of modern-day T'ang-yang in Honan.

192
Physicians Cannot Raise the Dead

Yeh Meng-te (12th century)

Hua-t'o was certainly a miraculous physician, but both Fan Yeh and Ch'en Shou, in their accounts of how he treated illness, stated that if it were actively concentrated internally where the effect of acupuncture needles and medi-cines could not reach it, he would first order the patient to take some

This text, included here out of chronological sequence and genre category, is a critique of the biography of Hua-t'o as presented in Fan Yeh's *History of the Later Han* and Ch'en Shou's (233–297) *History of the Three Kingdoms* (see selection 191, especially notes 5 and 6). It is noteworthy that, more than a thousand years after Hua-t'o's time, conventional wisdom still could not comprehend his methods and achievements. Yeh Meng-te was a high-ranking scholar-official of the late Sung period. He represents Confucian rationalism as against imagi-native Buddho-Taoist/Indian medical theorizing.

morphean powder in wine, whereupon the patient would become intoxicated to the point of unconsciousness, and then he would make an incision into the abdomen or the back, enabling him to pull out the diseased tissue that had accumulated and cut it away. If the illness were in the intestines or the stomach, he would dissect them, then wash and rinse them, before removing the diseased portions, after which he would sew them back together and apply a miraculous ointment. In four or five days the wound would heal, and within a month the patient would completely return to normal.

There is absolutely no principle whereby to account for this. That which makes a human being a human being is his physical form, and that which enlivens the physical form is the vital breath. I have no way of knowing whether Hua-t'o's medicine could make a person intoxicated to the point of unconsciousness so that he could endure being cut open and could fully recuperate, causing the damaged portions to grow back together again. However, once the abdomen, back, intestines, or stomach have been cut open and dissected, how can they again be infused with vital breath? Being in such a condition, how could they be brought back to life again? If Hua-t'o could do this, then whoever was subjected to the punishment of dismemberment could be brought back to life again and there would no longer be any reason for carrying out royal punishments.[1]

The discourses of the tutor of the heir apparent of the state of Kuo are recorded in the Grand Historian's[2] biography of Pien-ch'üeh.[3] He believed that sickness could be treated without decoctions, fluids, brandies, wines, pointed stones, or bending and extending.[4] Instead, incisions were to be made in the skin, the flesh separated, the blood vessels plucked out, the sinews tied up, the intestines and stomach washed and rinsed, and the five viscera irrigated and cleansed. In antiquity, Yü Fu[5] possessed these techniques. The

1. Because punishments involving physical mutilation required the consent of the ruler, they were referred to as "royal punishments."

2. Ssu-ma Ch'ien, author of the *Records of the Grand Historian* (see selection 160, unnumbered note and selection 173, note 10).

3. A renowned physician from the period of the Warring States. His precise dates unknown, he is thought to have lived during the fifth century B.C.E.

4. These are all traditional methods for the treatment of disease in China. The last named was apparently similar to osteopathic or chiropractic manipulations. "Pointed stones" is a traditional way of referring to acupuncture and suggests that this technique goes back to the Stone Age.

5. A legendary physician said to have lived in the time of the Yellow Emperor. He clearly subscribed to the same tradition of medicine as Hua-t'o, a tradition that seems to have disappeared in China for a couple of millennia during the interval between these two famous physicians and was lost again until more than a thousand years after the latter. The descriptions of their surgical techniques detailed by both Ssu-ma Ch'ien and Ch'en Shou are astonishingly similar to surgical techniques developed in the West. No adequate explanation of these similarities has yet been given. Pien-ch'üeh belongs in the mainstream of traditional Chinese medicine; Yü Fu and Hua t'o are almost preternaturally mysterious aberrations.

biography does not claim that Pien-ch'üeh could do these things, but later generations attributed them to Hua-t'o. How could it be that a single medical practitioner could increase or decrease a person's allotted life-span or determine whether he lives or dies? Unfortunately, there are those whose illness would not necessarily be fatal yet who are nevertheless killed by common physicians. But there has never been a case of someone with an incurable illness who was restored to life by a physician.

The fundamental purpose of medical books is to help the physician be prepared for curable illnesses and prevent him from harming the patient—that is all. Even Pien-ch'üeh himself said, "I, Yüeh-jen,[6] cannot bring dead people back to life. If a patient is supposed to live, I can bring him back to health." Therefore, it is better for someone in the course of an illness to know a little bit about how to cure the body himself rather than to be harmed by the fraudulent practices of a common physician with a fondness for strange but untested remedies. That way, they could conserve their health in happy, uneventful times so as to maintain themselves during the years allotted to them by heaven.

Translated by Victor H. Mair

6. Pien-ch'üeh's personal name. It could mean either "Viet Man" (i.e., man of Viet) or "Surpasses Others."

193
The Autobiography of Instructor Lu

Lu Yü (733–804)

Master Lu's name was Yü and his style was Hung-chien. It is not known where he was from. Some say that his style was Yü and that his name was Hung-chien, but it is impossible to know who is right. His appearance was as ugly as that of Wang Ts'an[1] or Chang Tsai[2] and he stammered like Ssu-ma Hsiang-ju[3] or Yang Hsiung,[4] but he was talented and persuasive and had a sincere and trustworthy character. He was narrow-minded and irritable, showing a great deal of subjectivity in his opinions. When his friends reproved him, however, he could be more open-minded and less suspicious. If he were living with another person and got the inclination to go somewhere else, he

This is the extraordinary self-account of the enormously influential founder of the tea cult.
1. A famous writer (177–217) from the kingdom of Wei during the Three Kingdoms period.
2. Another famous writer of the kingdom of Wei (third century).
3. See selection 129.
4. See selection 161.

would leave without saying anything, causing others to suspect that he was born full of anger. But if he had an agreement with another person, he would never fail to keep his word, even if it meant traveling a thousand tricents through ice and snow over roads infested by wolves and tigers.

At the beginning of the Superior Origin reign period (760–761), Lu Yü built a hut by the bank of Grandiflora Stream.[5] He closed his door and read books, refusing to mix with rogues, though he would spend whole days chatting and convivializing with eminent monks and lofty scholars. Often, he would travel back and forth between various mountains and monasteries in his little slip of a boat, clad only in a gauze kerchief, vine sandals, a short shirt of coarse wool, and a pair of underpants. He would frequently walk alone in the wilderness reciting Buddhist scriptures or chanting ancient poems. Striking the forest trees with his staff or dabbling in the flowing water with his hand, Lu Yü might dilly-dally hesitantly from morning until evening and on into the darkness of night after the sun had gone completely down, whereupon he would return home wailing and weeping. So the southerners would say to each other, "Master Lu must be today's Madman of Ch'u."[6]

An abandoned waif at the age of three, Lu Yü was taken in and raised in the Ching-ling meditation[7] monastery by the great teacher Chi-kung. From the age of nine he learned how to write and Chi-kung revealed to him the occupation of escaping from the world that was described in the Buddhist books. In reply, the lad said to him, "To be cut off from one's brothers, to have no further descendants, to wear a cassock and shave one's head, to call oneself an adherent of Śākyamuni[8]—if the Confucians were to hear of this, would they proclaim it to be filial behavior? Would it be all right if I request that you teach me the writings of the Confucian sages?"

"It's excellent," said the elder, "that you wish to show your filial devotion, but you have no idea at all how great is the meaning of the Way of the tonsure and cassock from the West." The elder obdurately insisted that Lu Yü study the Buddhist canon, and Lu Yü obdurately insisted that he study the Confucian canon. Consequently, the elder feigned not to love the youngster any longer and tested him with a series of demeaning tasks. He had him sweep the monastery grounds, clean out the monks' toilet, mix mud with his feet to plaster on walls, carry tiles on his back and build rooms, and herd thirty head of cattle. At Ching-ling and around West Lake, there was no paper for the lad to practice writing, so he would trace characters on the backs of the cattle with a piece of bamboo.

5. In the northern part of Chekiang, it rises in the vicinity of Celestial Eye mountain (T'ien-mu shan) and flows into Lake T'ai.

6. Chieh-yü, an eccentric of the Spring and Autumn period who is noted for having taunted Confucius with a wild song about the phoenix.

7. Sanskrit *dhyāna* = Japanese Zen, Chinese Ch'an.

8. The Buddha.

One day, Lu Yü asked a learned person about some characters and the person gave him a copy of Chang Heng's[9] "Rhapsody on the Southern Capital." The lad could not recognize the characters of the rhapsody, but there in the pasture he imitated the little boys who were students. He would sit up straight with the scroll unrolled before him and move his mouth, but that was all. When the elder learned of this, he was afraid that the lad was gradually becoming infected by heretical texts and thus daily growing more distant from the Way. So he confined him to the monastery and ordered him to cut away the overgrown bushes and weeds under the supervision of the head gateman.

From time to time, a character would come to mind, and then Lu Yü would fall into a stupor as though he were lost. He might spend a whole day standing there disheartened like a wooden post and doing nothing. The supervisor thought he was lazy and struck him with a whip. The result was that the lad sighed over the passing of the months and years, fearing that he would never acquire the knowledge that was in books, which caused him to sob uncontrollably. The supervisor thought that he harbored resentment and whipped him on the back until his cane broke. Because he was weary of these labors, the lad escaped from the supervisor and ran away. With only a few extra items of clothing rolled up in a bundle, he joined a variety troupe. While with them, he wrote "Jests" in three chapters. As an actor, he played the role of the phony blockhead clerk who hides a pearl.

Upon finding him, the elder said, "When I think how you have become lost to the Way, how sad it is! Our founding teacher had a saying that, in a twenty-four hour day, a disciple was only permitted to study two hours of non-Buddhist subjects so that heretical teachings might be overcome. Since there are so many people in our monastery, I'll let you do as you wish now. You may also study miscellaneous subjects and practice your calligraphy."

During the Heavenly Jewel reign period (742–755), some people from Ch'u held a feast in the circuit of Ts'ang-lang.[10] The district subofficial functionary invited Lu Yü to be the director of the entertainers who were hired for the occasion. At the time, Li Ch'i-wu, administrator of Honan, had been appointed governor of Ts'ang-lang and was in attendance at the feast. He considered Lu Yü to be someone of extraordinary talent, so he shook his hand and patted him on the back, then personally presented him with his own poetry collection. Thereupon the common people of the Han and Min valleys also considered Lu Yü to be extraordinary.

After that, Lu Yü carried his books to the villa of Master Tsou on Firegate Mountain. This happened to be just when the director of the ministry of

9. A famous writer, especially of rhapsodies (see selections 122 ff.), and inventor who lived during the Eastern Han period. His dates are 78–139.
10. In the modern-day province of Hupei.

rites, Ts'ui Kuo-fu,[11] was appointed adjutant of Ching-ling commandery. Altogether, Lu Yü and he enjoyed each other's company for three years. During this period, Lu Yü was presented with a white donkey, a jet-black pack ox, and a bookcase made of patterned pagoda tree wood. The white donkey and pack ox were given to him by Li Ch'eng, the governor of Hsiang-yang;[12] the bookcase of patterned pagoda tree wood was a present from the late vice-director of the chancellery, Lu. These three things were all much cherished by the recipient himself. Realizing that they are well suited for riding and storing by rural folk, that is why they gave me these items in particular.

At the beginning of the Highest Virtue reign period (756–757), refugees[13] from Shensi fled south of the Yangtze and Lu Yü also went south at that time. There he developed a friendship with the monk Chiao-jan[14] that ignored their difference in age and religious status.

From the time he was young, Lu Yü enjoyed writing, mostly in a satirical vein. If he saw people do something good, he would feel as though he himself had done it; but if he saw people do something bad, he would feel as though he were ashamed of himself. "Bitter medicine is hard to swallow; bitter words are hard to hear"—since there was nothing that he would shy away from saying, the average person kept out of his way. In response to An Lu-shan's[15] rebellion in the Central Plains, he wrote a poem entitled "Quadruple Sorrow" and, in response to Liu Chan's insurrection[16] in the region west of the Huai River, he wrote "Rhapsody on the Unclarity of Heaven." All these pieces were inspired by his passionate reaction to current events, which caused him to weep and snivel. His other writings include *The Contract Between Ruler and Subject* in three scrolls, *Genealogy of Four Surnames from South of the Yangtze* in eight scrolls, *An Account of Men of Distinction from North and South* in ten scrolls, *A Record of Successive Officials in Wu-hsing* in three scrolls, *A Historical Record of the Prefecture of Ch'ao-chou* in one scroll, *Tea Classic* in one scroll, and *The Divination of Dreams* in three scrolls (A, B, C), all of which he keeps in a coarse cloth sack.

> Composed during the second year of the
> Superior Origin reign period (761),
> when Lu Yü was twenty-nine years of age.
> *Translated by Victor H. Mair*

11. A T'ang poet and official.
12. In Hupei.
13. Escaping from the An-Shih rebellion (see selection 149).
14. A well-known Buddhist poet (730–799).
15. Roxsan the Arsacid, of Sogdian-Turkish ancestry, had been a favorite of the T'ang emperor Hsüan Tsung and his "precious consort," Yang Kuei-fei (see selections 149 and 150).
16. This occurred in 760.

194

Biography of the Child Ou Chi

Liu Tsung-yüan (773–819)

Mr. Liu[1] says that the people of Viet[2] are lacking in kindness. When they give birth to a child, whether boy or girl, they look upon it as a commodity. From the time children lose their baby teeth, their fathers and older brothers sell them off out of a desire for profit. If they do not earn enough from their own children, they snatch them away, bound and manacled, from other families. If they do not have the strength to resist, even those who are old enough to grow a beard are invariably forced to become slaves. It is common for such mutual depredations to occur right out on the main thoroughfares. Those children who are fortunate enough to grow up turn around and capture others who are smaller and weaker than they. Because the Han[3] officials themselves consider this trade profitable if they illicitly obtain a slave child through it, they let it go on freely and ask no questions. Consequently, the fertility of the Viet population is being squandered.

Few of the children manage to escape by themselves. That child Ou Chi was able to do so when he was only eleven years old is most extraordinary. Tu Chou-shih,[4] a retainer in the Kweichow surveillance commissioner's office, told me how it happened.

Child Chi was a herd-boy and woodcutter from Liu-chou.[5] Once when he was out herding and cutting firewood, a couple of ruffians kidnapped him. They tied his hands behind his back and gagged him with a piece of cloth, then took him to a market forty tricents away to sell him. Chi pretended to cry like a boy and trembled with fear, putting on the customary appearance of a little boy. The ruffians, thinking he would be easy to handle, drank together until they were tipsy. Then one of them went off to do some business and the other lay down after sticking his knife in the ground by the side of the road.

When child Chi stealthily noticed that the ruffian had fallen asleep, he backed up against the knife blade with his bound hands and moved them up and down vigorously until the rope broke, whereupon he grabbed the knife and killed the sleeping ruffian. Before the child was able to run very far away, however, the ruffian who had gone off to do some business returned and caught him. Greatly startled by what had happened to his partner, he was all

---

For a brief note on the author, see selection 44.
1. The author himself.
2. The area of modern-day Fukien and Chekiang. Vietnam means "south of Viet."
3. Chinese.
4. Received his Advanced Scholar's degree in 801.
5. In modern-day Hunan province.

set to kill the child when the latter spoke hastily, "How can being the servant of two masters compare with being the servant of one master? He was unkind to me. If you can honestly preserve my life and be kind to me, I'll do anything for you."

The ruffian who had come back from doing business thought about it for quite a while then said, "Rather than kill this slave, wouldn't it be better to sell him? And rather than sell him and then have to divide up the profits, wouldn't it be better for me to get them all for myself? So it's fortunate that the kid killed him after all. Excellent!" Thereupon the ruffian buried his partner's corpse and took the child along with him to the place where he was staying, making sure to tie his bonds still tighter.

In the middle of the night, the child rolled over by himself and burned through his bonds by getting close to the fire in the stove. Even though the fire singed his hands, he did not shrink from it. Once again, he grabbed a knife and killed the second ruffian. Then he began to yell so loudly that the whole town was alarmed. "I am the son of a man named Ou," said the child, "and should not have to be a slave. These two ruffians captured me, but luckily I was able to kill both of them! I request that you inform the courts of this matter."

The town subofficial functionary reported what had happened to the prefect and the prefect reported what had happened to the superior prefect. When the superior prefect summoned the boy, he saw before him an earnest young lad. The prefect Yen Cheng[6] marveled at Ou Chi and wished to retain him as a minor subofficial functionary, but the child was unwilling. The prefect gave him a set of clothing and sent a subofficial functionary to escort him back to his village.

All those in the village who were engaged in abduction looked at Ou Chi warily and dared not pass by his gate. "This boy is two years younger than Ch'in Wu-yang,"[7] they said, "but he's already put two ruffians to death. We'd better stay clear of him!"

Translated by Victor H. Mair

6. Appointed as prefect of Kweichow in present-day Kwangsi, a remote southern province.

7. A courageous youth of the state of Yen during the Warring States period who at age thirteen killed some thugs.

195

Biography of a Girl Surnamed Chao

P'i Jih-hsiu (c. 833–c. 883)

She was a young girl with the surname Chao who was from Salt Hill in Shan-yang commandery.[1] Her father was a salt merchant who stole some government salt for personal profit and failed to pay the statutory taxes on it.[2] He was arrested by officials and, according to the law, was to be put to death. He had already confessed and the execution date was imminent. His daughter, whom we will call the Chao girl, sought an audience with the commissioner for the salt and iron monopoly and told her tearful tale before the court.

"When I was seven, my mother died. Thanks to my father's salt-running, he was able to make enough money to provide me with food and clothing. Father's kindness in keeping me alive is truly immeasurable. Now that his crime has been exposed, I should be adjudged together with him. If the law cannot permit that, would your honor please forgive him? Please allow me to be adjudged together with him." The judge, Ts'ui Chü of Ch'ing-ho district, swayed by her righteousness, declared, "It is only fitting that I reduce the sentence."

The Chao girl burst into tears and said, "My life was previously preserved by my father. Now, sir, it has been saved by you. I swear that I shall shave my hair and become a Buddhist in order to repay your virtue." Concerned that others might not believe the words of a girl, she took out a stiletto that she carried in her bosom and forthwith cut off her ear to demonstrate that she would certainly keep her oath. Ts'ui Chü was all the more impressed by her and, in the end, preserved her father's life intact. After nursing her father back to health from the punishment he had received when he was arrested, the Chao girl bid him adieu and entered a Buddhist nunnery.

P'i Jih-hsiu comments: "In times of danger or disaster, many were the ancients who would make a show of their trustworthiness, but after their family or nation had been preserved whole, they would go back on their oath. Yet the Chao girl, who was still wet behind the ears, declared herself willing to die together with her father to plead for his life—such was her filial devotion. And she mutilated herself to seal her oath—such was her trustworthiness. Having a firm grasp both of filial devotion and trustworthiness, she strode loftily above the world. Not even fabled gems are adequate to describe

For information on the author, see selection 52.

1. In modern-day Kiangsu province.

2. The T'ang government strove to exercise total monopoly on the production and sale of salt. Naturally, this was achieved only through ruthless control over the sources of salt and those who actually extracted the salt from the land.

her spotless purity; not even redolent orchids are adequate to describe her luxuriant fragrance. She was far superior to those ancients who rescued their families or countries from disaster and danger, but then went back on their oaths.

"The gentleman of today, when faced with adversity, does not maintain his high moral principles and, when enjoying security, does not fulfill his pledge of trustworthiness. Let him take the Chao girl as his model! May those in the future who compile women's history not forget the Chao girl!"

Translated by Victor H. Mair

196
The Biography of A-liu [1]

Lu Jung (1436–1494)

A-liu was a servant boy in the house of Chou Yüan-su of T'ai-ts'ang.[2] By nature, he was doltish and unruly, but Yüan-su kept him around anyway.

Once Yüan-su asked him to do the sweeping and he spent the whole morning moving the broom but couldn't even finish a single room. When his master upbraided him, A-liu threw the broom on the floor and said, "If you're so good at sweeping, why bother me with it?"

Occasionally Yüan-su would go somewhere else and he'd have A-liu watch the gate. But he couldn't even remember the names of those visitors with whom he was familiar. If Yüan-su asked who had come, he'd invariably say, "One of 'em was short and fat; one of 'em was skinny and bearded; one of 'em was pretty good-looking; one of 'em was so old and crippled he had to lean on a cane." Later, he realized that it was too hard to remember what everybody looked like, so he closed the gate and refused to greet guests any longer.

Yüan-su's family had a collection of ancient bronze vessels.[3] Once when some guests came, he put them out on display. A-liu waited until the guests left and then secretly went up and tapped on the vessels. "This stuff is bronze,

---

The author became a Presented Scholar in 1466 and filled a succession of middle-level posts in the bureaucracy. He was known more for his erudition than for his literary ability, but wrote a number of perceptive and charming essays.

1. The name of the main character in this sketch probably means something like "hang around" or "stick around." The prefix "a" indicates that he is most likely of low birth.

2. Located in the modern-day province of Kiangsu.

3. These are specified as *tsun* (for wine), *yi* (also for wine), *ting* (tripot for cooking), and *tui* (for serving food).

isn't it?" he asked himself. "How come it's so black and tarnished?" So he went outside and got some sand and pebbles that he used along with water to give the vessels a good scrubbing.

Yüan-su had a couch with short legs that was missing one of them. He asked A-liu to cut off the branch of a tree to fix it. Grasping an ax and a saw, A-liu traipsed around the garden for an entire day. When he returned, A-liu held up two fingers like a forked branch and said, "All tree branches grow upward. I couldn't find any that point downward." The whole family burst into laughter when they heard him say this.

Once Yüan-su planted several new willows in front of his house. Afraid that the neighbor's children would tug at them, he asked A-liu to guard them. When the time came for A-liu to eat, he pulled up the willows and brought them into the house for safekeeping. The ridiculous things that A-liu did were mostly of this sort.

Yüan-su had an excellent calligraphic hand in the regular script and was a particularly good painter. One day as he was preparing his inks, he said playfully to A-liu, "Can you do this?" "What's so hard about that?" answered A-liu. Whereupon Yüan-su asked him to paint something. The density and consistency with which A-liu applied the inks were like those of someone who was long practiced in painting. Yüan-su tested him repeatedly, and everything he produced met with people's approval.

From that time on, Yüan-su employed A-liu especially as a painter, never abandoning him to the end of his life.

Translated by Victor H. Mair

197
The Biography of Actor Ma

Hou Fang-yü (1618–1654)

Actor Ma was a member of the theater world[1] in Chin-ling,[2] the former capital of the Ming dynasty. The altars to the earth and grain were still there, as were various government offices. Furthermore, since it was a time of great

The author was a Ch'ing period advocate of the ancient-style prose movement, especially as conceived by Han Yü (see selection 42) and Ou-yang Hsiu (see selection 174). He is the hero of the famous romance portrayed in K'ung Shang-jen's (1648–1718) drama "The Peach Blossom Fan."

1. The text has "Pear Garden," an old name for the acting profession that dates back to the T'ang dynasty.

2. Chin-ling is an old name for Nanking.

peace and prosperity, it was easy for people to make merry. The men and women who visited Peach Leaf Ferry and made excursions to Rain Flower Terrace[3] were so numerous that they stepped on each other's toes. In the theater world, there were roughly several dozen troupes that were famous for their skilled actors, but the two most outstanding troupes were called Reformation and Flower Grove.

One day, some Cantonese merchants from Hsin-an jointly hired the two troupes for a large party to which they invited all the leading men of letters and beautiful ladies of Chin-ling, none of whom refused. They had Reformation set up in East Market and Flower Grove in West Market; both troupes were to perform "Cry of the Phoenix,"[4] which tells the story of Yang Chi-sheng's accusation of Yen Sung.[5]

As the opera reached the halfway mark, the notes were being played to perfection and the rhythms varied exquisitely, so that everyone exclaimed how good both troupes were. At the point where the two ministers, Hsia Yen and Yen Sung, were discussing whether or not to take back Ho-t'ao[6] from the Tatars, the role of the minister Yen was being played by Actor Li in West Market and by Actor Ma in East Market. The audience turned toward the West Market and sighed with appreciation. Some of them shouted loudly as they ordered more wine or they moved in closer, till they no longer turned their heads toward East Market at all. Before long, the situation reached a point where the troupe in East Market could not go on with its performance. When they were asked why, they said that Actor Ma was so ashamed by his inferiority to Actor Li that he changed out of his costume and ran away.

Actor Ma was one of the best singers in Chin-ling. With him gone and the Reformation troupe unwilling to replace him immediately, they finally stopped performing and disbanded. Thus the Flower Grove troupe had the stage all to itself.

After he had been away for three years, Actor Ma returned. He went around to contact his old associates and then made the following request of the Cantonese merchants: "Please be so kind as to have another banquet today and invite all the guests who came that day three years ago. We'd like to perform 'Cry of the Phoenix' with the Flower Grove troupe once again for a day of enjoyment."

The performance was arranged and before long they came to the scene where the discussion over Ho-t'ao takes place. Actor Ma again appeared as the minister Yen Sung. Actor Li suddenly lost his voice and came crawling

3. Popular tourist attractions in Nanking.
4. *Ming feng chi*, attributed to Wang Shih-chen (1526–1590), a dominant poet and critic during the late sixteenth century (not the same person as the author of selection 81, whose name is similar and who played a similar literary role during the seventeenth century).
5. Two Ming dynasty officials involved in a power struggle.
6. The bend of the Yellow River as it passes through the Ordos Desert.

to declare himself the disciple of Actor Ma. That day the Reformation troupe far surpassed the Flower Grove troupe.

In the evening, the Flower Grove troupe went to call on Actor Ma, saying, "Sir, there are many fine performers under heaven, but none who can take the place of Actor Li. Actor Li's performance of minister Yen is the height of perfection. From whom did you learn how to overtake him?"

"Admittedly," said Actor Ma, "there's no one under heaven who can take the place of Actor Li, and Actor Li was unwilling to accept me as his student. But I heard that the current minister, Ku Ping-ch'ien of K'un-shan, bears a striking resemblance to minister Yen. So I traveled to the capital where I begged to serve as his doorman for three years. Every day I waited upon the minister from K'un-shan in his offices at court. I observed his movements and listened to his speech habits. After a long time, I finally mastered them. This is how I taught myself." The members of the Flower Grove troupe arrayed themselves around Actor Ma and did obeisance to him, then left.

Actor Ma's name was Chin and his style was Yün-chiang ("Cloud General"). His ancestors came from the Western Regions[7] and his contemporaries also called him "Moslem Ma."

Hou Fang-yü comments: How extraordinary was Actor Ma's manner of finding a teacher for himself! Because Actor Li's skill was unparalleled, there was no one whom he could ask to teach it to him. So he went to wait upon the minister from K'un-shan. Watching the minister from K'un-shan was just like watching minister Yen Sung, who was from Fen-yi. To use the living likeness of the minister from Fen-yi to instruct himself how to act the role of the minister from Fen-yi, how could he not succeed? Amazing! Ashamed that his skill was inferior, he journeyed several thousand tricents and served as a doorman for three years. If three years had not been enough, he still would not have returned. With such determination, one need not ask how refined his skills must have been.

Translated by Victor H. Mair

---

7. Central Asia and beyond, hence Ma was not of Chinese ancestry.

Fictional and Fictionalized Biographies and Autobiographies

198

The Biography of Fur Point

Han Yü (768–824)

Fur Point was a native of Central Mountain. His patriarch, Bright Sight,[1] aided Yü in bringing order to the lands of the East, and he had some success in nourishing nature, thus he was enfeoffed with the lands of Mao.[2] When he died, he became one of the twelve spirits. He once said, "My descendants will be the posterity of a spirit-illuminate and shall not be the same as normal

This is a humorous essay on a writing brush, couched in the form of a traditional biography in the standard histories as established by Ssu-ma Ch'ien (see selection 160, unnumbered note, and selection 173, note 10). The first level of the narrative camouflages a satirical statement on the nature of the relationship between the ruler and his ministers—which may refer directly to Han Yü's own career. This work and others of a similar nature fostered the relationship between the reformed "ancient-style prose" of the early ninth century and the then fledgling fictional genre known as *ch'uan-ch'i* (transmission of the strange; see selections 207 and 208).

For a note on the author, arguably the greatest essayist in Chinese literary history, see selection 42.

1. "Bright Sight," like many names in this piece, is taken from a classical, metonymic reference to the rabbit (here from the *Record of Rites* [*Li chi*]).

2. A fairly common surname in China, as in Mao Tse-tung, which also happens to mean "fur," as translated in the title.

beings. They will be born by being vomited."[3] And, indeed, that is how it was!

The eighth-generation descendant of Bright Sight was Bunny, who, so popular tradition has maintained for ages, lived in Central Mountain during the Yin dynasty and learned the artifices of the spirit-immortals so that he was able to hide in bright light and bring about alchemical changes in things. He had secret relations with Heng Ŏ and rode a toad to the moon.[4] His descendants, therefore, withdrew from government service.

One of them named Wiley, who lived near the eastern city-wall, was crafty and a skilled runner. He put his talents to a test against Blackie of Han, who could not catch him. Since he was angry, he plotted with Sung Ch'üeh to kill Wiley and then tore his family to ribbons.

During the time of the First Emperor of Ch'in,[5] General Meng T'ien[6] led an expedition south against Ch'u and camped at Central Mountain, intending to undertake a great hunt to intimidate Ch'u.

He summoned his stewards of the left and right and his staff to divine concerning the prospect of the hunt with the *Lien-shan*.[7] He obtained the oracles "heaven" and "human culture," and the diviner congratulated him:

> In today's catch,
> no horns or fangs to match,
> but one dressed in coarse clothes,
> with a harelip and long whiskers 'neath his nose.
> with eight orifices and his legs tucked in flat,
> you'll only take the hair from his head,
> and with it, on bamboo and wooden slat,
> unify the empire's scripts to be read;
> thus Ch'in will unite the feudal lords instead.

Then the hunt began. They surrounded all of Mao's clan, pulled out their best, and, taking up Point, returned. Meng T'ien presented him as a captive at the Patterned Platform Palace, along with his clansmen, gathered and bound. The Emperor of Ch'in ordered that he be granted a hot cleansing bath, and invested him in Tube City, naming him "Baron of Tube City." Daily he gained favor and was employed in more affairs.

Point was the sort of man who had a strong memory and an easy under-

---

3. A traditional notion of how rabbits are born.

4. Heng (later Ch'ang) Ŏ in ancient Chinese lore stole an elixir of immortality from her husband, the archer Yi, and fled to the moon. The story as Han Yü tells it is different from all classical text versions and may well be intended to refer allegorically to a contemporary set of events.

5. 246–210 B.C.E.

6. The supposed inventor of the writing brush (d. 210 B.C.E.).

7. One of the early divination works.

standing of things. From the "era of rope knots"[8] down to the events of Ch'in's rise to power, there was nothing he did not compile. The works of the yin-yang school, of the diviners, of the physiognomists, of physicians and pharmacists, genealogists, geographers, local historians, calligraphers, painters, of the nine schools, the one hundred philosophers, the gods, and even the theories of Buddha, Lao Tzu, and other foreigners, were all among those things he knew in detail. He was also versed in contemporary affairs, administrative records, accounts and records of market transactions, and whenever the emperor wanted to take note of something, he always stood at his service. Everyone from the emperor himself to the Crown Prince Fu-su and his son Hu-hai, the Grand Councilor Li Ssu, the Keeper of the Chariots Chao Kao, on down to the people, loved and respected him. He was, moreover, expert at following his master's intent and in demonstrating uprightness or crookedness, skill or clumsiness, always taking his cue from the other person. Even if forsaken by someone, he would not allow an inkling of anything to leak out. Soldiers alone he did not like; but, if invited, he would also go to them from time to time.

His rank rose until he was made "Officer Fit for Composition." He became even more intimate with the emperor, so that the latter took to calling him "Lord Fit for Composition." The emperor personally decided all matters, going through one hundred pounds of documents each day. Not even his personal staff was permitted to stand in attendance. Only Fur Point and Candle Holder served him always, put out only when the emperor retired.

Fur Point was a close friend of Spread-out Black[9] from Chiang, Porcelain Pool[10] from Hung-nung, and Mulberry Tree[11] from Kuei-chi. They recommended one another, and when one would go out or stay in, the others had to go along. If the emperor summoned Fur Point, the other three did not wait for a command, but came directly together and the emperor never reprimanded them for it.

Later during an audience, since the emperor had a task he wanted Fur Point to undertake and tried to rub up to him, Point removed his cap to express his gratitude. The emperor saw his bald spot, and, since in his copying of paintings he was no longer able to reach the standard desired by the emperor, the latter chided him: "Lord Fit for Composition, you are old and balding and can no longer perform useful service. I have called you 'Fit for Composition.' Can it be that you are now 'Not Fit?' " Fur Point replied, "I am one who has 'Worn out His Heart' for you." Thus he was called for no more, but returned to the city of his fief and came to his end there in Tube City.

8. A system of notation similar to the quipu of the ancient Peruvians.
9. Ink.
10. Ink reservoir.
11. Paper.

His descendants were very numerous. They spread out through the empire and into barbarian lands. All lay claim to the title of Tube City for themselves, but only those who lived in Central Mountain were able to continue their ancestor's profession.

The Grand Historian comments: In the Mao clan there were two lineages. The first took the surname Chi and were the sons of King Wen. They were enfeoffed in Mao and were the ones referred to in the expression "Lu, Wei, Mao, and Tan." During the Warring States period their lineage included Mao Kung and Mao Sui.[12] Although the origin of the Central Mountain lineage is unknown, its descendants were most numerous. But upon the completion of *The Spring and Autumn Annals* they all came to an end with Confucius, through no fault of their own. Since General Meng pulled out their heir on Central Mountain and the First Emperor installed him in Tube City, each generation has had someone well known. But as to the lineage surnamed Chi, nothing can be learned.

Fur Point was first presented as a captive and finally became a trusted servant. When Ch'in annihilated the feudal lords, he played a role in the success. But his rewards did not requite his toil and, because of his age, he was estranged. Ch'in was truly wanting of gratitude!

Translated by William H. Nienhauser, Jr.

12. Historical personages who happened to bear the surname Mao ("Fur").

199
Biography of the Vagrant of Rivers and Lakes

Lu Kuei-meng (?–c. 881)

A vagrant is someone who is dissolute. His mind wanders, his ideas wander, his form wanders, and his spirit wanders. Being completely unbridled, he is looked at askance by his contemporaries. People who are constrained by decorum distance themselves from him by saying, "This man is a vagrant."

Lu Kuei-meng was born into a family of moderate means from a town near Soochow. He was a learned student of the Confucian classics but had closer ties with Taoism. In fact, he was something of an alchemist and a fancier of mushrooms and herbs. An eccentric character, he wandered about the countryside visiting temples and monasteries while hunting for all sorts of oddities and observing local phenomena. Lu was a fervent devotee of the then newly popular beverage tea (see selection 193) and a friend of the poet and essayist P'i Jih-hsiu (see selections 52 and 195).

The vagrant does not consider this shameful, but goes right along with them in calling himself what they do.

People may ridicule him, saying, "Those who look upon you as a vagrant mean to fault you, yet you take this word as your own sobriquet. Why is this?"

The vagrant would reply, "Heaven and earth are quite large, but they are just a speck within the Great Vacuity. They labor themselves in covering and supporting the myriad objects; they labor themselves with the constant revolution of the spheres. If the inclination of the gnomon gets out of kilter, the seasons will be jumbled. Thus heaven and earth cannot hope for even a moment's vagrancy.

"Let us examine, however, whether the vagaries of water and soil are of any use. Water in its vagrancy becomes rain, dew, frost, and snow. When confined, it appears as ponds, rivers, puddles, or droughts. Soil in its vagrancy may be piled up to become high hills, may be dug out to become deep pits, may give life when things are planted in it, may harbor death when corpses are buried in it. When confined in the form of an ocarina, it can no longer be made into a pottery mold; when confined in the form of a brick, it can no longer be made into a basin. Is this not because when soil and water are in a vagrant state they are open to transformation, whereas when they are confined they are not?

"If a person does not adopt an attitude of vagrancy when he withdraws from public life, then he will still cling to those expedient devices which enable him to gain fame; if a person does not adopt an attitude of vagrancy when he enters public life, then he will strive to grasp ephemeral power. But can he cling to such devices forever and can he grasp such power forever?"

Therefore, I have composed some vagrant's songs and this vagrant's biography to celebrate the vagrancy of the man of the rivers and lakes.

Translated by Victor H. Mair

PART IV

Fiction

Rhetorical Persuasions and Allegories

200
Intrigues of the Warring States

Compiled by Liu Hsiang (77–6 B.C.E.)

Pien-ch'iao and the King's Carbuncle

The great physician Pien-ch'iao [1] visited King Wu of Ch'in and the king showed him the carbuncle on his face. Pien-ch'iao offered to remove it.

"Your majesty's carbuncle is forward of the ear and below the eye," cried

The *Intrigues of the Warring States (Chan-kuo ts'e)* consists of material from the Warring States period that was compiled by Liu Hsiang (77–6 B.C.E.) and reorganized by Kao Yu (fl. 200 C.E.). While it is generally agreed that the *Intrigues* is the largest pre-Han collection of historical anecdotes, fables, snippets of romances, and tales of famous persons, the uses to which it has been put by the Chinese are as varied as the ages through which it has passed. Their persistent view has been that the book is a piece of bad history, and from time to time it has joined that group of alluring, if slightly sinister, "secret books of the ancients" which, if studied diligently enough, would never make one a "True King" but might lead one to great secular power and wealth. An equally persistent, but very sound, conviction is that the *Intrigues* contains many of the finest examples of "ancient prose" extant. Hence avid readers ever since Han times have condemned its morality while praising its style. On a less subjective level, it appears in fact to be a heterogeneous collection of rhetorical pieces, which may have been used as grist by the wandering political persuaders of the times and may actually record some of their happier inspirations.

The fictionality of much of the *Intrigues* was long ago demonstrated by Henri Maspero. Thus, while the *Intrigues* itself may not be classified as fiction per se, with it begins the impulse toward fictionalization which achieves full bloom during the T'ang period, partly under the influence of Buddhism. The dividing line between fiction and nonfiction is, of course, notori-

the king's attendants. "If the physician should not cease soon enough while removing it he might cause your majesty to lose his hearing or the sight of an eye."

As a result the king excused Pien-ch'iao. Pien-ch'iao was furious and threw down his flint lancet.

"Your majesty planned this by consulting with one who had knowledge, but now he revokes it on the advice of those who know nothing! If the government of Ch'in were run in the same fashion, the country would perish with your first action."

---

ously difficult to draw. In general, however, the fictional component of those texts earlier in the prose section of this anthology is smaller than that of those which follow below.

For a note on the compiler, see selection 203.

1. A famous physician of antiquity (see selection 192, note 3). His name is also spelled Pien-ch'üeh.

A Dialect[1] Word

Marquis Ying[2] said, "In Cheng they call jade which has not been worked 'pure'; in Chou they call fresh-dressed rats which have not yet been preserved 'pure.'

"A man of Chou carrying fresh-dressed rats passed a Cheng merchant and asked him if he wanted to buy some 'pures.' The merchant replied that he did. But when he was shown dressed rats he declined them.

"Now Lord P'ing-yüan[3] is busy getting himself a name for virtue throughout the empire. It was he who banished his own ruler, the former king of Chao, to Sha-ch'iu in order to become minister, yet rulers everywhere still respect him. This merely proves that rulers are less intelligent than the Cheng merchant. They are so dazzled by the word 'pure' that they do not trouble to discover what reality lies behind it."

1. "Dialect," as used loosely in reference to Sinitic tongues, often signifies separate and mutually unintelligible languages according to usual linguistic standards. Also see selection 190, note 9 and selection 161, unnumbered note (last sentence).

2. Minister of Ch'in.

3. Kung-tzu Sheng.

The Handsome Man

Tsou Chi was tall and fair of face and figure. He put on his court robes and cap and looked in the mirror.

"Am I more handsome than Mr. Tardy of Northwall?" he asked his wife.

"You are much more so," replied his wife. "How can Mr. Tardy even be compared with you?"

Now, Mr. Tardy was a man known in Ch'i for his beauty, and Tsou Chi was not content, so he asked his concubine:

"Am I more handsome than Mr. Tardy?"

"How can there be any comparison?" she replied.

Next morning when guests, not members of his family, came and he sat with them and talked, he asked them:

"Who is the more handsome, Mr. Tardy or I?"

"Mr. Tardy is not as handsome as you are, sir," they replied.

The day after that Mr. Tardy himself came. Tsou Chi examined him closely and decided he was not as handsome as Mr. Tardy. Then he looked in the mirror at himself and decided he was much less well favored than was Mr. Tardy. When he went to bed that night he thought about it:

"My wife thinks me handsome because she is close to me, my concubine because she fears me, and my guests because they want something of me."

He then went to the court, had an audience with King Wei, and said:

"Your servant knows he is really not as handsome as Mr. Tardy. My wife is close to me, my concubine fears me, and my guests want something of me, so they all say I am more handsome than he. Now in the thousand square tricents of our country and in its one hundred and twenty cities there is no woman of the king or attendant who is not close to him. In the court there is no minister who does not fear him, and within the borders of the land there is no one who does not seek something of the king. If one looks at it this way, the king has been monstrously hoodwinked!"

"It is so," said the king, and he sent down an order:

"To all ministers, officers, and citizens who will criticize the king's faults to his face will go the highest reward; those who will remonstrate with the king in writing will be given the next highest reward; and to those who overhear criticism of the king and convey it to his ears will go the least reward."

As soon as the order had been given, ministers came in with remonstrations; the doorway to the chamber looked like a marketplace. In a few months there were occasional petitioners, and after a year none who spoke to the king had petitions to present.

When Yen, Chao, Han, and Wei heard of this, they all came to court at Ch'i. This is what is meant by "winning a battle from the throne room."

The Tiger and the Fox

"I hear that the North fears Chao Hsi-hsü," said King Hsüan to his ministers. "What say you to this?"

None of them replied, except Chiang Yi, who said, "The tiger hunts all the animals of the forest and devours them, but once when he caught a fox, the fox said, 'You dare not eat me. The Lord of Heaven ordained me chief among beasts; if you now kill me you will be disobeying the will of Heaven. If you doubt it, follow behind me through the forest and watch the animals flee when they see me.' The tiger did indeed doubt the fox and therefore followed him. Animals saw them and fled, but the tiger did not know that the animals ran because they feared him. He thought they were afraid of the fox.

"Now your majesty's country is five thousand tricents square and in it are a million first-class troops, all of whom are under Chao Hsi-hsü. Therefore when the North fears Hsi-hsü, in reality it fears your majesty's arms, just as the animals of the forest feared the tiger."

Translated by James I. Crump

201
The Donkey of Ch'ien

Liu Tsung-yüan (773–819)

There were no donkeys in Ch'ien [1] until someone who was fond of curiosities brought one in by boat. After the man got it there, he found the donkey was useless, so he let it loose near the hills. A tiger, upon seeing it, thought it was such a large beast that it took it for a god. So the tiger hid in the forest to spy on it. Bit by bit the tiger came closer to it, but carefully so that it wouldn't know.

One day the donkey brayed, and the tiger was so terrified that he ran far off. He thought that the donkey was going to eat him and was extremely

Allegories have a long tradition in China. They were originally linked to persuasive rhetoric and sometimes found in philosophical writings such as *Chuang Tzu*, *Lieh Tzu*, and *Han Fei Tzu*. By the T'ang dynasty, a number of writers, who were involved to varying degrees with the literary reforms known as the *ku-wen* (old-style prose) movement, experimented with different types of allegories. These works, written either in prose or in verse, often featured animals rather than people. Through descriptions of situations in the animal world with direct counterparts in the human sphere, writers were able to offer indirect criticism or moral instruction about general philosophical principles. Animal allegories were also used to illustrate the possible dangers of a given political situation or to express the author's dissatisfaction with events in his own life. Since the analogies in these works were often fairly subtle, authors had more freedom of expression than they did in more narrowly defined, constraining genres. T'ang animal allegories also present a fascinating look at how writers of this era envisioned the natural world and the role of man within it.

The first of a group of "Three Admonitions."

For a brief note on the author, see selection 44.

1. An old name for Kweichow.

frightened. Yet as the tiger kept observing it time and again, he realized there wasn't anything unusual about the donkey. The tiger had gotten increasingly used to hearing the braying. He now came out near the donkey circling it, but still dared not pounce. In a little while, he pressed even closer to it, and he nudged it unconcernedly. Overcome with rage, the donkey kicked out at the tiger.

Now the tiger happily reckoned to himself, "So this is the extent of its talents." Thereupon he leaped, roaring loudly, and ripped open the donkey's throat. He ate his fill and then left.

Alas! The donkey's larger size made it seem to be a creature of virtue; its loud voice made it seem to be a creature of ability. If it had never revealed the limit of its talents, the tiger, despite his own ferociousness, would still have been suspicious and fearful and in the end would not have dared attack it. Now, instead, things have come to this — how disheartening!

Translated by Madeline K. Spring

Anecdotal Fiction

202
A New Account of Tales of the World

Liu Yi-ch'ing (403–444)

When K'ung Jung[1] was in his tenth year, he accompanied his father to Loyang. At the time Li Ying[2] was at the height of his reputation there as commandant of the Capital Province. Those who came to his gate gained

A New Account of Tales of the World (Shih-shuo hsin-yü) consists of stories, conversations, and short characterizations. It covers the period from the second through the fourth centuries. In contrast to formal historical writing on this period, Tales of the World was written closer to the time when the events depicted actually occurred, hence it is likely to be more reliable; certainly it is more vivid. Nearly all 626 characters appearing in the pages of the Tales of the World are attested in the histories and other sources. Furthermore, for most incidents and remarks recorded therein, allowing for literary embellishment and dramatic exaggeration, there is no compelling reason to doubt their veracity. Only a small minority pose problems of anachronism, contradiction of known facts, gross supernatural intrusions, or apparent internal inconsistencies. And yet the Tales of the World was never considered by Chinese bibliographers as a work of history. Rather, it was always classed as "minor talk" (hsiao-shuo, i.e., "fiction"). Its main purpose was considered to be that of an aid to conversation, and another of its aims, so it was said, was to provide enjoyment. The bias against Tales of the World as a legitimate work of history undoubtedly stemmed from its failure to subscribe to the sanctioned conventions of historiography enshrined in the dynastic histories and from its inclusion of colorful dialogues and details normally not considered appropriate in the pages of a historical text. All of this, furthermore, is expressed in lively language that occasionally flirted with bits of colloquial, making it all the more unseemly to the staid Confucian arbiters of "proper" history-writing.

1. K'ung Jung (153–208) was a twentieth-generation descendant of Confucius.
2. Li Ying (110–169) was an implacable foe of eunuchs in government, but lost in his struggles against them.

admittance only if they were men of exceptional talent and unblemished reputation, or if they were relatives on their father's or mother's side. Jung arrived at Li's gate and announced to the gatekeeper, "I'm a relative of Commandant Li." After he was let in and seated before his host, Li Ying asked him, "And what relationship have you with me?"

He answered, "Long ago my ancestor K'ung Chung-ni (Confucius) had the respectful relationship of student to teacher with your ancestor Li Po-yang (Lao Tzu),[3] which means that you and I have carried on friendly relations for generations."

Li Ying and all the guests marveled at him.

The Great Officer of the Center, Ch'en Wei,[4] arrived later. Someone reported what Jung had said, and Wei remarked, "If a lad is clever when he's small it doesn't necessarily mean he'll be superior when he grows up."

Jung retorted, "I suppose when you were small you must have been clever?"

Wei was greatly discomfited.

3. Confucius's surname was K'ung and Lao Tzu's surname was supposedly Li. There are many apocryphal stories about Confucius receiving instruction from Lao Tzu, the ostensible founder of Taoism and the alleged author of the *Tao te ching* (see selection 9).
4. Active during the late second century.

Hsü Yün's wife was the daughter of Juan Kung and the younger sister of Juan K'an. She was extraordinarily homely. After the marriage ceremony was over, Yün had no intention of ever entering her apartment again. The members of her family were very upset over this. It happened once that Yün was having a guest come, and his wife had a female slave look to see who it was. She returned and reported, "It's Master Huan." Now "Master Huan" was Huan Fen.

The wife said, "Then there's nothing to worry about. Huan will surely urge him to come to my apartment."

As expected, Huan said to Hsü, "Since the Juan family gave you a homely daughter in marriage, they obviously did so with some purpose in mind. You would do well to look into it."

Accordingly, Hsü had a change of heart and entered his wife's apartment. But the moment he saw her he immediately wanted to leave again. His wife foresaw that if he went out this time there would be no further chance of his returning, so she seized his robe in an effort to detain him. Hsü took the occasion to say to his wife, "A wife should have four virtues.[1] How many of them do *you* have?"

1. According to the *Rites of Chou* (*Chou li*, 1.48), the nine preceptresses were in charge of the methods of womanly instruction by training the nine imperial concubines in proper womanly behavior, speech, appearance, and work. These later became known as the four womanly virtues.

His wife answered, "Where your bride is deficient is only in her appearance. But a *gentleman* should have a hundred deeds. How many have *you?*"

"I have them all."

"Of those hundred deeds, virtue is the first. If you love sensual beauty, but don't love virtue,[2] how can you say you have them all?"

Yün looked ashamed, and thereafter held her in respect and honor.

Translated by Richard B. Mather

2. In the *Analects* (see selection 6), 9.16, Confucius declares, "I have not seen any who love virtue as they love sensual beauty."

Tales of the Strange

203

Biographies of Transcendents

Attributed to Liu Hsiang (77–6 B.C.E.)

T'ao An-kung held the post of Superintendent of the Foundry at Liu-an,[1] where he kept many furnaces in full blast. From them one day flames shot forth and mounted upward to the sky in sheets of purple fire, whereupon T'ao An-kung cast himself prostrate upon the ground beside his smelting crucibles and begged for mercy. Hardly had he done so when the Scarlet Bird[2] alighted upon a crucible and thus spake: "An-kung! An-kung! Thy

The author was a Han polymath and statesman who was also a sort of magician. He was a distinguished bibliographer and ubiquitous editor-redactor of ancient texts, a compiler of anecdotal literature, and a poet and author in his own right, particularly of lamentations (see selection 200). The *Biographies of Transcendents* (*Lieh hsien chuan*) is the earliest extant Taoist hagiographical work and inspired many similar later collections. In all, it includes seventy brief accounts of Taoist adepts thought to have achieved immortality in one form or another.

Dragons are often depicted as aerial steeds of the transcendents. The short account above gives the legend connected with one such incident and also embodies several ancient religious beliefs.

1. In Anhwei.

2. One of the Four Supernatural Creatures that symbolize the four quadrants of heaven. It is also a group of constellations in the southern sky and a position in geomantic fields. As such, it stands for the south and, according to the notions of ancient Chinese philosophy, is associated with the element fire and with the number 7. It is to be noted that T'ao An-kung was carried off toward the southeast, which, together with the south, is that point of the compass where the element fire is located. Modern scholarship has attempted to identify the Scarlet Bird with the quail, but archaic representations show a crested bird with prominent tail feathers—a figure

flames have reached unto Heaven. On the seventh day of the seventh month I will send a red dragon to fetch thee."

When the appointed day arrived, the red dragon came in a deluge of rain, and An-kung rode off on its back toward the southeast. Thousands of the inhabitants of Liu-an had collected on one of the city walls to make votive offerings for a propitious journey; and all bade T'ao An-kung farewell.

Translated by W. Perceval Yetts

---

that might well be meant for a peacock or one of the pheasants and, indeed, is not unlike the traditional Chinese phoenix.

204
Search for the Supernatural

Kan Pao (fl. 318)

Preface

Even though we examine ancient fragments in the written documents and collect bits and pieces which have come down to the present time, these things are not what has been heard or seen by one person's own ears and eyes. How could one dare say that there are no inaccurate places? Note Wei Shuo's [1] losing the country. The two commentaries are at odds in what they have heard. Note Lü Wang's [2] serving Chou. In the *Shih chi* there exist two stories.[3] Things like this occur time and time again. From this standpoint we

---

Search for the Supernatural (Sou-shen chi) is a collection of over four hundred stories gathered by the Eastern Chin court historian Kan Pao. It is the best example of a genre of literary tale that contemporaries called "leftover history" and later scholars identified as the beginnings of Chinese fiction. The tales borrow an austere documentary style of official history writing, but their subjects reach beyond that range. Mixed together in the collection are tales of avenging ghosts, fox spirits, Taoist adepts, diviners and doctors, dreams and transformations, strange creatures of distant places, and odd customs of non-Han peoples. They demonstrate the profound interest of medieval literati in matters that were curious, bizarre, and remote.

The influence of Kan Pao's collection on later fiction and drama is tremendous. Many of the characters introduced so briefly here reappear as the protagonists of complete plays and short stories in later dynasties. And the genre of collecting brief tales of the supernatural continues as well, culminating in huge collections of thousands of stories, many in later times highly crafted and literary.

1. This refers to Duke Hui of Wei, a noble of the Spring and Autumn period. Kan Pao's point is that historical works are often at odds with each other about the interpretation of events.

2. I.e., Lü Shang, a minister to King Wen of the Chou dynasty.

3. The *Shih chi* is the *Records of the Grand Historian* by Ssu-ma Ch'ien (see selection 160,

can observe that the difficulties of hearing and seeing have come down from ancient times.

Even in writing the set words of a funerary announcement or following the manuals of the official historians, one finds places where it is difficult to write accurately. How much more difficult then is looking back to narrate events of a past one thousand years ago, writing down the characteristics of distant and peculiar ways of life, stringing together word fragments between textual faults and fissures, questioning the old people about things in former times! If one must have historical events without any discrepancies, have the words in every text agree, and only then regard them as veritable, then this point will surely seem a defect of previous historians.

Nonetheless, the state does not eliminate the office charged with writing commentaries on historical documents, and scholars do not cease in their recitations of the texts. Is this not because what is lost is inconsequential and what is preserved is vital?

As for what I am putting together now, when they are items gotten from previous accounts, then the fault is not mine. In the event they are recent happenings which I have collected or found out, should there be errors or omissions, I would hope to share the ridicule and condemnation with scholars and worthies of the past.

Coming now to what these records contain, it is enough to make clear that the spirit world is not a lie. On this subject, the countless words and hundred differing schools are too much even to scan. And what one perceives with his own eyes and ears is too much to write down. So I have lumped records together that are just adequate to express the main points of the eight categories[4] and provide some trivial accounts; that is all.

I will count myself fortunate if in the future curious scholars come along, note the basis of these stories, and find things within them to enlighten their hearts and fill their eyes. And I will be fortunate as well to escape reproach for this book.

Translated by James I. Crump and Kenneth DeWoskin

---

unnumbered note, and selection 173, note 10). In addition to better known historical records about Lü Shang, the *Shih chi* includes a hearsay story about his chance meeting with the king. Kan Pao's point here is that even the classic histories like the *Shih chi* saw fit to include information that was suspect but conveniently ready at hand.

4. The precise meaning of "categories" is not known. One possibility is that it refers to the addition of *chih-kuai* (tales of anomalies), such as those in the *Search for the Supernatural*, to the traditional seven categories of Liu Hsin's (?–23 C.E., son of Liu Hsiang, on whom see selection 203) seminal bibliographical scheme. In this case, it would imply "satisfying the needs of this [maverick] genre." Alternatively, and perhaps more likely, it refers to the classes of spiritual phenomena, meaning roughly "satisfying my purpose of displaying all eight types of spiritual phenomena."

Treasure Recovered Through the Classic of Changes

Huai Shao was a citizen of the Hung-shou relay station settlement well versed in the *Classic of Changes*. As he drew near death, he presented his copy of the *Changes* to his wife, saying, "When I am gone, there will be a great famine. Though this be so, I enjoin you never to sell the house. In the spring of the fifth year after my passing, an emissary surnamed Hung will stop at the relay station. This man owes me a debt; take the book to him and demand payment. You must give me your word and honor it."

After he died, there were in fact great troubles. Several times Huai's wife was tempted to sell off the house, but she remembered her husband's words and stopped herself. When the time came, a certain Hung did indeed stay at the relay station, whereupon Huai's wife presented him her copy of the *Changes* and taxed him with the debt. He accepted the book but was puzzled by her words.

"Never in my life did I contract such a debt," said he. "I wonder what is behind this?"

"As my husband neared death, he put his hand to his very book and saw what was to be. Truly, I would not deceive you," insisted the woman.

The emissary pondered and muttered to himself for some time until finally he understood. He ordered milfoil stalks to be brought so that a divination might be made. A while later, he clapped his hands together and sighed.

"Most wonderful, Mr. Huai," he exclaimed. "You have concealed your brilliance and hidden your tracks so that none of us had heard of you. But obviously you were one who could hold a mirror up to failure and success and fathom felicity and ill-fortune."

The emissary then turned to Huai's wife and said, "I never did incur such a debt. Your husband had the money. He knew that after his death you would temporarily find yourself in straitened circumstances so he hid the gold that it might wait upon better times. He deliberately told neither wife nor child about it for fear the money would disappear before the bad times had. He knew I was skilled in the *Changes* and therefore left this copy so that his intentions might become known. Now, five hundred catties of gold are buried in a black jar capped with a sheet of copper near the east wall of your house. It is exactly one rod from the wall and is buried nine feet deep."

The wife went home and dug. She recovered the gold and all was as had been divined.

Translated by James I. Crump and Kenneth DeWoskin

The Origins of the Man[1] Barbarians

In the times of Kao-hsin, an elderly woman attached to the palace had been suffering from an earache for some time. The physician treated her and removed an insect the size of a silkworm cocoon. When the woman had left, the physician placed the insect in a gourd pot (*hu*) and covered it with a dish (*p'an*). In no time it turned into a dog mottled with colorful patches. This dog was called P'an-hu and was reared by the physician.

At that time, the Wu barbarians had become numerous and strong and several times penetrated the borders. Generals were sent against them but could not gain victories. A declaration was sent throughout the kingdom: "Anyone bringing in the head of the Wu leader will be rewarded with a thousand catties of gold, an appanage of ten thousand households, and the hand of the emperor's youngest daughter."

Sometime later P'an-hu appeared carrying a head in its mouth and went straight to the king's palace. The king examined the head and concluded that it belonged to the Wu leader. What was he to do?

His officers all said, "P'an-hu is a domestic animal; he cannot be allowed to join the ranks of officials and certainly cannot be given your daughter to wed! Though he has acquired merit for the deed, he cannot be given the reward."

When his younger daughter heard of this, she addressed the king: "Since Your Majesty promised me to anyone in the world and P'an-hu brought you the head, ridding your kingdom of danger, we have here the will of Heaven. This is not something P'an-hu's intelligence could have contrived. Kings must keep promises, rulers must be believed. You cannot repudiate your word, clearly given to the world, for the sake of my humble person; that would result in calamity for your kingdom."

The king feared she was right and ordered her given to P'an-hu.

The dog took the girl into the southern hills where the undergrowth was so dense that the feet of men never trod. There she discarded her court robes, donned those of a common freeman, and bound herself to P'an-hu as his servant. He then led her over mountains and through valleys until they reached a cave in the rocks.

Now, the king sorely missed his daughter and he often sent men forth to search for her. However, the heavens would always rain, the mountain peaks would shake, and clouds would so darken the sky that they could not reach where she was.

Nearly three years passed. The princess had given birth to six boys and six girls when P'an-hu died. Their offspring married one another; they wove

---

1. The tribal name "Man" is completely unrelated to the English word designating a human being. The Man people lived in the southeast reaches of the Chinese empire.

cloth from the bark of trees dyed with the juices of berries and fruits— for they loved colorful garments— and they cut the cloth to fit their tails.

Later, their mother returned to the palace and the king sent envoys to welcome the children— this time the heavens did not rain. But their clothes were outlandish, their speech barbaric; they squatted on their haunches to eat and drink, and preferred mountain wilds to cities. The king acceded to their wishes and gave them famed mountains and broad swamps for their home. They were called Man barbarians.

The Man barbarians appear stupid but are in fact crafty. They are contented in the lands they inhabit and set store by their old ways. They believe they were given strange capacities by the will of Heaven and therefore they act under laws not common to others. They farm and they trade but have no documents to show at borders, no identifications or tallies, nor do they have rents or taxes of any sort. They live in small villages where the headmen are given tallies and wear crowns of otter-skin, for the Man secure their food from the waters.

Presently the commanderies of Liang, Han, Pa, Shu, Wu-ling, Ch'ang-sha, and Lu-chiang are all inhabited by Man barbarians. They eat rice-gruel mixed with the flesh of various fish; they pound on containers and howl to honor P'an-hu with sacrifices of gourds. This custom has lasted until the present day. These are the reasons for the saying:

> Red buttocks, yellow trousers do
> Reveal descendants of P'an-hu.
>
> *Translated by James I. Crump and Kenneth DeWoskin*

Liang Wen and Lord Kao-shan

During the Han, Liang Wen from the Ch'i area was given to Taoist practices. He added a room three or four beams wide onto his house as an offertory. His altar was covered with a large, dark drape and he spent much time in there.

This is how things went for more than a decade. Then, because of the numerous sacrifices directed to the shrine, one day the sound of a voice suddenly issued from beneath the altar cloth.

"I am the Lord Kao-shan," [1] it said. The god had quite an appetite for food and drink and was efficacious in curing illness. Liang Wen was very attentive and respectful toward it.

And so things went for several more years until one day the god invited Liang Wen to come under the altar drapes. There Wen found the god very drunk, but he respectfully asked if he could reverently look upon the sacred countenance.

---

1. Meaning "high hill," where goats are most often pastured.

"Stretch thy hand forth," said Kao-shan, and Liang Wen did as the god bade him. He was then allowed to finger the god's chin. His hand came in contact with quite a long beard. Gradually and carefully Wen wrapped the beard around his fingers— and suddenly gave a great tug!

There was the sound of a loud goat bleat. Wen's congregation all jumped to their feet in surprise and helped him drag the god forth. It was a goat belonging to the house of Yüan Shu! Seven or eight years before, the family goat had disappeared and the Yüan family had no idea where it had gone.

They slaughtered the goat and there were no manifestations after that.

Translated by James I. Crump and Kenneth DeWoskin

205
Strange Tales from Make-Do Studio

P'u Sung-ling (1640–1715)

The Mural

While staying in the capital, Meng Lung-t'an of Kiangsi and Master of Letters Chu once happened upon a monastery. Neither the shrine-hall nor the meditation room was very spacious, and only one old monk was found putting up within. Seeing the guests enter, the monk straightened up his clothes, went to greet them, and showed them around the place. An image of Zen

---

P'u Sung-ling, possibly of distant Persian, Turkic, or Arabic ancestry, passed the regional examinations for the Bachelor of Letters degree at age nineteen, but was repeatedly rejected in numerous subsequent provincial examinations, well into his seventies. P'u spent most of his life teaching in a country schoolroom. Through poverty and austerity, he learned to identify closely with the common people.

Most of the stories in *Strange Tales from Make-Do Studio* (*Liao chai chih yi*) were collected from various sources, while others were made up by the author himself. All of them were exquisitely created and elegantly constructed. Although the collection is extremely well known, few Chinese could read it in the original because of the difficulty of the allusive classical book language in which it was written. Instead, the recondite tales were made known to the wider public through dramatic presentations, oral storytelling, vernacular paraphrases, and other types of popularizations. Ironically, P'u was also the author of earthy, colloquial arias and plays of his own that were quite opposite in character to the highly classical *Strange Tales*. Indeed, so dissimilar are these two types of writing that it is hard to imagine they are from the same hand.

The comments by the Chronicler of the Tales that occur at the conclusion of most of the stories are by the author himself. These are modeled after the comments at the end of each chapter by the Grand Historian, Ssu-ma Ch'ien, in his *Shih chi* (see selection 160, unnumbered note and selection 173, note 10) and often give a wry twist to the narrative or offer bitter social criticism without being overtly and offensively didactic.

Master Pao-chih [1] stood in the shrine-hall. On either side-wall were painted fine murals with lifelike human figures. The east wall depicted the Buddhist legend of "Heavenly Maidens Scattering Flowers." Among the figures was a young girl with flowing hair [2] with a flower in her hand and a faint smile on her face. Her cherry-red lips were on the verge of moving, and the liquid pools of her eyes seemed to stir with wavelike glances. After gazing intently for some time, Chu's self-possession began to waver, and his thoughts grew so abstracted that he fell into a trance. His body went adrift as if floating on mist; suddenly he was inside the mural. Peak upon peak of palaces and pavilions made him feel as if he was beyond this earth. An old monk was preaching the Dharma on a dais, around which stood a large crowd of viewers in robes with their right shoulders bared out of respect. Chu mingled in among them.

Before long, he felt someone tugging furtively at his sleeve. He turned to look, and there was the girl with flowing hair giving him a dazzling smile. She tripped abruptly away, and he lost no time following her along a winding walkway into a small chamber. Once there, he hesitated to approach any farther. When she turned her head and raised the flower with a beckoning motion, he went across to her in the quiet, deserted chamber. Swiftly he embraced her and, as she did not put up much resistance, they grew intimate. When it was over she told him not to make a sound and left, closing the door behind her. That night she came again. After two days of this, the girl's companions realized what was happening and searched together until they found the scholar.

"A little gentleman is already growing in your belly, but still you wear those flowing tresses, pretending to be a maiden," they said teasingly. Holding out hairpins and earrings, they pressured her to put her hair up in the coiled knot of a married woman, which she did in silent embarrassment. One of the girls said, "Sisters, let's not outstay our welcome." At this the group left all in a titter.

Looking at the soft, cloudlike chignon piled atop her head and her phoenix ringlets curved low before her ears, the scholar was more struck by her charms than when she had worn her hair long. Seeing that no one was around, he began to make free with her. His heart throbbed at her musky fragrance but, before they had quite finished their pleasure, the heavy tread of leather boots was heard. A clanking of chains and manacles was followed by clamorous, arguing voices. The girl got up in alarm. Peering out, they saw an officer dressed in armor, his face black as lacquer, with chains in one hand and a mace in the other. Standing around him were all the maidens. "Is this all of you?" asked the officer. "We're all here," they answered. "Report

1. A monk who lived during the Northern and Southern dynasties (420–589).
2. Her hair was not bound up, signifying that she was unmarried.

if any of you are concealing a man from the lower world. Don't bring trouble on yourselves." "We aren't," said the maidens in unison. The officer turned around and looked malevolently in the direction of the chamber, giving every appearance of an intention to search it. The girl's face turned pale as ashes in fear. "Quick, hide under the bed," she told Chu in panic. She opened a little door in the wall and was gone in an instant. Chu lay prostrate, hardly daring to take a little breath. Soon he heard the sound of boots stumping into, then back out of, the room. Before long, the din of voices gradually receded. He regained some composure, though the sound of passersby discussing the matter could be heard frequently outside the door. After cringing there for quite some time, he heard ringing in his ears and felt a burning ache in his eyes. Though the intensity of these sensations threatened to overwhelm him, there was no choice but to listen quietly for the girl's return. He was reduced to the point that he no longer recalled where he had been before coming here.

Just then his friend Meng Lung-t'an, who had been standing in the shrine-hall, found that Chu had disappeared in the blink of an eye. Perplexed, he asked the monk what had happened. "He has gone to hear a sermon on the Dharma," said the monk laughingly. "Where?" asked Meng. "Not far," was the answer. After a moment, the monk tapped on the wall with his finger and called, "Why do you tarry so long, my good patron?" Presently there appeared on the wall an image of Chu standing motionless with his head cocked to one side as if listening to something. "You have kept your traveling companion waiting a long time," called the monk again. Thereupon he drifted out of the mural and down to the floor. He stood woodenly, his mind like burned-out ashes, with eyes staring straight ahead and legs wobbling. Meng was terribly frightened, but in time calmed down enough to ask what had happened. It turned out that Chu had been hiding under the bed when he heard a thunderous knocking, so he came out of the room to listen for the source of the sound.

They looked at the girl holding the flower and saw, instead of flowing hair, a high coiled chignon on her head. Chu bowed down to the old monk in amazement and asked the reason for this. "Illusion is born in the mind. How can a poor mendicant like myself explain it?" laughed the monk. Chu was dispirited and cast down; Meng was shaken and confused. Together they walked down the shrine-hall steps and left.

The Chronicler of the Tales comments: " 'Illusion is born in the mind.' These sound like the words of one who has found the truth. A wanton mind gives rise to visions of lustfulness. The mind dominated by lust gives rise to a state of fear. The Bodhisattva made it possible for ignorant persons to attain realization for themselves. All the myriad transformations of illusion are nothing but the movements of the human mind itself. The old monk spoke in earnest solicitude, but regrettably there is no sign that the youth found enlightenment in his words and entered the mountains with hair unbound to seek the truth."

Translated by Denis C. Mair and Victor H. Mair

The Taoist of Lao Mountain [1]

In our district lived scholar Wang, the seventh son of an old family. From youth onward he was attracted to Taoist arts. Hearing that immortals abounded on Lao Mountain, he packed his books on his back and set out there on an adventure. Climbing to the top of a peak, Wang came to a Taoist temple set in a wild, secluded spot. A Taoist with white hair hanging past his collar was sitting on a bast mat. He had about him an otherworldly air that was graceful and lofty. Scholar Wang made obeisance to him and struck up a conversation. The Taoist's talk impressed him as quite mysterious and subtle. Wang asked to be accepted as his disciple, to which he replied, "I am afraid you are too soft and lazy to work hard."

"Oh, but I can," answered Wang. The Taoist had a crowd of acolytes, all of whom came together at dusk. Having saluted each of them, Wang settled down in the hermitage.

At the crack of dawn the Taoist woke Wang, gave him an ax, and made him go to gather firewood with the others. Wang did exactly as he was told. After more than a month of this, his hands and feet had calluses on top of calluses. Unable to bear the toil, he nursed secret intentions of returning home. One evening on his return he saw two men drinking with his master. The sun had already set but no lamps or candles had yet been lit, so the master cut paper in the shape of a mirror and pasted it on the wall. Suddenly a light as bright as the moon's flooded the room, making the tiniest hairs visible. The acolytes in attendance ran back and forth at the guests' bidding. One of the guests said, "It's a beautiful night for good times. We ought to share them with everyone here." The Taoist picked up a pitcher of wine from the table and began to pour some for each acolyte, urging them to drink their fill. Wang thought to himself, "How can a pitcher of wine suffice for seven or eight people?" Each of them hunted up a drinking vessel. They vied to see who would be first to drain his cup. Their only fear was that the pitcher was empty, but when they went to pour from it again they were astonished to find that the wine had not gone down in the slightest. Soon another guest said, "You have been nice enough to give us moonlight to drink by, but there is still no entertainment. Why don't you call the goddess of the moon to come?" At this the Taoist tossed a chopstick into the moon and a beautiful woman appeared out of the circle of light. At first she was not even a foot

1. An old sacred spot for Taoists on the Shantung coast of Chiao-chou Bay.

tall, but she grew to normal size as she descended to the floor. Her slender waist and graceful neck moved through the fluttering gyrations of the Dance of the Rainbow Skirt and Feathered Blouse.[2] To the tempo of the dance she sang,

> Immortal of the mountains,
> Is it true you're bound for home?
> Will you leave me all alone
> In this icy crystal dome?

Her silvery voice was as piercing as a flute. At the end of the song she arose with a sweeping motion, jumped up on the table and, in the space of an astonished glance, was already a chopstick again. The three men laughed boisterously.

The other guest spoke up, "This evening has been wonderful, but the wine is getting the better of me. Would it be all right if we had a farewell drink in the palace of the moon?" The three men moved their mats and slowly floated into the moon. The acolytes saw the three seated in the moon drinking, their features distinct as reflections in a mirror. After a time the moon gradually dimmed. When the acolytes brought a lighted candle, they found the Taoist sitting alone, his guests nowhere to be seen. The delicacies on the table were just as before, and the moon on the wall was nothing more than a disk of paper.

"Did you have enough to drink?" the Taoist asked the acolytes.

"Enough," they said.

"Then you ought to go right to bed. Don't let this interfere with gathering wood and kindling."

The acolytes said "yes" and retired.

Wang's intention of leaving subsided out of heartfelt admiration. But after another month had passed the grinding toil became too much for him, and the Taoist would not pass on even a single magical technique. Unable to wait any longer, Wang took his leave, saying, "I came a hundred miles to study under such an immortal master as yourself. Even though I cannot learn the art of everlasting life, there may perhaps be some small skill you could impart that would appease my wish for learning. For the past two or three months all I have done is go out to gather wood in the morning and return in the evening. When I was at home, I was not used to this kind of hard work."

The Taoist answered with a laugh, "I said from the start that you would not be able to stand hard work, and you have proven me right. I will send you off tomorrow morning."

2. A famous dance which flourished in palaces during the T'ang dynasty (618–907).

"I have labored for many days. If you could just impart some insignificant part of your art, my coming would not be in vain." The Taoist asked what art he hoped to learn.

Wang answered, "I have often noticed that walls are no hindrance to your free motion. I would be satisfied to learn the method of such magic."

The Taoist gave his assent with a laugh. Then he taught Wang the words of a spell and told him to chant it through by himself, at which he cried, "Go through." Wang faced the wall, not daring to walk into it. Again the Taoist cried, "Try to go through it!" Doing as he was told, Wang gingerly approached the wall, but it proved unyielding to his forward movement.

"Lower your head and go through quickly. Don't hold back," instructed the Taoist. So Wang backed several steps away from the wall and ran toward it. When he came to the wall it seemed not be there at all. Turning around to look, he found that he was already outside the building. Overjoyed, he went back in to thank his master. The Taoist said, "You must live chastely after your return, or the spell will not work." Then he gave Wang money for the trip home and sent him off.

Upon reaching home Wang boasted that he had met with an immortal and that now his power was such that no solid wall could stop him. His wife found this hard to believe. Wang stood several feet from a wall and ran headlong against it as he had done before, but this time his head smacked against the hard wall and he tumbled backward. His wife helped him up and looked at the goose egg rising moundlike on his forehead. Shamed but incited by her ridicule into a fury, he raved that the old Taoist was nothing but a reprobate.

The Chronicler of the Tales comments: "No one who hears of this incident can keep from laughing out loud, but those who laugh do not realize that the Scholar Wangs of this world are by no means few and far between. Take the case of a worthless official who would 'rather swallow poison than medicines.' A 'boil-sucking, hemorrhoid-licking' sort of person might cater to his wishes by advocating brutal, self-aggrandizing policies and inveigle him, saying, 'You need only adhere to such and such a policy—nothing will stand in your way.' The first time he tries, it might yield some small measure of success, thus giving him the idea that such policy can be applied to all cases under heaven. Those who are taken in by this will not stop until they run headlong into a solid wall and topple over backward."

Translated by Denis C. Mair and Victor H. Mair

The Cricket

During the Hsüan-te reign period (1426–1435) of the Ming dynasty, cricket-keeping was a popular amusement in the palace. The insects were levied

annually from the populace. Live crickets were not originally a Shensi product until a magistrate in Hua-yin county who was anxious to win favor with
his superiors presented one, which was tried in the ring and found to be an
outstanding fighter. From then on Hua-yin county was charged with providing crickets to the court regularly. The magistrate delegated the responsibility
to the headman in each ward. Young idlers in the marketplace kept the best
of them in cages, forcing prices up by cornering the market. Cunning ward
administrators used this as an excuse to impose a head tax on the peasants.
For every cricket that was requisitioned, several families were driven into
bankruptcy.

In the district there was a man named Ch'eng Ming, a long unsuccessful
candidate for the Bachelor of Letters degree. The crafty ward administrator,
seeing that Ch'eng was impractical and slow of speech, recommended him
for the position of headman. Ch'eng made numerous futile attempts to free
himself from the obligations of this office. Before a year had passed his
meager resources were used up. Then came the cricket levy. Ch'eng did not
dare collect money from the households, nor could he fulfill the duty out of
his own funds. He was so despondent he wanted to kill himself.

"What good would killing yourself do?" said his wife. "It would be better
to look for a cricket yourself. There is a slight chance you might find one."

This made sense to Ch'eng. He went out in the mornings, and returned
at nightfall, bamboo pail and wire cage in hand, poking under stones and
opening burrows amid crumbling walls and thick growths of grass. There was
nothing he did not try, but it was no use. The few that he did manage to
catch were too puny to fit the regulations. The magistrate's deadline was
rigorously enforced, and he was given a total of a hundred strokes with a cane
over a period of ten days. Blood and pus oozed from his buttocks and, what
was worse, he was unable to go looking for the insects at all. He tossed and
turned on his bed, his mind filled with thoughts of suicide.

It was then that a hunchbacked shamaness who performed divinations
with the help of a spirit-familiar came to the village. Ch'eng's wife scraped
up a sum of money and went to call on her. Smartly dressed young women
and white-haired old ladies were milling around the door. Inside the house
was a curtained-off sanctum, with an altar standing outside the curtain.
Petitioners lit incense in the censer and kowtowed twice, while the shamaness
stood to one side looking off into space and pronouncing an invocation for
them, her lips contorted with unintelligible mutterings. Everyone stood stiffly
listening until shortly a piece of paper, bearing a message that dealt with the
petitioner's troubles, was thrown out from within the curtain. The messages
were never off by a hair.

Ch'eng's wife placed her money on the table, lit incense, and kowtowed
like those before. After the time it takes to eat a meal passed by, the curtain
moved and a slip of paper was tossed out onto the ground. Picking it up, she

saw not words but a drawing depicting a group of buildings, apparently those of a monastery. Behind it at the foot of a hill was a jumble of odd-looking boulders. There, at the edge of a dense bramble thicket, couched a shiny black cricket. Beside it was a toad that seemed to be on the point of leaping. She spread the drawing out and pored over it, unable to make out its meaning. Still, the cricket was just what she had been looking for. She folded the paper up, tucked it away, and took it back to show Ch'eng who, after much reflection, wondered if the picture were not telling him where to hunt for a cricket. Careful scrutiny of the scene in the drawing revealed a close resemblance to the Great Buddha Abbey east of the village.

Ch'eng dragged himself out of bed, propped himself up with a cane and proceeded, drawing in hand, to the rear of the monastery. The overgrown ruins of an ancient tomb stood before him. Following the edge of the tomb, he saw boulders squatting one on top of the other like fish scales, precisely as in the drawing. He walked slowly through a jungle of weeds, cocking his head to catch the slightest sound and looking for all the world as if he were searching for a needle or a mustard seed. He could no longer maintain the intentness of eyes, ears, and mind, but he had not yet seen or heard a cricket. He was still groping about, when suddenly to his great amazement a wart-headed toad leaped from underfoot. He stayed close behind it as it ducked into a dense growth of grass. He stepped gingerly into the grass, spreading the blades apart with his hands to get a better look. There, crouching at the base of a bramble-bush was an insect. He hurriedly grabbed for it, but it ducked into a hole in the stones. He poked at it with a sharp blade of grass, but it would not come out. Finally, by pouring water from his bucket into the hole, he was able to flush the robust-looking cricket out. He gave chase and caught it. A closer look showed it to have a thick torso, a long tail, a blue-green neck, and metallic wings. Great was Ch'eng's joy as he put it in the cage and returned home.

The whole family rejoiced as if he had found a treasure more precious than the legendary piece of jade worth fifteen cities.[1] They put it in a basin and nourished it on crabmeat and chestnuts, going to every extreme to give it the best of care. They planned to keep it until the deadline, when Ch'eng would use it to discharge his official duty.

But one day Ch'eng's nine-year-old son, seeing that his father was out, furtively lifted the lid off the basin. The cricket hopped straight out, so quickly that the boy could not grab it. He jumped and caught it in his hand,

---

1. An allusion to Pien Ho of the state of Ch'u during the Spring and Autumn period, who presented two kings successively with jade enclosed in an uncut stone and each time was accused of trying to pass off sham jade as genuine and punished by the loss of one of his feet. When the third king came to the throne, he summoned Pien, had the stone carved up, and found the jade inside. The jade was later claimed by a king to be worth the price of fifteen cities.

breaking off a leg and cracking its abdomen. In a few short moments it was dead. The terrified boy ran crying to tell his mother. Her face paled to the hue of ashes at what she heard.

"A bad seed, that's what you are!" she cursed him loudly. "Your day of doom will not be long now! When your father comes home he'll settle accounts with you." The boy ran out sniveling. Ch'eng soon returned. When his wife told him what had happened, it was as if a heap of freezing snow had been dumped on his head. He called angrily for his son but the boy was nowhere to be seen. Soon afterward, they found his body in a well. Ch'eng's rage turned to sorrow. Stricken half-dead with grief, he struck his head on the ground and cried out to heaven. Husband and wife went inside and each turned their sobbing faces toward separate corners. No cooking fire was lit in their thatched hut that night. They had come to their wit's end and could only stare dumbly at one another. As the day drew to an end, they prepared to wrap their son in a grass mat for burial. Touching him, they found that he was now breathing haltingly. Joyfully they placed him on the bed. In the middle of the night he regained consciousness, which relieved his parents somewhat, but his breath came in gasps and he had the vacant look of a sleepwalker. Looking at the empty cricket cage was enough to rob them of breath and make their voices die in their throats, but they dared not question their son again. Their eyes did not close for the whole night. When the sun in the east began its course through the heavens they lay down stiffly, brooding sleeplessly.

Suddenly there was a chirping outside their door. They got up in amazement to observe; there was the cricket looking as sound as ever. Jumping for joy, they ran to catch it, but it gave a chirp and hopped rapidly away. Ch'eng covered it with a cupped hand, but he seemed to have grasped nothing but thin air. As soon as he lifted his hand, the cricket leaped swiftly out from under it. He followed it closely, but lost it when it rounded the corner of a wall. As he walked about distractedly, looking all around him, he saw a cricket crouching on the wall. A careful look showed that it was short, small, and reddish-black in color—certainly not the one he had been chasing. It was worthless to him because of its small size. He went on walking aimlessly and staring in all directions for the one he had been chasing. All of a sudden the little cricket jumped off the wall and landed on the side of his robe. It was built like a mole cricket, with finely veined wings, a square head, and long neck. It impressed him as a good specimen, so he was glad to keep it. His plan was to present it at the yamen, but the thought that it might not meet the magistrate's expectations made him shudder, so he decided to observe how it would perform in a fight.

A young man known as a busybody in the village was keeping a cricket which he had named Crabshell Blue. He matched it daily with the crickets of other young men, and it always emerged victorious. He was holding onto it until he could turn a nice profit, but nobody would pay the high price he asked. One day this young man went to Ch'eng's house for a visit. Seeing the cricket Ch'eng was keeping, he had to stifle a laugh with his hand. He took out his cricket and put it into the cage. Ch'eng was discomfited at the sight of its huge build. He dared not pick up the gauntlet, but the young man insisted. It occurred to Ch'eng that keeping an inferior specimen would be useless anyway, and that he might as well set his cricket against the other for a laugh. Both insects were placed in a fighting basin. The small one crouched motionless, looking as foolish as a wooden chicken.[2] The young man guffawed once more as he used a boar bristle to poke at the cricket's antennae. Still it did not move, provoking the young man into another burst of laughter. He prodded it repeatedly. The insect exploded with rage and ran at its opponent. They attacked one another with flying leaps, rousing themselves to battle with defiant chirps. In an instant the small cricket jumped up, its antennae and tail stiffly erect, and bit down on its opponent's neck. The frightened young man pulled them apart and put an end to the fight. The small cricket drew itself up and chirped proudly, as if it were reporting victory to its master.

Ch'eng was overjoyed. As he and his guests were admiring the winner, a chicken caught sight of it, ran over, and delivered a peck at the small cricket. Ch'eng stood there numb with dread and cried out in alarm. Luckily the chicken's beak had missed its mark; the cricket leaped a foot and some inches away. The chicken lunged forward and bore down upon it. Before Ch'eng could come to its rescue, the insect was under the chicken's claws; he turned pale and stamped his feet helplessly. But in the next moment he saw the chicken stretching its neck and fluttering about. Much to his amazed delight, upon closer inspection he found the cricket hanging tenaciously onto the fowl's comb. He picked it up, put it in its cage, and presented it to the magistrate the next day.

The magistrate berated Ch'eng angrily for bringing such a puny cricket, and he was not convinced by Ch'eng's account of the cricket's extraordinary prowess. The cricket was tried in the ring against others of its kind: all were vanquished. When it was tried against a chicken, the outcome confirmed Ch'eng's story.[3] The magistrate thereupon rewarded him and presented the cricket to the provincial governor. The governor, greatly delighted, presented it to the emperor in a golden cage along with a memorial detailing its abilities.

After the champion was taken into the palace, all sorts of unusual crickets, such as "butterflies," "mantises," "oily beaters," and "silky green foreheads"

---

2. A fable in the *Chuang Tzu* (see selection 8) describes a superb gamecock as having such a placid exterior that it seemed to be made of wood.

3. Cockfighting was a popular betting sport in China from a very early period (see selection 17).

were tried against it, but none could get the better of it. When it heard the music of lutes and zithers it hopped to the beat, which made people marvel at it all the more. The emperor was so pleased that he called for the provincial governor and gave him thoroughbred horses and satins for clothing. The governor did not forget the source of his good fortune; before long word was going around that the magistrate was an "outstanding" official. The delighted magistrate released Ch'eng from his duties as headman and instructed the civil examiner to grant him admission to the district academy.

A little more than a year later Ch'eng's son regained his faculties, claiming that he had been transformed into an agile, combative cricket and that today his soul had finally reentered his body. The provincial governor rewarded Ch'eng generously. Within a few years Ch'eng possessed fifteen hundred acres of fields; pavilions and storied buildings in such number that thousands of rafters had been used to roof them over; and sheep and horses numbering in the hundreds. The furs he wore and the horses he rode when he went out could not have been equaled by an aristocratic family.

The Chronicler of the Tales comments: "The emperor may use something once on a whim and give it no more thought, but for the people who carry out his wishes it becomes a fixed article of tribute. With the greed of officials and the cruelty of administrators on top of this, there is no end to hardships which make peasants give up their wives and sell their children. Thus, every time the emperor takes a step, the lives of the people are affected. There is no room for carelessness. Ch'eng's case was unique: after being reduced to poverty by the depradations of corrupt officials, a cricket brought him wealth enough to go about flaunting furs and fine horses. Back in the days when he was beaten for failing to fulfill his duties as headman, how could he have foreseen that such a fortune was in store for him? Heaven made the provincial governor and magistrate enjoy the benefits of the cricket's favor as a means of rewarding one man's honesty. When the Taoist master in the old story perfected the elixir and rose to heaven, immortality redounded even to his dogs and chickens. There is much truth in this!"

Translated by Denis C. Mair and Victor H. Mair

206

A Chi Yün Sampler
Sketches from the Cottage for the Contemplation of Subtleties

Chi Yün (1724–1805)

I

The following was told to me by Wu Hui-shu, a member of the Royal Academy.

There was a certain doctor whose nature it was to be earnest. One night,

These stories are taken from a large collection of approximately twelve hundred stories, tales, anecdotes, and notes brought together by Chi Yün at the end of the eighteenth century. Its author was one of the three chief editors of the famous Ch'ing imperial library known as the "Complete Library in Four Divisions [classics, histories, thinkers, and collected works] of Literature" (Ssu-k'u ch'üan-shu) finished in 1782. The original was installed in the "Pavilion of the Pool of Literature" (Wen-yüan ko). Six copies were distributed to various parts of the empire, one of these being placed in the "Pavilion of the Ford to Literature" (Wen-chin ko) at Luan-yang, where the Ch'ing court maintained a summer retreat. The magnitude of the task of setting up these copies can be appreciated from the fact that the "Complete Library in Four Divisions" was composed of nearly eighty thousand fascicles. The catalog of this library, for which Chi Yün was largely responsible, is still recognized as the most complete and important bibliographical work on traditional Chinese literature.

The Sketches (Yüeh-wei ts'ao-t'ang pi-chi) originally appeared between 1789 and 1798 in a series of five parts (hence the five prefaces), which were assembled in their present form by one of Chi's students, Sheng Shih-yen, in 1800. The titles of the five parts convey the deceptively casual manner in which the sketches were composed, yet behind the facade of entertaining stories and anecdotes lies a serious moral purpose. They are: A Record of Whiling Away the Summer at Luan-yang, That's the Way I Heard It, Miscellany from the Old House West of the Scholar Tree, Listen If You Will, and A Sequel to the Record of Whiling Away the Summer at Luan-yang. Luan-yang was located in Ch'eng-te district of Hopei Province. The title of the second part is based on a Buddhist expression: ju shih wo wen, a standard Chinese translation of the Sanskrit evaṃ mayā śrutam ("Thus have I heard [from the Buddha]"). Chi Yün styled himself the "Man of the Way Who Kibitzes at Go."

The sketches are brief, seldom running to more than a page of Chinese text. The subject usually has ostensibly to do with the supernatural, but a hint of satire is almost always present. Virtually without exception, the supernatural forces in these tales adopt a favorable attitude toward virtuous people, genuine scholars, filial sons, and exemplary officials. On the other hand, these supernatural forces take a negative attitude toward immoral individuals, pedants, disrespectful youth, and evil officials. In effect, the supernatural agents ironically represent normative social values. It should be emphasized that this is accomplished without heavy-handed didacticism, a fatal error to which Chi's many imitators succumbed. These sketches conspicuously bear the mark of rich creativity and make for delightful reading. A relatively large sampling of Chi Yün's work is given here because it is virtually unknown outside China except by a few specialists. Even within China, Sketches is inadequately known, perhaps because it has long been overshadowed by the brilliantly allusive Strange Tales from Make-Do Studio by P'u Sung-ling (see selection 205) and the acerbically witty What the Master [Confucius] Would Not Discuss (Tzu pu yü) by Yüan Mei (see selection 84).

an old lady brought him a pair of gold bracelets with which she wished to buy an abortifacient. The doctor was appalled by the request and so steadfastly refused it. The next evening, she came again bringing an additional two pearl hairpins. The doctor was all the more appalled and so forcibly sent her away.

More than half a year later, he suddenly dreamed that he was arrested by an officer from the nether world. The officer stated that someone had accused him of killing a person. When they arrived in the nether world, a young woman with disheveled hair and a red strip of cloth bound about her neck tearfully made her plaint of being denied medicine that she had sought.

"Medicine," said the doctor, "is for the preservation of human life. How could I have dared to kill a person for personal gain? You ruined yourself through adultery. How am I at fault?"

"When I begged you for the medicine," said the woman, "the fetus had not yet developed. If I had been able to abort it, I would not have died. It was a matter of breaking up an unconscious clot of blood to preserve a life that was on the verge of extinction. Since I could not obtain the medicine, there was no way I could avoid childbirth. In the end, the fate of the baby was to suffer horribly by being strangled. And I was so beset that all I could do was hang myself. In wishing to preserve one life, you ended up destroying two lives! If the responsibility for this crime does not fall upon you, then upon whom does it fall?"

"What you have stated is a consideration of the particular circumstances of this case," the judge of the nether world declared with a deep sigh. "What he, the doctor, insists upon is the principle of the matter. Since the Sung dynasty, there has been a stubborn insistence upon a single principle without estimating the advantages and disadvantages of actual situations. It's not just this man alone! Case dismissed!"

The judge banged the table and the doctor awoke with a start.

II

The following was told to me by Wang Hsiao-yüan, a member of the Royal Academy.

There was an old monk whose tears began to fall freely as he was passing by a butchery. A bystander who was surprised by this asked him why he did so.

"It's a long story," replied the monk. "I can remember events from two other lives. In my first life, I was a butcher and I died when I was a little over thirty. My celestial soul was trussed up and pulled away by several persons. The judge in the nether world rebuked me for the enormity of my murderous karma and had me sent away in custody to the universal spiritual king[1] to

---

1. *Chuan-lun* (Shanskrit *cakravartī*). I suspect that this is an error for *lun-chuan* (Sanskrit *saṁsāra*), "transmigration," hence "to undergo transmigratory retribution for my evils."

receive retribution for my evil. My senses were blurred and confused, as though I were drunk or dreaming. And my brain was so hot that I could not endure it. Suddenly, it seemed to be cool and I found myself in a pigpen.

"After I had been weaned, I noticed that humans were unclean and realized that the food they were giving me was contaminated.[2] But my hunger pains were excruciating and my inwards felt as though they were being torn in shreds. There was nothing I could do but eat what they gave me.

"Later, I gradually learned pig language and often asked questions of my fellow creatures, many of whom could remember events from former incarnations. But we were quite incapable of talking to human beings. For the most part, we were aware that we would be slaughtered. At such times, we would grunt and groan with worry. Feeling sorry for ourselves, we would constantly have traces of tears on our eyelashes.

"The body of a pig is stiff and heavy so that, at the peak of summer, we suffered from the heat. Only by wallowing in the muddy water could we obtain a measure of relief, but we seldom got the chance to do that. A pig's bristles are sparse and stubby so that, in the dead of winter, we suffered from the cold. Compared to ours, the fur of dogs and sheep is as soft and thick as that of a mythical beast.

"When the time came for me to be seized, I knew that I couldn't escape. Nevertheless, I hopped about and ran away, hoping that I could delay for a while. After my pursuers caught up with me, they trampled upon my neck and head; they tore at my shanks and pettitoes. They tied up my legs with a rope which cut deeply into my bones. It was as painful as if I were being sliced with a knife.

"Sometimes we were transported by boat or cart and then, layer after layer, we'd press upon each other. My ribs were nearly broken; my veins and arteries surged and choked; my belly nearly burst. Sometimes they carried me by sticking a pole between my legs, which was even more painful than being shackled and fettered. When I arrived at the butchery, I was thrown upon the ground, which shook my heart and spleen so that they almost shattered. I might have died that very day or remained tied up for several days.

"What was even harder to endure was to see the cleaver and chopping board to the left, the pot full of water for scalding to the right—without knowing what pain they would cause when they touched my body. Whereupon I would be seized with paroxysms of uncontrollable fear. Then, again, I often looked at my own body and wondered into how many unknowable pieces I would one day be sundered and in whose cup I would serve for a soup. I was so despondent that I nearly expired.

---

2. *Hui* is an adjective which refers to the impurity of the world in contrast to the Pure Land of Mahāyāna Buddhism. It also refers to leftover food or food that has been touched by someone with an illness.

"When the time came for me to be slaughtered, my eyes went dim with fright as soon as the butcher tugged at me and all of my legs went limp. It felt as though my heart were surging wildly to left and right and that my soul flew right up out of my head and then fell back down. When I saw the gleaming light of the blade, I dared not look at it directly but only closed my eyes and waited for the cutting and cleaving. The butcher began by stabbing his knife-blade into my throat and then shook and twisted it, allowing my blood to drain into a basin. The pain was such that words cannot describe it. I hoped for death but it would not come, so all I could do was utter a long squeal. After the blood was emptied, the butcher pierced my heart, which caused me to suffer so greatly that I could no longer make any sound.

"Gradually, my senses blurred and I became confused as though drunk or in a dream. It was as though I were in the early stages of transmigration. A considerable time passed before I awoke sufficiently to see that I had taken on human form. The judge in the nether world allowed me to be a man again since I still had some good karma from previous lives.

"That is why in the present life, when I just now saw this pig, I lamented its suffering. So I thought of the past when I had undergone such suffering. I also felt sorry for this man who is wielding the knife and who in the future will undergo such suffering. I was so enwrapped by these thoughts of the past, present, and future that, before I knew what was happening, my tears began to fall."

Upon hearing this, the butcher threw his knife on the ground at once and changed his occupation to that of vegetable seller.

III

The following was told to me by Sung Meng-ch'üan.

A Mister Sun O-shan once fell ill aboard a boat at Kao-yu.[3] Suddenly, it seemed as if he had strolled over to the river bank and that his feelings had become exceedingly invigorated. Soon there was a man who led him as he walked along. Trancelike, he was not fully aware of what was happening to him nor did he ask any questions. He followed along until they came to a house, the gateway to which was neat and tidy. Gradually, they made their way into an inner chamber where he saw a young woman who was at that moment sitting on a mat of rushes used in childbirth. He wanted to retreat but a hand was pressing him from behind so that he fell into a dazed unconsciousness.

After a long while, he gradually revived but his body had shrunk to a small size. Nestled amidst the soft swaddling-clothes, he realized that he had been reborn and there was nothing he could do about it. He wished to speak but he felt a cold air enter through his fontanel which abruptly silenced him so that he could not utter a word. He looked around at the tables, couches, and

3. In Kiangsu province.

furnishings and saw clearly all the hanging couplets, calligraphy, and paintings.

On the third day, a maid picked up the baby to give him a bath, but her
hand slipped and he fell to the floor. Again he fell into a dazed unconsciousness. When he revived, he was still lying in the middle of the boat. A member
of his household told him, "You'd stopped breathing for three days but, since
your limbs were flexible and the area around your heart was still warm, we
didn't dare to prepare you for the coffin."

Mr. Sun hurriedly took a piece of paper and made a written statement on
it of all that he had seen and heard. He dispatched a messenger who was to
carry this, by way of a certain road, to such-and-such a house and who was to
tell them not to be unduly harsh in punishing the maid. Thereupon, he
leisurely related to his family all of the particulars.

He recovered from his illness that very day and went directly to the same
house. When he saw the maids and serving-women, they were all like old
acquaintances. The head of the house was old and childless. Face to face
with Mr. Sun, all he could do was sigh with regret and exclaim how strange
it was.

Recently, the same sort of thing happened to the Executive Agent, Meng
Chien-hsi. He too recalled the road to the gate of a certain house and, sure
enough, when he visited it, he found that a baby boy had been born there
that day but that the baby had died immediately. When I was on duty in the
palace not long ago, T'u Shih-ch'üan of the Royal Academy told me all the
circumstances in great detail. For the most part, it was similar to what Mr.
Sun O-shan had said, except that Sun recalled going but not returning
whereas Meng Chien-hsi was quite clear about both going and returning.
But there was the slight difference that Meng met his deceased wife on the
way and that, when he reached the house and went inside, he saw his wife
and the woman who was to be his new mother seated together.

Comment: The doctrine of transmigration of souls is disputed by the
Confucians. But the fact is that it happens all the time. The principle of
cause and effect is, of course, not to be falsified. It is just that these two
gentlemen momentarily entered the process of transmigration and then rapidly returned to their original bodies. For no apparent reason, this illusory
realm had been made manifest. Thus it cannot be explained on the basis of
principle alone. "The sages set aside without discussion what lies beyond the
world." [4] It is advisable to reserve judgment on that whereof one is uncertain.

IV

In the year 1784, there were many disastrous fires in the city of Tsinan. [5] At
the end of the fourth month of that year, a fire broke out again inside the

4. From chapter 2 of the *Chuang Tzu* (selection 8).
5. The capital of Shantung province.

south gate on West Cross Street. Spreading from east to west, the fire burned fiercely in the narrow alleys and raged violently through the cramped lanes.

There was a certain Mr. Chang who had a three-pillar hut on the north side of the road. He would have had time to get his family out before the flames reached it but, because his mother's coffin was inside, he tried first to think of a way to move it to safety. Soon, the situation was such that he, his wife, and their four children could not get out. They embraced the coffin and wept sorrowfully, swearing that they would perish with it.

At that very moment, a lieutenant-colonel of the governor's army was directing his troops in rescue operations. When he heard the faint sound of crying, he ordered his troops to climb up on the roofs in the alley behind. They followed the sound to its source and let down a strap with which to haul them out. But Chang and his wife called out together: "Our mother's coffin is here. How can we abandon it?"

The children called out likewise: "Our parents are willing to die for their parent. Shouldn't we be willing to die for our parents too?" Nor would they consent to go up.

Suddenly, the fire was upon them. The troops leaped over the roofs to flee from it and barely escaped with their lives. Imagining that the entire family had been reduced to ashes, all they could do was sigh in sympathy as they watched from a distance.

When the fire was extinguished and the inspectors came to their hut, amidst all the other houses, it alone remained unscathed. Most likely, a whirlwind had suddenly arisen and caused the fire to veer off to the north. It went around behind their hut and burned down a pawnshop belonging to their neighbor before it finally turned toward the west again. Were it not for some ghost or spirit protecting them, how could this have happened?

This matter was recorded and sent to me in the seventh month of 1793 by Mr. Chang Ch'ing-yüan, who is the principal of an academy in Te-chou.[6] It is similar to the matter about the widow which I included in the *Records of Whiling Away the Summer at Luan-yang*. But that a husband, his wife, and their children would all be of the same mind and will is even more so the rarest of the rare, for, "when two people are of the same mind, they have the strength to overcome the hardest obstacles."[7] How much more so with six people! "No sooner does the ordinary woman call out than thunder strikes down."[8] How much more so when there are six people, all of them truly devoted! "When the highest sincerity is attained, heaven, earth, and man are

6. Also in Shantung province.

7. From section eight of the first chapter of "The Great Appendix" in the *Classic of Changes* (see selections 3 and 4).

8. This sentence differs significantly from the sentence in the *Huai-nan Tzu*, whence it was borrowed, in having "calls out" instead of "invokes Heaven."

moved with sympathy."[9] Although one's life is fated, he cannot but try to reverse the tide of misfortune. "Human determination can transcend destiny."[10] This, too, is one way of putting it. Although the matter here related is "unusual news," one may aver that it bespeaks a common principle.

I am not acquainted with Chang Ch'ing-yüan and yet he has taken the trouble to send me this account through the mails. Inasmuch as he made certain that it was transmitted, one can get an idea of Chang's purpose. Consequently, I have edited what he wrote and recorded it here.

V

A man from Wu-yi[11] had gone flower-viewing with some of his friends and relatives at a Buddhist temple. Though the ground in front of the hall for storing the Tripiṭaka[12] was quite spacious and open, strange things often happened inside the hall. When night came, no one dared to sit next to the hall. But the man from Wu-yi, who was a self-appointed Neo-Confucian, calmly expressed his disbelief. In a state of drunken exhilaration, he was holding forth on the notion in Chang Tsai's "Western Inscription"[13] that all creation partakes of the same substance. While everyone present listened intently, night imperceptibly fell.

Suddenly, a stern voice railed at him from inside the hall: "At this very moment, many people are dying because of famine and pestilence. You are a local official. Since you have not considered advocating timely measures on behalf of the public such as distributing food and dispensing medicine, you should have availed yourself of this fine night to have a pleasant sleep behind the doors of your own house. At least that would not be out of character for the self-centered person that you are. Instead, here you prattle and twaddle away, lecturing on 'brotherhood with the people and identification with all creation.'[14] I wonder, even if you lecture straight on to daybreak, whether that can make any food for the people to eat or medicine for them to take? I'll just toss a brick at you and then we'll see if you lecture again on 'heresy not overcoming the truth'!"

Suddenly, a brick from the city wall came flying down with a crash like thunder, breaking the cups, plates, and the long, low table.

Startled, the man from Wu-yi went running out as he said: "May it not be

9. This is one variation of a frequently pronounced idea that, in part, goes back as early as the *Chuang Tzu.*

10. From the *Treatise on Reclusion* (*Kuei-ch'ien chih*).

11. In Hopei.

12. The Buddhist canon.

13. Perhaps the most succinct and authoritative statement of basic Neo-Confucian principles. Chang's dates are 1020–1077.

14. From the "Western Inscription" (see note 13).

that this apparition is an apparition simply because it does not believe in the theories of Ch'eng and Chu?" [15]

Slackening his pace, he sighed heavily and left.

VI

One summer night, Ma Ta-huan ("Great Return") [16] of Tung-kuang [17] had fallen asleep naked in the hall for storing the Tripiṭaka [18] of the Tzu-sheng ("Surpassing Aid") Temple when he felt someone tugging at his arm and saying: "Get up! Get up! Don't sully the Buddhist scriptures!"

When he awoke, he saw an old man at his side and asked, "Who are you?"

"I am the guardian spirit of the Tripiṭaka."

By nature, Ta-huan was both uninhibited and fearless. At the time, the light of the moon made it bright as day. So Ta-huan called the spirit to sit down and have a chat with him.

"Why, sir, are you protecting this canon?"

"Because I was so ordered by Heaven."

"The Confucian books are so numerous that they reach to the rafters and would spill out of an ox-cart, but I've never heard there's a spirit to protect them. May it be that Heaven is partial to the Buddhist scriptures?"

"Buddhism establishes its doctrine through the way of gods [19] in whom living beings either believe or not. Therefore it is protected by the gods. Confucianism establishes its doctrine through the way of men and all men ought to respect and protect it. This is also the reason why all men know they are to respect and protect it. There is no need to bother with spiritual powers. It is not because Heaven is partial to the Buddhist scriptures."

"Then does Heaven view the three doctrines as one?"

"Confucianism has as its substance the cultivation of self and, for its function, the government of men. Taoism has as its substance quietude and, for its function, flexibility. Buddhism has as its basis meditation [20] and, for its function, compassion. [21] Their fundamental purposes are each distinct and cannot be considered as one. But there is no difference with reference to their teaching men to do good, nor is there any difference in the assistance they afford to all creation. Since their ultimate aims are more or less the

15. The founders of Neo-Confucianism.

16. The usual understanding of this expression is that it is a reference to Taoist alchemical refining of cinnabar. Given the remarks which Mr. Ma makes about Taoism, it is ironic that he chose such a name for himself.

17. A district in Hopei.

18. See note 12.

19. This is a rather unusual application of a clause that occurs in commentaries to Hexagram 20 of the *Classic of Changes* (see selection 3).

20. *Ting* (Sanskrit *samādhi*).

21. *Tz'u* (Sanskrit *maitra* or *karuṇā*).

same, Heaven surely cannot but preserve them side by side. Yet the Confucian takes the people as the fulfillment of his Heaven-ordained being and exercises this basic principle in his own person. Buddhism and Taoism are both teachings that concentrate on the self and devote whatever energy remains to other beings. Therefore elucidation of the way of man is taken to be primary and elucidation of the way of spirits is taken to be supportive of that. Nor may all under heaven be ruled exclusively by Buddhism and Taoism. This is how they are not the same and yet the same, how they are the same and yet not the same. We may say that Confucianism is like the five staple grains; if one does not eat them for a single day, he will starve. If he goes several days without eating them, he will certainly die. Buddhism and Taoism are like medicines; one takes them at a crisis of life and death or when he is feeling overly strong emotions. They may be used to free one of grievance and grief or to dissipate melancholia. For these purposes, they are far more effective than Confucianism. Their concepts of calamity and good fortune, of cause and effect, may be used to incite the ignorant masses to goodness. For this purpose, too, they penetrate more readily than Confucianism. But once the illness has been treated, they should be discontinued. They are not to be used exclusively or administered frequently, for that would result in the misfortune of partiality.

"Some Confucians may idly talk of 'mind' and 'nature,' [22] thus confusing Confucius with Gautama [23] and Lao Tzu. Others may attack the latter two worthies, as though they were defending against their mortal enemies. But these are both limited viewpoints."

"The Taoist priests in their yellow caps and the Buddhist monks in their black robes indulge in supernatural foolishness. If we do not strenuously attack them, would this not beget trouble for manners and morals?"

"What I was talking about were the basic premises of these doctrines. If we focus on their decadent aspects, it's not Buddhism and Taoism alone that beget trouble for manners and morals. The trouble begot by Confucianism is by no means inconsequential. For example, sir, your getting drunk and falling asleep naked here, I suspect, is not necessarily in conformity with the rites and regulations of the Duke of Chou and Confucius."

After apologizing, Ta-huan freely carried on his conversation with the spirit until dawn, whereupon he departed. He never did find out which spirit it was. Some say it was a fox.

22. There are numerous possible interpretations of *hsin-hsing*, Buddhist and otherwise. That given in the translation might actually be construed as Mencian. The usual Buddhist understanding of the expression is "the immutable mind-nature" (*citta-dharmatā*). While it is difficult to identify precisely what Chi Yün intended here, he seems to be criticizing those Confucians who have adulterated the doctrine of the sages with concepts that are fundamentally Buddhist.

23. The Buddha.

VII

The following was told to me by a criminal named Kang Ch'ao-jung who had been banished to Urumchi.[24]

There were two men on a business trip to Tibet.[25] Each of them was mounted on a mule. As they were passing through the mountains, they lost their way and could not tell east from west. Suddenly, more than ten people jumped down from an overhanging cliff. The merchants suspected that they were bandits.[26] As they came closer, the merchants saw that they were all seven to eight feet tall.[27] Their bodies were covered with fine hair of a yellowish green color and their faces seemed human but not yet fully so. Their speech was so croaky that it was impossible to understand. Believing the approaching figures to be demons, the merchants thought that they would surely die, so they fell to the ground trembling. But the ten-odd people looked at each other and laughed, giving no indication that they would seize the merchants and devour them.

Instead, they clasped the merchants under their arms and went off driving the mules before them. When they reached a hollow in the mountains, they put the two merchants on the ground. Then they pushed one of the mules into a pit and butchered the other with a sharp knife. They built a fire and, having roasted the mule meat over it, sat down in a circle and began to gorge themselves. They picked up the two merchants and gave them places as well, putting meat before each of them. Perceiving that the men had no evil intentions and beset by hunger and exhaustion, the merchants decided they

24. Chi Yün himself had been banished to this remote city for one year (1770–1771). Many of his sketches are set in and around Urumchi or were told to him by people from that city. Urumchi is located in Sinkiang ("New Territory"), the westernmost region of modern China. The original inhabitants of this area were Indo-European peoples such as the Tocharians, Yüeh-chih (Ju-chih), and Sakas (Scyths). These were Caucasoid and Europoid peoples, many of whom had long noses, blond or reddish hair, and deep-set blue or greenish eyes. In further contrast to the people of the Middle Kingdom, they were also tall, dolichocephalic, and hirsute. Their existence has been proved by wall-paintings from this area dating to over a thousand years ago and by numerous extremely well-preserved, fully clothed corpses dating to approximately 4,000–2,300 years ago. In spite of the understandable amazement of the two merchants in this story, it would appear that Chi Yün is basically reporting reliable facts that are of great importance for history, linguistics, and anthropology. The data presented in this story have been repeatedly corroborated by other travelers in the Kunlun and Pamir ranges who have encountered such fantastic creatures. They could be the descendants of the original Indo-European inhabitants of the Tarim Basin and surrounding areas who have retreated into the mountains to evade more recently arrived groups such as the Altaic Uighurs, Kirghiz, and Kazakhs and the Sinitic Han peoples.

25. Trade between Tibet and what is now Sinkiang has flourished for thousands of years, the enormous difficulties of the terrain notwithstanding.

26. The text has *chia-pa*, said to be the Mandarin transcription of a Tibetan word (perhaps *kampa*).

27. About six feet according to the U.S. system of measurement. Many of the Europoid mummies of Sinkiang are this tall or taller.

might as well just go ahead and eat it. After they had eaten their fill, the ten-odd men patted their stomachs, raised their heads, and wheezed, making a sound like the whinny of a horse.

Two of the men then each clasped one of the merchants under their arms as before and sped off over three or four ridges as swiftly as a gibbon or a bird. After sending the merchants to the side of a main road, they gave each of them a stone and disappeared in a flash. The stones were as large as melons and were both turquoise. The merchants carried the stones back and sold them for a price worth double their losses.

This incident occurred sometime between 1765 and 1766. Ch'ao-jung had met one of the merchants who had told him about it in great detail.

One does not know whether these creatures were mountain specters or tree spirits. Judging from their actions, however, they were not demons. Perhaps they are simply a kind of feral human being that has always lived in isolated mountain valleys and has been cut off from communication with the rest of the world.

Translated by Victor H. Mair

Classical-Language Short Stories

207
The Story of Ying-ying

Yüan Chen (?) (779–831)

During the Chen-yüan period [1] there lived a young man named Chang. He was agreeable and refined, and good-looking, but firm and self-contained, and capable of no improper act. When his companions included him in one

"The Story of Ying-ying" (the name of the heroine means "Oriole") is perhaps the most celebrated of all classical-language short stories. It is also probably the best known of all Chinese love stories, regardless of genre or language. Extremely well crafted, this beautiful and moving story formed the basis for the medley entitled "Master Tung's Western Chamber Romance" (see selection 215) and the splendid Yüan drama *Record of the Western Chamber* (recently translated in full into English as *The West Wing*), by Wang Shih-fu (fl. 1234).

The writing of fiction, even in the classical language, was traditionally considered by Confucian purists to be a trivial pursuit, and literati would seldom publicly admit that they indulged in it (this was, of course, particularly the case with vernacular-language fiction). Nonetheless, there are good grounds for attributing the story of Ying-ying to the famous poet and statesman Yüan Chen. Among these is the long, stuffy poem by him that appears near the end of the story. Yüan was descended from Tabgatch royalty (the non-Han rulers of the Northern Wei dynasty). At the age of fourteen, he was already well versed in the classics and had passed the first of several competitive examinations. In 822 he was appointed to one of the highest bureaucratic offices in the empire but was removed from it shortly thereafter due to factional infighting at court. Yüan was a close friend of the renowned poet-official Po Chü-yi (see selection 149).

1. Chen-yüan (785–804) was the last of the three reign periods of Emperor Te Tsung of the T'ang dynasty.

of their parties, the others could all be brawling as though they would never get enough, but Chang would just watch tolerantly without ever taking part. In this way he had gotten to be twenty-three years old without ever having had relations with a woman. When asked by his friends, he explained, "Teng-t'u tzu [2] was no lover, but a lecher. I am the true lover—I just never happened to meet the right girl. How do I know that? It's because things of outstanding beauty never fail to make a permanent impression on me. That shows I am not without feelings." His friends took note of what he said.

Not long afterward Chang was traveling in P'u,[3] where he lodged some ten tricents east of the city in a monastery called the Temple of Universal Salvation. It happened that a widowed Mrs. Ts'ui had also stopped there on her way back to Ch'ang-an. She had been born a Cheng; Chang's mother had been a Cheng, and when they worked out their common ancestry, this Mrs. Ts'ui turned out to be a rather distant cousin once removed on his mother's side.

This year Hun Chen [4] died in P'u, and the eunuch Ting Wen-ya proved unpopular with the troops, who took advantage of the mourning period to mutiny. They plundered the citizens of P'u, and Mrs. Ts'ui, in a strange place with all her wealth and servants, was terrified, having no one to turn to. Before the mutiny Chang had made friends with some of the officers in P'u, and now he requested a detachment of soldiers to protect the Ts'ui family. As a result all escaped harm. In about ten days the imperial commissioner of inquiry, Tu Ch'üeh,[5] came with full power from the throne and restored order among the troops.

Out of gratitude to Chang for the favor he had done them, Mrs. Ts'ui invited him to a banquet in the central hall. She addressed him: "Your widowed aunt with her helpless children would never have been able to escape alive from these rioting soldiers. It is no ordinary favor you have done us; it is rather as though you had given my son and daughter their lives, and I want to introduce them to you as their elder brother so that they can express their thanks." She summoned her son Huan-lang, a very attractive child of ten or so. Then she called her daughter, "Come out and pay your respects to your brother, who saved your life." There was a delay; then word was brought that she was indisposed and asked to be excused. Her mother exclaimed in

2. Teng-t'u was an archetypal lecher. This allusion originates from the character ridiculed in Sung Yü's (fl. 3rd century B.C.E.) rhapsody, "The Lechery of Master Teng-t'u."

3. P'u-chou, also known as Ho-chung in T'ang times, was under the jurisdiction of Chiang-chou. It is modern-day Yung-chi district in Shansi province, located east-northeast of Ch'ang-an.

4. Hun Chen, the regional commander of Chiang-chou, died in P'u-chou in 799.

5. Tu Ch'üeh, originally prefect of T'ung-chou (in modern-day Shensi), was appointed, after the death of Hun chen, the prefect of Ho-chung as well as the imperial commissioner of inquiry of Chiang-chou.

207. Yüan Chen 509

anger, "Your brother Chang saved your life. You would have been abducted if it were not for him—how can you give yourself airs?"

After a while she appeared, wearing an everyday dress and no make-up on her smooth face, except for a remaining spot of rouge. Her hair coils straggled down to touch her eyebrows. Her beauty was extraordinary, so radiant it took the breath away. Startled, Chang made her a deep bow as she sat down beside her mother. Because she had been forced to come out against her will, she looked angrily straight ahead, as though unable to endure the company. Chang asked her age. Mrs. Ts'ui said, "From the seventh month of the fifth year of the reigning emperor to the present twenty-first year, it is just seventeen years."

Chang tried to make conversation with her, but she would not respond, and he had to leave after the meal was over. From this time on Chang was infatuated but had no way to make his feelings known to her. She had a maid named Hung-niang with whom Chang had managed to exchange greetings several times, and finally he took the occasion to tell her how he felt. Not surprisingly, the maid was alarmed and fled in embarrassment. Chang was sorry he had said anything, and when she returned the next day he made shame-faced apologies without repeating his request. The maid said, "Sir, what you said is something I would not dare repeat to my mistress or let anyone else know about. But you know very well who Miss Ts'ui's relatives are; why don't you ask for her hand in marriage, as you are entitled to do because of the favor you did them?"

"From my earliest years I have never been one to make any improper connections," Chang said. "Whenever I have found myself in the company of young women, I would not even look at them, and it never occurred to me that I would be trapped in any such way. But the other day at the dinner I was hardly able to control myself, and in the days since, I walk without knowing where I am going and eat without hunger—I am afraid I cannot last another day. If I were to go through a regular matchmaker, taking three months and more for the exchange of betrothal presents and names and birthdates [6]—you might just as well look for me among the dried fish in the shop.[7] Can't you tell me what to do?"

"Miss Ts'ui is so very strict that not even her elders could suggest anything improper to her," the maid replied. "It would be hard for someone in my position to say such a thing. But I have noticed she writes a lot. She is always reciting poetry to herself and is moved by it for a long time after. You might see if you can seduce her with a love poem. That is the only way I can think of."

6. To determine an astrologically suitable date for a wedding.
7. An allusion to the parable of help that comes too late in chapter 9 of the pre-Ch'in philosophical work *Chuang Tzu* (see selection 8).

Chang was delighted and on the spot composed two stanzas of spring verses which he handed over to her. That evening Hung-niang came back with a note on colored paper for him, saying, "By Miss Ts'ui's instructions." The title of her poem was "Bright Moon on the Night of the Fifteenth":

> I await the moon in the western chamber
> Where the breeze comes through the half-opened door.
> Sweeping the wall the flower shadows move:
> I imagine it is my lover who comes.

Chang understood the message: that day was the fourteenth of the second month, and an apricot tree was next to the wall east of the Ts'uis' courtyard. It would be possible to climb it.

On the night of the fifteenth Chang used the tree as a ladder to get over the wall. When he came to the western chamber, the door was ajar. Inside, Hung-niang was asleep on a bed. He awakened her, and she asked, frightened, "How did you get here?"

"Miss Ts'ui's letter told me to come," he said, not quite accurately. "You go tell her I am here."

In a minute Hung-niang was back. "She's coming! She's coming!"

Chang was both happy and nervous, convinced that success was his. Then Miss Ts'ui appeared in formal dress, with a serious face, and began to upbraid him: "You did us a great kindness when you saved our lives, and that is why my mother entrusted my young brother and myself to you. Why then did you get my silly maid to bring me that filthy poem? You began by doing a good deed in preserving me from the hands of ravishers, and you end by seeking to ravish me. You substitute seduction for rape—is there any great difference? My first impulse was to keep quiet about it, but that would have been to condone your wrongdoing, and not right. If I told my mother, it would amount to ingratitude, and the consequences would be unfortunate. I thought of having a servant convey my disapproval, but feared she would not get it right. Then I thought of writing a short message to state my case, but was afraid it would only put you on your guard. So finally I composed those vulgar lines to make sure you would come here. It was an improper thing to do, and of course I feel ashamed. But I hope that you will keep within the bounds of decency and commit no outrage."

As she finished speaking, she turned on her heel and left him. For some time Chang stood, dumbfounded. Then he went back over the wall to his quarters, all hope gone.

A few nights later Chang was sleeping alone by the veranda when someone shook him awake. Startled, he rose up to see Hung-niang standing there, a coverlet and pillow in her arms. She patted him and said, "She is coming! She is coming! Why are you sleeping?" And she spread the quilt and put the pillow beside his. As she left, Chang sat up straight and rubbed his eyes. For some time it seemed as though he were still dreaming, but nonetheless he waited dutifully. Then there was Hung-niang again, with Miss Ts'ui leaning on her arm. She was shy and yielding, and appeared almost not to have the strength to move her limbs. The contrast with her stiff formality at their last encounter was complete.

This evening was the night of the eighteenth, and the slanting rays of the moon cast a soft light over half the bed. Chang felt a kind of floating lightness and wondered whether this was an immortal who visited him, not someone from the world of men. After a while the temple bell sounded. Daybreak was near. As Hung-niang urged her to leave, she wept softly and clung to him. Hung-niang helped her up, and they left. The whole time she had not spoken a single word. With the first light of dawn Chang got up, wondering, was it a dream? But the perfume still lingered, and as it got lighter he could see on his arm traces of her makeup and the teardrops sparkling still on the mat.

For some ten days afterward there was no word from her. Chang composed a poem of sixty lines on "An Encounter with an Immortal" which he had not yet completed when Hung-niang happened by, and he gave it to her for her mistress. After that she let him see her again, and for nearly a month he would join her in what her poem called the "western chamber," slipping out at dawn and returning stealthily at night. Chang once asked what her mother thought about the situation. She said, "She knows there is nothing she can do about it, and so she hopes you will regularize things."

Before long Chang was about to go to Ch'ang-an, and he let her know his intentions in a poem. Miss Ts'ui made no objections at all, but the look of pain on her face was very touching. On the eve of his departure he was unable to see her again. Then Chang went off to the west. A few months later he again made a trip to P'u and stayed several months with Miss Ts'ui.

She was a very good calligrapher and wrote poetry, but for all that he kept begging to see her work, she would never show it. Chang wrote poems for her, challenging her to match them, but she paid them little attention. The thing that made her unusual was that, while she excelled in the arts, she always acted as though she were ignorant, and although she was quick and clever in speaking, she would seldom indulge in repartee. She loved Chang very much, but would never say so in words. At the time she was subject to moods of profound melancholy, but she never let on. She seldom showed on her face the emotions she felt. On one occasion she was playing her zither alone at night. She did not know Chang was listening, and the music was full of sadness. As soon as he spoke, she stopped and would play no more. This made him all the more infatuated with her.

Some time later Chang had to go west again for the scheduled examinations. It was the eve of his departure, and though he had said nothing about what it involved, he sat sighing unhappily at her side. Miss Ts'ui had guessed that he was going to leave for good. Her manner was respectful, but she spoke deliberately and in a low voice: "To seduce someone and then abandon her is perfectly natural, and it would be presumptuous of me to resent it. It would be an act of charity on your part if, having first seduced me, you were to go through with it and fulfill your oath of lifelong devotion. But in either case, what is there to be so upset about in this trip? However, I see you are not happy and I have no way to cheer you up. You have praised my zither-playing, and in the past I have been embarrassed to play for you. Now that you are going away, I shall do what you so often requested."

She had them prepare her zither and started to play the prelude to the "Rainbow Robe and Feather Skirt." [8] After a few notes, her playing grew wild with grief until the piece was no longer recognizable. Everyone was reduced to tears, and Miss Ts'ui abruptly stopped playing, put down the zither, and ran back to her mother's room with tears streaming down her face. She did not come back.

The next morning Chang went away. The following year he stayed on in the capital, having failed the examinations. He wrote a letter to Miss Ts'ui to reassure her, and her reply read roughly as follows:

I have read your letter with its message of consolation, and it filled my childish heart with mingled grief and joy. In addition you sent me a box of ornaments to adorn my hair and a stick of pomade to make my lips smooth. It was most kind of you; but for whom am I to make myself attractive? As I look at these presents my breast is filled with sorrow.

Your letter said that you will stay on in the capital to pursue your studies, and of course you need quiet and the facilities there to make progress. Still, it is hard on the person left alone in this far-off place. But such is my fate, and I should not complain. Since last fall I have been listless and without hope. In company I can force myself to talk and smile, but come evening I always shed tears in the solitude of my own room. Even in my sleep I often sob, yearning for the absent one. Or I am in your arms for a moment as it used to be, but before the secret meeting is done I am awake and heartbroken. The bed seems still warm beside me, but the one I love is far away.

Since you said good-bye the new year has come. Ch'ang-an is a city of pleasure with chances for love everywhere. I am truly fortunate that you have not forgotten me and that your affection is not worn out. Loving you as I do, I have no way of repaying you, except to be true to our vow of lifelong fidelity.

Our first meeting was at the banquet, as cousins. Then you persuaded my maid to inform me of your love; and I was unable to keep my childish

---

8. After this Brahman music was introduced into China, it was dignified by the elegant name given to it by Emperor Hsüan Tsung of the T'ang dynasty and by the performance of his favorite consort, Yang Kuei-fei (see selection 149).

heart firm. You made advances, like that other poet, Ssu-ma Hsiang-ju.[9] I failed to repulse them as the girl did who threw her shuttle.[10] When I offered myself in your bed, you treated me with the greatest kindness, and I supposed, in my innocence, that I could always depend on you. How could I have foreseen that our encounter could not possibly lead to something definite, that having disgraced myself by coming to you, there was no further chance of serving you openly as a wife? To the end of my days this will be a lasting regret—I must hide my sighs and be silent. If you, out of kindness, would condescend to fulfill my selfish wish, though it came on my dying day it would seem to be a new lease on life. But if, as a man of the world, you curtail your feelings, sacrificing the lesser to the more important, and look on this connection as shameful, so that your solemn vow can be dispensed with, still my true love will not vanish though my bones decay and my frame dissolve; in wind and dew it will seek out the ground you walk on. My love in life and death is told in this. I weep as I write, for feelings I cannot express. Take care of yourself; a thousand times over, take care of your dear self.

This bracelet of jade is something I wore as a child; I send it to serve as a gentleman's belt pendant. Like jade may you be invariably firm and tender; like a bracelet may there be no break between what came before and what is to follow. Here are also a skein of multicolored thread and a tea roller of mottled bamboo. These things have no intrinsic value, but they are to signify that I want you to be true as jade, and your love to endure unbroken as a bracelet. The spots on the bamboo are like the marks of my tears,[11] and my unhappy thoughts are as tangled as the thread: these objects are symbols of my feelings and tokens for all time of my love. Our hearts are close, though our bodies are far apart and there is no time I can expect to see you. But where the hidden desires are strong enough, there will be a meeting of spirits. Take care of yourself, a thousand times over. The springtime wind is often chill; eat well for your health's sake. Be circumspect and careful, and do not think too often of my unworthy person.

Chang showed her letter to his friends, and in this way word of the affair got around. One of them, Yang Chü-yüan,[12] a skillful poet, wrote a quatrain on "Young Miss Ts'ui":

9. An allusion to the story of the Han poet Ssu-ma Hsiang-ju (179–117 B.C.E.), who enticed the young widow Cho Wen-chün to elope by his zither-playing (see selection 129).

10. A neighboring girl, named Kao, repulsed Hsieh K'un's (280–322) advances by throwing her shuttle in his face. He lost two teeth.

11. Alluding to the legend of the two wives of the sage ruler Shun, who stained the bamboo with their tears.

12. The poet Yang Chü-yüan (fl. 800) was a contemporary of Yüan Chen.

For clear purity jade cannot equal his complexion;
On the iris in the inner court snow begins to melt.
A romantic young man filled with thoughts of love,
A letter from the Hsiao girl,[13] brokenhearted.

Yüan Chen [14] of Honan [15] wrote a continuation of Chang's poem "Encounter with an Immortal," also in thirty couplets:

Faint moonbeams pierce the curtained window;
Fireflies glimmer across the blue sky.
The far horizon begins now to pale;
Dwarf trees gradually turn darker green.
A dragon song crosses the court bamboo;
A phoenix air brushes the well-side tree.
The silken robe trails through the thin mist;
The pendant circles tinkle in the light breeze.
The accredited envoy accompanies Hsi Wang-mu; [16]
From the clouds' center comes Jade Boy.[17]
Late at night everyone is quiet;
At daybreak the rain drizzles.
Pearl radiance shines on her decorated sandals;
Flower glow shows off the embroidered skirt.
Jasper hairpin: a walking colored phoenix;
Gauze shawl; embracing vermilion rainbow.
She says she comes from Jasper Flower Bank
And is going to pay court at Green Jade Palace.
On an outing north of Loyang's [18] wall,
By chance he came to the house east of Sung Yü's.[19]

13. In T'ang times the term "Hsiao-niang" referred to young women in general. Here it means Ying-ying.

14. Yüan Chen was a key literary figure in the middle of the T'ang period.

15. The Honan Circuit in T'ang times covered the area to the south of the Yellow River in both the present provinces of Shantung and Honan, up to the north of the Huai River in modern-day Kiangsu and Anhwei.

16. Hsi Wang-mu, the Queen Mother of the West, is a mythological figure supposedly dwelling in the K'un-lun Mountains in China's far west. In early accounts she is sometimes described as part human and part beast, but since early post-Han times she has usually been described as a beautiful immortal. Her huge palace is inhabited by other immortals. Within its precincts grow the magic peach trees which bear the fruits of immortality once every three thousand years. This might be an allusion to Ying-ying's mother.

17. The Jade Boy might allude to Ying-ying's brother.

18. Possibly a reference to the goddess of the Lo River. This river, in modern-day Honan, is made famous by the rhapsody of Ts'ao Chih (192–232), "The Goddess of Lo."

19. In "The Lechery of Master Teng-t'u" (see note 2 above), Sung Yü tells about the beautiful girl next door to the east who climbed up on the wall to flirt with him.

His dalliance she rejects a bit at first,
But her yielding love already is disclosed.
Lowered locks put in motion cicada shadows; [20]
Returning steps raise jade dust.
Her face turns to let flow flower snow
As she climbs into bed, silk covers in her arms.
Love birds in a neck-entwining dance;
Kingfishers in a conjugal cage.
Eyebrows, out of shyness, contracted;
Lip rouge, from the warmth, melted.
Her breath is pure: fragrance of orchid buds;
Her skin is smooth: richness of jade flesh.
No strength, too limp to lift a wrist;
Many charms, she likes to draw herself together.
Sweat runs: pearls drop by drop;
Hair in disorder: black luxuriance.
Just as they rejoice in the meeting of a lifetime
They suddenly hear the night is over.
There is no time for lingering;
It is hard to give up the wish to embrace.
Her comely face shows the sorrow she feels;
With fragrant words they swear eternal love.
She gives him a bracelet to plight their troth;
He ties a lovers' knot as sign their hearts are one.
Tear-borne powder runs before the clear mirror;
Around the flickering lamp are nighttime insects.
Moonlight is still softly shining
As the rising sun gradually dawns.
Riding on a wild goose she returns to the Lo River,[21]
Blowing a flute he ascends Mount Sung.[22]
His clothes are fragrant still with musk perfume;
The pillow is slippery yet with red traces.
Thick, thick, the grass grows on the dike;
Floating, floating, the tumbleweed yearns for the isle.
Her plain zither plays the "Resentful Crane Song";
In the clear Milky Way she looks for the returning wild goose.[23]
The sea is broad and truly hard to cross;

20. Referring to her hairdo in the cicada style.
21. Again the theme of the goddess of the Lo River.
22. Also known as the Central Mountain, it is located to the north of Teng-feng county in Honan province. Here the one ascending the mountain may refer to Chang.
23. Which might be carrying a message.

The sky is high and not easy to traverse.
The moving cloud is nowhere to be found—
Hsiao Shih stays in his chamber.[24]

All of Chang's friends who heard of the affair marveled at it, but Chang had determined on his own course of action. Yüan Chen was especially close to him and so was in a position to ask him for an explanation. Chang said, "It is a general rule that those women endowed by Heaven with great beauty invariably either destroy themselves or destroy someone else. If this Ts'ui woman were to meet someone with wealth and position, she would use the favor her charms gain her to be cloud and rain or dragon or monster—I can't imagine what she might turn into. Of old, King Hsin of the Shang and King Yu of the Chou[25] were brought low by women, in spite of the size of their kingdoms and the extent of their power; their armies were scattered, their persons butchered, and down to the present day their names are objects of ridicule. I have no inner strength to withstand this evil influence. That is why I have resolutely suppressed my love."

At this statement everyone present sighed deeply.

Over a year later Ts'ui was married, and Chang for his part had taken a wife. Happening to pass through the town where she was living, he asked permission of her husband to see her, as a cousin. The husband spoke to her, but Ts'ui refused to appear. Chang's feelings of hurt showed on his face, and she was told about it. She secretly sent him a poem:

Emaciated, I have lost my looks,
Tossing and turning, too weary to leave my bed.
It's not because of others I am ashamed to rise;
For you I am haggard and before you ashamed.

She never did appear. Some days later when Chang was about to leave, she sent another poem of farewell:

Cast off and abandoned, what can I say now,
Whom you loved so briefly long ago?
Any love you had then for me
Will do for the one you have now.

After this he never heard any more about her. His contemporaries for the most part conceded that Chang had done well to rectify his mistake. I have often mentioned this among friends so that, forewarned, they might avoid

---

24. Hsiao Shih was a well-known flute-playing immortal of the Spring and Autumn period.

25. Hsin Chow was the infamous last ruler of the Shang dynasty, whose misrule and fall are attributed to the influence of his favorite concubine, Ta-chi. King Yu (reigned 781–771 B.C.E.), last ruler of the Western Chou, was misled by his consort Pao-ssu. The behavior of both rulers is traditionally attributed to their infatuation with the women they loved.

doing such a thing, or if they did, that they might not be led astray by it. In the ninth month of a year in the Chen-yüan period, when an official, Li Kung-ch'ui,[26] was passing the night in my house at the Pacification Quarter, the conversation touched on the subject. He found it most extraordinary and composed a "Song of Ying-ying" to commemorate the affair. Ts'ui's child-name was Ying-ying, and Kung-ch'ui used it for his poem.

Translated by James Robert Hightower

26. Kung-ch'ui was the style of the T'ang poet Li Shen (780–846; see selection 47).

208

An Account of the Governor of the Southern Branch

Li Kung-tso (c. 778–848)

Ch'un-yü Fen of Tung-p'ing was a man who wandered about the lower Yangtze region avenging wrongs as he saw fit. He was too fond of drinking

This is a typical example of the Tang classical-language short story (*ch'uan-ch'i*, literally "transmission of the strange"). "An Account of the Governor of the Southern Branch" belongs to a subgenre of dream stories in which the dreamer is allowed to see how his own life would develop if he could achieve his worldly goals. The form may originally have come from India in the collections of allegories which were translated into Chinese during the Period of Disunion (180–589 C.E.), and it certainly has strong Buddhist and Taoist overtones during the T'ang dynasty (618–907 C.E.). Many early Chinese short stories were derived from Indian tales, although the exact source is often difficult to pinpoint because of uncertainties surrounding the dating of Indian texts and because so many Indian tales either were only transmitted orally or, if written down, are no longer extant. It is revealing that tales of clearly Indian origin were often passed off as ostensibly Taoist pieces. This tells us much about the nature of the assimilation of foreign cultural elements in China.

Irrespective of the story's origins, its resonances are purely Chinese in the hands of its author, Li Kung-tso. The story may be based on a local legend in the Yangchow region, where Li served for a time. But the unusual surname Ch'un-yü would likely call to mind Ch'un-yü K'un, a tippler who, a millennium earlier, depended on his wife's family for support. Some scholars read the story as a topical allegory, intended to mock the practice of marrying royal princesses to local satraps to hold their loyalty, a practice particularly popular around the turn of the ninth century. The motif of messengers clad in hues of blue or purple coming to take an unsuspecting mortal to another realm for instruction is a hoary Taoist one. Other features of the story, such as the women of the court being so attracted to our protagonist, are familiar. In fact, their names identify them as Taoist "nuns" who oft-times plied the world's oldest trade in the T'ang demimonde and who were especially active on holidays (such as those mentioned in the story), when men and women encountered each other on the streets (these encounters were not normal at other times).

The tree translated as "locust" is actually the *Sophora japonica*. It is written with a sinograph

and given to impulse, paying little attention to the finer points of convention. He had amassed a great deal of property and supported a retinue of gallant men like himself. Once, because of his military skills, he had been appointed a general in the Huai-nan Army. But he drank too much, gave rein to his passions, and offended his commander. Thus he was dismissed and drifted about with nothing to do, spending all his time in unrestrained drinking.

His family lived a few miles east of Kuang-ling commandery. To the south of the house in which they lived was a grand, old locust tree, its branches and trunk long and interwoven, its cool shade spreading for nearly an acre. Ch'un-yü and his hearties would drink profusely beneath it every day.

In the ninth month of the seventh year of the Chen-yüan reign period [1] Ch'un-yü drank so heavily that he became ill. The two friends who were seated with him at the time carried him into his house and laid him in a room to the east of the main hall.

"You should get some sleep," they said to him. "We'll feed the horses, wash our feet, and wait for you to recover before we go."

When Ch'un-yü took off his headband and put his head on the pillow, everything went dark and seemed to spin about, as if in a dream. He saw two envoys clad in purple, kneeling before him, who said: "The king of the Nation of Locust Tranquility has sent us to deliver his message of invitation to you."

Ch'un-yü got down off the couch unconsciously, straightened his clothing, and followed the two envoys toward the gate. There he saw a black-lacquered carriage driven by four steeds and seven or eight attendants. They helped him up into the carriage and departed, pointing to an opening under the old locust tree as they went out the main gate. Then they sped into the opening. Ch'un-yü found this most strange, but he didn't dare to ask any questions.

Suddenly he saw that the landscape, climate, vegetation, and roadways were all markedly different from those of the world he knew. After they had gone a dozen or so miles they came to the suburbs and ramparts of a city. Here, vehicles and people both flowed along the road. To the left and right of him were runners who called out orders very sternly so that passersby on either side struggled to give way. Farther on they entered a great city wall with red gates and a high tower. On the tower "The Great Nation of Locust Tranquility" was written in golden letters. The gate guards made haste to pay

---

which, when broken into its basic components, means "tree of ghosts." (The "ghost" component is actually only a phonetic element.) Like its Western cousin, the acacia, the tree is often host to ants.

Li Kung-tso was one of the main authors of classical-language short stories during the T'ang period. Information concerning him is vague and scanty, but it is known that he successfully passed the Presented Scholar examination, perhaps sometimes around the mid-790s, after which he received several low-level administrative positions in the far southern regions.

1. 791 C.E.

their respects and perform their attendant duties. After a short period of time a rider called out, "Because the future royal son-in-law has traveled far, the king has ordered that you rest a while in the Eastern Flowery Lodge." Then he went ahead to clear the way. All of a sudden Ch'un-yü saw an open door and he descended from the carriage and went in. There were many-colored railings next to carved columns, flowering trees with rare fruits, row upon row beneath a dais. Benches and tables, cushions and mats, curtains and a feast were all arranged on the dais. He was most pleased. Again someone called out, "The Chief Minister of the Right is about to arrive." Ch'un-yü then descended the stairs to meet him properly. A man wearing purple and holding an ivory court-tablet came forward quickly, and they greeted each other according to all the rules of propriety.

"My Liege has not considered our humble land too far out of the way to welcome Milord," the Chief Minister began, "He is hoping to contract a formal marriage with you."

"How could this humble person dare to hope for such a thing?" Ch'un-yü replied.

The Chief Minister thereupon asked that Ch'un-yü accompany him to where the king was. After they had gone about one hundred paces, they entered a red gate. Guards with spears, shields, axes, and halberds standing in formation to the left and the right stepped back to let them pass. Chou Pien, a lifelong drinking companion of Ch'un-yü, was among them. Ch'un-yü was secretly pleased to see him, but didn't dare to step forward and greet him. The Chief Minister led the way up into a spacious hall, heavily guarded as if it were the king's. There he saw a man, large and imposing, sitting on the throne, dressed in a white silken gown and wearing a crimson-flowered crown. Ch'un-yü Fen trembled and didn't dare to look up. The attendants to the left and right told him to kneel down and do homage.

Then the king said, "Sometime before, I received your father's word that he wouldn't reject our small nation out of hand and he agreed to allow my second daughter, Jade Fragrance, to serve you respectfully as your wife."

Ch'un-yü could only continue staring at the ground. He didn't dare to say anything.

The king went on, "Take him back to the guest lodge first, we will carry out the ceremony later!" There was also a formal edict stating that the Chief Minister should also go back with him to the guest lodge.

Ch'un-yü thought this over. As far as he knew, his father had been a general on the border and because of that had fallen captive to the enemy, so that it wasn't known whether he was still alive. Had the king meant to say that after communicating with his father, who was among the northern barbarians, this matter had been concluded? His mind was very confused and he didn't really know how it had come about.

That evening everything for the ceremony was in complete readiness; the gifts of lambs, geese, monies, and silk, awe-inspiring attendants standing tall, female singers and musicians, wines and savory foods, lamps and candles, carriages and riding horses. There was a group of women, one calling herself Lady Flowery Slope, another Ms. Green Stream, another Higher Transcendent, and yet another Lower Transcendent. There seemed to be a large number of them, each with several thousand attendants. They wore kingfisher- and phoenix-feather hats, golden-cloud cloaks, gems of all colors, and golden jewelry, so that they overwhelmed the eye. Roaming about and enjoying themselves, they stopped by his door, competing to trifle with Master Ch'un-yü. Their manner was very bewitching, their speech seductive, so that he was unable to respond. There was another girl who said to him, "Once on the third day of the third month I went along with Madame Mithridate to the Wisdom of Zen Temple. In the India Hall we saw Shih-yen[2] dance the Brahman Dance. I sat on the stone bench under the north window with some of my companions. At that time you were still young, but you also dismounted and came to watch. You alone tried to force us closer, teasing and flirting. My little sister Hortensia Flower and I knotted a red scarf and put it on a bamboo pole.[3] How could you have forgotten? Another time on the sixteenth of the seventh month I was in the Filial Feelings Temple attending Lady Higher Purity and listening to the monk, Bound to Mystery, lecture on the *Lotus Sūtra*. I left a pair of golden-phoenix hairpins as an offering beneath the podium and Higher Purity left a box made of water-buffalo horn. At the time you were also on the lecture mat and you asked the monk for the hairpins and the box to examine them, sighing repeatedly with appreciation and uttering cries of admiration for some time. Turning to look at us you said, 'Both you and your things are not the sort we have in this world.' Then whether you asked about my family or where I lived, I refused to respond. Your heart was filled with love and you were loath to take your eyes off us. Can it be you don't remember?"

"I treasure the memory in my heart," Ch'un-yü replied. "How could I have forgotten it?"

The women in one voice said, "Who would have imagined that today you would become our relative?"

Three men, very grand in their official hats and sashes, also came forward to pay their respects. "We have received a command to serve the royal son-in-law as best men." Among them was a man who seemed to be an old friend of Ch'un-yü Fen. Fen pointed to him and said, "Aren't you T'ien Tzu-hua of P'ing-yi?" "Yes, I am," T'ien replied. Fen came forward, took his hands, and talked over old times for long while. Then he asked, "Why are you living here?"

---

2. A general from Sogdiana in Central Asia.
3. This is similar to dropping a handkerchief for a gentleman to pick up in Western society.

"I was wandering about at large, when the Chief Minister of the right, Mr. Tuan, the Marquis of Wu-ch'eng, recognized my abilities. Because of this I've joined up with him."

"Chou Pien is here. Did you know?" Fen went on to ask.

"Mr. Chou," Tzu-hua replied, "is a notable person. He is serving as Metropolitan Commandant, and great are his power and influence. Several times I have benefited from his protection." And so they chatted and laughed happily.

In a short time a messenger called out, "The Royal Son-in-law may go in now!" The three men then outfitted him in a sword, a belt, a cap, and clothes.

"I never thought the day would come when I could personally witness such a marriage," said Tzu-hua. "Don't forget about me once you're married!"

Then several dozen of those transcendent beauties played the most extraordinary music for them, sweet and pure, but with a melancholy melody, such that no mortal had ever heard. There were also several dozen of them holding candles and leading the way for him. To the left and right appeared cloth partitions of various hues and lusters, embroidered with kingfisher feathers and golden thread, which ran on for over a mile. Fen sat upright in the carriage, very agitated, unable to settle down. T'ien Tzu-hua often said something or smiled to help him dispel the tension. Those women he had just spoken with each rode in phoenix-wing carriages and were also coming and going in the palace. They came to a gate on which was written "Cultivation Palace." Those transcendent women all gathered on either side of the gate, telling him to get out of his carriage and bowing and making way, ascending and descending—all just as it is in the world of men. They removed the partitions and took away the screens and he saw a woman who was called "Princess of the Golden Branch." She was about fourteen or fifteen and was just like an immortal. Preparations for the rites of the wedding night were also evident.

From this time on, with each day Ch'un-yü Fen's affection for her grew deeper as his star shined brighter at court. The carriages and vestments in which he went about, on excursions or at banquets, were always inferior only to those of the king. The king ordered Ch'un-yü Fen and his fellow officials to ready the palace guard to go on a grand hunt at Efficacious Tortoise Mountain in the western part of the nation. There were mountains and hills steep and lofty, streams and marshes far and wide, forests of trees in abundance and luxuriance, and of the birds that fly and the beasts that run, there were none which were not bred there. The soldiers had a huge catch, and only when night fell did they go home.

One day Ch'un-yü Fen asked the king for instruction. "On that day when I got married, Your Majesty said he was following my father's orders. My father had served as a general on the northern frontier, but he was defeated in battle and fell into Tatar hands. Since then I haven't had a letter from him in nearly twenty years. As Your Majesty knows his whereabouts, I beg to be allowed to visit him."

"Your honorable father," the king quickly replied, "is serving guard over the northern lands. We haven't lost contact with him. You need only prepare a letter stating your news. There's no need to go to see him immediately!"

Then Ch'un-yü Fen ordered his wife to prepare presents to send with the letter to his father. In a few days a reply arrived. As Ch'un-yü Fen read over the general ideas in this letter, he found that they followed closely those his father had held all his life. In the letter instructions were recalled and emotions expressed indirectly, all as in the past. He also asked whether their relatives were still alive and about the prosperity of their village. And he said that the road between them was lengthy and blocked by winds and mists. The tone of his letter was sad and there was distress in his writing. Further, he would not allow Ch'un-yü Fen to come to visit him, explaining, "In the Ting-ch'ou year,[4] I will meet you again." Fen clasped the letter and choked back a sob, overcome with emotion.

Sometime later his wife said to him, "Why don't you ever think about politics?"

"I am a reckless sort who has no experience in politics," Fen replied.

"But if you were to pursue a political goal, I would support you," she said. Then she reported this conversation to the king. After some time had passed, he said to Fen, "Our province of Southern Branch is not well governed. The governor has been dismissed and I'd like to engage your talents. If you would condescend to take such a limited position, you could go there with our young daughter!"

Fen took these instructions to heart. The king then ordered those in charge of such things to outfit the new governor for his journey. For this reason they arrayed gold and jade, brocades and silks, baskets and boxes, servants and maids, carriages and horses along a broad thoroughfare for the princess to take with her.

As a youth, Ch'un-yü Fen had been a knight-errant and had never dared to have such hopes, so when he achieved this postion he was greatly pleased. Thereupon he submitted a memorial, saying:

> Your subject is the descendant of generals, just an ordinary man with no cultural refinement or administrative talent. He is too coarse to serve in such an important position and would certainly disrupt the regulations of the court. It would be like a common cart-puller changing places with his noble passenger, or like sitting idly while a caldron overturns. Now I want

4. 797 C.E.

to search far and wide for the worthy and the sagacious to assist me in areas I am unable to manage. Your Subject has found that the Metropolitan Commandant, Chou Pien from Ying-ch'uan, is loyal, upright, law-abiding, and has the talents to assist me. T'ien Tzu-hua from P'ing-yi, who is currently living in retirement, is honest, prudent, and understands government thoroughly. He would enable me to improve the effectiveness of my administration. I have been friends with these two for ten years. I understand fully their talents and can rely on them in political matters. I'd like to request that Chou be appointed Minister of Justice of Southern Branch and T'ien be appointed Minister of Agriculture. This would allow my administration to achieve merit and fame and our legal system to maintain order.

The king made the appointments completely in accordance with the memorial.

That night, the king and his wife gave them a farewell banquet in the southern part of the capital. The king said to Fen, "Southern Branch is the largest commandery in the nation. Its lands are fertile and rich, its people numerous and hearty. Without a gracious political policy, you won't be able to govern it. Moreover, you have your two assistants, Chou and T'ien, so we hope you will do your utmost to meet the nation's expectations."

Then his wife admonished the princess, "Mr. Ch'un-yü is by nature inflexible and intemperate, and besides he is young. You must act as is proper for a wife, valuing most compliance and obedience. If you can serve him well, I won't be concerned. Although the border to Southern Branch is not that far, mornings and nights we'll be separated.[5] Thus today since we must part, how could I hold back my tears?"

Ch'un-yü Fen and his wife paid their respects and left for the South, mounting their carriage and urging on their horses, all the while talking and joking in great happiness. After a few days they reached the commandery. Officials, clerks, Buddhists, Taoists, local elders, musicians, carriages, military guards, and horses with bells pressed forward to welcome them. People crushed around them and the sounds of bells and drums clamored for several miles. They could see parapets, towers, and lookouts. The place exuded an abundance of good auras.

As they entered the city-gate, it also had a large plaque written in golden characters which read: "The Seat of Southern Branch Commandery." The homes with red windows and ornamented halberds before their doors were as thick as trees in a forest.[6]

---

5. Children were expected to call on their parents every morning and evening.

6. Red windows and ornamented halberds arranged before the door were indications of wealth.

Ch'un-yü Fen "got out of his carriage"[7] and began to examine the local customs, to heal disease, and end suffering. Political matters he entrusted to Chou and T'ien, so that throughout the commandery things were gradually put in order. Twenty years after he took the position of governor, the people throughout the commandery had been reformed by his teachings and they all sang his praises. They erected a Meritorious Virtue Tablet in a shrine they set up for him.

The king greatly valued him and bestowed upon him further emoluments and land, also conferring him with rank and position, so that he became Prime Minister.

Chou and T'ien both became famous because they governed well and were steadily promoted to higher positions. Ch'un-yü Fen had five sons and two daughters. The sons received official positions through the hereditary rank system and the daughters were all married to members of the royal family.

His fame and glory were the highest of the era, beyond that of all his contemporaries.

In that year the Nation of Sandalwood Creepers came to attack this commandery. The king ordered Ch'un-yü Fen to train his officers and exhort his troops so that they could attack the invaders. Fen submitted a memorial asking that Chou Pien be put in command of thirty thousand foot soldiers to defend against the bandit host at Jade Tower City. Chou was too reckless and underestimated the enemy, so his troops were defeated. Under the cover of night he returned alone on horseback, having cast off his armor to flee the enemy. The rebels also collected the provisions and armor his troops had abandoned and withdrew. Ch'un-yü Fen for these reasons imprisoned Chou Pien and asked that he be punished as well, but the king pardoned them both.

In the same month the Minister of Justice, Chou Pien, got an ulcer on his back and died. Ch'un-yü Fen's wife, the princess, suddenly became ill and after ten days she also passed away. Ch'un-yü Fen therefore asked to be relieved of his governorship to escort her body back to the capital; the king granted his request. Then he entrusted the Minister of Agriculture, T'ien Tzu-hua, with the duties of Governor of Southern Branch. Ch'un-yü Fen set out, sadly accompanying her hearse. As they moved in a dignified manner along the road men and women wailed, people set out offerings of food, and those who obstructed the carriage or blocked the road were too numerous to count. When their procession reached the capital city, the king and his wife, weeping and clothed in white, were in the suburbs, awaiting the arrival of

---

7. A figurative expression indicating an official arriving to take up a new post. One of the first duties of such officials was to look into "local customs" to determine that the moral influence of the government was in force.

the hearse. The princess received the posthumous title of "The Princess of Mild Bearing." An honor-guard carrying feathered umbrellas and beating drums had been prepared, and she was buried a few miles east of the capital city at Coiled Dragon Tumulus. The same month the son of the former Minister of Justice, Chou Jung-hsin, also escorted his father's remains back to the capital city.

While Ch'un-yü Fen was stationed in Southern Branch, he got to know many personalities in the capital, so that all the noble and prominent families were on good terms with him. Since he had resigned from his position as governor and returned to the capital city, he went out constantly, numbering friends and retainers in his company, so that his prestige and fortune increased daily. The king began to suspect and fear him. At that time someone from the capital city submitted a memorial, which read:

> In the signs from heaven an error is evident, suggesting a great threat to the nation. The capital will be moved, and the ancestral temple will collapse. The cause of this strife came from another people, but the matter lies within Your Majesty's walls.

At the time it was agreed that this was an omen caused by Fen's extravagance. Then Fen's bodyguard was taken away, he was forbidden to see his band of friends, and he was placed under house arrest. Fen, certain that in his many years as governor of the commandery he had not failed in his policies and that rumors unjustly found fault with him, was melancholy and unhappy. The king knew this and said to Fen, "You have been related to us by marriage for more than twenty years. Unfortunately, my daughter died young and wasn't able to be with you in your old age. This is really hard to bear!"

For this reason his wife, the queen, kept her grandchildren in her charge to care for and to educate. A little later the king said to Fen, "You have been separated from your family for a long time. You ought to go home to your village for a time and see your relatives. You can leave your children here. They will want for nothing. After three years[8] we shall send them to you."

"But this is my home," Fen replied. "Where else would I go?"

The king laughed and said, "You come from the world of men—your home is not here!"

Suddenly Fen grew groggy with sleep and his sight was hazy for a while until he became aware of his former life again. Then he wept and asked to return there. The king turned to his attendants indicating they should see him off. Bowing repeatedly, Fen left, and again saw the two purple-clad envoys from before following him.

When they had walked through the main palace gate, he was astonished to see that the carriage he was to ride was dilapidated and there were no

---

8. I.e., in the Ting-ch'ou year.

diligent envoys or palace servants as when he had come. He got into the carriage and after a few miles they came out of the great city. It seemed to be the eastern road along which he had come to the capital in the past. The mountains, streams, plains, and fields on either side were all the same as before. But his two attendants were not as awe-inspiring, leaving him even less pleased. He asked them, "When will we arrive at Kuang-ling command-ery?" But the two went on singing and paid him no heed, until one of them, after a long time, answered, "We will be there soon."

Not long after, they emerged from a hole and he saw the lane through his village which had not changed from former days. Deeply moved, he could not hold back his tears. The two envoys helped Fen out of the carriage, into his gate, and up his stairs, where he saw his own body lying underneath the veranda east of the main hall. Fen was in great dread and didn't dare to advance farther. The two envoys for this reason called out his name in a loud voice a few times and Fen then came back to his senses as before. He saw one of the household servants sweeping the courtyard with a broom and one of his retainers sitting on a bench washing his feet. The setting sun had not yet sunk behind the western wall of his compound and the wine left in their goblets was still glistening by the eastern window. In the dream which flashed by him it was as if he had passed an entire lifetime.

As Fen recalled his dream, he was moved to sigh. Then he called his two friends to him and recounted what had happened. Amazed, they then went out with him to search for the hole beneath the locust tree. Fen pointed to it and said, "This is where I entered in my dreams." The two friends supposed he must have been struck by a fox spirit or a tree elf.

Subsequently they ordered servants to take axes to the knotted roots and newly sprouted secondary trunks and locate the mouth of the opening. Nearby the road running north to south was a large hole, cavernous but well lit, which was large enough to have accommodated a bench. The soil piled on the roots made it seem they were city walls, escarpments, towers, and palaces in which several bushels of ants were hiding. In their midst was a raised platform, its color a kind of crimson. Two large ants about three inches in length with white wings and red heads sat upon it. Several dozen large ants assisted them there, and all the other ants cowered before them. This was their king and it was none other than the capital city of Locust Tranquil-ity.

Farther on they followed another hole which ran straight up nearly two rods into a southern branch. Winding about within the hole were earthen walls and small towers. A swarm of ants was also there, which was none other than the Southern Branch Commandery which Fen had directed.

Farther on was another hole. It went west for over a rod, broad and expansive with tightly packed walls and a deep pit of strange shape. In it was a rotting turtle-shell as big as a peck measure. It was immersed in rainwater that had accumulated there. Small plants grew thick, providing shadows of luxuriance and overlapping each other as they swayed up and down in the wind. This was the Efficacious Tortoise Mountain where Fen had hunted.

They discovered another hole which ran east about a rod: old roots twisted about, shaped like dragons and snakes. In its midst there was a small earthen mound, a little over a foot tall. This, then, was the grave at Coiled Dragon Tumulus where Fen had buried his wife.

When he thought back to those former affairs he sighed and was moved, as those places they had discovered by opening the base of the tree all fit closely with those of which he had dreamed. Not wanting his two friends to destroy them, he quickly ordered them covered up as before.

That night there was a violent storm. In the morning, when he went to look into the hole, the ants had disappeared without a trace. Therefore the prediction made earlier—"When great disaster threatens the nation, the capital city must be moved away"—had its fulfillment.

Now Ch'un-yü Fen recalled the events of the campaign against Sandal-wood Creepers, and again asked his two friends to go out and look for traces of it. Not half a mile to the east of his home was an old dried-up brook. On its bank was a huge sandalwood tree covered with vines and creepers so that if you looked up you couldn't see the sun. There was a small hole in the side of the trunk in which indeed swarms of ants were concealed. Could the Nation of Sandalwood Creepers be anywhere else than here?!

Ah! If even the spiritual mystery of ants is unfathomable, how much more are the transformations of those who hide in the mountains or conceal themselves in forests.[9]

At the time Fen's drinking companions Chou Pien and T'ien Tzu-hua both lived in Six Harmonies county, but had not been by to visit for ten days. Fen anxiously sent his servant-boy to hurry and ask after them. Mr. Chou had suddenly taken ill and passed away, and Mr. T'ien was also bedridden with a disease. Feeling even more the transience of the Southern Branch and understanding man's life was only a sudden moment, Fen then rested his mind in the gate of the Tao, giving up wine and women. Three years later in the Ting-ch'ou year [10] Fen also died in his home at the age of forty-seven, just as predicted.

In the eighth month—the fall—of the eighteenth year of the Chen-yüan reign era,[11] the author of this piece, having sailed from Wu to Loyang and moored my boat for a short time at Huai-p'u, chanced to meet Master Ch'un-

9. Hermits and ascetics.
10. See notes 4 and 8.
11. This is the equivalent of 802 C.E.

yü. I inquired about these events and visited the places involved so that we went over them a number of times. As the events were all verifiable, I recorded and edited them into this account as matter for those fond of such things. Although it is all searching after spirits and speaking of the strange rather than matters involved with the classics, I hope it will be a warning to those young men who wish to steal their way into an official position. May you later gentlemen be fortunate to take the Southern Branch as an accident of life and may you not act so haughtily in this world because of fame or position!

The former Military Adviser of Hua prefecture, Li Chao, composed a coda:

> The noblest emolument and position,
> Power to overthrow cities and lands—
> The wise man regards these things
> As nothing different from swarming ants.

Translated by William H. Nienhauser, Jr.

Vernacular Short Stories

<hr>

209

The Shrew: Sharp-Tongued Ts'ui-lien

Anonymous (late 14th or early 15th century)

The Storyteller's Preamble:

> She declaims whole chapters extempore—
> > let no one despise her gift!
> Each speech brings her fresh enemies;
> > her fate moves men to pity.
> Though she lacks the persuasion of the wise Tzu-lu [1]
> May her tale yet win a laugh from you.

This highly colloquial short story harks back to the T'ang transformation texts (*pien-wen*) as preserved in tenth-century manuscripts at Tun-huang, in which verse and prose alternate in both narrative and dialogue (see selection 214). The form of its verse, in which heptasyllabic lines predominate, interspersed with trisyllabic lines and punctuated by a rough and ready rhyme (not reproduced in the translation), is similar to that of the Tun-huang stories, which it also resembles in its mixing of the serious with the grotesque, in its naive tone and incoherence, and in its homeliness of language and infelicitous allusions. When it is further remembered that the heroine ends up as a nun, the ultimate monastic origins of the story seem to be beyond doubt.

Although the present text of "The Shrew" probably dates to the early fifteenth century, it must have assumed more or less its present shape around the end of the thirteenth century, and many of the customs and motifs it portrays date back at least a century earlier. It is likely that the oral precursor of the present written text derives from Buddhist recitations held in fairgrounds during the eleventh century after monastic performances were forbidden by the government.

1. The disciple of Confucius noted more for fortitude than for wisdom or eloquence.

These lines refer to former days in the Eastern Capital,[2] where dwelled a gentleman by the name of Chang Eminent, who had in his house much gold and silver. Of his two grown-up sons,[3] the older was called Tiger, the younger Wolf. The older son had already taken a wife, the younger was not yet married. In the same city was another gentleman, Li Lucky, who had a daughter named Ts'ui-lien,[4] aged sixteen and uncommonly pretty, accomplished in the art of the needle and conversant even with the Classics, Histories, and Hundred Philosophers. She was, however, somewhat too ready with her tongue. In speaking to others, she composed whole essays, and the flow of her speech became a flood. Questioned about one matter, she answered about ten, and when questioned about ten, she answered about a hundred. There is a poem to prove it:

> Asked about one thing, she tells about ten—indeed a feat!
> Ask her ten things, she'll tell you a hundred—rare talent!
> Her speech is ready, her words come swift—truly a marvel!
> Regard her not as common; she is no ordinary maid.

The story went that in the same city was a Madam Wang who went to and fro between the two families to arrange about a marriage. The family stations corresponding, a match was agreed upon, and a propitious day and hour chosen for the wedding. Three days before the event, Li Lucky said to his wife, "Our daughter is faultless in most respects; only her tongue is quick and you and I cannot be easy about it. Should her father-in-law prove hard to please, it were no trifling matter. Besides, the mother-in-law is certain to be fussy, and they are a large family with older brother, sister-in-law, and numerous others. What shall we do?" And his wife said, "You and I will need to caution her against it." With this, they saw Ts'ui-lien come before them, and when she found that the faces of both her parents were clouded with grief, and their eyebrows closely knit, she said:

> "Dad as bounteous as heaven, Ma as bounteous as earth,
> To arrange this match for me today!
> The man finds a wife, the maid a mate,
> It's a time for rejoicing: be gay for luck!
> A fine husband, people all say,
> Possessed of riches and many precious things, and well connected,
> Clever and nimble,
> Good at Double-Six,[5] chess, and all the gentle arts.

2. I.e., the Northern Sung capital Pien, or Kaifeng.
3. The original merely says "two sons," but Wolf's younger brother is later mentioned.
4. The name means "Blue Lotus" and thus has Buddhist associations.
5. A dice game. Skill in the game was rated an accomplishment, certainly in the Yüan and Ming. In *Chin P'ing Mei* ([*Gold Vase Plum*], the celebrated late sixteenth-century erotic novel),

He composes verse, and antithetical couplets[6] on demand;
He even knows trade and commerce, selling and buying.
How do you like him for a son-in-law
That bitter tears should fall in drops?"

When Li Lucky and his wife had heard her to the end, they were exceedingly angry. They said, "We were grieving even because your tongue is as sharp as a blade. We feared that when you entered your husband's house you might talk too much and offend against the proprieties, and thus incur the displeasure of your parents-in-law and everyone else, and become a laughing-stock. So we called you to caution you to talk as little as possible. But higgledy-piggledy, you come out again with a long discourse! What a bitter lot is ours!" Ts'ui-lien, however, said in reply:

"Dad, ease your mind; Ma, be consoled;
Brother, rest assured; sister-in-law, stop worrying;
It is not that your daughter would boast of her cleverness
But from childhood she has been on her mettle:
She can spin, she can weave,
She makes dresses, does patching and embroidery;
Light chores and heavy duties she takes in her stride,
Has ready the teas and meals in a trice;
She can work the hand-mill and pound with the pestle;
She endures hardship gladly, she is not easily tired,
Thinks nothing of making dumplings and cookies,
Prepares any soup or broth, does to a turn some cutlet or chop.
At night she is vigilant,
Fastens the back door and bolts the gate,
Scrubs the frying pan, shuts the cupboard,
Tidies up the rooms both in front and behind,
Makes ready the beds, unrolls the quilts,
Lights the lamp, asks the mother-in-law to retire,
Then calls out 'Rest well' and returns to her room:
Thus shall I serve my parents-in-law,
And would they be dissatisfied?
Dear Dad and Ma, let your minds be at rest—
Besides these set tasks, nought matters more than a fart."

When Ts'ui-lien had finished, her father rose from his chair to beat her. But the mother pleaded with him, and loudly reproved her, saying, "Child, your father and I were worried just because of your sharp tongue. From now on,

---

go-betweens cataloging the virtues of prospective lovers and bridegrooms invariably mention a knowledge of chess and Double-Six.

6. Making up such couplets was part of the schoolboy's exercise in composition.

talk less. The ancients say, 'Loquacity earns the hatred of many.' When you enter your husband's house, be wary of speaking. A thousand times remember this!" Ts'ui-lien thereupon said, "I know now. From this time onward I will keep my mouth shut."

On the eve of the wedding,[7] Mrs. Li said to Ts'ui-lien, "Old grandfather Chang next door is a neighbor of long standing, and you grew up, as it were, under his very eyes. You should go over and bid him farewell." And Mr. Li also said, "That would be right." Ts'ui-lien then went over to the neighbors', crossed their threshold, and spoke in a loud voice:

> "Grandpa Chang, hearken; Grandma Chang, hearken;
> Hearken to my speech, you two old ones.
> Tomorrow at dawn I mount my bridal sedan;
> Today I am come to make the announcement.
> My parents are frail, they have no support;
> Pray keep an eye on them morning and night.
> If my brother and his wife offend you in any way,
> Forgive them for my parents' sake.
> When I return a month after the event,
> I shall myself come to ask your pardon."

Grandfather Chang replied, "Little lady, set your mind at rest. Your father and I are dear old friends. I shall certainly look after him morning and evening. And I shall ask my aged spouse to keep your mother company. On no account let it trouble you."

When Ts'ui-lien returned from bidding Grandfather Chang farewell, Li Lucky and his wife said to her, "Child, you should now tidy up and go to bed early. Tomorrow you have to rise before daybreak to attend to things." Ts'ui-lien then said:

> "Dad, retire first; Ma, retire first;
> You are not like us young ones.
> Sister-in-law and brother can keep me company
> While each part of the house I tidy up.
> The young can watch all through the night;
> Older folk, when they try it, fall a-dozing."

When Ts'ui-lien had spoken, the father and mother were greatly vexed. They cried, "Have done! Have done! As we were saying, you would never change. We will now retire. You can tidy up with your brother and sister-in-law, and then 'Early to bed and early to rise.' "

When Ts'ui-lien saw that her parents had gone to rest, she hurriedly went to the door of her brother's room and shouted aloud:

7. The time, not mentioned in the original, is inserted by the translator.

"Do not pretend to be drunk, sister-in-law and brother—
How distressing even to think of you two!
I am your own dear little sister
And shall be home just one more night.
However could you two act in this way,
Leaving all the chores to me,
Shutting your door, ready to fall asleep?
Sister-in-law, how ungracious of you!
I am at home but this short while—
Would it matter so much if you lent a hand?
You cannot wait to send me away
That the two of you may be free and easy."

Ts'ui-lien finished speaking, and the brother remonstrated with her, saying, "How could you still behave like this? With Dad and Ma there, I am not in a position to scold you. Go and rest now, and get up early tomorrow. Your sister-in-law and I will attend to whatever has to be done." So Ts'ui-lien went back to her room to sleep. In a little while the brother and sister-in-law had tided up each part of the house, and the entire family retired for the night.

Li Lucky and his wife woke up after a good sleep. They called out to Ts'ui-lien, saying, "Child, what time is it now? Is it fine or rainy?" Then Ts'ui-lien broke into speech:

"Dad, do not rise yet; Ma, do not rise yet;
I do not know if it be rainy or fine;
I do not hear the watch being sounded—or the cock crow.
The streets are quiet, none are conversing;
I only hear Mrs. Pai next door
    making ready to grind her bean-curd,
And old father Huang opposite pounding his sticky rice.
If not still the fourth watch,
Certainly it would be the fifth.
Let me rise first,
Start the fire, chop the wood, and fetch the water.
Next let me scrub the pot,
Boil water with which to wash my face,
And comb my hair till it is smooth and shining.
Let everyone else rise early too,
Lest the bridal procession find us all in a flurry."

Then father, mother, brother, and sister-in-law all rose from their beds. And the father and mother said in an outburst of rage, "All too soon it will be bright in the east. Yet instead of attending to your toilet, you are busy wagging your tongue." But Ts'ui lien said in reply:

"Dad, do not scold; Ma, do not scold;
See how cleverly I adorn myself in my room.
My raven-black hair I flatten around each temple,
Mix powder and rouge and rub them on my cheeks,
Then paint my red lips and pencil my eyebrows.
A golden earring I wear in each lobe,
Silver and gold, jade and pearl I pin all over my head,
Pendants of gems and tinkling bells I attach to my sides.
You are marrying me off today,
But, oh! my Dad and Ma, how could I leave you?
I bethink me of the favors of giving suck and rearing
And teardrops wet through my scented silk handkerchief.
Hark, I hear voices outside the house —
Despite myself I grow alarmed.
But today is my lucky day:
Why go on tattling and prattling like this?"

Ts'ui-lien stopped. However, when her toilet was done, she went straight into her parents' presence and said:

"Dad, hear my report; Ma, hear my report;
The dumplings are steamed, the noodles are cut,
The viands and box of delicacies are laid out.
I have them all ready, and now wait patiently
Even while the drumbeats give out the fifth watch.
Mark how our own rooster crows right on the hour!
We must send for the relatives who planned to see me off.
It would matter little if Ma's sister and Uncle's wife stayed away,
But how wicked of Dad's own sister!
She sets no store by her words.
She promised to be here by the fifth watch only yesterday;
The cock has crowed, yet there is no trace of her.
When, later, she enters our gate, I must just —
Instead of a final invitation —
Offer her a resounding slap with all five fingers outstretched." [8]

Angry though they were at her words, Li Lucky and his wife forbore to speak out. Mrs. Li said, "Child, go and ask your brother and sister-in-law to rise now and attend to things. The bridal procession will soon be here." When Ts'ui-lien heard her mother say this, she hurriedly went to the door of the brother and sister-in-law and shouted aloud:

"Dear sister-in-law, dear brother, you are no longer children.
From now on I shall seldom be home;

8. Presumably to give a harder smack.

You could at least have risen early today—
Will you sleep until broad daylight?
It's time to unbolt the gate and open the windows;
Next, you might light the candles and aromatic incense;
Then give the ground, within and without, a sweeping:
The bridal sedan is expected any moment,
And if the hour[9] be missed and my parents-in-law annoyed,
The pair of you shall hear from me!"

The brother and sister-in-law swallowed the affront and kept silent, and they attended to various tasks in the house. Then Li Lucky said to Ts'ui-lien, "Child, you should go before the family shrine, make obeisance to your ancestors, and bid them farewell. I have already lit the candles and incense; so do it while we wait for the bridal procession. May the ancestors protect you and you be at peace in your husband's home." Thus instructed, Ts'ui-lien took a bunch of lighted incense sticks and went before the shrine, and even as she made obeisance, she prayed aloud:

"Shrine that guides the household,
You sages that were our ancestors,
This day I take a husband,
Yet shall not dare keep my own counsel:
At the solstices and equinoxes and the beginning of each season,
I still will offer up the smoke of incense.
I pray to your divine wisdom
Ten thousand times that you pity and hearken!
The man takes a wife, the maid a mate—
This is in the nature of things—
May there be good fortune and rejoicing!
May husband and wife both remain sound and whole,
Without hardship, without calamity,
Even for a hundred years!
May they be merry as fish in water
And their union prove sweeter than honey,
Blessed with five sons and two daughters—
A complete family of seven children—
Matched with two worthy sons-in-law,
Wise and versed in etiquette,
And five daughters-in-law too,
Paragons of filial piety.
May there be grandsons and granddaughters numerous
To flourish generation after generation.
May there be gold and pearls in heaps,

9. The lucky hour fixed upon by the astrologer for the wedding ceremony.

And rice and wheat to fill a granary,
Abundance of silkworms and mulberry trees,
And cattle and horses drawn up neck to neck,
Chickens, geese, ducks, and other fowl,
And a pond teeming with fish.
May my husband obey me,
Yet his parents love and pity me;
May the sister-in-law and I live in harmony,
And the older and the younger brother be both easy to please;
May the servants show full respect,
And the younger sister take a fancy to me.
And, within a space of three years,
Let them die, the whole lot,
And all the property be left in my hands:
Then Ts'ui-lien would be happy for some years!"

When Ts'ui-lien had finished her prayer, there was a din outside the gate. It was a confused noise of many musical instruments, above which rose the shrill notes of pipes and singing. The procession from the bridegroom's family, carriage, horsemen and all, was at the gate. And the astrologer accompanying the procession chanted in verse:

"Roll up your bead curtain and fasten it with jade hooks;
A perfumed carriage, followed by noble horses,
    has reached your gate.
Be liberal in your happy-omened tips on this auspicious occasion
And in wealth, honor, and splendor pass a hundred autumns."

Li Lucky then asked his wife to fetch money to reward the astrologer, the matchmaker, the grooms, and other attendants. But when Mrs. Li came out with the banknotes, Ts'ui-lien snatched them from her, saying, "Let me distribute these notes—

Dad, you are not used to this; Ma, you are not used to this;
Brother and sister-in-law, you too are not used to this dealing.
Hey, all of you there, come and stand before me!
Be it less or more, it is as I shall apportion.
To the sedan-bearers, five thousand copper cash;
Mr. Astrologer and the matchmaker each get two and a half.
Keep your money well, do not start a row;
If any of you lose it, you have but yourself to blame.
Look, there's another thousand cash note remaining—
Take it, matchmaker, and buy a cake
To comfort your dotard of a husband at home."

The astrologer, the sedan-bearers, and the others were all aghast when they heard this. They said, "We have seen thousands of brides but never one so quick in speech." They gaped and put their tongues out and, swallowing their anger, crowded around Ts'ui-lien and helped her onto the bridal sedan.

While they were on their way, the matchmaker kept on admonishing Ts'ui-lien, "Little lady, when you reach the gate of the house of your parents-in-law, on no account open your mouth." Before long, the procession reached the gate of the Chang home and the sedan-chair was let down. The astrologer chanted:

> "The sound of nuptial music is heard all over the capital;
> The Weaving Maid this day weds the Divine Cowherd.[10]
> The relatives of this house come forth to receive the treasure;
> The bride in her finery accepts her mouthful of rice —
>
> > a custom from time immemorial."

To go on with the story, the matchmaker held up a bowl of rice and shouted loudly, "Little lady, open your mouth to receive the rice." [11] Upon this, Ts'ui-lien in her bridal sedan burst out in rage:

> "Shameless old bitch! Shameless old bitch!
> One moment you tell me to shut my mouth,
>
> > and the next you ask me to *open* it!
>
> Oh! the unfathomable glibness of matchmakers!
> However could you change your don'ts at once into do's?
> Are you drunk already so early in the day
> That foolishly you open *your* mouth,
>
> > lying and wagging your tongue?
>
> Just then while you walked by my sedan
> You warned me on no account to open my mouth.
> I have only now been set down before the gate —
> Why then do you ask me to open my mouth?
> Blame me not for calling you names —
> Really you are but a painted old bitch."

The astrologer then said, "Bride, cease your anger. She is the matchmaker. You go too far in your words. There is no precedent for such behavior in a bride." But Ts'ui-lien replied:

> "Mr. Astrologer, you are a man of learning;
> How then could you be so dull of apprehension?
> Not to speak when one ought to is, by definition, slow-witted.

---

10. The lovers who were transformed into two stars separated by the Milky Way, to meet only on the night of the seventh of the seventh moon each year.

11. The custom is not recorded in the accounts of Sung city life.

This bawd of a matchmaker will be the death of me!
She says the bridegroom's family is wealthy and high-ranking,
Possessed of riches and precious things, much silver and gold;
A calf or horse they would kill for their table;
Their gate is made of sandal and sapanwood;
They have silks, gauzes, brocades in numberless rolls,
And pigs, goats, cattle, and horses all in droves.
Yet even before I enter the house, they dish up this cold rice:
Better be poor than wealthy and high-ranking in *this* fashion.
Hard indeed to endure a family so uncouth
As would serve up cold rice and expect me to swallow it!
Had I no regard for the faces of both parents-in-law,
I could beat you till you saw stars!"

Ts'ui-lien having had her say, the matchmaker was so incensed that she tasted not a drop of wine but, like a whiff of smoke, vanished into the house, minding neither Ts'ui-lien's descent from the bridal sedan [12] nor the ensuing ceremony at the altar.

But the relatives of the bridegroom's family crowded around Ts'ui-lien and escorted her into the ceremonial hall, where they made her stand with her face to the west.[13] The astrologer, however, announced, "The bride will turn and face the east. The stars of good luck are all in the east today." At this, Ts'ui-lien again burst out:

"Just then it was west, and now I must face east.
Will you drag the bride about as you would lead a beast?
Having turned around and around, tending in no fixed direction,
I am so vexed, my heart is afire:
I cannot tell who my mother-in-law
Or who my father-in-law is
Amidst this noisy crowd of relatives even to the ninth degree,
With the younger brother and sister adding to the confusion.
The red paper tablet is placed in the center
And red silken lanterns, several pairs of them, are lit.
But, wait, my father-in-law and mother-in-law are not yet deceased.
Why then should there be a lamp for the dead?"

Old Chang Eminent and his wife were furious when they heard this. They exclaimed, "It was earlier agreed that our son would marry the daughter of a respectable family. Who would have known it would turn out to be this ill-

12. This involved much ceremony.
13. The customary position. The altar is in the north, and as seen by the guests, the bride would be on the right and the groom on the left.

mannered, ill-bred, long-tongued wayward peasant girl?" And all the relatives of the nine degrees gaped, utterly confounded.

Finally the astrologer said, "This child has been spoiled at home. She has only just arrived today. You will need to train her gradually. Let us proceed with the ceremony of bowing before the altar, to be followed by the bowing to the relatives." And when the ceremony was over and all the relatives, old and young, had been introduced, the astrologer, chanting in verse, requested the bride and groom to enter the nuptial chamber for the strewing of the bed-curtains:

> "The newly wed move their steps across the lofty hall;
> Nymph and god together enter the nuptial chamber.
> Be liberal in your happy-omened tips
>   on this auspicious occasion —
> Scatter the grain in all directions,
>   that yin and yang mingling may increase."

Wolf went in front, with Ts'ui-lien behind him. The astrologer, holding before him a peck containing a mixture of the five grains, followed them into the nuptial chamber.

The newly wedded couple sat on the bed while the astrologer chanted with the grain in his hand:

> "Scatter the grain east of the bed-curtains —
> Red candles cast their shadows where thick screens enfold.
> Long may youthful charms bloom, not fade;
> Eternal spring prevail in the painted hall!
>
> Scatter the grain west of the bed-curtains —
> Pennants and ribbons stream down the corners of the bed.
> Lift the veil and you will see the goddess's face;
> The godlike bridegroom attains his laurel branch.[14]
>
> Scatter the grains south of the bed-curtains —
> Nuptial bliss long to linger over!
> A gentle breeze in moonlight cools hall and bower,
> Flapping two belts adorned with the 'heir-bearing' plant.[15]

14. The goddess Ch'ang-o dwells alone with a white rabbit and a laurel tree in the moon, where her earthbound husband, Yi, eventually joins her. In other versions, she is visited by the woodcutter Wu Kang, who is, however, condemned to hack eternally at the laurel branches, which heal at once. T'ang examination candidates spoke of "breaking off a laurel branch" when they were successful. Since successful examination candidates were readily accepted as bridegrooms, "attainer of the laurel branch" and "moon-goddess's guest" came to be applied to both successful examinees and bridegrooms.

15. The day lily.

> Scatter the grain north of the bed-curtains—
> That overflowing beauty between her eyebrows!
> In the warmth of the embroidered curtains on a night in spring
> The moon goddess detains her favored guest.
>
> Scatter the grain above the bed-curtains—
> A pair of intertwining mandarin ducks!
> May you dream tonight of the bear [16]
> And the pearl-oyster falling onto your palm!
>
> Scatter the grain within the bed-curtains—
> A pair of jade hibiscus under the moon!
> It's as if one encountered a fair immortal,
> Wrapped in crimson clouds, alighting from Mount Wu. [17]
>
> Scatter the grain under the bed-curtains—
> Some say a golden light will shine in the room.
> Share now the lucky dreams of this night:
> Bring forth next year a man-child and win enhanced standing.
>
> Scatter the grain in front of the bed-curtains—
> Hovering in the air is neither mist nor smoke,
> It is the coiled-dragon incense fume:
> The student at last meets his fairy bride. [18]
>
> Scatter the grain behind the bed-curtains—
> Man and wife agreeing, long cherish each other.
> From of old 'Wife chimes in when husband sings';
> Do not then roar like the proverbial lioness." [19]

To go on with the story, the astrologer had not yet completed the ceremony of strewing the bed-curtains, when Ts'ui-lien sprang up and, groping about, found a rolling-pin, with which she dealt him two smart blows in the sides, and roundly abused him, "You skunk of a windbag. It's your own wife who would be the lioness." And without further ado she drove him out of the bridal chamber, shouting after him:

> "Scatter the grain indeed! I ask you, to what purpose?
> Having littered that way, again to litter this way—
> Beans, rice, wheat, barley all over the bed.

16. Omen of the birth of a son. The pearl-oyster is the symbol of pregnancy.

17. Mount Wu, whose goddess came to the Ch'u king, Huai, in a dream. Her presence, she told him, was to be felt in the morning clouds and evening rain. Hence the expression "clouds and rain" for a love encounter.

18. The legendary student Wen Hsiao met his fairy bride Wu Ts'ai-luan in the mountains.

19. Euphemism for wife's scolding.

Just pause to think: Ain't it a pretty sight?
The parents-in-law are rude and rash,
The bride's untidy and careless, they'll say.
And if the husband should pretend to be vexed,
He would say the wife was slatternly.
Off with you at once—out of the gate.
And spare yourself more blows from my rolling-pin."

The astrologer took his beating and went out through the gate. The bride-groom, Wolf, was now roused and exclaimed, "Of the thousands of misfor-tunes, to have married this peasant woman! Strewing the bed-curtains is an ancient ceremony." To this Ts'ui-lien said in reply:

"Husband, husband, be not angry,
Hear me and judge the right and wrong for yourself.
The mere thought of that man tries my patience,
Littering beans and barley all over the place.
Yet you ask no one to sweep them away;
Instead you say, I lack womanly obedience.
If you vex me any further,
You too I will drive out with him,
Shut my door, sleep by myself.
'Early to bed and early to rise' as I please,
And 'Amitābha' [20] chant my prayers
With my ears undisturbed in careless solitude."

And Wolf, at a loss what to do with her, went out to join in the feasting and toast his guests.

By nightfall the feast broke up and the relatives all went home. Sitting alone in the nuptial chamber, Ts'ui-lien thought to herself, "Soon my hus-band will come into the room and his hands are certain to rove in some wild ecstatic dance. I have to be prepared." So she stood up, removed her jewelry, undressed and, getting into bed, rolled herself tightly in a quilt and slept. Now, to go on with the story, Wolf came in and undressed, and was about to go to bed, when Ts'ui-lien stunned him with a thundering cry:

"Wretch, how ridiculously mistaken in your designs!
Of a truth, what an uncouth rustic!
You are a man, I a woman;
You go your way, I go mine.
You say I am your own bride—
Well, do not call me your old woman yet.

20. The Buddha of immeasurability who is associated with the paradise called Sukhāvati, or the Western Pure Land. Perhaps ultimately of Iranian origin.

Who was the matchmaker? Who the chief witness?
What were the betrothal presents? How was the gift of tea?
How many pigs, sheep, fowl, and geese? How many vats of wine?
What floral decorations embellished the gifts?
How many gems? How many golden head ornaments?
How many rolls of silk gauze, thick and thin?
How many pairs of bracelets, hatpins, hairpins?
With what should I adorn myself?
At the third watch late at night,
What mean you to come before my bed?
At once depart, and hurry away,
Lest you annoy my folk at home.
But if you provoke my fiery temper,
I will seize you by the ears and pull your hair,
Tear your clothes and scratch your face;
My heavy hand with outstretched fingers shall fall pat on your cheek.
If I rip your hairnet, don't say I did not warn you,
Nor complain if your neatly coiled hair gets disheveled.
This is no bawd's lane.
Nor the dwelling of some servile courtesan.
What do I care about silly rules like 'Two and two make four'?
With a sudden laying about of my fist
I'll send you sprawling all over the room."

When Wolf heard his bride declaim this chapter, he dared not approach her, nor uttered even a groan, but sat in a far-off corner of the room.

To go on with the story, soon it was indeed almost the third watch, and Ts'ui-lien thought to herself, "I have now married into his family. Alive, I shall remain one of their household; dead, I shall dwell among their ghosts. If we do not sleep in the same bed tonight, when tomorrow my parents-in-law learn about it, they will certainly blame me. Let it be, then! I will ask him to come to bed." So she said to Wolf:

"Dumb wretch, do not say you are drunk!
Come over, I will share the bed with you.
Draw near me and hear my command:
Fold your hands respectfully before you;
    tread on your toes; do not chatter.
Remove your hairnet and off with your cap;
Gather up your garments, socks, and boots;
Shut the door, lower the curtain,
And add some oil to the lamp grown dim.
Come to bed, and ever so softly;
We'll pretend to be mandarin ducks or intertwining trees.

Make no noise, be careful of what you say;
When our conjugal rites are completed,
    you'll curl up next to my feet,
Crooking your knee-joints, drawing in your heels.
If by chance you give even one kick,
Then know it's *death* for you!"

And the story went that the whole night through Wolf indeed dared not make the least noise. They slept until dawn, when the mother-in-law called out, "Wolf, you should ask your bride to rise early, finish her toilet, and come out to tidy up." So Ts'ui-lien spoke out:

"Do not hurry, do not rush;
Wait till I have donned my everyday clothes.
Now—vegetables with vegetables, ginger with ginger,
Each variety of nuts into a separate pack.
Pork on one side, mutton on the other;
We'll sort out the fresh fish from boiled tripe.
Wine by itself, away from the broth;
Salt chicken and smoked venison should not be mixed.
In the cool of this time of year
They will keep yet a good five days.
Let me set apart some neat slices
To serve on the third morn with tea for the aunts.
And if the relatives do not eat them all,
The parents-in-law can have the leftovers as a treat."

When the mother-in-law had heard this, she was a long while speechless. She wanted to scold Ts'ui-lien but was afraid she would only make herself a laughing-stock. So she swallowed her anger and endured in silence until the third morn,[21] when the bride's mother called in to present her gifts. And when the two mothers-in-law had met, Mrs. Chang could no longer contain herself: she recounted from beginning to end how Ts'ui-lien had inflicted blows on the astrologer and how she had abused the matchmaker, how she had insulted her husband and how she had slighted her parents-in-law. Upon hearing this account, Mrs. Li grew exceedingly ashamed. She went straight to her daughter's room and said to Ts'ui-lien, "What did I warn you against when you were still at home? I told you not to jabber and chatter when you entered your husband's house, but you never listened to me. It is only the third day, yet your mother-in-law made many complaints about you just then, causing me to be in fear and trepidation, and unable to utter a word in reply." Ts'ui-lien, however, said:

21. It was customary during the Sung period for the bride's family to send gifts of colored silks and honey cake or to call themselves, which was known as "comforting the daughter."

"Mother, don't start a row yet;
Listen while I relate it in each particular.
Your daughter is no untaught peasant woman;
There are some matters you little know about.
On the third morn the new daughter-in-law enters the kitchen [22]
(Ha ha, to relate this would but earn me ridicule!)
Two bowls of thin rice porridge with salt was all they provided
And, to serve with the meal, not even tea but plain boiling water!
Now you, their new relation, make your first call,
At once they start their tittle-tattle:
Regardless of white or black, true or false,
Harassing me is all they are bent on.
My mother-in-law is by nature too impetuous,
The things she says are none too proper.
Let her beware—lest driven to my last resource,
With a bit of cord and swing from the noose
I leave her to answer for my corpse."

When the mother found Ts'ui-lien talking in this way, she could not very well scold her. And without drinking her tea or tasting the wine, Mrs. Li instantly took leave of her new relations, mounted her sedan-chair, and returned home.

To go on with the story, Wolf's older brother, Tiger, now began to shout in the house, "What kind of a family are we now? It was said at first that brother would be marrying a well-behaved young woman. Who would have expected it to be this tavern waitress who chatters the whole day, wagging her tongue and declaiming sentences and maxims? It is quite outrageous!" Ts'ui-lien heard him and said in reply:

"Brother-in-law, you err against ritual;
I did not in the least provoke you.
A full-grown, manly pillar of society
To call his sister-in-law a glib tavern-waitress!"

Tiger then called to Wolf and said, "Haven't you heard the old saying: 'Teach a wife when she first comes to you'? Though you need not go so far as to beat her, you might at least lecture her now and then; or else go and tell her old bawd of a mother." At this, Ts'ui-lien exclaimed:

"Busybody of a brother-in-law!
I did not dip my fingers in your bowl of rice.
Though I may be a bit loquacious,
There's husband and mother-in-law, to keep me in order.

22. In accordance with custom, to prepare her first meal for the family.

Your new relations did not provoke you—
Why then do you call my mother a bawd?
Wait till I go back when the month is over;[23]
I will tell my own dear brother at home.
My brother is a hotheaded firebrand;
You will perhaps know me better
When his fist and hand shall both at once hit out,
And like a tortoise in a drought you'll crawl in vain for shelter."

Tiger was enraged by her speech and, laying hands upon Wolf, thought to give the brother a thrashing. But his wife, Mistress Ssu, ran out from her room and said, "To each his own; how should brother's wife concern you? It was said of old: 'Don't wear your clean shoes to tread on a dunghill.'" At once Ts'ui-lien burst out again:

"Sister-in-law, don't start trouble;
This kind of conduct would never do.
Was it not enough for brother-in-law to shout at me
But you must step forward to scold some more?
It ever has been: when the wife is dutiful, the man shuns all ills
And succeeds in the highest enterprise.
Go off then quickly, back to your room,
And sit in hiding in some secure corner.
Sister-in-law, I did not provoke you—
Why then do you liken me to dung?
Since we must die even if we lived to a hundred,
Shall you and I now fight it out?
And if any mishap befell me,
Before Yama, King of the Underworld, I would not let you off."

The daughter of the house, Wolf's younger sister, heard this. She went into her mother's room and said, "You are her mother-in-law. Why don't you keep her under control? How very unseemly it would be if she carried on like this unchecked! People would only laugh at us." But when Ts'ui-lien saw the younger sister thus engaged, she called out after her:

"Younger sister, how wicked of you
To sneak within to incite your mother!
If my mother-in-law should beat me to death,
I would carry you off with me to the king of hell.
My father is by nature pugnacious—
He's not one to endure wrongs meekly—
He would insist on a hundred priests, Taoist and Buddhist,

23. A month after the wedding, the bride visits her own home.

To conduct services seven nights and seven days,
And a pine-wood coffin with a solid block for base,
And mother-in-law and father-in-law to burn paper-money for me.
You, younger sister, and sister-in-law,
    would wear mourning headscarves,
And brother-in-law could prostrate himself as my heir,
And the relatives of the nine degrees would carry the bier.
The funeral ended, our troubles would start afresh:
Accusations would have sped to the local and high courts,
Whose judges with all your silver you would bribe in vain.
Even had you millions upon millions of strings of cash,
You would spend them all and still forfeit your lives."

The mother-in-law now came out and said to Ts'ui-lien, "Luckily you have been my daughter-in-law only these three days; had you been these three years, would any of us in this family, old ones and young ones, ever get to speak at all?" Ts'ui-lien replied:

"You are too easily swayed, my mother-in-law;
When older folk grow slack, they lose the respect of the young.
Dear younger sister, do not tempt fortune too far;
Must you splutter all before your mama,
Exaggerating heavily the lightest rumors?
To which the old fool, listening and readily believing,
Stings me to the quick with this remark or that
In words unfit for the ear.
If any mishap befell me,
Rest assured the old one would pay with her life."

When the mother-in-law heard this, she went straight back to her room. And she said to the old gentleman, "Just look at that new daughter-in-law of ours. Her tongue is as sharp as a blade, and she has insulted each member of the family in turn. You are her father-in-law. Don't be afraid to summon and reprimand her." The old gentleman said, "I am the father-in-law, and so hardly in a position to reprimand her. However, let me ask her for some tea to drink, and we can then see what happens." His wife then said, "When she sees you, she will not dare wag her tongue."

Thereupon Mr. Chang gave the order, "Ask Wolf's wife to brew some midday tea." When Ts'ui-lien heard the father-in-law calling for tea, she hurriedly went into the kitchen, scrubbed the pot, and boiled the water. She then went to her own room and took out a variety of nuts, and, returning to the kitchen, made bowls of tea, which she placed on a tray. Holding the tray before her, she went into the ceremonial hall, where she arranged the chairs. She then went before her parents-in-law, saying, "Pa and Ma will please have their tea in the hall." And she also went to the sister-in-law's room and said,

"Brother and sister-in-law will please have tea in the hall." Mr. Chang then remarked, "You were all saying the new daughter-in-law had a sharp tongue. Now when I order her to do something, she dare not raise her voice." His wife rejoined, "Since this is so, you shall give her all the orders."

In a little while, the entire family were gathered in the ceremonial hall and sat down in order of seniority. And they saw Ts'ui-lien come forward with her tray to address them:

> "Pa, have tea; Ma, have tea;
> Brother and sister-in-law, come and have your tea.
> If younger sister and younger brother would like tea,
> They can help themselves to the two bowls on the oven.
> But hold your bowls well, the pair of you, and tread with care
> Lest the hot tea scald your hands and you cry 'Oh! oh!'
> This tea we call Granny's Tea;
> The name is homely, the taste delicious.
> Here are two chestnuts freshly roasted brown,
> Half a pinch of fried white sesame seeds,
> Olives from south of the Yangtze, and mixed nut kernels,
> And walnuts from beyond the Great Wall, and shelled haws.
> You two venerable ones will eat them slowly
> Lest all unwares you lose a tooth or two."

When the father-in-law found her speaking in this manner, he said in a rage, "A female person should be gentle and staid, and sober in speech: only then is she fit to be a daughter-in-law. Was there ever a long-tongued woman like this one!" But Ts'ui-lien again spoke out:

> "Venerable Pa, venerable Ma,
> And brother and sister-in-law too, sit you down,
> You two old ones, do not scold me
> But listen to your daughter-in-law's account:
> She is not stupid nor is she sly;
> From childhood on, she was straight and blunt,
> And unkind words, once uttered, slip clean out of her mind.
> Pa and Ma, do not detest her overmuch;
> But if you really disapprove, then—repudiate her:
> She will not grieve nor be afraid;
> She will mount her sedan and return home.
> No new husband shall she think of—
>   neither one who would dwell with her parents
> Nor one who would take her to his own house.
> She will not put on powder and rouge, nor adorn herself,
> But, as in mourning, wear white from top to toe,
> And so wait on her parents and end her days.

I remember many ancient men of wisdom:
Chang Liang [24] and K'uai Ch'e were skilled in argumentation,
Lu Chia and Hsiao Ho ever ready with some learned allusion;
Ts'ao Chih and Yang Hsiu were no less ready in wit;
The eloquence of Chang Yi and Su Ch'in swayed the Warring States,
And Yen Tzu and Kuan Chung overcame mighty princes
    through persuasion;
And there were Ch'en P'ing with his six stratagems, and Li Tso-chü,
And the twelve-year-old official Kan Lo,
    and the disciple Tzu-hsia himself:
These ancients all excelled in making speeches;
They regulated their households, governed their kingdoms,
    and pacified the Empire.
If Pa would stop me from speaking,
Then you must stitch up my mouth."

Mr. Chang cried, "Have done! Have done! Such a daughter-in-law would one day bring down the family name and be a reproach to the ancestors." And he called Wolf before him and said, "Son, put your wife away. I will find you another, a better wife." Though Wolf assented to this, he could not find it in his heart to cast her off. And Tiger and his wife both pleaded with the father saying, "Let her be taught gradually." But Ts'ui-lien, having heard them, once more spoke up:

"Pa, do not complain; Ma, do not complain;
Brother and sister-in-law, do you not complain.
Husband, you need not persist in clinging to me;
From now on, each will do as he pleases.
At once bring paper, ink, slab, and brush,
Write out the certificate of repudiation and set me free.
But note: [25] I did not strike my parents-in-law
    nor abuse the relatives;
I did not deceive my husband nor beat the humble and meek;

24. Chang Liang, etc. All were eloquent and persuasive speakers, including the twelve-year-old Kan Lo, who belonged to the Warring States period, as also Chang Yi and Su Ch'in; still earlier, Yen Tzu and Kuan Chung were ministers of the Ch'i state, and Tzu-hsia, the disciple of Confucius. Chang Liang, K'uai Ch'e, Lu Chia, Hsiao Ho, Ch'en P'ing, and Li Tso-chü were of early Han; and Ts'ao Chih and Yang Hsiu were of the Three Kingdoms period.

25. According to the *Record of Ritual* (*Li chi*), a wife may be repudiated on any one of seven grounds: if she refused to obey her parents-in-law; if she produced no heir; if she was lewd; if she was jealous; if she suffered from foul disease; if she talked too much; or if she thieved or robbed. A wife may not, however, be repudiated if she no longer had her own family to return to; if she had mourned her parents-in-law for three years; or if her husband had been poor at the time of their marriage but since grown rich and important. In Ts'ui-lien's list of faults of which she is innocent there occurs one important omission.

I did not go visiting neighbors, west or east;
I did not steal nor was I cozened;
I did not gossip about this person nor start trouble with that one;
I was not thievish nor jealous nor lewd;
I suffer from no foul disease; I can write and reckon;
I fetched the water from the well, hulled the rice,
    and minded the cooking;
I spun and wove and sewed.
Today, then, draw up the certificate as you please,
And when I carry away my dowry, do you not resent it.
In between our thumbprints add these words:
'Never to meet again, never to see each other.'
Conjugal affection is ended,
All feelings dead;
Set down on paper many binding oaths:
If we chance upon each other at the gate of hell,
We shall turn our heads away and not meet."

Wolf, because his parents had decided for him, wrote out the document with tears in his eyes, and the two of them affixed their thumbprints. The family called for a sedan-chair, loaded the trousseau on it, and sent Ts'ui-lien home with the certificate of repudiation.

In the Li family, Ts'ui-lien's father, mother, brother, and sister-in-law all blamed her for her sharp tongue. But she said to them:

"Dad, do not shout; Ma, do not shout;
Brother and sister-in-law, do you not shout.
It is not that your lassie would sing her own praises,
But from childhood she has been of high mettle.
This day I left their household,
And the rights and wrongs of the affair I will leave off.
It is not that my teeth are itching to speak,
But tracing patterns and embroidering, spinning, and weaving,
Cutting and trimming garments, in all these I am skilled.
True it is, moreover, I can wash and starch, stitch and sew,
Chop wood, carry water, and prepare choice dishes;
And if there are silkworms, I can keep them too.
Now I am young and in my prime,
My eyes are quick, my hand steady, my spirits bold;
Should idlers come to peep at me,
I would give them a hearty, resounding slap."

Mr. Li and his wife cried, "Have done! Have done! The two of us are now old; we can no longer keep you under our control. What we are afraid of is

that some indiscretion or other would make you simply an object of ridicule.
Poor, pitiful one!" But Ts'ui-lien went on:

> "Your daughter was destined at birth to a lonely, wretched life—
> She married an ignorant, foolish husband!
> Though I might have endured the severity of his father and mother,
> How could I have borne those sisters-in-law?
> If I but moved my lips,
> Off they went and stirred up the old ones.
> Besides, such venom lay behind their scolding,
> It soon led to blows and kicks,
> From which began an incessant to-do;
> Then all at once they wrote the certificate of dissolution.
> My one hope was to find contentment and peace at home—
> How should I expect even Dad and Ma would blame me?
> Abandoned by the husband's family and my own,
> I will cut off my hair and become a nun,
> Wear a straight-seamed gown and dangle a gourd from a pole,
> And carry in my hands a huge "wooden fish." [26]
> In the daytime from door to door I shall beg for alms;
> By night within the temple I shall praise the Buddha,
> Chant my 'Namaḥ,' [27]
> Observe my fasts and attend to my exercises.
> My head will be shaven and quite, quite bald;
> Who then will not hail the little priestess?"

And having spoken, she removed her ornaments and changed out of her gay
garments into a suit of cotton clothes. She then went before her parents,
joined the palms of her hands to perform a Buddhist salute, and bade them
farewell. And she turned and bade her brother and sister-in-law farewell. And
the brother and sister-in-law said to her, "Since you have chosen to take the
vows, let us accompany you to the Clear Voice Temple in the street in front."
Ts'ui-lien however, replied:

"Brother and sister-in-law, do not accompany me; I will go by myself;
And when I am gone, you can be easy and free.
As the ancients put it well:
'Though here not welcome, elsewhere I shall be.' [28]

---

26. Skull-shaped block on which Buddhist priests beat time when chanting. As a religious
recitation, "Sharp-Tongued Ts'ui-lien" was probably accompanied by the "wooden fish" in the
first instance. Such performances eventually may have evolved into Cantonese *mukyu* (literally,
"wooden fish"), a popular type of prosimetric storytelling.

27. Expression of submission or reverence.

28. A fairly common saying.

Since I am renouncing the world
And shall have my head shaven,
All places may be my home—
Why only the Clear Voice Temple?
Uncncumbered and without a care,
I too shall be free and easy."

She would not cling to wealth and rank;
Wholeheartedly she embraced her vows.
She donned her nun's brocade robes
And constantly fingered her beads.
Each month she kept her fasts;
Daily she offered up fresh flowers,
A Bodhisattva [29] she might not become:
To be Buddha's least handmaid would still content her!

Translated by H. C. Chang

29. Characteristic savior figure of Mahāyāna Buddhism.

210
The Canary Murders

Feng Meng-lung (1574–1645)

A bird it was at the root of the trouble;
Seven lives lost—what a lamentable case!

This gripping tale was included in a collection entitled *Stories Old and New* or *Illustrious Words to Instruct the World*, edited by the indefatigable Feng Meng-lung (see selections 154 and 190). The story commemorates a series of incidents alleged to have taken place in the vicinity of Lin-an (modern-day Hangchow in Chekiang province) in 1121, six years before the city was made the capital of the Southern Sung court. Although there is no means of establishing the authenticity of the events recorded or the personages concerned, there is equally no reason to doubt that the story was based on an actual crime of local and contemporary notoriety, and written down while the public memory was fresh.

Our story is a forerunner of the detective story, which had its greatest vogue in the nineteenth century. Perhaps "detective" is a misnomer; more properly, these are stories of clever magistrates. Although the magistrate makes only a brief appearance in "The Canary Murders," he is the central figure in many other stories. The reason is that, as the highest civil authority in the district, the magistrate shouldered the manifold responsibilities for the maintenance of law and order. It was his duty in a criminal case to bring the offender to book, to conduct the trial, and to pronounce sentence. Since he alone was responsible for ascertaining the true facts

Note, all of you, this tragic lesson:
Do not let your sons and daughters neglect their home.

It is told how in the year 1121, the third year of the period Hsüan-ho in the reign of the Emperor Hui Tsung of the great Sung dynasty, a master-weaver named Shen Yü had his home in the prefecture of Hai-ning, near Hangchow. He lived below the New North Bridge, outside the Wu-lin Gate. This Shen Yü, styled Pi-hsien, was in a prosperous way of business, and he and his wife, Madam Yen, were devoted to each other. They had an only son, Shen Hsiu, who had reached the age of sixteen but had not yet married. The father made his living solely from weaving silk cloth, but to everyone's surprise Shen Hsiu took no heed of his duty to earn his keep. He devoted himself to pleasure and amusement and spent all his time breeding canaries,[1] and his parents doted on their only child and had no control over him. The neighbors gave him the nickname "Birdie" Shen. Every day at dawn he would take up one of his canaries and hurry off to match it against others in the park of willows inside the city.

This went on day after day, until it came to the end of spring, when the weather is neither too hot nor too cold, when the flowers bloom red and the willows are green. One morning at this time Shen Hsiu got up at the crack of dawn, washed and dressed and ate his breakfast, and made ready a cage, into which he put one matchless canary. This creature was the sort that is found only in heaven and not here below. He took it all over the place to fight, and it had never been defeated. It had won him over a hundred strings of cash, and he doted on it and held it dearer than life itself. He had made a cage for it of gold lacquer, with a brass hook, a green gauze cover, and a seed-pot and water-pot of Ko-yao porcelain.[2] This particular morning Shen Hsiu took up the cage and proudly hurried off through the city-gate to match his bird in the willow park. And who would have thought that Shen Hsiu, off on this jaunt of his, was going to his death? Just like

---

of the case, it followed that where there was any element of mystery he must function as his own detective. He could rely on his runners to make inquiries, detain witnesses, and arrest suspects, contenting himself with making deductions from the statements he heard or extracted in court; or, as often happens in such stories, he could leave his court incognito to conduct his own investigations. One of the most famous magistrate-detectives in Chinese history, Ti Jen-chieh (607–700), was the model for the main character in Robert van Gulik's popular "Judge Dee Mysteries."

1. "Canary" is used purely for the sake of familiarity to represent the bird *hua-mei*. There are, in fact, several points of resemblance. The *hua-mei* is a member of the oriole family: it is known to ornithologists as *Oreocinola dauma aurea*. It is 4–5 inches in length. Its plumage is grayish-yellow, speckled with black, the breast being yellowish-white. White markings above its eyes give rise to the name *hua-mei* (literally "painted eyebrows"). The male bird is both a singer and a fighter. The *hua-mei* is commonly found in North China, both wild and as a pet.

2. Ko-yao means "the elder brother's kiln," a term used to describe the work of the Sung potter Chang Sheng-yi, whose kiln was at Lung-ch'üan in Chekiang.

A pig or a lamb to the slaughter,
Seeking with every step the road to death.

Shen Hsiu took his bird into the willow park, but he was later than he had thought and the bird-fanciers had dispersed. The place was silent and gloomy, with not a soul about. Shen Hsiu, finding himself alone, hung the bird in its cage on a willow-branch, where it sang for a while. Then, disappointed, he took the cage down again and was just about to go back, when suddenly a bout of pain came surging up from his belly and forced him to his knees.

The fact was that Shen Hsiu was a sufferer from what is known as "dumplings of the heart," or hernia. Every attack sent him into a dead faint. It must have been that he had risen earlier than usual that morning, and then, arriving late to find no one there, he felt disappointed and miserable, so that this time the attack was particularly severe. He collapsed on the ground at the foot of a willow tree, where he lay unconscious for four whole hours.

Now, wouldn't you agree that "there is such a thing as coincidence"? This very day a cooper called Chang came walking through the park, his pack on his back, on the way to a job at the Ch'u household. He saw from a distance that there was someone lying at the foot of this tree, and so he came bounding up to the spot, set down his load, and had a look. Shen Hsiu's face was a waxy yellow, and he was still in a coma. There was nothing of any value on him, but at one side was the canary in its cage; and the canary chose just this moment to sing away more beautifully than ever. It was a case of "the sight of the treasure provides the motive," and "the plan is born when the man is poorest." Chang thought, "I might work all day for a couple of silver cents. What good would that do me?"

Shen Hsiu must have been doomed to die, for at the sight of Chang the canary began to sing harder than ever. Chang said to himself, "The rest doesn't matter, but this canary alone is worth two or three silver taels at least." So he picked up the cage and was just making off, when to his surprise Shen Hsiu came round. Shen opened his eyes to see Chang picking up the cage. He tried to get up but couldn't. All he could do was cry out, "Where are you off to with my canary, you old blackguard?"

"This little fool has too quick a tongue," Chang thought to himself. "Suppose I take it, and he manages to get up and comes after me—he'll make trouble for me. There's only one thing for it, one way or the other I'm in a mess." So he went to the barrel he had been carrying and took out a curved paring-knife, then turned to Shen Hsiu and struck at him. The knife was sharp and he used all his strength, and Shen Hsiu's head rolled away to one side.

Chang cast panic-stricken glances to left and right, fearful lest someone should have seen him. Then, looking up, he saw that to one side stood a hollow tree. Hurriedly he picked up the head and dropped it into the hollow trunk, returned the knife to the barrel, and hung the bird-cage from his pack. He did not go on to the job at the Ch'u house, but went off like a puff of smoke, through the streets and alleys of the town, looking for somewhere to hide.

Now, how many lives do you think were lost on account of this one live bird? Indeed,

> Private words among men,
> Heard in Heaven like thunder;
> A misdeed in a dark room,
> But the gods have eyes like lightning.

As Chang walked along, the thought came to him, "There is a traveling merchant who stays in an inn at Hu-chou-shu, and I have often seen him buying pets. Why not go there and sell the bird to him?" And he made straight for the suburb past the Wu-lin Gate.

The evil fate in store must have been determined from a previous existence, for there he saw three merchants with two youths at their heels, five persons all told. They had just packed up their goods to go back, and he met them coming in through the gate. The merchants were all men of the Eastern Capital, Pien-liang.[3] One of them was called Li Chi, a trader in herbs. He had always had a fancy for canaries, and seeing this lovely bird on the cooper's back, he called to Chang to let him see it. Chang set down his pack. The merchant examined the canary's plumage and eyes, and saw that it was a fine bird. It had a lovely singing voice, too, and he was delighted with it. "Would you like to sell him?" he asked Chang.

By this time Chang's only concern was to be rid of the evidence. So he said, "How much will you give me, sir?"

The longer Li Chi looked at the bird the more he liked it. "I'll give you a tael of silver," he said.

Chang realized the deal was on. "I don't want to haggle," he said. "It's just that this bird's very precious to me. But give me a little more and you can have him."

Li Chi took out three pieces of silver and weighed them: there was one tael and a fifth. "That's the lot," he said, handing it to Chang.

Chang took the silver, examined it, and put it in his wallet. He gave the canary to the merchant and took his leave. "That's a good deed done, getting rid of the evidence," he told himself. He did not go back to his work, but hurried straight home. But still he felt certain misgivings at heart. Indeed,

> The evil-doer fears the wrath of Heaven and Earth,
> The swindler dreads discovery by gods and demons.

3. Kaifeng.

Chang's home was in fact against the city-wall by the Yung-chin Gate. There was only himself and his wife; they had no children. When his wife saw him coming back, she said, "You haven't used a single splint. Why have you come home so early? What's the trouble?"

Chang said not a word until he had entered the house, taken off his pack, and turned back to bolt the door. Then he said, "Come here, wife, I've something to tell you. Today I've been to such-and-such and done such-and-such, and I've come by this ounce and a fifth of silver. I'm giving it to you so that you can enjoy yourself for a while." And the two of them gloated over the money.

But this does not concern us. Let us rather go on to tell how there was no one about in the willow park until late morning, when two peasants carrying loads of manure happened to pass through. The headless corpse blocking their path gave them a fright, and they began to kick up a fuss, quickly rousing the ward headman and all the citizens of the neighborhood. The ward submitted the matter to the district and the district to the prefecture, and the next day a coroner and other officers were sent to the willow park to investigate. They found no mark on the body: the only thing wrong was that the head was missing; nor had anyone come forward as plaintiff. The officers made their report to the authorities at the prefecture, who dispatched runners to arrest the criminal. Within the city and out in the suburbs, all was thrown into an uproar.

Let us now rather tell how Shen Hsiu's parents, when evening came and he still had not returned, sent people out in every direction to search for him, but without success. When again at dawn searchers were sent into the city, in the vicinity of the inn at Hu-chou-shu they heard a commotion about the headless corpse of a murdered man being found in the willow park. When Shen Hsiu's mother heard of this, she thought, "My boy went into the city yesterday to show his canary, and there's still no sign of him. Can it be him?" And at once she cried to her husband, "You must go into the city yourself and make inquiries."

Shen Yü gave a jump when he heard this and, filled with alarm, he hurried off to the willow park. There he saw the headless corpse, which, after a careful look at the clothing, he recognized as his own son. He began to wail in a loud voice. "Here is the plaintiff," said the ward headman. "Now all that is missing is the criminal."

Shen Yü went at once to make accusations before the prefect of Lin-an. "It is my son," he said. "Early yesterday morning he went into the city to show his canary, and he has been murdered, no one knows how or why. Your Highness, I demand justice!"

Runners and detectives were sent from the prefecture throughout the area, with orders to arrest the criminal within ten days. Shen Yü was ordered to prepare a coffin in the willow park to contain the corpse. He went straight home and said to his wife, "It's our son; he's been murdered. But no one knows where the head has been taken. I have made accusation at the prefecture, and they have sent runners out everywhere to arrest the criminal. I've been told to buy a coffin for him. What is best for us to do about it all?"

At this news, Madam Yen began to wail aloud and collapsed to the floor. "If you don't know how she felt inside, first see how she lies there motionless." Indeed,

> Body like the waning moon at cockcrow, half-hidden behind the hills;
> Spirit like a dying lamp at the third watch, the oil already gone.

They proceeded to revive her by forcing hot soup down her throat, and when she came to, she said through her tears, "My boy would never listen to good advice, and now he is dead and we cannot bury him.[4] O my son, so young, and dead in such a grievous manner. Who could have told that in my old age I should be left without support?" All the time she was speaking her tears flowed ceaselessly. She would take neither food nor drink, although her husband used every effort to console her. Somehow or other they got through the next fortnight, without any news. Then Shen Yü and his wife began to discuss the matter. "Our boy would never heed our words, and now this terrible thing has happened and he has been murdered. Nor can the murderer be found. There is nothing we can do about it. But at least it would be something if his corpse could be made whole. Our best plan is to write out a notice and inform people everywhere that if they find the head, so that the corpse can be made whole, they will be rewarded for it."

When the two had come to this decision, they promptly wrote out copies of a notice and went out to paste them up all over the city. The notice ran:

> To all citizens: One thousand strings of cash reward to anyone discovering the whereabouts of the head of Shen Hsiu. Two thousand strings of cash reward to anyone apprehending the murderer.

They informed the prefecture of this, and the authorities issued fresh orders to the runners to arrest the criminal within so many days, and put out an official notice, as follows:

> Official reward of five hundred strings of cash to anyone discovering the whereabouts of the head of Shen Hsiu. One thousand strings of cash reward to anyone apprehending the murderer.

We will leave the town in its ferment of excitement over the notices, and go on to tell how at the foot of the Southern Peak there lived an old pauper

---

4. It would be the gravest of misfortunes for Shen Hsiu in the next world if his corpse were buried while still incomplete. His parents were anxious to postpone the funeral for as long as possible in the hope that the head might be found.

whose name was Huang and who was known by the nickname "Old Dog." He was an ignorant man who had spent his life as a chair-coolie. With old age he had lost his sight, and he depended entirely on the support of his two sons, Big Pao and Little Pao. The three of them, father and sons, had neither enough clothes to wear nor enough food to eat. They lived from hand to mouth and their bellies were never full. One day Old Dog Huang called Big Pao and Little Pao to him and said, "I hear talk of some rich man or other called Shen Hsiu, who's been murdered, and his head is missing. And now they're offering a reward, and they say if anyone finds this head, the family will give them a thousand strings of cash and the authorities will give them another five hundred. I've called you together now just to say this: I'm an old man now anyway, and I'm no use, I can't see and I've no money. So I've decided to give you two a chance to make something and enjoy yourselves. Tonight you must cut off my head. Hide it in the water at the edge of the Western Lake, and in a few days it will be unrecognizable. Then you must take it to the prefecture and claim the reward, and altogether you'll get one thousand five hundred strings of cash. It's better than staying on here in misery. It's a very clever scheme, and you mustn't waste any time, because if somebody else gets in first, I'll have lost my life for nothing."

This "Old Dog" made this speech because he had given up in despair; moreover, his two sons were very stupid men and understood nothing of the law. Indeed,

> The mouth is the gateway of disaster,
> The tongue is an executioner's knife.
> Keep your mouth shut and your tongue well hidden,
> And you will live at peace and secure.

The two went outside to discuss the matter. "This is a brilliant idea of our father's," said Little Pao. "Not even a Commander-in-Chief or a Field Marshal could have thought up a plan like this. It's a very good one, although it's a pity we have to lose Dad."

Big Pao was by nature both cruel and stupid. He said, "He's got to die sooner or later anyway. Why shouldn't we seize this opportunity and do him in? We can dig a pit at the foot of the mountain and bury him, and there'll be no trace, so how can we be found out? This is what they call 'doing it while the water's hot,' and 'leaving no trace.' Men's hearts are governed by Heaven: it wasn't ourselves who forced him to it, he told us to do this of his own accord."

"All right then," said Little Pao, "only we'll not set to work until he's fast asleep."

Having laid their plans, the brothers went bustling off and bought two bottles of wine on credit. They came back to their father, and the three of them got good and drunk and sprawled about all over the place. The two brothers slept right through to the early hours of the morning, when they crept out of bed to watch the old man lying there, snoring. Then Big Pao took a kitchen-knife from in front of the stove, and with one powerful stroke at his father's neck cut his head clean off. Hurriedly they wrapped it in an old garment and hid it in the bed. Then they went off to the foot of the mountain and dug a deep pit. They carried the body there and buried it, and before it was daylight they had hidden the head in the shallow water at the edge of the lake, near the Lotus House at the foot of the Nan-p'ing Hills.

A fortnight later they went into the city and looked at the notice. First of all they went to Shen Yü's house to make their report, "The two of us were shrimping yesterday when we saw a human head by the edge of the lake near the Lotus House. We thought it must be your son's head."

"If it really is," said Shen Yü at this, "there is a reward of a thousand strings of cash for you, not a copper short." Then he prepared food and wine for them, and presently they took him straight to the point by the Lotus House at the foot of the Nan-p'ing Hills. There they found the head, lightly buried in the mud. When they picked it up and examined it, they found it had been under water so long that the features were bloated and past recognition. But Shen Yü thought, "It must be my son's head. If it isn't, how does another head come to be here?"

Shen Yü wrapped the head in a kerchief and accompanied the two of them straight to the prefecture, where they reported the discovery of Shen Hsiu's head. The prefect repeatedly questioned the two brothers, who replied, "We saw it when we were shrimping. We don't know anything else about it." Their word was accepted, and they were given the five hundred strings of cash. Then, taking the head with them, they accompanied Shen Yü to the willow park. They opened the coffin, set the head on the shoulders of the corpse, and nailed the coffin up again. Then Shen Yü took the brothers back to his home. When Madam Yen heard that her son's head had been found she was much happier, and at once set out food and wine to feast the brothers. They received the thousand strings of cash as their reward, and took their leave and returned home. There, they built a house, and bought farming implements and household goods. "We are not going to work as chair-coolies any longer," they said to each other. "We'll work hard at our farming, and we can make a bit extra by gathering firewood from the hillside and selling that."

But this does not concern us. Indeed, "time flew like an arrow" and "days and months passed like a weaver's shuttle." Several months passed unnoticed, and the authorities grew lax and concerned themselves less every day with the affair.

We will say no more of all this, but go on to tell how the time came for Shen Yü, who was a master-weaver for the Eastern Capital, to make a journey there to deliver a consignment of cloth. When all his weavers had completed their quotas, he went to the prefecture for the delivery permit, returned home to order his affairs there, and then started out. This journey, just because Shen Yü chanced to see a bird which had belonged to his own family, resulted in the forfeiture of another life. Indeed,

> Take no illegal goods,
> Commit no illegal acts.
> Here above the law will catch you,
> Down below the demons pursue you.

Let us now tell how Shen Yü, on his journey, ate when hungry and drank when thirsty, rested each night and set out again each morning, and after more than one day like this arrived in the Eastern Capital. He delivered each and every bolt of cloth, and collected his permit to return. Then he thought, "I have heard that the sights of the Eastern Capital are unique. Why shouldn't I stroll about for a while? This is an opportunity which doesn't come often." He visited all the historic sites and beauty spots, the monasteries both Taoist and Buddhist, and all the other celebrated sights. Then he chanced to pass by the gate of the Imperial Aviary. Now, Shen Yü was very fond of pets and he felt he would like to have a look inside. On distributing a dozen or so cash at the gate he was allowed in to have a look round. All at once he heard a canary singing beautifully. Taking a careful look at it, he realized it was his son's canary which had disappeared. When the canary saw Shen Yü's familiar face, it sang louder than ever and hopped about its cage jerking its head toward him. The sight of the bird reminded Shen Yü of his son. Tears streamed down his face and his heart filled with sorrow. Without reflecting where he was, he began to cry out and make an uproar, shouting, "Could such a thing come to pass?"

The guard who was keeper of the aviary shouted, "Here's a fool who doesn't know the regulations. Where do you think you are, making such a fuss?"

Shen Yü, unable to contain his grief, began to yell louder still, and the guard, fearful of bringing trouble on his own head, found nothing for it but to arrest Shen Yü and have him brought before the Grand Court. The officer of the Grand Court shouted, "Where do you come from, that you dare to enter a part of the palace itself and make a disturbance like this? If you have some grievance, come straight out with it like an honest fellow, and you'll be let off."

So Shen Yü told how his son had gone off to match his canary and had been murdered, the whole story from beginning to end. The officer of the Grand Court was dumbfounded by the story. Then he reflected that the bird had been presented as tribute by a man of the capital, Li Chi; but whoever had dreamed there could be all this business behind it? He sent off runners to arrest Li Chi and bring him to court on the instant. The questioning commenced, "What was your reason for murdering this man's son in Hai-ning, and bringing his canary here as tribute? Make a full and open statement, or you will be punished."

"I went to Hangchow on business," said Li Chi, "and as I was going through the Wu-lin Gate I chanced to see a cooper who had this canary in a cage hanging from his pack. When I heard it singing and saw that it was a fine bird I bought it, for an ounce and a fifth of silver. I brought it back with me; but I did not dare to keep it for myself, because it was such a fine specimen, and so I presented it as tribute for the emperor's use. I know nothing about any murder."

"Who are you trying to implicate?" said his interrogator. "This canary is concrete evidence. Tell the truth!"

Li Chi pleaded again and again, "It is the truth that I bought it from an old cooper. I know nothing about a murder. How would I dare to make a false statement?"

"This old man you bought it from," went on the interrogating officer, "what was his name and where did he come from? Give me the true facts and I will have him brought in. Then we shall get at the truth, and you will be released."

"I simply bought it from him when I ran into him on the street," said Li Chi. "I really don't know what his name is or where he lives."

The interrogating officer began to abuse him, "You're only trying to confuse the issue. Are you hoping to make someone else pay for this man's life? We must go by the concrete evidence, this canary. This rascal won't confess until he's beaten."

Li Chi was flogged over and over until his flesh was ripped open. He could not bear the pain and had no alternative but to make up a story that, when he saw what a fine bird this canary was, he had killed Shen Hsiu and cast his head away. Thereupon Li Chi was committed to the main jail, while the officer of the Grand Court prepared his report for submission to the emperor. The imperial rescript ran: "Li Chi was beyond doubt the murderer of Shen Hsiu, the canary being evidence of this. The law requires that he shall be executed." The canary was returned to Shen Yü, who was also given a permit and allowed to return to his home; while Li Chi was sent under escort to the execution-ground, and there beheaded. Indeed,

> When the old turtle won't turn tender,
> You shift the blame onto the firewood.

At this time, the two merchants who had accompanied Li Chi to Hai-ning on business could hardly keep still for indignation. "How could such an injustice be done," they complained, "when it was plain for all to see that he had bought the canary. We would have pleaded for him, but what could we do? Although we would recognize the man who sold Li Chi the canary, we don't know his name any more than Li did. Moreover, he is in Hangchow. We would not have been able to clear Li Chi, and we would have implicated ourselves. How can the truth be brought to light? A man has been executed when he was obviously innocent, and all because of one single bird. The only thing is for us to go to Hangchow and, when we get there, to wring the truth out of this fellow."

Let us say no more of this, but rather tell how Shen Yü packed his baggage, picked up his canary, and hurried home, traveling day and night. He reported to his wife, "When I was in the Eastern Capital, I succeeded in avenging our son."

"How did that come about?" asked Madam Yen. Shen Yü told her the whole story right through, beginning with his seeing the canary in the Imperial Aviary. When Madam Yen saw the canary she burst out weeping, for the sight of things brings back sad memories; but we will say no more of this. The next day Shen Yü took up the canary again and went to the prefecture to have his permit canceled, and there he reported all that had happened. "What a lucky coincidence," cried the delighted prefect. Indeed,

> Do nothing of which you need feel ashamed:
> Who, throughout time, has been allowed to escape?

And murder, needless to say, is the concern of Heaven, not to be taken lightly. The prefect dismissed Shen Yü with the words, "Since the criminal has been caught and executed, you may have the coffin cremated." Shen Yü had the coffin cremated and the remains scattered, and we will say no more of this, but go on to tell how of the two merchants who had accompanied Li Chi to Hangchow on that former occasion to sell herbs, one was called Ho and the other Chu. These two got some more herbs together and went straight to Hangchow, to stay in the inn at Hu-chou-shu. They quickly sold off their herbs, then, their hearts filled with a sense of injustice, they went into the city to look for the cooper. They searched all day without finding a trace of him, and returned, weary and dispirited, to the inn to sleep. The next morning they returned to the city, and as luck would have it, they chanced to see a man with a cooper's pack. "Tell us, brother," they said, calling to him to stay, "is there another cooper here, an old man who looks like this?" And they described him. "We don't know his name, but perhaps you know him?"

"Gentlemen," said the cooper, "there are only two old men here in the cooper's trade. One is called Li, and he lives in Pomegranate Garden Street; the other is called Chang, and he lives by the city-wall on the west side. I don't know which one it is that you want."

The two merchants thanked him and carried their search straight to Pomegranate Garden Street. As it happened, the man named Li was sitting there cutting splints. The two took a look at him, but he was not their man. Then they found the house by the western wall and, coming up to the door, they asked if Chang was at home. "No, he isn't," replied Chang's wife. "He's gone out to a job."

The two men turned away again without more ado. It was now early afternoon. They had gone no more than a few hundred yards when they saw in the distance a man carrying a cooper's pack. And this man's fate it was to pay for the life of Shen Hsiu and to clear the name of Li Chi. Indeed,

> Let mercy and righteousness everywhere prevail,
> And you will meet with them at every turn of your life;
> Never make an enemy,
> For when you meet him in a narrow path it is not easy to turn back.

Chang was walking south toward his home, and the two men were walking toward the north, so that they met face to face. Chang did not recognize the pair, but they recognized him. They stopped him and asked his name, "My name is Chang," he replied.

"It must be you who lives by the western wall," they continued. "That is so," replied Chang. "What do you want of me?"

"We have some things at the inn that need repairing," said the merchants, "and we are looking for an experienced man to do the job. That's why we want you. Where are you going now?"

"I'm on my way home," said Chang. The three of them talked as they went along, until they came to Chang's door. "Please sit down and have some tea," said Chang.

But the others replied, "It is getting late. We'll come again tomorrow."

"Then I won't go out tomorrow, but will wait for you here," said Chang.

The two men took their leave of him, but they did not return to the inn: they went straight to the prefecture to inform on him. The court had just begun its evening session, and the two men went straight in and knelt down. They told the whole story of Shen Yü's recognition of the canary and Li Chi's execution, and of Li's earlier meeting with Chang when he bought the canary. "We two are filled with a sense of injustice, and with the desire to avenge Li Chi. We entreat your honor to question Chang thoroughly and to find out how he came by the canary."

"The Shen Hsiu case has been wrapped up," said the prefect. "The criminal has been executed—what more remains to be done?"

So the two merchants made accusation, "The officer of the Grand Court was misled. He took the canary as evidence, but did not look carefully into the details of the case. It is plain for all to see that Li Chi was wrongfully executed. We have 'found injustice in our path,' and are determined to avenge Li Chi. If we were not speaking the truth, how would we dare to make a nuisance of ourselves with this accusation? We beg your honor in your mercy to intervene in this matter."

Observing how earnestly they pleaded, the prefect at once sent out runners to arrest Chang that very night. It was just like

Vultures chasing a purple swallow,
Fierce tigers slavering over a lamb.

That night the men from the court hurried to the western wall. They tied Chang's arms behind his back and delivered him up to the prefecture, where he was committed to the main jail. When court opened the next day, Chang was brought from the jail and forced to his knees. The prefect said, "What was your reason for murdering Shen Hsiu and making Li Chi pay for it with his life? Today the facts have come to light, and the right must prevail." The prefect shouted to his men to flog the prisoner, and Chang received thirty strokes to begin with, till his flesh was ripped open and the blood came soaking out. Over and over again he was flogged, but he would not confess.

The merchants and the two youths who had been with them shouted at him, "Although Li Chi is dead, we four are still here, and we were with him when he bought your canary for an ounce and a fifth of silver. Who are you going to put the blame on now? If you say it wasn't you who did it, then tell us where the canary came from. Tell the truth: you can't lie your way out of this, and it's no use trying to make excuses."

But Chang continued to defy them, and at last the prefect roared at him, "The canary is genuine evidence of the theft, and these four are eyewitnesses. If you still refuse to confess, we'll have the finger-press out and torture you." Terrified, Chang had no choice but to confess everything, how he had stolen the canary and cut off Shen Hsiu's head.

"When you had killed him, where did you put the head?" asked the prefect.

"I was seized by panic," Chang answered, "and seeing a hollow tree nearby I dropped the head into the hole. Then I picked up the bird and went straight to the Wu-lin Gate. There I happened to come across three merchants with two youths. They wanted to buy the canary, and I got an ounce and a fifth of silver for it. I took the money home and spent it, and this is the truth."

The prefect ordered Chang to make his mark on his deposition, and sent men to summon Shen Yü. Then they all proceeded, with Chang under escort, to the willow park to search for the head. Hundreds of people on the streets, all agog, gathered round and followed them to the willow park to look for it. They found that there was indeed a hollow tree, and when they had sawn it down they gave a shout of excitement, for there inside the trunk was a human head. When they examined it, they saw it to be completely unaffected by the passage of time.[5] When Shen Yü saw the head, he took a close

---

5. The religious explanation for this is that corruption would not set in until the spirit had departed. The spirit of the murdered boy was waiting for the murderer to be brought to justice. In actuality, the head was probably preserved by the resins of the hollow tree.

look and recognized it as that of his son. He cried out in a loud voice and fainted to the ground, remaining unconscious for a long time. Then they wrapped the head in a cloth and returned to the prefecture, with Chang still under escort.

"Now that the head has been found," said the prefect, "the facts are clear and the guilt established." They put a large wooden cangue round Chang's neck, fettered his hands and feet, and dragged him off to the condemned cells, where he was put under close guard. The prefect then put a question to Shen Yü. "Those two Huang brothers, Big Pao and Little Pao: where did they get that human head when they came to claim the reward? There is some mystery here. Your son's head has been found now: whose head was that?"

Runners were immediately ordered to bring in the Huang brothers for interrogation. Shen Yü led the runners to the Huangs' house in the southern hills. The two brothers were arrested and brought to court, where they were forced to kneel.

"The murderer of Shen Hsiu has been arrested," the prefect told them, "and Shen Hsiu's head has been recovered. Who was it that you two conspired together to murder, so that you could claim the reward for his head? Confess or you will be tortured!"

Big Pao and Little Pao were dumbfounded and bewildered and could make no reply. The prefect, enraged, ordered them to be strung up and flogged, but for a long time they refused to confess. But then they were branded with red-hot irons. This was more than they could bear, and they fainted away. When water was spurted over them and they revived, they saw there was nothing for it but to blurt out the truth. "Seeing that our father was old and sick and miserable," they said, "on an evil impulse we got him drunk and cut off his head. We hid it at the edge of the Western Lake near the Lotus House, and then made up a story to claim the reward."

"Where did you bury your father's body?" asked the prefect. "At the foot of the Southern Peak," they replied. When the brothers were taken there under escort and the ground was dug, there did indeed prove to be a headless corpse buried at the spot. The two men were taken back to the prefecture and the guards reported, "There is indeed a headless corpse, in a shallow grave in the southern hills."

"That such a thing should happen!" said the prefect. "It is a most abominable crime. If there really are such evil men in this world, I want neither to speak nor hear nor write of them. Let them be flogged to death here and now, and we shall be rid of them; how can this evil deed ever be expiated?" He shouted to his men to flog them without keeping count of the strokes. The two brothers were flogged unconscious and revived again many times, then large cangues were placed on them and they were taken off to the condemned cells to be closely guarded.

Shen Yii and the original plaintiffs returned to their homes to await events, while a report on the wrongful execution of Li Chi was at once submitted in the form of a memorial. The imperial rescript ordered the Board of Punishments and the Censorate to investigate the conduct of the officer of the Grand Court who had originally questioned Li Chi, and to reduce him to the status of commoner and banish him to Ling-nan.[6] Li Chi was declared to have been innocent and wrongfully convicted. The imperial sympathy was expressed, and his family was granted one thousand strings of cash in compensation and his descendants exempted from compulsory service. Chang, for premeditated murder for gain and for wronging an innocent man, was to be executed in accordance with the law. In view of the seriousness of the crime, the execution was to be performed by the slow process, with two hundred and forty cuts, and his corpse dismembered. The Huang brothers, convicted of patricide for gain, were both without distinction to be executed by the slow process, with two hundred and forty cuts, their corpses dismembered, and their heads publicly exposed as a warning. Indeed,

> Heaven, clear and profound, is not to be deceived,
> Before the design appears to you it is already known.
> Do nothing of which you need feel ashamed:
> Who, throughout time, has been allowed to escape?

When the rescript reached the prefecture, officers and executioners and the rest mounted the three criminals on "wooden mules," and it was broadcast throughout the city that in three days' time they were to be executed by the slow process, their corpses dismembered, and their heads publicly exposed as a warning.

When Chang's wife heard that her husband was to be sliced to death, she went to the execution-ground in the hope of catching a glimpse of him. Who would have thought it possible?—when the executioners were given the signal to start, they all began to slice their victims, and it was indeed a frightful sight: Chang's wife was frightened out of her wits, and she turned to go, her body bent with grief. But by accident she tripped and fell heavily, injuring her whole body, and when she reached home she died. Indeed,

> Store up good deeds and you will meet with good,
> Store up evil and you will meet with evil.
> If you think about it carefully,
> Things usually turn out right.

Translated by Cyril Birch

6. In the southernmost province of Kwangtung.

Novels

211
The Journey to the West

Chapter 7

Attributed to Wu Ch'eng-en (c. 1506–1582)

From the Brazier of Eight Trigrams the Great Sage escapes;
Beneath the Five Phases Mountain the Monkey of the Mind [1] is stilled.

The Journey to the West (*Hsi-yu chi*) is a comic fantasy based on the pilgrimage of the monk Hsüan-tsang (596–664), also known as Tripiṭaka ("Three Baskets," i.e., the Buddhist Canon), to India for the purpose of collecting Buddhist scriptures. His journey lasted seventeen years altogether in real life, although the novel only has him spending fourteen years on the road. From the factual travelogue written by the monk himself and a biography of him written by his disciples, the story of Hsüan-tsang's passage to India underwent a long period of development through various forms of popular literature, culminating in the one-hundred-chapter novel of which the present selection is the seventh.

As portrayed in the novel, Hsüan-tsang is accompanied by four disciples of superhuman ability. Foremost among them is Sun Wu-k'ung, whose name may quite literally be interpreted as "The Monkey Who Is Enlightened to Vacuity." In many ways, the novel may be said to be more about Sun Wu-k'ung than about Hsüan-tsang, ostensibly the main character. Next comes Chu Pa-chieh, whose revealing name may be rendered as "The Pig of Eight Prohibitions." He is the epitome of sensuality, slothfulness, and gargantuan appetite. Sha Ho-shang ("Sand Monk"), a cannibalistic monster symbolizing the dangers of the desert, is converted by Kuan-yin (Avalokiteśvara), the salvific Bodhisattva of Compassion. Lastly, there is the faithful white horse who was originally a dragon prince.

On their way, the pilgrims encounter all sorts of demons and monsters who are determined to devour Tripiṭaka, in part because it was thought that consuming his flesh would make them

Fame and fortune,
All predestined;
One must ever shun a guileful heart.
Rectitude and truth.
The fruits of virtue grow both long and deep.
A little presumption brings on Heaven's wrath;
Though yet unseen, it will surely come in time.
If we ask the Lord of the East [2] for reasons why
Such pains and perils now appear,
It's because pride has sought to scale the limits,
Confounding the world's order and perverting the law.

We were telling you about the Great Sage, Equal to Heaven, who was taken by the celestial guardians to the monster-execution block, where he was bound to the monster-subduing pillar. They then slashed him with a scimitar, hewed him with an ax, stabbed him with a spear, and hacked him with a sword, but they could not hurt his body in any way. Next, the Star Spirit of the South Pole ordered the various deities of the Fire Department to burn him with fire, but that, too, had little effect. The gods of the Thunder Department were then ordered to strike him with thunderbolts, but not a

---

immortal. Tripiṭaka is repeatedly captured and in danger of being eaten or otherwise destroyed, but he is invariably rescued by his disciples, especially by Sun Wu-k'ung, who are assisted by various protective deities.

The first seven chapters of the novel tell of the birth and acquisition of magical powers of Sun Wu-k'ung. He represents the human mind and, as such, is resourceful and intelligent, but at the same time is unbridled and wild unless controlled. In the novel, we see Sun Wu-k'ung being tamed by the powerful discipline of Buddhism. This selection is one of the chapters dealing specifically with Sun Wu-k'ung and his subjugation. He is hatched from a stone egg that for eons had absorbed the essences of Heaven and Earth and the Sun and the Moon. In this connection, we should note the cosmogonic symbolism of stone in Chinese mythology. The Monkey King raises turmoil in Heaven until the Jade Emperor entitles him Great Sage Equal of Heaven. Eventually, Sun Wu-k'ung becomes possessed of formidible powers of transformation and a magic rod with which he can conquer any opponents. He is kept in check, however, by the tight fillet which has been fastened around his head and which ensures that his awesome powers are harnessed for Buddhism. The chapters dealing with Sun Wu-k'ung could well stand alone as an independent story cycle, but they are an essential underpinning for the rest of the novel.

Readers of the *Journey to the West* who are familiar with the *Rāmāyaṇa* will note many striking correspondences between Sun Wu-k'ung and Hanumat, the famous monkey-chief of that great Indian epic.

1. This is the first of several instances in the chapter (e.g., the second poem on p. 570) and in the book (e.g., the titles of chapters 14, 30, 35, 36, and 41) where reference is made to the phrase "Monkey of the Mind and Horse of the Will." Bridling these symbols of restless human intelligence and impetuous self-assertiveness is a theme central to the entire narrative. Sun Wu-k'ung is the very embodiment of the Monkey of the Mind; it is necessary for Tripiṭaka to control this wayward and forceful creature if he is to achieve his religious and spiritual goals.

2. Possibly a reference to the sun god.

single one of his hairs was destroyed. The demon king Mahābāli and the others therefore went back to report to the Throne, saying, "Your Majesty, we don't know where this Great Sage had acquired such power to protect his body. Your subjects slashed him with a scimitar and hewed him with an ax; we also struck him with thunder and burned him with fire. Not a single one of his hairs was destroyed. What shall we do?" When the Jade Emperor heard these words, he said, "What indeed can we do to a fellow like that, a creature of that sort?" Lao Tzu [3] then came forward and said, "That monkey ate the immortal peaches and drank the imperial wine. Moreover, he stole the divine elixir and ate five gourdfuls of it, both raw and cooked. All this was probably refined in the stomach by the Samādhi fire [4] to form a single solid mass. The union with his constitution gave him a diamond body which cannot be quickly destroyed. It would be better, therefore, if this Taoist takes him away and places him in the Brazier of Eight Trigrams, where he will be smelted by high and low heat. When he is finally separated from my elixir, his body will certainly be reduced to ashes." When the Jade Emperor heard these words, he told the Six Guardians of Darkness and the Six Guardians of Light to release the prisoner and hand him over to Lao Tzu, who left in obedience to the divine decree. Meanwhile, the illustrious Sage Erh-lang [5] was rewarded with a hundred gold blossoms, a hundred bottles of imperial wine, a hundred pellets of elixir, together with rare treasures, lustrous pearls, and brocades, which he was told to share with his brothers. After expressing his gratitude, the Immortal Master returned to the mouth of the River of Libations, and for the time being we shall speak of him no further.

Arriving at the Tushita Palace,[6] Lao Tzu loosened the ropes on the Great Sage, pulled out the weapon from his breastbone, and pushed him into the Brazier of Eight Trigrams. He then ordered the Taoist who watched over the brazier and the page-boy in charge of the fire to blow up a strong flame for the smelting process. The brazier, you see, was of eight compartments corresponding to the eight trigrams of Ch'ien, K'an, Ken, Chen, Sun, Li, K'un, and Tui.[7] The Great Sage crawled into the space beneath the compartment

3. The legendary founder of Taoism (see selection 9).

4. The fire that is said to consume the body of Buddha when he enters Nirvāṇa. But in the Buddhism of popular fiction, this fire, possessed by many fighters or warriors who have attained immortality, is often used as a weapon.

5. The supernatural creature who was able to subdue the not yet fully developed Sun Wu-k'ung in a fantastic battle of transformations. Erh-lang was an extremely powerful deity in folk religion. His name literally means "Second Young Gentleman" because the historical personage out of whom the deity evolved was the second son of Li Ping. Together, father and son were responsible for the construction of the celebrated large-scale irrigation system outside Ch'engtu (in Szechwan) called Tu-chiang-yen. The cult devoted to Erh-lang was first centered in the temples at the site that were dedicated to Li Ping and his son.

6. A heaven ruled over by Maitreya, the Buddha of the future.

7. See selection 3.

which corresponded to the Sun[8] trigram. Now Sun symbolizes wind; where there is wind, there is no fire. However, wind could churn up smoke, which at that moment reddened his eyes, giving them a permanently inflamed condition. Hence they were sometimes called Fiery Eyes and Diamond Pupils.

Truly time passed by swiftly, and the forty-ninth day[9] arrived imperceptibly. The alchemical process of Lao Tzu was perfected, and on that same day he came to open the brazier to take out his elixir. The Great Sage at the time was covering his eyes with both hands, rubbing his face, and shedding tears. He heard noises on top of the brazier and, opening his eyes, suddenly saw light. Unable to restrain himself, he leaped out of the brazier and kicked it over with a loud crash. He began to walk straight out of the room, while a group of startled fire tenders and guardians tried desperately to grab hold of him. Every one of them was overthrown; he was as wild as a white-brow tiger in a fit, a one-horn dragon with a fever. Lao Tzu rushed up to clutch at him, only to be greeted by such a violent shove that he fell head over heels while the Great Sage escaped. Whipping the compliant rod out from his ear, he waved it once in the wind, and it had the thickness of a rice bowl. Holding it in his hands, without regard for good or ill, he once more careened through the Heavenly Palace, fighting so fiercely that the Nine Luminaries[10] all shut themselves in and the Four Devarājas[11] disappeared from sight. Dear Monkey Monster! Here is a testimonial poem for him. The poem says:

> This cosmic being perfectly fused with nature's gifts
> Passes with ease through ten thousand toils and tests.
> Vast and motionless like the One Great Void,
> Perfect and quiescent, he's named The Primal Depth.
> Refined a long while in the brazier, though not of mercurial stuff,[12]
> He's the very immortal, living ever above all things.
> Knowing boundless transformations, he changes still;
> The three refuges and five commandments[13] he all rejects.

8. Pronounced *soon*, this is the name of a trigram and has nothing whatsoever to do with the English word "sun" or the surname of Wu-k'ung, which means "monkey."

9. The time is calculated according to the sacred number 7. In popular Buddhism, forty-nine days is the usual amount of time it takes for a soul to be reincarnated after death. This accounts for the customary length of a complete cycle of funeral services.

10. The sun, moon, Mars, Mercury, Jupiter, Venus, Saturn, the spirit that causes eclipses, and the comet Ketu.

11. Guardian generals of the god Indra, who dwell on the four sides of Mount Meru (the *axis mundi*) and who ward off the attacks of evil spirits.

12. Mercury is one of the crucial elements in alchemy.

13. The "three refuges," or Triśaraṇa, refer to three kinds of surrender: to surrender to the Buddha as master, to the Law (*Dharma*) as medicine, and to the community of monks (*Saṅgha*) as friends. The "five commandments" (*pañca veramaṇī*) are prohibitions against killing, stealing, adultery, lying, and intoxicating beverages.

Here is another poem:

> Just as light supernal fills the boundless space,
> So does that cudgel serve his master's hand.
> It lengthens or shortens according to the wish of man;
> Upright or recumbent, it grows or shrinks at will.

And another:

> A monkey's transformed body weds the human mind.
> Mind is a monkey—this, the truth profound.
> The Great Sage, Equal to Heaven, is no idle thought.
> For how could the post of pi-ma [14] justly show his gifts?
> The Horse works with the Monkey—this means both Mind and Will
> Must firmly be harnessed and not be ruled without.
> All things return to Nirvāṇa, taking this one course:
> In union with Tathāgata [15] to live beneath twin trees. [16]

This time our Monkey King had no respect for persons great or small; he lashed out this way and that with his iron rod, and not a single deity could withstand him. He fought all the way into the Hall of Perfect Light and was approaching the Hall of Divine Mists, where fortunately Wang Ling-kuan, aide to the Immortal Master of Adjuvant Holiness, was on duty. He saw the Great Sage advancing recklessly and went forward to bar his way, holding high his golden whip. "Wanton monkey," he cried, "where are you going? I am here, so don't you dare be insolent!" The Great Sage did not wait for further utterance; he raised his rod and struck at once, while the Ling-kuan met him also with brandished whip. The two of them charged into each other in front of the Hall of Divine Mists. What a fight that was between

> A red-blooded patriot with reputation great,
> And a defier of Heaven with notorious name!
> The saint and the sinner gladly do this fight,
> To test the skills of two warriors brave.
> Though the rod is brutal
> And the whip is fleet,
> How can the hero, upright and just, forbear?
> This one is a supreme god of vengeance with thunderous voice;

---

14. A minor position in the stables of Heaven to which Sun Wu-k'ung had been appointed and which he found terribly insulting.

15. Tathāgata ("Thus Come/Gone"): one of the highest titles of Buddha. It may be defined as: "He who comes as do all other Buddhas"; or, "He who took the absolute way of cause and effect, and attained perfect wisdom."

16. The twin Sāl trees in the grove in which Śākyamuni entered Nirvāṇa.

The other, the Great Sage, Equal to Heaven, a monstrous ape.
The golden whip and the iron rod used by the two
Are both weapons divine from the House of God.
At the Treasure Hall of Divine Mists this day they show their might,
Displaying each his prowess most admirably.
This one brashly seeks to take the Big Dipper Palace.
The other with all his strength defends the sacred realm.
In bitter strife relentless they show their power;
Moving back and forth, whip or rod has yet to score.

The two of them fought for some time, and neither victory nor defeat could yet be determined. The Immortal Master of Adjuvant Holiness, however, had already sent word to the Thunder Department, and thirty-six thunder deities were summoned to the scene. They surrounded the Great Sage and plunged into a fierce battle. The Great Sage was not in the least intimidated; wielding his compliant rod, he parried left and right and met his attackers to the front and to the rear. In a moment he saw that the scimitars, lances, swords, halberds, whips, maces, hammers, axes, gilt bludgeons, sickles, and spades of the thunder deities were coming thick and fast. So, with one shake of his body, he changed into a creature with six arms and three heads. One wave of the compliant rod, and it turned into three; his six arms wielded the three rods like a spinning wheel, whirling and dancing in their midst. The various thunder deities could not approach him at all. Truly his form was

Tumbling round and round,
Bright and luminous;
A form everlasting, how imitated by men?
He cannot be burned by fire.
Can he ever be drowned in water?
A lustrous pearl of maṇi [17] he is indeed,
Immune to all the spears and the swords.
He could be good;
He could be bad;
Present good and evil he could do at will.
Immortal he'll be in goodness or a Buddha,
But working ill, he's covered by hair and horn. [18]
Endlessly changing he runs amok in Heaven,
Not to be seized by fighting lords or thunder gods.

At the time the various deities had the Great Sage surrounded, but they could not close in on him. All the hustle and bustle soon disturbed the Jade

17. The maṇi pearl, said to give sight to the blind, is known for its luster.
18. I.e., he is reduced to an animal.

Emperor,[19] who at once sent the Wandering Minister of Inspection and the Immortal Master of Blessed Wings to go to the Western Region and invite the aged Buddha to come and subdue the monster.

The two sages received the decree and went straight to the Spirit Mountain. After they had greeted the Four Vajra-Buddhas [20] and the Eight Bodhisattvas [21] in front of the Treasure Temple of Thunderclap, they asked them to announce their arrival. The deities therefore went before the Treasure Lotus Platform and made their report. Tathāgata at once invited them to appear before him, and the two sages made obeisance to the Buddha three times before standing in attendance beneath the platform. Tathāgata asked, "What causes the Jade Emperor to trouble the two sages to come here?"

The two sages explained as follows: "Some time ago there was born on the Flower-Fruit Mountain a monkey who exercised his magic powers and gathered to himself a troop of monkeys to disturb the world. The Jade Emperor threw down a decree of pacification and appointed him a pi-ma-wen,[22] but he despised the lowliness of that position and left in rebellion. Devarāja Li and Prince Naṭa were sent to capture him, but they were unsuccessful, and another proclamation of amnesty was given to him. He was then made the Great Sage, Equal to Heaven, a rank without compensation. After a while he was given the temporary job of looking after the Garden of Immortal Peaches, where almost immediately he stole the peaches. He also went to the Jasper Pool and made off with the food and wine, devastating the Grand Festival. Half-drunk, he went secretly into the Tushita Palace, stole the elixir of Lao Tzu, and then left the Celestial Palace in revolt. Again the Jade Emperor sent a hundred thousand heavenly soldiers, but he was not to be subdued. Therefore Kuan-yin [23] sent for the Immortal Master Erh-lang and his sworn brothers, who fought and pursued him. Even then he knew many tricks of transformation, and only after he was hit by Lao Tzu's diamond snare could Erh-lang finally capture him. Taken before the Throne, he was condemned to be executed; but, though slashed by a scimitar and hewn by an ax, burned by fire and struck by thunder, he was not hurt at all. After Lao Tzu had received royal permission to take him away, he was refined by fire, and the brazier was not opened until the forty-ninth day. Immediately he jumped out of the Brazier of Eight Trigrams and beat back the celestial guardians. He penetrated into the Hall of Perfect Light and was approaching the Hall of Divine Mists when Wang Ling-kuan, aide to the Immortal Master of Adju-

19. It is interesting to observe that the chief deity in the Taoist pantheon here invites the Buddha to restore order to his own heaven.

20. Diamond Buddhas, the same as the Four Heavenly Kings (Devarājas), on which see note 11.

21. Eight saviors.

22. See note 14.

23. Avalokiteśvara, the all-seeing, all-hearing Bodhisattva (savior) of compassion.

vant Holiness, met and fought with him bitterly. Thirty-six thunder generals were ordered to encircle him completely, but they could never get near him. The situation is desperate, and for this reason, the Jade Emperor sent a special request for you to defend the Throne."

When Tathāgata heard this, he said to the various bodhisattvas, "All of you remain steadfast here in the chief temple, and let no one relax his meditative posture. I have to go exorcise a demon and defend the Throne."

Tathāgata then called Ānanda and Kāśyapa, his two venerable disciples, to follow him. They left the Thunderclap Temple and arrived at the gate of the Hall of Divine Mists, where they were met by deafening shouts and yells. There the Great Sage was being beset by the thirty-six thunder deities. The Buddhist Patriarch gave the dharma [24] order: "Let the thunder deities lower their arms and break up their encirclement. Ask the Great Sage to come out here and let me inquire of him what sort of divine power he has." The various warriors retreated immediately, and the Great Sage also threw off his magical appearance. Changing back into his true form, he approached angrily and shouted with ill humor, "What region are you from, monk, that you dare stop the battle and question me?" Tathāgata laughed and said, "I am Śākyamuni, the Venerable One from the Western Region of Ultimate Bliss. I have heard just now about your audacity, your wildness, and your repeated acts of rebellion against Heaven. Where were you born? When did you learn the Great Art? Why are you so violent and unruly?"

The Great Sage said, "I was

> Born of Earth and Heaven, immortal magically fused,
> An old monkey hailed from the Flower-Fruit Mount.
> I made my home in the Water-Curtain Cave;
> I sought friend and teacher to gain the Mystery Great.
> Perfected in the many arts of ageless life,
> I learned to change in ways boundless and vast.
> Too narrow the space I found on that mortal earth;
> I set my mind to live in the Green Jade Sky.
> In Divine Mists Hall none should long reside,
> For king may follow king in the reign of man.
> If might is honor, let them yield to me.
> Only he is hero who dares to fight and win!"

When the Buddhist Patriarch heard these words, he laughed aloud in scorn. "A fellow like you," he said, "is only a monkey who happened to become a spirit. How dare you be so presumptuous as to want to seize the honored throne of the Exalted Jade Emperor? He began practicing religion when he was very young, and he has gone through the bitter experience of one

---

24. The Buddhist law or doctrine.

thousand, seven hundred and fifty kalpas, with each kalpa lasting a hundred and twenty-nine thousand, six hundred years. Figure out yourself how many years it took him to rise to the enjoyment of his great and limitless position! You are merely a beast who has just attained human form in this incarnation. How dare you make such a boast? Blasphemy! This is sheer blasphemy, and it will surely shorten your allotted age. Repent while there's still time and cease your idle talk! Be wary that you don't encounter such peril that you will be cut down in an instant, and all your original gifts will be wasted."

"Even if the Jade Emperor has practiced religion from childhood," said the Great Sage, "he should not be allowed to remain here forever. The proverb says, 'Many are the turns of kingship, and next year the turn will be mine!' Tell him to move out at once and hand over the Celestial Palace to me. That'll be the end of the matter. If not, I shall continue to cause disturbances and there'll never be peace!" "Besides your immortality and your transformations," said the Buddhist Patriarch, "what other powers do you have that you dare to usurp this hallowed region of Heaven?" "I've plenty of them!" said the Great Sage. "Indeed, I know seventy-two transformations and a life that does not grow old through ten thousand kalpas. I know also how to cloud-somersault, and one leap will take me a hundred and eight thousand miles.[25] Why can't I sit on the Heavenly throne?"

The Buddhist Patriarch said, "Let me make a wager with you. If you have the ability to somersault clear of this right palm of mine, I shall consider you the winner. You need not raise your weapon in battle then, for I shall ask the Jade Emperor to go live with me in the West and let you have the Celestial Palace. If you cannot somersault out of my hand, you can go back to the Region Below and be a monster. Work through a few more kalpas before you return to cause more trouble."

When the Great Sage heard this, he said to himself, snickering, "What a fool this Tathāgata is! A single somersault of mine can carry old Monkey a hundred and eight thousand miles, yet his palm is not even one foot across. How could I possibly not jump clear of it?" He asked quickly, "You're certain that your decision will stand?" "Certainly it will," said Tathāgata. He stretched out his right hand, which was about the size of a lotus leaf. Our Great Sage put away his compliant rod and, summoning his power, leaped up and stood right in the center of the Patriarch's hand. He said simply, "I'm off!" and he was gone—all but invisible like a streak of light in the clouds. Training the eye of wisdom on him, the Buddhist Patriarch saw that the Monkey King was hurtling along relentlessly like a whirligig.

As the Great Sage advanced, he suddenly saw five flesh-pink pillars supporting a mass of bluish air. "This must be the end of the road." he said. "When I go back presently, Tathāgata will be my witness and I shall certainly take up residence in the Palace of Divine Mists." But he thought to himself,

25. Seventy-two and one hundred and eight thousand are both sacred Buddhist numbers.

"Wait a moment! I'd better leave some kind of memento if I'm going to negotiate with Tathāgata." He plucked a hair and blew a mouthful of magic breath onto it, crying, "Change!" It changed into a writing brush with extra thick hair soaked in heavy ink. On the middle pillar he then wrote in large letters the following line: "The Great Sage, Equal to Heaven, has made a tour of this place." When he had finished writing, he retrieved his hair, and with a total lack of respect he left a bubbling pool of monkey urine at the base of the first pillar. He reversed his cloud-somersault and went back to where he had started. Standing on Tathāgata's palm, he said, "I left, and now I'm back. Tell the Jade Emperor to give me the Celestial Palace." "You stinking, urinous ape!" scolded Tathāgata. "Since when did you ever leave the palm of my hand?" The Great Sage said, "You are just ignorant! I went to the edge of Heaven, and I found five flesh-pink pillars supporting a mass of bluish air. I left a memento there. Do you dare go with me to have a look at the place?" "No need to go there," said Tathāgata. "Just lower your head and take a look." When the Great Sage stared down with his fiery eyes and diamond pupils, he found written on the middle finger of the Buddhist Patriarch's right hand this sentence: "The Great Sage, Equal to Heaven, has made a tour of this place." A pungent whiff of monkey urine came from the fork between the thumb and first finger. Astonished, the Great Sage said, "Could this really happen? Could this really happen? I wrote those words on the pillars supporting the sky. How is it that they now appear on his finger? Could it be that he is exercising the magic power of foreknowledge without divination? I won't believe it! I won't believe it! Let me go there once more!"

Dear Great Sage! Quickly he crouched and was about to jump up again, when the Buddhist Patriarch flipped his hand over, and tossed the Monkey King out of the West Heavenly Gate. The five fingers were transformed into the Five Phases of metal, wood, water, fire, and earth. They became, in fact, five connected mountains, named Five-Phases Mountain, which pinned him down with just enough pressure to keep him there. The thunder deities, Ānanda, and Kāśyapa all folded their hands and cried in acclamation: "Wonderful! Wonderful!"

> Taught to be manlike since hatching from an egg that year,
> He set his aim to learn and walk the Way of Truth.
> He lived in a lovely region by ten thousand kalpas unmoved.
> But one day he changed, dissipating vigor and strength.
> Craving high place, he flouted Heaven's dominion;
> Mocking sages, he stole pills and upset the great relations.
> Evil, full to the brim, now meets its retribution.
> We know not when he may hope to find release.

After the Buddhist Patriarch Tathāgata had vanquished the monstrous monkey, he at once called Ānanda and Kāśyapa to return with him to the Western Paradise. At that moment, however, T'ien-p'eng and T'ien-yu, two heavenly messengers, came running out of the Treasure Hall of Divine Mists and said, "We beg Tathāgata to wait a moment, please! Our Lord's grand carriage will arrive momentarily." When the Buddhist Patriarch heard these words, he turned around and waited with reverence. In a moment he did indeed see a chariot drawn by eight colorful phoenixes and covered by a canopy adorned with nine luminous jewels. The entire cortege was accompanied by the sound of wondrous songs and melodies, chanted by a vast celestial choir. Scattering precious blossoms and diffusing fragrant incense, it came up to the Buddha, and the Jade Emperor offered his thanks, saying, "We are truly indebted to your mighty dharma for vanquishing that monster. We beseech Tathāgata to remain for one brief day, so that we may invite the immortals to join us in giving you a banquet of thanks." Not daring to refuse, Tathāgata folded his hands to thank the Jade Emperor, saying, "Your old monk came here at your command, Most Honorable Deva. Of what power may I boast, really? I owe my success entirely to the excellent fortune of Your Majesty and the various deities. How can I be worthy of your thanks?" The Jade Emperor then ordered the various deities from the Thunder Department to send invitations abroad to the Three Pure Ones, the Four Ministers, the Five Elders, the Six Women Officials,[26] the Seven Stars, the Eight Poles, the Nine Luminaries, and the Ten Capitals. Together with a thousand immortals and ten thousand sages, they were to come to the thanksgiving banquet given for the Buddhist Patriarch. The Four Great Imperial Preceptors and the Divine Maidens of Nine Heavens were told to open wide the golden gates of the Jade Capital, the Treasure Palace of Primal Secret, and the Five Lodges of Penetrating Brightness. Tathāgata was asked to be seated high on the Spirit Platform of Seven Treasures, and the rest of the deities were then seated according to rank and age before a banquet of dragon livers, phoenix marrow, juices of jade, and immortal peaches.

In a little while, the Jade-Pure Honorable Divine of the Origin, the Exalted-Pure Honorable Divine of Spiritual Treasures, the Primal-Pure Honorable Divine of Moral Virtue, the Immortal Masters of Five Influences, the Star Spirits of Five Constellations, the Three Ministers, the Four Sages, the Nine Luminaries, the Left and Right Assistants, the Devarāja, and Prince Naṭa all marched in leading a train of flags and canopies in pairs. They were all holding rare treasures and lustrous pearls, fruits of longevity and exotic flowers to be presented to the Buddha. As they bowed before him, they said, "We are most grateful for the unfathomable power of Tathāgata, who has subdued the monstrous monkey. We are grateful, too, to the Most Honorable Deva, who is having this banquet and asked us to come here to offer our thanks. May we beseech Tathāgata to give this banquet a name?" Responding

26. According to the *History of the Sui*, the Six Women Officials were established in the Han dynasty. They were in charge of palace upkeep, palatial protocol, court attire, food and medicine, banquets, and the various artisans of the court.

to the petition of the various deities, Tathāgata said, "If a name is desired, let this be called 'The Great Banquet for Peace in Heaven.'" "What a magnificent name!" the various immortals cried in unison. "Indeed, it shall be the Great Banquet for Peace in Heaven." When they finished speaking, they took their seats separately, and there was the pouring of wine and exchanging of cups, pinning of corsages [27] and playing of zithers. It was indeed a magnificent banquet, for which we have a testimonial poem. The poem says:

> That Feast of Peaches Immortal disturbed by the ape
> Is now surpassed by this Banquet for Peace in Heaven.
> Dragon flags and phoenix chariots stand glowing in halos bright,
> As standards and blazing banners whirl in hallowed light.
> Sweet are the tunes of immortal airs and songs,
> Noble the sounds of panpipes and double flutes of jade.
> Incense ambrosial surrounds this assembly of saints.
> The world is tranquil. May the Holy Court be praised!

As all of them were feasting happily, the Lady Queen Mother also led a host of divine maidens and immortal singing-girls to come before the Buddha, dancing with light feet. They bowed to him, and she said, "Our Festival of Immortal Peaches was ruined by that monstrous monkey. We are beholden to the mighty power of Tathāgata for the enchainment of the mischievous ape. In the celebration during this Great Banquet for Peace in Heaven, we have little to offer as a token of our thanks. Please accept, however, these few immortal peaches plucked from the large trees by our own hands." They were truly

> Half red, half green, and spouting aroma sweet,
> Of luscious roots immortal, and ten thousand years old.
> Pity those fruits planted at the Wu-ling Spring! [28]
> How do they equal the marvels of Heaven's home:
> Those tender ones of purple veins so rare in the world,
> And those of matchless sweetness with pale yellow pits?
> They lengthen your age and prolong your life by changing your frame.
> He who has the luck to eat them will never be the same.

After the Buddhist Patriarch had pressed together his hands to thank the Queen Mother, she ordered the immortal singing-girls and the divine maidens to sing and dance. All the immortals at the banquet applauded enthusiastically. Truly there were

---

27. Supposedly a custom of the Sung dynasty. After offering sacrifices at the ancestral temple of the imperial family, the emperor and his subjects would pin flowers on their clothes or on their caps.

28. Wu-ling is the prefecture in which is located the town of Ch'ang-te, in Hunan province. Its fame rests on the utopian "Peach-Blossom Spring," poems written by T'ao Ch'ien (365–427) and later by Wang Wei (701–761). The spring is said to be near the town (see selection 172).

Whorls of heavenly incense filling the seats.
And profuse array of divine petals and stems.
Jade capital and gold arches in what great splendor!
How priceless, too, the strange goods and rare treasures!
Every pair had the same age as Heaven.
Every set increased through ten thousand kalpas.
Mulberry fields or vast oceans, let them shift and change.
He who lives here has neither grief nor fear.

The Queen Mother commanded the immortal maidens to sing and dance, as wine-cups and goblets clinked together steadily. After a little while, suddenly

A wondrous fragrance came to meet the nose,
Rousing Stars and Planets in that great hall.
The gods and the Buddha put down their cups.
Raising his head, each waited with his eyes.
There in the air appeared an aged man,
Holding a most luxuriant long-life plant.
His gourd had elixir of ten thousand years;
His book listed names twelve millennia old.
Sky and earth in his cave knew no constraint;
Sun and moon were perfected in his vase.[29]
He roamed the Four Seas in joy serene,
And made the Ten Islets [30] his tranquil home.
Getting drunk often at the Peaches Feast
He woke; the moon shone brightly as of old.
He had a long head, short frame, and large ears.
His name: Star of Long Life from South Pole.

After the Star of Long Life had arrived and had greeted the Jade Emperor, he also went up to thank Tathāgata, saying, "When I first heard that the baneful monkey was being led by Lao Tzu to the Tushita Palace to be refined by alchemical fire, I thought peace was surely secured. I never suspected that he could still escape, and it was fortunate that Tathāgata in his goodness had subdued this monster. When I got word of the thanksgiving banquet, I came at once. I have no other gifts to present to you but these purple agaric, jasper plant, jade-green lotus root, and golden elixir." The poem says:

Jade-green lotus and golden drug are given to Śākya.
Like the sands of Ganges is the age of Tathāgata.

---

29. A metaphoric expression for the alchemical process.
30. Legendary home of the immortals.

The brocade of the three wains [31] is calm, eternal bliss.
The nine-grade [32] garland is a wholesome, endless life.
In the School Mādhyamika [33] he's the true master,
Whose home is the Heaven both of form and emptiness. [34]
The great Earth and cosmos all call him Lord.
His sixteen-foot [35] diamond body abounds in blessing and life.

Tathāgata accepted the thanks cheerfully, and the Star of Long Life went to his seat. Again there was pouring of wine and exchanging of cups. The Great Immortal of Naked Feet also arrived. After prostrating himself before the Jade Emperor, he too went to thank the Buddhist Patriarch, saying, "I am profoundly grateful for your dharma which subdued the baneful monkey. I have no other things to convey my respect but two magic pears and some fire dates, [36] which I now present to you." The poem says:

Fragrant are the pears and dates of the Naked-Feet Immortal,
Presented to Amitābha, whose count of years is long.
Firm as a hill is his Lotus Platform of Seven Treasures;
Brocadelike is his Flower Seat of Thousand Gold adorned.
No false speech is this—his age equals Heaven and Earth;
Nor is this a lie—his luck is great as the sea.
Blessing and long life reach in him their fullest scope,
Dwelling in that Western Region of calm, eternal bliss.

Tathāgata again thanked him and asked Ānanda and Kāśyapa to put away the gifts one by one before approaching the Jade Emperor to express his gratitude for the banquet. By now, everyone was somewhat tipsy. A Spirit Minister of Inspection then arrived to make the report, "The Great Sage is sticking out his head!" "No need to worry," said the Buddhist Patriarch. He took from his sleeve a tag on which were written in gold letters the words *Oṁ maṇi padme hūṁ.* [37] Handing it over to Ānanda, he told him to stick it on the top of the

31. The three vehicles (*triyāna*), drawn by a goat, a deer, and an ox to convey the living across the cycles of births and deaths (*saṁsāra*) to the shores of Nirvāṇa.

32. The nine classes or grades of rewards in the Pure Land.

33. The Mādhyamika or San-lun School advocates the doctrine of formlessness or nothingness (*animitta, nirābhāsa*).

34. "Form is emptiness and the very emptiness is form" is the famous statement of the *Heart Sūtra* (the *Prajñāpāramitāhṛdaya*).

35. Buddha's transformed body is said to be sixteen feet tall, the same height as his earthly body.

36. Pears and dates are the traditional fruits of religious Taoism.

37. Said to be a prayer to Padmapāṇi (Kuan-yin/Avalokiteśvara holding a lotus flower), this Lamaistic charm begins with the universal sacred syllable *Oṁ*. Each syllable is supposed to have its own mystic power of salvation, but the prayer is often translated as meaning "Oh, jewel in the Lotus."

mountain. This deva[38] received the tag, took it out of the Heavenly Gate, and stuck it tightly on a square piece of rock at the top of the Mountain of Five Phases.[39] The mountain immediately struck root and grew together at the seams, though there was enough space for breathing and for the prisoner's hands to crawl out and move around a bit. Ānanda then returned to report, "The tag is tightly attached."

Tathāgata then took leave of the Jade Emperor and the deities, and went with the two devas out of the Heavenly Gate. Moved by compassion, he recited a divine spell and called together a local spirit and the Fearless Guards of Five Quarters to stand watch over the Five-Phases Mountain. They were told to feed the prisoner with iron pellets when he was hungry and to give him melted copper to drink when he was thirsty. When the time of his chastisement was fulfilled, they were told, someone would be coming to deliver him. So it is that

> The brash, baneful monkey in revolt against Heaven
> Is brought to submission by Tathāgata.
> He drinks melted copper to endure the seasons,
> And feeds on iron pellets to pass the time.
> Tried by this bitter misfortune sent from the Sky.
> He's glad to be living, though in a piteous lot.
> If this hero is allowed to struggle anew,
> He'll serve Buddha in future and go to the West.

Another poem says:

> Prideful of his power once the time was ripe,
> He tamed dragon and tiger, exploiting wily might.
> Stealing peaches and wine, he roamed the House of Heaven.
> He found trust and favor in the Capital of Jade.
> He's now imprisoned, for his evil's full to the brim.
> By the good stock[40] unfailing his spirit will rise again.
> If he's indeed to escape Tathāgata's hands.
> He must await the holy monk from T'ang court.

We do not know in what month or year hereafter the days of his penance will be fulfilled, and you must listen to the explanation in the next chapter.

Translated by Anthony C. Yu

38. Divine being.

39. The five elements of Chinese cosmology: earth, wood, fire, metal, water.

40. Good stock (Sanskrit *kuśala-mula*): the Buddhist idea of the good seeds sown by a virtuous life which will bring future rewards.

212
Wu Sung Beats the Tiger

from *Water Margin*

Anonymous
Commentary by Chin Sheng-t'an (1610?–1661)

Now we'll divide the story and tell of how Wu Sung, after he left Sung Chiang, put up at an inn that evening. The next morning he lit up the fire and had breakfast, and after settling the account he packed, carried his club [*Club: the fifth time.*] and set out again. He thought to himself, "I have heard much about the Opportune Rain, Sung Kung-ming,[1] among men of rivers and lakes. It is really not false talk. To become a sworn brother with such a person is not in vain." [*Flowers in the mirror and the moon in water. An ordinary writer wouldn't be able to paint such a picture. This is truly a piece of writing concocted out of thin air.*]

After traveling on the road for a few days, Wu Sung came to the district of Yang-ku. There was still some distance to the district town. That day, toward noon, Wu Sung walked until he was both hungry and thirsty. He saw in the distance a wine-shop with a pennant sticking out in front of the door. On the pennant were written five characters: No Crossing After Three Bowls. [*Extraordinary writing.*] [Comments on upper margin: *The next few chapters from here on all describe Wu Sung's supernatural valor. The wine drinking here should be read as one section, the fight with the tiger as another.*]

This famous and exciting episode involving a life-and-death struggle between man and beast is taken from *Water Margin* (*Shui-hu chuan*), one of the earliest Chinese novels written in the vernacular language. Greatly indebted to a rich oral tradition, the novel came into existence probably during the fourteenth century and is attributed variously to Shih Nai-an (late Yüan–early Ming) and Lo Kuan-chung (c. 1330–c. 1400). It celebrates the exploits of a band of a hundred and eight colorful, daredevil bandit-heroes who dare to rob the wealthy and powerful and fight against government troops. In this excerpt, the hero, Wu Sung, fights with the tiger in the days before he joined the band.

Most of the old editions of the novel were printed with comments made by later readers. Of all the running commentaries for the novel, the one by Chin Sheng-t'an is the most widely known. As can be seen in the episode here, Chin's comments (italicized and enclosed in brackets) are lively and idiosyncratic, and at their best they enhance the reader's appreciation of the dazzling narrative skill demonstrated by the author. The celebrated modern essayist Chou Tso-jen (1885–1967) put it best when he explained why he liked to read the novel together with Chin's commentary: "Of all commentaries on fiction, Chin Sheng-t'an's are of course the best. . . . When I read *Water Margin*, I pay equal attention to the main text and to the comments. It is like eating white fungus [*pai mu-erh*, a Chinese delicacy]; they taste even better eaten with soup."

1. I.e., Sung Chiang.

Wu Sung entered the wine-shop and sat down; leaning the club to the side [*Club: the sixth time.*], he called, "Shop owner, bring out your wine right away so I can drink." [*Wu Number Two was fond of wine all his life. From this very first sentence spoken by him, it is as though we can hear his voice and see his person.*] Then we see the shop owner bring three bowls [*Extraordinary writing.*], a pair of chopsticks, and a plate of freshly cooked vegetables and set them out in front of Wu Sung. He then poured wine to fill one bowl to the brim. [*The first bowl. In this, the first segment, the author describes the action bowl by bowl. In the second, third, and fourth segments, he writes segment by segment. In the fifth and sixth segments, he writes both at once.*] Wu Sung took up the bowl and downed it at one gulp. "What potent wine!" he cried out. [*We know what the wine is like.*] "Shop owner, if you have anything that's filling, I want to buy some to go with the wine." [*He calls for wine first and then meat. So we can understand which one is more important to him. I have heard that meat-eaters are despicable. As for wine, no person of an unconventional bent doesn't like it.*] "There is only cooked beef," said the owner. "Bring me two or three catties² of the best part to eat," said Wu Sung.

The shop owner went inside to cut up two catties of cooked beef. Putting everything on a big platter, he brought it out and placed it before Wu Sung. At the same time he poured another bowl of wine. [*The second bowl.*] "Excellent wine," said Wu Sung after finishing it. [*Again he praises the wine. We know therefore it is good wine.*] The shop owner again poured a bowl. [*The third bowl.*] After Wu Sung finished drinking the third bowl of wine, the shop owner never came out again. [*Extraordinary writing.*] Knocking on the table, Wu Sung cried out, "Shop owner, why aren't you coming to pour more wine?" The owner replied, "If you want more meat, sir, I will bring some." [*The reply doesn't match the question. Hilarious!*] "I also want wine," said Wu Sung, "and cut more meat too." "I will cut the meat and bring it to you," said the owner. "As for wine, I will not add any more."

"What is the meaning of all this?" said Wu Sung, perplexed, and he proceeded to ask the shop owner, "Why don't you want to sell wine to me?" "Sir," said the owner, "surely you can see the pennant in front of the door. On it is clearly written 'No Crossing After Three Bowls.'" "What do you mean by 'No Crossing After Three Bowls'?" asked Wu Sung. "Although my wine is the rustic kind," said the owner, "it is as tasty as the old brews. All the guests who come to my shop get drunk after three bowls and are not able to cross the mountain ridge ahead. Hence, we say 'No Crossing After Three Bowls.' Traveling guests who pass by here never ask for more after three bowls." [*Ordinary folks are not worth mentioning.*]

Wu Sung laughed and said, "So that's what you mean. I have had three bowls; how come I am not drunk?" "This wine of mine is called 'Bottle

2. A catty is equal to about 1⅓ pounds.

Penetrating Fragrance' [*Good name*.]. It is also known as 'Fall Down Outside the Door' [*Good name*.]. It tastes rich and mellow when you first sip it, but in a short while you will fall down." "Don't talk nonsense," said Wu Sung. "It is not like I am not paying. Pour me three more bowls."

Seeing that Wu Sung was not affected at all, the owner poured three more bowls. [*The fourth bowl, fifth bowl, and sixth bowl.*] "Truly fine wine," said Wu Sung after finishing. [*Again he praises the wine profusely. We know it is good wine.*] "Shop owner, every time I finish one bowl I will give you money for it. So just keep pouring." "Sir," said the owner, "please don't keep drinking. This wine will really make you drunk and there is no antidote for it." "Stop your cursed talk," said Wu Sung. "I'll be able to smell it even if you put a narcotic in the wine." Unable to gainsay him, the shop owner again poured three bowls in a row. [*The seventh bowl, eighth bowl, and ninth bowl.*]

"Bring me two more catties of meat," Wu Sung demanded. [*The author writes about Wu Sung's capacity for food while writing about his drinking ability. All this is to show his valor.*] After cutting two more catties of cooked beef, the owner again poured three bowls of wine. [*The tenth bowl, eleventh bowl, and twelfth bowl.*] His appetite now fully activated, Wu Sung kept asking for more. Fishing out some loose silver that he carried with him, he called, "Shop owner, come and look at my silver. Is it enough to pay for the wine and meat?" [*The author switches to another way of writing. I cannot help roaring with laughter in reading this.*] Taking a look, the owner said, "More than enough. You should get some change back." [*Marvelous thought and marvelous writing. We can see that the wine-shop owner doesn't want to sell any more wine.*] "I don't want your change," said Wu Sung. "Just keep the wine coming." "Sir," said the owner, "if you want more wine, there are only five or six bowls left. But I am afraid you cannot take any more." "If you still have as many as five or six bowls," Wu Sung demanded, "pour them all out for me." "If a tall fellow like you falls down drunk," said the owner, "who can prop you up?" [*All of a sudden, as though out of nowhere, Wu Sung's features are revealed through the eyes and mouth of the wine-shop owner. How can an ordinary writer describe this?*] "I am no brave man if I need you to prop me up," replied Wu Sung. But the owner refused to bring the wine out.

Agitated, Wu Sung said, "I am not drinking for nothing. Don't get your old Daddy upset, or I will smash up everything in this room and turn your cursed shop upside down." The owner said to himself, "This fellow is drunk. I'd better not provoke him." He poured six more bowls for Wu Sung. [*The thirteenth bowl, fourteenth bowl, fifteenth bowl, sixteenth bowl, seventeenth bowl, and eighteenth bowl.*] Altogether Wu Sung drank eighteen bowls of wine. [*A concluding sentence.*]

Picking up his club, Wu Sung stood up [*Club: the seventh time. Throughout this episode the author singles out the club for special description at every turn. His intention is to make the reader feel that when later on Wu Sung suddenly confronts the tiger he can rely on this thing completely without any fear. Who could anticipate that something unexpected is going to happen that would frighten the reader to death? Picking up his club—the first posture he assumes with the club.*] [Comments on upper margin: *In writing about the club, the author has Wu Sung assume countless postures.*] and said, "I am not drunk." Walking out the door, he laughed and said, "Who says 'No Crossing After Three Bowls'?!" [*Amusing.*] Carrying his club, he walked away. [*Club: the eighth time. Carrying his club—the second posture he assumes with the club.*]

The wine-shop owner ran after him and called out, "Where are you going, sir?" [*Extraordinary writing.*] Wu Sung halted and asked, "What are you calling me for? I don't owe you any wine money. Why do you beckon me?" [*The author again creates waves.*] "I mean well," the owner called out. "Please come back to my house and see an official proclamation copied on a piece of paper." [*Extraordinary writing.*] "What proclamation?" Wu Sung asked. "Nowadays," said the owner, "there is a tiger with slanting eyes and a white forehead on the Ching-yang Ridge ahead. At night it comes out to harm people. It has already killed twenty or thirty big, stout fellows. The authorities now have given a deadline to the hunters to capture the tiger on pain of flogging. The proclamation is posted on every road near the ridge instructing passing travelers to cross the ridge in groups and during the hours from mid-morning to mid-afternoon. They are not allowed to cross the ridge during hours immediately before and after. Single travelers especially must wait to form groups before they can cross. It's going to be late afternoon pretty soon. Seeing you leave without asking people, I am afraid you might lose your life in vain. Why don't you put up at my place for now? Tomorrow, when twenty or thirty people have gathered, you may cross the ridge together."

Upon hearing this, Wu Sung laughed and said, "I am a resident of nearby Ch'ing-ho district. I must have crossed this Ching-yang Ridge at least ten or twenty times. Whoever has heard of a tiger? Don't scare me with this cursed talk of yours. I am not afraid even if there is a tiger." "I am trying to save you out of compassion," said the wine-shop owner. "If you don't believe me, come in and read the official proclamation." "You are just making some cursed noise," said Wu Sung. "Your old Daddy is not afraid even if there is really a tiger. You want me to put up at your place—could it be because you want to rob and kill me in the middle of the night and therefore scare me with this cursed tiger?" "Look, you," said the owner. "I do this completely out of compassion and yet you think I harbor evil intentions. If you don't believe me, just go as you please." While saying this, he shook his head and went back into his shop. [*The owner's change of countenance is described as vividly as a painting.*]

Wu Sung carried his club [*Club: the ninth time. Carried his club—the third posture he assumes with the club.*], and in big strides went toward the

Ching-yang Ridge. After having gone about four or five tricents, he came to the foot of the ridge. There he saw a huge tree, the bark of which had been scraped away, so that there was a patch of white wood. On the white patch were written two columns of characters. Wu Sung could recognize quite a few characters, so when he raised his head to look, he saw there written: "Because of the tiger on the Ching-yang Ridge that has been inflicting harm on the people recently, if there are travelers passing, they should cross the ridge in groups and between the hours from mid-morning to mid-afternoon. Please do not endanger yourselves." [*Extraordinary writing.*]

After having read the notice, Wu Sung laughed and said, "This is a trick played by the innkeeper to frighten the travelers so that they will stay in his inn. What cursed thing should I be afraid of?" Holding his club sideways [*Club: the tenth time. Holding his club sideways—the fourth posture he assumes with the club.*], he walked up the ridge.

At that time it was already late in the afternoon, and the red sun, like a wheel, was slowly rolling down the side of the mountain. [*Frightening scenery.*]

Wu Sung walked up the ridge heedlessly on the strength of the wine. In less than half a tricent, he came upon an abandoned shrine to the mountain spirit. [*Extraordinary writing. Were it not for this shrine, there would be almost no place for pasting the proclamation.*] Approaching the front of the shrine, he saw pasted on the door a proclamation with an official seal. When Wu Sung stopped to read, he saw there written: "A Proclamation from the district of Yang-ku: On Ching-yang Ridge, recently a tiger has taken the lives of people. At present, the heads of various villages as well as hunters have been given a deadline for capturing the tiger on pain of flogging. They have not yet succeeded. For this reason, if there are any passing travelers, they are instructed to cross the ridge in groups and during the hours from mid-morning to mid-afternoon. No one is allowed to cross the ridge by himself, or at other times, lest he lose his life. Everyone should take note of this. Proclaimed on such a day in such a month of such a year in the reign period Cheng-ho." [*Extraordinary writing.*]

After finishing the proclamation, Wu Sung began to realize that truly there was a tiger. He was about to turn around to go back to the wine-shop [*With this sign of weakness, Wu Sung's valor is brought out even more clearly. Otherwise, it would mean that things happened too suddenly, and Wu Sung simply could not avoid meeting the tiger, and that he was lucky to have escaped from the mouth of the tiger*],[3] when he thought to himself, "If I go back, I shall be ridiculed by him for not being a brave man. I will not turn back." [*Is it not extraordinary to stake one's life for the sake of fame?*] After

---

3. Wu Sung, after hesitating, deliberately chose to confront the tiger rather than simply being forced to meet it. This shows his courage and valor.

debating with himself for a while, he said, "What cursed thing am I afraid of? Let me just go up and see what will happen." [*Wu Sung's valor is vividly portrayed.*]

As Wu Sung walked, the fumes of the wine rose up in his head. [*See how methodically the author writes about drunkenness!*] So he whisked away his felt hat to hang on his back [*This is wintertime, but the author insists on describing the great heat felt by Wu Sung. Later when the tiger jumps at him, he is so scared as to shed cold sweat. A superb writer!*], tucked the club underneath his arm [*Club: the eleventh time. Tucked the club underneath his arm—the fifth posture he assumes with the club*], and step by step went up the ridge. He turned his head around to look at the sun, and saw that it was gradually going down. [*Frightening scenery. If I were there at that time, even if there were no tiger coming out, I would cry aloud.*] This was right in the midst of the tenth month. The days were short and the nights long, and it grew dark very quickly. [*This is the author's own explanatory note.*] Wu Sung mumbled to himself, "What tiger is there? People just scare themselves and dare not climb the hill." [*Again the author lets Wu Sung comfort himself.*] After Wu Sung had walked for a while, the strength of the wine became apparent. [*Drunk.*] He began to feel scorchingly hot inside. [*Hot.*] With one hand carrying the club [*Club: the twelfth time. Again he carries the club— the sixth posture he assumes with the club*] and the other opening up his coat at the chest [*A superb picture.*], he stumbled and staggered, and blundered straight through a forest of tangled trees. [*Frightening scenery. We know it is a forest for tigers.*] He saw a high, smooth, bluish rock. [*After having Wu Sung pass the tangled trees, the author might be expected to let the tiger jump out. Instead, he conjures up a piece of blue rock, and almost lets Wu Sung fall asleep on it. After having caused the reader to be worried to death, he then brings out the tiger. How incorrigible is the man of genius!*] He leaned his club against the side of the rock [*The club was leaned to the side—the seventh posture Wu Sung assumes with the club. Club: the thirteenth time.*] and was just about to lay himself down upon the rock to sleep [*The reader is frightened to death.*], when there rose a violent gust of wind. After the gust of wind had passed, Wu Sung heard a great crash behind the tangled trees, and out leaped a tiger with slanting eyes and white forehead. [*The tiger came out with force and power.*] Seeing it, Wu Sung cried, "Ah-ya!" and rolled down from the blue rock. [*With this sign of weakness, Wu Sung's valor is brought out even more clearly. Otherwise, it would be like the story of Tzu-lu [4] told in a small village, extremely untrue to life.*] Grasping the club in his hand [*Club: the fourteenth time. Grasping the club—the eighth posture he assumes with the club.*], he dodged to the side of the blue rock. [*The first dodging. From here on the man becomes a superman and the tiger a live tiger. The reader must*

---

4. One of Confucius' disciples, known for his physical strength and impetuosity.

pay very close attention from paragraph to paragraph. I have often thought that there are places to see a painted tiger, but none to see a genuine one; one can see a genuine tiger that is dead, but not one that is living; a living tiger walking can probably be seen occasionally, but a living tiger battling with a man—there are never places to see such a thing. Now suddenly in an almost casual way, Nai-an[5] *with his playful pen has painted a complete picture of a living tiger battling with a man. From now on those who want to see a tiger can all come to the Ching-yang Ridge in* Water Margin *to stare to their satisfaction. Moreover, they need not be frightened. What a great kindness Nai-an has rendered to his readers! It is said that Chao Sung-hsüeh*[6] *was fond of painting horses. In his latter years, his technique became even more penetrating. Whenever he wished to meditate on how to paint a new picture, he would loosen his clothes in a secluded room and crouch on the floor. He would learn first how to be a horse, and then order a brush. One day Lady Kuan*[7] *came upon him in this process, and Chao even appeared to be a horse. Now when Nai-an was writing this passage, could it be that he too had loosened his clothes, and while crouching on the ground, assumed the postures of a pounce, a kick, and a cut?*[8] *Su Tung-p'o in a poem on a painting of geese wrote:*

> *When wild geese see the approach of a man,*
> *They appear startled even before taking off.*
> *From what hidden place have you observed them,*
> *To catch this natural pose of theirs so oblivious of man?*

I really don't know where in his mind Nai-an obtained this method of painting a tiger eating a man. When I say that of all writers of the past three thousand years he alone is a genius, is this mere empty praise?]

The tiger was both hungry and thirsty. With just a light touch on the ground with its two front paws, it gathered itself and sprang through the air. [*The tiger.*] Wu Sung was frightened and the wine in him came out in a cold sweat. [*Subtle and marvelous writing. As I was reading this under the lamp, the light seemed to shrink into the shape of a bean, and its color became green.*][9] In less time than it takes to tell it, when Wu Sung saw that the tiger was coming down upon him, with one quick move he dodged behind it. [*The man. The second dodging.*] Now it is most difficult for a tiger to see

5. The putative author of the novel.

6. 1254–1322. A famous painter of the Yüan period whose given name was Meng-fu (see selection 61).

7. Chao's wife.

8. As will soon be seen in the following narrative description, these are the three things the tiger did in its efforts to seize Wu Sung. Chin's claim about Chao Meng-fu's emulation of the horse and Shih Nai-an's complete success in bringing to life Wu Sung's fight with the tiger is what we today would call "empathy."

9. A sure sign of the presence of a powerful ghost or spirit

someone behind its back. [*In the midst of this turmoil the author takes time out to provide an explanatory note.*] It therefore dug its front paws into the ground, and with one sweep lifted up its back and rear parts to kick. [*The tiger.*] With a single quick move Wu Sung dodged to one side. [*The man. The third dodging.*] Seeing that it could not kick Wu Sung, the tiger let out a tremendous roar which, like a thunderclap in the sky, shook the whole mountain ridge. It then erected its tail like an iron staff and slashed down. [*The tiger.*] But Wu Sung again dodged to one side. [*The man. The fourth dodging.*] Ordinarily when a tiger tries to seize a man, it does so only with a pounce, a kick, and a cut. If after these three maneuvers it cannot seize a man, half of its heart and temper desert it. [*In the midst of this turmoil the author takes time out to provide an explanatory note. A genius, commanding a wide acquaintance with things, certainly does not speak falsely. However, there is no place to verify this statement of his. This passage brings all the previous action to an end. In what has gone above, Wu Sung only used the method of dodging four times. In what follows he will apply his strength.*]

Unable to cut Wu Sung with its tail, the tiger roared again and swiftly circled round. [*The tiger.*] Seeing that the tiger had again turned, Wu Sung whirled his club with both hands [*Whirled his club—the ninth posture he assumes with the club. Club: the fifteenth time.*] and with all his strength brought it down from mid-air in one swift blow. [*The man. After this blow, who would not think that the tiger will be done away with? And yet unexpected things are going to take place.*] There was a crashing sound, and leaves and branches scattered down over his face. When he fixed his eyes to see, Wu Sung found that he had not hit the tiger [*He had marshaled all his strength and yet he did not hit the tiger. What a hair-raising sentence!*]; instead in his haste he had hit a withered tree. [*In this turmoil the author again takes time out to provide this explanatory note.*] The club broke in two, and he was only holding half of it in his hand. [*Club: the sixteenth time. The author has been busy writing about the club for a long while. We all thought that Wu Sung could rely on it to strike the tiger, but all of a sudden it comes to nought here: we are absolutely stunned and hardly dare read on. After the club is broken, Wu Sung's extraordinary power of fighting the tiger with his bare hands can be revealed. However, the reader is so frightened that his heart and liver have jumped out of his mouth.*]

The tiger roared, its wrath fully aroused. Turning its body around, it again leaped toward Wu Sung. [*The tiger.*] Wu Sung again jumped away and retreated ten steps. [*The man.*] No sooner had he done so than the tiger planted its two forepaws right in front of him. [*The tiger.*] Seizing the opportunity, Wu Sung threw away the broken club [*The club is gotten rid of. Club: the seventeenth time.*], and with the same motion both his hands clutched the tiger's spotted neck and pressed the head down. [*The man.*] The tiger in desperation attempted to struggle loose [*The tiger.*], but Wu Sung forced it down with all his strength, unwilling to relax his grip even for a moment. [*The man.*] Then he kicked the tiger's face and eyes wildly. [*Kicking with a foot—marvelous. For he cannot loosen his hands. Kicking the eyes—marvelous. For it would be hard to kick any other spot.*] The tiger began to roar, and clawed up two heaps of yellow mud underneath its body, forming a mud pit. [*The tiger. How did Nai-an know that the man who kicks at a tiger must kick its eyes, and that when a tiger is being kicked at, it will make a mud pit? All this is improbable writing, and yet the matter must be a certainty. How absolutely extraordinary! How absolutely marvelous!*] [10] Wu Sung pressed the tiger's mouth straight into the pit. [*The man.*] Being so mauled by Wu Sung, the tiger became completely worn out. [*The tiger.*]

Wu Sung then used his left hand to grasp tightly the tiger's spotted neck, and freeing the right hand, lifted up his hammerlike fist and bludgeoned the tiger with all his strength. [*The man.*] After fifty or seventy blows, blood began to gush out from the tiger's eyes, mouth, nose, and ears. The tiger, unable to stir any more, could barely gasp for breath. [*The tiger.*] Wu Sung let go of the beast, and went among the pine trees in search of his broken club. Grasping the broken club in his hand and fearing lest the tiger was not yet dead, he struck it again. [*Club: the eighteenth time. This is the last mention of the club.*] Only after he saw the tiger's breathing cease did he finally throw down the club. [*The club ends here.*] He then thought to himself, "I'll just pick up the tiger and drag it down the ridge." [*His first thought is to take it away. Marvelous.*] But when he tried to pull the tiger from its pool of blood with both his hands, he couldn't! The truth was he had completely used up his strength, and all his limbs were weak and powerless. [*With this sign of weakness his powers of a moment ago become even more evident.*]

Wu Sung returned to the blue rock and sat there for a while. [*Wu Sung's extreme weariness depicted here brings out more clearly through contrast his great prowess of a moment ago. The narrative comes back to the blue rock again. Absolutely marvelous!*] He thought to himself, "It is getting dark. Suppose another tiger leaps out, how will I subdue it? I'd better get down the ridge somehow, and come back tomorrow morning to take care of the beast." [*The sentence is specially designed so as to make what follows appear surprising.*] [11] He then found his felt hat by the side of the rock [*With a cry "Ah-ya!" he rolled down from the blue rock. At that moment he was so frightened out of his wits that he hadn't noticed where his hat had dropped. Penetrating writ-*

10. What Chin seems to mean here is that the account is more convincing *because* it departs from literal truth—an indication of Chin's love of paradox. Or perhaps he is saying that, unlikely as it would be to invent or observe such details, they really must be true.

11. As we shall see shortly, Wu Sung runs into two hunters disguised as tigers when he is going down the ridge, which creates another moment of high suspense. What Chin means here is probably that when Wu Sung's fear (the possibility of encountering another tiger) seemingly comes true later in the story, the surprise felt by the reader is even greater.

ing.], went through the tangled trees [*The author comes back to the tangled trees*], and dragged himself down the ridge a step at a time.

Wu Sung had not traveled more than half a tricent when two tigers leaped out of the withered grass. [*Extraordinary writing that will frighten people to death.*] "Ah-ya!" he cried. "This is the end of me." [*Extraordinary writing that will frighten people to death.*] But suddenly the two tigers stood upright in darkness. [*Extraordinary writing that will frighten people to death.*] When Wu Sung looked closely at them, he saw that they were none other than two people wrapped tightly in clothes sewn together from tiger skins. They each had a five-pronged pitchfork. [*Extraordinary writing.*] Seeing Wu Sung, they were startled and said, "You . . . you, have you eaten a crocodile's heart, or a leopard's gall, or a lion's leg, that you are not afraid of anything? How dare you walk over the ridge alone in the darkness of the approaching night without any weapon? You . . . you, are you a man or a ghost?" [*Although the fight with the tiger is over, the author comments on the event through the mouths of the hunters.*] "Who are you two?" asked Wu Sung. "We are local hunters," replied one of them. "What are you doing on the ridge?" asked Wu Sung. [*These are words that will make people split their sides. I am on the ridge to kill the tiger, but what are you up here for? Absolutely marvelous!*]

Greatly surprised, the two hunters said, "So you still don't know. Nowadays, there is a huge tiger on the Ching-yang Ridge. It comes out every night to harm people. Even we hunters have lost seven or eight of our own. Countless passing travelers have been eaten by this beast. The district magistrate has instructed the village leaders and us hunters to capture it. But the evil beast is powerful and hard to get near. [*We know therefore that a pounce, a kick, and a cut were unusual things.*] Who dares approach it? Because of it we don't know how many floggings we have received for our failures in our mission. Still we cannot capture it. Tonight is our turn again to try. We are here with a dozen or so villagers. Spring-bows and poisoned arrows are set up all over the place to await its arrival. We were waiting in ambush when we saw you nonchalantly [*Four characters (in the original). Wu Sung's valor is described unintentionally.*] walking down the ridge. You gave us a start. But who are you? Have you seen the tiger?"

"I am from Ch'ing-ho district, surnamed Wu and number two among siblings. [*In the midst of this turmoil the author fixes our attention on the case of Wu Sung's going to see his elder brother. Therefore these four characters ('number two among siblings') are planted everywhere.*] A while ago, I bumped into that tiger by the tangled trees up on the ridge and killed it by punching and kicking." [*His first recapitulation.*] The two hunters looked stunned upon hearing this and said, "You are making it up!" "If you don't believe me," said Wu Sung, "look at the bloodstains on my clothes." [*Too bad he is wearing a red jacket.*] "How did you kill it?" asked the two. Wu Sung repeated his story of killing the tiger. [*His second recapitulation. Actually, it is something he is most proud of. Therefore he cannot help saying it over and over again. I too want to say it over and over again, but unfortunately there isn't anything I have to say that is worth speaking about.*]

Upon hearing this, the two hunters were both joyous and astonished. They called out to gather the ten villagers. The ten villagers, all carrying pitchforks, crossbows, knives, and spears, gathered around right away. "Why didn't they come up the hill with you?" Wu Sung asked. "That beast was just too ferocious," said the hunters. "How dared they come up?"

The dozen or so villagers now all stood in front. The two hunters asked Wu Sung to tell the crowd how he killed the tiger. [*His third recapitulation. It is also marvelous that the hunters should ask Wu Number Two to speak. Even others felt proud, let alone Wu Sung himself.*] None of the group believed it. "If you don't believe me," said Wu Sung, "come with me and see for yourselves." They all carried steel and flint with them, so they struck fire and lit five or six torches. [*Fine. Like a picture.*] Tagging after Wu Sung [*These four characters read like a picture.*], they again ascended the ridge. Seeing that the tiger was dead there in a heap, they were all overjoyed. They dispatched someone ahead to report to the village leader and the responsible prominent family. Meanwhile five or six villagers tied up the tiger and carried it down the ridge.

Translated by John Wang

213

A Burial Mound for Flowers

from *Dream of Red Towers*

Ts'ao Hsüeh-ch'in (1718?–1764)

To return now to Queen Yüan-ch'un in the Palace,[1] when she had read over the poems written on the occasion of her visit to the Garden of Pomp and

"A Burial Mound for Flowers" is taken from chapter 23 of *Dream of Red Towers* (*Hung-lou meng*), originally called *A Record of the Stone* (*Shih-t'ou chi*). Generally recognized as China's greatest novel, *Dream* was left unfinished in eighty chapters by its young author, Ts'ao Hsüeh-ch'in. The novel was continued for another forty chapters by Kao Ô (fl. 1792).

Ts'ao Hsüeh-ch'in was the descendant of a once fabulously wealthy family that had its roots in Sung dynasty officialdom and had ably served the Manchus for nearly a century. By the time the author had achieved maturity, however, the family had suffered serious financial setbacks due to dramatic political changes at court. As a consequence, he was forced to live in much reduced circumstances. Brooding melancholily over the lost grandeur of the family, he poured his soul into the writing and rewriting of his masterwork.

The novel is so complex and is peopled with so many major and minor characters that it would be futile to attempt to summarize it in a paragraph or two. It is the story about the decay

State [2] and rearranged them as a collection with her own comments on their respective merits, it occurred to her that the Garden with its arbors and rockeries would be utterly desolate if, after her own visit, her father, Secretary of the Board of Works Chia Cheng,[3] as he was in duty bound, had the gates locked and sealed, thus hiding it from the view of all. Besides, there were all her literary female cousins at home, and who better than they to inhabit a place so delightful? They need never feel their inspiration dry up; nor could the flowers and willows languish in such lovely company. She then thought of her own younger brother, Pao-yü,[4] who, unlike her male cousins, had been brought up with the girls—how that, if he should be left out, he would certainly feel lonely and neglected, which in turn might affect the spirits of her own mother and grandmother, the Dowager Duchess: she therefore considered it best to allow Pao-yü to move into the Garden with the female cousins.

Having thus decided, Yüan-ch'un sent the Steward of the Palace, the eunuch Hsia Chung, to the Jung Residence [5] with the order that Pao-ch'ai

---

of an aristocratic family affiliated with the Manchus and gives an intimate picture of upper-class life as in no other Chinese work. The external world, however, is seen as reflected in the hero's heart, and the book has a symbolic scheme. The stone of the original title is as old as the world itself and for one brief lifespan it was transformed—with the help of a mangy Buddhist monk and a crazy Taoist priest—into a young man and lover and tasted the joys and sorrows of the human lot before reverting to its stone-hearted existence. The young man, who is the hero, was born with a piece of jade in his mouth and named Pao-yü ("Precious Jade"), jade being stone carved, polished, and rendered artificial. His family, among the noblest in the land, bears the surname Chia (punningly interpreted as "Unreal").

The present episode is one of the most memorable of the novel. It is highly symbolic in that the beautiful and flowerlike Tai-yü ("Lustrous Jade"), who laments the fallen petals and prepares a burial mound for them, may seem to be tending her own grave. The passage also shows something of the love tradition under which novelists and romancers labored. Upon looking into the famous Yüan drama, The West Chamber (see selections 207 and 215, unnumbered notes), Pao-yü is suddenly emboldened in his love prattle; and the stray lines from The Peony Pavilion (selection 217), overheard by Tai-yü while the tunes were being rehearsed on the other side of the garden wall, define and give shape to her own feelings. In the context of this book, the passage also reveals the reading habits of the young in rich households and the insidious influence—so greatly dreaded by their elders—of novels and plays.

1. Yüan-ch'un, i.e., Prime of Spring, was born on New Year's Day; hence her name. She is the daughter of Chia Cheng (Pao-yü's father) and is one of the emperor's consorts. To enable her to visit her parents in comfort and seclusion, the family built for her sole use the Garden of Pomp and State adjoining their residence. Yüan-ch'un is a dozen or more years older than her brother Pao-yü, whom as a child she taught to read.

2. Ta-kuan-yüan, by which is meant "world in a nutshell," including, as it does, buildings in various styles, an artificial village, and a temple in a varied landscape setting. The name has also been rendered as "Grand Prospect Garden."

3. Chia Cheng, grandson of Duke Jung and son of the Dowager Duchess, is only Junior Secretary in chapter 2, but is made Senior Secretary of the Board of Works in chapter 85.

4. In this part of the story, he is about thirteen years of age.

5. Residence of Duke Jung, now inhabited by his descendants. The residence of Jung's brother, Duke Ning, is similarly referred to as the Ning residence.

and the other female cousins[6] should take up their abode in the Garden, which was on no account to be locked up with entry debarred to all, and that Pao-yü was also to move in, to pursue his studies along with the cousins. Secretary Chia and his lady respectfully received the Queen's command and, when the eunuch had made his departure, reported the matter to the Dowager Duchess before ordering the servants to enter the Garden and sweep and tidy up each corner of it, and outfit the various buildings with curtains, screens, beds, and hangings.

While all who heard the news rejoiced, Pao-yü alone was in raptures: he began at once to demand this or that piece of her furniture from the Dowager. But his animated conference with his grandmother was interrupted by a servant girl entering to announce: "The master wants Pao-yü." The effect of this upon Pao-yü was like a thunderbolt[7]—his countenance fell, almost as if his face was charred; all his newly raised hopes seemed dashed; and like a stick of gum he attached himself to the Dowager, turning and twisting in every direction and refusing to come unstuck. The Dowager, however, said soothingly, "My precious! Go to your father, who won't eat you! Remember, there's always Grandmamma behind you. Besides, you've just written that good essay for him! Since the Queen would have you and the girls housed in the Garden, I suppose your father will have a few things to say to you, only so as to keep you out of mischief. Be a good boy and agree with whatever he might say." And even as she calmed Pao-yü, she called two of her own serving women and told them to accompany Pao-yü and not let the master scare him.

Pao-yü was now obliged to obey his father's summons and came away with the old women, though advancing no more than a few inches with each step he took. Eventually, however, he reached his mother's apartments[8] where, a family council being in progress, the servant girls Gold Bangle, Rainbow Cloud, Sunset, Bird of Paradise, and Embroidered Phoenix stood waiting outside, under the eaves. At the sight of Pao-yü crawling along, they puckered up their mouths and sniggered. Suddenly Gold Bangle pulled Pao-yü toward her and announced with a chuckle, "I've just smeared my lips with rouge soaked in fragrant oil. Lick me! Now's best!"[9] Rainbow Cloud hurriedly pushed Gold Bangle aside and, herself giggling, said below her breath, "We

6. Pao-ch'ai ("Precious Hairpin") is the daughter of Aunt Hsüeh, sister of Mrs. Secretary Chia; she is aged fifteen and a rival to the heroine, Tai-yü, who is mentioned below with the other female cousins. As a relative, rather than one of the Dowager Duchess's granddaughters, Pao-ch'ai is given precedence over the others.

7. The strange antipathy between Pao-yü and his father is a recurrent theme in the novel.

8. As the lady of the house, Mrs. Secretary Chia occupies the center courtyard with a main suite of five stately rooms, but lives for the most part in three smaller rooms constituting the east wing. The center courtyard is connected by a rear passage to the Dowager Duchess's courtyard, situated to its west.

9. It is Pao-yü's habit to lick the rouge off the lips of the servant girls.

aren't in the mood. No teasing!" And turning to Pao-yü, she continued, "You'll find the master in a good temper—better go in at once!"

Pao-yü dragged himself into the room, only to learn that his parents were in the inner room. Madam Chao, the concubine,[10] who had remained in the outer room, now lifted the door curtain for Pao-yü, who entered the bedroom and made his bow. Secretary Chia and his lady were seated opposite each other on the heated brick-bed, talking. A row of chairs facing the brick-bed was occupied by the girls, Ying-ch'un, T'an-ch'un, and Hsi-ch'un,[11] and Pao-yü's half-brother Huan; [12] the three last, being all younger than Pao-yü, stood up upon his entering. Secretary Chia raising his head, saw before him Pao-yü with his lofty and graceful air and his strikingly handsome appearance, which showed up all the more the drooping hangdog look and ill-bred, clownish manners of the son of the concubine—Huan, who stood beside him. Secretary Chia then remembered his eldest boy,[13] Chu, now dead, and realized with a twinge of remorse how deeply his wife loved and cherished her sole surviving son. He himself, too, was aging, his beard already turned gray. All these considerations combined to militate against his aversion for his son and his inclination to chastise him. After indulging for some time in this musing, which left him nine-tenths mollified, Secretary Chia said, not unkindly, "It is the Queen's wish that you, who are in the habit of following your idle whims day after day outside the house, should now be confined to the Garden, where you will carry out your reading and writing in the company of your sister and cousins. Ply well at your books, my lad. If you persist in your dawdling, rest assured that you will hear about this."

Pao-yü responded with a whole string of yeses, and his mother pulled him on to the brick-bed beside her. The others, too, sat down again. Gently rubbing her hand against Pao-yü's neck,[14] Mrs. Secretary Chia asked, "Have you finished the pills, my boy?" Pao-yü said, "There is one left still." His mother continued, "I'll send for another ten tomorrow, and remind Bombarding Scent [15] to make you take it at bedtime." Pao-yü protested, "Why, Bombarding Scent does give it to me every night! She has not once forgotten ever

10. Secretary Chia's concubine, regarded as an inferior, is kept out of the family council, though her two children are not.

11. Ying-ch'un ("Welcome Spring") is the daughter of Pao-yü's uncle, the Duke, noted below; Hsi-ch'un ("Pity Spring") is descended from Duke Ning and not one of the Dowager's granddaughters; T'an-ch'un ("Seek Spring") is Pao-yü's half sister, i.e., the daughter of the concubine, but unlike her brother, Huan, she is in no way handicapped by her birth.

12. Huan, Pao-yü's half brother, is the son of the concubine.

13. Chu, Pao-yü's older brother, does not appear in the story but leaves a widow, Li Wan, mentioned below, and a son.

14. To detect any glandular swellings the pills were expected to cure.

15. A demure and level-headed girl who was one of the Dowager's own maids before she is assigned to Pao-yü, whom she jealously guards and protects. Her surname is Hua (Flower). Pao-yü alters her own name, Pearl, to Bombarding Scent. She is a few years older than Pao-yü.

since you, Mother, told her to." At this point, Secretary Chia broke in with some impatience, "Who is this Bombarding Scent?" Mrs. Chia replied blandly: "Oh, one of the maids." The head of the family went on contemptuously, "A servant girl might of course be called anything. But why such a name? Whose farfetched conceit was this?" His manner alarmed his lady, who, to shield Pao-yü, declared: "It was our gracious mother who gave the girl the name." Secretary Chia sneered, "Mother? Would Mother even dream of such an expression? It could only be Pao-yü." Pao-yü saw that concealment no longer availed; slipping off the brick-bed, he justified himself thus before his father: "In reading the old poets, I chanced upon the line—'The flowers' bombarding scent proclaims a sultry morn' [16] which came pat when I learned that the girl's surname was Flower; so I gave her that name." Mrs. Chia hurriedly added, "You had better hunt out another name for her, Pao-yü, as soon as you get back to Grandmamma." [17] Then, turning to Secretary Chia, she said, "I should not have thought it necessary, my lord, to lose one's temper over a thing like that." Secretary Chia conceded, "There is no real harm in that name and certainly no need to change it now. But it does serve to show that Pao-yü wastes all his time on precious verse compositions to the detriment of his proper studies." And suddenly rounding upon his son, he barked, "Wretch! Be off with you!" Mrs. Chia, anxious for Pao-yü to be gone, also said, "Go now. Don't let Grandmamma keep waiting for you to come to dinner."

Pao-yü assented gravely and slowly withdrew from his father's presence. But when he found himself among the servant girls outside, he remembered their joke and stuck his tongue out at Gold Bangle before scurrying off, followed by the two old women. At the end of the corridor leading to the Dowager's courtyard, he noticed Bombarding Scent herself leaning against the door, waiting for him. When Bombarding Scent saw Pao-yü return, safe and unscathed, she asked, beaming, "What was it about?" Pao-yü said, "Oh, hardly anything at all. Merely that I was to keep out of scrapes in the Garden, the usual words to that effect." As he spoke, he started for the room of his grandmother, to whom he reported the interview with his father. His cousin Tai-yü [18] happening also to be there, he now asked her, "Which house would you rather have?" Tai-yü, whose mind had been engaged on the same subject, responded to his question with a smile; she said, "I was thinking of

16. The line is derived from Lu Yu, "Joys of Village Life" (see selection 59).

17. Pao-yü, being the Dowager Duchess's favorite grandchild, lives in his grandmother's courtyard, as does Tai-yü, who, at least in the earlier part of the story, enjoys a position of privilege.

18. Tai-yü is the daughter of Aunt Lin, the Dowager's daughter. When Aunt Lin dies, Tai-yü is taken, at the age of six, from her father's official residence in Yangchow to live with her grandmother in the capital. In chapter 3, Tai-yü describes herself as being a year younger than Pao-yü, whose favorite cousin she fast becomes.

Hsiao-Hsiang Hermitage. I love those bamboos screening the curved railing—it's so much quieter there than anywhere else." Upon hearing this, Pao-yü grinned and clapped his hands in glee, crying, "Just as I thought! And it's just where I wanted you to stay! I'll live in Crab Red Court, where we shall be near each other and both in secluded spots."

As the two of them went on planning in this fashion, a woman-servant entered with a message from the head of the household to the Dowager: "The cousins are to move on the twenty-second of the second month, an auspicious day, into the Garden, which is being swept. The houses will be got ready in the few intervening days." Pao-ch'ai chose for her abode Aromatic Herb Rockery; Tai-yü, Hsiao-Hsiang Hermitage; Ying-ch'un, Tapestry Tower; T'an-ch'un, Autumn's Breath Studio; Hsi-ch'un, Smartweed Bank Loggia; Li Wan,[19] Sweet Paddy Village; and Pao-yü himself, Crab Red Court. At each of the dwellings, two older women and four girls were to be in attendance, not counting the wet nurse and the personal maid, cleaners and gardeners being additionally provided. Thus on the twenty-second, the entire company took possession of the Garden of Pomp and State: embroidered waistbands now brushed against the flowers, and perfumed breezes intoxicated the willows, so that the place was no longer desolate.

Pao-yü dwelt in the Garden and found everything to his heart's content and longed for no other happiness than that of spending each day in the company of the female cousins in reading or practicing calligraphy, in playing the guitar or games of chess, in painting or composing verse. And in such pastimes of theirs as the tracing of embroidery patterns, perhaps of some phoenix or bird of paradise, and the embroidery itself, or the hunting out of rare plants[20] and the arranging of flowers as part of their headdress, or singing or humming tunes, or word-games and riddles, he too joined with zest. And Pao-yü wrote some poems in which he described scenes in the Gardens at various times of year, of which four are quoted below, not, to be sure, for their excellence, but because they were based on his actual experience:

Night in Spring

Shut in by rainbow-colored silk bed-curtains,
I fancy I hear frogs croaking beyond the wall.
A chill creeps up my pillow; rain taps at the window.
Before my eyes, lo, she whom I wooed in my dream—
"The candle drips tears—tears shed for whom?

19. Li Wan, the widow of Chu, Pao-yü's older brother. She is the only adult among the seven, her son Lan being only two or three years younger than Pao-yü.

20. A competitive game in which each participant produces an unusual plant or flower, or a branch or shoot notable for its shape or color, and sets forth the claims of his/her particular specimen in poetical or horticultural terms.

The flowers in the vase seem a cluster of griefs — my griefs!"
"Let alone a simple nurse-maid, poor sleepyhead me!
When lying abed, I can't abide jesting and teasing." [21]

Night in Summer

The girl has fallen asleep at her embroidery;
The parrot in its gold cage [22] renews its call for "tea";
The full moon shines through the open window — a rounded mirror;
Sandalwood fumes from rival censers circle about the room.
Amber cups overflow with sparkling "Dew on Lotus";
Breezes rustling the willows spread cool through the glass verandah.
Silk fans now wave all over the water pavilion:
Roll up the curtain — my lady's evening toilet is done.

Night in Autumn

A breathless hush reigns within the Crimson Library,[23]
But shimmering moonlight *will* peep through gauze curtains.
Sheltered by the moss-grown rockery, the cranes curl up in sleep;
Crows perch on the well-curb wet with dew.
A drowsy maid brings a quilt, unrolling a golden phoenix; [24]
The beloved one returns from the window, her hairpin undone.
Awake in the still night, athirst with too much wine,
I poke at the smoldering embers and infuse fresh tea.

Night in Winter

Flowering plums [25] and bamboos engulf each other's dreams at the
   third watch:
But embroidered coverlet and kingfisher-down would still induce no
   sleep.

21. Personalities are deliberately vague in Chinese verse, and the apportioning of the lines to two speakers is the translator's own. The more favored servant girls slept in the same beds as the children, often even when they ceased to be children.

22. The cloistered part of Crab Red Court is filled with exotic birds in cages of various colors, thus further adding to the "maze" and "trap" symbolism; and Tai-yü has a parrot that recites verses.

23. Crimson Library is used as an alternative name for Crab Red Court. It is to be regarded as the name of Pao-yü's study rather than any specific part of Crab Red Court.

24. A golden phoenix embroidered on the quilt.

25. The Chinese plum (*mei-hua*) with its five-petaled flower blooms in winter and early spring. The plum, the bamboo, and the pine are designated the "Three Friends of Winter," symbolizing hardiness and purity.

Amidst shadows of pines in the courtyard, a lonely crane flaps;
Frost, like pear blossoms, bestrews the ground, though no oriole sings.
The girl with the green sleeves tosses off verses about the cold;
His golden sable pledged for wine,[26]
　　the gay young lord declares it insipid.
Luckily my lord's page is thoroughly adept in blending tea—
Sweeping up the new snow, he makes an instant brew.[27]

It being then known that these verses were by a scion of the Jung branch of the Chia ducal house, aged but twelve or thirteen, the crowd of sycophants made copies of them and took every opportunity of reading them aloud and praising them. Flippant young men, attracted by the showy, amatory diction, wrote them on their fans and on the walls of their rooms, reciting them repeatedly with undiminished pleasure. It thus came about that, through intermediaries, strangers would approach Pao-yü with requests for a poem or a piece of calligraphy or an inscription on some picture, which he, being much flattered, willingly obliged, spending days on end upon such extramural activities.

Nevertheless, the very tranquility of the Garden became a source of vexation. One day, Pao-yü suddenly felt out of sorts and declared himself dissatisfied with one thing after another, and wandered in and out of the place, moody and dispirited. For the Garden was inhabited mostly by young ladies in a state of primordial innocence, given over to childish candor and oblivious as yet of the proprieties, neither shunning one another while sitting or lying down nor intending by a smile or laugh more than the spontaneous expression of gladness or merriment. How indeed could they divine what went on in Pao-yü's mind? For his part, being continually in an ill humor, he would no longer remain within the Garden but loafed away his time outside its precinct, looking all the while blank and abstracted.

When the library page, Tea-Tobacco,[28] saw his young master thus preoccupied, he took it upon himself to devise some means of diverting him. Tea-Tobacco considered one expedient after another, but Pao-yü seemed already familiar with them all, and tired of them all, unlikely to be amused by any of them. There remained, however, a source of delight not yet known to Pao-yü, which having at last hit upon, Tea-Tobacco went straight to the booksell-

26. Yüan Fu (279–327) exchanged his official cap of golden sable for wine, for which he was impeached, though later pardoned.

27. In chapter 41, the nun Miao-yü makes a special brew of tea with snow gathered from plum blossoms five winters earlier and sealed in a jar buried in the ground.

28. Tea-Tobacco (Ming-yen), whose duty it is to accompany Pao-yü to school during the fitful periods of the latter's attendance and generally to wait upon his young master in and about the library. He would be a few years older than Pao-yü.

ers and bought many volumes of stories old and new,[29] and the Intimate and Revealing Histories of Chao Fei-yen and her sister Ho-te,[30] and of the Empress Wu,[31] and of the beauteous Yang Kuei-fei,[32] and the texts of numerous plays, and showed them to Pao-yü, who, never having read such books before, rejoiced exceedingly in the new discovery. Tea-Tobacco then warned Pao-yü not to take the books into the Garden,[33] for if they should be seen, the wrath that would descend upon him, Tea-Tobacco, would be great and terrible. Pao-yü, however, would not now hear of being deprived of their company. After prolonged debate with himself, he picked out a few sets of elegant diction and refined sentiment, and these he brought with him into Crab Red Court, where he hid them above his bed[34] and read them when no one was about. But the ones that were low and coarse he kept in the library outside.

It being now the middle of the third month,[35] Pao-yü took with him after breakfast one day a copy of *The Meeting with Fay*, otherwise known as *The West Chamber*, and sat on a stone under the peach tree by the bridge above Soaking Fragrance Weir.[36] Opening the book, he read slowly from the beginning, drinking in each line. When he reached the lines:

> "A fresh shower of red petals descending,
> Ten thousand flakes of melancholy!"[37]

a sudden gust shook the boughs and robbed the peach tree of a good half of its blossoms, the falling petals alighting all over Pao-yü and the pages of his

29. Light reading was anathema to Confucian orthodoxy and regarded as a source of corruption, which it often was. *Stories Old and New* was the title of Feng Meng-lung's first collection of colloquial stories of about 1621, and a general title to all his three collections, but the reference here would seem to be to stories generally rather than specifically Feng's collections (see selection 210).

30. Chao Fei-yen and her equally beautiful sister Ho-te were ladies in the harem of Emperor Ch'eng-ti of the Han dynasty. In such "intimate histories" (*wai-chuan*), the secrets of the harem are recounted with undisguised relish.

31. A fictional narrative bearing the title *Tse-t'ien wai-shih* (*Intimate History of Wu Tse-t'ien*) seems not to have survived, but the intrigues of the Empress Wu are part of traditional lore. Wu Tse-t'ien (624–705) was the only woman in Chinese history to found her own dynasty.

32. The celebrated favorite of Emperor Hsüan-tsung of the T'ang dynasty (see selection 149).

33. In spite of the fourth poem, "Night in Winter," Tea-Tobacco is not allowed into the Garden.

34. I.e., above his four-poster bed, concealed by the bed-curtains.

35. About the middle of April.

36. The bridge is directly above Soaking Fragrance Weir, below which the stream flows into a river outside the garden.

37. Only the first line is quoted in the original, but the full force of the allusion is lost without the second line (itself taken from a poem by Tu Fu), which has therefore been supplied in the translation.

open book and the surrounding earth. Pao-yü was on the point of dusting himself off but, at the thought of the flowers being scattered and trodden upon, he desisted; instead he lifted the skirt of his robe and, moving forward a few steps, emptied the blossoms into the pond. The red petals floated and whirled on the water until, drifting with the current, they disappeared down the weir. Returning to the spot where he had sat before, he now noticed the blossoms on the ground, and when he paused to consider what to do with them, a voice from behind called to him—"And what business brings *you* here?"

Pao-yü turned round: it was Tai-yü, who came up, shouldering a small hoe, from which hung a dainty silk bag, and holding a besom [38] in her hand. Pao-yü shouted with joy, "Well met! The very thing I wanted! Come and sweep up the blossoms so that we may throw them into the pond! I have already thrown a whole lot in." Tai-yü, however, said, "It would be a pity to do that! The water is clear enough here, but once it leaves the Garden and flows through the crowded part of town, it will be polluted and the poor blossoms themselves outraged. Over there, in that corner, I have prepared a tomb for the flowers. I shall sweep up these petals and put them in my silk bag and consign the whole to earth so that the flowers may return to dust, a clean and proper end for them." Struck by the idea,[39] Pao-yü was in transports; he agreed eagerly and then added: "Let me put down my book first. Then I can help you to gather them up." Tai-yü asked, "What book?" At the recollection of which, Pao-yü tried hastily to conceal the book he had been reading and stammered, "Ah, well, only *The Doctrine of the Mean and The Great Learning.*[40] Why, what else could it be?" Tai-yü laughed, saying, "I know your tricks! Now surrender that book at once!" Pao-yü then said sheepishly, "Dearest cousin! It's not that I am afraid of your seeing the book, but don't—for heaven's sake!—tell anyone. In truth, its style is inimitable! I wager you'll be forgetting your meals when you're reading it." And with that he handed over the text of the plays.

Tai-yü laid down her gardening tools and took the book. Reading from the beginning, she became more and more absorbed in it as she went on, so that within a short while she had read through all sixteen scenes.[41] Being herself enthralled by its arresting tropes and frothy eloquence, she laid the book aside and, looking vacant and pensive, repeated in her mind many of its lines and

38. Broom made of twigs.

39. The sanctity of earth does not readily occur to Pao-yü, who places his trust in the purity of water.

40. Forming, with the *Analects* and *The Book of Mencius*, the Confucian "Four Books" studied by every schoolboy.

41. Strictly speaking, sixteen acts (*che*). The term "scene" (*ch'ü*) is taken over from the Southern drama, and the four plays regarded as one long play.

phrases. Pao-yü ventured to smile; he asked, "Did you like it, cousin?" And when Tai-yü returned his smile and said, "Yes, I really have enjoyed it," Pao-yü suddenly giggled and started to quote from the plays: " 'The melancholy and sickly lover'—*that* I am assuredly! And yours—yours, 'the face that overthrew cities and kingdoms'!" Tai-yü instantly flushed, her cheeks, neck, and ears turned a furious crimson; she frowned, then half raised her eyebrows; [12] her sparkling eyes narrowed to two slits, then opened wide again in a disdainful stare: her exquisite features were now the picture of anger and reproach. Pointing her finger accusingly at Pao-yü, she exclaimed, "How dare you! It's death that you deserve for this! Foisting lewd verses upon me and using such rude language too! What an affront! I'll tell my uncle and aunt."

At the word "affront," two red rings showed around her eyes, and she turned abruptly to go. Pao-yü started up in a panic and barred her way, pleading: "Forgive me this once, dearest cousin! I was at fault in giving utterance to such absurdities, but if I really had intended any affront, then let me fall into the pond tomorrow and be swallowed by a monstrous turtle, and so be reborn as a large turtle myself that I might bear the stone tablet on your tomb [43] when one day you die, the lady of some great minister or other!" This grotesque protestation caused Tai-yü to burst out laughing again. Hurriedly rubbing her eyes, she cried triumphantly, "That scared the daylights out of you, didn't it? I won't stand any more nonsense from you:

'Tut! A weak sapling—
A spearhead of tinfoil—that you are!' " [44]

The allusion did not escape Pao-yü, who broke into hilarious laughter, saying, "What about yourself then? I'll go and tell on you too!" Tai-yü, however, refused to be intimidated. She answered playfully, "But it did come out of *your* book. If—like the prodigy you are—you can memorize and recite whole essays after a single reading, will you not allow that I may be able to take in ten lines at a glance?"

Pao-yü now put away the book and, with a happy grin, declared, "To our task! Let us bury the flowers and forget the other part." So the two of them swept up the fallen petals, which they placed in the silk bag and solemnly deposited in a hollow in the earth. When finally they had covered up the hollow

42. Tai-yü is noted for her frown, which is regarded as a sign of her poor health and for which she is nicknamed "Miss Eyebrows." Here Pao-yü has already had more than his share of her smiles and laughter.

43. Stone steles often had for their pedestal the figure of a tortoise; "turtle" and "tortoise" are words of abuse which readily occur in oaths. Pao-yü's momentary fancy of himself as a stone tortoise at Tai-yü's tomb is, however, the foreboding of an unhappy end for both.

44. A quotation from near the end of *The West Chamber* which alludes to a line from the *Analects* about a plant that does not blossom.

with a tiny mound,[45] Bombarding Scent rushed up and said reproachfully to Pao-yü: "Here of all places! As if I haven't looked all over the Garden for you! The cousins have gone across to ask after your uncle, the Duke,[46] who is indisposed, and the old mistress has ordered you to go, too. Come back now for a change of clothes." Pao-yü thereupon picked up his book and, having excused himself to Tai-yü, returned with Bombarding Scent to Crab Red Court to dress for the visit to his uncle, which forms no part of our story.

Being now left alone and having heard that the female cousins were all away, Tai-yü turned her steps sadly toward the Hermitage.[47] As she reached the corner of Pear Courtyard, from across the wall came the sweet notes of pipes, now loud, now muted, blending with the melodious voices of singers, and it occurred to her that the troupe of twelve girls from Soochow were rehearsing the airs of their Southern repertory.[48] Only Tai-yü had never cared much for the Southern drama and, paying no regard to the music, she walked on.[49] But borne by the breezes, two lines of a song assailed her ears, each word falling clear and distinct:

45. "Which they placed . . . tiny mound" is the translator's own version. The original merely reads: "So the two swept up the fallen petals, and just when they had buried them, Bombarding Scent . . . ."

46. The Duke is Chia She, elder brother to Secretary Chia, who lives in a separate part of the Jung residence, entered through its own street gate. Being neither learned nor a man of affairs, he is content with a role secondary to his more ambitious younger brother.

47. The Hsiao-Hsiang Hermitage, which is her own residence. The Hsiao and Hsiang, two rivers of Hunan province, are the subject of numerous misty landscapes by painters and are redolent of tragic, suicidal poets and ethereal goddesses. These and other evocative aspects of the Hermitage make it perfectly suited for Tai-yü.

48. The twelve girls were brought to the capital from Soochow to give musical and dramatic performances on the occasion of the queen's visit. They are appropriately housed in Pear Courtyard adjoining the Garden, Emperor Hsüan Tsung of T'ang having trained his three hundred musicians in a pear orchard.

49. Tai-yü's native place is Soochow and, in spite of her lack of interest, her ear would be attuned to southern melodies. Aside from *Peony Pavilion*, which is mentioned in the following notes, two of the most famous southern dramas were Kao Ming's (c. 1305–1359) *The Lute (P'i-p'a chi)* and K'ung Shang-jen's (1648–1718) *The Peach Blossom Fan (T'ao-hua-shan)*.

Southern-style plays typically have a large cast of characters instead of just the four in Yüan drama that focus primarily on a single lead role. Contrasting groups of characters alternate in different scenes. They may sing solo, duet, or in chorus; the singing role is by no means restricted to a single character. There are also many more scenes in a southern-style play than in northern plays. *The Peach Blossom Fan*, for example, has forty plus a Prologue and Epilogue. Often four or five evenings would be required for the complete production of a southern-style drama. The scenes in southern drama vary greatly in length and complexity though there are standard themes that make love scenes, martial scenes, and comic scenes almost obligatory. *The Lute* was one of the very first plays written in the romance (*ch'uan-ch'i*; for the origin of this term, see selection 208), a form of drama that emerged during the fourteenth century from Southern drama (*nan-hsi*) to become a model for later playwrights of this genre. In contrast to Northern plays such as Yüan drama (*tsa-chü*), which are livelier and somewhat raucous, Southern romances tend to be slower and more languorous, both musically and theatrically.

"Gay purple and exquisite red abloom everywhere,
But all abandoned to a dried-up well and crumbled walls." [50]

The words filled Tai-yü with a deep melancholy and longing. She stopped and, inclining her head, listened intently. The song now went:

"That glorious moments amidst this splendid scene
    should enshroud despair!
In whose courtyard do hearts still rejoice in the present?"

These last two lines caused her to sigh and nod inadvertently in agreement. She thought to herself: "It is true, then, that one may come across fine verse even in the theater, but I suppose most people simply follow the action and do not pause to savor the language."

The next moment, however, she blamed herself for letting her mind wander instead of attending to the song. And when she listened again, she heard:

"Because of your flowerlike beauty
And tender years like a rushing stream," [51]

and almost trembled with excitement. She then heard the lines that followed:

"I sought you in each nook and corner
But find you dejected in your chamber."

Being now quite overcome with emotion, she could hardly remain on her feet but sank on to a rock to brood over the words,

"Because of your flowerlike beauty
And tender years like a rushing stream,"

alert to their every nuance and suggestion. Suddenly she recalled a line she had read in the T'ang poets only the other day:

"Faded blossoms borne on a plaintive stream: lovelorn both"; [52]

and also from among the lyric compositions:

"The water rushing, the blossoms falling: Spring is gone forever!
Alas, heaven above and man's despair!" [53]

50. The song is from *Peony Pavilion*, scene 10: it is sung by the heroine, Bridal Tu; see selection 217.
51. *Peony Pavilion*, scene 10; sung by the hero, Willow.
52. From Ts'ui T'u (late ninth century), "Evening in Spring."
53. The last two lines of Li Yü, "Lang t'ao sha." Li Yü (937–978, see selection 91) was the last ruler of the Southern T'ang kingdom, and the poem, written after he was deposed by the

and the lines, too, she had just read in *The West Chamber:*

> "The stream speckled with red petals falling,
> Each speck a grain of sorrow." [54]

Buoyed up from the depths of memory, all these lines floated in her mind, juxtaposed as in some conspiracy. She pondered over each passage and her heart was touched to the quick; her crowding fancies raced one another; and tears dropped from her eyes. While Tai-yü was thus enveloped in her thoughts, she felt a sudden pat on her back, and when she turned to look. . . .[55]

Translated by H. C. Chang

Sung in 976, contrasts his state of captivity with his regal past. The two concluding lines, which point out the contrast, lend themselves to a variety of interpretations. An alternative version reads:

> "The water rushing, the blossoms falling—gone forever!
> Alas, heaven above and man's despair!"

54. These lines are from the introduction.

55. This is followed by "but as to who it was that she saw, it shall be told in the next chapter" and two lines of verse which end chapter 23.

PART V

Oral and Performing Arts

Prosimetric Narratives

214

Transformation Text on Mahāmaudgalyāyana Rescuing His Mother from the Underworld, with Pictures, One Scroll, with Preface

Anonymous (late 9th–early 10th century)

Now, on the fifteenth day of the seventh month, the heavens open their doors and the gates of the hells are flung wide. The three mires dissipate, the ten virtues increase. Because this is the day when the company of monks end

This tale is about the Buddist saint Mu-lien (the Chinese version of his Sankrit name, which is given in the title), who saves his mother from the tortures of hell. It belongs to the popular genre called *pien-wen* (transformation text). This genre had a close relationship to pictures that were used as illustrations for oral storytelling, a trait evident even in the formula that occurs before the verse portions. Transformation texts constitute the earliest extended vernacular narratives in Chinese. The manuscript on which this translation is based was discovered around the turn of this century in a cave in the Chinese part of Central Asia at Tun-huang (far western Kansu province). The copying was completed on a date equivalent to May 26, 921, although the original composition occurred approximately 150 or more years before that date. Other manuscripts discovered at Tun-huang contain abbreviated versions of the tale, but this one offers the complete story.

Roughly 40,000 manuscripts were unearthed from one of the Caves of the Thousand Buddhas at Tun-huang, where they had been sealed up sometime during the first half of the eleventh century. Written in about twenty different languages, a number of which are now extinct, the Tun-huang manuscripts represent one of the most important archeological recoveries of written texts in history. Their reemergence in this century has revolutionized our

their summer retreat, the deity who confers blessings and the eight classes of supernatural beings all come to convey blessings. Those who undertake to make offerings to them in the present world will have a supply of blessings and those who are dead will be reborn in a superlative place. Therefore, a purgatorian feast[1] is spread before the Three Honored Ones[2] who, through the grace of their welcoming the great assembly, put a priority upon saving those who are distressed by hanging in limbo.

Long ago, when the Buddha was in the world, he had a disciple who was styled Maudgalyāyana. When he was still a layman and had not yet left home to become a monk, his name was Turnip. He believed deeply in the Three Precious Ones[3] and had a high regard for Salvationism.[4] Once he wanted to go to another country to engage in trade. So he disposed of his wealth, ordering his mother later on to arrange for vegetarian food to be provided for the many members of the Buddhist Trinity and the numerous beggars who would come. But after Turnip departed, his mother became stingy and hid away for herself all the riches which had been entrusted to her.

Before many months had elapsed, the son had completed his business and returned home. "As you had charged me," the mother said to her son, "I held vegetarian feasts which shall bring us blessings." Thus did she deceive commoners and saints so that, when her life came to an end, she fell into the Avīci Hell,[5] where she endured much harsh suffering.

After Turnip finished observing the three full years of mourning, he immediately surrendered himself to the Buddha and left home to become a monk. Having inherited the good deeds of his former lives, he actualized these inherent causes by paying heed to the Law and attaining arhatship.[6] Whereupon he sought his mother in the six paths of transmigration with his unlimited vision, but nowhere did he see her.

Maudgalyāyana awoke from meditation full of sadness. "In which place is my dear mother enjoying happiness?" he inquired of the World-Honored.

The World-Honored then informed Maudgalyāyana: "Your mother has

---

understanding of medieval Chinese literature, religion, politics, institutions, economics, society, dance, music, art, and other areas of human endeavor.

The dots under some of the words in the translation indicate places where sinographs are missing on the manuscript and have had to be restored. Three dots equal roughly one sinograph.

1. The presumed source of the Yü-lan-p'en ("All Souls") festival.
2. Amitābha Buddha and his two attendant bodhisattvas (saviors).
3. The Three Precious Ones or the Buddhist Trinity are the Buddha, dharma (his doctrine), and sangha (Buddhist community).
4. Mahāyāna, the Greater Vehicle of Buddhism.
5. The deepest of the eight hot hells.
6. Sainthood.

already dropped down into the Avīci hell, where she is now undergoing much suffering. Although you have attained the fruit of the saintly life, your knowledge will be to no avail. You can save her only if you employ the might of the assembly on the day when the companies of monks in all directions disband at the end of the summer retreat." Therefore, the Buddha in his compassion instituted this expedient method. This, then, is the story of how the purgatorian offerings were founded.

> From the time when Turnip's father and mother had passed away,
> After three full years of ceremonial sorrow, the period of mourning
>   came to an end;
> Listening to music did not make him happy—his appearance became
>   emaciated,
> Eating fine foods gave him no pleasure—he wasted away to skin and
>   bones.
> But then he heard that the Tathāgata [7] was in the Deer Park,
> Where he comforted and cared for all men and deities;
> "Now I shall study the Way and seek the Tathāgata!"
> And so he journeyed to the twin trees [8] to visit the Buddha.
> At that time, the Buddha came immediately to receive him,
> The monk prostrated himself before him who is most honored among
>   men and deities;
> To his right and left were the mighty Indra and Brahmā with their
>   hosts,
> To his east and west were the great generals and other sundry spirits.
> The sauvastika [9] on the front of his breast had a crystalline glow,
> The halo behind his neck was like the disc of the moon;
> Don't you know, the hundreds of gems and the thousands of flowers on
>   his throne,
> Were just like the five-colored clouds at the edge of the horizon.
> "I, your disciple, am a mediocre person who is limited by his desires,
> Neither can I renounce nor free myself from desire and anger;
> Just because the sinful karma of my whole life was of such enormity,
> It extended to my dear mother, causing her to enter the gates of Hades.
> I only fear that impermanence will press upon her,
> And that she will sink in the ocean of misery beside the ford of births
>   and deaths;
> May you, oh Buddha, show compassion by saving your disciple,
> Allowing me to concentrate on studying the Way so that I may repay
>   my parents."

7. The "Thus-come/gone," an epithet of the Buddha.
8. The pair of *śāla* trees under which the Buddha entered nirvāṇa.
9. The Buddha's lucky mark, which is a reversed form of the swastika

As soon as the World-Honored heard what Turnip was saying,
He knew that he was upright and was not being deceitful;
He began by enumerating and explaining the doctrine of the Four Noble Truths,[10]
Then lectured him on the necessity of avoiding the seven rebellious acts.[11]
Even though one amasses so much treasure that it towers to the Milky Way,
This is not as good as urgently persuading others to leave home and become monks;
It is precisely the same as a blind turtle bumping into a floating log,
Or yet like a lotus blossom issuing from a great expanse of water.[12]
It is difficult to escape from a house which is wrapped in flames,[13]
The raging sea of misery is so broad that it has no shores;
Just for the reason that all living beings are different,
The Tathāgata established three types of conveyances to nirvāṇa.
The Buddha summoned Ānanda to perform the tonsure,
And his clothing was then exchanged for a monk's cassock;
Instantaneously, Maudgalyāyana achieved sainthood,
And subsequently he received the commandments for monks.
During the time that Turnip was there in front of the Buddha,
Incense smoke curled up in wreaths from a golden censer;
The fabulous forest shaken by the six kinds of earthquakes[14] moved heaven and earth,
The four divine flowers were wafted on the air and scattered through the clear skies.
A thousand sorts of elegant brocades were spread on the couches and seats,
Ten thousand styles of pearled banners hung in the air.
The Buddha himself proclaimed: "Now you are my disciple!"
And he styled him "Mighty Maudgalyāyana of Supernatural Power."

At that moment, Maudgalyāyana achieved sainthood beneath the twin trees. How did it happen like this? It is just as in the *Lotus Sūtra:* "The

10. These are: 1. misery is a condition of life, 2. origination of misery, 3. stopping of misery, and 4. the eightfold path that leads to the stopping of misery.

11. Shedding a Buddha's blood; killing one's father or mother, a monk, teacher, or arhat (saint); disrupting religious organizations.

12. Both this and the preceding line are metaphorical expressions of the improbability of a man being reborn as a man or meeting with a Buddha and his teaching. The implication is that one should accumulate as much good karma as possible to better his chances of a happy rebirth.

13. This is the famous parable of the burning house in the *Lotus Sūtra.*

14. Auspicious signs of the Buddha's power.

prodigal son first received his worth, then later was cleansed of his impurities." This is precisely the same in that he first obtained the fruit of sainthood and afterward engaged in the study of the Way.

Look at the place where Maudgalyāyana sits meditating deep in the mountains—how is it?

> After Maudgalyāyana's beard and hair had been shaved away,
> Right away he took himself into the depths of the mountains;
> It was a remote and quiet place where there was no one else,
> Right away, he contemplated unreality and sat in meditation.
> He sat in meditation and contemplated unreality, learning good and
>   evil,
> He subdued his mind, he settled his mind, until nothing more
>   adhered to it;
> Facing a mirror, its image was clear and unwavering,
> And all the while he pressed his right foot down upon his left foot.[15]
>> He sat with his body erect on a large rock,[16]
>> And with his tongue touching the roof of his mouth;
>> White bones became for him completely empty,[17]
>> His breathings no longer were intertwined.[18]
> Just at that time, a herd of deer stopped to drink in the woods,
> They drew near to the clear pool and looked across its waters;
> Beneath the bright moon in front of the courtyard, he listened to
>   religious discourses,
> Under the pines on the green hills, he sat meditating.
> The lake air on the horizon was like colored clouds,
> The watchtowers on the green hills outside the frontier were visible;
> The autumn wind soughed as it passed through the center of the
>   forest,
> Yellow leaves drifted down and floated on the water.
> Maudgalyāyana sat reposefully in a state of incorporeality,
> Gradually he cultivated his internal and external experiential mind;
> By realizing discipleship, he occupied his hoped-for position,
> He entered and left the mountains [19] as free as he pleased.
>> Maudgalyāyana awoke from abstract meditation,
>> Then swiftly exercised his supernatural power;
>> His coming was quick as a thunderclap,

15. The posture for overcoming evil spirits.
16. To symbolize solidity.
17. The ninth and final stage of meditation on the decomposition of a corpse for the purpose of curbing desire.
18. He had achieved carefully controlled yogic breathing.
19. In Buddhist parlance, "mountain" oftens stands for monastery.

His going seemed like a gust of wind.
Wild geese honked at the hunter's darts,
Gray hawks escaped from nets and cages;
The mist in the center of the pond was greenish,
The sky was clear, the distant road was red.
With his supernatural power, he gained freedom,
So he hurled up his begging-bowl and leaped into space;
Thereupon, instantaneously,
He ascended to the heavenly palace of Brahmā.
In an instant, Maudgalyāyana arrived at the heavenly court,
All that he heard in his ears was the sound of music and drums;
Red towers [20] were faintly reflected on the golden halls,
A profusion of green lattices opened on white jade walls.
With his metal-ringed staff, he knocked at the gate three or four times,
Unaware of the tears which were crisscrossing his breast;
An elder came out from within to have a talk with him,
He brought his palms together [21] and began to speak of his sincere
     filiality.
"I wonder if you know me?" he inquired of the elder,
"I, a poor monk, am an inhabitant of Jambūdvīpa.
When I was still young, I was bereft of my father and mother;
Although our family was quite wealthy, it was lacking in sons and
     grandsons,
I was orphaned and, furthermore, had no future before me.
The dear mother of this poor monk was styled Nīladhi,
     My father's name was Śūlakṣaṇa;
All his life was spent in doing kind and charitable works,
After he died, it would have been fitting for him to be reborn in this
     heaven.
This is such a delightfully splendid and charming place,
Just gazing at it brings happiness to the hearts of men;
Bells and drums resound in harmony with elegant music,
The sound of harps being strummed is also loud and clear.

How sad it is that they never relaxed from their parental chores!
The affection she showed in nursing me is not easily forgotten;
I wonder whether they have been peaceful and well since leaving me,
And that is why I am now searching for them in this place."

When the elder heard these words, he seemed to be sympathetic,
But his mind was in a whirl and he spoke haltingly:

20. Means "splendid mansions" (compare with selection 213).
21. In salutation.

"I, your disciple, had a son in Jambūdvīpa,
But I wasn't aware that he had left home to become a monk.
Do not blame me, Your Reverence, if I question you closely,
There are so many different types of people in the world;
As I observed you speaking for the first time, I took you for a stranger,
But now that I reflect upon it, I am somewhat nonplussed.
Among laymen, there are many people who have the same name and
        surname,
And there are hundreds of types of faces which are similar;
Your appearance and disposition are familiar,
But then when I think about it, I cannot place you.
If, oh Teacher, you insist on seeking to be recognized,
Please tell me some more about your family matters."

Maudgalyāyana went to the palaces of heaven in search of his father. He arrived at a gate where he met an elder. "When I was young," he informed the elder, "my name was Turnip. After my parents died, I surrendered myself to the Buddha and left home to become a monk. My whiskers and hair were shaved off and I was given the title 'Mahāmaudgalyāyana, Preeminent in Supernatural Power.' "

When the elder heard him say his childhood name, he knew right away that it was his son. "We have long been separated. Have you been well?"

After Turnip-Maudgalyāyana had been acknowledged by his dear father and had inquired about how he was getting along, he asked: "In what place is my dear mother enjoying happiness?"

The elder replied to Turnip: "Your mother's activities while she was alive were different from mine. I practiced the ten virtues and the five commandments, so that, after I died, my soul was reborn in heaven. Throughout her life, your mother committed a large number of sins and, at the end of her days, she fell into hell. If you search for your mother along the infernal paths of Jambūdvīpa, you'll soon find out where she has gone."

After hearing these words, Maudgalyāyana took leave of the elder. He vanished and descended to Jambūdvīpa. There he searched for his mother along the infernal paths but could not find her. However, he did see eight or nine men and women wandering about aimlessly with nothing to do.

This is the place where he goes forward and asks the reasons for this situation:

> "Please do not pay me any reverence.
> Who are you, my good friends,
> That have all gathered here in this place —
> Wandering about aimlessly with not a thing to do,
> Roaming around outside the walls of the city?

I, who am a humble monk, only arrived here today,
To my mind, it is really quite extraordinary."
The men and women answered the reverend one with these words:
"It's only because we had the same name and same surname as
    someone else,
Our names were mixed up with theirs and so we were escorted here;
The interrogation lasted just four or five days,
We were judged 'not guilty' and released to return to our homes.
Long since sent to the grave by our wives and sons,
Our solitary bodies were flung into the wilderness;
On all four sides, there were neither relatives nor companions,
Foxes, wolves, crows, and magpies competed to divide us up.
Our houses fell into disrepair leaving us with no place to take refuge,
We appealed to the King of the Underworld with plaintive voices;
His judgment was that we be released as wandering ghosts with
    nothing to do,
Having received this supplemental verdict, what more is there to say?
Today, we have already been cut off from the road of births and
    deaths,
Once the gates of Hades slam shut, they never open again.
Though there be a thousand kinds of food placed on our grave-
    mounds,
How can they alleviate the hunger in our stomachs?
All our wailing and weeping, in the end, will be to no avail,
In vain do they trouble themselves to make folded paper money.[22]
Take a message to the sons and daughters in our homes telling them:
'We entreat you to save us from infernal suffering by performing good
    deeds.' "

Maudgalyāyana waited a long while before speaking. "I wonder whether you know of a Lady Nīladhi?"

"None of us know her," the men and women replied.

"Where does the Great King Yama dwell?" Maudgalyāyana continued with his questioning.

"Reverend sir!" the men and women replied. "If you walk several steps farther toward the north, you'll see in the distance a tower with triple gates where there are thousands and ten thousands of stalwart soldiers, all holding swords and cudgels. That is the gate of the Great King Yama."

Upon hearing these words, Maudgalyāyana walked several steps farther toward the north. From there he could see the tower with its triple gates into which stalwart soldiers were driving countless sinners. Maudgalyāyana went forward and made inquiries but could not find his mother, so he sat by the

22. Chinese still present such offerings to the dead.

side of the road and cried loudly. When he had finished crying, he went forward again and was taken in to see the King by functionaries.

This is the place where Maudgalyāyana is led in by the gatekeepers to see the Great King who asks him his business:

> When the Great King saw Maudgalyāyana enter,
> He quickly joined his palms in salutation and was about to stand up:
> "What is your reason for coming here, reverend sir?"
> Hurriedly, he bowed respectfully from behind his table.
> "Your coming here embarrasses me, oh Exemplar!
> I, your disciple, am situated here in this infernal region,
>> Where I flog sinners to determine whether they shall remain dead
>> or be reborn;
>> Although I do not recognize you, reverend sir,
>> It was long ago that I had heard of your name.
> It must be either that the Buddha has sent you here on a mission,
>> Or that there is some private family business;
> The Lord of Mount T'ai's [23] verdicts are, in the end, difficult to alter,
> For all were sanctioned by heaven's bureaucrats and earth's pen-
>> pushers.
> A sinner's karmic retribution is in accord with conditional causation,
> Who is there that could rescue them on the spur of the moment?
> Fetid blood and congealed fats stink through the Long Night,[24]
> Leaving an offensive stain on your clothing, which is so pure.
> These infernal paths are no place for you to spend much time,
> It is my humble wish that you, oh Exemplar, make an early
>> departure."
> Maudgalyāyana replied to him as best as he could:
>> "Perhaps you may be aware, oh Great King,
> That I, poor monk, had a father and mother who, when alive,
> Day and night observed the laws of abstinence, never eating after
>> noon?
> Based on their behavior while in the World of Mankind,
> After their deaths, they should have been reborn in the Pure Land.
> My father alone is dwelling in the mansions of heaven,
> But I cannot locate my dear mother in any of the heavens;
> In my estimation, she should not even have passed through hell,
> My only fear is that she may have been unjustly punished by High
>> Heaven.
> I have followed her traces to the edges of heaven and earth,

---

23. T'ai-shan Lao-chün, the Taoist counterpart of Yama.
24. Of transmigration (*saṃsāra*).

Filled with sorrowful vexation, I heave a long sigh;
If she has come to this realm because of her karmic retribution,
Perhaps you, oh Great King, would have been made aware of it."

When Maudgalyāyana had finished speaking, the Great King then summoned him to the upper part of the hall. There he was given audience with Kṣitigarbha Bodhisattva, [25] to whom he quickly paid obeisance.

"Have you come here in search of your mother?"

"Yes," replied Maudgalyāyana, "I am searching for my mother."

"In the days when your mother was still alive, she committed a large number of sins. So limitless and boundless were they that she must have fallen into hell. Would you please come forward? My duty-officer will be here in just a moment."

The King then summoned his karma-watcher, fate-investigator, and book-keeper, who came immediately.

"The name of this reverend monk's mother is Lady Nīladhi. How long has it been since she died?"

The karma-watcher replied to the Great King: "Three years have already passed since Lady Nīladhi died. The legal records of the criminal proceedings against her are all in the casebook of the Commandant of Mount T'ai, who is Recorder for the Bureau of the Underworld."

The King summoned the two Good and Evil Boys and told them to examine the books at Mount T'ai to find out which hell Lady Nīladhi was in.

"Reverend sir," the Great King said, "Follow along with the Boys. If you ask the General of the Five Ways, you should be able to find out where she has gone."

After Maudgalyāyana had heard these words, he took leave of the Great King and went out. He walked several steps and soon came to the banks of the Whathellwedo River.[26] There he saw numberless sinners taking off their clothes and hanging them on trees. There were many sounds of loud crying by those who wished to cross but could not. Distraught and apprehensive, they clustered in groups of threes and fours. They held their heads as they wept and wailed.

This is the place where Maudgalyāyana asks them the reason for this:

The waters of the Whathellwedo River flow swiftly to the west,
Broken stones and precipitous crags obstruct the road they walk on;
They take off their clothes and hang them on the sides of tree
     branches,

25. Overlord of Yama, he is guardian of the earth.
26. The Styx of the Chinese Buddhist underworld.

Pursued, they are not allowed to stand still for even a moment.
At the edge of the river, when they hear their names being called out,
They are unaware of the tears which are drenching their breasts;
Today, at last, they know that their bodies have really died,
They stand next to trees in pairs and weep sorrowfully for a long time.
"When I was alive, I was in thrall to my prized possessions,
I went out in a golden four-in-hand carriage with crimson wheels;
Saying that it would never change in ten thousand ages,
Who would have thought that it long ago was transformed into dust?
Oh! Alas and alack! What pain there is inside my heart!
In vain have my white bones been buried in a tall tumulus.
My sons and grandsons ride the dragon-horses in the southern stables,
My wives and concubines use the scented carriage outside the
     northern window."
Their many mouths all said the same thing—"It is inexpressible!"
Long did they sigh but all their complaining went for nought;
Every person who commits sins will fall into hell,
He who does good will certainly be reborn in heaven.
Now each must follow his own circumstantial karma,
It is certain that it will be difficult to meet again later on;
They grasp each other's hands and repeatedly enjoin, "You must cheer
     up!"
Looking back, they wipe away their tears as they look longingly at one
     another.
In their ears, all they hear are cries of "Hurry along!"
As they are driven forward by the thousands and ten thousands;
On the river's southern bank, ox-head guards hold their truncheons,
At the water's northern edge, hell's jailers raise their pitchforks.
The eyes of the people in the water are filled with distress,
The tears of those who are on the banks flow copiously;
If only they had known earlier that they were to sink in a place of
     hardship,
Now all they can do is regret that they had not done good works while
     they were still alive.

Maudgalyāyana asked a man who was beneath a tree at the side of the
Whathellwedo River:

"Heaven's Mansions and Hell's Halls are not insubstantial;
It goes without saying that Heaven punishes those who do evil,
The minions of the underworld also promptly join in prosecution.
This poor monk's dear mother did not accumulate goodness,
So that her lost soul fell into the three mires leading to hell;
I have heard tell that she has been taken inside hell,

All I want to ask is whether or not you have any news of her?"
As all the sinners looked at Maudgalyāyana the teacher,
Together they wept mournfully and knitted their brows:
"It is only recently in time that we, your disciples, died,
Truly, we do not know of your dear mother, reverend sir.
While we were alive, we committed numerous sins,
Now, today, that we endure such suffering, we at last begin to feel
 regret;
Even though one has wives and concubines enough to fill the
 mountains and rivers,
Who among them would be willing to die in his place?
Whenever you are able to depart from the underworld gates,
Inform those sons and grandsons of ours who are still at home
That it is unnecessary to make coffins and caskets of white jade,
And that gold is spent in vain when it is buried in the grave.
Endless sorrow and sighs of resentment are ultimately to no avail,
For we hear not the sacred drum music and songs to string
 accompaniment;
If they wish to obliterate the suffering of the dead,
Nothing is better than cultivating blessedness to save these souls from
 darkness."

"When you go back, reverend sir, pass this news to all men. Instruct them
to create blessings whereby they may save the dead. Except for the Buddha
and him alone, there is no other way to be saved. We wish, reverend sir, that
you achieve perfect wisdom and nirvāṇa, which, even on ordinary occasions,
is not concealed, and that it will serve as a conveyance for all living beings.
May your blade of knowledge be assiduously sharpened and not be obstructed
by the forest of moral affliction. Thus will your awe-inspiring mind be active
everywhere throughout the world and so realize the great vow of all the
Buddhas. If we are to escape from this joyless place, it will be due to the
universal bestowal of your compassionate regard, reverend sir."

After Maudgalyāyana heard this, he went forward once again and, within
a short period of time, he arrived at the seat of the General of the Five Ways.

This is the place where he asks for news of his mother:

The General of the Five Ways had a frightful disposition,
The bright gleam of his golden armor intersected with the light from his
 sword;
  To his left and his right, there were more than a million men,
  And assistants who were continuously flying back and forth.
 His yelling and shouting were like the terrifying rumble of thunder,
 His angry eyes resembled the dazzling flash of lightning.

There were some whose bellies were being rent and whose chests
    were being opened,
And others whose faces were being skinned alive;
Although Maudgalyāyana was a holy person,
Even he was completely frightened out of his wits.
Maudgalyāyana wept mournfully as he thought of his dear mother,
He exercised his supernatural powers with the speed of the windborne
    clouds;
If you ask which is the most crucial place on the infernal paths,
None exceeds that of the great General of the Five Ways.
To the left and the right, a concentration of spears blocks the way,
To the east and west, there are more than ten thousand men with
    staves erect;
All together, they raise their eyes and gaze toward the southwest,
What they see is the imposing Spirit of the Five Ways.
He has been guarding this road for numerous eons,
He fixes the type of punishment for thousands and ten thousands;
Starting with the very first one, each of them follows his own karmic
    conditions.
"The dear mother of this poor monk deviated from the practice of
    almsgiving
So that her souls were sent drifting along these infernal roads;
Whenever I ask which of the three mires leading to hell is the most
    painful place,
Everyone says that it is the devils' barrier of the Five Ways.
Men mill everywhere about the evil way to rebirth as an animal,
But the good way to the heavenly mansions is vacant morning and
    night;
All of those who are sinners must pass along this way,
It is my humble wish that you, General, will make a check of them."
The General brought his palms together in salutation and said to the
    exemplar,
"You must not weep so mournfully that you do harm to your appear-
    ance.
The crowds on this road are usually as numberless as the sands of the
    Ganges,
But you have, on the spur of the moment, asked me if I know who
    Nīladhi is.
In Mount T'ai's regency, there are many sections dealing with names,
Investigations include heaven's bureaus and earth's offices;
Each of the overseers of documents also has these names,
And all warrants which come down pass through this place.
Today, it just so happens that I, your disciple, am the officer of names,

I shall spend a few moments trying to check up on this for you, oh
   Teacher;
If we are so fortunate as to come across her name,
It will not be very difficult to locate her whereabouts."

"Have you seen a Lady Nīladhi or not?" the General asked his attendants
to the left and right.

On the left side there was an officer-in-charge who informed the General:
"Three years ago, there was a Lady Nīladhi who was summoned away by a
warrant sent up from the Avīci Hell. She is at this very moment in the Avīci
Hell undergoing torture."

When Maudgalyāyana heard these words, he spoke to the General, who
replied to him: "Reverend sir, all sinners receive their sentences from the
King and only then do they descend farther into hell."

"Why didn't my mother see the King face to face?" Maudgalyāyana im-
portuned him.

"Reverend sir," replied the General, "there are two kinds of people in the
world who do not get to see the King's face. The first are those people who,
during their lifetimes, cultivate the ten virtues and the five commandments.
After they die, their souls are reborn in heaven. The second are those people
who, during their lifetimes, do not cultivate good karma but commit a large
number of sins. After their lives come to the end, they enter hell forthwith
and they, too, do not get to see the King's face. Only those people who are
half-good and half-bad are taken into the presence of the King to be sentenced. Then they are reincarnated, receiving their retribution in accordance
with conditioning causes."

This is the place where Maudgalyāyana, when he hears these words, goes
forthwith to the various hells in search of his mother:

Maudgalyāyana's tears fell, his thoughts wandered aimlessly,
The karmic retribution of sentient beings is like being tossed on the
   wind;
His dear mother had sunk into a realm of suffering,
Her souls had already by that time long since dissipated.
Iron discs continuously plunged into her body from out of the air,
Fierce fires, at all times, were burning beneath her feet;
Every place on her chest and belly had been stripped to shreds,
Every inch of her bones and flesh had charred to a pulp.
Bronze-colored crows pecked at her heart ten thousand times over,
Molten iron poured on the top of her head a thousand repetitions;
One might ask whether the tree of knives up ahead were the most
   painful,

But can it compare with the cleaving mill which chops men's waists in
    two?
                                     Beyond description
Is the congealed fat and ground flesh so like a broad ferry-crossing;
There are wild mountains all around for several hundred miles,
Which, from their jagged peaks, plummet downwards for a league.
Ten thousand iron lances are installed at the bottom,
A thousand layers of smoke and fire obscure the four gates;
Should one ask what sort of crimes are being punished herein,
It is just for those who have killed others in the world of men.

After Maudgalyāyana had finished speaking, he went forward again. Before
long, he came to another hell. "Is there a Lady Nīladhi in this hell?" he
asked the warden. "It is because she is my mother that I have come hunting
for her."

"Everyone in this hell is a man, reverend sir," replied the warden. "There
are no women at all. If you go on ahead and ask whether she is in the hell
with the hill made of knives, I am sure that, through your inquiry, you will
get to see her."

Maudgalyāyana went forward and again he came to another hell. The left
side of it was named Knife Hill and the right was named Sword Forest. Inside the hell, spear tips and swords were pointed from opposite sides and
blood flowed copiously. He saw the warden driving countless sinners into this
hell.

"What is the name of this hell?" Maudgalyāyana asked.

"This is the Knife Hill and Sword Forest Hell," answered an ogre.

"What sinful karma did the sinners who are in this hell produce that they
should have fallen into *this* hell?" Maudgalyāyana asked.

"While they were alive," the warden informed him, "the sinners who are
in this hell trespassed upon and damaged the perpetual property of the
assembly of monks. They befouled the monastery gardens, were given to
eating the fruit of the orchards held in perpetuity by the monasteries, and
stole firewood from the forests held in perpetuity by the monasteries."

Here is the place where they are now being made to climb up the trees of
swords with their hands, causing them to be stripped bare of every limb and
joint.

> The white bones on Knife Hill were strewn chaotically every which
>   way,
> The human heads in Sword Forest numbered in the thousands and
>   ten thousands;
> Those who wish to avoid clambering up the hill of knives,

> Should never pass by the monastery holdings without adding good
>   earth.
> Propagate fruit trees and present them to the monastery orchards,
> Contribute seeds to increase the crops from the fields held in
>   perpetuity.
> Oh, you sinners! it is absolutely indescribable,
> How you will endure punishment through eons as numerous as the
>   sands of the Ganges.
> Even when the Buddhas achieve nirvāṇa, you still will not get out.
> This hell stretches for hundreds of miles from the east to the west,
> The sinners race through it wildly, bumping against each other's
>   shoulders;
> The winds of karma blow upon the fire which advances as it burns,
> The jailers holding pitchforks jab at them from behind.
> Their bodies and heads are all like so many broken tiles,
> Their hands and feet immediately become like powder and froth;
> Boiling iron, light leaping from its surface, is poured into their
>   mouths,
> Whomever it touches is pierced to the left and penetrated to the right.
> Bronze arrows fly beside them and shoot into their eyes,
> Wheels of swords come straight down, cutting them in mid-air;
> It is said that it will be a thousand years before they are reborn as men,
> With iron rakes they are scraped together and revivified.[27]

When Maudgalyāyana heard these words, he wept mournfully and sighed with grief. He went forward and asked the warden: "Is there a Lady Nīladhi inside this hell?"

"What relationship has she to you, reverend sir?" the warden answered in reply.

"She is the dear mother of this poor monk," Maudgalyāyana informed him.

"Reverend sir, there is no Lady Nīladhi inside this hell," the warden told him. "Inside those hells which are on ahead, there are some which are all for women. You ought to be able to find her there."

After Maudgalyāyana had heard these words, he went forward again. He came to a hell which was about a league in depth. Great clouds of black smoke issued from it and malodorous vapors reeked to the heavens. He saw a horse-head ogre standing there arrogantly and holding a pitchfork in his hands.

"What is the name of this hell?" Maudgalyāyana asked him.

To which the ogre answered, "This is the Copper Pillar and Iron Bed Hell."

---

27. This does not constitute genuine rebirth. It is only part of the torture process.

"Of the sinners who are in this hell," asked Maudgalyāyana, "what sinful karma did they create while they were alive that they should have fallen into this hell?"

To which the warden answered, "While they were alive, be it the woman who led on the man or the man who led on the woman, they indulged their sexual passions on their parents' beds. Those who were disciples did so on their masters' beds, and slaves did so on their owners' beds. Thus they were bound to fall into this hell."

The breadth from east to west was immeasurable and, in it, men and women complemented each other half-and-half.

> Women lay on the iron beds with nails driven through their bodies,
> Men embraced the hot copper pillars, causing their chests to rot away;
> The iron drills and long scissors were sharp as lance-tips and sword-
>   edges,
> The teeth of the plows with their sharp metal points were like awls.
> When their intestines are empty, they are at once filled with hot iron
>   pellets,
> If they cry out that they are thirsty, molten iron is used to irrigate
>   them;
> The metal thorns which enter their bellies rend them like knives,
> Swords and halberds shoot by wildly like stars in mid-air.
> Knives scrape the flesh from their bones, pound by pound it breaks,
> Swords cut the liver and intestines, inch by inch they are severed;
>   Indescribable,
> How opposite to each other are heaven and hell!
> In heaven's mansions, morning and night there is resounding music,
> But there is not one who can beg his way out of hell.
> Although parents in this present existence may have blessings created
>   for them,
> They receive only one-seventh out of the total;[28]
> Even though the eastern sea be transformed into mulberry orchards,[29]
> Those who are suffering punishment will still not be released.

After Maudgalyāyana had finished speaking, he again went forward. Before long, he came to another hell. "Is there a Lady Nīladhi inside this hell or not?" he asked the warden.

To which the warden asked in reply, "Is Lady Nīladhi your mother, reverend sir?"

"Yes, she is my dear mother," Maudgalyāyana answered him.

28. This reflects the folk-Buddhist concept that one who "pursues the departed with rites for their happiness" will receive a full complement of blessings while those for whom the ceremony is held will receive one seventh of the total.

29. I.e., "a long, long time."

"Three years ago," the warden informed the venerable monk, "there was a Lady Nīladhi who arrived in this hell. But she was summoned away by a warrant sent up from the Avīci Hell. She is at this very moment inside the Avīci Hell."

Stifled with sorrow, Maudgalyāyana collapsed. It was quite a long while before he revived.

This is the place where he slowly goes forward and soon happens upon an ogre who is guarding the road:

> Maudgalyāyana was greatly distressed as he walked along,
> The knives and swords by the side of the road were like wild grass;
> He inclined his ear to listen for noises of the hells in the distance,
> Abruptly, there was the howling sound of a strong wind.
> For thinking of his dear mother, his heart was on the verge of breaking,
> Walking without stopping along the road in front of him, he soon arrived;
> Suddenly, he happened upon a prince of demons,
> Hand resting on his sword, he sat there blocking the main way.

Maudgalyāyana addressed him, saying: "I am a poor monk,

> A disciple of the Tathāgata, Śākyamuni Buddha,
> I have witnessed the three insights[30] and have escaped from the cycle of
>   birth and death.
> How pathetic is my dear mother whose name was Nīladhi;
> After she passed away, her souls descended into this place.
> I have just now come from inspecting in order all the other hells,
> Everyone whom I asked all said, 'No, this is the wrong place' —
> But lately they've been saying that she was taken into Avīci,
> Surely Great General, you are aware of this matter.
> Do not hesitate to tell me truthfully whether she is here or not,
> For the most profound human kindness is that of suckling one's child;
> When I hear talk of my mother, it pains me to the marrow of my bones,
> Yet there is no one who can readily understand this poor monk's heart."
> Upon hearing these words, the demon's heart started to waver,
> He spoke directly and, moreover, without mincing his words:
> "Your filial devotion, reverend sir, is rare in all ages,
> You have not shirked making a personal search along these infernal
>   paths.
> It seems as though there may be a Lady Nīladhi,

30. Three types of knowledge of an arhat (saint): 1. memory of past lives, 2. supernatural insight into the future, and 3. knowledge of present mortal sufferings.

But I can't quite put my finger on what sort of appearance she has;
Poured steel has been used to make the outer walls, copper for the inner—
With a thunderous roar, the winds of karma abruptly begin to blow,
Turning the carcasses of those who enter to smithereens.
I advise you, oh Teacher, to return early to your own home,
In vain do you trouble yourself by seeking her in this place;
It would be better to leave early to see the Tathāgata—
What good is it for you to beat your chest in vexation?"

When Maudgalyāyana heard of the difficulties of this hell, he immediately turned around. Hurling up his begging-bowl, he leaped into space. Before very long, he had arrived at the Teak Tree Grove. Three times he circled around the Buddha, then withdrew and sat off to one side. He looked reverently upon the countenance of the Honored One, not averting his eyes for even a moment.

This is the place where he speaks to the World-Honored:

"For many days have I been negligent in my services to you, oh
    Tathāgata,
Because I was following my parents' traces to the ends of heaven and
    earth;
Only my father obtained rebirth in heaven above,
So I was unsuccessful in reuniting myself with my dear mother.
I have heard it said that she is suffering punishment in Avīci,
When I think of it, before I know what has happened, I become
    deeply aggrieved;
Due to the fierce fires, dragons, and snakes, it was difficult to go
    forward,
Nor was I able to come up with a suitable plan on the spur of the
    moment.
Your supernatural strength, oh Tathāgata, can move mountains and
    seas,
For which you are much admired by all living beings,
'Always has it been that a subject in distress unburdens himself to his
    lord'—
How will I be able to see my dear mother again?"
The World-Honored called out to him, saying, "Mahāmaudgalyāyana!
Do not be so mournful that you cry yourself heartbroken;
The sins of the world are tied to those who commit them like a string,
They are not stuck on clay-fashion by anyone else.
Quickly I take my metal-ringed staff and give it to you,

It can repel the eight difficulties[31] and the three disasters,[32]
If only you remember diligently to recite my name,
The hells will certainly open up their doors for you."

Having received the Buddha's awesome power, Maudgalyāyana flexed his body and went downward as swiftly as a winged arrow. In an instant, he had arrived at the Avīci Hell. In mid-air, he met fifty ox-headed and horse-faced guards. They were ogres and demons with teeth like knife-trees, mouths similar to blood-basins,[33] voices like the peal of thunder, and eyes like the flash of lightning. They were headed for duty in the Bureau of the Underworld. When they met Maudgalyāyana, they informed him from a distance: "Don't come any farther, reverend sir! This is not a good way; it is the road to hell. In the middle of the black smoke[34] on the western side are all the poisonous vapors of hell. Should you be sucked up by them, reverend sir, you will turn into ashes and dust."

This is the place:

"Haven't you heard tell, reverend sir, of the Avīci Hell?

Even iron and steel, should they pass through it, would be disastrously affected;
If you're wondering where this hell is situated,
It's over there on the west side in the midst of the black smoke."
Maudgalyāyana repeated the Buddha's name as often as there are sands in the Ganges,
And said to himself, "The hells are my original home—"
He wiped his tears in mid-air, and shook the metal-ringed staff,
Ghosts and spirits were mowed down on the spot like stalks of hemp.
Streams of cold sweat crisscrossed their bodies, dampening them like rain,
Dazed and unconscious, they groaned in self-pity;
They let go of the three-cornered clubs which were in their hands,
They threw far away the six-tined pitchforks which were on their shoulders.
"The Tathāgata has sent me to visit my mother,
And to rescue her from suffering in the Avīci Hell."

31. Situations in which it is difficult to see a Buddha or hear his dharma: in hell; as a hungry ghost; as an animal; in the comfortable northern continent of *uttarakuru*; in the long-life heavens; as someone deaf, blind, and dumb; as a worldly philosopher; in the interim between a Buddha and his successor.

32. Major: fire, water, and wind. Minor: war, pestilence, and famine.

33. There is a hell in which women who die in childbirth are tortured by having to bathe in an enormous pool of blood.

34. Similar black gasses are also mentioned by Dante in Canto V of the *Inferno*.

Not to be stayed, Maudgalyāyana passed by them with a leap,
The jailers just looked at each other, not daring to stand in his way.

Maudgalyāyana walked forward and came to a hell. When he was something over a hundred paces away from it, he was sucked in by the fiery gasses
and nearly tumbled over. It was the Avīci Hell with lofty walls of iron which
were so immense that they reached to the clouds. Swords and lances bristled
in ranks, knives and spears clustered in rows. Sword-trees reached upward for
a thousand fathoms with a clattering flourish as their needle-sharp points
brushed together. Knife-mountains soared ten thousand rods in a chaotic
jumble of interconnecting cliffs and crags. Fierce fires throbbed, seeming to
leap about the entire sky with a thunderous roar. Sword-wheels whirled,
seeming to brush the earth with the dust of starry brightness. Iron snakes
belched fire, their scales bristling on all sides. Copper dogs breathed smoke,
barking impetuously in every direction. Metal thorns descended chaotically
from mid-air, piercing the chests of the men. Awls and augers flew by every
which way, gouging the backs of the women. Iron rakes flailed at their eyes,
causing red blood to flow to the west. Copper pitchforks jabbed at their loins
until white fat oozed to the east. Thereupon, they were made to crawl up
the knife-mountains and enter the furnace coals. Their skulls were smashed
to bits, their bones and flesh decomposed; tendons and skin snapped, liver
and gall broke. Ground flesh spurted and splattered beyond the four gates;
congealed blood drenched and drooked the pathways which run through the
black clods of hell. With wailing voices, they called out to heaven—moan,
groan. The roar of thunder shakes the earth—rumble, bumble. Up above are
clouds and smoke which tumble-jumble; down below are iron spears which
jangle-tangle. Goblins with arrows for feathers chattered-scattered; birds with
copper beaks wildly-widely called. There were more than several ten
thousands of jailers and all were ox-headed and horse-faced.

This is the place where, though your heart be made of iron or stone, you too
will lose your wits and tremble with fear:

> Staff in hand, Maudgalyāyana went forward, listening,
> As he thought about Avīci, he became more and more preoccupied;
> Inside all of the other hells, there are periods of rest,
> But within this Avīci, they never see a pause.
> Crowds as numerous as the sands of the Ganges simultaneously enter,
> Together their bodies are transformed into a single shape;
> Supposing that, there being no one else, someone entered alone,
> His body itself would fill up the surrounding iron walls.
> Relentlessly, lamentlessly, iron weapons are flourished;
> Querulous, perilous, the cloud-filled sky is turbulent,
> Howling, growling, the wind which blasts the ground is terrifying.

There are long snakes which glisten and have three heads that are
    black,
There are large birds which glare and have pairs of wings that are dark-
    green;
In ten thousand red-hot ovens, heaped-up coals are fanned,
From a thousand tongues of crimson flames, shooting sparks explode.
On the east and the west, iron augers stab at the muscles of their
    chests,
To the left and the right, copper scissors puncture the pupils of their
    eyes;
Iron spears descend chaotically like the wind and the rain,
Molten iron from out of mid-air seems to be a baptismal sprinkling.
Lackaday! Welladay! How difficult it is to bear!
And to top it all off, long spikes are lowered into their bellies and
    backs.

When Maudgalyāyana saw this, he cried out "Horrors!"
Steadfastly he invoked the Buddha many thousands of times.
Though one breathe the poisonous vapors borne on the wind at a
    distance,
Right while you're watching, his body will become a pile of ashes.

With one shake of his staff, the bars and locks fell from the black
    walls,
On the second shake, the double leaves of the main gate flew open;
Before Maudgalyāyana there even had a chance to call out,
The jailers came right out, carrying pitchforks in their hands.
"About whom, reverend sir, do you wish to find information?"
The gates in the walls of this hell were ten thousand leagues wide,
What sort of person could open and close them so easily?
Inside, knives and swords cluttered with a brilliant light,
The people undergoing punishment were remorsefully sad;
Great fires flamed and flared making the entire ground luminous,
Misty fog spread everywhere, filling the sky with blackness.
"Suddenly we saw an exemplar standing here in hell,
And furthermore, one with whom we have never been acquainted;
From the looks of things, it would appear that there is no one else,
It must be due to the compassionate power of the Three Jewels."

"For what reason, reverend sir, did you open the gates of this hell?" the
warden asked him.

"If this poor monk didn't open them, who would?" he replied. "The
World-Honored entrusted me with an object for opening them."

"What object did he entrust to you for opening them?" asked the warden.

"He entrusted me with his twelve-ringed metal staff to open them," Maudgalyāyana informed the warden.

"For what purpose have you come here, reverend sir?" a jailer asked again.

"The name of this poor monk's mother is Lady Nīladhi," Maudgalyāyana informed him. "I have come in order to see if I might find her."

Upon hearing this, the warden went back inside hell and climbed up on a tall tower from which he signaled with a white flag and beat a steel drum.

"Is there a Lady Nīladhi inside the first compartment?" he called out. There was none in the first compartment, so he went on to the second compartment. The warden signaled with a black flag and beat a steel drum.

"Is there a Lady Nīladhi inside the second compartment?" Neither was there any in the second compartment, so he went on to the third compartment. He signaled with a yellow flag and beat a steel drum.

"Is there a Lady Nīladhi inside the third compartment?" Again there was none. So he went on to the fourth compartment and again there was none When he reached the fifth compartment and asked, the answer there was also "none." He went on to the sixth compartment, where again the answer was: "No Lady Nīladhi." The jailer walked to the seventh compartment, where he signaled with a green flag and beat a steel drum.

"Is there a Lady Nīladhi inside the seventh compartment?"

At that very moment, Lady Nīladhi was inside the seventh compartment. All up and down her body, there were forty-nine[35] long spikes nailing her to a steel bed. She dared not respond.

The warden repeated the question: "Is there a Lady Nīladhi in the seventh compartment or not?"

"If you're hunting for Lady Nīladhi, this sinful body is she."

"Why didn't you speak up earlier?"

"I was afraid, warden, that you'd take me away to another place to receive punishment so I didn't dare to respond."

"There is a Buddhist monk outside the gate," the warden informed her. "His hair and beard have been shaved off and he wears a monastic robe. He claims to be your son and that is why he has come to visit you."

After Lady Nīladhi heard these words, she thought for quite a while and then replied: "Warden, I don't have any son who left home to become a monk. Isn't there some mistake?"

Upon hearing this, the warden turned around and walked back to the tall tower. "Reverend sir!" he said. "Why do you pretend to recognize a sinner in hell as your mother? For what reason do you tell such a lie?"

When Maudgalyāyana heard these words, tears of sadness fell like rain. "Warden," he said, "when I explained things just now, my message was

---

35. This number was probably suggested by the length of the funeral service (forty-nine days).

garbled. When I, poor monk, was a child, my name was Turnip. After my father and mother died, I surrendered myself to the Buddha and left home to become a monk. The title given me upon receiving the tonsure was Mahāmaudgalyāyana. Do not be angry, warden. Go and ask her once again."

After hearing these words, the warden turned around and went to the seventh compartment. "Sinner!" he announced. "As a child, the name of the monk outside the gate was Turnip. After his parents died, he surrendered himself to the Buddha and left home to become a monk. The title given him upon receiving the tonsure was Mahāmaudgalyāyana."

"If the name of the monk outside the gate as a child was Turnip, then he is my son," said Lady Nīladhi when she heard his words. "He is the precious darling of this sinful body."

When the warden heard Lady Nīladhi say this, he helped her up by pulling out the forty-nine long spikes. With steel chains locked about her waist and surrounded by gyves, she was driven outside the gate.

This is the place where mother and son see each other:

> The interlocking links of the gyves were as numerous as gathering clouds;
> A thousand years of punishment is beyond comprehension,
> Trickles of blood flowed from the seven openings[36] of her head.
> Fierce flames issued from the inside of his mother's mouth,
> At every step, metal thorns out of space entered her body;
> She clanked and clattered like the sound of five hundred broken-down chariots,
> How could her waist and backbone bear up under the strain?
> Jailers carrying pitchforks guarded her to the left and the right,
> Ox-headed guards holding chains stood on the east and the west;
> Stumbling at every other step, she came forward,
> Wailing and weeping, Maudgalyāyana embraced his mother.
> Crying, he said: "It was because I am unfilial,
> You, dear mother, were innocently caused to drop into the triple mire of hell;
> Families which accumulate goodness have a surplus of blessings,
> High Heaven does not destroy in this manner those who are blameless.
> In the old days, mother, you were handsomer than P'an An,[37]
> But now you have suddenly become haggard and worn;
> I have heard that in hell there is much suffering,
> Now, today, I finally realize, 'Ain't it hard, ain't it hard.'[38]
> Ever since I met with the misfortune of father's and your deaths,

36. Eyes, ears, nose, and mouth.
37. P'an An-jen (P'an Yüeh). The story goes that the ladies of Loyang were so taken by his beauty that they tossed fruit at him when he went out on the street.
38. The title of a popular ballad during the Six Dynasties and T'ang periods.

I have not been remiss in sacrificing daily at your graves;
Mother, I wonder whether or not you have been getting any food to eat,
In such a short time, your appearance has become completely haggard."
Now that Maudgalyāyana's mother had heard his words,
"Alas!" she cried, her tears intertwining as she struck and grabbed
    at herself:
"Only yesterday, my son, I was separated from you by death,
Who could have known that today we would be reunited?
While your mother was alive, she did not cultivate blessings,
But she did commit plenty of all the ten evil crimes;
Because I didn't take your advice at that time, my son,
My reward is the vastness of this Avīci Hell.
In the old days, I used to live quite extravagantly,
Surrounded by fine silk draperies and embroidered screens;
How shall I be able to endure these hellish torments,
And then to become a hungry ghost for a thousand years?
A thousand times, they pluck the tongue from out of my mouth,
Hundreds of passes are made over my chest with a steel plow;
My bones, joints, tendons, and skin are everywhere broken,
They need not trouble with knives and swords since I fall to pieces
    by myself.
In the twinkling of an eye, I die a thousand deaths,
But, each time, they shout at me and I come back to life;
Those who enter this hell all suffer the same hardships,
It doesn't matter whether you are rich or poor, lord or servant.
Though you diligently sacrificed to me while you were at home,
It only got you a reputation in the village for being filial;
Granted that you did sprinkle libations of wine upon my grave,
But it would have been better for you to copy a single line of a sūtra."
Maudgalyāyana choked and sobbed, his tears fell like rain,
Right away, he turned around and petitioned the warden:
"Although I, poor monk, did leave home so that I could take orders,
How can I rescue my mother with my small strength?
One should cover up for the faults of those to whom he has
    mourning obligations,
This has been the teaching of sages and saints since ancient times;
My only wish, warden, is that you release my mother,
And I myself will bear the endless suffering for her."
But the warden was a man of unyielding temperament,
He glared silently and vacantly at Maudgalyāyana;
"Although I, your disciple, do serve as a warden,
All of the decisions come from the Impartial King.
If your mother has sinned, she will receive the punishment for it,

And if you, oh Teacher, have sinned, you will bear the punishment for it;
The records of sins on the gold tablets and jade tokens cannot be wiped
    or washed away,
In the end, there is no one who can readily alter them.
It is simply that, today, the time has already arrived for her to be
    punished,
I must lead her back to the hall of punishments and apply the knife
    and spear;
If, reverend sir, you wish to obtain your mother's release,
You cannot do better than return home and burn precious incense."
The words of Maudgalyāyana's mother sounded plaintive,
But jailers holding pitchforks prodded her from both sides;
Just as she was about to reach the front of the hell, she nearly fell over,
Quickly she called out long and sad, "Take good care of yourself!"

With one of her hands, Lady Nīladhi held fast to the gate of hell and turned back to gaze at him. "Take good care of yourself!" she said. "Oh precious darling of this sinful body!"

"In the old days, your mother behaved avariciously.
I failed to provide myself with grace for the karmic retribution of the next
    life;
The things which I said deceived heaven and denied hell,
I slaughtered pigs and goats on a grand scale to sacrifice to ghosts
    and spirits.
My only concern was for the pleasures of the moment,
How could I have known that on these infernal paths they flog lost souls?
Now that I have already suffered the hardships of hell,
I finally learned to awaken to repentance of my own person.
But even though I do repent, what good does it do me?
'There's no use crying over spilt milk,' so says the well-known proverb;
When shall I be able to escape from this horrible suffering?
And how can I dare to hope that I'll ever again be a human being?
You, oh Teacher, are a disciple of the Buddha,
And are capable of understanding the kindness of your parents;
If, one day, you should attain the enlightenment of a sage,
Do not forget your mother who suffers so grievously here in hell."
After Maudgalyāyana had watched his mother depart,
He wished with all his heart that he could destroy himself;
Then, like Mount T'ai collapsing, he fell to the ground and
    pummeled himself,
Blood spattered from all the seven openings of his head.
"Mother, do not go back in for a while yet!" he said to her,

"Turn back and listen again to a word from your son;
The affection between a mother and her son is innate,
The kindness of her suckling him is a natural impulse.
Today, mother, you and I shall take leave of each other,
No one can tell for certain when we shall meet again;
How can I bear to listen to this horrible suffering?—
Sharp is the pain in my heart from the anxiety which weighs upon me.
Hell does not allow one to substitute for another,
All I can do is weep and wail and state my grievance loudly;
Since there is nothing at all I can do to save you,

"I too, will follow you, mother, and myself die before the gate of hell."

Maudgalyāyana watched his mother go back into hell. Grief-stricken and brokenhearted, he sobbed until his voice became hoarse. Then, as though he were five Mount T'ais collapsing, he fell to the ground and pummeled himself. Blood flowed with a gush from all of the seven openings of his head. After quite a long time, he died, and then he revived again. He got up by pressing against the ground with both hands.

This is the place where, having rearranged his clothing, he leaps into space and goes to the World-Honored.

Maudgalyāyana's consciousness was all hazy,
It seemed he could not hear people's voices, they were so indistinct;
After quite a long time, he moaned deeply and came to his senses,
Hurling up his begging-bowl, he leaped into space and called upon
    the World-Honored.
Facing the Buddha, Maudgalyāyana stated his bitter grievances,
He spoke both of the knife-mountains and of the sword-trees;
"I received supernatural strength from you, oh Buddha, and borrowed
    your surplus majesty,
Thus was I enabled to visit my dear mother in Avīci.
Smoke and flames flared up from the fires atop the iron walls,
The forests of sword blades were in ranks many ten thousands deep;
Human fat and ground flesh mixed together with molten copper,
The spattering flesh collected in pools of coagulated blood.
How can my dear mother's features endure such harsh treatment?
The whole night long she confronts the assault of knives and swords;
Her white bones climb the sword-trees ten thousand times over,
Her red face ascends the knife-mountains, making hundreds of passes.
In all the world, what is the most important thing?
It is the affection of one's parents and their kindness most profound;
You, oh Tathāgata, are the compassionate father and mother of all
    living beings,

I beseech you to illuminate this ignorant and trifling heart of mine!"
The Tathāgata was by nature of great mercy and compassion,
When he heard these words, he knitted his brows with sorrow:
"All living beings emerge and disappear in the net of transmigration,
Just like chaff-gnats which have rushed against a spider's web.
In times past, many were the sins your mother committed,
As a result, her souls fell headlong into Avīci;
For these crimes of hers, an eon will elapse before she can get out,
An ordinary person, one who is not a Buddha, cannot understand
    this."
The Buddha then summoned Ānanda and the company of his
    followers:
"I will go to the infernal regions and save her myself!"

    The Tathāgata led the eight classes of supernatural beings who surrounded him, front and back.

This is the place where, radiating light and shaking the earth, they rescue the sufferers in hell:

The Tathāgata in his holy wisdom was, by nature, impartial,
Out of mercy and compassion, he rescued all the beings of hell;
A numberless host composed of spirits of the eight classes,
Following each other, they went forward as a group.
               Such pomp and circumstance!—
In heaven above and on earth below, it was an incomparable sight;
    Sinking on the left, disappearing on the right,
They were like mountains projecting high above the clouds.
            Precipitous—   precarious—
Heaven's mansions and hell's halls opened their doors at once;
    Like driving rain—   like rumbling thunder—
They made as full a circle as the moon rising over the ocean.
Commandingly, he walked by himself with a lion's pace,
Confidently, he moved alone with an elephant king's gait;
Amidst the clouds, there were strains of the "Willow Branch" tune,
In space, there fluttered "Plum Blossoms Falling."
Sovereign Śakra went forward carrying a jade token;
Brahmā followed behind holding a jade tablet;
It was a sight indescribably indescribable!—
The Tathāgata, with supernatural strength, rescued them from the
    gates of Hades.
To his left and right, there were deities and the host of the eight spirit
    realms.

To his east and west, there were attendant guards and the generals of
  the four directions;
Between his brows appeared a tiny hair that had a thousand different
  forms,
Behind his neck was a halo of five-colored clouds.
Saturated by the light, hell dissolved completely,
The sword-trees and knife-forests crumbled as though they were dust;
Saturated by the light, all of the jailers fell to their knees,
They joined their palms in heartfelt respect and prostrated themselves
  at his feet.
This day, the Buddha's mercy and compassion were aroused,
He destroyed hell, leaving it completely in ruins;
The steel pellets were transformed into luminous jewels,
The knife-hills were transformed into sheets of lapis lazuli.
Molten copper was changed into the water of merit and virtue;
Meandering round pools and in currents, it was refreshing and clear,
Mandarin ducks and other waterfowl nestled together like beads on a
  necklace.
Every night, emerald mists lifted from the red waves,
Every morning, purple clouds rose above the green trees;
All of the sinners obtained rebirth in heaven above,
There was only Maudgalyāyana's mother who became a hungry ghost.
Everything within hell was utterly transformed,
And it was all because of the might of the holy Śākyamuni Buddha.

Having been granted the awesome power of the Buddha, Maudgalyāyana
was enabled to visit his mother. But the roots of her sin were deep and fast;
the karmic forces difficult to eliminate. Thus, although she was freed of the
torments of hell, she fell upon the path of hungry ghosts. Here the sorrow
and suffering were dissimilar, for misery and joy were completely polarized.
When placed next to her previous existence, the difference was intensified
hundreds, thousands, even ten thousands of times. Her throat was like the
eye of a needle, through which a drop of water could not pass. Her head
seemed to be Mount T'ai, which the three rivers could hardly fill. She never
even heard the words "broth" or "water." Months would accumulate and
years would pass while she endured the miseries of hunger and emaciation.
She might see in the distance some clear, cool water but, when she came
near, it would turn into a river of pus. Even though she obtained delicious
food and tasty meals, they would immediately be transformed into fierce
flames.

  "Mother, now you are so distressed by hunger that your life is as though it
were hanging by a thread. If your plight does not arouse in me compassion
and mercy, how can I be called a filial son? Once we are separated by the

road between life and death, it will be hard to expect that we shall meet again. If I wish to rescue you from this precarious danger, the urgency of the situation demands that I not delay. The way of those who have left home to become monks is to rely upon the donations of the faithful to maintain themselves. Even though you had a constant source of food and drink, I am afraid that it would be difficult for you to digest.

"I shall take leave of you now, mother, and go toward the center of Rājagṛha. There I will get some rice and then come to see you again."

Maudgalyāyana took leave of his mother. He hurled up his begging-bowl and leaped into the air. Within an instant, he had already arrived in the center of Rājagṛha. As he went from house to house begging for rice, he walked up to the gate of a householder.

This is the place where the householder detains and questions Maudgalyā-yana when he sees that he is begging for food at the wrong time:

"The morning meal is already over, reverend sir. Since the time for eating has already past, for what purpose do you intend to use this food which you are begging?"

Maudgalyāyana replied to the householder:

> "After this humble monk's mother had passed away,
> Her souls[39] fell straightaway into the Avīci Hell;
> Recently, I obtained her release with the help of the Tathāgata,
> Her body was like a bunch of dried bones, her breath was wispy.
> This poor monk's heart was rent in many tiny pieces,
> How can anyone else understand the pain which afflicts me?—
> Even though I realize that it is inappropriate, I am begging out of
>   time.
> Because it is to give to my dear mother to feed her."
> When the householder heard these words, he was greatly startled,
> Reflecting on the impermanence of things, he began to feel unhappy.
> "Her golden countenance is forever deprived of being made up with
>   rouge and mascara,"
> Her jade-like appearance has no cause for entering the dressing-room.
>   We sing for a while—   we are happy for a while—
> Human life is frittered away like a sputtering candle.
> We seek not the mansions of heaven where we could enjoy happiness,
> Even though all we hear of is how numerous are the sinners in hell;
>   Sometimes to eat—   sometimes to clothe ourselves—
> We should not imitate those stupid people who accumulate much.
> It would be better to create many good works for the future,

39. Celestial (yang) and terrestrial (yin).

For who can guarantee that his life will be preserved from morning to
   evening?
While two people are looking at each other, death steals upon them,
After which their riches are certainly no more to be grudged by their
   bodies.
When, one fine morning, we breathe our last and enter our eternal
   coffins,
Who knows what good are the libations sprinkled vainly upon our
   graves?
The wise man uses his money to create many blessings,
The fool spends his gold by purchasing fields and houses.
Throughout our lives, we search laboriously for riches,
But, after we die, it is all divided up by someone else."
When the householder heard these words, he was suddenly surprised,
It is not often that one has the opportunity to make offerings to a
   monk;
Hurriedly, he urged his assistants not to delay,
They brought rice from inside the house to give to the exemplar.
"From the sudden and complete dissolution of hell,
The ineffableness of the Buddhas is clearly perceived."
The householder held in his hand the rice which he had obtained,
And gave it over to the exemplar while making a grand vow:
"May this serve not only for you to present to your dear parent,
   reverend sir,
But may it serve, as well, to fill all the sinners in the whole of hell!"
Maudgalyāyana was successful in begging for table-rice;
He picked up his begging-bowl and took it to present to his dear
   mother.
Thereupon, he walked as far as the deserted outskirts of the city;
Holding a golden spoon in his hand, he fed her himself.

Although she had undergone the hardships of hell, Lady Nīladhi's avarice
had, after all, not been eradicated. When she saw her son bringing the bowl
of rice, the mere expectation of his approach excited her greed.

"The monk who is coming is my own son! He has fetched rice for me
from the world of men. The whole lot of you others shouldn't get any ideas!
I've got to appease my own hunger right now. There won't be enough extra
to help anybody else!"

Maudgalyāyana offered up the rice which was in the begging-bowl. His
mother, afraid that it might be snatched away, raised her eyes and looked
about continuously on all four sides. She shielded the bowl with her left
hand and scooped up the food with her right. But, before it entered her
mouth, the food was transformed into a fierce fire. Although the house-

holder's vow was a solemn one, unfortunately the obstructiveness of her greed was even greater.

Seeing his mother like this, Maudgalyāyana felt as though his heart were being sliced with a knife. "The strength of my doctrinal understanding is still inferior. I am a wretched person of little wisdom. The only thing I can do is address my questions to the World-Honored. Then I shall surely learn the way to extricate her."

Look, now, at the place where he gives his mother the rice:

> When the Lady saw the rice, she went forward to receive it,
> Because of her avarice, she senselessly bickered before she began to eat:
> "My son brought this rice from far away in the world of men,
> I intend to take it to cure my own bottomless pit;
> If I eat it all by myself, it still looks like it won't be enough to satisfy me,
> All you others should give up your ideas of getting any—go slow with your hopes!"
> The karmic force of Nīladhi's avarice was strong,
> As the food entered from her mouth into her throat, fierce flames erupted.

When Maudgalyāyana

> Saw the rice his mother was eating become a fierce fire,
> He pummeled himself all over and fell to the ground like a mountain collapsing;
> Blood began to flow from both his ears and his nostrils,
> Tearfully, he cried out to high heaven: "Oh, my mother!"
> This rice was given as charity in the world of mortal men,
> Above the rice, there was a spirit-light seven feet high;
> They took it to be a savory, flavorsome sustenance,
> But before the food entered her mouth, it had already turned into fire.
> Her appetite was avaricious and her heart had not changed,
> With the result that, year after year, she underwent punishment;
> Now he was painfully afflicted that he had no further means to save her,
> But karmic retribution did not allow that one substitute for another.
> The people of the world should not entertain jealous envy,
> For, once they fall into the three mires of hell, the punishment is endless;
> Before the savory rice had even entered her throat,
> Fiery flames began to issue from his mother's mouth.
> Though the sins of the mundane world fill the universe,

It is this very sin of avarice which is most frequent;
Unexpectedly, the flames issued from her mouth,
Which shows clearly that karmic retribution does not devolve upon
    others.
One should always exercise impartiality toward everything,
And should, furthermore, single-mindedly recite the name of
    Amitābha;
If only one can rid himself of his greedy heart,
The heavenly mansions of the Pure Land will be gained at his
    pleasure.
"My obedient son," Nīladhi called out to him,
"I cannot discard this sinful body by myself;
If I am not favored by *your* exercise of filiality, oh Teacher,
Who would be willing to exert themselves to save your mother?
I saw the rice but, before I could scoop it into my mouth,
It unexpectedly burst into flames and burned me;
Thinking over in my mind this display of avarice,
It simply must be due to the leftover ill effects of my past.
You, oh Teacher, who are your mother's obedient son,
Give me some cold water to relieve the hollowness in my stomach."

Maudgalyāyana listened to his mother's request for water, her breath catching and her voice harsh. While he was considering what to do, he suddenly recalled that, south of the city of Rājagṛha, there was a great river. Its waters were so wide as to be boundless and it was called by the name Ganges. Surely it would be sufficient to rescue his mother from the torment of her fiery calamity.

When the living beings of the mortal world saw the river, to them its waters were refreshing and cool. When the various deities saw the river, to them it was a precious pond of greenglass. When fish and turtles saw this river, to them it was either torrent or marsh. But when Nīladhi saw the river, to her it was a stream of pus and fiery flames. She walked up to the water's edge and, without waiting for her son to utter the requisite vows, immediately supported herself against the bank with her left hand in consequence of her selfishness and scooped up the water with her right hand in consequence of her greed. Her avaricious heart was simply not to be restrained. Before the water entered her mouth, it had already become fire.

Maudgalyāyana had seen how the rice his mother started to eat had become a fiery fire and how the water she was drinking became a fiery fire. He beat his chest and struck his breast, moaning sorrowfully and weeping. He came before the Buddha and circled three times around him. Then, standing off to one side, he addressed him with these words: "Your disciple's mother, oh World-Honored, did many things which were not good, and so she fell down into the three mires. Having been blessed by your mercy and compassion, I was able to rescue my mother from her suffering there. But now the rice which she eats becomes fire and the water she drinks becomes fire. How can I rescue my mother from the torment of her fiery calamity?"

"Maudgalyāyana!" the World-Honored called out to him, "it is true that your mother, up to now, has not been able to eat any food. She will obtain food to eat only if you observe annually, on the fifteenth day of the seventh month, the provision of a purgatorian feast on a large scale."

Maudgalyāyana looked at his starving mother and then spoke: "World-Honored, may it not be held monthly on the thirteenth and fourteenth? Must she wait each year for the fifteenth day of the seventh month before she gets any food to eat?"

"Not only is this the prescribed date on which to provide a purgatorian feast on a large scale for your mother," the World-Honored replied to him, "it is also the day on which those who have been sitting in meditation in the monasteries end their summer retreat, the day on which arhats achieve the fruit of their religious practice, the day on which Devadatta's[40] sins are annihilated, the day on which King Yama rejoices, and the day on which all hungry ghosts everywhere get to eat their fill."

Having received the Buddha's clear instructions, Maudgalyāyana went to the front of a temple which was near the city of Rājagṛha. There he read aloud the Mahāyāna sūtras and performed the good deed of providing a purgatorian feast on a large scale. It was from these basins of food that his mother was finally able to eat a full meal. But after she received the food, he did not see his mother again.

Maudgalyāyana searched for his mother everywhere but could not find her. Tears of sorrow falling like rain, he came before the Buddha and circled three times around him. Then, standing off to one side, he joined his palms in reverent greeting and knelt respectfully. "World-Honored," he addressed him, "when my mother ate rice, it became fire; when she drank water, it became fire. Having been blessed by your compassion and mercy, I was able to rescue my mother from the torment of her fiery calamity. But, ever since the fifteenth day of the seventh month, when she received the meal, we haven't seen each other again. Perhaps she has fallen into hell. Or perhaps she went toward the path of hungry ghosts?"

"Neither has your mother fallen into hell nor is she on the path of hungry ghosts," the World-Honored replied. "Having obtained the merit of your reading the sūtras and the good deed of providing a purgatorian feast, your mother's body as a hungry ghost has been transformed. She has gone into the

40. The son of King Droṇodana and a cousin of Śākayamuni with whom he competed by cultivating supernatural powers. He was said to have been swallowed up in hell for his evil behavior toward the Buddha. Later, however, a tradition emerged which predicted that he would be a future Buddha known as Devarāja.

center of Rājagṛha, where she has taken on the body of a black dog. If you wish to see your mother, go from house to house begging for food, seeing that your mind and actions are impartial and that you do not question whether they are rich or poor. When you walk up to the gate of a certain very wealthy householder, a black dog will come out. It will tug at your cassock and, holding it in its mouth, will make human sounds. That will be your mother."

Having been granted the Buddha's clear instructions, Maudgalyāyana immediately took up his begging-bowl in one hand and a basin in the other and went in search of his mother. Without asking whether they were for the rich or the poor, he walked a complete circle through the city's wards and alleys, but nowhere did he see his mother. He walked up to the gate of a certain householder where he saw a black dog which came out from the house. It tugged at Maudgalyāyana's cassock and, holding it in its mouth, started to make human sounds.[41]

"Oh, obedient son of your mother!" it said, "if you could rescue your mother from the infernal paths of hell, why do you not rescue her from the torment of having the body of a dog?"

"My dear mother!" Maudgalyāyana addressed her, "because your son was unfilial, you met with misfortune and fell into the three mires. But wouldn't you prefer to be living here in the form of a dog rather than existing as a hungry ghost?"

"Obedient son!" his mother called out, "I have received this body of a dog and my dumbness as a due reward. I spend my life walking, standing, sitting, or lying. When I'm hungry, I eat human excrement in the latrines. When I'm thirsty, I drink the water which drips from the eaves to relieve the hollow feeling. In the morning, I hear the householder invoking the Three Treasures. In the evening, I hear his wife reciting the esteemed sūtras. I would rather have the body of a dog and endure the filth of the earth than hear in my ears the name of hell."

Maudgalyāyana led his mother away to the front of a Buddhist stupa in Rājagṛha. There, for seven days and seven nights, they read aloud the Mahāyāna sūtras, confessing and repenting, and reciting the prohibitions. Availing herself of this merit, she was transformed out of her dog-body. She sloughed off her dogskin and hung it on a tree. Then, getting back her body of a woman, she was once again in complete possession of a perfect human form.

"Mother," Maudgalyāyana said to her, "it is difficult to obtain a human body, difficult to be born in the Central Kingdom,[42] difficult to hear the Law of the Buddha, and difficult to manifest a good mind. I call upon you,

---

41. Dogs are, of course, normally dumb. That the dog is able to speak to Maudgalyāyana in this particular case is due to a special dispensation of the Buddha.

42. The "Central Kingdom" here refers to India, not China.

mother, now that you have regained human form, swiftly to cultivate blessings."

Maudgalyāyana took his mother to the twin Sāl trees. He circled three
times around the Buddha and then, standing off to one side, addressed him
in these words: "Oh World-Honored! Would you look over for me the path
of my mother's karma up to the present, examining it from the very beginning
to see if she has any other sins?"

The World-Honored was not opposed to Maudgalyāyana's request. Observing her from the standpoint of the three types of karma, he found that there
were no further individual sins.

Seeing that his mother's sins had been annihilated, Maudgalyāyana rejoiced greatly at heart. "Mother," he said to her,

> "Let us go back!
> The world of mortal men is not fit to remain in;
>   Birth, life, death —
> It wasn't really a place to stay in anyway.
> It is the Kingdom of Buddha in the West which is the finest!"

Deities and dragons were moved to lead the way in front and heavenly
maidens came to welcome her. She was received forthwith into the Trayas-
triṁśā Heaven to enjoy happiness.

In the very beginning,[43] the Buddha uttered the stanzas with which he
converted the first five disciples. At the time (the time this sūtra was
preached) there were 84,000 [44] bodhisattvas, 84,000 monks, 84,000 laymen,
and 84,000 laywomen, all circling around the Buddha and making obeisance
to him. They rejoiced in the receptivity and obedience of their faith.

Transformation Text on Mahāmaudgalyāyana, One Scroll
Written on the sixteenth day of the fourth month in the seventh year of
the True Brightness reign-period by Hsüeh An-chün, lay student [45] at the
Pure Land Monastery.

Chang Pao-ta's copy
Translated by Victor H. Mair

43. Of the transmission of the Law of the Buddha after his enlightenment.

44. The supposed number of atoms in the human body. As such, it was a frequently used
figure for a large number of various phenomena or objects.

45. Lay students pursuing a largely secular curriculum under the auspices of various monasteries at Tun-huang were primarily responsible for the copying of transformation texts. They
were thus extremely important in the creation of a written vernacular for China.

215

Master Tung's Western Chamber Romance

Tung Chieh-yüan (fl. c. 1190–1208)

Chapter 2

(Hsien-lü-tiao mode)

Trimming the Silver Lamp

Stopping before the steps, the young monk gushed:
"What a fearful sight:

This text is an example of a genre called the medley (*chu-kung-tiao*, literally, "various modes"). The medley is a dramatic type of storytelling that developed toward the end of the eleventh century and flourished particularly under the Chin dynasty of the Jürchen. Like so many other genres of popular literature that came after the Buddhist-influenced transformation texts (see selection 214) of the T'ang and Five Dynasties periods, the medley was prosimetric in form, the verse portions being sung and the prose portions being spoken. The medley was a solo performance in which a single artist, accompanied by percussion or a string instrument, both told the story and spoke all of the quoted dialogue. The verse portions of the medley were sung to various tunes or arias (*ch'ü-tiao*) arranged in a sequence according to fixed musical rules. A group of tunes in one mode (*kung-tiao*) were considered to be a suite (*t'ao-shu*). Several mode names and tune titles reflect the ultimate Buddhist and western (i.e., Central and South Asian) origins of the musical elements of the genre. For example, Master Wen-hsü was a T'ang period monk who gave popular lectures, and *p'an she* is the Chinese transcription of the Sanskrit word for "five" (*pañca*), hence *P'an-she-tiao* means "Fifth Mode." In spite of their once great popularity as an oral performing art, only three, or perhaps four, written medleys are extant. The majority of these survive only in fragments and were recovered only in this century, demonstrating once again the usual fate of folk and popular literature in a society that was so thoroughly dominated by the elitist values of Confucian literati.

Master Tung's Western Chamber Romance (Tung Chieh-yüan hsi-hsiang chu-kung-tiao), in contrast to the rough, earthy quality of the medley on Liu Chih-yüan (unearthed from the sands of Kharokhoto, by the Russian explorer Petr Kuzmitch Kozlov, during his expedition of 1907–1908), is of exceptional literary value and shows how the medley can also exist in a more refined form. The contrast between these two medleys demonstrates a recurring paradigm: Chinese literary genres tend to be created in the popular milieu but are later taken up by the literati and become increasingly polished.

The present medley, based on the famous T'ang period classical-language short story, "The Story of Ying-ying" (see selection 207), is very different from its source in language, form, and style. The medley version is written in a mixture of vernacular and classical language, and is much more elaborate and detailed than the short story. For example, the entire second chapter given here is a vivid and lengthy description of a battle that is barely alluded to in the T'ang short story. The author's fertile imagination is demonstrated in his creation of the warrior monks who are instrumental in quelling the rebellion of local troops that threaten the safety of Ying-ying and her mother, who have taken refuge in their temple. The monks are particularly interesting, yet unprecedented in the tradition of the short story and its subsequent adaptations.

Next to nothing is known of the author. Indeed, we do not even know his real name,

Tumultuous dust seals the sky;
Fluttering banners conceal the sun;
A shower of fine earth rains down from all directions!
Gongs are clashing; drums are rolling;
Lances and swords surge pell-mell
All around our temple!

"One glimpse at the chief bandit
Is enough to freeze you with terror.
He wears a scarlet turban covered with
Pearls, like rice clinging to the sides of a vat,
Two suits of lion-hide armor,
A pair of green boots
And his mount is a dragonlike
Curly-maned Ch'ih-t'u.[1]

Coda

"A yellow birch crossbow arches over his arm,
A mountain-cleaving ax, big as a winnowing fan,
    rests on his shoulder,
He's none other than Flying Tiger Sun, the bridge-guarding
    general!"

[Prose]

During the T'ang dynasty, troops were stationed in the P'u prefecture. The year of our story, the commander of the garrison, Marshal Hun, died. Because the second-in-command, Ting Wen-ya, did not have firm control of the troops, Flying Tiger Sun, a subordinate general, rebelled with five thousand soldiers. They pillaged and plundered the P'u area.

How do I know this to be true? It is corroborated by "The Ballad of the True Story of Ying-ying." The "Ballad" says:

Bridge-side garrison loses its chief,
Banners and halberds topple in a heap.
Ere a new head is announced,
Soldiers mutiny and crowd into town.
Husbands proffer silk and jade,
So wives from injury may escape.
But how can the beauties flee and hide
When everywhere rebels gallop and riot?

Chieh-yüan being but an honorific title (nominally Prefectural [Provincial] Graduate with Highest Honors).

1. The name of a famous charger owned by Lü Pu (second century C.E.), the Three Kingdoms warrior.

Mothers cry and wail to heaven;
Holding daughters they part with ornaments.
Abandoning rouge to lessen their charm,
Maidens seem effigies, pale and wan.

(Cheng-kung mode)

Master Wen-lısü, ch'an

[The young monk continued:]
    "Reverend elders,
Cease your commotion, and
Hear me while I explain:
Marshal Hun Chen
Recently passed away.
The bridge-guarding Wen-ya is a profligate.
He's incompetent;
His troops mutinied and
Proceeded to terrorize the countryside.
City walls and moats, one after the other, are overrun and
    destroyed.

"The insurgents loot and plunder; they
Seize women and girls.
None dare oppose them, since
Rioters don't know right from wrong,
White from black.
In the town of P'u, the southern district and the northern ward have
    been burned to ashes;
Booty is carted away;
Highways and byways
Are mounds of corpses and seas of blood.

Licorice Root

    "They wreak a terrible havoc.
Oh, they wreak a terrible havoc.
The rebel chief's
Crimes are as vast as the sky.
Intrepid, fearless,
He does battle in a heavy coat of mail.
With his military might
He thinks he can overthrow the T'ang.
It will be pure luck if he leaves us alone.
But if not, how can we resist?

Removing the Cotton Garment

> "How can we resist?
> The thought confounds me.
> We're really in a fix—
> Do I hear more troops approach? . . ."

Coda

> Within an hour,
> Waves of soaring dust have fully eclipsed the sun;
> Five thousand bandits throng outside.

[Prose]

The monks had no time to make any preparations. All they could do was to close the temple gate. The bandits beat on the gate with their swords and sent arrows into the temple. One of them shouted: "We don't want anything else; we just want a meal." The abbot said to the monks: "I think we had better open the gate and invite them in. They can stay in the prayer halls and on the verandahs. After giving them a meal, we can soften them up with bribes so that they will not hurt us. Otherwise, I am afraid they may force their way in and kill us all. Does my suggestion appeal to you?"

The monk Chih-shen, the superintendent, replied: "Inviting the bandits in will not harm *us* in any way. But at present we have in the temple Madam Ts'ui's daughter Ying-ying, who is a beautiful girl. If the bandits saw her, they would certainly kidnap her. Minister Ts'ui had many relatives and friends who enjoy imperial favors and occupy important positions. Once Ying-ying is captured, we shall certainly suffer for it. For, although it would be the bandits who had seized her, the fault would be ours for having opened the gate to them. When we are charged with complicity, what can we say in our own defense?"

(Ta-shih-tiao mode)

Kun Section of [the Elaborate Melody] Yi-chou

> In the prayer hall
> The monks discussed
> Whether they should invite the bandits in.
> The superintendent said no,
> And gave his reasons in detail:
> "What shall we do
> If the rebels
> Should capture Ying-ying?
> When the news becomes known
> We're sure to share the fate of vanishing waters."

"What can be done then?" the abbot asked.
"The bandits are at the gate, and
We've no way to fight them."
From the ranks a monk
Thundered out his angry cry:
"Have no fear, abbot.
You other monks, you three hundred and more,
Jabbering is all you do.
Despite your size, you're helpless babes.
Your chow has been wasted on you, you good-for-nothings."

Coda

Lifting his frayed Buddhist robe,
Raising his three-foot consecrated sword,
He said: "Let me put my life on the line and fight this horde of
    thieves."

[Prose]

Who was this monk? He was none other than Fa-ts'ung. Fa-ts'ung was a descendant of a tribesman from western Shensi. When he was young he took great pleasure in archery, fencing, hunting, and often sneaked into foreign states to steal. He was fierce and courageous. When his parents died, it suddenly became clear to him that the way of the world was frivolous and trivial, so he became a monk in the Temple of Universal Salvation.

"My mind is made up. As long as we are menaced, I will not sit back and watch. For such is not the way of a humane person. If my valiant brothers will help me, we can easily defeat the rebels. In fact, they will dissolve on their own, like a shaken grain stalk snapping into bits. Actually, only two or three mutineers have a seditious intent; the rest have been tricked into following. While they see the spoils before their eyes they are blind to the dire consequences waiting around the corner. If I can explain to them the gains and the losses, most of them will lose their desire to fight and will disperse."

(Hsien-lü-tiao mode)

An Embroidered Belt

He didn't know how to read sūtras;
He didn't know how to follow rituals;
He was neither pure nor chaste
But was indomitably courageous . . . .
Formerly he had often killed
Without batting an eye.

After becoming a monk,
He left his iron cudgel
Unsharpened for years.
His consecrated sword
Had slain tigers and dragons.
But once he tired of shedding blood,
It hung neglected
On the wall.

The sword's ram-horn hilt was sealed to the sheath by grime,
Its icy blade and point had dulled.
Fa-ts'ung called out: "Fellow monks,
Who will follow me?
Have no fear,
I guarantee there'll be no risk."
To himself he thought:
"Today I'll have meat to eat and
My cudgel will sharpen itself on the thieves."
He stood by the verandah
And counted the gathering monks:
"Tough and fierce men
Who dare to fight.
You need only shout to cheer me on.
No danger will befall you.

Coda

"Just open the gate and aid me with war yells,
And I'll mow down the thieves with my sword.
Let them be pastry fillings for our meal!"

[Prose]

A penchant to kill
Has changed into a desire to save;
A former ruffian
Is now a praiseworthy hero.

Fa-ts'ung urged loudly: "For our religion and for each other, we should do our utmost. Those who dare help me fight, go to the right of the hall." In a short time nearly three hundred monks gathered by the hall with cudgels and swords in their hands. They said to Fa-ts'ung: "We are willing to follow you and fight to the death."

(Shuang-tiao mode)

Wen-ju-chin

When you looked close you'd see
Fa-ts'ung had a ferocious mien:
Defiant, bold,
Somewhat irregular and somewhat strange.
His bull-like torso was hefty,
His tiger waist supple and long.
He wore a three-foot consecrated sword and
Carried an iron cudgel.
His horse was
An elephant without tusks.
Wearing a tight-fitting cloth corselet, he had
No armor, no helmet.
A full eight feet,
He was splendidly imposing.
A Buddhist Tzu-lu! [2]
A tonsured Chin-kang! [3]

His followers, more than two hundred,
Used weapons
Rarely seen.
Some had deep-set eyes;
Some looked savage and fierce.
Some brandished kitchen cleavers,
Rolling pins;
Some banged on temple drums and gongs.
They wore prayer pennants for armor,
Begging-bowls as helmets.
A few novices with disheveled hair
Dashed out of their cells in
Dark brown clerical gowns.
Giving rein to pent-up valor,
They shouted: "We too want
To fight on the battleground till the bitter end."

Coda

Unwilling to follow Tripiṭaka to search for scriptures, [4]
This lot shouldered brooms and canes to
Trail a homicidal monk!

2. Confucius' disciple. In *The Analects*, the Master says: "Yu [Tzu-lu] is more inclined to bravery than I."
3. A protective deity.
4. See selection 211.

[Prose]

Before the superintendent could caution prudence, Fa-ts'ung had already led his followers to the gate. Seeing the impressive enemy strength, he knew he could not defeat them easily. At once he dismounted and ascended the belfry to address the rebels in the hope of undermining their morale.

(P'an-she-tiao mode)

Spring in the Chin Garden

> Closely dotting the vast fields,
> Iron halberds pierced the sky;
> Embroidered banners reflected the sun;
> They formed the backdrop for
> A mounted officer
> Whose red brocade military cape covered
> A suit of oil-glossy, jet-black armor.
> Flat-nosed, hare-lipped, with
> Thick eyebrows and large eyes,
> The general carried on his shoulder a gigantic Ku-ting sword,[5]
> Magnificent as a god,
> He had a barrel chest, a bulky torso,
> Massive thighs, thick buttocks and waist.
>
> Virile, alert,
> He playfully prodded with his sword the jeweled stirrup of his
>   mount.
> And the warriors in his command?—
> It's always difficult to describe
> The panache of true heroes—
> Some were short, some were tall,
> Some thin, some fat,
> But all were flawlessly stalwart and brave.
> If you counted carefully,
> They were less than six thousand,
> But certainly five thousand and more.

Flowers Above the Wall

> In neat formations,
> They tightly encircled
> The temple's five-mile estate.
> A third of them wore black cotton leggings;
> Half had yellow silk wadded jackets.

5. A sword wrought in Ku-ting, near P'u-yang district in Hopei.

Their drums rumbled *tung-tung.*
The din of their horns spiraled and whirled.
Their banners danced in the wind, like brilliant tongues of fire.
The combat-urgers made earth-stunning, deafening roars;
The battle-criers uttered sky-lifting yells and shouts.

How could the temple withstand such an onslaught?
Solidly built,
Its walls were like stone ramparts.
The iron-bound gate was impregnable.
An almost impossible feat to get inside
And molest the monks.

Song of Che Tree Branches

Steel axes and swords hacked and hewed.
What cacophony, what confusion.
Politely Fa-ts'ung said to
The rebel general:
"We have no treasures,
Or food or fodder,
How can we offer adequate hospitality
To the immense troops in your command?

Kun Section of [the Elaborate Melody] God of Longevity

"The court will soon hear of
Your treasonous deeds.
Armies will be dispatched
To quell you.
You're making a grave mistake.
When it's too late, even remorse won't help.
Think over what I say."

The rebel general
Was outraged by these words.
"You bald-pated criminal, fit to be flogged,
How dare you contravene your lord's will?
We don't mean to
Impose on you monks.
Why should your unchaste lips make such a fuss?

A Fast Melody

"We don't want to take your temple.
We don't want to get your gold.
My men are tired and need a rest.

So why close your gate?
Of all the monks only you behave like a tiger, a leopard, and
Plague your father with tiresome chatter.

Coda

"Your hands should be cut off,
Brains knocked out,
Ears chopped off, and with legs tied,
You ought to be hung upside down from the lintel till doomsday!"

[Prose]

Fa-ts'ung said: "Compose yourself, compose yourself. We shall comply with your wishes. Since there are a few thousand of you, I shall be grateful if you would retreat about a hundred paces, so that when the food is ready you can file in slowly, in an orderly way."

The general said: "Now that you agree to help us, I would be in the wrong if I didn't cooperate."

Thereupon he ordered his troops to retreat a hundred paces. In the meantime, Fa-ts'ung came down from the belfry and mounted his horse.

(Huang-chung-tiao mode)

The Restless Oriole, ch'an-ling

When the soldiers heard the order
They retreated two or three hundred paces.
Someone removed the crossbar, the padlock,
    and threw open the two panels of the temple gate.
Fa-ts'ung shouted:
"Follow me!" and
With this call
All the monks plunged through the gate.
Such a bizarre army was never seen before.

Rash,
Fearless,
They thought nothing of their five thousand foes.
Fa-ts'ung, holding his cudgel level with the ground,
Raised his voice and menacingly yelled:
"Treasonous rebels!
Send someone out to fight!
There's no need for you to sink staves,
    drive in posts, and make camp.

Ssu-men-tzu

> "Our country hasn't treated you ill.
> Reckon for yourselves:
> The emperor gives you your uniforms, your food, and your pay.
> You don't know how lucky you are.
> Shame! Disgrace!
> The time is peaceful with no strife.
> Shame! Disgrace!
> You receive your wages without having to work.
>
> "At Marshal Hun's death,
> You broke into a lawless mob.
> You terrorized the people; you robbed them
>   of their wealth and goods.
> Now you want to ransack my temple.
> Shame! Disgrace!
> The food you demand I'll refuse—
> Shame! Disgrace!—
> I'd rather feed it to my ass.

Willow Leaves

> "Why make a racket here?
> You'd be better off guarding your mother's tomb.
> I know what I say, I don't mean to frighten you,
> My sons, it's time to surrender and yield.

Coda

> "Wise or unwise,
> I'll let you go.
> If you don't leave
> You'll taste the gall of my sixty-pound cudgel."

[Prose]

Fa-ts'ung, galloping on his horse, shouted: "I wish to see the commanding general." An officer rode forth from the ranks and said to him: "You are a Buddhist monk, you should be chanting sūtras and meditating. Why are you here threatening and menacing us?"

Fa-ts'ung replied: "You are soldiers and officers; our country pays you to keep peace on the frontier. You and your families receive food rations at the end of every month, and every season you are given new clothes. Not only are you spared the pain of hunger and cold, you are allowed to enjoy the bliss of family life. Now, temporarily deprived of guidance, you forget the great favor our country has conferred upon you; mercilessly you persecute innocent people and leave the whole prefecture in ruins. The court is not far; it will be informed presently; troops will arrive any moment. You yourselves will be reduced to pools of blood on the battlefield and your families will be condemned for complicity. After you are dead and your clans exterminated, what good is the loot? I think it would be wise for you to reflect on this."

Spurring his horse forward, the rebel officer retorted: "So, besides refusing us food, you have the impudence to harangue my men!"

(Ta-shih-tiao mode)

Jade-Winged Cicada

> When the officer heard Fa-ts'ung's words,
> Even if he had been a Buddha, he would have been enraged.
> He ground and nearly broke his great wolflike teeth.
> He scanned his men:
> "Trusted soldiers,
> Do as I bid.
> Help me with just one shout, and
> In one round I'll capture the bald-pated lout."
> At this the rebels
> Rolled their drums and
> Vigorously waved their multicolored flags.
>
> Their yells penetrated the sky.
> In unison they blew their decorated horns.
> Worried clouds shielded the sun as
> The air of battle reached the firmament.
> The officer growled: "You, monk,
> Quit your madness and just wait:
> Hold on to your cudgel;
> Sit tight on your saddle;
> Meditate on the Western Paradise.
> In seconds I'll perform the charitable deed
> Of sending you there
> With ten thousand strokes of my sword."

Coda

> Before you could cover your ears, his horse had dashed ahead.
> A rainbow of dust trailed behind the hooves.
> The rebel aimed his sword straight at the monk's nose.

[Prose]

A clashing sound was heard. Was the monk dead?

(Ta-shih-tiao mode)

Kun Section of [the Elaborate Melody] Yi-chou ch'an-ling

> Hell wind rises.
> The field is packed with lances and armor.
> The air of battle darkens the sky.
> Soldiers of six divisions yell and shout.
> Before the banners, two mounted warriors fight.
> The monk Fa-ts'ung,
> Deftly defending himself,
> Raises his cudgel to his eyebrow.
> A clashing sound—
> He wards off the slashing Ku-ting sword.
>
> Dragonlike chargers, tigerlike warriors.
> The cudgel twirls, the sword strikes,
> In ways prescribed by *Martial Arts*.[6]
> This combat will separate
> The victor from the loser.
> After three rounds
> The rebel begins to tire.
> What does he do?
> He adopts a defensive posture and hides behind his sword.
> It will be impossible now for him to overcome the monk.

A Red Gauze Garment

> Doggedly he fights on,
> Desperately he perseveres.
> He's like a rabbit facing an eagle,
>   a mouse running into a cat.
> When finally he manages
> A slight advantage
> He tries to
> Escape to his ranks.
> Just then another mounted warrior flies forth,
> Holding a spear twelve feet long,
> Dressed with bizarre extravagance that seems to
> Add to his brutal ferocity.

6. *Six Scabbards* (*Liu t'ao*), a pre-T'ang work on military craft.

The valiant monk
Has mastered the military arts well.
Though the moment he fends off the spear the sword is upon him,
He remains confident, relaxed,
Calm, undaunted,
Serene, and cool.
His eyes are sharp, his movements brisk;
His steed charges swiftly, his blows are precise and sure.
Circling round him, the two rebels pant and gasp.
They want to quit
But dread their men's jeers.

Coda

Fa-ts'ung's heart pounds violently.
He's furious; his eyes are heptagons, octagons.
The two rebels dare not approach him.

[Prose]

Six arms,
The one holding the cudgel is the strongest.
Three warriors,
The one wearing a helmet withdraws to rest.
The sword-wielder leaves the struggle,
The spear-thruster carries on the fight.

(Cheng-kung mode)

Master Wen-hsü

Having recovered his strength,
The sword-wielder puts on his armor again.
No threats are exchanged,
No question asked,
He lunges toward the monk to unhorse him.
The monk dodges and grasps the rebel's belt.
With no pity and
All his strength
He yanks the rebel over to his own horse
And smashes him down across the pommel of his saddle.

A shrill wail —
The rebel is sliding, head down, through his belt!
Too weary to
Remount his tired horse,
Unable to keep up even the pretense of a hero,

He decides to flee.
Steering clear of
The monk,
He sprints south to save his skin.

Licorice Root

How to catch him?
How to catch him?
When Fa-ts'ung sees him escape,
His anger flares up.
Feigning to give chase,
He screams and yells thunderously.
Actually he doesn't budge;
His screams alone are terrifying enough.
All the rebels stare with unblinking eyes:
"This bald monk is unbelievably fierce!"

Coda

The monk now noisily taunts:
"You bandits, you criminals, how dare you rebel?
If anyone else is crazy enough to fight, come out this instant."

[Prose]

Embroidered vanguard banners
Set loose in the wind hundreds of miles of morning clouds.
Rousing military drums
Exploded from the ground a thousand claps of thunderbolts.
One general was so incensed that he took up the challenge. Who was he?
Who was he?

(Hsien-lü-tiao mode)

Adorning Crimson Lips

This general
Is famous for his bravery.
Dissatisfied with his rank
He wants to rule the whole country.

Robust, ferocious:
People freeze when he appears.
Fa-ts'ung says to himself:
"I'll bet he always looks
Annoyed and angry."

The "Hai-Hai" Song

> Roly-poly, a portly belly,
> Triangular eyes, enormous nose, thick fleshy lips,
> His forehead is wide, his chin is broad, he has winged eyebrows,
> And a red beard.
> *Hai-hai.*

Wind Blowing Lotus Leaves

> Wearing a military cape with clouds and geese embroidered in
>   gold,
> A pair of green, wolf-skin boots,
> He's superbly fitted out.
> The scarlet turban
> On his head
> Is decorated profusely with pearls.

The Inebriated Tatar Woman

> He wears two suits of armor.
> His courage is unsurpassed—
> Single-handedly he'd take on ten thousand foes.
> He's nicknamed Flying Tiger Sun.

Coda

> Carrying an iron-shafted crossbow,
> A quiver with a hundred pairs of steel arrows,
> He shoulders a mountain-cleaving ax as big as a winnowing fan.

[Prose]

> A moment ago this bandit held sway on the highway;
> Suddenly a challenger entered the chess game.[7]

(P'an-she-tiao mode)

A Pock-Marked Old Lady

> Flying Tiger is brave,
> Fa-ts'ung is stalwart.
> Flying Tiger likes to fight,
> Fa-ts'ung refuses to yield.
> Flying Tiger's out to sack the temple.

---

7. Similar parallel-line descriptions occur frequently in Chinese stories of the Robin Hood type. The lines are inappropriate here as neither Fa-ts'ung nor Flying Tiger Sun is a highwayman. Master Tung seems to have simply borrowed them from the other tradition.

Fa-ts'ung's determined to crush the rebels.
Fa-ts'ung has a plan to subdue the insurgents,
Flying Tiger has a scheme to overthrow the throne.

Fa-ts'ung uses an iron cudgel,
Flying Tiger uses a steel ax.
One smites the monk with his ax,
One attacks the Tiger with his cudgel.
Flying Tiger excels in offensive jabs,
Fa-ts'ung's superb with defensive parries.
Fa-ts'ung has the upper hand,
Flying Tiger tries to escape.

Coda

Fa-ts'ung wins;
Flying Tiger loses.
Fa-ts'ung shouldn't have pursued—
Flying Tiger draws his crossbow.

[Prose]

Fa-ts'ung thought he really had won, but actually Flying Tiger feigned defeat. Flying Tiger thrust his ax into the saddle, put his boots through the stirrups, and raised his dragon-tendon crossbow. He oiled the release and cranked the brass gear. Even in the wind his arrows could pierce an aspen tree from a hundred paces, so how could he possibly miss the seven-foot monk? [8]

(Cheng-kung mode)

Master Wen-hsü

The general's flight
Is a ruse.
Fa-ts'ung shouldn't have given chase.
In chasing
He falls into a trap. . . .
Pressing his feet on the stirrups,
Flying Tiger rears nimbly.
A clap of thunder—
An arrow leaves the bowstring and
Flies forward like a lightning bolt.

---

8. Earlier, Fa-ts'ung is said, variously, to be seven-and-a-half and eight feet tall. Such inconsistency is not infrequent in this medley.

Fa-ts'ung
Sees this
From afar.
Truly a seasoned
Fighter, he's
Completely unruffled.
With quick reflexes,
He pulls at the reins,
Leans forward on his saddle, and
Halts his white-bellied bay.

Coda

Opening wide his murderous eyes,
He lifts, his *ta-chiang* whip.[9]
Crash—the whip intercepts and breaks the arrow.

[Prose]

An iron whip was raised: a great python leaped into the air.

A steel arrow was blocked: a meteor plummeted to the ground.
The rebels were petrified. Flying Tiger said to them: "The monk has no armor. Although I failed to defeat him at close range, you can overpower him from where you are. If he chases after me again, shoot your arrows at him in unison; that will certainly finish him off."

Fa-ts'ung thought: "The bandits seem to have something up their sleeves. Moreover, my horse is exhausted and cannot fight on much longer." He told his followers: "Retreat and guard the temple: I shall break through the lines to carry out a plan I have."

(Chung-lü-tiao mode)

Catching a Snake in a Comical Way

Looking ahead, Fa-ts'ung
Sees a tremendous throng of rebels
Brandish their spears and lances on the field
In a threatening way.
Before the ranks, a general sits on a stallion,
An ax on his shoulder and
A peevish scowl on his face.

The rebels press forward to
Cut at the passing monk.

---

9. "Beat-the-[opposing]-general whip." The term seems to be a coinage expressing the purported use of this weapon.

But every thrust is cleverly warded off.
Fat-ts'ung is invulnerable.
No one can match his skills.
Flying Tiger despairs at his
Dexterity, his sharp vision,
              his ability to slither away and escape.

Coda

The rebels muse:
"Before we can stretch out our hands,
This damned quick, shaven-headed criminal
Has slipped by."

[Prose]

The fierce monk:
          Fighting singly,
          Is as brave as Hsiang Yü at Nine-Mile Mount.[10]
          Battling alone,
          Is as bold as Kuan Yü at White Horse Hill.[11]
He charges into the thick of Flying Tiger's troops without giving a thought to
his life.

(Hsien-lü-tiao mode)

Yi-hu-ch'a

The rebels are numerous,
They promptly fall back before the monk.
They are like lambs confronting a tiger,
Beasts surprised by a wolf.
Their arrows are useless,
The monk's cudgel is an impenetrable shield.
Sky-rocking wails shoot up in the wake of his horse's hooves,
Bile and blood splash on the dusty ground.

In half an hour the monk breaks the lines;
His fearlessness is truly magnificent.
Covered with spilled blood—
In emergencies certain things can't be helped—
He looks like the monk of Yao-chou,

10. Hsiang Yü, the Prince of Ch'u (third century B.C.E.), contended for the throne against Liu Pang and was besieged by his enemies at Nine-Mile Mount, near present-day T'ung-shan district in Kiangsu.
11. Kuan Yü, a general of the third century C.E., slew his opponent, Yen Liang, in a battle at Pai-ma kang (White Horse Hill), near present-day Hua district in Honan.

After a bout with the fierce Scholar Meng.[12]
Perhaps I shouldn't say this—he's exactly like
A cock having just
Emerged from a cunt.

[Prose]

Unable to defeat the rebels alone, Fa-ts'ung broke out through the enemy lines. The rebels then surrounded the temple and Flying Tiger Sun cried at the gate: "First, I want to give my men some food. Second, I know Madam Ts'ui and her family are here and I want Ying-ying. If you give her to me, we shall withdraw; otherwise, calamity will befall you this instant." His words were reported to the Ts'uis. Ying-ying was terrified.

(Ta-shih-tiao mode)

Jade-Winged Cicada

Braving the lines, whipping his horse,
Fa-ts'ung flees to the southwest.
He hasn't time to worry
That his followers
Aren't protected
By cuirasses or armor.
The rebels shower arrows at them
Without a moment's respite.
Of more than three hundred monks
Seventy or eighty percent are
Killed before they can knock on the temple gate.

A few senior monks
Die serenely from their wounds.
The prior is stricken by a sword;
His blood oozes through his muslin robe.
A number of injured cenobites,
Though at first buoyed up by the Buddha,
        are finally trampled to death by the horses.
One slow-moving priest,
Captured by a lieutenant,
Turns ashen
In fright,
Like a figure of wax.
From under the banners Flying Tiger bawled:
        "Drive him hither for interrogation."

12. Apparently this alludes to a story popular in Tung's time. The story is no longer extant.

Coda

> The rebels think to drag him by the hair, but alas,
>> his head has been shaved.
> Pulling him by his mendicant robe,
> They yank him toward their general's horse.

[Prose]

Flying Tiger asked: "Why do you refuse me a single meal?"

The monk replied: "The abbot was willing to invite you, but the superintendent argued that you might kidnap the beautiful Ying-ying, who is keeping vigil in our temple over her deceased father, the late Prime Minister Ts'ui. He said that if this happened, there would be grave consequences as the minister had many influential friends."

Flying Tiger laughed: "What Fa-ts'ung just said was true, then; there really is a Ying-ying!"[13] He thought to himself: "Since Ting Wen-ya likes nothing better than wine and women, if I have Ying-ying put on makeup and a gorgeous dress, and offer her to Ting, I am sure he would be overjoyed. We can join forces to occupy the entire P'u area, and once this is done, we can defeat any troops the court may dispatch against us."

(Cheng-kung-tiao mode)

Licorice Root

> Having heard the monk,
> Having heard the monk,
> Flying Tiger strokes his blond beard[14] and
> Relaxes his peevish frown.
> A few underlings transmit his order
> To the men to quicken their attack.
> He himself shouts at the gate:
> "Listen, you monks,
> Obey me and I'll withdraw; otherwise
> You'll have to suffer the consequence.

Removing the Cotton Garment

> "If you give me Ying-ying, I'll remove my troops;
> If not, I'll destroy you instantly.

13. This is curious as nowhere has Fa-ts'ung mentioned the existence of Ying-ying. An exchange between Fa-ts'ung and Flying Tiger Sun might have been inadvertently left out by the copyist who made what was to become the origin of all existing editions of this medley.

14. Earlier, the beard is red (see p. 658). Flying Tiger must be from northwest China and of Central Asian (Indo-European or Indo-Iranian) extraction.

> I've wasted enough time
> And enough words with you!

Coda

> "Even if your temple were wrapped in steel
> And couldn't be broached, I could always
> Block the gate and set it on fire."

[Prose]

The monks are frightened. Fa-pen takes the injured monks to Madam Ts'ui to tell her what has happened. When she hears the report, she faints. Alarmed, Hung-niang [15] and Ying-ying try to revive her. After a long time they succeed. Ying-ying weeps and says: "Please do not worry about me, Mother, as you have Father's coffin to care for. Allow me to give myself up to the rebels. Though I shall be humiliated, you will be left your remaining years, and the temple, the monks will likewise be spared. You must not let others be harmed just so that I may be saved from shame."

(Tao-kung mode)

Chieh-hung

> The sudden report
> Frightened Ying-ying's soul away from her body.
> "It seems inevitable that
> My family will be torn apart.
> Father has died, and
> While we mourn him, we're besieged by these rebels.
> Alas,
> Brother Huan-lang is still a boy. . . ."
> Just then she heard strident voices
> Clamor for her.
> A thousand knives cut into her heart.
> The widowed mother and her daughter
> Had no place to seek help.
>
> Ying-ying reflected on the situation:
> "Only by a miracle
> Could I escape.
> As things stand,
> There's little hope of that.
> If I go with the rebels
> Who'd care for

15. Ying-ying's maid.

My aged mother?
This worries me even more.
Though the earth is wide, the sky is high, there's no shelter for me.
I'm completely at the mercy of a horde of bandits.
I can worry about neither chastity nor filial piety.
I must make clear to Mother
That if she tries to save me
There'll be three calamities:

Coda

"One, her life will be in danger;
Two, the monks will be killed;
Three, the magnificent temple will be burned."

[Prose]

Madam Ts'ui wept: "It is proper that a mother love her children with all her might, and it is natural that she care for them with the most profound affection. If you give yourself up to the rebels, what would be the good of my living on? I am sixty; if I die now I would have had a long life. But you are still young and unmarried. If you die, you would die a spinster, leaving no one behind." When she had finished, she let go of herself and wailed.

(Ta-shih-tiao mode)

Music for Returning to the Capital

Ying-ying and her mother
Held on to each other and cried.
Their loud wailing
Threw the monks into great confusion.
"It's more than likely that
Mother and I will both be killed this time.
I'd like to commit suicide,
But I'm afraid the rebels,
Frustrated in their desires,
Would burn the temple in revenge.
If I give myself up,
Posterity will learn of my shame;
Not only will I be
A laughing-stock for thousands of years to come,
My father's name will be disgraced as well.

"What am I
To do?
While Mother and the abbot

Discuss and ponder,
Some of the monks
Are urging reverently—
With touched palms—
For my delivery to the thieves.
It'd be difficult to dissuade them.
They're so insistent. . . .
All right, I will die, and
To appease
The rebels
My corpse can be offered
To their lawless swords.
They can strike me ten thousand times.
At least in death
My reputation will be intact!"

Coda

She lifted her gown and prepared to jump from the steps.
All became immobile, dazed with alarm—
Someone laughed and clapped his hands.

[Prose]

Fa-ts'ung's valor
Fails to defeat the rebels,
A weakling's plan
Succeeds in subduing the bandits.

Ying-ying was about to jump; she was about to jump! Madam Ts'ui and
Hung-niang restrained her. Suddenly, peals of laughter were heard; everyone
looked around. Who laughed?

(Huang-chung-kung mode)

Year of Happiness

Ying-ying and her mother were beside themselves with anguish;
Others shared their grief.
Suddenly someone spoke out claiming that
He could defeat the rebels.
All turned and looked.
A young scholar
Matchless in beauty
Emerged from the crowd of monks

Over twenty years old,
Five feet tall,

Trim eyebrows, lovely eyes,
Straight nose, strong teeth.
His lips were red as rouge,
His face, a luminous moon.
Compared with him
P'an An and Sung Yü [16] were ugly ruffians.

Dancers' Exit

All recognized him to be Chang.
A monk tugged at his robe and
Whispered: "Young gentleman,
This is not like chanting poetry in your study!
You should've seen the rows and rows of rebels.

"Are you mad or insane?
How can you make good your boastful claim?
You saw how hard Fa-ts'ung fought
With Flying Tiger on the battleground.
And even he had to flee before he was overcome.

Willow Leaves

"Your muscles and bones are as delicate as a girl's,
How can you wield a sword?
You have no strength in your arms or legs,
How can you ride a horse?

"Your fingers are like bamboo shoots,
How can you let fly an arrow?
You are slight and frail,
How can you support a hauberk?

Coda

"Even holding a brush tires you out,
Yet you claim you can make the troops withdraw.
Tell me, what's your plan?"

[Prose]

Who laughed? Who laughed? Everyone looked around; it was Chang. Chang
said: "Women have no presence of mind; whenever danger arises, they only
weep. And you monks, you, too, have not been very resourceful. Obviously
you have not come up with a way to deter the rebels; you merely wait to be
slaughtered. But if you follow my suggestion, you can certainly defeat them."

16. Epitomes of masculine beauty and literary talent.

The abbot Fa-pen knew that Chang was endowed with a rare intelligence, so that he might well have an unusual plan. He went up to Chang and said: "Indeed we have no way to escape our predicament. Since you, sir, have an unusual scheme, please help us."

Chang smiled and replied: "You and your followers are disciples of the Buddha; do you not understand that life is the origin of death and death paves the way for your next life? Life and death are natural phenomena of human existence. Even Shakyamuni [17] himself had to die! Moreover, the concept of retribution is indigenous to Buddhism; it is expounded clearly in your scriptures. If, in your previous incarnation, you did evil to the bandits, it is natural that they should seek revenge now, and there is no escape for you. But, if, on the other hand, you never harmed them, then they are not your enemies in this life, and you have no reason to be afraid."

The abbot said: "You are quite right, sir. Actually, I only begrudge the destruction of our temple. When they were built, the gate, prayer halls, verandahs, bell towers, and library cost more than one million pieces of silver. A fire would reduce them to a heap of ashes. I wish that, just for the sake of accumulating merits, you would prevent this from happening."

Chang smiled even more broadly: "When you preach, reverend abbot, you explicate the *Diamond Sūtra*. You seem, however, to be ignorant that even our bones, our flesh, our skin and hair are not our own. Our spirit is our true self; our body is but a temporary abode. When death arrives, our spirit leaves, and the four elements which make up our body disintegrate. Those who are dearest to us, our wives and children, cannot follow us; possessions most precious to us, our gold and pearls, must be left behind. And now you manifest such a proprietary attachment to the prayer halls and bell towers!"

The abbot retorted: "True, true, we who preach the Dharma do not care whether we live or die, and we are actually quite indifferent to the destruction of a temple. But it does pain us to see a daughter forcibly taken away from her mother. It is only for this reason that I am asking for your help."

Chang then said: "Madam Ts'ui has never bestowed any kindness upon me, and I was not acquainted with the late minister. There has never been any communication between the Ts'ui family and me, so why should I save them?"

"If you do not save Ying-ying, and Madam Ts'ui refuses to surrender her, the enraged rebels will no doubt attack us with great force. What will *you* do then?"

"You need not worry about me, I can protect myself. You would do well to devise a way to protect *yourself*."

The abbot tried another tack: "You are a Confucian, sir, and you uphold

17. The historical Buddha.

the principle of charity and justice. A charitable person loves humanity and abhors that which threatens it; it thus follows that you would want to remove this present threat. An upholder of justice respects order and detests those who subvert it; so, clearly, you would want to dispel the unruly rabble. Now a young woman and her widowed mother are both at the point of committing suicide, yet you sit here and laugh at them. Is this a charitable person's manifestation of love for humanity? On a different plane, these mutinous soldiers have ruthlessly harried innocent people; you see it but make no attempt to curb them. Is this how an upholder of justice shows his respect for order? In antiquity, Duke Chung of Cheng did not restrain Shu-tuan when Shu-tuan behaved incorrectly as a younger brother; [18] the Marquis of Wei did not save the Marquis of Li when the latter was attacked by Ti barbarians; [19] they were both censured in the *Spring and Autumn Annals*. Sir, you have a scheme to repel the mutineers, but you refuse to disclose it. Judged by the criterion implicit in *Spring and Autumn*, your conduct is greatly amiss. Decide for yourself whether I am right."

Chang smiled again and said: "Reverend abbot, your knowledge of Confucian teaching is indeed superficial. The Master once said: 'When a gentleman is brave but behaves improperly, confusion will result. When a small man is brave but behaves improperly, banditry will result.' Thus, a gentleman shuns actions that are brave but lack propriety. In the present situation, although I am fearless, so long as the parties involved do not ask for it, it would be improper for me to offer help. Furthermore, the Master said: 'When propriety is observed, pupils seek their teachers; teachers do not go about looking for pupils.' Clearly, it is beneath a gentleman to recommend himself."

(P'an-she-tiao mode)

A Pock-Marked Old Lady

> Again and again the abbot tried to persuade Chang:
> "Sir, you're being perverse.
> Everyone is distressed
> But you; you're in high spirits."
> Chang laughed with glee:
> "Reverend teacher, how dense you are!

18. Shu-tuan attempted to usurp the dukedom from his older brother Duke Chung, who for a long time took no action to stop him.

19. During the Spring and Autumn period (770–481 B.C.E.), the state of Wei had hegemony for a time over nine other states, of which Li was one; the Marquis of Wei was therefore bound by treaty to render whatever help he could to the Marquis of Li. When Ti barbarians invaded the state of Li, not only did the Marquis of Wei refuse to dispatch troops to expel the invaders, but he also treated the Marquis of Li shabbily when the latter fled to Wei.

Surely you must know, since it's recorded
    in your Buddhist scriptures and not
In my Confucian books:

Where there is life, there is death;
Only when birth desists will extinction cease!
Death, like life, is part of human existence.
It needn't be feared. . . .
There are more than five thousand rebels outside.
But even if they were as fierce as the God of Water and the God of
    Wrath,
So long as I'm alive
You'll not be captured.

Coda

"I don't need to mount a horse,
I don't need an inch of weapon,
I don't need to fight in battles,
One look from me will reduce the five thousand bandits
    to messes of fat and blood."

[Prose]

When the abbot transmitted Chang's words to Madam Ts'ui, she replied: "Is that so?"[20] With decorum she introduced herself to Chang and said, sobbing:

(Hsiao-shih-tiao mode)

The Center of the Flower Moves

"The rebels
Demand my daughter Ying-ying, and
Whatever can we do?
We, piteous
Widow and orphan,
Put ourselves in your hands."
Chang responded with a smile:
"Honorable Madam, pray sit down.
Set your heart at ease.
There's nothing to fear.

"I'm not boasting;
I do have a plan which will
Defeat the rebels immediately.

---

20. This, of course, refers to the previous prose passage, in which Chang says that it is beneath a gentleman to recommend himself.

The troops will withdraw,
The temple will stay intact,
The monks will be spared, and
You, your family and servants—all fifty of you—
Will not be hurt in any way. . . .
But when this is done
You mustn't start treating me like a stranger again."

[Prose]

Madam Ts'ui said: "Of course not, of course not; your apprehension is quite unnecessary. I only hope you will not consider my offer unworthy: once the catastrophe is averted and we are safe, I should like to have you as a son." [21] (etc., etc.) [22]

Chang told the abbot: "Send a messenger to inform the rebels that Ying-ying has agreed to their demand. She is taking leave of her mother and her father's coffin, and making herself presentable. She will be ready in a moment. Ask them to be patient and to please relax their attack somewhat."

The rebels slackened their harassment.

Chang then said: "Mutinous troops cannot be swayed with words; insurgent hordes should not be tackled with mere force. They must be subdued by authority."

The abbot and Madam Ts'ui asked simultaneously: "Who has authority?"

"I have a friend who was a Confucian scholar in his youth. Later, he distinguished himself in military campaigns and suppressed many rebellions. He has a just heart and an awe-inspiring countenance. When he was made a governor, all the thieves and brigands left his province. When he was appointed to the frontiers, barbarian horsemen ceased to encroach on our land. From these accomplishments one knows that he must be an invincible warrior replete with goodness and virtue, and that he must command devotion from the people and respect from his troops. Though his surname is Tu, and his given name Ch'üeh, people call him 'White Horse General,' since he often rides a white stallion on the battlefield. He is at present the Commanding General of P'u pass. And because of the unwavering loyalty his men have for him, no one has dared to offend him. General Tu and I are intimate friends, and I have here a draft of a letter addressed to him. Please read it, Madam."

In brief the letter said:

21. The term may mean making someone a son by giving him the hand of one's daughter, or adopting someone as a son and hence making him the brother of one's daughter. The ambiguity, fully intended by Master Tung, makes later events possible.

22. "Et cetera," and "and so forth," set in smaller print than the rest of the text is probably meant to indicate to the performing singer-narrator that at this point he may or is expected to add further elaboration.

Your humble friend Chang Kung sends this missive to Your Excellency, the Commanding General:

In haste, I shall not embellish my prose; before Your Excellency, I shall come immediately to my entreaty. An unfortunate event has occurred: Marshal Hun of P'u prefecture recently passed away. His brigadier general, Ting Wen-ya, lost control of the troops, so that certain regiments mutinied and proceeded to ravage the countryside. As villages and towns are burned, moaning and wailing reverberate throughout the entire region. All citizens are threatened with death and torture; they are in desperate straits like a man hung from his heels. Your Excellency is blessed with unusual farsightedness; you are revered by all who know you. You are famous for your protection of the people and for your courage in combat. In face of the present upheaval, I know you will not stay behind in your fortress and allow the rebels to indulge their savagery. Indeed, Your Excellency seems the only one who can stop this menacing anarchy. Please make haste, since undue hesitation may cause widespread chaos. Once you come, you will easily destroy the rebel leaders and the rest will surrender; the people will be saved and peace will be restored. When the court hears of this, an imperial edict will commend you for your meritorious achievement. If, on the contrary, you refuse to dispatch your troops, then surely you will be censured for your cowardice. At present the insurgents have surrounded the Temple of Universal Salvation, and I have no way to escape. So it is with some urgency that I beseech you to serve your country and to save your unworthy friend. Trapped in the mouth of death I look forward eagerly to your reply. I shall be exceedingly grateful to you for vouchsafing me a second life.

Once again your humble friend Chang Kung salutes Your Excellency, the Commanding General.[23]

Translated by Li-li Ch'en

23. In the next chapter, we learn that Chang had already given a copy of the letter to Fa-ts'ung when he went forth to fight the rebels. After breaking through their lines, Fa-ts'ung gives the letter to General Tu. The latter arrives in due course with his troops, who swiftly subdue the rebels.

Drama

216
Injustice to Tou Ŏ

Kuan Han-ch'ing (c. 1220–c. 1307)

DRAMATIS PERSONAE [1]

(listed in the order of their appearance)

MISTRESS TS'AI, a widow
TOU T'IEN-CHANG, a poor scholar, later a surveillance commissioner

This is a complete Yüan drama (*tsa-chü*) showing all the typical features of the genre. The verses are sung by a single actor per act (a vestige of its origins in prosimetric storytelling) to various standard arias (*ch'ü*), the names of which are not always completely transparent and hence left untranslated here. Instead, they are simply indicated serially by number.

The story of Tou Ŏ has been told in many different versions and is still presented in Peking opera under the title *Snow in Midsummer*. All of the supernatural phenomena that occur when Tou Ŏ dies are taken from earlier sources, but through his literary artistry, Kuan Han-chi'ing (see selection 105) first brought them together in a fashion that has made this the most memorable work in which they are to be found. The verse portions of Kuan's play are especially fine. *Injustice to Tou Ŏ* is written in early Mandarin, as is all Yüan drama, which means that it is full of colloquial speech.

A brief synopsis of the play is as follows: Scholar Tou sells his only daughter, age seven, to Mistress Ts'ai, a money-lender, for a few ounces of silver so that he can travel to the capital to sit for the imperial examinations. Thirteen years later, Tou Ŏ, who was married to Mistress Ts'ai's son, is now mourning his death as a young widow of twenty. Old Chang and his son, Donkey Chang, come courting Mistress Ts'ai and Tou Ŏ respectively. The two men force their way into the house and demand compensation for having previously saved Mistress Ts'ai from being strangled by an evil quack doctor. Mistress Ts'ai seems willing to remarry, but Tou Ŏ refuses out of faithfulness to the memory of her late husband. Donkey Chang plans to do away with Mistress Ts'ai so that he can have his way with Tou Ŏ after the old lady is dead. When Tou Ŏ makes some mutton-tripe soup for her mother-in-law, Donkey Chang puts poison in it. Old Chang drinks the poisoned soup by mistake and dies. Donkey Chang accuses Tou Ŏ of

TOU Ŏ (Tuan-yün), Tou T'ien-chang's daughter
DOCTOR LU
OLD CHANG
DONKEY CHANG, Old Chang's son
PREFECT T'AO WU
ATTENDANT to a magistrate
THE OFFICER in charge of executions
YAMEN RUNNERS
EXECUTIONER
CHANG CH'IEN, attendant to Tou T'ien-chang
MAGISTRATE succeeding T'ao Wu
THE GUARD escorting prisoners

1. The *Dramatis Personae*, as is the convention of traditional Chinese drama, is absent in the Chinese text.

Arousing Heaven Stirring Earth Is Tou Ŏ's Injustice [1]

Kuan Han-ch'ing of Ta-tu [2] in the Yüan Dynasty

Prologue [3]

(*Enter the old woman* MISTRESS TS'AI.)

---

having murdered his father and has her dragged into court. There a forced confession is extracted from her after she is flogged. She is sentenced to death and executed. The three-year drought brought on by Tou Ŏ's unjust execution brings to the district a high official, who happens to be Tou Ŏ's father, on an inspection tour. As he reviews the documents of her trial by candlelight, Tou Ŏ's ghost appears to him and asks for retribution. The unfortunate young woman's case is reopened, she is cleared of guilt, and the real culprit is punished.

The third act is the execution scene. In it Tou Ŏ passionately calls on Heaven and Earth to rectify the great injustice inflicted upon her. The supernatural phenomena that come to pass in response to her invocation transform a single woman's fight against her enemies into a battle of good and evil, thus enlarging the scope of the play and endowing it with cosmic significance. It is particularly renowned for exemplifying the skill and power of Kuan as a playwright.

1. This is also the second line of the couplet at the end of the play. A Yüan drama conventionally concludes with two or four seven-character lines, generally summing up the story of the play. One of the lines usually appears also as the full title of the play. The title refers to the play as a *tsa-chü*, a term that Yüan playwrights presumably borrowed from the name of the Sung dynasty four-act "Variety Play" (*tsa-chü*), a term no longer fitting for a play based on a plot.

2. Peking.

3. The term used for "prologue" here is *hsieh-tzu* (literally, "wedge") and may also signify an interlude in Yüan drama. The *hsieh-tzu* has only one or two songs in it, unlike a regular act, which has a song-sequence.

TS'AI:

(*Recites.*[4])

Flowers will bloom again,
But men may never regain their youth.
One need not always be rich and noble;
To have peace and happiness is to be like the immortals.

I am Mistress Ts'ai, a native of Ch'u-chou. There were three of us in the family. Unfortunately my husband passed away some time ago, and I have only this one child, who is now eight years old. We two, mother and son, live together and are fairly well off. Hereabouts is a Scholar Tou, who last year borrowed twenty taels of silver from me, and now owes forty taels in capital and interest. I have asked several times for the money. But Scholar Tou only claimed that he was poor and unable to pay. He has a daughter, who is seven this year. She was born cute and has grown to be lovely. I have a mind to make her my daughter-in-law. Then I would cancel the forty taels of silver. Isn't it a case of "both sides getting some benefit out of it?" He has said that today is an auspicious day and he would bring his daughter to me in person. I shall not, for the time being, go out to collect from my debtors, but wait for them at home. Now Scholar Tou must soon arrive. (*The supporting actor impersonating* TOU T'IEN-CHANG, *guiding the female lead impersonating* TUAN-YÜN, *enters.*)

TOU:

(*Recites.*)

Having read ten thousand books of great profundity,
Ssu-ma Hsiang-ju still remained as poor as he could be.
When the Emperor summoned him to the court of Han one day,
He spoke no more of wine but of his "Sir Fantasy." [5]

---

4. The notation "recites" occurs before the mannered declamation of a poem.

5. Title of a famous rhapsody by Ssu-ma Hsiang-ju (c. 179–118 B.C.E., see also selection 129). In his youth, Ssu-ma Hsiang-ju served at the court of King Hsiao of the state of Liang, a prince of the Han imperial house. King Hsiao had gathered around him an illustrious group of poets and rhetoricians, which included Mei Ch'eng (see selection 124). Ssu-ma wrote the first part of this rhapsody while attached to the court of King Hsiao, and it subsequently came into the hands of Emperor Wu, who exclaimed, "What a pity that I could not have lived at the same time as the author of this!" When informed that the author was still alive, the emperor summoned Ssu-ma to the capital and provided him with writing materials so that he could continue his literary labors. The poet thereupon revised and expanded his earlier rhapsody to produce "Sir Fantasy"—sometimes treated as a single piece under that title and sometimes as two items, the second entitled "Rhapsody on the Shang-lin (Hunting Park)."

Like many early rhapsodies, "Sir Fantasy" is cast in the form of a debate, the participants being three officials with names that emphasize their fictitious nature, each speaking in praise

My family name is Tou, and my given name is T'ien-chang. My ancestral home is in the Ching-chao District of Ch'ang-an.[6] I have studied
the classics since childhood and have learned a great deal. However,
the times have not been favorable, and fame has not yet come to me.
Unfortunately too, my wife has died, leaving me this daughter, whose
name is Tuan-yün. She lost her mother when she was three and now
she is seven. I am as poor as if I had been scoured; now I have drifted
aimlessly here to Ch'u-chou to live. Around here is a Mistress Ts'ai,
who is quite well off. Lacking traveling money, I once borrowed from
her twenty taels of silver. Now I should repay her forty taels including
interest. She has asked for the money several times, but with what am I
supposed to pay her back? Who would have thought that she would
often send people over to say that she wants my daughter to be her
daughter-in-law? Since the spring examinations will soon start, I should
be going to the capital. However, I have no traveling money. I have no
other choice; I just have to send my daughter Tuan-yün to Mistress
Ts'ai to be her future daughter-in-law.[7] (*He sighs.*) Hai! How can one
say that this is marrying her off to be a daughter-in-law? It is clearly the
same as selling the child to her. If Mistress Ts'ai would cancel the forty
taels she has lent me, and if I can get a little something extra for my
expenses while taking the examination, it would be more than I can
hope for. While talking, I have come to her gate already. Is Mistress
Ts'ai at home? (*Enter* MISTRESS TS'AI.)

TS'AI: Will the scholar please come in. I have been waiting for you for a long
time. (*They see each other.*)

TOU: I have brought you my daughter, madam. How dare I presume to
present her to be your future daughter-in-law; I am giving her to you
only to serve you day and night. Presently I have to go to the capital to
take the examination. Leaving my daughter here, I only hope that you
will look after her.

TS'AI: Now you are my in-law. As to the forty taels you owe me, including
interest, here is your promissory note, which I am returning to you. In

---

of his master. In the first part of the rhapsody, presumably composed at an earlier date, Sir
Fantasy of the fief of Ch'u and Master No-such of Ch'i describe the hunts and outings of their
respective lords. In the second part, Lord Not-real, spokesman for the supreme ruler, the Son
of Heaven (i.e., the emperor), overwhelms his companions with a magnificent description of
the Shang-lin Park on the outskirts of Ch'ang-an and the imperial hunts and entertainments
that take place there. Surprisingly, the work ends with a passage in which the emperor is shown
renouncing such pleasures, opening his parks and ponds to the use of the common people, and
adopting a policy of frugality in government.

6. Ch'ang-an (in Shensi province) was several times the capital in ancient China, and
Ching-chao was one of its districts.

7. In old Chinese society, it was customary for a family to take in a girl, usually from a poor
family, to be a future daughter-in-law.

addition, I am presenting you with ten taels of silver for your traveling expenses. In-law, I hope that you do not find this too little. (TOU T'IEN-CHANG *thanks her.*)

TOU: Many thanks, madam. Not only have you cancelled the amount I owe you, but you have also presented me with traveling money. Someday I shall greatly repay you for your kindness. Madam, when my little girl acts silly, for my sake, please look after her.

TS'AI: In-law, you need not worry. Now that your worthy beloved daughter has come to my family, I shall look after her just as though she were my own daughter. You may leave with your mind at ease.

TOU: Madam, when Tuan-yün deserves a beating, please, for my sake, just scold her. When she deserves to be scolded, please just speak to her. My child, now it won't be like staying with me anymore; I, as your father, can be tolerant of you. Now if you are naughty here, you will be asking for a scolding and a beating. My child, I do what I do because there is no other way. (*He becomes sad.*)

(*Sings.*[8])

Having no way to make a living,
I am surrounded by four bare walls;
Therefore I must make a sacrifice and be separated from my child.
Today I shall travel afar to the dust of Loyang.[9]
Not knowing the date of my return,
I become speechless, pale, and listless.

(*Exit.*)

TS'AI: Scholar Tou has left his daughter to be my daughter-in-law. He has gone straightaway to the capital to take the examination. (TOU TUAN-YÜN *is grieved.*)

TOU TUAN-YÜN: Father, you really can bear to leave me, your child, behind!

TS'AI: Daughter-in-law, you are now in my house. I am your mother-in-law. You are my daughter-in-law and will be treated as my own flesh and blood. Don't cry. Follow me and we will go to the front and to the back of the house to attend to things. (*Exeunt.*)

Act 1

[*Thirteen years later*]

(*Enter* DOCTOR LU.)

---

8. The notation "sings" occurs before lyrics set to various fixed tunes.
9. In Honan province, Loyang was several times capital of ancient China.

LU:

(*Recites.*)

I diagnose disease with care,
And prescribe according to the medicine book.
I cannot bring dead men back to life,
But the live ones by my doctoring often die.

My name is Lu. People say that I am good at doctoring, and call me "Sai Lu-yi." [1] I keep an apothecary shop at the South Gate of Shan-yang District. In town there is a Mistress Ts'ai from whom I borrowed ten taels of silver. With interest I now owe her twenty taels. She has come several times for the money, but I have none to repay her. If she doesn't come again, then there's an end to it. If she comes, I have an idea. Now I'll just sit down in the apothecary shop here and see who will come. (*Enter* MISTRESS TS'AI.)

TS'AI: I am Mistress Ts'ai. Some time ago, I moved to Shan-yang to live. It is pretty quiet here. Since that time thirteen years ago when Scholar Tou T'ien-chang left his daughter Tuan-yün behind to be my daughter-in-law, I have changed her name to Tou Ŏ. Not quite two years after the marriage, my son unexpectedly died of consumption. My daughter-in-law has already been a widow for three years and will soon be out of mourning. I have just told her that I am going outside the city gate to collect a debt from Sai Lu-yi. (*She performs walking gesture.*) I stride along the walls and go around the corners of many houses. I have already come to the door of Sai Lu-yi's house. Is Sai Lu-yi at home?

LU: Come in, madam.

TS'AI: You have kept my few pieces of silver for a long time. How about paying them back to me?

LU: Madam, I have no money at home. Come with me to the village, and I shall get the money for you.

TS'AI: I shall go with you. (*They start walking.*)

LU: Well, here we are—nobody to the east, nobody to the west. If I don't do the job here, what am I waiting for? I have some rope with me. Hey, Mistress, who is calling you?

TS'AI: Where? (DOCTOR LU *tries to strangle her.* OLD CHANG *and* DONKEY CHANG *rush forward;* DOCTOR LU *hurries away.* OLD CHANG *revives* MISTRESS TS'AI.)

DONKEY CHANG: Father, it's an old woman nearly strangled to death.

---

1. "Lu-yi" refers to the famous doctor Pien Ch'üeh of the District Lu in the Warring States period (see selection 192, note 3). "Sai" means "to rival"; in Yüan plays, the term "Sai Lu-Yi" is often used ironically for incompetent doctors.

OLD CHANG: Say, Mistress, where are you from, what is your name? Why did that man want to strangle you?

TS'AI: My name is Ts'ai. I live in town and I have only one widowed daughter-in-law, who lives with me. Because Sai Lu-yi owes me twenty taels of silver, I went to ask it back from him today. Who would have thought that he'd lure me to a deserted place in order to strangle me to escape a debt? Had it not been for you and this young man, how could I have come out of it alive?

DONKEY CHANG: Father, did you hear what she said? She has a daughter-in-law at home. We have saved her life; she will have to reward us. The best thing would be for you to take this old woman, and I'll take her daughter-in-law. What a convenient deal for both sides! Go and talk to her.

OLD CHANG: Hey, old lady, you have no husband and I have no wife; how about you being my old woman? How does that strike you?

TS'AI: What talk is this? Wait till I get home; I shall get some money to reward you.

DONKEY CHANG: You must be unwilling and want to bamboozle me with money. Doctor Lu's rope is still here; perhaps I had better strangle you after all. (*Takes up rope.*)

TS'AI: Brother, how about waiting till I think it over slowly?

DONKEY CHANG: Think what over? You go with my old man, and I'll take your daughter-in-law.

TS'AI: (*Aside.*) If I don't go along with him, he will strangle me. All right, all right, all right, you two, father and son, come home with me. (*Exeunt. Enter the female lead.*)

TOU Ŏ: My family name is Tou; my humble name is Tuan-yün. My ancestors came from Ch'u-chou. When I was three, I lost my mother; at seven I was separated from my father. He gave me away to Mistress Ts'ai to be her daughter-in-law, and she changed my name to Tou Ŏ. When I reached the age of seventeen, I was married. Unfortunately my husband died, and it has already been three years.[2] Now I am twenty years old. Outside the South Gate there is a Sai Lu-yi, who owes my mother-in-law twenty taels of silver in principal and interest. Although he has been

---

2. Tou Ŏ was married when she was seventeen; not quite two years later, her husband died and she has remained a widow for three years already. In the Western way of reckoning, she should be about twenty-two or at least twenty-one years old by this time, when she claims, "I am now twenty years of age." In Chinese, *san nian* ("three years") may refer to three different years; thus after three years of mourning, Tou Ŏ can still be twenty, as seen below:

Tou Ŏ's age

17—married at seventeen

18—husband died, not quite two years later

19

20—Tou Ŏ at twenty, being widowed for three years already.

asked several times for the money, he has not returned it. Today my mother-in-law has gone to ask for it herself. Ah, Tou Ŏ, this life of yours, how miserable!

(*Sings first lyric.*)

Of my heart full of sorrow,
Of my years of suffering,
Is Heaven aware?
If Heaven only knew my situation,
Would it not also grow thin?

(*Second lyric.*)

I just want to ask:
To go without eating or sleep both day and night–
When is this to end?
What appears in last night's dream often lingers in the mind today.
Embroidered flowers lying across the door call forth tears;
The full moon hanging above the lady's chamber breaks one's heart.
I have long been anxious and unable to suppress my worries;
Deeply depressed, I cannot relax my knitted brows.
More and more my heart grows heavy,
And my thoughts become anxious and long.

(*Speaks.*) There is no knowing when this sorrow will end!

(*Sings third lyric.*)

Is it my fate, to be unhappy all my life?
Who else knows such endless grief as I?
We all know that human feelings, unlike water, cannot flow endlessly.
When I was three years of age, my mother died;
At seven, I was separated from my father.
And then I married a man who died young,
Leaving my mother-in-law and me to keep to our lonely chambers.
Who is there to care for us, who is there to look after us?

(*Fourth lyric.*)

Is it because I did not burn enough incense in my last life,
That in this life I have to suffer?
I urge people to do good deeds to cultivate a better next life.
I serve my mother-in-law and mourn for my husband:
My words must be fulfilled.

(*Speaks.*) Mother has gone to collect the debt. Why hasn't she come back by now? (*Enter* MISTRESS TS'AI *with* OLD CHANG *and* DONKEY CHANG.)

TS'AI: You two, father and son, stay here at the gate while I go in first.

DONKEY CHANG: Mother, you go in first and say that your son-in-law is at the door. (MISTRESS TS'AI *sees* TOU ŏ.)

TOU ŏ: Mother, you're back. Have you eaten?

TS'AI: (*Crying.*) Child, how can I tell you?

TOU ŏ:

(*Sings fifth lyric.*)

Why are tears flowing down unceasingly?
Is it because while collecting debts she provoked a quarrel with
   someone?
I hurry over to greet and inquire after her,
And she is about to give her reasons.

TS'AI: It's all so embarrassing; how can I ever say it?[3]

TOU ŏ: She looks half hesitant and half embarrassed.

(*Speaks.*) Mother-in-law, why are you so upset and crying?

TS'AI: When I went to Sai Lu-yi to ask for my money, he lured me to a deserted place and tried to strangle me. Fortunately an old man named Chang and his son, Donkey, saved me. Now Old Chang wants me to take him as a husband. That's why I am so upset.

TOU ŏ: Mother-in-law, I am afraid this won't work out. How about think-ing it over again? We are not starving, and we do not lack clothing or owe money. We are not pressed by creditors. Besides, you are advanced in years. You are over sixty years old; how can you take another hus-band?

TS'AI: Child, what you said is right. But I owe these two my life. I also told them, "Wait till I get home, I'll give you a lot of money to thank you for your kindness in saving my life." I don't know how he found out I had a daughter-in-law at home. He argued that since we did not have husbands and they did not have wives, truly ours would be matches made in Heaven; and that if I did not agree with him, he still would strangle me to death. At the time I became frantic; and it wasn't just myself I promised them, but you also. My child, there was nothing else I could do.

TOU ŏ: Mother, you listen to me.

(*Sings sixth lyric.*)

To avoid evil spirits, one must select auspicious days;
For a wedding ceremony, one must offer incense-burning.

---

3. Tou Ŏ's next line is sung. The breaking up of the song text with prose dialogue is a convention in Yüan drama and helps to reduce the distance between song and speech.

> Now your knot of hair is as white as snow,
> How can you wear the colorful silk veil?[4]
> No wonder people say,
> You cannot keep a grown girl at home.[5]
> Now you are about sixty years of age,
> Isn't it said that "when middle age arrives, all is over"?
> With one stroke, you mark off the memories of former love;
> Now you and this man act like newlyweds.
> To no purpose you make people split their mouths with laughter.

TS'AI: These two saved my life. Since it has come to this, I don't care if other people laugh at me.

TOU Ŏ:

(Sings seventh lyric.)

> Though indeed you had him, had him save you,
> You are no longer young like a bamboo shoot, like a bamboo shoot;
> How can you paint your eyebrows fine to make another match?[6]
> Your husband left you his property;
> He made plans for you;
> He bought fertile land to provide food for morning and evening
> And clothing for summer and winter,
> Fully expecting his widowed wife and orphaned son,
> To remain free and independent till old age.
> Oh, father-in-law, you labored for nothing!

TS'AI: Child, he is waiting to get married. He is so excited, how can I refuse him?

TOU Ŏ:

(Sings eighth lyric.)

> You say that he is excited and happy.
> I, however, am worried for your sake.

---

4. At a Chinese wedding, red is predominantly used, whereas white, traditionally used in a Western wedding, is worn at a Chinese funeral.

5. There is a proverb: "A grown girl is not to be kept at home; if you try, you only make an enemy out of her."

6. Chang Ch'ang of the Han dynasty, in his devotion to his wife, painted her eyebrows for her. Although later the allusion "Chang Ch'ang painting eyebrows" is used to signify affection between husband and wife, the story, as told in the *History of Han*, always suggests a slightly improper intimacy. Since the painting of a wife's eyebrows by a husband is considered an excessive gesture according to traditional Chinese taste, the thought of Mistress Ts'ai at her age contemplating such an intimate gesture with a stranger is outrageous.

I worry that you, in waning spirit, cannot swallow the wedding wine;
I worry that you, with failing vision, cannot tie the same-heart knot;
I worry that you, sleepy and feeling dim, cannot rest secure under the
flower-quilt.
You want to be led by songs and music to the wedding hall;
I would say that this match[7] certainly will fall short of others.

TS'AI: Oh child, scold me no more. They are both waiting at the gate. Since
things have come to this, it is better that you too take a husband.

TOU Ŏ: If you want to take a husband, go ahead. I definitely do not want a
husband.

TS'AI: Who wants a husband? But what can one do when both, father and
son, squeezed past the door of their own accord? What am I to do?

DONKEY CHANG: Today we are going to be married and be taken into our
wives' family.

Bright are our hats,
Today we are going to be bridegrooms;
Handsome are our sleeves,
Today we are going to be guests of honor.[8]

What good husbands, what good husbands! Not bad, not bad! (*He and*
OLD CHANG *enter and salute.*)

TOU Ŏ: (*Refuses to salute.*) You wretch, stand back!

(*Sings ninth lyric.*)

Women should not, I think, believe what men say;
My Mother-in-law, I am afraid, will not maintain her chaste
widowhood.
Now she takes as a husband an uncouth old fellow,
Who brings along with him a half-dead convict.

DONKEY CHANG: (*Making a grimace.*) You can see that we two, father and
son, cut such fine figures that we fully qualify for being selected as
husbands. Don't let your good days go to waste. You and I, let's get on
with the wedding ceremonies.

---

7. *Yin-yüan:* generally used to mean the fate that brings about a marriage, or "causes" a
man and a woman to marry. The expression is derived from the Buddhist technical term *yin-
yüan,* which was a translation of the Sanskrit term *hetu-pratyaya,* meaning "cause" and "condition." *Hetu* is the primary cause, or internal cause, such as a seed is to a sprout, and *pratyaya*
is the condition or secondary cause or causes, such as rain, dew, etc., are to a sprout.

8. This verse describing the neatness of a groom's attire and his happy mood appears several
times in Yüan plays, usually quoted by others to the groom. Donkey Chang's quoting of the
verse in praise of himself and his presumptuous behavior here further expose his boorish
character and strengthen the audience's sympathy for Tou Ŏ when she rejects him.

TOU Ŏ:

> (*Refusing to salute, sings.*)

> You really can kill a person!
> Swallows and orioles in pairs! [9]
> Mother-in-law, don't you feel shame?
> My father-in-law worked in different prefectures and states;
> He amassed a solid fortune, lacking in nothing.
> How can you let the wealth he secured be enjoyed now by Donkey
>   Chang?

> (DONKEY CHANG *pulls* TOU Ŏ *to kneel for the wedding ceremony.* TOU Ŏ
> *pushes him over.*)

TOU Ŏ:

> (*Sings.*)

> Isn't this the outcome of us widowed women! (*Exit.*)

TS'AI: You, sir, don't be annoyed. You saved my life; I cannot but think of
repaying you. Only that daughter-in-law of mine is not to be provoked
and easily prevailed upon. Since she does not want to take your son as
a husband, how can I take you, sir, as my husband? Now I shall provide
good wine and good food to keep you both here at my house. Wait till
I take time to persuade my daughter-in-law. When she has changed her
mind, we can again make arrangements.

DONKEY CHANG: Such a perverse bone! Even if she were a virgin, just to be
pulled by someone, she need not be so cross and push me to the ground
for no reason. Will I let this go? I shall swear to your face that if I do
not get her to be my wife in this life, I shall not be considered a man.

> (*He recites.*)

> Beautiful women I have seen by the thousands,
> But none so perverse as this wench.
> I saved your mother-in-law's life;
> How can you be unwilling to make a sacrifice to serve me with your
>   body? (*Exeunt.*)

Act 2

(*Enter* DOCTOR LU.)

LU:

> (*Recites.*)

> I am a physician.
> There is no knowing how many have died from my doctoring.

9. A traditional image of happy couples.

But when have I been afraid of accusation,
And closed my door once for apprehension?

There is a Mistress Ts'ai in town. I owe her twenty taels of silver. She has been here often to claim the money. I almost broke her back. Indeed, I was stupid for a moment; I led her to the deserted countryside. Then we ran into two strangers. They shouted, "Who dares commit a murder, a violent deed, under the open sky, disregard the law and strangle a citizen!" It frightened me so much that I threw away the rope and ran. Although nothing happened during the night, I was scared out of my wits. Now I know that a human life is tied to Heaven and Earth. How can one treat it like mere dust on the wall? From now on I shall change my profession and try to wipe out my guilt and cultivate a better Karma. For each life that I killed by my doctoring, I shall offer the reading of a scripture to release the soul from suffering. I am Sai Lu-yi. Merely for wanting to default on a loan of twenty taels of silver, I lured Mistress Ts'ai to a deserted place. When I was just about to strangle her to death, two strangers turned up and saved her. If she comes again to ask for her money, how am I to face her? It is well said by the proverb "Of the thirty-six schemes, the best is to run away." Fortunately, I am by myself, not burdened by a family. It is better that I pack my valuables and luggage, tie up a bundle and quietly go to another place to hide and to start a new life. Won't that be a clean break? (*Enter* DONKEY CHANG.)

DONKEY CHANG: I am Donkey Chang. But alas! Tou Ǒ is still unwilling to yield to me. Now the old woman is sick. I shall get a dose of poison to give to her. When the old woman is poisoned, that little wench, for better or for worse, must be my wife. (*He walks.*) Wait a bit! There are too many eyes and ears and too much gossip in town. If they see me buying poison, they will make noise and cause trouble. The other day I saw an apothecary shop outside the South Gate, where it was quiet and just right for getting the drug. (*He arrives and calls out.*) Brother doctor, I came to get some medicine!

LU: What medicine do you want?

DONKEY CHANG: I want a dose of poison.

LU: Who dares mix poison for you? This wretch certainly has a lot of gall! [1]

DONKEY CHANG: You really refuse to give me the medicine?

LU: I will not give it to you. What are you going to do to me?

DONKEY CHANG: (*Seizes* DOCTOR LU.) Fine! Aren't you the one who tried to strangle Mistress Ts'ai the other day? Do you think that I don't recognize you? I'll take you to the magistrate.

---

1. The "gall" is said to be the seat of courage.

LU: (*Panics.*) Big brother, let me go. I have the medicine, I have the medicine. (*Gives him the poison.*)

DONKEY CHANG: Since I now have the drug, I will let you off. Indeed, it is: "When one can set others free, it is better to set them free; when one is able to forgive, it is better to forgive." (*Exit.*)

LU: This is surely bad luck. The fellow who has just asked for the medicine is the one who saved that old woman. Now I have given him a dose of poison; if anything happens, I shall be in more trouble. I'd better close this store before it's too late. I'll go to Cho-chou to sell rat poison. (*Exit DOCTOR LU. Enter* MISTRESS TS'AI, *sick, holding onto a table. Enter* OLD CHANG *and* DONKEY CHANG.)

OLD CHANG: I came to the house of Mistress Ts'ai hoping to be her second husband. But her daughter-in-law stubbornly refuses to give in. The old woman has kept the two of us, father and son, here at her house. She keeps on saying that a good thing should not be rushed, and we should wait until she succeeds in persuading her daughter-in-law to change her mind. Who would have thought that the old woman would fall sick? Son, have you had our horoscopes read? When will the lucky star and the auspicious day enter into our life?

DONKEY CHANG: Why wait for the auspicious day to arrive? One can only gamble on his ability. If you are able to do something, go ahead and do it.

OLD CHANG: Son, Mistress Ts'ai has been sick for quite a few days. Let us go inquire after her sickness. (*Sees the old woman and inquires.*) P'o-p'o,[2] how do you feel today?

TS'AI: I don't feel well at all.

OLD CHANG: Would you want a little something to eat?

TS'AI: I'd like to have some mutton-tripe soup.

OLD CHANG: Son, you tell Tou Ŏ to prepare some mutton-tripe soup for p'o-p'o.

DONKEY CHANG: (*Calling toward the stage door.*) P'o-p'o would like to have some mutton-tripe soup. Hurry to prepare some and bring it here. (*Enter* TOU Ŏ, *carrying the soup.*)

TOU Ŏ: I am Tou Ŏ. My mother-in-law doesn't feel well and she wants to have some mutton-tripe soup. I myself have made some for her, and I am going to take it to her now. Mother-in-law, we widows should be discreet in all things. How can we keep Donkey Chang and his father, who are not relatives or members of our family, here in the house with us? Won't that make people talk? Mother-in-law, do not promise them your hand secretly and involve me also in impro-

---

2. Mother-in-law.

priety. I can't help thinking how hard it is to keep watch over a woman's heart.[3]

(*Sings first lyric.*)

She wants to rest behind lovebird curtains all her days,
Unwilling to sleep in an empty chamber for half a night.
First she was Mr. Chang's woman, now she is Mr. Li's wife.
There is a type of woman, who, following each other's fashion,
Speak not of household matters, but pick up all idle gossip.
They vaguely talk of catching-phoenix adventures,
And display knowledge of trapping-dragon tricks.[4]

(*Second lyric.*)

"This one is like Lady Cho, who worked in a tavern;[5]
This one is like Meng Kuang, who raised her tray as high as her
    eyebrows."[6]
Behind these clever words they hide their true selves.
Their words do not reveal, only their deeds.
Old love is easily forgotten, and new love is favored.
Upon the grave the earth is still wet;
On the rack new clothes are hung.
Where would one find a woman who would weep down the Great
    Wall at her husband's funeral?[7]
Where would one find a girl who, while washing her yarn, would
    willingly plunge into the Big River?[8]

---

3. Here Tou Ŏ turns aside from the immediate situation to a general reflection that will become the subject of the following two arias.

4. "Catching a phoenix" or "trapping a dragon" is usually interpreted as "to hurt a good person."

5. Refers to Cho Wen-chün, the wife of Ssu-ma Hsiang-ju. When they were poor, they kept a small tavern in Chengtu, where she served as a barmaid. See selection 129.

6. Meng was the wife of Liang Hung of the Later Han. She showed her respect and love by bringing in the dinner tray raised as high as her eyebrows.

7. This refers to the folk tale about Meng Chiang-nü, whose husband, Fan Ch'i-liang, died while a conscript laborer working on the Great Wall during the reign of the first emperor of Ch'in. Later she went to seek her husband and wept so bitterly at the foot of the Wall that part of it crumbled and exposed her husband's body.

8. During the Spring and Autumn period, the minister Wu Tzu-hsü fled from the state of Ch'u to Wu. A woman washing by the river took pity on the refugee and fed him. Upon leaving, he asked her not to tell his pursuers which way he had gone. She drowned herself in the river to assure him that no word of his escape could come from her. Another reason for her drowning was that, although she helped the refugee out of compassion, she nonetheless failed in chastity in dealing with a man who was a stranger. Tou Ŏ made the allusion here evidently on account of this second reason.

Where would one find a wife turning into stone while waiting for her
    husband's return? [9]
How pitiable and shameful!
Women today are not virtuous but wanton and lacking in purpose.
Fortunately, there were faithful women of old;
Thus say not that "human nature is hard to change." [10]

(*Speaks.*) Mother, the mutton-tripe soup is ready. How about eating
    some?

DONKEY CHANG: Let me take it to her. (*He tastes the soup.*) There is not quite
    enough salt and vinegar in this; go get some. (*Exit* TOU ŏ. *He puts the*
    poison in the soup. Enter TOU ŏ.)

TOU ŏ: Here are the salt and vinegar.

DONKEY CHANG: You put some in the soup.

TOU ŏ:

(*Sings third lyric.*)

You say that, lacking in salt and vinegar, the soup has no taste;
Only if I add spice and pepper will it be good.
All I hope is that mother will soon recover.
Drinking one cup of soup is better than filling yourself with medicine;
When you get well, I shall greatly rejoice.

OLD CHANG: Son, is the soup ready?

DONKEY CHANG: Here is the soup. You take it to her. (OLD CHANG *takes the*
    soup.)

OLD CHANG: Eat some soup, *p'o-p'o.*

TS'AI: Thanks for the trouble. (*She vomits.*) I feel nauseated; I don't want this
    soup now. Why don't you eat some?

OLD CHANG: This was prepared especially for you. Even if you don't feel like
    it, eat a mouthful anyway.

TS'AI: I don't want it anymore. You eat some. (OLD CHANG *eats.*)

TOU ŏ:

(*Sings fourth lyric.*)

9. This refers to a legend that a faithful wife, during her husband's absence from home,
climbed a hill every day to watch for his return, until finally she was transformed into a large
stone, which was called "Watching-for-husband Stone."

10. A stock phrase. Here it means: "Do not say that women are born to be fickle, because
many women in the old days were chaste and faithful."

One says, "Please eat this."
One says, "You eat first."
This kind of talk is hard to take,
And how can I help getting angry?
What relation is there between him and us!
How could she forget the love of her former husband,
Who used to indulge her many wishes?
Oh, mother, is it because you regard gold as but a fleeting treasure,
And a friend in old age a rare thing,[11]
That you value your new find more than your former love?
You want even in death to share a grave with a mate;
Where is any thought of going a thousand miles[12] to deliver winter
    clothes?

OLD CHANG: After eating the soup, why do I begin to feel dizzy? (*He falls.*
    MISTRESS TS'AI *panics.*)
TS'AI: You, sir, get hold of yourself. Make an effort to stay awake! (*Cries.*) He
    is dead!
TOU Ŏ:

(*Sings fifth lyric.*)

It's no use grieving; you really have no understanding.
Birth and death are part of transmigration.
Some fall sick, some encounter hard times,
Some catch a chill, some suffer rheumatic fever,
Some die of hunger, overeating, or overwork;
Each knows his own lot.
Human life is ruled by Heaven and Earth;
How can one substitute years for another person?
Our life-span is not determined in this world.
You and he were together only for a few days;
What is there to speak of in terms of one family?
Besides, there is neither sheep, wine, silk, money, nor other wedding
    gifts.

11. The meaning of these two lines is ambiguous. The saying here is evidently proverbial, and loosely applicable to the situation; a literary sense perhaps is not to be looked for.

12. A Chinese "mile," or "tricent" (three hundred paces), is about one-third of an English mile. Here Tou Ŏ is contrasting her fickle mother-in-law to the faithful Meng Chiang-nü, who traveled a thousand "miles" to deliver warm clothing to her conscript husband in the construction of the Great Wall under the first emperor of Ch'in (see note 7 above). Mistress Ts'ai evidently wants to enjoy companionship with her mate even in death, but cannot remain faithful when deprived of the companionship.

Clenching our hands, we work and go on,
Letting loose the hand, it is the end of life.
It is not that I am contrary; only I fear what others may say.
It is better to heed my advice and regard the whole thing as poor luck.
Sacrifice for him a coffin and secure several pieces of cotton and silk;
Get him out of our house and send him to his grave.
This one is not a marriage contracted from your young age;
I really do not care and cannot shed half a drop of tears.
Do not be so overcome with grief,
Sigh or wail like this!

DONKEY CHANG: Fine! You have poisoned my father; yet you expect to get out of it clean!

TS'AI: Child, how is this going to end?

TOU Ŏ: What poison would I have? When he was asking for salt and vinegar, he put the poison in the soup himself.

(*Sings sixth lyric.*)

This fellow tricked my old mother into keeping you.
You yourself have poisoned your father.
Whom do you think you can frighten?

DONKEY CHANG: My own father—to say that I, the son, poisoned him, nobody would believe it. (*Shouts.*) Neighbors, neighbors, listen! Tou Ŏ has poisoned my father!

TS'AI: Stop! Don't get so excited. You scare me to death.

DONKEY CHANG: Are you afraid?

TS'AI: Indeed I am afraid.

DONKEY CHANG: You want to be let off?

TS'AI: Indeed, I want to be let off.

DONKEY CHANG: Then you tell Tou Ŏ to give in to me, to call me dear, beloved husband three times; then I shall let you off.

TS'AI: Child, you had better give in now.

TOU Ŏ: Mother, how can you say such a thing?

(*Sings.*)

One horse cannot wear two saddles.[13]
When your son was alive we were married for two years;
Yet now you ask me to marry another.
This is indeed something I cannot do.

---

13. A proverb meaning that one woman cannot serve two husbands.

DONKEY CHANG: Tou Ŏ, you have poisoned my father. Do you want to settle the matter officially or privately?

TOU Ŏ: What do you mean by officially or privately?

DONKEY CHANG: If you want to settle the matter officially, I shall drag you to court, where you will be thoroughly interrogated. Frail as you are, you will not be able to stand the beating and will have to confess to the murder of my father. If you want to settle privately, you had better become my wife soon. After all, you will benefit.

TOU Ŏ: I did not poison your father. I am willing to go with you to see the magistrate. (DONKEY CHANG *drags* TOU Ŏ *and the old woman out. Enter the prefect with an attendant.*)

PREFECT:

(*Recites.*)

I am a better official than many another.
Whoever comes to file a suit is asked to pay in gold and silver.
If a superior official comes to investigate,
I stay at home, pretending to be under the weather.

I am the prefect of Ch'u-chou. My name is T'ao Wu. This morning I am holding court. Attendants, summon the court. (*Attendant shouts. Enter* DONKEY CHANG *dragging in* TOU Ŏ *and* MISTRESS TS'AI.)

DONKEY CHANG: I want to lodge a charge! I want to lodge a charge!

ATTENDANT: Then bring them over here. (DONKEY CHANG *kneels; the prefect also kneels.*)

PREFECT: Please rise.

ATTENDANT: Your honor, he is the plaintiff. Why do you kneel to him?

PREFECT: Don't you know that these who come to file a suit are like my parents who pay for my clothing and food? (*Attendants shout.*)

OFFICIAL: Which of you is the plaintiff? Which is the defendant? Now tell the truth.

DONKEY CHANG: I am the plaintiff, Chang Lü-erh, who accuses this young woman, called Tou Ŏ, of preparing poison, putting it into mutton-tripe soup and poisoning my father. This one is Mistress Ts'ai, who is my stepmother. I ask your honor to render a decision on my behalf.

PREFECT: Which one of you put in the poison?

TOU Ŏ: It had nothing to do with me.

TS'AI: And it had nothing to do with me.

DONKEY CHANG: It had nothing to do with me either.

PREFECT: It wasn't any of you. It must have been I who put in the poison?

TOU Ŏ: My mother-in-law is not his stepmother either. His family name is Chang; ours is Ts'ai. When my mother-in-law was asking a loan back from Doctor Lu, she was led by him to the countryside to be strangled. However, my mother-in-law's life was saved by these two, father and son. Therefore my mother-in-law took both father and son into our house to stay permanently as a reward for their favor. Who could have known that the two of them would begin to have evil thoughts? One boldly claimed to be my mother-in-law's second husband; the other wanted to force me to become his wife. I had a husband, and my mourning for him was not yet over. I firmly refused the proposal. It just happened that my mother-in-law was sick and asked me to prepare some mutton-tripe soup. I don't know where Donkey Chang got the poison that he carried with him. He took the soup, and, saying that it lacked salt and vinegar, he managed to send me away. Meanwhile he secretly put the poison in the soup. It was indeed a piece of heaven-sent good fortune that my mother-in-law suddenly began vomiting. She didn't want the soup anymore. She gave it to his father to eat. No sooner had he eaten a few mouthfuls than he died. His death had absolutely nothing to do with me. I hope your honor will raise high the clear mirror [14] and act on my behalf for justice.

(Sings seventh lyric.)

Your honor, you, bright as a mirror and clear as water,
Can discern whether I am inwardly true or false.
The soup had the five flavors all properly blended;
Besides this I know nothing else.
He pretended to taste it;
His father swallowed it and became unconscious.
It is not that I answer evasively in court,
Your honor, what could I say groundlessly when I am innocent? [15]

DONKEY CHANG: Your honor, please examine the matter carefully. Her name is Ts'ai and my name is Chang. If her mother-in-law did not take my father as her second husband, why did she keep us two, father and son, in her house? This woman, though young, is bad and stubborn, unafraid of a beating.

---

14. This is an idiom for politely asking an official "to discern wrongs and justice." As a clear mirror reflects things lucidly, a discerning judge sees through motivation and can detect false intentions. A clear mirror is thus associated with a wise judge; cf. the first line of the following verse section and the first line of the concluding couplet of the play.

15. This foreshadows her later forced confession and suggests that she senses that the case will go against her.

PREFECT: People are mean worms. If you don't beat them, they will not confess. Attendants, select a heavy stick and beat her. (*The attendants beat* TOU Ŏ. *Three times they sprinkle water on her to revive her.*)

TOU Ŏ:

(*Sings eighth lyric.*)

This heartless stick is more than I can endure.
Oh mother, this indeed is your own doing;
Who else can be blamed?
Here I urge all women in the world, married or remarried,
To take note of my case as a precedent.[16]

(*Ninth lyric.*)

Ah! Who is shouting so fiercely?
I cannot help being frightened out of my wits.
No sooner does the noise stop and scarce do I revive,
Than once again I faint.
A thousand beatings and ten thousand punishments;
One blow falls—one streak of blood, one layer of skin!

(*Tenth lyric.*)

They beat me till pieces of my flesh fly about,
And I am dripping with blood.
Who knows the bitterness in my heart?
Where could I, this insignificant woman, have secured poison?
Oh Heaven, why don't the sun's rays
    Ever reach underneath an overturned tub? [17]

PREFECT: Are you going to confess or not?
TOU Ŏ: Really, I did not put in the poison.
PREFECT: Since it wasn't you, let's just beat the old woman.
TOU Ŏ: (*Hastily.*) Stop! Stop! Stop! Do not beat my mother-in-law; rather, I'll confess. It was I who poisoned my father-in-law.
PREFECT: Since she has confessed her crime, have her make her mark on her confession. Fasten her in the cangue [18] and throw her in the cell for the

---

16. In making sentences, magistrates, besides resorting to the law of the land, often used decisions made in other district courts as precedents.

17. Meaning that justice does not exist in a dark court.

18. A frame used to confine the neck and hands: an old Chinese punishment. The English and French "cangue" is from the Portugese *canga*, which in turn is from the Vietnamese *gong* (yoke).

condemned. Tomorrow I shall sentence her to death and have her taken to the marketplace to be executed.

TS'AI: (*Weeps.*) Tou Ŏ, it is I who am costing you your life. Oh, this pains me to death!

TOU Ŏ:

(*Sings eleventh lyric.*)

When I become a headless ghost, suffering great injustice,
Do you think I would spare you,
    A lustful, lecherous, brazen-faced thief?
Men cannot be long deceived;
Injustice escapes not the eyes of Heaven and Earth.
I struggled to the end and fought to the finish,
Now why should I wait any longer?
I willingly admit poisoning my father-in-law and sign a confession.
Oh mother, if I do not die,
How can I save your life?

(*Exit* TOU Ŏ *following the attendant.*)

DONKEY CHANG: (*Kowtows.*) Thank you, heavenly magistrate, for acting on my behalf. When Tou Ŏ is executed tomorrow, my father's death finally will be avenged.

TS'AI: (*Weeps.*) Tomorrow at the marketplace they are going to kill Tou Ŏ, my child. Oh, this pains me to death!

PREFECT: Donkey Chang and Mistress Ts'ai, get yourselves securities. I would have you at the court's disposal at all times. Attendant, sound the drum for the court's dismissal. Bring my horse. I am going home. (*Exeunt.*)

Act 3

(*Enter the officer in charge of execution.*)

OFFICER: I am the officer in charge of execution. Today we are putting a criminal to death. Officers, guard the roads. Do not let any passersby loiter. (*Enter attendant. They beat the drum and gong three times. The executioner enters, waving a flag, carrying a sword, and guarding* TOU Ŏ *in a cangue.*)

EXECUTIONER: Move faster, move faster! The officer in charge of execution has long since gone to the place of execution.

TOU Ŏ:

> (*Sings first lyric.*)

> For no reason, I am found guilty by Imperial law;
> Unexpectedly, I suffer punishment.
> My cry of injustice startles Heaven and Earth!
> In a moment, my drifting soul goes to Yama's palace.[1]
> Why shouldn't I blame Heaven and Earth?

> (*Second lyric.*)

> The sun and moon hang aloft by day and by night;
> Ghosts and spirits hold the power over our lives and deaths.
> Heaven and Earth should distinguish the pure from the foul;
> But how they have mixed up Bandit Chih and Yen Yüan![2]
> The good suffer poverty and short life;
> The wicked enjoy wealth, nobility, and long life.
> Even Heaven and Earth have come to fear the strong and oppress the
> weak.
> They, after all, only push the boats following the current.[3]
> Oh Earth, as you fail to discriminate between good and evil,
> How can you function as Earth?
> Oh Heaven, in mistaking the sage and the fool,
> You are called Heaven in vain!

EXECUTIONER: Move on faster; we are late.
TOU Ŏ:

> (*Sings third lyric.*)

> I am twisted by this cangue
> Till I tilt to the left and stagger to the right;
> The crowd pushes me backward and forward.
> I, Tou Ŏ, wish to say something to you, brother.

EXECUTIONER: What do you want to say?
TOU Ŏ:

> (*Sings.*)

> If we go through the main street, I shall bear you a grudge;
> If we go through the back street,

---

1. The palace of Yama, king of the nether world in popular Buddhism.
2. Both were of the Spring and Autumn period. Chih was a notorious robber, and Yen Yüan, a Confucian disciple, was a virtuous person who died young in poverty. Later these two persons represented the extreme bad and good.
3. Meaning "to help without sincerity; to offer help to those who are already lucky."

I will have no grievance, though I die.
Do not refuse me by saying, "The back road is too long."

EXECUTIONER: Now that you are going to the execution ground, if you have any relatives you would like to see, it would be all right for you to see them.

TOU Ŏ:

(*Sings fourth lyric.*)

Unhappily I am all alone and have no relatives;
So I can only endure in silence, and sigh in vain.

EXECUTIONER: Do you mean to say that you don't even have parents?

TOU Ŏ: I have only a father, who went to the capital thirteen years ago to take the Examination. There has not been any word from him since.

(*Sings.*)

I have not seen my father for over ten years.

EXECUTIONER: Just now you asked me to take you by the back street. What is your reason?

TOU Ŏ:

(*Sings.*)

I fear that on the main street my mother-in-law would see me.

EXECUTIONER: You cannot even take care of your own life now. Why should you worry about her seeing you?

TOU Ŏ: If my mother-in-law sees me in a cangue and lock, going to the execution ground to be killed,

(*Sings.*)

Won't she die from anger for nothing?
Won't she die from anger for nothing?
I tell you, brother,
It is good to do favors for people in times of peril.

TS'AI: Oh Heaven, isn't this my daughter-in-law?

EXECUTIONER: Old woman, stand back.

TOU Ŏ: Since my mother-in-law is here, ask her to come closer. Let me say a few words to her.

EXECUTIONER: You old woman over there, come near. Your daughter-in-law wants to say something to you.

TS'AI: My child, this pains me to death!

TOU Ŏ: Mother, when Donkey Chang put the poison in the mutton-tripe soup, he really wanted to kill you and then force me to be his wife. He never expected you to give the soup to his father to eat, and thus kill him instead. Because I was afraid you would get into trouble, I confessed, under pressure, to murdering my father-in-law. Today I am going to the execution ground to be killed. Mother, in the future, during the winter season, on New Year and other festivals, and on the first and fifteenth of each month, if you have any spare gruel, pour half a bowl for me; and if you have paper money to spare, burn some for me. Do this for the sake of the personal dignity of your late son.

(*Sings fifth lyric.*)

Think of Tou Ŏ, who wrongly was found guilty;
Think of Tou Ŏ, whose head and body were severed;
Think of Tou Ŏ, who, in the past, worked in your house.
Oh mother, do all of these for the sake of Tou Ŏ's face,
    Since she has no father or mother.

(*Sixth lyric.*)

Think of Tou Ŏ, who served you all these years;
At festivals, offer me a bowl of cold gruel,
Burn some paper money for my headless corpse.
Regard this as offering sacrifice to your own late son.

TS'AI: (*Weeping.*) Child, don't worry. I shall remember all this. Ah Heaven, this kills me.
TOU Ŏ:

(*Sings.*)

Oh mother, do not cry or fret or complain to high Heaven.
It is I, Tou Ŏ, who has no luck,
And who has to suffer in confusion such great injustice.

EXECUTIONER: (*Shouts.*) You old woman over there, stand back! The hour has come. (TOU Ŏ *kneels and the executioner unlocks the cangue.*)
TOU Ŏ: I wish to say to your honor, that if you would agree to one thing, I would die content.
EXECUTION OFFICER: Say what you have on your mind.
TOU Ŏ: I want a clean mat to stand on. Also, I want a piece of white silk, twelve feet long, to hang on the flagpole. If I have really been wronged, when the knife strikes and my head falls, a chestful of warm blood, without a drop staining the ground, will fly up to the piece of white silk.

EXECUTION OFFICER: I agree to this; it's nothing of importance. (*The execu-tioner fetches the mat and* TOU Ŏ *stands on it. He also fetches a piece of white silk and hangs it on the flagpole.*)

TOU Ŏ:

(*Sings seventh lyric.*)

It is not that I, Tou Ŏ, make irrational wishes;
Indeed the wrong I suffer is profound.
If there is no miraculous sign to show the world,
Then there is no proof of a clear, blue Heaven.
I do not want half a drop of my blood to stain the earth;
All of it will go to the white silk hanging on the eight-foot flagpole.
When people see it from four sides,
It will be the same as the blood of Ch'ang Hung [4] turning into a green
    stone,
Or the soul of Wang-ti [5] residing in a crying cuckoo.

EXECUTIONER: What else do you have to say? If you don't tell his honor now,
    when are you going to tell?

TOU Ŏ: (*Kneels again.*) Your honor, this is the hottest time of summer. If Tou
    Ŏ has been truly wronged, after her death Heaven will send down three
    feet of auspicious snow to cover her corpse.

EXECUTION OFFICER: In such hot weather, even if you had grievances reach-
    ing to Heaven, you still couldn't call down one snowflake. Surely this
    is talking nonsense!

TOU Ŏ:

(*Sings eighth lyric.*)

You say that hot summer is not a time for snow.
Have you not heard that frost formed in June because of Tsou Yen? [6]
If I have a chestful of wronged feelings that spurt like fire,
It will move snow to tumble down like cotton,
And keep my corpse from exposure.

---

4. Ch'ang Hung was an official of the Chou dynasty who was unjustly killed. According to legend, after his death his blood turned into a green stone.

5. According to legend, Tu Yü, styled Wang-ti, was king of the Shu state toward the end of the Chou dynasty. He abdicated in favor of his prime minister because of the latter's success in controlling the flood. Wang-ti himself then retired to the Western Mountain and later turned into a cuckoo that cries in the spring, and people grieve for it.

6. Frost formed in the sixth month of the year because of Tsou Yen's unjust death. Tsou Yen was a loyal official of the Warring States period. When he suffered unjust imprisonment, he cried to Heaven; frost occurred—even in the warm month of June. This unnatural event is understood to be a sign of Heaven's displeasure.

What need is there of white horses and a white carriage,[7]
To escort my funeral through the ancient path and wild trail?

(TOU Ŏ *again kneels.*) Your honor, I, Tou Ŏ, truly die unjustly. I ask that from this day this Ch'u-chou[8] district should suffer from drought for three years.

EXECUTION OFFICER: Slap her! What a thing to say!

TOU Ŏ:

(*Sings ninth lyric.*)

You say that Heaven cannot be counted on,
It has no sympathy for the human heart;
You don't know that Heaven does answer men's prayers.
Otherwise, why did sweet rain fail to fall for three years?
It was all because of the wrong suffered by the filial daughter at Tung-hai.[9]
Now is the turn of your Shan-yang district! [10]
It is all because officials care not for justice,
People in turn are afraid to speak out.

EXECUTIONER: (*Waving a flag.*) Why is the sky suddenly overcast? (*Sound of wind is heard from backstage.*) What cold wind!

TOU Ŏ:

(*Sings tenth lyric.*)

The wandering clouds darken for my sake,
The mournful wind whirls on my behalf.
My three prayers will make things completely clear.

(*Weeps.*) Mother, wait till snow falls in June and drought lasts for three years;

(*Sings.*)

Then, and only then, the innocent soul of Tou Ŏ will be revealed.

(*The executioner strikes, and* TOU Ŏ *falls.*)

EXECUTION OFFICER: What! It is indeed snowing. How strange!

EXECUTIONER: I, for my part, say that usually, when I execute people, the

---

7. In the Later Han period, Chang Shao died, and his friend Fan Shih came from afar and attended the funeral in a white (the color of death and mourning in China) carriage drawn by a white horse. Later this allusion comes to mean a funeral.

8. The area from which Mistress Ts'ai hails.

9. An allusion to the source of the basic story in *Injustice to Tou Ŏ*, which is taken from the biography of Yü Ting-kuo in the *History of the Han*.

10. Where the action of this play occurs.

ground is full of blood. The blood of this Tou Ŏ, however, all flew onto the twelve feet of white silk and not a single drop is on the ground. This is truly wondrous.

EXECUTION OFFICER: There must be injustice in this death sentence. Two of her wishes have already come true. There is no knowing whether her talk of a three-year drought will come true or not. We shall wait and see how it turns out. Attendants, there is no need to wait for the snow to stop; now take her corpse away and return it to Mistress Ts'ai. (*All answer. Exeunt, carrying the corpse.*)

Act 4

(*Enter* TOU T'IEN-CHANG *in cap and sash, followed by* CHANG CH'IEN [1] *and attendants.*)

TOU:

(*Recites.*)

As I stand alone in this empty hall, my thoughts are dark.
The moon appears above the cliff-top, the woods are shrouded in mist.
It is not because of cares that I cannot sleep;
It's just that my startled spirit cannot rest at night.[2]

I am Tou T'ien-chang. It has been sixteen years since I left my child Tuan-yün. I went to the capital, passed the Imperial Examination on the first try, and was made a State Councilor in the Secretariat. Because I am incorruptible, able, moderate, and strong, the emperor kindly appointed me concurrently to the post of Surveillance Commissioner to the two circuits of the Huai River area.[3] I have traveled from place to place to inspect prisons, check court records, and to discover and investigate corrupt officials. I have been given authority to execute the guilty before reporting to the throne.[4] I am both happy and sad. I am happy because I hold high posts in the Censorate and Secretariat and have the power to see that justice is done. With the sword from the emperor and a golden tablet, my authority is extensive. I am unhappy because of my child, Tuan-yün. When she was seven years old, I gave her to Mistress Ts'ai to be her daughter-in-law. After I had become an official, I sent messengers to Ch'u-chou for news of Mistress Ts'ai. Her

---

1. A conventional name for a male servant in Yüan drama.

2. He is probably haunted, as his next reference to his daughter indicates.

3. The Circuit to the west of the Huai River and north of the Yangtze River and the Circuit to the east of the Huai River and north of the Yangtze River.

4. Note here the extraordinary power given to Tou to carry out a death sentence without the usual mandatory review by a higher (in this case, the central) judicial authority.

neighbors said that she moved away that same year; no one knew where she went, and there had been no word since. I have wept for my child, Tuan-yün, till my eyes are dim and blurred, and I have worried so much that my hair has turned white. I have come south of the Huai River and I wonder why it hasn't rained here in Ch'u-chou for three years. Today I shall rest in this district office. Chang Ch'ien, tell the local officials they need not call today. I shall see them early tomorrow.

CHANG CH'IEN: (*Calling toward the stage door.*) Officials of all ranks! You are excused from attendance today; his honor will see you early tomorrow.

TOU: Chang Ch'ien, tell the secretaries of the six departments to bring over all the files that ought to be reviewed. I shall study some under the lamp. (CHANG CH'IEN *hands him the files.*)

TOU: Chang Ch'ien, light the lamp for me. You must be tired; you may retire now. You need not come unless I call. (CHANG CH'IEN *lights the lamp. He leaves with other attendants.*) Let me go through a few cases. Here is a criminal by the name of Tou Ŏ, who poisoned her father-in-law. This is the first thing I read and I come upon someone with the same family name as my own. To poison one's father-in-law is one of the ten unpardonable crimes.[5] Thus, among my clan too, there are some who

---

5. The Criminal Law Section in the *History of Yüan* lists the "ten crimes" as the following:

(1) "to contemplate rebellion": more specifically, to conspire against and to put into danger the gods of soil and grain [to endanger one's country];

(2) "to contemplate a greatly subversive act": more specifically, to conspire to destroy the imperial ancestral temples, tombs, and palaces;

(3) "to contemplate treason": more specifically, to renounce one's country and to put oneself in the service of a foreign power;

(4) "a detestable, subversive act": more specifically, to beat or murder grandparents or parents; to kill a paternal uncle, paternal uncle's wife, paternal aunt, older brother, older sister, maternal grandparents, husband, husband's grandparents, or husband's parents;

(5) "to lack moral rules": more specifically, to massacre three persons of one family not guilty of a capital crime; to mutilate someone [for making medicine]; to concoct violent poisons and to conjure up evil spirits;

(6) "to be extremely disrespectful": more specifically, to steal any of the sacred vessels consecrated to divine purpose, the ornaments on carriages or sedan chairs and other objects used by the emperor; to steal or to counterfeit the imperial seal; to make a mistake in a remedy prepared for the emperor, not following the prescriptions of the formula; to present things erroneously in the secret reports to the emperor; in the preparation of the emperor's meals, to present him forbidden food [because of religion or of health]; or to put at the emperor's disposal boats that are not strong. . . .

(7) "to lack filial piety": more specifically, to accuse in court, or curse and revile one's grandparents, father, or mother, or the husband's grandparents, father, or mother; while one's grandparents and parents are still living, to establish a different household and to store property there; to be lacking in providing for one's parents; during the mourning

are lawless. Since this is a case that has been closed, I shall not read any more of it. I shall put this at the bottom of the pile, and look at another case. (*Yawns.*) I am drowsy. It must be that I am getting old and tired from traveling. Let me lean on the desk and take a little rest. (*Sleeps. Enter the ghost of* TOU Ŏ.)

TOU Ŏ:

(*Sings first lyric.*)

Daily I weep at the Homegazing Terrace;[6]
Anxiously I await my enemy.
Slowly I pace in darkness,
And quickly I am borne along by the whirlwind;
Enveloped in fog and clouds,
I come fast as a ghost.

(*The ghost of* TOU Ŏ *looks about her.*)

The door-guards[7] will not let me pass. I am Surveillance Commissioner Tou T'ien-chang's daughter. Because I died unjustly, and my father does not know it, I come especially to visit him in his dreams.

---

period for one's father or mother, to marry, to make music, or to discard mourning clothes; upon learning of the death of one's grandparents, father, or mother, to feign ignorance and abstain from showing grief; to falsely report the death of one's grandparents, father, or mother.

(8) "to lack concord": more specifically, to contemplate the murder or the sale of a relative for whose death one should wear fifth-degree mourning; to beat, or to accuse in court one's husband or a relative of an older generation for whom one should wear third-degree mourning, or a relative of an older generation for whose death one should wear fourth-degree mourning.

(9) "to be unrighteous": more specifically, the crime of a subordinate who kills his prefect, governor, or magistrate; the crime of a soldier who kills his officer; the crime of a clerk or employee of a court of justice who kills an official of the fifth or higher rank; the crime of a disciple who kills his teacher; the crime of a wife, who, learning of the death of her husband, feigns ignorance and abstains from showing grief, finds joy in music, discards mourning clothing, and remarries.

(10) "to commit incest": more specifically, to have carnal relations with relatives for whose death one should wear fourth-degree mourning, with the concubines of one's father or grandfather, or with any other woman with whom the father or grandfather has had intimate relations.

Tou Ŏ was accused of the crime of "a detestable, subversive act," listed as item (4) here.

6. According to Chinese folklore, there is a terrace in the nether world for the dead to ascend to watch their families in the human world.

7. On the New Year, pictures of the god of the left door and of the god of the right door are hung to ward off evil spirits.

(*Sings second lyric.*)

I am the executed daughter of the Surveillance Commissioner;
I am not an evil spirit.
Why prevent me from going near the lamp shadow?
Why do you stop me outside the gate?

(*Calls.*) Oh, that father of mine,

Useless are his powerful sword and golden tally.
How is he to redeem my innocent, three-year rotting bones,
From the boundless sea of sufferings?

(*She enters the gate, weeping.* TOU T'IEN-CHANG *also weeps.*)

TOU: Tuan-yün, my child, where are you? (TOU Ŏ's *ghost vanishes.* TOU T'IEN-CHANG *wakes up.*) How strange! As soon as I closed my eyes, I dreamed of Tuan-yün, my child, who seemed to appear right in front of me. Where is she now? Let me go on with these cases. (TOU Ŏ's *ghost enters and adjusts the lamp.*)

TOU: How strange! I was just about to read a case when the lamp flickered. Chang Ch'ien is asleep. I had better fix the lamp myself. (*He trims the lamp.* TOU Ŏ's *ghost rearranges the file.*) Now the lamp is brighter. I shall read a few more cases: "A certain criminal, Tou Ŏ, who poisoned her father-in-law. . . ." (*He is puzzled.*) I read this case first, and put it under the other documents. How has it again come to the top? Since this case has already been closed, let me again put it at the bottom and study a different one. (TOU Ŏ's *ghost again adjusts the lamp.*) Why is this light flickering again? I shall trim it once more. (*He trims the light.* TOU Ŏ's *ghost again turns over the file.*) Now I have made the lamp brighter. Let me read another case. "A criminal Tou Ŏ poisoned her father-in-law." Ah! How strange. I had definitely put this paper at the bottom of the file, and I have just trimmed the lamp. How is it again put on the top? Can it be that there is a ghost in the hall? Even if there is no ghost, there must be some injustice involved in this case. Let me again place this underneath and read another case. (TOU Ŏ's *ghost again adjusts the lamp.*) How is it that the light dims again? It must be a ghost who is adjusting this light. Let me again trim the wick. (*He trims the wick.* TOU Ŏ's *ghost enters. They unexpectedly see each other.* TOU T'IEN-CHANG *takes out his sword and strikes the desk.*) Ah! I said, "There is a ghost." Hey, you ghost over there, I am the Imperial Surveillance Commissioner who wears the golden tally[8] and has access to the government's horses and posting stations. If you advance toward me, I shall

---

8. A symbol of power that enables an official to execute first and report to the throne later (see note 4).

cut you in two with my sword. Chang Ch'ien, how can you be sound
asleep? Get up at once. There is a ghost. There is a ghost. This frightens
me to death!

TOU Ŏ'S GHOST:

(*Sings third lyric.*)

Full of doubts, he makes random guesses;
Upon hearing my cry, he becomes frightened.
You, Tou T'ien-chang, are indeed powerful;[9]
Let me, Tou Ŏ, bow to you.

TOU: Ghost, you say that Tou T'ien-chang is your father and should receive
the greetings of his child, Tou Ŏ. You must be mistaken. My daughter
was called Tuan-yün. When she was seven, I gave her to Mistress Ts'ai
to be her daughter-in-law. You are Tou Ŏ; the name is different. How
can you be my daughter?

TOU Ŏ'S GHOST: Father, after you gave me to Mistress Ts'ai, she changed my
name to Tou Ŏ.

TOU: You are then my child Tuan-yün. Let me ask you this: Was it you who
poisoned your father-in-law?

TOU Ŏ'S GHOST: It was.

TOU: Be quiet, you wretched girl! I have wept for you till my eyes have grown
dim, and I have worried for you till my hair has turned white. How did
you come to commit one of the ten unpardonable crimes and be
executed? Now I hold high official posts in the Censorate and the
Secretariat, and am in charge of criminal law. I have come here to the
Huai River area to investigate criminal cases and to expose corrupt
officials. You are my own daughter. If I could not govern you, how can
I govern others? When I gave you in marriage to that family, I expected
you to observe the Three Obediences and the Four Virtues. The Three
Obediences are obedience to your father before marriage, obedience to
your husband after marriage, and obedience to your son after your
husband's death. The Four Virtues are service to your parents-in-law,
respect for your husband, being on good terms with your sisters-in-law,
and living in peace with your neighbors. You have disregarded the
Three Obediences and the Four Virtues, and, on the contrary, have
committed one of the ten unpardonable crimes. In our Tou family for
three generations there has been no male who has broken the law, and
for five generations there has been no woman who has remarried. Now

---

9. The daughter would not, in actual speech, pronounce her father's given name, especially
in his presence; nor would she use the pronoun for "you." This is a license allowed in arias; it
could also be a freedom accorded a ghost.

you have disgraced our ancestors and dishonored my good name. Tell me at once the truth in detail, and do not try to make excuses. If your account varies in the slightest from the truth, I shall send you to the temple of the city god, and you will never be able to re-enter human form, and will be exiled to a dark mountain and remain forever a hungry ghost.

TOU Ǒ'S GHOST: Father, please, for the time being, rest your anger and your "wolf and tiger"–like bearing. Listen to me tell the whole story slowly. At three I lost my mother, and at seven I was separated from my father. You gave me to Mistress Ts'ai to be her future daughter-in-law. At seventeen I married. Unfortunately, after two years, my husband died. I remained a widow and lived with my mother-in-law. Outside the South Gate of the Shan-yang District there was a Sai Lu-yi. He owed my mother-in-law twenty taels of silver. When my mother-in-law went to ask for the money, she was lured by him to the country, where he intended to strangle her to death. Unexpectedly Donkey Chang and his father came upon them. The two of them saved my mother-in-law's life. When Donkey Chang learned that there was a young widow in our family, he said, "You two, mother-in-law and daughter-in-law, do not have husbands. Why don't you two marry us, father and son?" My mother-in-law was unwilling at first. Donkey Chang said, "If you refuse, I shall strangle you again." My mother-in-law was afraid. Because there was no way out, she haphazardly consented and brought the two of them, father and son, home, to provide for them for life. Donkey Chang tried several times to flirt with your daughter and to seduce her. I firmly resisted him. One day my mother-in-law was not well and wanted some mutton-tripe soup. When I had the soup ready, Donkey Chang happened to be there with his father to inquire after my mother-in-law's sickness. He said, "Bring the soup and let me taste it." Then he said there was not enough salt and vinegar. Having tricked me into fetching salt and vinegar, he secretly put poison in the soup. He actually expected to poison my mother-in-law and to force me into marrying him. Quite unexpectedly, however, my mother-in-law started to vomit. Not wanting the soup any more, she gave it to Old Chang to eat. Then blood spurted from the old man's mouth, nostrils, ears, and eyes, and he died. Donkey Chang then said, "Tou Ǒ poisoned my father. Do you want to settle this officially or privately?" I then said, "What do you mean by settling this officially or privately?" He said, "If you want it settled officially, I shall take the case to court, and you will pay for my father's death with your life. If you want it settled privately, then be my wife." Your child then said, "A good horse will not have two saddles; a chaste woman will not serve two husbands. I would rather die than be your wife. I would rather go to court." He dragged me to court, where

I was questioned again and again, hanged, beaten, stripped, and bound. I would rather have died than make a false confession. How could I stand it when the prefect, seeing that your child would not confess, was going to beat my mother-in-law? I was afraid that she was too old to stand the torture, so I could not but make a false confession. Thereupon they took me to the execution ground and executed me. Your child made three vows to Heaven. First, I asked for a twelve-foot piece of white silk to be hung on a flagpole. I swore that if I were falsely accused, when the knife struck and my head fell, a chestful of warm blood would not stain the ground, but would fly up to the white silk. Second, I asked that, although it was mid-summer, Heaven would send down three feet of snow to cover my corpse. Third, I vowed that this Ch'u-chou would suffer three years of severe drought. Indeed, my blood flew up to the white silk, snow fell in June, and there was no rain for three years. All these came to pass because of your child.

(*Recites.*)

I appealed not to the court, but to Heaven.
The grievance in my heart cannot be put into words.
To save my old mother from torture,
Without argument I willingly confessed to the crime.
Three feet of snow fell to cover my corpse;
A chestful of blood stained the silk streamer.
Not only did frost fly because of Tsou Yen's wrong,
Today the injustice to Tou Ŏ is also revealed.

(*Sings fourth lyric.*)

Look at the record and see whether it reveals anything!
How am I to endure this injustice?
I would not yield to another;
Instead, I was sent to the execution ground.
I refused to disgrace my ancestors;
Instead, I lost my life.

(*Fifth lyric.*)

Ah! Today I lean on the Summoning-souls Terrace,
A lonely spirit, grievous and sad.
Ah, father, you have the law in your hand
And are sent by the Emperor;
Study this case with care.
That wretch, violating the moral order, deserves ruin;

Even if he is cut into pieces,
My wrongs can never be fully avenged.

TOU: (*Weeps.*) Ah, my wrongly slain child. For you, I shall die from grief. Let me ask you this: is it really because of you that Ch'u-chou has had no rain for three years?

TOU Ŏ'S GHOST: It is because of your child.

TOU: That such things could happen! Wait until tomorrow; I shall act on your behalf.

(*Recites.*)

A white-headed father is suffering great pain,
Because you, a young girl, have been wrongly slain.
I am afraid that dawn is breaking, and you had better go.
Tomorrow I shall set right your case and make it plain.

(TOU Ŏ's *ghost leaves.*)

TOU: Ya! It's dawn. Chang Ch'ien, last night when I was reading these cases, a ghost came to complain of her grievance. I called you several times, but you did not answer. You really slept well!

CHANG CH'IEN: I never closed my nostrils all night long. However, I did not hear any woman ghost complain of her grievance, nor did I hear your honor call me.

TOU: (*Scolding.*) Be quiet. The court is to be in session this morning. Call the court to order.

CHANG CH'IEN: (*Speaking aloud.*) People and horses in this courthouse be still; bring in the desk. (*To the Commissioner:*) The magistrate presents himself. (*The magistrate enters and presents himself.*) The clerk presents himself. (*The clerk enters and presents himself.*)

TOU: Why is it that there has been no rain in Ch'u-chou for three years?

MAGISTRATE: This is a drought decreed by Heaven. It is a calamity of the people of Ch'u. We know no guilt.

TOU: (*Angrily.*) You know no guilt? In the Shan-yang District there was a criminal, Tou Ŏ, who poisoned her father-in-law. When she was executed, she made a vow that if she were wrongly accused, there would be no rain in Ch'u-chou for three years, and not an inch of grass would grow on the ground. Is this true or not?

MAGISTRATE: This conviction of the criminal was effected by the former magistrate T'ao, who has since been promoted to the position of prefect. We have the documents.

TOU: That such a muddle-headed official should have been promoted! You are his successor. During these three years, have you offered any sacrifice to the wronged woman?

MAGISTRATE: Her crime was one of the ten gravest. No one has ever performed sacrificial services for a person guilty of such a crime; so I have not made sacrificial offerings to her.

TOU: Formerly in the Han dynasty there was a widow who showed great filial piety. When her mother-in-law hanged herself, the mother-in-law's daughter brought accusation that this widow was the murderess. The governor of Tung-hai had the woman executed. Because she was wronged, for three years there was no rain in the district. Later, when Lord Yü was reviewing cases of persons confined in the prisons in the area, he seemed to see the widow weeping in front of the courthouse, with papers in her hands. After Lord Yü rectified her court records and personally offered sacrifice to her in front of her grave, rain poured down. Now your Ch'u-chou is suffering severe drought. Isn't the situation comparable to the Han case? Chang Ch'ien, ask the Department to sign a warrant and go to the Shan-yang District to arrest criminals Donkey Chang, Sai Lu-yi, and Mistress Ts'ai. Quickly bring them here for questioning. Do not delay.

CHANG CH'IEN: Yes, your honor. (*Leaves. Enter the guard, escorting prisoners* DONKEY CHANG *and* MISTRESS TS'AI, *accompanied by* CHANG CH'IEN.)

OFFICER: The Shan-yang District has arrested and brought here the criminals, waiting to be called.

TOU: Donkey Chang.

DONKEY CHANG: Present.

TOU: Mistress Ts'ai.

TS'AI: Present.

TOU: How is it that Sai Lu-yi, who is a key criminal, is not here?

OFFICER: Sai Lu-yi fled three years ago. An order has been issued to search widely for him and to arrest him. As soon as he is taken, he will be brought here for trial.

TOU: Donkey Chang, is Mistress Ts'ai your stepmother?

DONKEY CHANG: How can a mother be falsely claimed? She is truly my stepmother.

TOU: In the court file there is no mention of the person who mixed the poison that killed your father. Whose poison was it?

DONKEY CHANG: It was the poison mixed by Tou Ŏ herself.

TOU: There must be an apothecary shop that sold this poison. Tou Ŏ was a young widow; where could she have gotten it? Donkey Chang, could it be that you mixed the poison?

DONKEY CHANG: If I had mixed the poison, why didn't I poison someone else instead of my own father?

TOU: My wrongly slain child, this is an important court case. If you do not come to defend yourself, how can things be made clear? Where is your wronged ghost anyway? (*Enter the ghost of* TOU Ŏ.)

TOU Ŏ'S GHOST: Donkey Chang, if you did not mix the poison, who mixed it?

DONKEY CHANG: (*Terrified.*) There is a ghost! There is a ghost! Put salt in the water. "God on high! Come quickly, as commanded. An Imperial Order."

TOU Ŏ'S GHOST: Donkey Chang, when you put the poison in the mutton-tripe soup, you planned to kill my mother-in-law and force me to be your wife. Unexpectedly my mother-in-law did not eat the soup and gave it to your father. He then died of poisoning. How dare you deny this today?

(*Sings sixth lyric.*)

Suddenly I see you, cursed knave.
I only want to know where the poison came from.
Your original scheme was to secretly arrange things, forcing me to
    marry;
However, you poisoned your own father.
How could you have let me shoulder your guilt?

(TOU Ŏ's *ghost strikes* DONKEY CHANG.)

DONKEY CHANG: (*Dodging.*) "God on high! Come quickly, as commanded. An Imperial order." Your honor has just said that there must have been a store that sold the poison. If your honor can find the seller to confront me, I shall die without further words. (*Enter the clown as guard, escorting* DOCTOR LU.)

OFFICER: The Shan-yang District has brought here under guard another criminal, Sai Lu-yi.

CHANG CH'IEN: (*Calls.*) Face His Honor!

TOU: Three years ago you wanted to strangle Mistress Ts'ai to escape a debt. How are you going to explain this?

DOCTOR LU: (*Kowtows.*) It is true that I attempted to escape the debt that I owed Mistress Ts'ai, but two men rescued the old woman; she did not die.

TOU: As to these two men, could you recognize them? What are their names?

DOCTOR LU: I would recognize them all right. But in that moment of excitement, I did not ask their names.

TOU: There is one at the foot of the stairs. Go and identify him. (DOCTOR LU *goes down to identify.*)

DOCTOR LU: This is Mistress Ts'ai. (*Pointing at* DONKEY CHANG.) I think it must be that the poison case has been discovered. (*Speaks to the official.*) It is this one. Let me respectfully report to your honor the story. That day when I was going to strangle Mistress Ts'ai, those two, father and son, came upon us and rescued the old woman. A few days later, he came to my store asking for a dose of poison. I am one who is

devoted to reciting Buddha's name and who observes a vegetarian diet;
I did not dare to do anything against my conscience. I said to him that
we only had legal medicine in the store; we did not have any poison.
He opened his eyes wide and said, "Yesterday in the country you wanted
to strangle Mistress Ts'ai. I shall drag you to see the magistrate." All my
life what I have dreaded the most is seeing an official. There was
nothing I could do but give him the poison. I saw that he had an evil
look and surely would use the poison to kill someone. For fear that
later the murder would be exposed and I would be involved, I fled to
the Cho-chou area, where I sold rat poison. It is true that recently I
poisoned quite a few rats, but in all truth, I have never even once mixed
poison for killing people.

TOU Ŏ'S GHOST:

(*Sings seventh lyric.*)

Merely to escape a debt, you employed deception;
You deserve to be punished.

(*Speaks.*) Oh, this poison!

(*Sings.*)

It was sold by Sai Lu-yi and bought by Donkey Chang.
For no reason at all,
They wrote the crime on my criminal plaque.
Now the judge is gone, only the courthouse remains.

TOU: Bring Mistress Ts'ai up here. I see that you are over sixty years of age;
your family is quite well off. How is it that you were married to Old
Chang and were involved in all this?

TS'AI: Because the two of them, father and son, saved my life, I took them
home to provide them with food and lodging for life. Donkey Chang
often suggested that I marry his father, but I never consented to it.

TOU: In that case, your daughter-in-law should not have confessed to poisoning her father-in-law.

TOU Ŏ'S GHOST: At the time the judge wanted to beat my mother-in-law. I
was afraid that she was too old to stand torture, so I confessed to
poisoning my father-in-law. It was truly a false confession made under
pressure.

(*Sings eighth lyric.*)

You say that I should not have signed the confession.
It all started with my feeling of filial piety,
Which, however, became the root of all my troubles.

I thought the officials would re-examine the case;
How could I know they would wrongly execute me in the street?
First, I vowed my blood would stain the white silk flying on the
    flagpole;
Second, I vowed that three feet of snow would cover my corpse;
Third, I vowed a three-year drought would visit as a divine
    punishment.
My vows were indeed comprehensive.

(*Ninth lyric.*)

Ah, it is true that from olden times, courthouses have faced the
    south,[10]
None inside has not suffered injustice.
It pains me that for over three years,
My fragile body has been locked in the netherworld.
All I have left is my deep sorrow flowing on like the long Huai River.

TOU: Tuan-yün, my child, I am fully aware of the injustice you have suffered.
Now you had better return. After I sentence these criminals and the
officials who originally handled your case, I shall offer a Buddhist
sacrifice to release your soul from suffering and enable you to ascend
to Heaven.

TOU Ŏ'S GHOST:

(*Sings tenth lyric.*)

Hereafter the golden tally and the sword of authority
Are to be displayed prominently in the first place.
They are to kill corrupt officials and dishonest clerks,
To relieve the Son of Heaven of his worries,
And to rid the people of evils.

(*Speaks.*) I almost forgot one thing. Father, my mother-in-law is old and
has no one to look after her. Please, out of compassion, keep her in
your house and provide her with her daily needs and give her a funeral
on behalf of your child. Then I shall be able to close my eyes in peace
in my grave.

TOU: What a filial and obedient daughter!

---

10. There is a Chinese jingle reflecting the people's cynical attitude toward the court:

    Courthouses open to the south;
    Whether you are right or wrong,
    Just bring the money along!

TOU Ŏ'S GHOST:

(*Sings.*)

I ask you, father, to care for my mother-in-law;
Take pity on her who has no son or daughter-in-law.
Who is to care for her, old and feeble?
Furthermore, re-open my case.

(*Speaks.*) Father, also under my name Tou Ŏ,

(*Sings.*)

Clear the criminal charges of the wrongly executed one,
Who had confessed under torture. (*Exit.*)

TOU: Call Mistress Ts'ai to come up here. Do you recognize me?
TS'AI: My eyes are bad; I do not recognize you.
TOU: I am Tou T'ien-chang. The ghost who has just been here is my wrongly
slain daughter, Tuan-yün. Now all of you listen to the sentence. Donkey
Chang, who murdered his own father and attempted to seduce a widow,
deserves to be sentenced to "slicing alive." Take him to the marketplace, nail him on a "wooden donkey," [11] and let him be sliced one
hundred twenty times and die. T'ao Wu, who has been promoted to
the post of governor, and the clerks in his department, all responsible
for the wrong handling of criminal law, should each receive a hundred
strokes and never again be employed in the government service. Sai
Lu-yi should not have repudiated his debt, tried to strangle a citizen, or
mixed poison that cost a human life. He is to be permanently exiled to
a malarial district to work under the surveillance of military authority. [12]
Mistress Ts'ai is to come to stay in my house. The guilt of Tou Ŏ is to
be cleared.

(*Recites.*)

Say not that for the thought of my late daughter,
I wipe out her guilt and wrongs;
It was only because of the pity for Ch'u-chou Prefecture,
Which has suffered a severe three-year drought.
Formerly Lord Yü revealed the innocence of the filial daughter of
Tung-hai; [13]

---

11. A wooden stake used as an implement of cruel punishment. The "Donkey's" being
punished by a "donkey" adds a macabrely ironic twist to the sentence that has been imposed.
12. This was part of a banishment sentence.
13. This is the story told by Tou T'ien-chang on p. 708.

Then rain was moved to fall like a fountain.
Do not make the excuse that natural disaster occurs in every
     generation;
The will of man can move Heaven to respond.
Today I shall correct the records,
To show that Royal law allows no one to suffer injustice.

Theme: Holding a mirror and carrying a scale[14] is the way of the
     Surveillance Commissioner.
Title: Arousing Heaven and stirring Earth is Tou Ŏ's Injustice.[15]

Translated by Chung-wen Shih

14. "Holding a mirror" and "carrying a scale" are images associated with a discerning and just law officer.
15. At the conclusion of a Yüan play, two or four seven-character lines are used to give a brief summary of the story and repeat its title.

217
The Peony Pavilion

Scene 7: The Schoolroom

T'ang Hsien-tsu (1550–1616)

CH'EN TSUI-LIANG:

     Droning verses, re-revising
          lines composed last spring,

The Peony Pavilion (*Mu-tan t'ing*), written in 1598, is a southern-style drama (see selection 213, note 49) consisting of fifty-five scenes. It celebrates the power of passion and was part of the new, humane current of thought that appeared during the waning years of the Ming dynasty. The schoolroom scene selected here is one of the two most famous scenes of the play and one of the few that is still performed. The play is much too long to be performed in toto for modern audiences.

The plot is that of a typical romantic comedy: boy meets girl; there are obstacles to their love due to family opposition coupled with a fortuitous separation or the machinations of some boorish rival; the obstacles are overcome; and the play concludes with a celebration of reunion. The theme of *The Peony Pavilion* is especially fantastic: Bridal Tu, the heroine, is resurrected from death by her lover, for whom she has pined away and died. She first experiences love only in dreams, then as a shade in the nether world, and finally as a real wife in the flesh. Bridal Tu's lover is Liu Meng-mei ("Dreaming of Plum," the name he has taken in memory of his dreamy assignation with her), who comes from a good family. He is a handsome, gifted scholar, but not simply conventional, for he also has the courage to follow his instincts borne of his

pondering, my belly filled,
    the taste of the noontime tea;
ants climb up the table leg
    to skirt the inkslab pool,
bees invade the window
    to raid the blooms in my vase.

Here in the Prefect's residence I, Ch'en Tsui-liang, have "hung my bed curtain" so that I may instruct the daughter of the house, following family tradition, in the *Classic of Odes*. The mistress, Madam Tu, is treating me with the greatest kindness. Now that breakfast is over I shall immerse myself for a while in the *Odes*.

(*He intones.*)

"*Kuan-kuan* cry the ospreys
on the islet in the river.
So delicate the virtuous maiden,
a fit mate for our Prince," [1]

"Fit," that is to say, "fit"; "mate," that is to say, "seeking." (*He looks about.*) How late it gets, and still no sign of my pupil. Horribly spoiled. Let me try three raps on the cloud board. (*He raps the cloud board.*) Fragrance, summon the young mistress for her lesson.

(*Enter* BRIDAL TU, *followed by* SPRING FRAGRANCE *bearing books.*)

BRIDAL TU:

Jao Ti Yu

Lightly adorned for morning,
to library leisurely strolling,
unconcerned I face
table's gleam by window's brightness.

---

devotion to Bridal Tu. Her father is Tu Pao, an official who is a Confucian rationalist and cannot believe that his daughter could come back to life through the strength of love.

The romanized transcriptions before the verse portions of the text refer to different aria patterns.

T'ang Hsien-tsu, the playwright, passed the metropolitan examinations at age thirty-three and began his career as a dramatist while serving in Nanking as a secretary under the board of ceremony. For more information concerning him, see selection 77.

1. The first stanza of the first poem in the *Classic of Odes* (see selection 16). Actually a folk love lyric, this, like many more of the *Odes*, was traditionally interpreted in didactic fashion as expressing popular esteem for a benevolent prince. James Legge's Victorian period translation is used here both to accord with this kind of interpretation and for the sake of its by now somewhat fustian quality.

SPRING FRAGRANCE:

> *Words of Worth from the Ancients*
> —What a deadly thought
>
> but when I'm through
>
> I'll be able to teach the parrot to order tea.

(*They greet* CH'EN.)

BRIDAL: Our best respects, esteemed sir.

FRAGRANCE: We hope you're not vexed, esteemed sir.

CH'EN: As the *Rites* prescribe, "It is proper for a daughter at first cockcrow to wash her hands, to rinse her mouth, to dress her hair, to pin the same, to pay respects to her father and mother." Once the sun is up then each should attend to her affairs. You are now a pupil and your business is to study: you will need to rise earlier than this.

BRIDAL: We shall not be late again.

FRAGRANCE: We understand. Tonight we won't go to bed so that we can present ourselves for our lesson in the middle of the night.

CH'EN: Have you rehearsed the portion of the *Odes* I presented yesterday?

BRIDAL: I have, but await your interpretation.

CH'EN: Let me hear you.

BRIDAL: (*Recites.*)

> "*Kuan-kuan* cry the ospreys
> on the islet in the river.
> So delicate the virtuous maiden,
> a fit mate for our Prince."

CH'EN: Now note the interpretation.

> "*Kuan-kuan* cry the ospreys":

the osprey is a bird; "*kuan-kuan,*" that is to say, its cry.

FRAGRANCE: What sort of cry is that?

> (CH'EN *imitates the call of the osprey;* FRAGRANCE *ad libs an imitation of* CH'EN *imitating the osprey.*)

CH'EN: This bird being a lover of quiet, it is on an island in the river.

FRAGRANCE: Quite right. Either yesterday or the day before, this year or last year some time, an osprey got trapped in the young mistress's room and she set it free, and I said to myself, if I try to catch it again, I *land* in the river.

CH'EN: Rubbish. This is a "detached image."

FRAGRANCE: What, a graven image? Who detached it?

CH'EN: To "image," that is to say, to introduce thoughts of. It introduces the thought of the "delicate virtuous maiden," who is a nice, quiet girl waiting for the Prince to come seeking her.

FRAGRANCE: What's he seeking from her?

CH'EN: Now you are being impudent.

BRIDAL: My good tutor, to interpret the text by means of the notes is something I can do for myself. I should like you rather to instruct me in the overall significance of the *Classic of Odes.*

CH'EN:

Tiao Chiao Erh

Of all six Classics
the *Classic of Odes* is the flower
with "Airs" and "Refinements" most apt for lady's chamber:
for practical instruction
Chiang-yüan[2] bears her offspring
"treading in the print of God's big toe";
warning against jealousy
shine the virtues of queen and consort.

And then there are the

"Song of the Cockcrow,"
the "Lament for the Swallows,"
"Tears by the Riverbank,"
"Longings by the Han River"
to cleanse the face of rouge:
in every verse an edifying homily
to "fit a maid for husband and for family."

BRIDAL: It seems to be a very *long* classic!

CH'EN: "The *Odes* are three hundred, but their meaning may be expressed in a single phrase":

no more than this,
"to set aside evil thoughts,"
and this I pass to you.

End of lesson. Fragrance, fetch the "four jewels of the scholar's study" for our calligraphy.

FRAGRANCE: Here are paper, ink, brushes, and inkstone.

CH'EN: What sort of ink is this supposed to be?

BRIDAL: Oh, she brought the wrong thing. This is "snail black," for painting the brows.

2. See selection 16, poem no. 245.

CH'EN: And what sort of brushes?

BRIDAL: (*Laughing.*) Mascara brushes.

CH'EN: Never did I see such things before! Take them away, take them away. And what sort of paper is this?

BRIDAL: Notepaper woven by the Tang courtesan Hsüeh T'ao.[3]

CH'EN: Take it away, take it away. Bring such as was woven by the noble inventor of paper, the ancient Ts'ai Lun. And what sort of inkstone? Is it single or double?

BRIDAL: It's not single, it's married.

CH'EN: And the "eye" patterns on it—what sort of eyes?

BRIDAL: Weeping eyes.[4]

CH'EN: What are they weeping about?—Go change the whole lot.

FRAGRANCE: (*Aside.*) Ignorant old rustic! (*To* CH'EN.) Very well. (*She brings a new set*) Will these do?

CH'EN: (*Examines them.*) All right.

BRIDAL: I believe I could copy some characters. But Fragrance will need your hand, sir, to guide her brush.

CH'EN: Let me see how you write. (*As* BRIDAL *writes, he watches in amazement.*) Never did I see writing of this quality! What is the model?

BRIDAL: The model is "The Beauty Adorns Her Hair with Blossoms," the style transmitted by the Lady Wei of Chin times.

FRAGRANCE: Let me do some characters in the style of "The Maid Apes Her Mistress."

BRIDAL: Too early for that.

FRAGRANCE: Master, I beg leave to be excused—to leave the room and excuse myself. (*She exits.*)

BRIDAL: Esteemed tutor, may I inquire what age your lady has attained?

CH'EN: She has reached exactly sixty.

BRIDAL: If you would let me have the pattern, I should like to embroider a pair of slippers to congratulate her.

CH'EN: Thank you. The pattern should be from *Mencius,* "To make sandals without knowledge of the foot."

BRIDAL: Fragrance isn't back yet.

CH'EN: Shall I call her?

(*He calls thrice.*)

FRAGRANCE: (*Enters.*) Clapping like that—I'll give him the clap!

BRIDAL: (*Annoyed.*) What have you been doing, silly creature?

3. See selection 43.

4. Inkstones of a highly prized variety made at Tuan-hsi in Kwangtung were decorated with patterns of "eyes" carved to follow the natural grain of the stone. If the "eyes" were not clear-cut "bright eyes," they were known as "weeping eyes," or, worse, "dead eyes."

FRAGRANCE: (*Laughing.*) Peeing. But I found a lovely big garden full of pretty flowers and willows,[5] lots of fun.

CH'EN: Dear, dear, instead of studying she is off to the garden. Let me fetch a bramble switch.

FRAGRANCE: What do you want a bramble switch for?

Tiao Chiao Erh

How can a girl
take the examinations and fill an office?

All it's for is to

read a few characters and scrawl a few crow's-feet.

CH'EN: There were students in ancient times who put fireflies in a bag or read by the moon.

FRAGRANCE: If you use reflected moonlight
you'll dazzle the toad up there;
as for fireflies in a bag
just think of the poor things burning!

BRIDAL: Then what about the man who tied his hair to a beam to keep from nodding off, or the scholar who prodded himself awake with an awl in the thigh?

FRAGRANCE: If you were to try

tying your hair to a beam
you wouldn't have much left
and pricking your thighs
you'd be even scabbier than you are.
What's so glorious about that?

(*A flower vendor's cry comes from within.*)

Listen, young mistress,

a flower vendor's cry
drowns out the drone of studies.

CH'EN: Again she distracts the young lady. This time I shall really beat her. (*He moves to do so.*)

FRAGRANCE: (*Dodging.*)

---

5. "Flowers and willows": this euphemism for "syphilis" reinforces the "clap" of her previous speech. We are no doubt to assume that Bridal remains innocent of these suggestions of her maid, aimed at Tutor Ch'en.

Try and beat me then,
poor little me—
tutor to young ladies
scaring this poor malefactor
within an inch of her life!

(*She grabs the bramble switch and throws it to the floor.*)

BRIDAL: You wicked creature, kneel at once for such rudeness to the tutor. (FRAGRANCE *kneels.*) Since this is her first offense, sir, perhaps it will be enough if I give her a scolding:

Tiao Chiao Erh

Your hands must not touch the garden swing,
nor your feet tread the garden path.

FRAGRANCE: We'll see about that!
BRIDAL: If you answer back, we shall have to

scorch with an incense stick
these lips of yours that blow breezes of malice,
blind with a sewing needle
these eyes that blossom into nothing but trouble.

FRAGRANCE: And what use would my eyes be then?
BRIDAL: I insist that you

hold to the inkstone,
stand fast by the desk,
attend to "It is written in the *Odes*,"
be there when "the Master says,"
and do not let your thoughts wander.

FRAGRANCE: Oh, do let's wander a little!
BRIDAL: (*Seizes her by the hair.*) Do you want as many

weals on your back
as there are hairs on your head?
I'll have you show respect for the "comptroller of the household"
—the stick Madam Tu my mother keeps in her room!

FRAGRANCE: I won't do it again.
BRIDAL: You understand then?
CH'EN: That will be enough, we shall let her go this time. Get up.

(FRAGRANCE *rises to her feet.*)

Except she lacks ambition for the fame of office,
instruction of the girl pupil parallels the boy's.

Only when your lessons are completed may you return to the house.
Meanwhile, I shall exchange a few words with your father.

BRIDAL, FRAGRANCE, CH'EN: What a waste of

this new red gauze on the sunlit window.

(CH'EN *exits*; FRAGRANCE *points scornfully at his retreating back.*)

FRAGRANCE: Ignorant old ox, dopey old dog, not an ounce of understanding.

BRIDAL: (*Tugs at her sleeve.*) Stupid creature, "a tutor for a day is a father for a lifetime"; don't you understand he has the right to beat you? But tell me, where is this garden of yours?

(FRAGRANCE *refusing to speak*, BRIDAL *gives an embarrassed laugh and asks again.*)

FRAGRANCE: (*Pointing.*) Over there, of course!

BRIDAL: What is there to look at?

FRAGRANCE: Oh, lots to look at, half a dozen pavilions, one or two swings, a meandering stream one can float wine cups down, weathered T'aihu rocks on the other bank. It's really beautiful, with all those prize blooms and rare plants.

BRIDAL: How surprising to find such a place! But now we may go back to the house.

(*Envoi.*)

BRIDAL:

Catkins floated on the breeze
in the Hsieh family court

FRAGRANCE:

thwarted is my desire to become
a butterfly in the western garden.

BRIDAL:

Ask not what sorrows follow spring
for they are limitless.

BRIDAL, FRAGRANCE:

Take for a while this loan
of green shade for your strolling.

Translated by Cyril Birch

218

The Mortal Thoughts of a Nun

from a popular drama

Anonymous (before 1700)

A young nun am I, sixteen years of age;
My head was shaven in my maidenhood.

For my father, he loves the Buddhist sūtras,
And my mother, she loves the Buddhist priests.

Morning and night, morning and night,
I burn incense and I pray, for I
Was born a sickly child, full of ills.
So they sent me here into this monastery.

Amitābha! Amitābha![1]
Unceasingly I pray.
Oh, tired am I of the humming of the drums and the tinkling of the
 bells;
Tired am I of the droning of the prayers and the crooning of the priors;
The chatter and the clatter of unintelligible charms,
The clamor and the clangor of interminable chants,
The mumbling and the murmuring of monotonous psalms.
Prajñāpāramitā, Mayura-sūtra,
  Saddharmapuṇḍarīka [2]
   Oh, how I hate them all!

While I say Mitābha,
  I sigh for my beau.
While I chant *saparah,*
  My heart cries, "Oh!"
While I sing *tarata,*
  My heart palpitates so!

Ah, let me take a stroll,
Let me take a stroll!

(She comes to the Hall of the Five Hundred Lohan,[3] where there are clay

This is a traditional scene from K'un-ch'ü (southern-style opera) that appears in several of
the better-known plays of the repertoire.
 1. The Buddha of the Western Pure Land (paradise).
 2. The names of important Buddhist scriptures.
 3. Saints; worthies; advanced disciples of the Buddha Śākyamuni. *Lohan* is an abbreviated
Chinese transcription of Sanskrit *arhat.*

figures of the Buddhist saints, known for their distinctive facial expressions)

Ah, here are the Lohan,
What a bunch of silly, amorous souls!
Every one a bearded man!
How each his eyes at me rolls!

Look at the one hugging his knees!
His lips are mumbling my name so!
And the one with his cheek in hand,
As though thinking of me so!
That one has a pair of dreamy eyes,
Dreaming dreams of me so!

But the Lohan in sackcloth!
What is he after,
With his hellish, heathenish laughter?
With his roaring, rollicking laughter,
Laughing at me so!
—Laughing at me, for
When beauty is past and youth is lost,
Who will marry an old crone?
When beauty is faded and youth is jaded,
Who will marry an old, shriveled cocoon?

The one holding a dragon,
He is cynical;
The one riding a tiger,
He is quizzical;
And that long-browned handsome giant,
He seems pitiful,
For what will become of me when my beauty is gone?

These candles of the altar,
They are not for my bridal chamber.
These long incense containers,
They are not for my bridal parlor.
And the straw prayer cushions,
They cannot serve as quilt or cover.

Oh, God!
Whence comes this burning, suffocating ardor?
Whence comes this strange, infernal, unearthly ardor?
I'll tear these monkish robes!
I'll bury all the Buddhist sūtras;

I'll drown the wooden fish,[4]
    And leave all the monastic *putras!*[5]

I'll leave the drums,
    I'll leave the bells,
        And the chants,
           And the yells,
And all the interminable, exasperating, religious chatter!

I'll go downhill, and find me a young and handsome lover—
Let him scold me, beat me!
    Kick or ill-treat me!
I will *not* become a Buddha!
I will *not* mumble *mita, prajna, para!*

Translated by Lin Yutang

4. Carved, hollow wood blocks for beating time in Buddhist ceremonies.
5. Some of the Sanskritic-sounding terms used by the young nun are intentional deformations meant to express contempt for the religion which constrains her.

PRINCIPAL CHINESE DYNASTIES AND PERIODS

Hsia (not fully verified)	c. 2100–c. 1600 B.C.E.
Shang or Yin (largely verified)	c. 1600–c. 1028
Chou	c. 1027–256
Western Chou	c. 1100–771
Eastern Chou	c. 770–256
Spring and Autumn period	722–468
Warring States period	403–221
Ch'in	221–207
Han	206 B.C.E.–220 C.E.
Western or Former Han	206 B.C.E.–8 C.E.
Hsin (New)	9–23
Liu Hsüan (Han)	23–25
Eastern or Later Han	25–220
Three Kingdoms	220–265
Wei (North China)	220–265
Shu (Szechwan)	221–263
Wu (Lower Yangtze Valley)	222–280
Chin	265–420
Western Chin	265–316
Eastern Chin	317–420
Southern and Northern Dynasties	420–589
Sixteen Kingdoms (North China)	304–439
Northern Dynasties[1]	386–581
Northern Wei (Tabgatch)	386–534
Eastern Wei	534–550

Note: B.C.E. and C.E. stand for Before the Common Era and the Common Era. They coincide with B.C. and A.D.

1. The Northern Dynasties were dominated by non-Sinitic groups.

Western Wei	535–557
Northern Ch'i	550–577
Northern Chou	557–581
Southern Dynasties[2]	420–589
Sung (Former or Liu)	420–479
Ch'i	479–502
Liang	502–557
Ch'en	557–589
Sui	581–618
T'ang	618–684, 705–907
Chou (Empress Wu)	684–705
Five Dynasties[3]	907–960
Later Liang	907–923
Later T'ang	923–936
Later Chin	936–946
Later Han	947–950
Later Chou	951–960
Sung (Later or Chao)	960–1279
Northern Sung	960–1127
Southern Sung	1127–1279
Liao (Khitan)	916–1125
Western Liao	1125–1201
Western Hsia (Tangut)	1032–1227
Chin (Jürchen)	1115–1234
Yüan (Mongol)	1260–1368
Ming	1368–1644
Ch'ing (Manchu)	1644–1911 C.E.

2. Wu and Eastern Chin plus the Southern Dynasties are collectively known as the Six Dynasties.

3. The Five Dynasties, dominated by non-Sinitic peoples, coexisted with a series of smaller and even more ephemeral Ten Kingdoms.

ROMANIZATION SCHEMES FOR MODERN STANDARD MANDARIN

Wade-Giles	Pinyin	Wade-Giles	Pinyin
a[h]	a	ch'iao	qiao
ai	ai	chieh	jie
an	an	ch'ieh	qie
ang	ang	chien	jian
ao	ao	ch'ien	qian
cha	zha	chih	zhi
ch'a	cha	ch'ih	chi
chai	zhai	chin	jin
ch'ai	chai	ch'in	qin
chan	zhan	ching	jing
ch'an	chan	ch'ing	qing
chang	zhang	chiu	jiu
ch'ang	chang	ch'iu	qiu
chao	zhao	chiung	jiong
ch'ao	chao	ch'iung	qiong
che	zhe	cho	zhuo
ch'e	che	ch'o	chuo
chei	zhei	chou	zhou
chen	zhen	ch'ou	chou
ch'en	chen	chu	zhu
cheng	zheng	ch'u	chu
ch'eng	cheng	chü	ju
chi	ji	ch'ü	qu
ch'i	qi	chua	zhua
chia	jia	ch'ua	chua
ch'ia	qia	chuai	zhuai
chiang	jiang	ch'uai	chuai
ch'iang	qiang	chuan	zhuan
chiao	jiao	ch'uan	chuan

Wade-Giles	Pinyin	Wade-Giles	Pinyin
chüan	juan	hsiu	xiu
ch'üan	quan	hsiung	xiong
chuang	zhuang	hsü	xu
ch'uang	chuang	hsüan	xuan
chüeh	jue	hsüeh	xue
ch'üeh	que	hsün	xun
chui	zhui	hu	hu
ch'ui	chui	hua	hua
chun	zhun	huai	huai
ch'un	chun	huan	huan
chün	jun	huang	huang
ch'ün	qun	hui	hui
chung	zhong	hun	hun
ch'ung	chong	hung	hong
e[h], ě	e	huo	huo
ei	ei	i	yi
en	en	jan	ran
erh	er	jang	rang
fa	fa	jao	rao
fan	fan	jeh	re
fang	fang	jen	ren
fei	fei	jeng	reng
fen	fen	jih	ri
feng	feng	jo	ruo
fo	fo	jou	rou
fou	fou	ju	ru
fu	fu	juan	ruan
ha	ha	jui	rui
hai	hai	jun	run
han	han	jung	rong
hang	hang	ka	ga
hao	hao	k'a	ka
hei	hei	kai	gai
hen	hen	k'ai	kai
heng	heng	kan	gan
ho	he	k'an	kan
hou	hou	kang	gang
hsi	xi	k'ang	kang
hsia	xia	kao	gao
hsiang	xiang	k'ao	kao
hsiao	xiao	ke, ko	ge
hsieh	xie	k'e, k'o	ke
hsien	xian	ken	gen
hsin	xin	k'en	ken
hsing	xing	keng	geng

WADE-GILES	PINYIN	WADE-GILES	PINYIN
k'eng	keng	lun	lun
kou	gou	lün	lün, lyun
k'ou	kou	lung	long
ku	gu	ma	ma
k'u	ku	mai	mai
kua	gua	man	man
k'ua	kua	mang	mang
kuai	guai	mao	mao
k'uai	kuai	me	me
kuan	guan	mei	mei
k'uan	kuan	men	men
kuang	guang	meng	meng
k'uang	kuang	mi	mi
kuei	gui	miao	miao
k'uei	kui	mieh	mie
kun	gun	mien	mian
k'un	kun	min	min
kung	gong	ming	ming
k'ung	kong	miu, miou	miu
kuo	guo	mo	mo
k'uo	kuo	mou	mou
la	la	mu	mu
lai	lai	na	na
lan	lan	nai	nai
lang	lang	nan	nan
lao	lao	nang	nang
le[h]	le	nao	nao
lei	lei	ne	ne
leng	leng	nei	nei
li	li	nen	nen
lia	lia	ni	ni
liang	liang	niang	niang
liao	liao	niao	niao
lieh	lie	nieh	nie
lien	lian	nien	nian
lin	lin	nin	nin
ling	ling	ning	ning
liu	liu	niu	niu
lo, luo	luo	no	nuo
lou	lou	nou	nou
lu	lu	nu	nu
lü	lü, lyu	nü	nü, nyu
luan	luan	nuan	nuan
lüan	lüan, lyuan	nüeh	nüe, nyue
lüeh	lüe, lyue	nung	nong

WADE-GILES	PINYIN	WADE-GILES	PINYIN
o, ŏ, e	e	shan	shan
ou	ou	shang	shang
pa	ba	shao	shao
p'a	pa	she	she
pai	bai	shei	shei
p'ai	pai	shen	shen
pan	ban	sheng	sheng
p'an	pan	shih	shi
pang	bang	shou	shou
p'ang	pang	shu	shu
pao	bao	shua	shua
p'ao	pao	shuai	shuai
pei	bei	shuan	shuan
p'ei	pei	shuang	shuang
pen	ben	shui	shui
p'en	pen	shun	shun
peng	beng	shuo	shuo
p'eng	peng	so	suo
pi	bi	sou	sou
p'i	pi	ssu, szu	si
piao	biao	su	su
p'iao	piao	suan	suan
pieh	bie	sui	sui
p'ieh	pie	sun	sun
pien	bian	sung	song
p'ien	pian	ta	da
pin	bin	t'a	ta
p'in	pin	tai	dai
ping	bing	t'ai	tai
p'ing	ping	tan	dan
po	bo	t'an	tan
p'o	po	tang	dang
p'ou	pou	t'ang	tang
pu	bu	tao	dao
p'u	pu	t'ao	tao
sa	sa	te	de
sai	sai	t'e	te
san	san	tei	dei
sang	sang	teng	deng
sao	sao	t'eng	teng
se	se	ti	di
sen	sen	t'i	ti
seng	seng	tiao	diao
sha	sha	t'iao	tiao
shai	shai	tieh	die

WADE-GILES	PINYIN	WADE-GILES	PINYIN
t'ieh	tie	ts'un	cun
tien	dian	tsung	zong
t'ien	tian	ts'ung	cong
ting	ding	tu	du
t'ing	ting	t'u	tu
tiu	diu	tuan	duan
to	duo	t'uan	tuan
t'o	tuo	tui	dui
tou	dou	t'ui	tui
t'ou	tou	tun	dun
tsa	za	t'un	tun
ts'a	ca	tung	dong
tsai	zai	t'ung	tong
ts'ai	cai	tzu	zi
tsan	zan	tz'u	ci
ts'an	can	wa	wa
tsang	zang	wai	wai
ts'ang	cang	wan	wan
tsao	zao	wang	wang
ts'ao	cao	wei	wei
tse	ze	wen	wen
ts'e	ce	weng	weng
tsei	zei	wo	wo
tsen	zen	wu	wu
ts'en	cen	ya	ya
tseng	zeng	yai	yai
ts'eng	ceng	yang	yang
tso	zuo	yao	yao
ts'o	cuo	yeh	ye
tsou	zou	yen	yan
ts'ou	cou	yin	yin
tsu	zu	ying	ying
ts'u	cu	yu	you
tsuan	zuan	yü	yu
ts'uan	cuan	yüan	yuan
tsui	zui	yüeh	yue
ts'ui	cui	yün	yun
tsun	zun	yung	yong

LIST OF PERMISSIONS

The editor and publisher acknowledge with thanks permission granted to reproduce in this volume the following material previously published elsewhere. Every effort has been made to trace copyright holders, but if any have been inadvertently overlooked, the publisher will be pleased to make the necessary arrangement at the first opportunity.

In an anthology of this magnitude, which includes nearly four hundred published and unpublished items by some eighty contributors, keeping track of copyrights and permissions has been an insurmountable task. A few of the previously published translations have appeared in several places, have been out of print and then back in print again, or have been retranslated expressly for this volume. Other translations that were prepared for this anthology have since appeared elsewhere. Some copyrights are held by the translators or their heirs, others by the publishers, and still others have changed ownership one or more times. Several of the older works are in the public domain. Some translators required only attribution at the conclusion of their works; others requested identification in the list of permissions.

Special thanks go to Anne Birrell for permitting generous use of her translations and notes for the following: Anon., "Crows on City Walls," from *Popular Songs and Ballads of Han China* (Honolulu: Hawaii University Press, 1993); and Ssu-ma Hsiang-ju, "Cock-Phoenix, Hen-Phoenix," Li Yen-nien, "A Song," attributed to Hsi-chün, "Lost Horizon," Anon., "Song of the Viet Boatman," Anon., "Mulberry up the Lane," Anon., from the "Nineteen Old Poems," Anon. or attributed to Ts'ai Yung, "Watering Horses at a Long Wall Hole," Fu Hsüan, "Pity Me!," Anon., "A Peacock Southeast Flew," and Pao Chao, "Magic Cinnabar," from *New Songs from a Jade Terrace* (Penguin Classics, 1986).

Li Po, "Late Bloomer at the Front of My Garden," "To Send to Tu Fu as a Joke," "Drinking Alone in the Moonlight," "A Suite in the Ch'ing-p'ing Mode," and Meng Hao-jan, "Spring Dawn," from Elling O. Eide, *Poems by Li Po* (Lexington, KY: Anvil Press, 1984), are reprinted by kind permission of Elling O. Eide.

Li Shang-yin, "Master Chia," from *The Poetry of Li Shang-yin: Ninth Century Baroque Chinese Poet* (1969), trans. James J. Y. Liu, reprinted by permission of the University of Chicago Press.

Selection from *Journey to the West,* trans. Anthony C. Yu, reprinted by permission of the translator and the University of Chicago Press.

Selections from *The Collected Songs of Cold Mountain,* trans. Red Pine. Copyright 1983 by Copper Canyon Press. Used by permission of Copper Canyon Press, Port Townsend, WA.

Selections from *Tao Te Ching: The Classic Book of Integrity and the Way,* trans. and ed. Victor H. Mair, are used by permission of Bantam Books, a division of Random House.

Selections from *Wandering on the Way: Early Taoist Tales and Parables of Chuang Tzu,* trans. and ed. Victor H. Mair, are used by permission of University of Hawaii Press.

K'ang-hsi, "Lines in Praise of a Self-chiming Clock," from *Emperor of China: Self-Portrait of K'ang-hsi,* trans. Jonathan Spence and published by Knopf, appears courtesy of Jonathan Spence.

Selections of P'u Sung-ling, *Strange Tales from Make-Do Studio,* trans. Victor H. Mair and Denis C. Mair, appears by permission of Foreign Languages Press, Beijing, China.

"On the Cicada: In Prison," by Lo Pin-wang, from *The Poetry of the Early T'ang,* trans. Stephen Owen, copyright 1977 by Yale University Press, is reprinted by permission of Yale University Press.

A chapter from the *Kuan Tzu,* attributed to Kuan Chung, "Duties of the Student," trans. W. Allyn Rickett, from *Guanzi: Political, Economic, and Philosophical Essays from Early China, Volume Two,* is used by permission of Princeton University Press.

Liu Hsiang, comp., *Intrigues of the Warring States,* appears with kind courtesy of James I. Crump, Jr.

"Songs of Depression" and "Watching a Village Festival," from *Heaven My Blanket, Earth My Pillow: Poems by Yang Wan-li,* trans. Jonathan Chaves, are reprinted by permission of Tanko Sha, New York.

Su Shih, "Red Cliff," number 1, Wang Hsi-chih, Preface to *Collected Poems from the Orchid Pavilion,* and Chou Mi, "Observing the Tidal Bore," from *Reminiscences of Wu-lin,* appear by kind permission of translator Richard Strassberg and the University of California Press. The selections appear in *Inscribed Landscapes,* edited by Richard Strassberg, the University of California Press.

Yang Wei-chen, "Mating" and Yang Hsün-chi, "Inscribed on the Doors of My Bookshelves," from Yoshikawa Kōjirō, *Five Hundred Years of Chinese Poetry (1150–1650),* trans. John Timothy Wixted, copyright 1989 by Princeton University Press, is reprinted by permission of Princeton University Press.

Yang Hsüan-chih, "The Establishment of the White Horse Temple," from Yi-t'ung Wang, *Record of Buddhist Monasteries in Loyang,* copyright 1983 by Princeton University Press, is reprinted by permission of Princeton University Press.

"A Poem on Wandering at the Stone Gate, with Introduction," from Susan Bush and Christian Murck, eds., *Theories of the Arts in China,* copyright 1983 by Princeton University Press, is reprinted by permission of Princeton University Press.

Nara Singde, "As If in a Dream" from David R. McCraw, *Chinese Lyricists of the Seventeenth Century,* is reprinted by permission of University of Hawaii Press.

Ou-yang Hsiu, "The Three Zithers," from Ronald C. Egan, *The Literary Works of Ou-yang Hsiu,* is reprinted with the permission of Cambridge University Press.

Scene 7 of *The Peony Pavilion (Mudan Ting)*, trans. Cyril Birch, published by Indiana University Press (1980).

"Dreaming of Southland" is from Kang-i Sun Chang, *The Late-Ming Poet Ch'en Tzu-lung: Crises of Love and Loyalism*, published by Yale University Press (1991).

"Singing of the Source of Holy Church" and "Happily Flitting Oriole" are from Jonathan Chaves, *Singing of the Source: Nature and God in the Poetry of the Chinese Painter Wu Li*, published by University of Hawaii Press (1993).

Selections from *Mencius: A New Translation Arranged and Annotated for the General Reader*, trans. by W. A. C. H. Dobson and published by University of Toronto Press (1963).

The Literary Review (Fairleigh Dickinson University) for a poem translated by Sam Hamill.

Various poems from *Sunflower Splendor*, eds. Wu-chi Liu and Irving Yucheng Lo, originally published by Indiana University Press (1975) and reprinted by Anchor.

Two poems from James Robert Hightower, trans. and comm., *The Poetry of T'ao Ch'ien*, published by Clarendon Press (1970).

Two poems from Jeanne Larsen, trans., *Brocade River Poems: Selected Works of the Tang Dynasty Courtesan Xue Tao*, published by Princeton University Press (1987).

"Letter in Reply to Liu Yi-chang," trans. Victor H. Mair, is reprinted by permission from *Renditions*, 9 (Spring 1978), pp. 81–84.

"The Sins of Mahādeva," trans. Victor H. Mair, formerly appeared in *Asian Folklore Studies*, 45.1 (1986) (Nagoya), pp. 19–32.

Poems by Juan Chi, Ch'en Tzu-ang, Chang Chiu-ling, and Li Po, trans. Victor H. Mair, are from the translator's *Four Introspective Poets*, published by Arizona State University Center for Asian Studies (1987).

"The Story about K'ung Jung" is from Richard B. Mather, trans., *Shih-shuo Hsin-yü: A New Account of Tales of the World*, published by University of Minnesota Press (1976).

"Written on Seeing the Flowers, and Remembering My Daughter" is from F. W. Mote, *The Poet Kao Ch'i, 1336–1374*, Princeton University Press (1962).

"To Meng Hao-jan," "Climbing Pien-chüeh Temple," and "Second Song for the Worship of the Goddess" from *The Great Age of Chinese Poetry: The High T'ang* by Stephen Owen copyright 1981 by Yale University Press.

"On a Visit to Ch'ung-chen Taoist Temple," trans. Kenneth Rexroth and Ling Chung, is from their *Women Poets of China*, published by New Directions (1972).

Injustice to Tou O, trans. Chung-wen Shih, is included here with the permission of Cambridge University Press (1972).

Various selections trans. by Lin Yutang have been taken from *The Importance of Living* (John Day).

Book 2, *Confucian Analects*, trans. Ezra Pound, was published in 1933 by Peter Owen.

"The Ballad of Mulan" is from Arthur Waley, trans., *The Temple and Other Poems*, published by George Allen and Unwin (1923).

The following appear by permission of Columbia University Press:

"The Shrew" and "A Burial Mound for Flowers" from *Chinese Literature: Popular Fiction and Drama* (1973), trans. and ed. H. C. Chang.

"Merchant's Joy," "Carefree Mood," and "To Show My Sons," from *The Old Man Who Does as He Pleases: Lu Yu* (1973), trans. by Burton Watson.

"Reading the Poetry of Meng Chiao," from *Su Tung-p'o: Selections from a Sung Dynasty Poet* (1965), trans. Burton Watson.

"The Stupid Old Man Who Moved a Mountain," from *The Book of Lieh-tzu*, trans. A. C. Graham (1990).

"Deva-like Barbarian," and "Offering Congratulations to the Enlightened Reign," from *Among the Flowers* (1982), trans. Lois Fusek.

"Two Brothers of Cheng and the Mother Who Doted on the Younger," from *The Tso Chuan* (1989), trans. Burton Watson.

Various poems from Jonathan Chaves, trans. and ed., *The Columbia Book of Later Chinese Poetry* (1986) and Burton Watson, trans. and ed., *The Columbia Book of Chinese Poetry: From Early Times to the Thirteenth Century* (1984).

Chapter 2 from *Master Tung's Western Chamber Romance*, trans. and ed. Li-li Ch'en (1994).

Other Works in the Columbia Asian Studies Series

TRANSLATIONS FROM THE ASIAN CLASSICS

Major Plays of Chikamatsu, tr. Donald Keene   1961

Four Major Plays of Chikamatsu, tr. Donald Keene. Paperback ed. only. 1961; rev. ed.   1997

Records of the Grand Historian of China, translated from the Shih chi of Ssu-ma Ch'ien, tr. Burton Watson, 2 vols.   1961

Instructions for Practical Living and Other Neo-Confucian Writings by Wang Yang-ming, tr. Wing-tsit Chan   1963

Hsün Tzu: Basic Writings, tr. Burton Watson, paperback ed. only. 1963; rev. ed. 1996

Chuang Tzu: Basic Writings, tr. Burton Watson, paperback ed. only. 1964; rev. ed. 1996

The Mahābhārata, tr. Chakravarthi V. Narasimhan. Also in paperbvack ed. 1965; rev. ed.   1997

The Manyōshū, Nippon Gakujutsu Shinkōkai edition   1965

Su Tung-p'o: Selections from a Sung Dynasty Poet, tr. Burton Watson. Also in paperback ed.   1965

Bhartrihari: Poems, tr. Barbara Stoler Miller. Also in paperback ed.   1967

Basic Writings of Mo Tzu, Hsün Tzu, and Han Fei Tzu, tr. Burton Watson. Also in separate paperback eds.   1967

The Awakening of Faith, Attributed to Aśvaghosha, tr. Yoshito S. Hakeda. Also in paperback ed.   1967

Reflections on Things at Hand: The Neo-Confucian Anthology, comp. Chu Hsi and Lü Tsu-ch'ien, tr. Wing-tsit Chan   1967

The Platform Sutra of the Sixth Patriarch, tr. Philip B. Yampolsky. Also in paperback ed.   1967

Essays in Idleness: The Tsurezuregusa of Kenkō, tr. Donald Keene. Also in paperback ed.   1967

The Pillow Book of Sei Shōnagon, tr. Ivan Morris, 2 vols.   1967

Two Plays of Ancient India: The Little Clay Cart and the Minister's Seal, tr. J. A. B. van Buitenen   1968

The Complete Works of Chuang Tzu, tr. Burton Watson   1968

The Romance of the Western Chamber (Hsi Hsiang chi), tr. S. I. Hsiung. Also in paperback ed.   1968

The Manyōshū, Nippon Gakujutsu Shinkōkai edition. Paperback ed. only.   1969

Records of the Historian: Chapters from the Shih chi of Ssu-ma Ch'ien, tr. Burton Watson. Paperback ed. only. 1969

Cold Mountain: 100 Poems by the T'ang Poet Han-shan, tr. Burton Watson. Also in paperback ed. 1970

Twenty Plays of the Nō Theatre, ed. Donald Keene. Also in paperback ed. 1970

Chūshingura: The Treasury of Loyal Retainers, tr. Donald Keene. Also in paperback ed. 1971; rev. ed. 1997

The Zen Master Hakuin: Selected Writings, tr. Philip B. Yampolsky 1971

Chinese Rhyme-Prose: Poems in the Fu Form from the Han and Six Dynasties Periods, tr. Burton Watson. Also in paperback ed. 1971

Kūkai: Major Works, tr. Yoshito S. Hakeda. Also in paperback ed. 1972

The Old Man Who Does as He Pleases: Selections from the Poetry and Prose of Lu Yu, tr. Burton Watson 1973

The Lion's Roar of Queen Śrīmālā, tr. Alex and Hideko Wayman 1974

Courtier and Commoner in Ancient China: Selections from the History of the Former Han by Pan Ku, tr. Burton Watson. Also in paperback ed. 1974

Japanese Literature in Chinese, vol. 1: Poetry and Prose in Chinese by Japanese Writers of the Early Period, tr. Burton Watson 1975

Japanese Literature in Chinese, vol. 2: Poetry and Prose in Chinese by Japanese Writers of the Later Period, tr. Burton Watson 1976

Scripture of the Lotus Blossom of the Fine Dharma, tr. Leon Hurvitz. Also in paperback ed. 1976

Love Song of the Dark Lord: Jayadeva's Gītagovinda, tr. Barbara Stoler Miller. Also in paperback ed. Cloth ed. includes critical text of the Sanskrit. 1977; rev. ed. 1997

Ryōkan: Zen Monk-Poet of Japan, tr. Burton Watson 1977

Calming the Mind and Discerning the Real: From the Lam rim chen mo of Tson-kha-pa, tr. Alex Wayman 1978

The Hermit and the Love-Thief: Sanskrit Poems of Bhartrihari and Bilhana, tr. Barbara Stoler Miller 1978

The Lute: Kao Ming's P'i-p'a chi, tr. Jean Mulligan. Also in paperback ed. 1980

A Chronicle of Gods and Sovereigns: Jinnō Shōtōki of Kitabatake Chikafusa, tr. H. Paul Varley 1980

Among the Flowers: The Hua-chien chi, tr. Lois Fusek 1982

Grass Hill: Poems and Prose by the Japanese Monk Gensei, tr. Burton Watson 1983

Doctors, Diviners, and Magicians of Ancient China: Biographies of Fang-shih, tr. Kenneth J. DeWoskin. Also in paperback ed. 1983

Theater of Memory: The Plays of Kālidāsa, ed. Barbara Stoler Miller. Also in paperback ed. 1984

The Columbia Book of Chinese Poetry: From Early Times to the Thirteenth Century, ed. and tr. Burton Watson. Also in paperback ed. 1984

Poems of Love and War: From the Eight Anthologies and the Ten Long Poems of Classical Tamil, A. K. Ramanujan. Also in paperback ed. 1985

The Bhagavad Gita: Krishna's Counsel in Time of War, tr. Barbara Stoler Miller 1986

The Columbia Book of Later Chinese Poetry, ed. and tr. Jonathan Chaves. Also in paperback ed. 1986

The Tso Chuan: Selections from China's Oldest Narrative History, tr. Burton Watson 1989

Waiting for the Wind: Thirty-six Poets of Japan's Late Medieval Age, tr. Steven Carter 1989

Selected Writings of Nichiren, ed. Philip B. Yampolsky   1990

Saigyō, Poems of a Mountain Home, tr. Burton Watson   1990

The Book of Lieh Tzu: A Classic of the Tao, tr. A. C. Graham. Morningside ed. 1990

The Tale of an Anklet: An Epic of South India—The Cilappatikāram of Iḷaṅkō Aṭikaḷ, tr. R. Parthasarathy   1993

Waiting for the Dawn: A Plan for the Prince, tr. and introduction by Wm. Theodore de Bary   1993

Yoshitsune and the Thousand Cherry Trees: A Masterpiece of the Eighteenth-Century Japanese Puppet Theater, tr., annotated, and with introduction by Stanleigh H. Jones, Jr.   1993

The Lotus Sutra, tr. Burton Watson. Also in paperback ed.   1993

The Classic of Changes: A New Translation of the I Ching as Interpreted by Wang Bi, tr. Richard John Lynn   1994

Beyond Spring: Tz'u Poems of the Sung Dynasty, tr. Julie Landau   1994

The Columbia Anthology of Traditional Chinese Literature, ed. Victor H. Mair   1994

Scenes for Mandarins: The Elite Theater of the Ming, tr. Cyril Birch 1995

Letters of Nichiren, ed. Philip B. Yampolsky; tr. Burton Watson et al.   1996

Unforgotten Dreams: Poems by the Zen Monk Shōtetsu, tr. Steven D. Carter   1997

The Vimalakirti Sutra, tr. Burton Watson   1997

Japanese and Chinese Poems to Sing: The Wakan rōei shū, tr. J. Thomas Rimer and Jonathan Chaves   1997

A Tower for the Summer Heat, Li Yu, tr. Patrick Hanan   1998

The Classic of the Way and Virtue: A New Translation of the Tao-te ching *of Laozi as Interpreted by Wang Bi,* tr. Richard John Lynn   1999

The Four Hundred Songs of War and Wisdom: An Anthology of Poems from Classical Tamil, The Puranāṇūṟu, eds. and trans. George L. Hart and Hank Heifetz   1999

Original Tao: Inward Training (Nei-yeh) *and the Foundations of Taoist Mysticism,* by Harold D. Roth   1999

Lao Tzu's Tao Te Ching: A *Translation of the Startling New Documents Found at Guodian,* Robert G. Henricks   2000

MODERN ASIAN LITERATURE

Modern Japanese Drama: An Anthology, ed. and tr. T. Takaya. Also in paperback ed. 1979

Mask and Sword: Two Plays for the Contemporary Japanese Theater, by Yamazaki Masakazu, tr. J. Thomas Rimer   1980

Yokomitsu Riichi, Modernist, Dennis Keene   1980

Nepali Visions, Nepali Dreams: The Poetry of Laxmiprasad Devkota, tr. David Rubin 1980

Literature of the Hundred Flowers, vol. 1: *Criticism and Polemics,* ed. Hualing Nieh 1981

Literature of the Hundred Flowers, vol. 2: *Poetry and Fiction*, ed. Hualing Nieh   1981

Modern Chinese Stories and Novellas, 1919 1949, ed. Joseph S. M. Lau, C. T. Hsia, and Leo Ou-fan Lee. Also in paperback ed.   1984

A View by the Sea, by Yasuoka Shōtarō, tr. Kären Wigen Lewis   1984

Other Worlds: Arishima Takeo and the Bounds of Modern Japanese Fiction, by Paul Anderer   1984

Selected Poems of Sŏ Chŏngju, tr. with introduction by David R. McCann   1989

The Sting of Life: Four Contemporary Japanese Novelists, by Van C. Gessel   1989

Stories of Osaka Life, by Oda Sakunosuke, tr. Burton Watson   1990

The Bodhisattva, or Samantabhadra, by Ishikawa Jun, tr. with introduction by William Jefferson Tyler   1990

The Travels of Lao Ts'an, by Liu T'ieh-yün, tr. Harold Shadick. Morningside ed.   1990

Three Plays by Kōbō Abe, tr. with introduction by Donald Keene   1993

The Columbia Anthology of Modern Chinese Literature, ed. Joseph S. M. Lau and Howard Goldblatt   1995

Modern Japanese Tanka, ed. and tr. by Makoto Ueda   1996

Masaoka Shiki: Selected Poems, ed. and tr. by Burton Watson   1997

Writing Women in Modern China: An Anthology of Women's Literature from the Early Twentieth Century, ed. and tr. by Amy D. Dooling and Kristina M. Torgeson   1998

American Stories, by Nagai Kafû, tr. Mitsuko Iriye   2000

STUDIES IN ASIAN CULTURE

The Onin War: History of Its Origins and Background, with a Selective Translation of the Chronicle of Ōnin, by H. Paul Varley   1967

Chinese Government in Ming Times: Seven Studies, ed. Charles O. Hucker   1969

The Actors' Analects (Yakusha Rongo), ed. and tr. by Charles J. Dunn and Bungō Torigoe   1969

Self and Society in Ming Thought, by Wm. Theodore de Bary and the Conference on Ming Thought. Also in paperback ed.   1970

A History of Islamic Philosophy, by Majid Fakhry, 2d ed.   1970

Phantasies of a Love Thief: The Caurapañcāśikā Attributed to Bilhaṇa, by Barbara Stoler Miller   1971

Iqbal: Poet-Philosopher of Pakistan, ed. Hafeez Malik   1971

The Golden Tradition: An Anthology of Urdu Poetry, ed. and tr. Ahmed Ali. Also in paperback ed.   1973

Conquerors and Confucians: Aspects of Political Change in Late Yüan China, by John W. Dardess   1973

The Unfolding of Neo-Confucianism, by Wm. Theodore de Bary and the Conference on Seventeenth-Century Chinese Thought. Also in paperback ed.   1975

To Acquire Wisdom: The Way of Wang Yang-ming, by Julia Ching   1976

Gods, Priests, and Warriors: The Bhṛgus of the Mahābhārata, by Robert P. Goldman   1977

Mei Yao-ch'en and the Development of Early Sung Poetry, by Jonathan Chaves   1976

The Legend of Semimaru, Blind Musician of Japan, by Susan Matisoff   1977

Sir Sayyid Ahmad Khan and Muslim Modernization in India and Pakistan, by Hafeez Malik 1980

The Khilafat Movement: Religious Symbolism and Political Mobilization in India, by Gail Minault 1982

The World of K'ung Shang-jen: A Man of Letters in Early Ch'ing China, by Richard Strassberg 1983

The Lotus Boat: The Origins of Chinese Tz'u Poetry in T'ang Popular Culture, by Marsha L. Wagner 1984

Expressions of Self in Chinese Literature, ed. Robert E. Hegel and Richard C. Hessney 1985

Songs for the Bride: Women's Voices and Wedding Rites of Rural India, by W. G. Archer; eds. Barbara Stoler Miller and Mildred Archer 1986

A Heritage of Kings: One Man's Monarchy in the Confucian World, by JaHyun Kim Haboush 1988

COMPANIONS TO ASIAN STUDIES

Approaches to the Oriental Classics, ed. Wm. Theodore de Bary 1959

Early Chinese Literature, by Burton Watson. Also in paperback ed. 1962

Approaches to Asian Civilizations, eds. Wm. Theodore de Bary and Ainslie T. Embree 1964

The Classic Chinese Novel: A Critical Introduction, by C. T. Hsia. Also in paperback ed. 1968

Chinese Lyricism: Shih Poetry from the Second to the Twelfth Century, tr. Burton Watson. Also in paperback ed. 1971

A Syllabus of Indian Civilization, by Leonard A. Gordon and Barbara Stoler Miller 1971

Twentieth-Century Chinese Stories, ed. C. T. Hsia and Joseph S. M. Lau. Also in paperback ed. 1971

A Syllabus of Chinese Civilization, by J. Mason Gentzler, 2d ed. 1972

A Syllabus of Japanese Civilization, by H. Paul Varley, 2d ed. 1972

An Introduction to Chinese Civilization, ed. John Meskill, with the assistance of J. Mason Gentzler 1973

An Introduction to Japanese Civilization, ed. Arthur E. Teidemann 1974

Ukifune: Love in the Tale of Genji, ed. Andrew Pekarik 1982

The Pleasures of Japanese Literature, by Donald Keene 1988

A Guide to Oriental Classics, eds. Wm. Theodore de Bary and Ainslie T. Embree; 3d edition ed. Amy Vladeck Heinrich, 2 vols. 1989

INTRODUCTION TO ASIAN CIVILIZATIONS

Wm. Theodore de Bary, General Editor

Sources of Japanese Tradition, 1958; paperback ed., 2 vols. 1964

Sources of Indian Tradition, 1958; paperback ed., 2 vols., 1964; 2d ed., 2 vols. 1988

Sources of Chinese Tradition, 1960; paperback ed., 2 vols., 1964; 2d ed., 2 vols. 1999

Sources of Korean Tradition, ed. Peter H. Lee and Wm. Theodore de Bary; paperback ed., vol. 1 1997

Sources of Chinese Tradition, 1999; 2d ed., vol. 1, compiled by Wm. Theodore de
   Bary and Irene Bloom; vol. 2, compiled by Wm. Theodore de Bary and Richard
   Lufrano

NEO-CONFUCIAN STUDIES

*Instructions for Practical Living and Other Neo-Confucian Writings by Wang Yang-
   ming*, tr. Wing-tsit Chan   1963
Reflections on Things at Hand: The Neo-Confucian Anthology, comp. Chu Hsi and
   Lü Tsu-ch'ien, tr. Wing-tsit Chan   1967
Self and Society in Ming Thought, by Wm. Theodore de Bary and the Conference
   on Ming Thought. Also in paperback ed.   1970
The Unfolding of Neo-Confucianism, by Wm. Theodore de Bary and the Conference
   on Seventeenth-Century Chinese Thought. Also in paperback ed.   1975
Principle and Practicality: Essays in Neo-Confucianism and Practical Learning, eds.
   Wm. Theodore de Bary and Irene Bloom. Also in paperback ed.   1979
The Syncretic Religion of Lin Chao-en, by Judith A. Berling   1980
The Renewal of Buddhism in China: Chu-hung and the Late Ming Synthesis, by
   Chün-fang Yü   1981
Neo-Confucian Orthodoxy and the Learning of the Mind-and-Heart, by Wm. Theo-
   dore de Bary   1981
Yüan Thought: Chinese Thought and Religion Under the Mongols, eds. Hok-lam
   Chan and Wm. Theodore de Bary   1982
The Liberal Tradition in China, by Wm. Theodore de Bary   1983
The Development and Decline of Chinese Cosmology, by John B. Henderson   1984
The Rise of Neo-Confucianism in Korea, by Wm. Theodore de Bary and JaHyun Kim
   Haboush   1985
Chiao Hung and the Restructuring of Neo-Confucianism in Late Ming, by Edward T.
   Ch'ien   1985
Neo-Confucian Terms Explained: Pei-hsi tzu-i, by Ch'en Ch'un, ed. and trans. Wing-
   tsit Chan   1986
Knowledge Painfully Acquired: K'un-chih chi, by Lo Ch'in-shun, ed. and trans. Irene
   Bloom   1987
To Become a Sage: The Ten Diagrams on Sage Learning, by Yi T'oegye, ed. and trans.
   Michael C. Kalton   1988
The Message of the Mind in Neo-Confucian Thought, by Wm. Theodore de Bary
   1989